Sir Arthur Bryant

THE AGE
OF CHIVALRY

THE ATLANTIC SAGA

A PLUME BOOK from
NEW AMERICAN LIBRARY
TIMES MIRROR
New York, Toronto and London

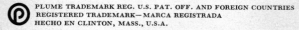 PLUME TRADEMARK REG. U.S. PAT. OFF. AND FOREIGN COUNTRIES
REGISTERED TRADEMARK—MARCA REGISTRADA
HECHO EN CLINTON, MASS., U.S.A.

SIGNET, SIGNET CLASSICS, MENTOR AND PLUME BOOKS
are published *in the United States* by
The New American Library, Inc.,
1301 Avenue of the Americas, New York, New York 10019,
in Canada by The New American Library of Canada Limited,
295 King Street East, Toronto 2, Ontario,
in the United Kingdom by The New English Library Limited,
Barnard's Inn, Holborn, London, E.C. 1, England

First Printing, March, 1970

PRINTED IN THE UNITED STATES OF AMERICA

To
Alec Myers

Contents

Maps

The greatest theme of history still is, and perhaps always will be, the unending story of men's efforts to reconcile order and liberty, the two essential ingredients of a truly great civilization.

B. WILKINSON

THE TOWER OF MEMORY

"Walk there awhile, before the day is done,
Beneath the banner and the battered casque,
Where graven heraldry in bronze and stone
With lily and with cross and leopard's mask
Spandrils the arch. Thou shalt not walk alone;
There dead men walk again and dead lips ask,
'What of the isles of England and her sea?'
Till whispers fill the tower of memory."

MURIEL STUART

WHEN TEN YEARS AGO, with the publication of *Makers of the Realm*, I completed the first volume of "The Story of England" I had hoped its successor would bridge the gap between the ages of de Montfort and Shakespeare. After I had begun to condense the vast mass of material needed for an understanding of those three and a half centuries, I realized that I had been far too ambitious and that, if my narrative was to be more than a catalogue of names, dates and generalizations, I should need more space.

The Age of Chivalry, as I have called this book, deals only with the comparatively brief period known as the high Middle Age. That crowded and formative time saw the first evolution of parliament, the beginnings of the legal profession, the legislative reforms of Edward I—"the English Justinian"—and the beginnings of an English "establishment." It witnessed that great king's attempt to unify Anglo-Saxon and Celtic Britain under a single law and monarchy, successful after a heroic resistance in Wales but in Scotland defeated in an epic war of independence that ensured, happily for mankind, the continued nationhood of the Scottish people. It was the time recorded by Froissart, of Arthurian chivalry and the foundation of the Order of the Garter, when England fought her giant neighbour, France, for

the Plantagenets' hereditary dukedom of Aquitaine: a contest
in which, through her national cohesion and the development of
a new weapon, the English vanquished and, until retribution
caught up with them, subjected to their greedy and imperious
pleasure the richest kingdom in Europe.   From 1294 until
Richard II's marriage with a French princess more than a century
later England was almost continuously at war with either France,
Scotland or Castile, and, at times, with all three.

These years were fraught for her with alternating achievement and disaster.   They saw her greatest military defeat,
Bannockburn, and her most astonishing victory, Crécy.   On the
morrow of that triumph she was struck down by a calamity comparable to that which would today follow a nuclear war.   Recurring three times in a generation, the Black Death halved England's
population.   By the injury it did to the Church's prestige it led
indirectly to that appeal to scripture and the individual conscience
which, under the name of Lollardry, foreshadowed the Reformation.   By undermining an economy already strained by war
taxation and the over-rapid expansion of capitalist wealth, it
brought about in the Peasants' Revolt an explosion of working-
class feeling surpassing in revolutionary violence and nearness to
success any other in our history.

Of England's six kings during the thirteenth and fourteenth
centuries, two were dethroned and murdered, two suffered defeat
in civil war, and only one escaped armed dictation by his
subjects.   Yet the same period saw the building of our
Decorated and early Perpendicular cathedrals and churches—of
the naves of Winchester and Canterbury, the Crécy window and
cloisters at Gloucester, and the roof of Westminster Hall; the
emergence of English as the national speech and its expression
in the poetry of Langland and Chaucer; the genesis of the Inns
of Court and the Oxford and Cambridge colleges, the foundation of the first City Companies and of William of Wykeham's
school at Winchester.

Between the accession of Edward I and the deposition of
Richard II, England became what under changing forms she has
ever since remained, a parliamentary monarchy.   By finding a
constitutional means to reconcile a strong centralized authority
with the liberty of the subject and his right to oppose and

reform government, she made a contribution of supreme importance to mankind. It was this that later enabled her, as the
maritime champion of Protestant Europe, to defeat the authoritarian power-states of Spain and France, to found in her image
the ocean nations that grew into the United States, Canada,
Australia and New Zealand, and to evolve out of the global
commercial empire created by her traders and administrators that
unique, at present precarious, yet infinitely precious conception
of inter-racial brotherhood, the Commonwealth.

The creation of parliament, with its triple components of
Crown, Lords and Commons, makes this century and a half vital
to an understanding of all that followed. We see a land of
obstinate men winning rights by trial and error that were to
become the basis of the laws and institutions by which free men
still live. In the early part of that struggle the championship of
private liberties and of the right to oppose arbitrary power
rested with the greater lords and churchmen; later the knights
of the shire and still humbler burgesses of the towns began to take
a share in that process. Out of that conflict between the expanding power of central government and the medieval tradition of
feudal and religious liberty was wrought the first great English
reconciliation between order and freedom. When twice in three
quarters of a century a successful revolution ended in the dethronement of a tyrannical king and the recognition by parliament of
his successor, the victors in both cases had the wisdom to preserve
the continuity of a strong royal government. This combination
of respect for central national authority with insistence on individual rights and liberties has remained the dominating political
motive of English history.

Because all this is so important I have left to my third volume,
The Island Kingdoms, the story of the fifteenth and sixteenth centuries, one of which Shakespeare made the theme of his historical
plays and in the other of which he lived—a period that, despite
the discovery of a new oceanic world, the Reformation and three
changes of dynasty, possessed, as historians now see, an essential
unity. Without breaking the continuity of history one cannot
separate the age in which Falstaff's tavern in Eastcheap was set
from that in which its author drew it from his contemporary
experience. As we watch those wonderful scenes in the Boar's

Head and see the stout knight and commissioner of array sitting in the Cotswold orchard with Justices Silence and Shallow, we are living simultaneously in the reigns of Henry IV and Elizabeth, of the first Lancastrian and the last Tudor.

The rest of my story will follow in two further volumes, *Liberty and the Sea* and *The Ocean Nations*. My problem in this, as in its predecessor, has been to present a composite picture, however imperfect, of an evolving nation in all its manifold activities —politics, law, administration, religion, agriculture, trade, war, social life, art and literature—and to do so, not in separate water-tight compartments, but as a living whole set in its context of passing time. I have tried, without being monotonous or didactic, to make it both a chronicle and an explanation: an explanation of how, within the setting of the period, we came to be what we are.

In these days of specialized and cumulative scholarship, for one man to try to survey a nation's history in all its aspects is an act of great presumption. It involves problems of arrangement and writing so baffling that it is seldom attempted, and with reason, since, through compression and generalization on the one hand and the selection of misleading detail on the other, it can so easily lead to over-simplification and misrepresentation. I am very conscious of the imperfections of a work that seeks to cover a field of knowledge so much wider and deeper than any single mind can master. Yet, if my work has any virtue, it is that it attempts, however imperfectly, just this. For if the ordinary reader is to understand his country's past, someone must essay the task or the truth will go by default. Because of this I had thought of calling my book *The Tower of Memory*. Unless those responsible for a nation's policy—in a parliamentary democracy the electors—can climb that tower, they cannot see the road along which they have come or comprehend their country's continuing destiny.

II

Before Plantagenet England can be understood its background must be realized. England was part, though an isolated part, of western Europe, and her king and nobles were of the same stock and spoke the same language as the French on the other side of the Channel. She has to seen in the context of that wider world. It was one both smaller and larger than ours—smaller because its furthest limits were the Atlantic and the Mediterranean coasts of North Africa and Asia Minor, larger because even a journey from London to York took five or six days and one to Rome or Avignon many weeks. Beyond every horizon were mystery and romance; the man from the next town was a foreigner if not an enemy: from the next country a being almost from another world. Each of the hundreds of little kingdoms, principalities and free cities of Europe had its separate laws and customs, though many were linked to one another by their rulers' feudal allegiances, and all belonged to the supranational polity over which the Church presided.

At the time of Edward I's accession by far the largest kingdom in Europe was France. It was about two-thirds of its present size, with the Rhone, Saone, Lower Meuse and Lys forming its eastern frontier. The part governed by the French king was only about half this, for the rulers of Flanders, Champagne, French Burgundy and Gascony, the fiefs on its circumference, owed him only a limited homage. Gascony even belonged to the King of England in his capacity as Duke of Aquitaine.

South of the Pyrenees were the little crusading kingdoms of the Iberian peninsula—mountain Navarre, tawny Castile and Leon, the rising Mediterranean sea-power of Aragon lately enlarged by the absorption of Catalonia and Valencia, and on the Atlantic coast the new-won kingdom of Portugal. Before the institution of feudal chivalry had given Christendom a new strength against Islam, they had been only a cluster of tiny hill states barely surviving in the northern mountains; now, together, they had driven the Moors back almost to Africa, leaving only the inaccessible hill caliphate of Granada under the Crescent. Bordering France to the east was the nebulous middle realm which the tripartite division of Charlemagne's empire had left between the tribal lands of the Franks and Germans. In the north of this indeterminate corridor, where the Rhine flowed into the North Sea, were Brabant and Hainault, whose thriving cloth-cities, with those of the neighbouring French fiefs of Flanders and

Artois, provided the market for England's raw wool. Further south were the duchies of Luxemburg and Lorraine, the "kingdom" of Burgundy or Franche Comté, Alpine Savoy, and Provence.

Beyond the Alps lay the Lombardy plain and the so-called kingdom of Italy, the richest, most populous and progressive region in Europe. Germanic emperor and Italian pope, contending for mastery, had failed to give it political unity—a blessing the peninsula had not known, save for a short time in the Norman-ruled Sicilian south, for nearly a thousand years. Behind their walls the cities of northern Italy had developed a commercial, civic and artistic life far in advance of any other land. For ever contending and leaguing with one another for control of the surrounding countryside, they had won for themselves complete independence, maintaining armies which, though usually aligned against one another, in association had proved a match for the feudal levies brought against them by successive German emperors. Some, like the great cloth-manufacturing and banking republic of Florence, head of the Tuscan League, had traditionally sided with the popes; others like Milan more usually with the emperors. Yet, though rival factions warred perpetually within their walls, they fought one another, not for the interests of pope or emperor but for their own, and it had been the Lombard League, led by Milan, that, more than any other single force, had broken the power of the Hohenstauffens.

To the north, beyond the head waters of the Rhine, lay Germany over which, as over northern Italy, the titular successors of Charlemagne nominally presided. Though the rulers of the greater German states still went through the old form of electing an Emperor and "King of the Romans," since the fall of the Hohenstauffens the imperial title had meant little. In theory the "Roman" emperor was the temporal head of Christendom, and his imperial mantle was competed for by rival princes eager for prestige. But power in Germany, with its three-hundred or more independent fiefs, now lay with the larger princely families—the Wittelsbachs of Bavaria, the Welfs of Brunswick, the Wettins of Saxony, the hereditary rulers of Brandenburg, the Palatinate and Bohemia, and with the great Rhineland ecclesiastics—the archbishops of Cologne, Mainz and Trier—on whom, in the hope of countering the power of their lay rivals, the Hohenstauffen emperors had bestowed vast territories. Here, too, in the absence of central authority, the "free" cities had gained not only independence, but, by forming leagues for mutual support, a power that rivalled that of any prince. Recently the Hansa or Hanseatic League, centering round the ports of Lübeck, Wisby, Rostock and Hamburg, had arisen to protect the carrying trade of the Baltic and North Sea, in both of which it sought to establish a monopoly. These German traders were known in England as easterlings, and their guildhall or factory in London was the centre of an expanding trade in timber, furs, cloth, stockfish, Rhenish wine and shipbuilding materials, and a source of perennial jealousy and envy among the turbulent city apprentices.

Far to the east, in the lands of the heathen Prussians, crusading Teutonic Knights, merchants and peasant settlers from Swabia and Saxony were pushing ever deeper into the Baltic pine-forests and the Polish and Lithuanian plains. Other colonisers from Bavaria in the Danube valley, driving back the Magyars, had already created a new province for the empire, the mark of Austria or Östmark. Beyond this slowly expanding frontier lay the sparsely-populated lands of the Viking north, the plains of Slavonic Poland and, south of the Carpathians, of Magyar Hungary, where under the influence of Christianity the fierce nomadic habits of the past were giving place to agriculture and a feudal organization of society. Further east still were the republic of Novgorod and the half-barbaric Russian princedoms whose Christianity, like that of the southern Slavs of the Balkans, stemmed from the Greek Orthodox Church of Byzantium. Here, beside the Bosphorus, precariously poised between the Islamic Turks of Asia Minor and the acquisitive Venetian traders of the West—now in possession of Greece and the Grecian isles—the descendants of the Eastern Roman emperors still maintained, in a capital only lately regained from marauding crusaders, an ancient culture more civilized and luxurious than any known to the Franks and Teutons.

This was the farthest horizon of a thirteenth century Englishman's world. Beyond that dark rim, where far-travelled trading-men exchanged goods along the golden road to Samarkand, no

westerner had ever penetrated save an occasional friar eager
for martyrdom or a Venetian merchant so curious for gain that
all the deserts of the East could not daunt him.[1] Out of that
remote other world had swept half a century earlier the terrible
nomadic Tartars or Mongols—the Golden Horde of Ghengis
Khan—overrunning for a time all southern and central Russia,
Poland, Hungary and Silesia as well as Asian Turkestan and the
great Abbasid Caliphinate of Baghdad. Since then, though
Russia still paid them tribute of gold and slaves, they had
receded into the eastern steppes, settling partially in China
whose ancient civilisation their khans had conquered, and arousing, as they grew more tolerant, fantastic dreams in the West of
an ultimate conversion to Christianity and an alliance against
the fanatic Moslems who, entrenched along the eastern and
southern shores of the Mediterranean, had for seven centuries
denied Christendom access to the Orient.

．　　．　　．　　．　　．　　．　　．　　．

This world of medieval Europe was far more harsh and cruel
than ours, though some cruelties and strains familiar to us were
unknown to it. In many ways it resembled that of feudal and
tribal Africa before the coming of modern civilisation. Men had
their hands, tongues and ears cut off in the processes of justice;
dungeons were dreadful places in which prisoners putrefied
or starved to death in pools of their own ordure; felons caught
in the act were beheaded on the spot, even though in England
a royal officer had to be present to make this lawful. Such
punishments were matched by the brutality of the populace;
in a single year Edward I had to pardon four hundred and fifty
murderers.[2] Yet on the borders of that violent world were the
marches of Heaven and Hell; it was this that made it for its
people exciting and significant. Most of the things they created

[1] In the middle of the century, after terrible hardships, two Franciscans
had reached the camp of the Mongol Great Khan at Karakorum, and in the
year before Edward's accession the seventeen-year-old Marco Polo set out
with his Venetian uncle and father on his famous journey to China and the
court of Kubla Khan, ruler at that time of most of Asia.

[2] *Salzman*, 215. Dr. Coulton reckoned that there were between ten and
twenty times more murders per head of the population than today. *Medieval
Panorama*, 371, 377-8.

and lived by have been destroyed. Yet some remain, a towering testimony to the strength and permanence of the greatest of their beliefs: their intense and abiding sense of the grandeur and immutability of God. To this day their vast cathedrals, made with puny tools and child's machinery, tower above the cities of modern Britain; there is nothing in Salisbury that compares with the tower and spire that Richard of Farleigh built in the time of the Black Death or with the choir and nave that his predecessors raised a century before. There was just as much folly, credulity, greed and vain glory in the age of faith as in any other; the sons of men do not change. It was a good time to live in for the fortunate so long as their fortunes lasted, and a bad time for those whom fortune passed by. Yet, when all is said that can be charged against them, there was something that the Middle Ages had that we have not. Stand beneath the west front of Wells or Lincoln or under the tower of Ely and think. And then look at the piled boxes of concrete, glass and girder erected today with one object and one alone, and that the most transient of objects, and think again.

III

My debt to those whose research and scholarship have made this book possible is incalculable. As in my earlier volume I am standing on the shoulders of giants. I am not a medievalist, but have been fortunate that in the present century England has been, and still is, so rich in great medieval historians. What appears in these pages is only a minute fraction of all they have made known by their researches and writings. In this it resembles the small portion of an iceberg which appears above the water-line that conceals the infinitely greater mass supporting it.

I am also deeply in the debt of friends; of those who so generously made copies and transcriptions of the countless extracts that had to be assembled from hundreds of different sources before the work of writing could be begun; of my secretary and publishers; of Wyndham Ketton-Cremer and Bertram Brooke who read the proofs of the book and Lord Goddard who corrected its legal passages. Above all I owe an obligation I can never repay to two who repeatedly criticized it at every stage of its writing and re-writing; to Milton Waldman and to Dr. A. R. Myers to whom in gratitude this book is dedicated.

Wincombe
August 1963

Chapter One

SO GREAT A KING

His broad, clear brow in sunlight glow'd;
On burnish'd hooves his war-horse trod;
From underneath his helmet flow'd
His coal-black curls as on he rode,
*   As he rode down to Camelot . . .*
And from his blazon'd baldraik slung
A mighty silver bugle hung,
And as he rode his armour rung,
*   Beside remote Shalott.*

All in the blue unclouded weather,
Thick-jewelled shone the saddle-leather,
The helmet and the helmet feather
Burn'd like one burning flame together.

TENNYSON

The laws of England . . . since they have been approved by the consent of those
who use them, and have been confirmed by the oath of kings . . . cannot be changed
or destroyed without the common consent of all those by whose counsel and
consent they were promulgated.

BRACTON

ON AUGUST 2nd, 1274, Edward of Westminster the crusader landed at Dover. He had been absent from England for more than four years and for nearly half that time had been its king. Before him lay a rich, well-ordered realm, over which his Angevin race had reigned for a hundred and twenty years and his Norman and English ancestors for four centuries.

Like all the rustic lands of Europe it was studded with castles, churches and monasteries, and small walled cities. They symbolised the might of the three classes who ruled Christendom—two of them ancient and firmly established, the other still new and unsure of itself. Earls, barons and knights, bishops, abbots and monks were the leading pieces on the chessboard of power with, far below them in status but less so in wealth, the merchant-

burgesses of the half-rustic trading-towns that had grown up in the
shadow of the castles and abbeys. From the castles the king's constables and sheriffs, and the greater feudal lords who were his
tenants-in-chief, enforced the peace and common law which his
judges administered. With their mounds and inner keeps, their
wide green baileys and encircling curtain-walls, their moats, portcullises and barbicans, wells,[1] granaries and dungeons, they represented an ultimate force that could only be challenged by an army
with catapults and battering-rams and the ability to maintain
itself for long periods in the field. Within their draughty, rush-
strewn halls and tiny stone-walled closets lived in mingled
splendour and discomfort the French-speaking lords whose trained
battle-horses, forged armour and hereditary skill in fighting from
the saddle had given them two centuries of unchallenged ascendancy over the native population.

Yet in England that ascendancy could only be exercised in
association with the Crown—a power which no earl or baron
could safely defy. Three civil wars fought in a century by
Edward's father, grandfather and great-grandfather had proved
it. It was this as much as the sea that set his realm apart from the
continental kingdoms. Since his victory over de Montfort in his
father's day most of the chief castles in England had been held by
the Crown or its dependents. Above him, as he landed, towered
the island's royal gateway, Dover, with its twenty-foot thick walls,
double lines of ramparts and vast rectangular keep built by the
first Plantagenet. Forty miles to the north-east along the road to
the capital lay Rochester, guarding the passage of the Medway,
where sixty years before the rebel barons had barred King John's
march after Magna Carta. Above London's Roman wall rose the
Conqueror's Tower, dominating the capital's thatched and red-
tiled roofs and tidal river. A further thirty miles up the Thames,
guarding another crossing, was Windsor, where Edward's children
had been born and beneath whose strong-walled hill stretched the
water-meadows of Runnymede. Still higher up, where the river
emerged from the Midland forests, lay Wallingford and Oxford.
Beyond them, ruling the sheep-walks and chalk downs of the

[1] At Dover Harold's well is 350 feet deep, lined with stone to a depth of
172 feet. From it and a tank adjoining, water was piped to every part of the
castle. Sidney Toy, *The Castles of Great Britain*, 100.

west, lay other royal keeps—Newbury in the Kennet valley, Marlborough and Old Sarum on the Plain, the fortresses of the Severn valley and Forest of Dean. And along the Channel shore, protecting its anchorages and estuaries, stood Pevensey, Porchester, Carisbrooke and Corfe, and, in the remote Celtic southwest, Exeter, Tremarton and Restormel.

North of London were the fastnesses that ensured the king's peace in the East Anglian and Midland shires—the wooded clay lands of the old Anglo-Saxon settlements and the heart of the country's agricultural wealth. Colchester and Framlingham, Berkhamsted and Northampton, Lincoln and Newark had all played, and might play again, a decisive part in defending the realm from rebellion and invasion. Their control by the Crown was the sanction on which the supremacy of the law depended. No one knew this better than the king; he ruled by writ of castle. Eight years before, the possession of Kenilworth had enabled his father's foes to prolong their rebellion for many months. Since then, though the local lord's tower rising above the trees was everywhere part of the landscape, the standards that flew over the masterpieces of the military engineer's art were those of the king and his kinsmen.

Only in the far north and west on the marches of Scotland and Wales were there castles of the first rank in the hands of the feudal nobles. There lay the strongholds of the prince bishop of Durham and the warrior lords of the Pennine dales, of the great Marchers of Clun and Oswestry, Brecon, Radnor and Montgomery, Glamorgan and palatine Pembrokeshire. The Clares at Cardiff and Caerphilly and the Mortimers at Wigmore and Ludlow could still withstand a royal army behind their walls. But in the face of the Welsh tribesmen, king and noble alike had an interest that needed no unifying sanction. They had to stand together or see their estates engulfed in pillage and massacre.

Yet England was not ruled by keep and lance alone. Like all the kingdoms of the Roman West she was swayed by an ideal whose symbol was the Cross, whose expression was justice and whose repository was the Church. An international organisation, administering under its own laws nearly a third of the kingdom's wealth, owed prior allegiance, not to king or feudal lord, but to Christ's vice-regent, the pope and bishop of Rome. In the governance of Edward's kingdom as of every western State there was a duality. Men were the subjects of their king and the lieges or serfs of their feudal lord, but they were all alike members of Holy Church and as such owed obedience to its prelates and ministers. The great stone monasteries and cathedrals whose towers and spires broke every horizon, and the parish churches whose roofs and belfries rose above village and town, were as much features of the landscape as the cities and castles of the king and his magnates. Before the homecoming crusader lay the shrines of the saints and martyrs he had so often visited with his father and to which, like every prince of the age, he delighted to offer relics and vessels of gold and silver, gems, statues and crucifixes, splendid embroideries. Under the Syrian skies his mind must often have turned to the grey stones and cool green garths, the ever-sounding bells and chanting, the stately monastic routine that surrounded the resting-places of St. Thomas at Canterbury, St. Edmund the king at Bury, and that other English king at Westminster after whom he had been named.

There were nearly seven hundred monasteries, canonries and nunneries in England and more canonries, friaries, colleges and chantries almost than anyone could count. Some of the monasteries were so rich that their abbots sat among the earls and barons in the king's council and parliaments. So did the secular bishops whose huge cathedral churches[1] rivalled the monastic cathedrals of their fellow prelates of the cloister. Crowning Edward's vision of England were Canterbury, Westminster and St. Albans; the island monasteries of Ely and Peterborough, Croyland and Thorney rising above the interminable fen skyline; the great East Anglian abbeys of Norwich, Colchester and Bury, within whose liberties, marked by four crosses, even the king's judges dared not come; and, at the far sandy end of Norfolk close to the North Sea, the shrine of Our Lady of Walsingham, whose celebrated reproduction of the holy family's house at Nazareth— built after a vision vouchsafed to a rich Saxon widow—drew pilgrims from every part of Britain. In the south-west lay Romsey and Sherborne; the convent beside the Avon at Ames-

[1]London, York, Lincoln, Salisbury, Exeter, Lichfield, Hereford, Wells, Chichester. The monastic cathedrals were Canterbury, Durham, Winchester, Norwich, Ely, Worcester, Rochester and Carlisle.

bury where Edward's mother, Queen Eleanor, had taken the veil,
and the hill-top abbey of Shaftesbury with the shrine of Edward
the Martyr and its long succession of aristocratic abbesses.
Beyond, where the foliage of Penselwood forest sank into the
Somerset marshes, rose the splendid new cathedral of Wells. Its
great western facade glittered with painted and gilded statues of
English kings and martyrs, and in the neighbouring vale of Avalon
beneath its haunted tor stood the holiest place in England
—Glastonbury. Here, according to legend, Joseph of Arimathea
had planted his staff of flowering thorn and the first seeds of
British Christianity. Here Arthur, it was said, had held his court
of paladins, and here, eighty years earlier, the monks had discovered his bones and those of his queen Guinevere. Further
north lay Malmesbury and Gloucestershire's four mitred houses[1]
and, beyond, the golden abbeys of the Severn valley and Welsh
border. And in the far north, beyond Lincoln and Kirkstead and
the forest abbeys of Rufford and Newstead, towered the lonely
Cistercian houses of the Yorkshire wolds—Rievaulx, Byland,
Fountains, Jervaulx—the minsters of York and Ripon and the
great Benedictine shrine of St. Cuthbert at Durham.

. . . .

It had been to fight for the creed these dear places enshrined,
and to guard and redeem the soil of "Outremer" or the Holy Land
that, four years before, Edward had followed his saintly uncle,
Louis of France, on crusade and, commanding the army of
Christendom, won by his victory over the Saracens at Haifa
a ten years' truce and respite for the Christian fortresses of
Syria. At the time of his return he was thirty-five years old.
Towering above his fellows[2] he was a magnificent-looking creature
—the beau-ideal of a medieval king. Longshanks, men called him
from his height in the stirrups. His feats at jousting, hunting,
falcony and wrestling were famed throughout Christendom; the

[1]Cirencester, Winchcombe, Gloucester and Tewkesbury. No other county
in England had so many. It also boasted the magnificent new foundation of
Hailes with its philtre of Christ's blood brought from Germany by Edward's
uncle, the King of the Romans.

[2] When in 1774 his tomb was opened by the Society of Antiquaries he was
found to measure 6 ft. 2 ins.—at least half a foot taller than the average man
of his time. Ackermann's *History of Westminster Abbey*. II. 207.

story of his youthful duel with the outlaw chief, Adam of Gurdon, in the wooded defile of Alton[1] and his victory in the great tournament or "little war" of Chalons on his way home from the crusade, were national legends. On his horse "Ferraunt, black as raven," he could leap, it was said, any chain.

The flaxen Plantagenet hair of his youth had now darkened and his skin was bronzed by eastern suns. His distinguishing attributes were perfect health and the vitality and good humour that sprang from it. " Never," a contemporary wrote, " was the king sad at heart save at the death of those dear to him." The round head under the crisp, curling locks, the large expressive eyes —dove-like when pleased but fierce as a lion's in anger—the small commanding mouth with brilliant teeth that remained unimpaired in age, the wide brow and beaked nose all spoke of fitness for rule in a warlike society. Upright, broad-shouldered, with lithe, sinewy limbs, Edward was everything the men of his time admired.

From his father he had inherited a drooping left eyelid and a slight stammer. When aroused, the impediment vanished and he spoke with an intensity that could move men to tears. A warrior from boyhood he had read few books but he wrote French and, rather less certainly, Latin, and corresponded with his Castilian brother-in-law in Spanish. His mastery of legal argument was as formidable as his prowess in arms, and he excelled at chess—the subtle oriental game brought back by the crusaders that well expressed the complexities of medieval kingship. He loved music and versification, splendid buildings and sculpture, paintings and illuminated manuscripts. His household accounts contain references to the English trumpeters, Welsh harpers and German fiddlers whom he kept in his service. It was a Welsh harper who was his companion when he was attacked by an assassin at Acre, and in his last campaign against Bruce he halted, a dying man, by the roadside to hear the Scots women singing the songs of their native land.

For all his imperious will, there was something noble and magnanimous about him; a great soul, *"animus magnificus,"* he

---

[1] A famous place for robbers on the road to Winchester.
   " Yea through the pass of Alton
   Poverty might pass without peril of robbing."
                                    Piers Plowman.

seemed to the Somerset born Nicholas Trevet who served him. In youth he had been reproached for his violent, overbearing temper —the legacy of his Angevin race derived, men said, from the devil. Yet he was easily appeased and swift to forgive; "a king terrible to all the sons of pride, but gentle to the meek of the earth." "Pardon," he once exclaimed, "why I will do that for a dog if he seeks my grace!" His harsh early experience of civil war had taught him to understand the point of view of others and to be patient and conciliatory. He knew, as his father had never known, how to work with men of different opinions and make them his friends.

In these gentler traits, so at variance with his fierce Plantagenet temper, Edward was helped by an ideal marriage. Eleanor of Castile was the great-granddaughter of the Castilian king who had led the crusading armies of northern Spain in the great victory of Las Navas de Tolosa. Her father had won Cordova, Seville and Cadiz for the Cross; her half-brother, Alfonso the Learned—a patron of Moorish and Jewish culture—was one of the first astronomers and mathematicians of the age. A crusader's daughter, Eleanor had accompanied her husband to Acre where her devoted care had saved his life when he was struck by an assassin's poisoned dagger.[1] Edward's love for this noble, stately woman, with her long, dark Spanish tresses and calm Gothic features that still look down from her carved head in the Abbey, was the guiding star of his life. Betrothed at Burgos when he was a youth of fifteen and she a child, she brought to his side the placid virtues he lacked and, so long as she lived, made them his. Their court was an orderly and decorous place, free from vice and grossness.

Beneath his majestic exterior Edward had the rough, hearty camp-manners of the first Plantagenet. Like him he preferred to dress in simple soldier fashion and to wear the "roba" and furred "collobium" of the *plebs*, the modest knightly and merchant class, "caring nothing for strange dyes, purple or welk-red." "What," he once asked, "could I do more in royal robes than in this plain gabardine?" He loved to be hail-fellow-well-met with his soldiers and humbler subjects, to jest with them and share their rough

[1] The Arabic word assassin is said to have been introduced into the English language through this incident.

humours. He once gave his horse to a washerwoman on condition that she won a race on it.

Hard-working and orderly, this French-speaking king with an English name brought to his task habits of the strictest business. He disliked every form of waste and extravagance. In his father's feckless embarrassed court he had seen the humiliations that attended a prince who failed to make both ends meet, and he was resolved to avoid his example. While on crusade he had been forced to add to the Crown's indebtedness by borrowing heavily from the Italian bankers who, by circumventing the Christian ban on usury, had succeeded the Jews as the moneylenders of Christendom. Once back in England he applied himself with all the vigour of his clear, categorical mind to enforcing his financial rights and making every rent, revenue and service go as far as possible. For he knew that only by rigid economy could he ensure, without sacrificing his freedom, the fine things that every thirteenth-century ruler needed to enhance his prestige and dignity: castles, horses and armour, embroideries and tapestries, jewels and sculpture, feasts and tournaments, splendid benefactions to shrines, churches and monasteries.

Edward's first care was to be master in his own house. Having no fear of his feudal nobles, he did not try, like his father and grandfather, to set himself apart from them. Most of them were men of his own age or younger, who had fought with him against the Welsh, rallied to his side against de Montfort, or campaigned under him in Syria. Four of the eleven earls were of royal blood: his brother, Edmund "Crouchback," of Lancaster, Derby and Leicester; his cousin, Edmund of Cornwall—son of the late King of the Romans—who ruled the south-west from Exeter to Land's End; his brother-in-law John of Brittany earl of Richmond; and his uncle William de Valence earl of Pembroke. Of the other seven only John de Warenne earl of Surrey and Sussex, was his senior. A few years before Warenne had figured in a dramatic episode in which his followers had attacked and wounded a rival litigant in Westminster Hall. Edward had pursued him to his castle at Reigate, threatened him with a siege and forced him to submit to his father's justices who had fined him for his offence against the royal peace the enormous sum of 10,000 marks or well over a quarter of a million in modern money. Yet, though a hot-

tempered man and a stickler for his feudal rights, Warenne bore
no malice against his new sovereign by whose side he had fought
at Lewes and Evesham. Bound, too, to Edward by close friendship
were William Beauchamp earl of Warwick, young Henry de Lacy
earl of Lincoln and Salisbury, and Robert de Vere earl of Oxford,
whose estates, under England's paradoxical feudal system, lay
mainly in Essex. The most powerful of all was the thirty-year-old
Marcher, Gilbert de Clare earl of Gloucester, who owed the
Crown the service of more than 450 knights—a landowner in
twenty-two English counties and " lord of the land of Morgan "
in South Wales, where he kept his own chancery, great seal, courts,
chancellor and sheriffs. This arrogant, impulsive, red-headed
warrior—a great-grandson of William the Marshal—had twice
changed sides during the civil wars. But Edward could usually
manage him, and he had been the first to proclaim his accession
and to greet him on his return to his kingdom.

Only two of the earls, Roger Bigod of Norfolk, the hereditary
marshal, and Humphrey de Bohun of Hereford, the constable—
both young—stood outside the royal circle. They alone represented the older baronial tradition of independence and, on
occasion, opposition to the Crown. The other earldoms were
either extinct or in abeyance. The greatest of all, Chester, had
been in royal hands since the death of the last of Hugh of
Avranches' line in 1237.[1]

Edward felt at home in these magnates' company. He had
grown up, jousted, fought and worshipped with them. For all his
business-like habits he was essentially the product of a chivalric,
aristocratic society. He was at his happiest in the tournament-
field, hunting in the forests or hawking along the rivers, feasting
in castle hall or hunting-lodge while minstrels and harpers
recalled the romantic tales of battle, courtesy and love which, with
returning civilisation, had become the staple fare of the rough
feudal warriors who had conquered the old Roman or romance
lands of western Europe. He loved the legends of King Arthur
and his knights which the French-speaking aristocracy of France
and England had adapted from the Celtic bards of Brittany, Wales
and Cornwall, and thought of himself as a descendant of Brutus of

---

[1] There had been seven of the line in all—a fierce brood, from whom, in
the female line, most of Cheshire's ancient families are descended.

Troy[1] and other fabulous paladins of antiquity. Both he and Gilbert of Gloucester established Round Tables on the Arthurian pattern at which, on special occasions, the lords of the realm, ruddy and bruised from the tournament-lists, sat at feast as equals in the fashion of fabled Camelot.

Yet though Edward lived on terms of social equality with his earls, stayed in their castles and shared their lives of jousting, hunting and feasting, he had no favourites among them. His intimates were men of birth but not the highest power whom he had learnt to trust during his perilous youth. They were drawn from every land from the Rhine to the Irish Channel: men like the Burgundian, Otto de Granson, Geoffrey de Genevill of Vaucouleurs in Champagne, Robert Tybetot or Tiptoft who had held Bristol for him in the civil war and witnessed his will at Acre; Thomas de Clare—brother of the Earl of Gloucester—who had ridden with him on his flight from Hereford before the battle of Evesham. He employed them as seneschals and constables of his wide English, French, Welsh and Irish dominions, on judicial commissions and on embassies to foreign courts. In council chamber or in the field one or more of them was always with him.

Even more important in his management of his kingdom were the great clerks or clerics of the State departments that had grown out of the royal *familia* or household. To the Chancery and Exchequer of the Anglo-Saxons and Normans had been added under the Angevins the Wardrobe, which in a century had evolved from a royal clothing-closet into a major financial and administrative office. Though some of their officials, especially in the older Exchequer, were nominees of hereditary office - holders whose functions they performed by deputy, public responsibility and the traditions and semi-collegiate life of their departments tended to unite them in devotion to the Crown. As in the past, most of them were Church-trained, but they were also drawn from the rising, vigorous class of knights of the shire. With their ink and green-wax, tallies, rolls and treasure-chests, their chambers at Westminster and wagons for following a perambulating court, they constituted a professional civil service that could function even when the king

---

[1] Who according to the popular historian and romancer, Geoffrey of Monmouth, had given his name to Britain "in the days of the prophets Eli and Samuel."

was absent or the country divided by civil war. Their expertise and public spirit made them a stabilising force in England's life and a permanent repository of her administrative tradition—stronger at that time than that of any other western land.

Edward was well served by this national bureaucracy. Shrewder and bolder than his father, he was neither misled by his servants nor afraid to trust them. At their head was the chancellor, Robert Burnell, who since the days of Evesham had been his secretary. This genial clerical administrator and lawyer—the younger son of a Shropshire knight—was a worldling who became, through his master's favour, a great landowner.[1] Yet of his devotion to the royal interests there was never any doubt. His bluff and not always over-scrupulous method of doing business admirably suited the purposes of a prince of chivalry who had learnt that the first need of kingship was a tight hold on the purse-strings. On his return to his kingdom Edward made him chancellor in place of his father's old adviser, William de Merton. He also conferred on him the bishopric of Bath and Wells, and, but for the pope's opposition, would have made him primate.

The most richly rewarded of the king's clerks, Burnell was only one among many. Like his great-grandfather, Edward maintained a whole school of officials dependent on his favour and obedient to his will. He used them as keepers and controllers, treasurers and secretaries, judges, assessors and commissioners and day-by-day counsellors in the steadily expanding business of a State whose northern march was the Cheviots and whose southern the Pyrenees. The names of more than a hundred of them are recorded in the official rolls: men like John Kirkby archdeacon of Coventry, the indispensable Chancery official and Exchequer baron whom he made his treasurer; William of Louth, cofferer and, later, keeper of the Wardrobe who had won his confidence in his youth when, as his father's deputy, he was governing Gascony; Antony Bek, his secretary; John Langton who succeeded Burnell as chancellor and his still more important namesake, Walter, a poor Wardrobe clerk who became treasurer

[1] At the time of his death in 1292 he held 82 manors in 19 counties, as well as a large number of ecclesiastical preferments. He built the episcopal hall at Wells with its battlemented wall, towers and gatehouse, and entertained both king and parliament in his Shropshire home, Acton Burnell, which he raised with timber from the royal forests.

and chief adviser of Edward's latter years. Several of these administrative familiars had begun their careers as graduates of the young universities of Oxford and Cambridge;[1] many were students of the civil and canon law; nearly all were clerks in Holy Orders. Yet their interests were secular rather than ecclesiastical, and they became the forerunners of a new class and profession. In disputes between Church and Caesar they took the part of Caesar, for it was he who paid them and gave them preferment. Several were rewarded with bishoprics, including Burnell, Kirby, both Langtons, and the two noble brothers Bek of Eresby, one of whom Thomas, received the see of St. David's and the other, Antony, the great palatine bishopric of Durham. It was the latter, a notable warrior and hunter, who built Eltham palace and restored the hall of Durham castle, where, though himself an austere liver, he maintained a magnificence strangely at variance with the simplicity of the see's founder, St. Cuthbert.

.   .   .   .

Of the same type, half cleric, half layman, were the lawyers who served the king as judges or pleaded as *servientes* or serjeants-at-law in his courts. With the growing complexity of legal procedure the royal justices had become something more than temporary deputies delegated from baronial or episcopal bench to try particular cases in their sovereign's place. They were now permanent royal officials. They still performed a multitude of services, hearing assizes, delivering county gaols on eyre, acting as commissioners of array, supervising the collection of subsidies and sitting on the royal Council. Some were in clerical orders like John le Breton or Britton, the bishop of Hereford who is believed to have written a condensation of Bracton's treatise on the laws of England, the much-used Martin of Littleburn, and the Norfolk-born Ralph de Hengham, canon of St. Paul's and arch-deacon of Worcester, who began his legal career as a clerk to one of Henry III's judges and rose to be chief justice both of the Common Pleas and King's Bench, leaving behind two important tracts on procedure and pleadings. Others were laymen, county knights and local notables or legal specialists who had practised as lawyers in the courts before they became judges. Of

[1] In the next reign one of them, Adam of Brome, became the founder and first provost of Oriel College.

the fifteen members of the King's Bench appointed during the reign seven were clerics and eight laymen, including both the chief justices of Edward's latter years.

Below them were the attorneys, who represented clients, prosecuting their writs and entering their pleas by proxy, and the skilled narrators, pleaders and serjeants-at-law—successors of the professional champions of trial by battle—who composed the pleas and narrated and argued the pleadings, so saving suitors from the verbal slips which could so easily unsuit the untrained.[1] For the rules of an action-at-law before the king's judges were most strictly enforced; the very language, a kind of bastard French interlaced with Latin and designed to ensure the utmost precision of meaning, was almost impossible for a layman to understand. At the time of Edward's accession the common law—the law of the royal courts common to the whole country—had been evolving for more than a century. Based in theory on an immemorial *corpus* of unwritten customary and local law on which it had been superimposed but which it was slowly superseding, it had been the creation of the first Plantagenet and the professional judges to whom he and his sons and grandson had entrusted their judicial powers. Their object had been to enforce the king's peace after anarchy and civil war and bring under the jurisdiction of the central royal courts all major crimes, violence and dispossessions of freehold land—the form of wealth on which the political organization of a feudal State depended. They had done so by making representatives of every county, hundred and township responsible for presenting suspected felons at periodic assizes before the royal justices, and by offering those dispossessed of their land remedies more certain, just and expeditious than could be obtained in the local courts of shire and hundred or in the private jurisdictions of feudal society. By substituting for the older methods of trial by battle, ordeal by fire and water and compurgation or "wager-of-law" the

[1] " Pleaders are serjeants wise in the law of the realm who serve the commonalty of the people, stating and defending for hire actions in court for those who have need of them. . . . When the declaration of the plaintiff has been heard, the adversary is concerned to make a good answer. And because folk do not generally know all the 'exceptions' which can be used by way of answer, pleaders are necessary who know how to set forth causes and to defend them according to the rules of law and the usage of the realm." *The Mirror of Justices*, (Selden Society) VII. 47, 90.

more rational and humane device of an inquest of neighbours under the supervision of professional jurists, they had found a new way of discovering the truth. The whole practice of law had been revolutionised by the king's power of ordering his sheriffs to summon juries of local freeholders to answer in their corporate capacity questions of right or fact put to them in a court of law by his judges.

In England, alone among the feudal kingdoms of Europe, it had become an established principle that no man need answer for his freehold without a royal writ and that no suit affecting a free tenure could be begun without one. Any freeholder who had been dispossessed or kept out of his land could buy from the Chancery clerks a writ addressed to the sheriff of his county directing him to summon the dispossessor to answer the plaintiff in an action-at-law. The number of such writs— *novel disseisin, mort d'ancestor*,[1] *darrein presentment*—had been steadily increasing in order to cover all conceivable causes of action over freehold-land. Yet, unless the one appropriate to the wrong complained of was chosen, the action was bound to fail. The forms of pleading and procedure of the particular remedy sought had to be meticulously observed by both plaintiff and defendant, even to the minutest details of wording. How essential this was can be seen from the defence made on behalf of the Bishop of Lichfield to a writ of *darrein presentment* affecting the right of presentation to a Cheshire church. Because the words "who is dead" had been omitted, the plaintiff would have been unsuited had not "a certain John of Wettenhall, who was sitting among the doomsmen of the county court, made answer that the Earl Ranulf "—the owner of the Palatine court before it had lapsed to the Crown—"delivered to them a register of original writs, and in that register that word neither was nor is, nor up till now has it been used in the county court of Cheshire, wherefore, if that word had been put in the writ, by that addition the writ must according to the custom of Chester be quashed."[2]

The Exchequer enforced the king's fiscal rights, the King's Bench tried pleas of the Crown and heard appeals from other

---

[1] See *Makers of the Realm*, 188-95, 312-16.
[2] *Select Cases in the Court of King's Bench under Edward I*. Vol. i. 43. (Selden Society, 1936.)

courts, the Common Pleas sat permanently in Westminster Hall to adjudicate, with the help of local juries from the shires, disputes between the owners of freehold land. Below them, though also subject to the king's overriding writ, were local courts of an older kind, administering the customary law of the neighbourhood. The most important of these was the shire court, presided over by the sheriff, which met once a month in the south and every six weeks in the wilder north. Held in some spot hallowed by immemorial usage and dating back to days when the shire had been almost an independent province, it was attended, not only by litigants, but by all, either in person or deputy who, holding freehold land in the county, owed it suit. For it was the basis of Anglo-Saxon and Danish law—long adopted by England's French-speaking kings and lords—that all freemen should by "witness of the shire" share responsibility for the administration of justice in the county where their lands lay.

At this great concourse of neighbours and men of substance, held either in the open air or, more often now, in a fine new hall of plea, like the one Edward's cousin, Edmund of Cornwall, had built for his duchy at Lostwithiel, royal ordinances and statutes were proclaimed, officers and bailiffs were sworn in, inquests were held into disputed rights, and presentments made on matters relating to pleas of the Crown for trial by the itinerant justices. The suitors of the court also elected those required by the king to "bear the record of the shire" in the courts at Westminster or in parliament, and the coroners whose business it was to keep a record, independently of the sheriff, of all crimes and incidents affecting the Crown's rights and to hold inquests on sudden deaths, shipwrecks and discoveries of treasure trove. Sentence of outlawry was passed, too, in the shire court on anyone who had failed on four successive occasions to answer a summons to a criminal charge. Though its work was being increasingly superseded by the king's courts, it still had cognizance of cases in which the accused elected to be tried by the older methods of compurgation. Sometimes, too, when neither party wanted a jury, a plea of land would remain in the county court to be resolved by two professional champions contending all day with minute horn-tipped pickaxes until one or other yielded as "craven."[1]

[1] *Cam.*

Below the sheriff's court was the hundred court, held once every three weeks by a bailiff to whom the sheriff or the owner of the hundred jurisdiction had sublet its profits, but who, as a royal officer, was responsible to the sheriff or, in a few special cases, directly to the Crown. It was usually held in the open air, the suitors of the court—freehold tenants of certain parcels of land —sitting on benches round a table occupied by the bailiff and his clerk. Its business was of a petty kind—claims for services arising out of land, detention of chattels and small debts, complaints about the maiming of beasts, and personal assaults and brawls not amounting to felony. More serious offences like theft or murder were automatically transferred by sheriff or coroner to the king's courts. The most common plea was trespass—an elastic offence which it was often easier to bring home to a neighbour in the hundred court than to compass in the rigid limits of a Chancery writ. It is doubtful, for instance, if Robert Kite could have obtained redress at Westminster from Stephen Winter whom he sued in the court of Milton hundred for coming into his garden, breaking down his hedges and carrying off his roses "against the peace," or John Malkin secure the justice he sought against Maud atte Hythe and her son for beating his pig and egging on their dogs till they bit off its tail.[1] There were other pleas, like verbal contracts and slander, for which the royal courts offered as yet no remedy, but under which rustic litigants could sue one another in those of the hundred.

Twice a year, at Easter and Michaelmas, the sheriff visited every hundred in the shire—some of the larger counties like Norfolk and Yorkshire had as many as a dozen—to hold a tourn or criminal court. Everyone who held freehold land in the hundred, except—after the Statute of Marlborough—magnates, lay and clerical, had to attend or be fined for absence. In the tourn or "law-hundred," peasants of villein blood as well as freemen, played an essential part. For by Anglo-Saxon law every layman without land that could be forfeited for felony had to belong to a tithing—a group of neighbours responsible for one another's good conduct. Before the sheriff's annual view of frankpledge, as it was called, the bailiff checked the tithing lists of every village in his hundred, crossing out the names

[1] *Idem*, 181-2.

of those who had died since the last view and swearing in any lad
who had reached the age of twelve and so become, in the eyes of
the law, a responsible citizen. With his hand on the Bible the boy
had to promise to keep the peace and be neither a thief nor helper
of thieves. " I will be a lawful man," he swore, " and bear loyalty
to our lord the king and his heirs, and I will be justiciable to my
chief tithing man, so help me God and the saints." Then he and
every other villager paid his tithing-penny, which constituted,
with the various court fees and assized rents, the profits of the
hundred jurisdiction. In southern and western counties this often
belonged to some private person to whose ancestor or predecessor
in title it had been granted by the Crown.[1]

At the sheriff's tourn every township or village was represented by its reeve and four men who answered for any omission in
its public duty, such as failing to keep the watch and ward or to
raise the hue and cry when a crime was committed or to arrest
suspicious persons who "walked by night and slept by day,"
and for offences like ploughing up the king's highway or execut-
ing a thief caught red-handed without first securing the official
witness of bailiff or coroner. They were responsible, too, for
the township's payment of any fines imposed on it for breaches
of the royal regulations for baking of bread and brewing of ale.
They also had to report to twelve freeholders called the jury of
presentment all crimes that had been committed within the township. The town dealt, too, with nuisances like washing clothes in
wells and polluting drinking-water. The more serious offences
were presented by the jury to the royal justices for trial on their
next visit. When this happened the humble representatives of
the village found themselves answering questions put to them
under oath by the king's chief legal officers. For in thirteenth-
century England the chain of law stretched from monarch to
peasant.

Like his famous great-grandfather, Henry II, Edward took his
legal responsibilities very seriously. As a boy he had studied law

[1] At the time of Edward I's accession there were 270 royal hundreds and
358 in private hands. In Sussex, a woodland county, every hundred was held
privately. Quite a number of hundreds were held by more than one lord.
The average revenue of a hundred and its court was about £5 a year—say,
between £250 and £300 p.a. in our money.

under his tutor, Hugh Giffard, one of his father's justices. On his leisurely journey home from the crusade he had been given a degree by the law school of Padua and had brought back from Italy to advise him—probably on matters of ecclesiastical or canon law—a distinguished jurist, Francis of Accursi, appointing him to his council and settling him with a pension at Oxford. The hero of his youth had been his uncle, the great French king, St. Louis, who had loved to sit under the oak at Vincennes dispensing justice to his subjects. His ideal and that of his age was of a delicately poised balance between conflicting claims, one in which every man's right to his own could be ascertained, weighed and enforced. For to the medieval mind, haunted by the memory of dark centuries of barbarism, justice was the highest earthly good, a mirror of the heavenly state in an imperfect world. It had nothing to do with equality, a conception then unknown. Its purport was expressed by a phrase in a legal treatise called *The Mirror of Justices*, written, it is believed, by a London fishmonger who held the office of city chamberlain: that "folk should keep themselves from sin and live in quiet and receive right according to fixed usage and holy judgments." The goal was a society in which every man was offered by law the peaceful means of enjoying his particular rights. Law was the mechanism provided by the Crown for ensuring him that opportunity.

Edward's sense of justice was of a narrower, less altruistic nature than that of St. Louis. He was resolved to do justice to all, but he did not except himself. Lordship to him was the first prerequisite of a Christian society—a right to be exercised justly and firmly and, wherever possible, extended. His duty to God and his people, he conceived, was to hold fast to his royal prerogative. He was always appealing to his coronation oath against suggestions that he should part with any of his rights, real or imagined; he held them, he said, in trust for his people. While endorsing the dictum of his subject, Andrew Horn, that "the law requires that one should use judgment, not force," he saw it as a contest, like the older trial-by-battle, in which a man was justified in using every technical nicety. He observed the full rigour of the game. Of its hard, intricate rules he showed himself as much a master as of war, seizing every advantage and never yielding a point without the clearest necessity. The courts were his, established to ensure not only that justice was done but that the kingdom was firmly ruled. Though after one or two early attempts he refrained from insisting that his judges should act as his advocates in disputes with the subject, he kept special pleaders or serjeants to "sue for the king," like William of Gisleham and Gilbert of Thornton, the earliest-known king's serjeant. They and his attorney, Richard de Bretteville—forerunner of our attorney-general—were kept incessantly busy. "O Lord," wrote a clerk at the foot of a membrane recording that officer's many activities, "have pity on Bretteville!"

Yet Edward abided by his own rules. He used them to further his kingly ends but respected them. His favourite motto was, "Keep troth." And though he was a strict upholder of his legal rights, his judges were not afraid to take their stand on his law rather than on his will. There is a story of Chief Justice Hengham turning in the royal presence on two of his fellow judges who had upheld a royal writ of summons which failed to specify the charges against the defendant—an incorrigibly litigious countess. "The law wills," he declared, " that no-one be taken by surprise in the king's court. If you had your way this lady would answer in court for what she has not been warned to answer by writ. Therefore, she shall be warned by writ of the articles of which she is to answer, and this is the law of the land." Though thwarted, the king accepted his chief justice's objection, adding characteristically, " I have nothing to do with your disputations but, by God's blood, you shall give me a good writ before you arise hence! "[1]

It was this growing acceptance of law by king and subject that made justice a more realisable commodity in England than in any other land. If Edward was resolved to have his way, he was equally resolved to find a legal justification for it. The pursuit of naked force—the barbarian's creed that might is right—made no appeal to him. Justice rested on Christianity; it was because Christianity discountenanced violence and slaughter that the fierce warriors of the Frankish West had come to substitute law, with its bloodless processes of formal verbal combat, for the arbitrament of sword and lance. By the standards of his

---

[1] *Select Cases in the Court of King's Bench under Edward I.* Vol. I. LXX (Selden Society, 1936).

age Edward was a true Christian king—a just and chivalrous paladin of Christendom.

．　　．　　．　　．　　．　　．　　．　　．

It was in pursuit of justice for all and his royal rights for himself that Edward after his return to his kingdom set about its reform. On Sunday August 19th, 1274, he was crowned in his father's abbey church of Westminster with all the traditional rites of Christian kingship, swearing to "confirm and observe the laws of ancient times granted by just and devout kings unto the English nation" and to minister equity and justice. Next day, while the conduit in Cheapside ran with wine and largesse was thrown about the tapestried streets, he received the homage of the magnates of the realm, including the King of the Scots. As each great feudatory rode into Westminster Hall to kneel before him, his attendant knights, clattering after, dismounted and let their horses loose for the scrambling populace to seize. In the coronation feast, which continued for fifteen days, four hundred oxen and as many sheep, pigs and wild boars, and twenty thousand fowls were consumed.

Long before the junketing was over the king had left the capital. He spent a month at Windsor, making a progress through Surrey, and, after a further visit to London in October, set out to travel the more populous parts of his kingdom. With him went his court of King's Bench, with its judges, pleaders and attorneys, to hear local pleas and petitions. That winter he visited Northampton, where he stayed for ten days, Luton, Fotheringay, Warwick, Silverstone and Brackley. Thence by way of Woodstock, Marlborough, Amesbury and Clarendon he travelled to Ringwood and Beaulieu, and back again by Caversham and Aylesbury to Bury St Edmunds and Lavenham. Wherever he stopped, the pleas of his court were proclaimed. Everywhere he seems to have been received with enthusiasm and to have been touched by his people's welcome.

He was moved, too, by their complaints. During his absence there had been much misgovernment. In a medieval State without a police force and with only a minute administrative service, and where most villages were several days' journey from the capital and in winter almost completely cut off from it, corruption was inevitable. It was one thing for the king in his council chamber to issue commands and ordinances, another to get them obeyed, even by his own officials. The most he could offer was remedial justice for abuses committed. And there had been many. Sheriffs and their officers had taken bribes, been extortionate, refused writs or sold them at inordinate prices. And though the country had settled down after the long years of baronial strife, it had done so only superficially. During the civil war much property had been violently seized; "when King Henry was in prison," it was said, "inasmuch as the governor and head of the law was in prison, the law itself was in prison,"[1] The protection which the first Plantagenet had given to the possessor of land against the disseisor had been twisted by the ingenuity of pleaders to allow the tortuous title of the man who had taken forcible possession to mature into a legal one. There was widespread resentment between lord and tenant, neighbour and neighbour—a state of affairs which invited disorder in an age when men were swift to anger and violence.

For, from the industrious, frugal peasant to the extravagant, indebted baron, everyone seemed to be trying to enlarge his rights at someone else's expense and to take advantage of the complexities of the law to do so. If, thanks to England's strong line of kings, the law and its subtle complex processes had taken the place of the sword, it was being employed with the ruthlessness of the battlefield. There was so much uncertainty about it and so many ways in which a man might employ unscrupulous means to obtain his ends that something approaching legal civil war existed. Lords were enclosing commons and commoners casting down enclosures at night, tenants taking advantage of their lords' absence or

[1] Y.B., 20 and 21 Edward I. (Rolls Series) 193. cit. *Plucknett*, 74. "Master William and Master Richard le Clifford and Geoffrey of Mores . . . in the time of the lord King Henry, father of the present lord king . . . whilst the aforesaid plea was pending . . . came in hostile fashion, armed and with barded horses and a multitude of armed men, on horse as well as on foot, crossbowmen and archers, to the dwelling of that William Gereberd in Thorley and break in the doors and gates of his dwellings there and assaulted him and made him fly within his chamber there and afterwards dragged the same William Gereberd out of his chamber and ejected him from his dwellings and his land there and took and carried away (and still do keep) the horses and other goods and chattels of that William Gereberd found there." *Select Cases in the Court of King's Bench under Edward I.* Vol. 1. 10. (Selden Society.)

infancy to cheat them of dues and services, lords using the weapon
of distraint against tenants' beasts and chattels, often to their ruin,
without resort to judgment. Thus it was reported by the jurors of
the Wiltshire hundred of Chalke to the king's justices in eyre that
" Richard earl of Gloucester, father of the earl that now is"—
tenant-in-chief of the Crown for the manor and chase of Cranborne
—had afforested to himself the woods of Chettle and Fernditch
and the whole country towards the borough of Shaftesbury as far
as the Nadder head by placing there seven foresters who attached
men for Vert and Venison, forced them to attend his court at
Cranborne and, imprisoning them until they paid fines, grievously
amerced them. They alleged that he took cheminage—the
customary toll for a way through the forest—from country folk
carrying wood and market-produce to Salisbury and that his
foresters, "exceeding the metes and bounds of the chase by ten
miles to the great damage of the whole county," had seized a
cartload of thorns belonging to the parson of Bishopstone and a
sumpter horse with a boy going towards the water in that place,
"maliciously charging the parson with stealing the thorns in the
forest until he gave them half a mark for the sake of peace."[1] On
another occasion, it was said, they had pounced on a man in the
village of Martin and, charging him with felony, carried him to
Cranborne "and there hung him without any reason at their will,"
afterwards confiscating his neighbours' horses, oxen and silver on
the ground that they had belonged to their victim.

Soon after the start of his progress the king appointed commissioners to enquire into the abuses and usurpations, particularly
of royal rights and revenues, that had occurred during his absence.
Throughout the winter they toured the shires, taking evidence on
oath from the juries of every hundred, borough and liberty. Their
returns, made on slips of parchment from the seals of the testi-
fying jurymen which hung from them, became known as the
"ragman" rolls. They provided a wealth of information about
the malpractices of landowners, sheriffs and bailiffs and about
encroachments on Crown rights. They listed the king's possessions,

[1] *A Chronicle of Cranborne* (1841), 154-61. The Earl of Gloucester contended
in his reply "that his ancestors had used all the aforesaid liberties from the time
whereof the memory of man is not to the contrary and neither he nor his
ancestors made any usurpation upon our lord the king." *Idem,* 168.

the number of his manors, the value of his "farms" and rentals, the private "liberties" or jurisdictions that hindered impartial justice or impugned his power, the cheats of officials who had taken bribes to conceal felonies, oppressed the innocent or embezzled public funds.

In no less than nineteen counties Edward found it necessary to dismiss the sheriff for extortion or abuse of the law. A sheriff's power to act unjustly was very great. Appointed by the Exchequer and answerable to it for all taxes and fines levied in the shire, he was also responsible for all suspects and prisoners and had to produce them in the courts on pain of heavy penalties. His castle in the county town, where he kept his office and records, contained, as well as a range of wooden cages in the courtyard for malefactors, a particularly deep and noisome dungeon into which he could cast anyone he chose. The processes of law against a royal official were slow, costly and uncertain, and, unless the king himself intervened, an action for unlawful imprisonment was seldom successful. By threatening to use his powers it was easy for a sheriff to make well-to-do persons pay large sums to avoid incarceration under conditions that all too often imperilled life and health. Among the charges brought against sheriffs and their underlings in the course of that winter's inquest were that they indicted men more than once for the same offence, that they took bribes to release them and then re-arrested them, that they delayed and suppressed writs, so denying litigants justice, and that they connived at felonies and let men charged with them roam the country committing more. They were accused, too, of keeping "approvers"—rogues who lived by denouncing accomplices or alleged accomplices—to "appeal" honest men so that they could extract fines from them. In some cases they were even accused of using torture.

Charges of the same kind were brought against the bailiffs and bedels of the hundreds who, living on the fees of jurisdiction and far from central control, were under heavy temptation to use the law to feather their nests. One of their favourite devices was to impanel a jury and then take bribes, described as fines, for letting their victims off a long and costly journey. With their white wands—symbols of royal office—and pompous, bullying ways, many bailiffs were real tyrants, like the one who "caused all the free tenants of Hatfield, to the number of eighty or more, to come before the king's justices at Waltham Cross to make a recognition in a certain assize and, when they were come, said to them, ' Now you know what the bailiffs of the lord king can do,' and that was all he did.''[1]

Carried out in the depth of winter and completed in the almost incredible space of just over four months, the " Ragman quest " was an administrative miracle, second only in English medieval annals to the Conqueror's Domesday survey. From the bundles of rolls with their pendant seals, still preserved in the Record Office, we can watch the commissioners at their work as, in groups of two and three, they travelled the country, taking down, first in one place, then in another, the testimony of the jurors. " We have commanded our sheriffs," ran the words of their commission, " to bring before you, at the fixed days and places which you shall signify to them, such and so many good and lawful men of their bailiwick that by them the truth of the above-mentioned matters may be well ascertained."[2] Taken down by their clerks and then read back to them before they affixed their seals, the jurors' replies provided the king with an accurate account of the working of the kingdom's legal machinery on the ground level and of the abuses and usurpations of jurisdiction that he would have to deal with to restore it to justice and order. Attempts were made in some cases to impede the commissioners' work by intimidating the jurors. One Yorkshire bailiff, Gilbert of Clifton of the wapentake of Staincliff, went so far as to threaten the commissioners themselves. " He used," they reported, " the most shameful words against William de Chatterton, justice assigned to take these inquests, because he told the jurors of the countryside fearlessly to tell the whole truth . . . Gilbert said that if he had been present when this announcement was made he would have pulled the justice down by his legs and that before a year was up the justice would be wishing that he had lost all his lands rather than be a commissioner."[3]

In the spring of 1275, as soon as the reports of the commissioners had been digested by his chancery officials and judges, the king called his first parliament or grand council and court of the nation. It was a judicial eyre or inquest of the whole realm.

[1] *Cam*, 160.   [2] *Idem*, 36.   [3] *Cam*, 43.

To it he summoned the magnates, lay and ecclesiastical—the earls
and barons, archbishops, bishops and abbots who were his tenants-
in-chief—and, through the sheriffs, four elected and representative
knights, "discreet in law", from the shire-court of every county and
four merchants or burgesses from the burgemote or borough court
of every important town. They were to come without arms and
under the king's peace and protection and to be immune from
the ordinary processes of law while the court of parliament was in
session. "And because elections ought to be free," ran the writ
to the sheriffs, "the king commandeth upon great forfeiture that
no man by force of arms nor by malice nor menacing shall disturb
or hinder any to make free election."[1]

For, having learnt through his inquest what was wrong with
his realm, Edward had resolved on great changes. For these he
needed his subjects' witness and approval. A king who was content
to leave ancient customs untouched did not need his people's co-
operation. One who was passionate for real justice and reform
could not do without it. For in the Middle Ages there were laws
that were seen, not as something that could be changed at will,
but as sacred and immutable. However unquestioned a king's
right to act, ordain and give judgment, the ancient law of the kingdom was a public inheritance which it was his duty to preserve and
enforce.[2] His ordinances might have the force of law but only while
he himself could impose them. After his death, if they were contrary to custom, they could be ignored or forgotten. Even in
England, where the power of the locality had been far more
strictly subordinated to the State than on the continent, the king's
word was law only in his lifetime. And though, on Henry III's
death, for almost the first time the succession itself had been

[1] "If we seek the origins of the parliamentary privileges of later times, like
freedom of speech and freedom from arrest, it is in the peculiar sanctities
accruing to a court of law that we must look for them." G. O. Sayles, *The
Medieval Foundations of England*, 453.

[2] "The only law recognized in the Middle Ages, Professor Kern has shown,
was the 'good old law,' the inherited custom of the people which was above
and superior to the State and which none, not even the king, could alter. The
business of the State was to maintain and to preserve the law, to restore it where
it had fallen into disuse, and even to 'declare' it; but none, save God, could
'make' the law, which had existed from time immemorial, concrete, all-
embracing and beyond human touch." G. Barraclough, "Law and Legislation
in Medieval England." *Law Quarterly Review*, LVI 76.

unchallenged, the conception of an unbroken sovereignty vested in an undying Crown had still to take root in men's minds.

If society was to progress, some authority, associated with the Crown yet more enduring than the king's life, was needed to register the nation's acceptance of major changes in the law. In an age of isolated and intensely localised communities the tendency of custom to ossify was a mountain in the path of a reforming king. "*Nolumus leges Angliae mutare*"—"we do not wish the laws of England to be changed"—Henry III's barons had replied at the Council of Merton to Bishop Grosseteste's plea for a more humane attitude towards children born out of wedlock.

Edward could not overcome this traditional inertia merely by devising ingenious legal writs and directives to his judges as his great-grandfather, Henry II, had done. With his strong practical sense he was seeking for some other instrument to achieve his end. He found it in the sessions or parliaments of the *magnum consilium* —that supreme national council and court of royal officials and judges, feudal tenants-in-chief, prelates, and magnates which his father, under pressure, had from time to time summoned for "colloquy and treating" and to which, in his latter years, he had increasingly referred the vast mass of petitions and appeals to the Crown from those unable to obtain justice from the regular courts.[1] Derived from the formal meetings of the Anglo-Norman *curia regis* at the Easter, Ascension and Christmas feasts, and possibly from the still earlier Anglo-Saxon witans or moots of "wise men," these gatherings had come to be called parliaments after similar national courts held by Edward's uncle, Louis of France. But in England, though closely linked to the more regular courts of law to which they often referred petitions, these parliaments had become occasions of a rather more representative and general kind than their counterparts in other European kingdoms. This had arisen partly from Henry III's financial extravagance and his consequent need of consultation with his subjects, and partly from the growing delegation of royal authority to local worthies like the knights of the shire, who from time to time had been summoned to his parliaments to

---

[1] " In the king's great council in parliament," wrote the author of the law book, *Fleta*, "judicial doubts are determined, new remedies are prescribed for new injuries and justice is done to everyone according to his deserts." *Powicke*, 356.

answer questions on oath. During the civil war, when de Montfort was ruling England in the king's name, he had even called to one parliament representatives of the merchant-communities or chartered towns. And after Evesham, Edward, as his father's lieutenant, had continued to summon both knights and burgesses whenever the support of the local communities seemed for any particular reason advisable.

An ordinance or judgment given by the king under seal and publicly witnessed and approved in a parliament of the nation's supreme council and court could thus have a sanction more than ordinarily binding. And in the course of Henry's last years, when first the reforming barons and then the young Edward were ruling the country, royal enactments issued during parliaments had been employed, not merely to define and adjudicate law at the highest level, but—in order to meet the needs of an evolving society—to reform it. In the Provisions of Oxford in 1258 the barons had laid it down that parliaments should "have the power of advising the king in good faith concerning the government of the kingdom . . . in order to amend and redress everything that they shall consider in need of amendment and redress." Under stress of bankruptcy and civil war a great council of the nation had assumed a partial legislative authority. The attempt of de Montfort to make such authority independent of the Crown had failed, as, in an intensely monarchical age and country, it was bound to fail. But in the Statute of Marlborough of 1267 Edward, in his father's name, had legalised the baronial reforms of the past decade by a solemn public act of the Crown, issued in parliament under the great seal and enrolled in writing as a permanent national record. By this means he had given to the royal decisions that resolved the controversies of the civil war an enduring validity which, despite, his unchallenged right to declare law by ordinance, they could have had in no other way. Henceforward such statutes, as they became called, were cited in pleadings in the royal courts. Like Magna Carta they became part of the continuing life of the nation.

When after their slow, laborious and reluctantly undertaken journeys the magnates and the representatives of the local communities met the king and his council at Westminster, they were presented with a document drafted by the royal judges in French

—the speech of their knightly class—and read to them by Chancellor Burnell. Its object was to define, clarify and, where found necessary, reform the law. " Because," ran its preamble, " our lord the king hath great desire to redress the state of the realm in such things as require amendment for the common profit of holy Church and the realm, and because the state of holy Church hath been evil kept and the people otherwise entreated as they ought to be, and the peace less kept and the laws less used and offenders less punished than they ought to be, the king hath ordained by his council and the assent of the archbishops, bishops, earls, baróns and all the commonalty of the realm the acts under-written."

The fifty-one clauses of this royal enactment in parliament covered a vast field. They set forth, in easy, almost conversational, speech, a legal remedy for many of the worst abuses the king's commissioners had noted in their winter's visitation. Like the Great Charter, they began by redressing the wrongs of the Church —the common concern of all. They forbade lords to abuse monastic hospitality, to quarter themselves and their servants on religious houses without invitation, to commandeer their corn or fish or course in their parks and ponds uninvited. They forbade the various forms of venality and oppression practised by sheriffs, unjust judges and bailiffs, and imposed penalties on keepers of gaols who made an excessive profit out of prisoners. They restricted, too, the rights of foreshore lords to cargoes wrecked on their property[1]—a sign of the growing importance of commerce— and abolished it altogether in the case of ships cast-away on Crown land.

Even more important were the provisions for safeguarding the rights of owners and occupiers of land—the chief source of liveli-hood of most Englishmen. No less than thirteen clauses dealt with the remedies open to freemen in disputes about real property. The statute offered redress to those who during the civil wars had been dispossessed by force and stopped tortuous seisin from ripening into legal right. It took a firm line—at the instance of the judges of assize, who were always being confronted by the

[1] Nothing was henceforward to be forfeit if a single man, dog, or cat escaped, though this had the unintended effect of sometimes causing wreckers to murder the survivors.

problem—with those who claimed dues and services to which they had no right and then impounded beasts and produce until their victims, faced with ruin, conceded their unjust demands.[1] Sheriffs were directed, even within private liberties, to execute writs of *replevin*—the legal reply to forcible distraint by which impounded chattels were returned pending court proceedings. They were authorised to call out the countryside against those who ignored such writs and batter down their pounds and castles.

The effect of this great reforming and defining code was to preserve, though at the cost of much change in customary law, the rights of both lords and tenants against those who had taken advantage of troubled times to seize an unfair advantage. Infant wards were protected against alienating guardians, and reasonable tariffs were fixed for feudal aids and fines at every level of the landed hierarchy. Thus the "aid" which could be levied from a knight's fee when the lord knighted his eldest son or married off his eldest daughter was fixed at twenty shillings—the equivalent of rather over fifty pounds in modern money. Such aids, it was laid down, were only to be taken when the lord's son had reached the age of fifteen or his daughter that of seven. The ideal of securing, by a specific remedy, the just rights of every man according to his status ran through the whole enactment. Drafted by practising judges, it reflected the preference, already marked in English law, for concrete remedies over abstract principles.

Copies of the act—the "new provisions and statutes . . . ordained for the good of the realm and relief of the people" and known as the first Statute of Westminster—were sent, like Magna Carta, to the sheriffs. It was proclaimed in the courts of every county, hundred, city, borough and market-town, and all judges, sheriffs and bailiffs were ordered to enforce it.[2] It was the first of a long succession of parliamentary statutes enacted by Edward

---

[1] "A wicked ribald of a bailiff or hayward may cause a poor man by coercion to do a suit, and thereby he stays charged with it for all time through that false possession." Bereford, C. J. *Year Books of Edward II*. (Selden Society) IV 161. cit. *Plucknett*, 52.

[2] That they did so with zeal is suggested by a later remark of Judge Mallory, " I saw a case before Sir John de Vaux in the eyre of Leicester where one R., because his rent was in arrears, took the farmer's corn and carried it away and disposed of it at his pleasure; *and he was hanged for it*." *Y.B.* 33-35. *Edward I* (Rolls Series) 503. cit. *Plucknett*, 58.

in council in the presence of the assembled magnates and representatives of the nation. Such statutes both changed and became
part of the common and customary law. They derived their
authority, not from verbally transmitted custom, but from a
written document issued under royal seal and preserved in the
rolls or records of parliament, which, before the end of his reign,
Edward ordered to be kept at Westminster. Copied by pleaders
into handbooks that became part of every practising lawyer's
equipment, they were cited in the courts and accepted as evidence
of law by the judges.

．　　．　　．　　．　　．　　．　　．　　．

The parliament which Edward held at Westminster in the
spring of 1275 was not only summoned to endorse his proposals
for reforming legal procedure. It was called to approve a new
kind of tax. With changes in the landed and economic structure of
the country most of the older feudal sources of revenue were drying
up, and the king, to support the growing charges of State, needed
new and extraordinary aids. He had returned from the crusade
heavily in debt and had had to borrow at high interest rates from
the merchant-bankers of the North Italian cities. It was partly his
wish to pay these off that had caused him to investigate so closely
the rights and claims of the Crown against its tenants and debtors.

Sixty years earlier the Great Charter had forbidden the levying
of additional aids on land save by consent of the assembled
magnates—a thing always hard to obtain. In its search for new
revenue the Crown had been forced to turn increasingly to the
taxation of moveable or personal wealth, which had not the same
sanctity as land in the eyes of the ruling class. Its chief possessors
in a taxable form were the merchants of the chartered towns and
the flock-masters and wool-exporters who during the past century
had been creating a new form of national wealth out of the
downland sheep.

Legally the king was not obliged to consult merchants before
taxing their goods. From time immemorial feudal lords had
tallaged the towns and markets of their demesnes; it was for this
that they had founded them. But times had changed, and
merchants were no longer the helpless, half-emancipated villeins
they had been before the crusades had introduced the feudal

nobility of Europe to the luxuries of the East. Ever since they had been driven into the rebel ranks by his father's insistence on his right to tax them at will, Edward had wooed the traders of the capital and south-eastern ports, seeing with his realist's eye the power that came from control of cash and credit. He saw that a freely-negotiated agreement under which the merchant community assumed corporate responsibility for its own taxes was likely to prove more valuable to the Crown and, in the elementary administrative conditions of the time, provide a more readily accessible revenue than any forced imposition.

It was this that had caused him to follow de Montfort's revolutionary precedent and to summon to his first parliament the proctors or representatives of all the cities, boroughs and "towns of merchants." He did not call upon them to take part in the discussions about his new land-laws—matters far above them— but to grant him a share of the increased trading profits which his strong rule and wise foreign policy were helping to create. He had already benefited them by negotiating, at their request shortly before his return to England, a treaty with an old crusading comrade, Count Guy de Dampierre, to end a three years' embargo on the export of wool to Flanders—the principal market for the country's fleeces. In return for a standing duty of half a mark, or 6s. 8d., on every sack of wool exported and 13s. 4d. on every last of leather, he now offered to surrender the royal prerogative of imposing direct taxation on merchandise. This gesture was as far-reaching as it was imaginative and generous. The "Great and Ancient Custom," as it became called, "granted at the instance of the merchants" and approved by the magnates, was the beginning of the Crown's permanent customs revenue.[1] Henceforth it took its place, with the older "tonnage" on wine-imports, beside the feudal aids and dues, the rents of the royal estates—now much reduced by the grants of earlier sovereigns—the sheriff's "farms" of the shires and the proceeds of justice.

Later that year, in a second parliament summoned to Westminster at Michaelmas and attended by knights-of-the-shire as well as by the feudal and ecclesiastical magnates, the king obtained an "aid" of a fifteenth on all other lay moveables. The idea of representation, of the right of those present to bind the absent and

[1] *Power, 75-7. A sack was 26 stone.*

of the majority to outvote the minority—a conception which the friars in their provincial assemblies had first introduced into England[1]—was beginning to take shape under Edward's guidance. In his writs to the sheriffs he insisted that elected knights and burgesses should have full power of attorney to bind their fellows to "whatever should be ordained by common counsel." Needing his subjects' co-operation, he pursued every means of obtaining it. It may have been as part of a bargain between him and his lords that he issued the statute *Districciones Scaccarii*, limiting his own royal right of distress against Crown tenants. He also, in 1276, confirmed Magna Carta and his father's Forest Charter. Another royal concession granted at this time was the Statute of Jewry, an ordinance to prevent Jews from obtaining more than half a debtor's goods and chattels and limiting the rate of interest they could charge to 42 per cent for three years only. The hated instruments by which Edward's forebears obtained for the Exchequer the forbidden proceeds of usury, they were no longer indispensable, for the Crown which had hitherto protected them found it could obtain credit more readily from the merchant-bankers of Italy. To please an orthodox, insular people these once privileged and now helpless aliens were ordered to wear a distinguishing badge of yellow on their garments.

The records of Edward's movements show how much of his time was devoted to national discussions between his counsellors and the nation's representatives. Throughout May and June 1275 he was at the palace of Westminster—their usual meeting-place— and again during October and November. Part of May and June and October and November of the following year were spent in the same way. Between these meetings of his parliaments, save for an occasional sojourn at Windsor, the court travelled incessantly. It had to, both to feed itself from the royal manors and to bring the king's law and peace into every part of a country in which a journey from the capital could take a week and even longer. Thame, Oxford and Woodstock, Kenilworth, Lichfield, Burton-on-Trent, Macclesfield, Chester and Birkenhead and many smaller places were all visited in the autumn of 1275.

[1] Enunciated seventeen years earlier in the baronial Provisions of Oxford —" If they cannot all be present, that shall be firm and established which the majority of them shall enact." *Annals of Burton*. cit. *Wilkinson*, I, 171.

That winter the king stayed at Reading and Marlborough, at Wimborne, Gillingham, Wareham and Canford, at the new Cistercian abbey of Bindon among the Frome water meadows, at Southampton, Winchester and in the Cotswolds. In the following winter he toured the whole of southern England from Yarmouth to Worcester.[1] The discomfort of such itineraries, traversing miry grass tracks and unbridged rivers, must have been very great. They were diversified by hunting and hawking—at Inglewood in the Staffordshire forest Edward and his companions once killed two hundred stags in a day—and by visits to monasteries, shrines and places of pilgrimage. There were also occasional tournaments, like the splendid one held in Cheapside in the autumn of 1276 for such an assemblage of young lords and knights as had never before been seen in England. But the real object of all the king's journeys was the ordering and unification of his realm. As through mud, fog, rain and snow this tall royal man rode about his business with his following of knights and men-at-arms, judges and clerks, ushers and pages, armourers, saddlers, smiths and tent-makers, he bore the image of kingship to a scattered, bucolic people.

[1] H. Gough, *Itinerary of Edward I. passim*

Chapter Two

THE CONQUEST OF WALES

An old and haughty nation proud in arms.

MILTON

Ruin seize thee, ruthless king!
Confusion on thy banners wait,
Though fanned by conquest's crimson wing
They mock the air with idle state.

GRAY

THOUGH an England growing increasingly conscious of nationhood responded to the unifying rule of her king, there were parts of the British island—Albion as it was still sometimes called—to which he could give neither lordship nor law. The right of his ancestors, heirs of the ancient Roman *imperium* claimed by the House of Wessex, to a vague suzerainty over all the princes of Britain had never been either implemented or seriously challenged. It was a claim to which Edward attached far more importance than any of his immediate predecessors, for, half Frenchman though he was, he had never shared his father's and grandfather's dream of regaining their Norman and Angevin patrimony in northern France. The only empire outside Gascony he coveted was that of the British isles. Nursed in the new courtly fashion of regarding the legendary King Arthur and his knights as the champions of Britain and the Roman west, he thought of himself as their heir.

This, however, was not how the real descendants of Arthur's warriors saw him. To the Celts of western Britain Edward was merely the king of the Saxons who had slaughtered and dispossessed their forebears. He was the lord, too, of the armoured horsemen from France who, by giving the Saxons discipline and leadership, had raised so many outposts of England in the valleys

54

of central and southern Wales. To the fierce tribesmen beyond the Severn the stone castles of the Normans seemed as alien as the Roman legionary camps a thousand years before.

Yet there was still little counterpart among them to the sense of common interest that the Norman and Plantagenet kings had awoken in their English subjects. In the Welsh and Scottish highlands loyalty still centred on the tribe and tribal leader. In lowland Scotland an Anglo-Norman baronage and institutions and a dynasty of able princes had created during the past century and a half the embryo of a feudal kingdom in the unconquered peninsula of moor and mountain that the Romans called Caledonia. Descended from the pirate princes who had invaded its western shores from Ireland and from the aboriginal Pictish chieftains and the petty Celtic "kings" of the once Romanised south-west, Kenneth MacAlpin's royal successors had given their Scots' name to the whole of this wild, mist-soaked region and, with it, the beginning of a unity it had never known before. In the last fifty years they had forced even the Viking settlers of Sutherland and the Western Isles to acknowledge their sovereignty. Under their strong rule there had been an almost complete cessation of the age-long raids on the farms and monasteries of northern England. Their policy had been to be friends with their Plantagenet kinsmen and titular suzerains, and, under cover of their benevolent neutrality, to impose order on the turbulent tribal lands and islands of the far north and west.

In Wales there was nothing comparable. Divided by tribal and dynastic feuds and far nearer to the heart of Anglo-Norman military power, its southern and central valleys had been colonised soon after the Conquest by Norman adventurers who had brought them under the overlordship, though not the direct rule, of the kings of England. From the upper reaches of the Severn in Powys to the ancient princedoms of Deheubarth and Morgannwy along the Bristol Channel, the great Marcher lords—Clares and Mortimers, Bohuns and Fitzalans, Braoses, Chaworths and Giffards—ruled by the sword, the king's licence and their own wits. With their castles and mounted knights they dominated the lowlands, leaving the bare uplands of sheep and heather to the migrant Celtic tribes.

For their penetration was only valley deep. Around them the

ancient life of mountain Cambria, half warlike, half pastoral, continued as it had done for a thousand years. Its people lived by raiding and keeping cattle and sheep. In the summer they fed them on the hill-pastures or *hafod*, in the winter on the lowlands or *hendre*. So wild was that sparsely populated countryside that two pilgrimages to St. David's were regarded by pious Englishmen as the equal in peril and hardship of one to Jerusalem. Its few minute towns huddled for safety around the Marchers' castles; its very churches, squat and austere and crowning tactical vantage-points, resembled forts. Its petty "kings" or brenins spent their summer days in forays on one another and the Saxon, and their winters listening to their bards and harpers nostalgically commemorating the glories of old. With their golden torques and white horses, their bands of young warriors and proud memories of ancient victory, they deemed it "ignoble to die in bed and an honour to fall on the field of battle." Every spring at their summons the clansmen set out along the cloud-hidden tracks above the valleys to burst in a torrent on some rival tribe or distant English farm. It had been so as long as men could remember.

So long as the Marchers left them to follow this immemorial life the Welsh, preoccupied with tribal and family feuds, made no attempt to combine against them. Only when England was weakly ruled or divided was any concerted effort made to drive the Anglo-Norman lords from the country. For outside their castle walls the latter seldom had the last word against the tribesmen of the hills. Plunder and arson could always be met by plunder and arson, and, as their farms offered tempting booty, their presence was accepted philosophically. In their turn the Marchers entered into the life of Wales.[1] They married the native chieftains' daughters and took sides in their tribal affrays. The inconveniences of cattle-raiding and seasonal war were offset for them by the freedom they enjoyed, unknown in judge-ridden England, of living under their own, not the king's law. Theirs was an independence that existed nowhere else in Edward's island dominion. No writ ran in their liberties and no appeal lay from their courts. They raised private armies to harry their neighbours' lands and guard their own, as in the far days before the Planta-

---

[1] A few of the smaller lords of the March were themselves Welsh, like the Owens of Pool whose name is commemorated in Welshpool.

genet kings had made feudalism a political strait-jacket for their warlike class.

In the same way the Cistercian monks and their monasteries became naturalised and part of the life of Wales. Their solitude and austerity recalled to a primitive hill people the lives of their own early evangelists. To the Welsh of the thirteenth century, it has been said, the Cistercian abbot seemed a St. David or a St. Te⸱ ⸱ returned to earth.[1] Despite their Latin affiliations and the splendid churches with which the Marchers and the Welsh princes endowed them, the Cistercian houses in Wales were far more Celtic than Roman, conforming increasingly to a traditional pattern in which personal piety and local loyalty counted for more than dogma and the regimentation of an international order. What little Lantwit and Llancarfan had been in the centuries of Rome's eclipse, Margam and Tintern, Abbey Dore and Strata Florida, Aberconway and Valle Crucis became in the new age of Rome's ecclesiastical grandeur. Yet though they formed centres of native learning and culture, they also helped to link Wales to the wider world of Christendom and to render possible her peaceful co-existence with her more orderly neighbour.

Had it not been for one circumstance the absorption of Wales into the Anglo-Norman kingdom might have come about in the end with as little violence as that of Celtic Cornwall. In 1237, with the death of its last hereditary earl, there lapsed to the Crown the greatest of all the Marcher lordships—the palatine earldom of Chester whose historic function it was to guard the Cheshire and Shropshire plains from the raiders of the Snowdon hills. Though still a separate legal entity, its administration passed into the hands of royal officials whose orderly minds, schooled in the discipline of the Exchequer and common law, abhorred such time-hallowed Cymric customs as cattle-raiding and the blood-feud. And confronting them across a no-man's land of little wooded hills and uncertain lordships lay the principality of Gwynedd, the last of the old independent "kingdoms" of Wales and the one place where, guarded by the precipices of Snowdonia, there existed a Welsh royal court, a body of Welsh law administered by native judges and a focus for a sentiment that was not only tribal but national.

[1] J. E. Lloyd, *History of Wales to the Edwardian Conquest*, 596.

A century earlier, after the civil wars of Stephen and Matilda, another semi-independent Welsh principality had flourished on the southern shores of Cardigan Bay under Rhys ap Gruffydd, a prince of the ancient house of Tewdwr or Tudor. Having seized Cardigan castle from the Marcher, Roger de Clare, he had kept it by a shrewd mixture of resistance and subservience to Henry II, whose supremacy he acknowledged and whose vice-regent he claimed to be. In 1176, at his Christmas feast, he had held the first recorded *eisteddfod* at which entrants from every part of Wales contested for the bardic crowns of music and poetry.[1]

After his death Rhys's dominion had disintegrated, and the primacy among the native chieftains had passed to the heirs of his northern ally, Owen prince of Gwynedd. The latter's grandson, Llywelyn ap Ioworth—Llywelyn the Great, as the bards called him—took advantage of King John's difficulties to seize Marcher territory on the upper Dee and Severn and later, by siding with his fellow tenants-in-chief in England, to win concessions from the Crown. Three of the clauses of Magna Carta were inserted at his instance. At one time he even captured Shrewsbury and, controlling two-thirds of Wales, aroused a surge of national pride in his countrymen. Yet, conscious of their incorrigible separatism, he made no attempt to flaunt his power, and, dividing his conquests among the lesser chieftains, chose to reign over his fellow Welshmen's hearts rather than their lands. Recognising the strength of a reunited England, he did homage for Gwynedd to the young king, Henry III, and lived in peace for the rest of his days.[2]

It was this prince's grandson, Llywelyn ap Gruffydd, who was now, after many vicissitudes, lord of Gwynedd. He, too, had taken advantage of England's troubles to impose his suzerainty on the Welsh chieftains of Powys, to seize the Mortimer stronghold of Builth on the upper Wye, and to overrun with his fierce spearmen the cantrefs of Perfeddwlad, as the Crown fiefs in the disputed

---

[1] The former was won by a southerner from the land of Morgan, the latter by a northerner from Gwynedd. A. L. Poole, *Domesday Book to Magna Carta*, 294.

[2] He died in 1240 at Aberconway abbey. The village of Beddgelert is said to commemorate the name and grave of a favourite dog who saved his infant son from a wolf.

coastal borderland between Chester and Gwynedd were called. But by allying himself too closely with de Montfort he had united the royal earl of Chester, Prince Edward, with the other Marcher lords. After they had overthrown de Montfort they compelled him to make his peace with King Henry, who in return for homage and military service acknowledged Llywelyn's lordship of Gwynedd and his self-chosen title of prince or pendragon of Wales. Since then the English power had again been rising, and the Marchers, resolved to prevent further raids from the north, had been building new and stronger castles, like the mighty Caerphilly which Gilbert de Clare, the red earl of Gloucester, raised near Cardiff in the closing years of Henry's reign.

The prince of Gwynedd and the English king were thus old rivals. Llywelyn, whose father had been killed trying to escape from the Tower, had tasted triumph over the English when Edward was a raw untried youth. He resented his supremacy and thought of himself as the overlord of all the native chieftains of Wales, whose allegiance he was always trying to deflect to himself. Even more fiercely he resented any legal control from Westminster, Chester or Shrewsbury, not only over his own rocky acres in Snowdonia and Anglesey—where for geographical reasons there had never been any—but over the disputed borderlands in the Marches.

Edward had no wish to deprive Llywelyn of what was lawfully his. But he was a feudal king, brought up in the strict tradition of feudal rights and obligations. He thought of the Prince of Gwynedd as the Welsh equivalent of an Anglo-Norman earl. By ancient prescription and a solemn treaty made after the barons' wars, Llywelyn owed him homage and fealty. And by the English conception of feudalism all lordship under the Crown involved subjection to the Common Law except where a clearly defined liberty had been granted. What stuck in Edward's gullet was the Welsh prince's claim, not merely to a feudal liberty like those of his forebears and the Marchers, but to a completely self-governing lordship like the Scottish kingdom which, under the kings of England's nominal suzerainty, had been independent from time immemorial.

For Llywelyn sought to be ruler, not only of Gwynedd, but of Wales. Nursed in bardic lore and deeply conscious of his countrymen's right to nationhood, he voiced his claim in a letter to Edward in 1273, after the royal authorities had refused to allow him to build an unlicensed castle on land of his own in the Marches near Montgomery. " We are sure," he wrote, " that the writ was not issued with your knowledge and would not have proceeded from the Chancery if you had been in your kingdom, for you know well that the rights of our principality are entirely separate from the rights of your kingdom . . . and . . . that we and our ancestors had the power within our boundaries to build castles and forts and create markets without prohibition by anyone or any announcement of new work. We pray you not to listen to the evil suggestions of those who seek to exasperate your mind against us."[1]

This was the inevitable reaction of a Welsh chieftain to any scheme of centralised control: one that was bound to arouse the challenge of a reforming king with a passion for legal definition and unity. Both men unconsciously wanted something new— Llywelyn the sovereignty of an independent Welsh nation, Edward the adminstration of the country on the closely-knit pattern of England. It was natural that, alarmed by the castles the Marchers were building against his power, Llywelyn should wish to see not only Gwynedd, but his new fiefs in the Marches guarded by castles of his own. Yet it was by now a principle of English law that a vassal's right to erect a military fortress could only be granted by royal licence.

Shortly after Edward's coronation, which Llywelyn failed to attend, a new dispute arose. The latter's brother, David, suspected of a plot to dethrone him, fled to England with the leading Welsh chieftain of the disputed border March of Powys. Instead of handing them back to Llywelyn for punishment, the king's officers, contending that the matter must first be investigated by law, allowed them refuge at Shrewsbury. To Llywelyn this seemed proof that their treachery was being condoned by Edward so that they might plot his death from English soil. Not until they were returned to him, he declared, would he do homage to an overlord who so criminally wronged his own vassal.

According to his lights, the king behaved with considerable restraint. Alone of his tenants-in-chief Llywelyn had failed to do homage on his accession. By feudal law the price of such con-

[1] F. M. Powicke, *Henry III and the Lord Edward*, 622.

tumacy was forfeiture of the fief. After waiting for nearly a year, and after the prince had ignored a further summons to West-minster, Edward invited him to meet him at Chester under safe conduct. To this and the royal journey to the Dee, Llywelyn's only response was to summon a parliament of his own vassals to endorse his refusal. Before he would meet the king, he announced, the latter must surrender as hostages his eldest son, his chancellor Burnell, and the Marcher earl of Gloucester.

Even this demand did not exhaust Edward's patience. He did not wish to incur the cost of a Welsh campaign or to be deflected from his work of reform in England. Yet he was determined to have his relationship with Llywelyn clarified. Three times he summoned him to do homage: at Westminster in November 1275, at Winchester in the New Year of 1276, and again at Westminster that Easter. It was characteristic of his habit of crossing the t's of his legal claims that the proposed meeting-places were no longer on the Welsh border but in the heart of his own realm.

This made Llywelyn still more indignant. Again he refused save on conditions to which no overlord could agree. He appealed to the pope for justice, declaring that the king was harbouring traitors, and, as though to underline the breach between them, sent to France for the daughter of Simon de Montfort, with whom ten years earlier, when they were in arms against the English Crown, he had made a treaty of marriage. This was a double offence against feudal law, for not only was Eleanor de Montfort the daughter of a traitor but, as a member of the royal house, she could not marry without the king's consent. By chance the ship bringing her and her brother to Wales was intercepted in the Bristol Channel and she was taken prisoner. Hence-forward her release became an added condition of Llywelyn's homage.

At the Easter parliament of 1276 the prelates asked if they might make a last appeal to the stubborn Welshman. A trained canonist was sent as envoy, and the summer passed in fruitless negotiation. When a new parliament met in November neither its members nor Edward were in a mood for parleying. They agreed that Llywelyn's contumacy must be punished and that the king should "go upon him as a rebel and disturber of his peace." The Marches were ordered to be put into a state of war and the feudal host summoned to meet at Worcester at midsummer 1277. A warning was also sent to Llywelyn by the Archbishop of Canterbury—metropolitan of the see in which Wales lay[1]—that unless he submitted he would be excommunicated.

Llywelyn treated the excommunication like the king's summonses. The English had never conquered Gwynedd, neither before nor after their subjection to the Normans, and it was natural for its brave, half-barbaric chieftains to regard it as unconquerable. Its ruler was taking no very apparent risk in defying his overlord. He was prince of the mountains and mountain tribes and despised the English host. His forebears had repelled it under Henry Plantagenet and John and, more lately, under the young Edward himself. He had only to withdraw into the trackless hills to ambush the heavily cumbered invaders in some forest defile or, lying concealed amid mists and precipices, starve them and their horses into retreat. Inspired by the prophecies of the legendary Merlin, he even dreamt of driving them out of Britain altogether and ruling, like his Roman ancestors, over the whole island. For the triumphs won by himself and his grandfather during England's baronial wars suggested to his enthusiastic, mercurial mind that what a few thousand Norman knights had done, the Cymri under his leadership might do again.

Though they could never refrain from quarrelling with one another the Welsh tribesmen were magnificent fighters. War was their occupation, and training for it their education. Under their laws six weeks of every summer were spent in maurauding expeditions and their entire youth was ready for instant service at their chieftains' call. Unlike the English, they were not pinned down by husbandry and harvest; they were used to living hard and travelling light. Able to subsist on the whey of their mountain goats and the cheese of their herds, they needed no commissariat. Some of them, in the hills of the south had evolved a new and terrifying weapon: the longbow of Gwent, "made of wild elm, unpolished, rude and uncouth,"[2] whose arrows, fired faster than a crossbow's, could pierce the mailed shirt, breeches and saddle of

---

[1] At the end of the previous century the Norman-Welsh ecclesiastic and topographer, Giraldus Cambrensis, had vainly tried to get the papacy to recognise St. David's as an independent metropolitan see for Wales.

[2] Giraldus, Vol. VI, 54 (Rolls Series) cit. *Morris*, 16.

an armoured knight and pin him to his horse's side. Their sudden, swift-footed charge with javelin, sword and war-horn down glen or hillside could break the nerve of all but the hardiest, and, though quickly discouraged if withstood, their recovery after defeat had again and again turned the tables on their victors. With their bare, sinewy legs, their squat bodies wrapped in scarlet plaids, their capacity to live out of doors in the depth of winter, they seemed as impervious to weather as the rocks among which they lay in ambush. Their trackless terrain and climate of mist, snow and driving rain made any prolonged campaign against them profitless. Punitive expedition after expedition of English knights had advanced up their mountain valleys only to withdraw, famished, horseless and empty-handed, after a few months in that starve-acre land.

> " Grevouse est la guerre et dure à l'endurer
> Quand ailleurs est l'été, en Galles est hiver,"

wrote a disgusted Anglo-Norman poet.

Yet Llywelyn had forgotten that times had changed. Under its new ruler England was no longer divided as in the days of de Montfort. Its whole administrative effort was now directed to bringing Gwynedd to heel; " the sheriff," ran the record of the King's Bench, " did not return any writ because the lord king was with the army in Wales and the justices were not hearing pleas." Nor was Edward the raw youth who had fought against the Welsh twenty years before. He was a commander of international fame who had led the armies of Christendom and rivalled the fame of his great-uncle Coeur-de-Lion. He was no amateur like his dilettante father.

His preparations for the coming campaign left nothing to chance. During the winter and spring of 1277, while the Marchers took the offensive against Llywelyn's supporters in Powysland and Cardiganshire, Edward was gathering, not only the largest English army since the Conquest, but the best-equipped. Agents were sent to France to buy up the huge war-horses[1] that would

---

[1] The *destriers* or trained battle-chargers, able to carry the immense weight of the heaviest armed nobles, cost around £100, or as much in modern purchasing-power as a high-powered limousine. Less powerful horses capable of carrying a less elaborately armoured knight could be obtained for between £15 and £30, while the rouncys of the mounted troopers or men-at-arms cost somewhere between £5 and £10. *Morris*, 82.

be needed as remounts for the cavalry of his household guard, and, with the help of the feudal levy, nearly a thousand heavily armoured horsemen were assembled in support of the Marchers along the Welsh borderland. But most of the troops Edward raised were infantry. They came from Cheshire, Lancashire and Derbyshire, from Rutland, Shropshire and Worcestershire, from Radnor and Brecon. Some were conscripted by commissioners of array from the fyrd or *posse comitatus*, others were volunteers recruited by indenture by veterans who had fought under Edward in the Barons' war or on crusade, like Reginald de Grey and Otto de Granson, the Northumbrian John de Vesci and Robert Tybetot who for his services he later made justiciar of South Wales. In all, over 15,000 foot soldiers were brought together, more than half of them Welsh. To these the king added a small force of professional crossbowmen, mostly Gascons, and a contingent of archers from Macclesfield forest.

It was not an experienced army, for it was twelve years since Evesham, and few young Englishmen outside the March had taken part in a campaign. But their commander was the greatest military organiser of the age, and he knew what was necessary for a campaign in a barren land. He took his time, for success depended on everything being ready and at hand when it was needed. He had set himself to do what no-one had yet succeeded in doing—not merely to drive the Welsh into the mountains, which was comparatively easy, but to hold them there and wear them down till they yielded. Hitherto it had always been the invaders of Snowdonia who had starved and given up the struggle. This time, by organizing a massive commissariat and transport train, Edward meant to see that the defenders did so.

Long before he was ready to strike, two things had become apparent. One was the strength of England under his leadership, the other the divisions of the Welsh. As Pain de Chaworth, lord of Kidwelly and keeper of the royal "munition" in the south-west, moved against Llywelyn's allies in Cardiganshire, and Roger Mortimer and the Marcher earls against his vassals in central Wales, from the head-waters of the Dee to those of Usk, Taff and Towy thousands of Welsh "friendlies" threw in their lot with the English. By the summer of 1277 all Llywelyn's conquests outside

the principality had vanished. Yet the hard core of an unconquered Gwynedd remained.

Early in July the king took command of the host at Worcester.
Attended by the hereditary constable the Earl of Hereford, the
marshal the Earl of Norfolk, and Llywelyn's brother Prince
David, he marched up the Severn and Dee to Cheshire, where, to
invoke a blessing on his campaign, he laid the foundation stone of
a new Cistercian abbey at Vale Royal.[1] His plan was to advance
by stages along the coast from Chester to Flint, Rhuddlan and the
mouth of the Conway, driving clearings through the forests—a
bowshot's width—through which his knights and their war-horses
and baggage could move in safety. At each point at which the
army halted to consolidate before tackling the next stage, he
planned to build a castle on or near the coast. For this he employed—impressing where necessary and paying the customary
rates of wages—thousands of craftsmen and labourers, drawn from
every county of western England, woodmen and carpenters,
masons, carters, charcoal-burners, quarrymen, blacksmiths, lime-
burners, hodmen—guarding them as they worked by relays of
archers.[2]

But the king's trump-card was sea-power. With a fleet to
protect his flank and bring up supplies as he moved along the
coast, he meant to drive a wedge, not into the high mountains,
where the odds would be all in favour of the defenders, but
between the Prince of Gwynedd and the rich isle of Anglesey, the
granary on whose crops he depended to maintain his tribesmen
and their flocks during the winter. Under the terms of their feudal
service the Cinque Ports of Kent and Sussex had to furnish the
Crown in time of war with ships and seamen at their own expense
for fifteen days; by taking their crews into his pay Edward had
secured a weapon that offset all his adversary's geographical
advantages. By the time he was ready to strike, he had assembled
in the Dee twenty-seven ocean-going ships, including one from
Southampton and another from Bordeaux, together with tenders

[1] It was the largest Cistercian church in England, larger even than
Fountains. Scarcely a stone now remains.

[2] Skilled men received 3d. or 4d. a day, and foremen 5d. or 6d.; unskilled
labourers were paid 2d., the same rate as the lowest grade of soldier. Bonuses
for good work—usually at the rate of 1d. a day—were also given to drink the
king's health. *Morris*, 139. 1.

and small craft, under the command of Stephen of Penecester, warden of the Cinque Ports.[1]

The advance from Chester began in the middle of July. The king was everywhere, supervising the transport and organising the relays of soldiers and workmen as they drove steadily forward through the densely wooded hills. By the 26th he was at Flint, where a century before his great-grandfather, Henry II, had been ambushed and had all but lost his life in an attempt to conquer Gwynedd. Three weeks later he moved forward to Rhuddlan, establishing his headquarters there on 20th August. On the 29th he reached the mouth of the Conway at Deganwy.

The moment had now come for which he had been preparing. Using his fleet to ferry an expeditionary force to Anglesey under Lord de Vesci and Otto de Granson, he overran the island just as the harvest was being got in and robbed Llywelyn of his winter's supplies. By doing so he also threatened a further landing in the rear of his impregnable position on the west bank of the Conway at Penmaenmawr. In two months Edward had completely out-manœuvred the Welsh.

Llywelyn saw that he was checkmated. He did not wait for the end, but surrendered at once and threw himself on Edward's mercy. By the treaty of Conway on November 9th, 1277, he restored the four cantrefs of Perfeddwlad, accepted the old frontier of Gwynedd on the Conway and abandoned all claims to suzerainty in the Marches. He also agreed to give hostages for his behaviour, to pay an indemnity for the war and a rent for Anglesey. Next day he swore fealty to the king in his new castle at Rhuddlan.

Edward had won what he sought—the recognition of his lordship and law. He at once remitted the indemnity and rent and within a year released the hostages. At the Christmas feast at Westminster, where Llywelyn again did homage, he gave him the kiss of peace. Ten months later, satisfied by his peaceful conduct, he permitted his marriage to Eleanor de Montfort and himself presided over their wedding feast.

* * * * * * *

[1] An office now held by Sir Winston Churchill. The two chief captains were paid a shilling a day, the forty-eight masters and constables sixpence, and the 608 sailors threepence. *Morris*, 128.

After overcoming one obstacle to his work of unifying his realm, Edward turned to others. As before, he sought support for his measures by taking "counsel and consent" of his chief men. On his way home from Wales he held a parliament at Gloucester to regulate the private franchises and jurisdictions and the encroachments on royal rights revealed by the Ragman inquest. To ensure what its preamble called "the fuller administration of right as the royal office demands," the Statute of Gloucester summoned all franchise-owners to appear before his judges to show by what warrant—*quo warranto*—they held them. Those who failed to appear were to forfeit their jurisdictions to the sheriffs until they had proved their claims. Edward was not seeking to deprive subjects of their legitimate courts and fees, for that would have been to deny the feudal principle in which, like everyone else, he believed. But he was resolved not to tolerate any jurisdiction that was not clearly defined and lawfully constituted and that was not, in the last resort, responsible to the Crown. Thus he asked to know by what right the Bishop of Norwich claimed a market at Crossmarket in Lynn—"which belongs to the king and his Crown and was alienated without licence and will of the king or his predecessor"—and by what warrant he maintained a prison in the same town.

How thorough and wide-ranging were these *quo warranto* inquests—not only into the jurisdictional powers of the great but into the lapse of the smallest royal right—and how deep down they went into the social strata is shown by a writ sent some years later to the constable of Bristol castle. "Whereas," it stated, "there ought to be taken for the king's use, as being the right and ancient prise of the king, two conger eels from every boat bringing fresh eels to the king's town of Bristol to be exposed for sale, eight hake from every boat bringing fresh hake, eight haddocks from every boat bringing fresh haddocks, eight plaice from every boat bringing plaice and four skate from every boat bringing skate, and some forgetful of their fealty to the king have withheld that prise, . . . the lord king has appointed his beloved and faithful Ralph of Hengham"—chief justice of the King's Bench—"and Nicholas of Stapleton to make enquiry by the oath of upright and lawful men of Bristol, by whom the truth of the matter can best be known, what person or persons caused the king to be so deprived, and of how many and of what kind of fish that deprivation consisted, and how and in what way."[1]

These enquiries of the royal judges caused a good deal of heartburning in the next few years. One indignant magnate, Earl de Warenne of Surrey, being asked for his title to some liberty, is said to have produced an old rusty sword in court, crying, "Here is my warrant! My ancestors came with William the Bastard and won their lands with this sword. With this I will defend them against all usurpers!" It was with just this that the king was concerned, for he was not so much trying to deprive overmighty subjects of their jurisdictions but of their claim to hold them by any other warrant than a royal grant. Yet his lawyers pressed their claims too ruthlessly, arguing that time never could run against the Crown and that no usage, however ancient, could avail without a charter. The pages at court, sons of the nobles whose rights were being so closely scrutinised, summed up their fathers' feelings in a song:

> " The king he wants to get our gold,
> The queen would like our lands to hold,
> And the *quo warranto*
> Shall make us all to do." [2]

.   .   .   .

Edward had a tougher nut to crack than the private jurisdictions of his lords. At a time when it was believed that the Church alone stood between mankind and damnation, its rights were the common concern of all. Men felt about it as patriots feel today about their country. During the past century the Church had reached the summit of its might. Claiming a "plenitude of power" over earthly rulers, its popes had broken their rivals, the "Roman" emperors of Germany, leaving them only a shadowy sovereignty over the Teuton north. They had established direct rule over part and a dominating influence over the rest of the Italian peninsula— the richest and most peopled land in Europe. The kingdoms of Aragon, England, Sicily, Portugal, Hungary and Bulgaria were their nominal fiefs and paid them tribute. Even the patriarch of

---

[1] *Select Cases in the Court of King's Bench under Edward I* (Selden Society) 1, 133-4.
[2] Cit. *Cam*, 237

the Greek Orthodox Church had acknowledged their suzerainty as the price of restraining the French king of Sicily from making a new assault on Constantinople. " The Lord left to Peter," the great Pope Innocent III had proclaimed, "the government not only of all the Church but of all the world."

Yet as Rome's temporal power grew its spiritual influence declined. The empire of the Caesars proved a delusive heritage. In trying to grasp it, the papacy lost the wider empire of the human heart. So long as it was content to rule men's minds its authority expanded; when it sought to command their bodies it began to contract. Its descent into the political arena had made it the rival instead of the arbiter of princes. By using religious weapons for secular ends it had blunted and tarnished them.

For by its reckless excommunication of political opponents the Holy See had narrowed and debased the conception of the Church as a universal fellowship in Christ's love and service. The great evangelical organisation that had brought the rule of peace and justice to the rude Gothic tribes, now, in pursuit of transient and —by its own eternal measure—trivial ends, divided the kingdoms of the West instead of uniting them. The armies and mobs it hired to enforce its secular policies had unloosed war and revolution on the Italian cities and kept Germany in permanent disunion. Its bankers and lawyers, levying toll on every country's ecclesiastical revenues, had become the chief tax-collectors of Europe. Even the universal awe in which St. Peter's throne was held could not stay the rising tide of resentment as the endowments of native churches were appropriated to provide for an extravagant foreign court and its often irresponsible and absentee nominees. At one time seven of England's abbeys, including Christ Church, Canterbury, were under excommunication for arrears of papal taxes, and twenty-eight of Salisbury's fifty prebends were held by aliens, only three of them resident.

Edward was a devout and orthodox prince—a crusader, a friend of the Holy See, a benefactor of monasteries and churches. He loved to go on pilgrimage and take part in religious processions and services. Among his first acts after his return from Wales were to attend the consecration of the rebuilt Norwich cathedral and to help carry the bones of King Arthur and his queen to their new resting-place before the high altar of Glastonbury. When during the ceremonies there his judges infringed the abbey's rights by attempting to hold an assize within its boundaries, he at once ordered the court's removal to less sanctified ground and handed over to the abbot, for the Church's milder justice, a prisoner who had committed the unforgivable sin against the royal peace of drawing a knife on one of his bodyguard.

Yet Edward would not brook dictation by priests or let them interfere with his lawful concerns. As the Lord's anointed and the son and nephew of the two most pious princes of the age, he regarded himself as the consecrated protector of the Church in England. In 1278, the year after the Welsh war, Robert Kilwardby, the Dominican friar and scholar who for the past six years had been Archbishop of Canterbury, resigned his see on being made a cardinal. To bring the administration of Church and State into closer association Edward used the royal prerogative to direct the Canterbury monks to elect in his place his chancellor, Burnell—an attempt in which earlier, while still a prince, he had been unsuccessful. But Burnell, though now Bishop of Bath, was a worldling who had caused scandal by having a family. For all his gifts as statesman and lawyer, this was too much for the pope. Instead the latter chose an Oxford friar named John Pecham,[1] who had been Provincial of the Franciscans in England and was now lector in theology at the papal university in Rome.

As the archbishop was the Crown's chief constitutional adviser and richest vassal,[2] Edward protested. " It seems to the king and his council," he wrote, " that in this respect there may be prejudice to himself and to the Church of which he is the patron and defender, especially if the example is followed with regard to other churches in England." Yet, having registered his objection, he took the papal intervention in good part. He was proud of the distinction of the English episcopal bench, and Pecham was a famous theologian and something of a saint. Instead of rejecting him as his grandfather had rejected Langton, he greeted him on

[1] Named after the little Sussex village of Patcham, near Brighton, where his father was a freeholder.

[2] The Archbishop of Canterbury was the lord or part-lord of thirty-five hundreds and of thirty-one knight's fees in Kent alone, where he possessed more than a dozen official residences. Among his sub-tenants was the Earl of Gloucester, the greatest lord in the kingdom.

his arrival "with benignity" and went out of his way to win his friendship.

Like Langton, the new archbishop came of modest English landowning stock and not from the Anglo-French military aristocracy. He had been educated by the monks of Lewes in one of the grammar schools which had sprung up all over Europe to teach clever lads to think and reason in Latin. At Oxford he had joined the Minorites and sat at the feet of the Franciscan scholars who had made the university renowned for mathematical and scientific studies. Here and at the still more famous university of Paris, where he was known as " Brother John the Englishman," he had established a European reputation as a biblical commentator and a writer of philosophical and scientific manuals.[1] At one time he had even crossed words with the great Dominican schoolman, Thomas Aquinas, defending the orthodox faith against the heretical tendencies which the Franciscans, with their distrust of pure intellect, discerned in their Dominican brethren.

Yet, though Pecham had showed himself an able administrator, he was no Stephen Langton. He was a man of the study—a perfectionist happiest on the rostrum or with the pen in his hand, and happiest of all in the life of contemplation from which, with his acceptance of the primacy, he cut himself off. In an age when the friars had ceased to be the evangelists of the very poor to become the advisers of kings and the confessors of the rich middle-class, he clung to the early Franciscan belief in poverty, defending it against those who regarded the mendicants' renunciation of wealth as an attack on the Church's endowments. He loved to wear his shabby old friar's gown in palace and cathedral, to fast and do penance, and had once walked barefoot across Europe to

[1] He was also, like Langton, a hymn-writer and poet. Two of his hymns on the Eucharist, the *Rhythmus de Corpore Christi*, and *Ave vivens hostia*, became part of the heritage of the Catholic Church. " A young Flemish clerk found a poem on the same theme and another in praise of the Virgin on a scroll hanging before the pope's special altar at St. Peter's. He loved them so much that he made copies of them, and fifty years later, when he was an old priest in a Flemish parish, he had them recopied and distributed as a precious legacy to his fellow parish priests, ... beseeching them to hang them in their churches for the profit of the faithful who could read and copy them, and begging them to remember in their prayers the author, brother John the Englishman." *Douie*, 45.

attend the chapter-general of his Order. He was not only a very sincere man—a mystic and poet deeply stirred by the example of Christ's love and sacrifice—but a rather dogmatic one, whose denunciations of his more worldly brethren left unforgettable wounds. With his tall austere figure, his earnest face, high cheek-bones and slightly petulant mouth, he was an unbending advocate of ecclesiastical reform and a castigator of all the petty frailties and abuses to which churchmen and laymen were inclined. His aim was not so much to make the world as righteous as circumstances admitted, but to change it altogether. For this reason he believed in the complete subordination of the civil to the canon law.

What was a graver drawback in the administrator-designate of the kingdom's richest estate was that Pecham's life of lecturing had unfitted him for the compromise and give-and-take that are the currency of the world of affairs. He was so famous a master that when he entered his lecture-room at Rome even the cardinals rose. Scholarship had made his mind acute but had made it also irritable and hypersensitive. In him the theologian seldom merged into the statesman. He could argue and denounce yet, for all his genuine goodness and capacity for Christian love, could scarcely ever persuade. A stickler for the Church's rights in their most extreme form, he might a century earlier have gone down to posterity as a saint and martyr. In a more complex age he soon got out of his depth.

Within a few days of landing, the new archbishop, like a second Becket, summoned his suffragans to a synod to institute a thorough-going reform of the Church's relations with the State. At its meeting that July and August in the great Benedictine abbey of Reading, he presented proposals for abolishing pluralism and non-residence among the clergy and for stopping, by wholesale excommunication, the writs of prohibition with which the Crown courts were wont to remove from the jurisdiction of the Church cases directly affecting the State and the maintenance of civil justice. By both he directly challenged the government.

For with his schoolman's logic Pecham saw the problems of human society in terms too simple. The most notorious pluralists were the king's ministers and judges who were rewarded for their services to the State by ecclesiastical preferment. They held, as the archbishop bluntly told his royal master, "a damnable multitude of benefices." Yet in an age when almost every educated man was a cleric, there was no-one else whom the king could employ if the kingdom was to be properly administered. And in a feudal society, where the basis of public service was the tenure of land, the only source from which they could be remunerated was the Church's endowments. As these constituted so large a share of the nation's wealth, it seemed reasonable that part of it should be used to maintain churchmen who served the State.

As for the archbishop's threats against those who issued writs of prohibition, this struck at the roots of public law and order. In a well-knit realm like England where Church and State were closely interwoven, the same man might be a vassal of the king and the owner of an advowson, a bishop and a member of the Great Council, a churchwarden and a juryman. There had to be some demarcation between the jurisdiction of the lay and clerical courts, and only anarchy could result from leaving the ecclesiastical authorities free to excommunicate any judge or sheriff who enforced the king's law in a case over which the Church chose to claim cognisance. And though it might be logical to argue that all cases affecting churchmen should be tried by the courts Christian, experience had shown that this merely enabled ecclesiastical malefactors to commit offences with impunity. With its civilised penalties and prohibition of judicial bloodshed, the canon law was too mild an instrument to enforce order in an age of habitual violence—a violence in which churchmen indulged almost as much as laymen. Nor was such violence confined to the disorderly hangers-on—the poor clerks, unbeneficed priests and ragged scholars—over whom the Church, with its vast numbers, cast its protecting cloak. Even a great prelate like Pecham, for all his genuine Christian humility, constantly embroiled himself with his fellow clerics. He denounced the monks of his cathedral chapter as "idlers, dunces, blockheads" and "demoniacs," his Order's critics as "barking dogs rising like sulphurous stink from the abyss," and his opponents as "robbers shooting poisoned arrows" and "witches suckling their greed with the milk of contention." When his suffragans, most of whom were men of the same distinction and piety as himself, complained of his high-handed ways, he placed them under suspension and interdict in the name of

God, the Virgin and St. Thomas of Canterbury. He even ex-communicated his own cathedral city because its bailiffs seized some brushwood from one of his carts.

Such clerical irascibility did not end only in words and litigation. It often resulted in blows. Pecham himself was struck in the face during divine service by the sacristan of Westminster; when his fellow metropolitan, reviving an old claim, had his cross borne before him through the province of Canterbury, the out-raged primate placed every town on his route under interdict and encouraged his officers to smash his cross in the streets of Rochester. A far worse scandal occurred a few years later when one of the canons of Exeter murdered the bishop's chief adherent in the cathedral precincts. In the ensuing cloister-vendetta a parish church was burnt and two men killed.

It was against this background of ecclesiastical intemperance that the archbishop flung down his gauntlet to the Crown over ministerial pluralities and writs of prohibition. Simultaneously he ordered copies of the sixty-year-old and now legendary Magna Carta, with its guarantee of clerical "liberties," to be nailed to the door of every cathedral and collegiate church. In resisting such a challenge Edward knew that he would have his magnates, and not only the magnates, behind him. The Church's power of dis-ciplining laymen depended on the secular power's readiness to enforce such discipline, and it was only reasonable that the Crown, as the Church's upholder and partner, should have the right of defining what spiritual jurisdiction it should enforce. The arrogance of the consistory and archdeacons' courts, and the petty and often corrupt blackmail that their summoners levied on lay-men for moral offences, made them unpopular with all classes.[1] The lightness of their sentences on rogues able to claim benefit of clergy outraged, too, the growing national sense of order. In such matters the interests of Crown and public were one.

[1] See a contemporary song giving the point of view of a peasant who, after a hearing in one of these courts, is forced by "a priest as proud as a peacock" to marry a wench called Mal whom he has made "un-comely under petti-coat." "No unclerkly person," he says, "may live in the land, the clerkly so lead us about. . . . First there sits an old churl in a black gown—and of all who sits there he seems to be most the lord—and lays his leg along. They pink with their pens on the parchment and say I am briefed and brought in of all my fair wealth . . . Herdsmen hate them." *Wright, Political Songs.*

In a parliament held that November the king sought the approval of his "chief men" for retaliatory measures. He summoned the archbishop before the council and forced him to revoke his order for posting copies of Magna Carta and to annul, "as though never issued," the threats of excommunication against his pluralist ministers and those who applied for writs of prohibition. He also sent a message to the prelates warning them, "as they loved their baronies, not to meddle with his prerogative."

Nor did he stop here. With the assent of the magnates he issued a statute, at first known from its opening words as *de Religiosis*, forbidding the alienation of land to the Church or any religious corporation without the licence of the Crown or other feudal superior of such land. By collusive conveyances into the dead hand or "mortmain" of some ecclesiastical body which, by never dying, escaped the ordinary "incidents" or fines of feudal tenure, sub-tenants had for some time been cheating the king and the greater magnates of the customary reliefs on death, marriage and knighthood and of the wardships, escheats and forfeitures that were part of the feudal contract and the fiscal structure of the State. Edward used the archbishop's attack on his prerogative not only to remind him of who was master of the realm but to stop an abuse of ecclesiastical authority that was robbing the Crown and its tenants-in-chief of revenue. The Statute of Mortmain, as it was later called, did not end the endowment of religious houses and corporations by private individuals, which continued under royal licence and fine as before. But it enabled the Crown to control the process.

Edward was careful not to press his advantage too far. He did not wish to quarrel with the Church, only to keep its powers within what he and his subjects regarded as legitimate bounds. Moreover he wished to tax its wealth to help pay for the Welsh war, and he could only do this with the consent of its clergy. He had already taken scutage on the fee of every knight who had not served in the campaign in person, a fine from all substantial freeholders who refused knighthood and a parliamentary grant of a tenth on lay personal property. He had carried through, too, a reform of the currency, with drastic punishments for coiners and coin-clippers—a measure which had fallen with particular ferocity on the Jews who, already subjected to a crushing tallage

and forbidden their hereditary craft of usury, had taken to specu-
lating in the coinage and, according to popular belief, clipping
it.[1]

Yet even these additions to his revenue could not enable
Edward to meet all the expenses of his kingdom without the aid
of the international estate that held so much of its wealth. He,
therefore, asked the archbishops to summon the representatives
of their provinces to consider his financial needs—a step normally
only taken before a crusade. At the same time he let it be
understood that his resistance to attacks on his ministers and
judges did not mean that he was unsympathetic to religious reform.
Nor, he intimated, was he against any ecclesiastic liberty that did
not prejudice the good order of the realm. He made no attempt
against the Church's right—unchallenged since Becket's day—to
punish criminous clerks. He conceded, or appeared to concede,
the claim of its courts to jurisdiction over offerings, oblations and
burial-dues, and, where the rights of lay patrons were not impugned, over tithes. He also promised that the clergy's beasts and
carts should be free from purveyance, and that malefactors
who had been granted sanctuary should not be arrested on their
way to exile. And to save the primate's face he agreed to submit
disputed writs of prohibition to a committee of royal clerks, whose
decision, however, in such matters was to be final.

Though most of the Council of Reading's demands were
shelved or rejected, the head-on clash of a century earlier
between king and archbishop did not recur. Edward was wiser
than Henry II, and Pecham less fanatical than Becket. Since the
Church in England could no longer undermine the jurisdiction
and administration of the State, the king could afford to be
magnanimous. Beyond a warning that any discussion by the
prelates of matters affecting his person or estate might endanger
their temporalities, he ignored Pecham's further threats of excommunication against violators of ecclesiastical liberties. The
archbishop, meeting no attempt to force him to retract, accepted

---

[1] The reform was carried out at the end of 1279, new dies being made and
the "pollarded" square coinage being superseded by a circular one. Among
the new coins was a fourpenny-piece which became known as a groat. *Powicke*,
632-3; J. Ramsay, *Dawn of the Constitution*, 326-7; C. Roth, *History of the
Jews in England*, 74-6.

the *status quo* and showed no resentment against his royal master.
" His excellent lord," he continued to call him.

The weakness of Pecham's position was that his clerical
colleagues were not united behind him. Much of the bitterest
opposition to his reforms came from churchmen—from monastic
chapters whose privileges were threatened or from aristocratic
pluralists like Bogo de Clare, the Earl of Gloucester's brother, who
held preferments in thirteen dioceses and, enjoying the revenues
of nearly thirty ecclesiastical offices, performed the duties of none.
The Bishop of Bath, the chancellor, was the Crown's chief
protagonist against the Church courts and a flagrant pluralist who
conferred benefices on his bastards. And even the most saintly of
Pecham's suffragans became embroiled with him over his insistence
on his right to carry out visitations in their dioceses and the
encroachments of his archiepiscopal court[1] on their local jurisdictions—the same centralising process against which the archbishop
himself protested so furiously when it was employed by the Crown
against the Church courts. Indeed, in his dealings with his fellow
churchmen he was more authoritarian than the king who at least
usually sought the assent of his "chief men" to his measures.
Regardless of canon law Pecham repeatedly issued the most
sweeping decrees without calling a provincial council.

Even the papal bureaucracy was not behind the archbishop
and was ready, at a price, to support his opponents. At one time
he had to sustain six simultaneous lawsuits at the Roman *curia*.
And the merciless insistence with which the Italian papal bankers
with threats of excommunication dunned him for the debts of his
province reduced the poor man to despair.[2] A generous almsgiver,

---

[1] The Court of the Arches, which six centuries later afforded employment
to the father of David Copperfield's Dora.

[2] "There has lately come to me a letter of execution horrible to look at and
terrible to hear." S. C. Carpenter, *The Church in England*, 104. As a friar
Pecham had no property of his own, yet at his enthronement feast he had
to provide in fish alone, 300 ling, 600 cod, 40 fresh salmon, 7 barrels of salt
salmon, 5 barrels of salt sturgeon, 600 fresh eels, 8000 whelks, 100 pike, 400
tench, 100 carp, 800 bream, 1400 lampreys, 200 large roach, besides seals,
porpoises and "pophyns"! He also had to make customary gifts to the chief
vassals of the see who acted as hereditary butler, pantler, chamberlain and
cup-bearer. The Earl of Gloucester, for instance, "received the archbishop's
cup, seven scarlet robes, thirty gallons of wine, thirty pounds of wax, provision

burdened like every other feudal magnate with a fantastic train of office-holders and dependents, he described himself as "crushed and weighted down" by the money he owed. He was even forced to borrow from the king—an accommodation which, though graciously granted, did nothing to strengthen his hands in attacks on uncanonical prerogatives.

Only in the realm of internal ecclesiastical reform was Pecham's zeal for Christian perfection able to achieve anything permanent. His enduring legacy to his country were the provisions that in 1281 the Council of Lambeth made at his instance for educating the parish clergy. In his ordinances he left behind rules for giving religious instruction and hearing confession, for repairing and maintaining churches and churchyards, and for preserving the host from neglect and misuse. Like all the great churchmen of his age he was profoundly moved by the doctrine of "transubstantiation"—the schoolman's attempt to define the mystery of the Eucharist adopted earlier in the century by the Lateran Council. That men should know, as he put it, "the King of Glory under the appearance of bread" he laboured incessantly to impress on the ignorant and superstitious parish clergy the importance of guarding the consecrated host or wafer from sacrilegious neglect or abuse by sorcerers and magic-makers. He insisted that it should always be kept in a pyx inside a locked box or tabernacle[1] and, when borne through the streets to the bedside of the sick and dying, be reverently preceded by bell and candle.

With the king and his lords, with his fellow prelates, with the cardinals, lawyers and all-devouring bankers of the papal *curia*, Pecham achieved little or nothing. He did not succeed in stopping clerical pluralism or lay interference with the Church, which remained, in England as elsewhere, riddled with abuses and corruption. Nor was he more successful in preventing clerical incontinence, the farming of benefices and the squandering by

---

for eighty horses and three days' free entertainment at one of the archiepiscopal manors whilst he recovered from the blood-letting necessitated by the festivities." *Douie*, 66.

[1]A few of these tall and beautifully decorated wooden tabernacles still survive in our parish churches. A magnificent example, delicately carved in wood like a cathedral tower and spire, can be seen hanging in the south transept of Milton abbey in Dorset.

worldly-minded ecclesiastics of the Church's endowments on pomp and luxurious living—the agelong tragedy that he once described as the priesthood's fall from the spirituality of Melchisideck to the carnality of Aaron. In the last year of his life, sickened by frustration, he wrote of his countrymen as "a stiff-necked people, kicking against the pricks and determined to resist all exhortations to obey the word of God." Yet because of his labours—though their fruits only became apparent after his death —thousands of humble English men and women were made more aware of the inner truths of the Christian life. Pecham's decree, *Ignorantia Sacerdotum*, outlining the religious instruction which parish priests were to give their parishioners on the articles of the Christian faith, the Ten Commandments and the Seven Deadly Sins, was still being observed long after his name had been forgotten.[1] So was the custom he revived of tolling the church bells at the elevation of the host so that passers-by in the street and the peasants in the fields might kneel or bow their heads in awareness of the mystery being enacted within.

.   .   .   .

The king received his grant from the clergy—a tenth from the convocation of York for two years and a fifteenth from Canterbury for three. Before these sums had been collected he became involved in another Welsh war. On the eve of Palm Sunday 1282, his former ally David fell by night on Hawarden castle, massacred the garrison and carried off the royal justiciar who had hanged one of his men for an offence unpunishable by Welsh law. Forgetting earlier wrongs at his brother's hands, Llywelyn threw in his lot with him. Everywhere the Welsh rose in sympathy, laying siege to the hated new castles of Flint and Rhuddlan, storming Llanbadarn—the modern Aberystwith—and carrying fire and sword to the walls of Chester and through the lands of the Marchers to the Bristol Channel. Everywhere, in that spring of Celtic fury and vengeance, the king's fortresses, except the very strongest, went up in flames. This time almost the entire race seemed united against the English.

---

[1] Cases of individual clergy being ordered to memorise Pecham's *Ignorantia Sacerdotum* occur in Wykeham's register in the later fourteenth century. "Wykeham's Register," *Hampshire Record Society* (1896) xi, cit. *Douie*, 139.

The rising took Edward completely by surprise. The pope and the kings of France, Castile, Aragon and Sicily were all at that moment seeking his arbitration. His mind was full of projects for a crusade against the sultans of Egypt and had little room for the squabbles of a remote and backward western province. He had showered favours on David, forgiven and befriended Llywelyn, and thought that he had done with the barren hills of Wales and its petty princes for ever. And the immediate aftermath of the treaty of Conway had seemed full of promise; "the prince of Wales," he had written three years earlier, "has appeared before our justices in the March and seeks and submits to justice and judgment in the most agreeable manner."[1]

Yet difficulties had arisen over the crucial clause in the treaty that disputes about Llywelyn's lands outside his own principality should be decided by the law of the locality where the land lay. Llywelyn contended that this must be Welsh law and should be governed by the code of the famous tenth century Welsh legislator, Hywel Dda or the Good. But, though calculated to favour him in actions against his Welsh and English neighbours, this was an over-simplification of a complex situation. Except in Gwynedd there was no regular Welsh court and the interpretation of Cymric law was left to private judges voluntarily hired by the litigants. In many parts even of Wales Hywel's three-hundred-year-old code was regarded as antiquated and obsolete. And for more than a century English as well as Welsh law had operated in the Marches. The greatest of all the Welsh chieftains—Llywelyn's rebellious vassal, Gruffyd ap Gwenwynwyn, lord of Pool—flatly refused to have his dispute over the ownership of Arwystli in the Severn highlands tried by Welsh law, claiming that as a Marcher he should be judged as an English baron. He was prepared, he said, to answer any man according to the common law, but in no way according to Welsh law.

This was too hard a poser for the justices of the March, and the matter was referred to the king. He laid it, as was now his custom with all baronial pleas, before his council at the next meeting of parliament. Here it was held—and, after an unsuccessful attempt to get agreement between the parties by arbitration,

[1] Foedera I, ii, 554, cit. F. M. Powicke, *Henry III and the Lord Edward*, 672.

Edward upheld the contention—that justice could only be done according to the law that parliament administered. The supreme royal court could not give judgment by rules that it regarded as unjust, barbarous or unchristian. The Crown, the indignant Welsh prince was informed, must "according to God and justice do what the prelates and magnates of the realm shall advise, especially as no-one supposes that such prudent men will give the king advice dissonant with or contrary to reason."[1] Instead of having the matter decided out of hand and in his favour by a Welsh judge interpreting a highly elastic local law, Llywelyn was forced to apply for a writ like an English baron and endure the long formalities and delays attendant on a parliamentary suit. The matter was still undecided when, in the spring of 1282, he threw in his lot with his brother.

It was not only Llywelyn and David who felt the iron of subordination to English law. The men of the Four Cantrefs bitterly resented being placed by the treaty under the jurisdiction of the justiciar of Chester and the Cheshire shiremoot. It was not like that of the princes of Gwynedd, or even of their earlier Anglo-Norman rulers, the palatine earls—swift, rough and ready and framed for a warlike society. A nomadic people, who for centuries had viewed cattle-stealing as a branch of agriculture, and war against one another and the Saxon as the poetry of life, did not take kindly to the common law. Its slow and elaborate processes seemed to them only tricks for evading justice, its pursuit of truth by the laborious interchange of pieces of parchment an affront to hot-blooded men in search of their rights. They could only respect judgment given instantly and on the spot.

Edward had declared that he would uphold Welsh law and custom in the Four Cantrefs so far as they were not barbarous or at variance with reason and the Ten Commandments. Yet this was just how they seemed to any Englishman trained in the royal courts. The officials of the county palatine who took over the administration of the conquered borderland had nothing but contempt for Welsh law. To them the code of Hywel Dda seemed as archaic and savage as the laws of their remote Anglo-Saxon forebears. How, they asked, could they be expected to administer

[1] J. G. Edwards, *Calendar of Ancient Correspondence concerning Wales*, 59-60, cit. *Powicke*, 382.

a legal system that treated civil war as a legitimate activity, that regarded a judge as private arbitrator hired by a criminal's kinsman to compound with his avengers, that punished the murder of a bard with a fine of a hundred-and-twenty-six cows? And how could they keep order in a violent land without a death penalty?

It was hard for the English, with their comparatively law-abiding and stable society, to regard the Welsh as anything but savages. To them, as to the sheriff of Shropshire who offered a shilling for every scalp taken during a Welsh raid on Strattondale, they were wolves' heads outside the law. Unlike the Marchers, with their half-Welsh ancestry and love of fighting, the farmers of the Cheshire plain could not appreciate the virtues of a people who burnt homes instead of making them and preferred robbery and idleness to honest husbandry. Archbishop Pecham, visiting Gwynedd in an eleventh-hour attempt to reason with Llywelyn, was horrified by the universal laziness, drunkenness and incontinence, by the pagan failure to distinguish between the offspring of wedlock and sin, by the illiteracy of the Welsh clergy with their bare legs, bright-coloured cloaks and concubines. Even the splendid Cymric heritage of poetry and legend that so appealed to England's knightly Norman rulers seemed to sober, home-keeping English yeomen only a barbarous tissue of lies.[1]

This assumption that everything Welsh was beneath contempt aroused deep resentment. During the years immediately after the conquest everyone in the Four Cantrefs who had a suit in the Palatine courts became a passionate nationalist. Every departure from ancient custom, every legal and administrative innovation was seen as an affront. Though far more efficient than any rulers Wales had known, and convinced that they were bringing civilisation and justice to a backward people, the bureaucrats of the County Palatine imposed a strait-jacket on the life of an ancient community. They divided the land into unfamiliar administrative patterns and cited men to appear in distant courts

[1] " The assertion of the Britons that the island was made subject in obedience to Arthur is a fable like the other stories which they have wantonly invented concerning him out of pure lust of lying." William of Newburgh, *English Historical Documents*, II, 340.

before judges who could not understand their tongue and who applied rules that appeared to them incomprehensible. They allowed no outlet for native pride, no safety-valve for local turbulence.

Under the rule of the great athelings and the Norman and Angevin kings the English had mastered political lessons far in advance of the Welsh or even of their most civilised continental neighbours. They had learnt to keep the king's peace, to pay taxes, to abide by a single law, to take personal part in an administrative and legal hierarchy that stretched from the parish and manorial court to the council of the realm in parliament. But their system was far too centralised and complex to be intelligible to a primitive, pastoral race. Everything had to be referred to distant authority or remote precedent. And the rules they imported to the Celtic borderland were too often applied in a narrow, pedantic spirit. When Llywelyn, in full cry after a stag, accidentally crossed the frontier-stream between Gwynedd and the Marches, "the king's officers came to the huntsmen and immediately called out with horns and cries almost the whole countryside," seizing the hounds and imprisoning the riders.[1] On another occasion the Welsh prince was goaded to fury by the justiciar of Chester pedantically impounding his honey at the instance of a Leicester merchant whose goods had been seized many years before under the Welsh law of wreck. Yet the very officials who slighted native custom to do justice to Englishmen cut down Welshmen's woods to make highways, requisitioned their beasts and carts to build castles and granted land to English merchants on which to raise towns from which native traders and shopkeepers were excluded.

Nor were the administrators England sent to govern the borderland always honest. The theory of thirteenth century law was one thing, its practice another. Those who served the State in an age of elementary organisation were allowed, and expected, to use the power they wielded to secure personal advantages. King Edward's judges and bailiffs enforced law and order and did justice as they were trained to do, but they also feathered their own nests. Many subordinate officials took bribes and falsely

[1] *Cal. of Ancient Correspondence concerning Wales*, 88-9, cit. F. M. Powicke, *Henry III and the Lord Edward*, 657.

accused the innocent. In the light of their conduct high-sounding talk about the moral superiority of English law struck the Welsh as nauseating.

Above all, the new rulers of the Four Cantrefs were English, not Welsh. The Welsh did not like Englishmen; they had been accustomed from time immemorial, not to nationhood, but to governing themselves. Most of them preferred to be ruled by an unjust fellow countryman than by an upright foreigner—a thing no Englishman could understand. As the Marchers had always recognised but as the administrators of the borderland had still to learn, only a Welshman could understand Welshmen.

For though Wales had never been a kingdom, and only a handful of her people yet thought of her as a nation, the Welsh loved their country. They loved its land, its traditions, its speech, its faith. " I am persuaded," an old Welshman had told Henry II a century before, " that no other race than this and no other tongue than of Wales, happen what may, will answer in the great day of judgment for this little corner of earth." Since then, under the two Llywelyns, a growing number of Welshmen, including for a time the inhabitants of the Four Cantrefs, had learnt what it was to live as members, not merely of a Welsh tribe, but of a Welsh State. With its impenetrable mountain barrier to the east and its rich island-granary of Anglesey, Gwynedd had become something more than a group of loosely-knit tribes. In its prince's wooden hall or *neuydd*, where native bards sang the glories of Wales in the presence of a ruler who claimed the allegiance of all Welshmen, the institutions of a modern national kingdom were beginning to take shape. Already it had a royal household on the Anglo-French pattern with a chancellor[1] and chancery, an exchequer collecting taxes in cash as well as in kind, a great and a privy seal, and even an embryonic high court that sought to formulate, though still only in theory, a single law for all Welshmen founded on western jurisprudence. The rude rule of the tribe and blood-feud was

---

[1] By the laws of the court of Gwynedd he enjoyed the first place in hall and sat next the king at table, receiving on his investment "a gold ring, a harp and a chess board." T. Jones-Pierce, *The Age of the Princes*. Lecture at the University of Bangor, January, 1945, printed in *The Historical Basis of Welsh Nationalism*, Cardiff, 1950, 54.

being modified; for the first time men were being taught, and by their fellow Welshmen, to distinguish between civil wrong and public crime, and homicide—for so long a normal incident in the life of the country—was being restrained and punished by the State. Private property was even in places growing up beside clan ownership, and settled agriculture beside the pastoral life of the past.

It was this that made Llywelyn regard the denial of Welsh law in the Marches as a monstrous injustice and affront. Because as lord of Gwynedd he enjoyed his own law under the titular sovereignty of the imperial Crown, he felt that that law should be equally valid in every part of the land of which he called himself prince. With indignation he brooded over the slights that he and his people suffered. " Each province," he wrote to Edward, " under the *imperium* of the king of England has its own customs and laws according to the mode and use of their respective parts where they are situated, such as the Gascons in Gascony, the Scots in Scotland, the Irish in Ireland and the English in England. I, therefore, seek, being a prince, that I likewise shall have my Welsh law and proceed according to that law. By common right we ought to have our Welsh law and custom, as the other nations in the king's empire have—and in our own language."[1]

But, though in Gwynedd no-one denied him that right, Llywelyn forgot that, whatever he might call himself, he was not the ruler of Wales as the Scots king was of Scotland and Edward of Gascony. Wales was not, and had never been, like Gwynedd, a single State. Yet though on false ground legally, in a wider, poetic sense Llywelyn was right. Because her people were aware of their separateness, even though politically divided, Wales was already one in spirit. Her bards sang of her now as *Cymru*—the land of all the Cymri—and of Llywelyn as "the great chieftain of fair Wales." Those who heard them shared his belief that to be punished by English judges in accordance with English-made law was for Welshmen a kind of servitude. "All Christians," wrote one of them, " have laws and customs in their own lands. The Jews among the English have laws. We and our ancestors in our lands had immutable laws and customs until after the last war the

[1] *Idem.* 52.

English took them from us.''[1] It was this conviction that made the second Welsh rising against Edward such a passionate affair.

It made it, too, a cruel one. The Welsh tribesmen did not spare the English in their path. And in those early weeks of the rising they travelled far. Ruthin Castle was captured, the Earl of Gloucester ambushed in the hills near Llandeilo Fawr, the valleys as far south as Builth and Cardigan harried. Many perished in cold blood, churches and farms were sacked, atrocious acts done. And these were exaggerated in the telling.

This time the English as well as their king were thoroughly aroused. They were resolved to be done with the Welsh, their raids and broken truces, and to subject them to government. While from Devizes, where news of the rising reached him, Edward called on the archbishops to excommunicate the rebels for sacrilege and treason, his officers and tenants-in-chief called the shires to arms. Once more it was a professional rather than a feudal army that took the field. While Gloucester in the south and Roger Mortimer in central Wales led the men of the March and the Welsh "friendlies," the royal host that met in May at Worcester was raised mainly by indenture. In place of a glittering but ill-disciplined horde of tenants-in-chivalry serving under the magnates at their own expense for the customary forty days but free thereafter to do as they pleased, most of its ten or twelve thousand fighting-men were raised by lesser barons or knights of the household who contracted with the Crown to pay them for agreed periods. Even a great magnate like the Earl of Lincoln accepted the king's wages, though Norfolk the marshal and Hereford the constable, standing on their feudal dignity, refused to do so and insisted on their ancient independent status and the formal summoning of the host. The advantage of such a system was that it enabled Edward to select the kind of force he needed— a vital consideration in a mountain campaign—instead of being forced to rely on masses of heavily armoured knights. For war in Snowdonia he required, as before, light horse or *hobelars*, cross-bowmen and archers, infantry in disciplined companies to contend with the Welsh spearmen; artificers, woodcutters, wagoners and labourers to make and maintain forts and communications.

[1] *Epistolae Johannis Peckham*, II 454, cit. F. M. Powicke, *Henry III and the Lord Edward*, 664.

Even in its heyday the feudal levy had never been able to produce a composite army. Though in deference to the marshal and constable it was summoned to join the king at Rhuddlan in August, it amounted to only a small fraction of the royal force. Most of the original knights' fees granted by the Conqueror and his tenants-in-chief to provide fighting-men for the Crown had been broken up through sale or divided inheritance; an eighth of a fee was a fiscal unit but not a military one. And the elaborately armed knight of Edward I's day was a far more costly article for a tenant to equip than the simple mail-coated *miles* or trooper of the Conqueror's day. A knight now was a fine gentleman, not a rough soldier. He was handsomer to look at, but there were not so many of him. Only a few hundred answered to the Rhuddlan muster-rolls compared with the five or six thousand whom the Norman kings had been able to put into the field. Nor had the policy of employing the holders of knights' fees in administrative and judicial tasks enhanced their efficiency as soldiers. Like the feudal lords to whom they owed service, they still regarded prowess in battle as the highest human accomplishment, but it was no longer their only, or even principal, activity. They were as brave as their ancestors. But, with the growing complexity of war, they were no longer professional warriors but amateurs.

To pay his army Edward needed cash. Since the Crown rents, feudal dues and customs barely sufficed for peace time, pending another parliament he sent his financial expert, John Kirkby, the vice-chancellor, round England to beg individual magnates and corporations for contributions—"courteous subsidies," he called them. It was all done with the utmost politeness, for Edward always sought to co-operate with and be on good terms with his subjects, provided, that is, they did as he wished. Nor did anyone refuse. Though the cash took a long time to come in and he had to borrow 12,000 marks from the Italian bankers—half a million of our money—it enabled him, with the help of scutage, to raise a disciplined force. " We are exceedingly grateful to you," he wrote to those who had contributed, "and through the grace of God we will indemnify you . . . at an opportune time."[1]

The strategic problem was the same as in 1277. But it was harder to solve because Llywelyn's successes in the south-west had

[1] *Stephenson and Marcham,* 155.

widened the area of fighting. During July the king worked his way along the coast from Chester to his besieged castles at Flint and Rhuddlan, both of which had held out since the spring against David's attacks. Meanwhile he sent Grey and the Earl of Surrey to clear his left flank in the Vale of Clwyd and to drive David from the Four Cantrefs. His aim was, by encircling Snowdon from the south, to force Llywelyn to abandon his conquests in central and south-western Wales in order to save the principality.

Once again sea-power proved decisive. With forty ships from London and the Cinque Ports, including two great galleys sent by Romney and Winchelsea, each with a crew of fifty compared with the usual ship's complement of twenty, Edward was able to turn the enemy's northern flank. As his army advanced slowly through the wooded defiles to the Conway, a seaborne force under a former seneschal of Gascony, Luke de Tany, landed in Anglesey to knock, in the king's words, the feathers out of Llywelyn's tail. It took a month's fighting to clear the island, for this time the Welsh were expecting the blow, but by the middle of October de Tany had almost completed a bridge of boats across the Menai Strait to enable him, at the decisive moment, to take the Welsh position at Penmaenmawr in the rear. Ruthin and Denbigh had already fallen in the south, and in the centre Edward had reached the Conway.

Faced by this triple threat to Snowdonia, Llywelyn abandoned his southern offensive and hurried back to defend his base. Archbishop Pecham had also arrived on the scene and was trying to negotiate an honourable surrender for the Welsh, but Edward gave him very little encouragement. Feeling that they were now at his mercy, he insisted that, since they had taken the law into their own hands and appealed to violence instead of to his justice, they must first submit unconditionally.[1]

Then, just as victory seemed certain, de Tany's impatience precipitated disaster. On November 6th, on the very day on which Edward had made it known that he would grant no terms but unconditional surrender, in disobedience to his orders and without

---

[1] He privately intimated, however, through the archbishop, that he would provide honourably for David on condition that he went on crusade, and would grant Llywelyn an English earldom in return for the cession of Gwynedd—terms which the Welsh prince indignantly rejected.

waiting for the concerted attack which had been planned, his lieutenant crossed the Menai Strait at low tide, expecting to surprise the Welsh. Instead he was ambushed near Bangor and overwhelmed, losing his life and his entire force as it tried to escape across the rising waters.

It seemed as though Gwynedd had been miraculously saved. Llywelyn was jubilant and, leaving his brother in command in the north, set off on a punitive raid against England's Welsh allies in the Marches. But Edward was never more dangerous than when fortune turned against him. Withdrawing to Rhuddlan he resolved to continue the campaign through the winter. Calling for new levies from the shires and for fifteen hundred horseman and professional crossbowmen from Gascony, he summoned two provincial parliaments—one for the south at Northampton and the other at York. " Whereas Llywelyn, son of Griffith," his writ to the sheriffs ran, " and his accomplices the other Welshmen, to us enemies and rebels, have so often in our time and in the time of our progenitors disturbed the peace of our kingdom, . . . we command and firmly enjoin you to summon . . . four knights from each of the aforesaid counties, having full authority on behalf of the communities of the said counties; also from each city, borough or trading town two men similarly empowered on behalf of their communities in order to hear and do what on our behalf we shall cause to be explained." Both assemblies voted a thirtieth, bringing in roughly twice as much as Kirkby's voluntary loans had done. Meanwhile the latter was told to remit cash in all haste. " Strive especially to prevent such an occurrence," he was enjoined, " as that we and our army should presently retreat from the region of Wales through default of that payment of money on which we are placing full reliance."

Six weeks after the disaster at Bangor and while the king and his men were steeling themselves for a winter campaign in the Welsh mountains, dramatic news arrived from the headwaters of the Wye. For taking advantage of his death to plunder the lands of his uncle, the great Marcher baron, Roger Mortimer—one of Edward's closest friends—Llywelyn had been surprised by the former's sons and John Giffard at Orewin bridge "in the land of Builth." On December 11th, 1282, while he was conferring with some local chieftains, his phalanx of spearmen was decimated by the volleys of Giffard's archers and then charged and broken by the English horse. Llywelyn himself was killed, as he hurried to the scene of the fight, by a centenar or lieutenant of Shropshire infantry named Stephen de Frankton. His body, found next day, was taken to the Cistercian abbey at Cwm Hir and his head sent to the king, who, to make a mockery of Merlin's prophecy that a Welsh prince should be crowned in London with the diadem of Brutus the Trojan, ordered it to be borne, crowned with ivy, through the streets of the capital and set on a pike above the Tower.

With Llywelyn's death the soul went out of the nationalist rising. David, who claimed his principality, had been too long in the English camp to take his place in his fellow Welshmen's hearts. For half a year he fought on in the northern mountains with the remorseless ring of Edward's men and the Marchers closing round him. In June 1283, a fugitive in the barren hills around Cader Idris, he was betrayed by his own countrymen and handed over to Edward who refused even to see him. His fate was left to an English parliament called to try him at Shrewsbury. For his treachery to the king who had knighted him he was condemned to be dragged to the gallows by horses, for his homicide to be hanged, for shedding blood in Passion week to be disembowelled, and for plotting the king's death to have his body quartered and distributed to the cities of Winchester, Northampton, Chester and York. The atrocious sentence was carried out in its entirety and his head set beside his brother's over the Tower.

So perished the princes of North Wales. The rebellion—for it was as such that Edward and every Englishman regarded it—ended the last hope of a self-governing Welsh state within the island *imperium*. Had Llywelyn been prince of Wales in fact and not merely of Gwynedd, it might have been achieved, for, as the treaty of Conway showed, Edward was willing to allow him virtual sovereignty in his hereditary dominions. But the lords of the rest of Wales were not Llywelyn but the Marchers, and by feudal and English law alike their rights were as good as his and could not be overriden. It had been, indeed, the insistence of a native Welsh Marcher on his rights that had provoked Llywelyn to his fatal defiance. And, as the event had proved, so long as there were two Wales, one wholly Welsh and one anglicised, war between them was inevitable. In so small and combative a land two independent sovereignties could scarcely co-exist without conflict. And in that conflict the weaker was bound to suffer.

That this was Edward's belief seems certain. Having grown up in the March and absorbed its warlike traditions, he had more understanding of the Welsh than his English subjects. He remained in Wales with his court of King's Bench for nearly eighteen months after his victory and threw himself, with his usual passionate mastery of detail, into the settlement of the country. He did not merge the principality with England but preserved its separate existence under the Crown and royal law. In his Statute of Wales, issued from Rhuddlan castle in March 1284, he divided Gwynedd into three counties on the English model—Caernarvon, Anglesey and Merioneth—and appointed a justiciar of Snowdon, with a treasury and capital at Caernarvon. At the same time he made a fourth county, Flintshire, out of part of the Four Cantrefs, placing it under the justiciar of Chester. Two other counties, Carmarthenshire and Cardiganshire, already created out of Llywelyn's former fiefs in the Marches, were provided with the usual English administrative hierarchy of sheriffs, bailiffs and coroners.

The settlement would not have been Edward's without the hard cement of a uniform system of law. It was for this that the war had been fought. Welsh and Anglo-Norman law were now made one. A body of law, half English, half Welsh,[1] and current throughout the six shires, took the place of the old law of Gwynedd and of the many contending laws around its borders. The Welsh were allowed to keep their system of inheritance by which all a man's sons shared his property equally, but, in deference to the orthodox Christian view of marriage, the illegitimate were excluded. Compurgation was retained in civil suits between Welshmen but was dropped, as it had long been in England, from criminal jurisdiction. Civil law remained Welsh, criminal law was anglicised.

[1] " It was a codification of the rules of English law made for the purpose of introducing that law into Wales. It reminds us of our Indian codes and other codifying Acts of the 19th century. Perhaps, indeed, it is more than a coincidence that it is only in the reign of Edward I and the 19th century—our two most important periods of matters legal—which have seen statutes of this nature." W. Holdsworth, *Makers of English Law*, 28-9.

For the rest Edward left Wales much as he found it. He left to the Marchers, who had helped him with the war, their feudal jurisdictions and martial lordships. Without civil war and a radical repudiation of the aristocratic society in which he had grown up, he could not do otherwise. He left the people of the former principality and the Cantrefs as much of their customary law as was compatible with peace and order and of the standards of morality and justice prevailing in Latin Christendom. He left them—the most precious thing of all—their language and, with a few exceptions, their Welsh officers and chieftains to fill the English legal and administrative posts which he imposed on them for their better ordering. He left them, in other words, not a Welsh State, which under provocation he had taken from them, but the wherewithal of Welsh nationhood.

The bards, the repositories of Cymric culture and learning who had shared Llywelyn's dream, bitterly lamented his death. And many Welshmen, who hated all government, including some who had fought on Edward's side, felt the iron of the new law enter into their souls. Twice in the decade after the conquest of the north the Welsh rose, once in 1287—when Edward was in Gascony—under a former ally of the English king, Rhys ap Mareddud, who took up arms rather than appear in the Carmarthenshire county court, and again in 1294. Yet such risings could achieve little in the face of the castles which Edward raised after the conquest to hold down the north. Four great fortresses were built—Conway and Caernarvon on strategic promontories on the northern coast and Criccieth and Harlech on the hills dominating the western coastal corridor round the shores of Cardigan bay. A fifth followed—after Madog's rebellion—at Beaumaris to control the Menai Strait. Built by the king's castle builder, Master James of St. George, in the new concentric style learnt by the crusaders from the Greeks and Saracens in the Syrian wars, with their cunningly placed towers, posterns and barbicans and their successive tiers of walls[1] they were so arranged that archers standing at different levels behind arrow-loops and machicolated battlements could enfilade an attacking force from every direction. Together with the Tower of London and the Earl

[1] The 1400-yard wall round the new castle and town of Conway had three great gates and twenty-two towers. *Brieger*, 254.

of Gloucester's Caerphilly—both newly rebuilt—they formed the greatest expression of the medieval military engineer's art raised in Britain before that art was superseded.

Around his Welsh castles, with his habitual thoroughness Edward laid out trading-towns built on the model of his new *bastides* in Gascony and his uncle Louis's city of Carcassonne. He gave them the same straight streets radiating from the castle which commanded and guarded them, and peopled them with colonists from England to whom he granted lands and special privileges of burgesship: the right to elect their own bailiffs and regulate their trade by merchant-gilds, weekly markets and annual fairs, exemption from royal tolls and from Welsh jurisdiction. As at Rhuddlan and Flint in the Four Cantrefs, he encouraged settlers by allowing them to build their houses from the royal forests and by remitting the rent of their burgages during the early years.[1] He kept them, however, under military control by appointing in every case as mayor the constable of the adjoining castle.

Edward was very proud of his new principality. For he was not merely king of the English, he was a prince of Christian chivalry. And Celtic Wales, at least in legend, was the most romantic of all the lands of chivalry: the fabled home of Arthur and his Round Table knights, of Gawain and Perceval and Galahad. Four weeks after the proclamation of the Statute of Wales Queen Eleanor gave birth at Caernarvon to a son who, on his elder brother's unexpected death a few months later, became heir to the English throne. The king, who christened him with his own name, gave the boy a Welsh nurse and attendants and, sixteen years later, the title of Prince of Wales—a compliment which is said to have pleased the Welsh people.

Later in the summer of 1284 he held a "round table" tournament at Nevin at which the most famous knights of Christendom jousted in his presence. With the last of the Welsh princes gone there was no-one now to challenge his claim to be the representative of King Arthur and Brutus of Troy. Just as a few years earlier he had helped to carry the bones of Arthur and Queen Guinevere, miraculously discovered at Glastonbury, to a new

[1] There is an account of Edward's town-planning activities in Wales and elsewhere in the American journal of medieval studies, *Speculum*, Vol. 22, 297-301. English towns were also established at Bala and Newborough.

place of entombment, he now, with equal solemnity, transferred to Westminster the supposed iron crown of Arthur and the bones of the Roman father of Constantine the Great, which had been found, together with a fragment of the true cross—the " Rood of St. Neot"—among Llwelyn's captured treasures. The idea of nationhood in the thirteenth century centred on the possession of such hallowed relics of the Christian and Roman past. By making them his, Edward hoped to win the Welsh people's hearts as well as their land.

Chapter Three

THE ESTABLISHMENT

The law has failed in many cases: divers additions to it and new provisions are needed to avoid grievous damage and disherisons.

STATUTE OF GLOUCESTER

The law he framed is barely obsolete today; the liberties that he worked into his system of administration still determine the forms of local government; the keepers of the peace and the constables whom he set alongside the sheriff were destined to rule the English countryside for five hundred years.

HELEN CAM

I**N DECEMBER** 1284 the king kept the Christmas feast at Bristol. After a pilgrimage to the monastery shrine of Bury St. Edmunds he returned to Westminster for the first time in three years. He reached London, wrote the Norwich chronicler, "on the vigil of the Ascension, and on the following Friday went in solemn procession with Queen Eleanor, magnates of the realm and fourteen bishops; John Pecham, the archbishop, bore the cross captured in Wales. On that day the king opened his parliament at Westminster; it lasted seven weeks and in it he established very many new laws and confirmed many charters of his ancestors. . . . Again in that year he published new statutes at Winchester against thieves, road brigands, receivers and concealers of malefactors, about setting watches in the country, townships and cities and the cutting away of woods by the king's highways. He also forbade the holding of pleas on Sundays and of fairs and markets in the burial grounds of churches."[1]

In this way a contemporary described the most intensive piece of lawmaking in medieval history. The summer and autumn of 1285 saw the statutes of Merchants and of Winchester and the famous collection of enactments known as the second Statute of

[1] *Bartholomaei de Cotton Historia Anglicana* (ed. Luard) 166, cit. *Powicke*, 369.

Westminster. They crowned the work, interrupted by the Welsh wars, of the first Statute of Westminster and the Statute of Gloucester. Drafted by the chancellor and judges, they bore the impress of the king's authoritative, unifying mind. In accordance with the adage that "that which touches all should be approved by all," they were submitted to the magnates and representatives of the counties and boroughs at his Whitsun and Michaelmas parliaments.

These statutes were the consequences of flaws in the law which had come to the notice of Edward and his judges in the course of administering it. They were designed to remedy abuses, too, brought to light by the great national inquest of ten years before and were based on the complaints and petitions for redress which flowed into Westminster. For days before a meeting of parliament the king sat in council considering these, while panels of "triers" sorted and arranged them. The work of devising detailed remedies and drafting statutes to give them effect fell on the royal judges who had to apply them in the courts and, in particular, on the chief justice of the King's Bench, Ralph de Hengham, the greatest English lawyer of his time.

To offer relief to the subject and strict and impartial justice to all in their degree, to ensure that under the Crown both the obligations and rights of a feudal society were observed, to unify and strengthen the realm, these were Edward's objects, tirelessly pursued. His instruments were the prerogative, the common law and royal courts of justice that had grown out of it and the periodic assemblies or parliaments of magnates, prelates, shire knights and burgesses that he had taken to summoning whenever he needed common counsel and consent in support of his measures. The statutes of Westminster of 1275, 1285 and 1290 were the crowning heights of his achievement. Each was a comprehensive code framed to amend, clarify and supplement the law and enable him to control the many-sided life of a passionate, turbulent and conservative people, rooted in ancient ways and divided by regional loyalties, rights and customs.

First place, in that hierarchical age, was given to the grievances of the larger landowners. At a time when revenue from land was almost the sole source of livelihood for everyone except a few merchant speculators, its owner had to make provision during his lifetime, not only for his heir, but for his other children, and his widow after his death. To prevent them from being left penniless he had to carve out of the family inheritance subsidiary estates to support them and their children and children's children. Yet if his own heirs were not to suffer, he had to ensure that such off-shoots from his main estate should revert to it after they had fulfilled the purpose for which they were intended. In his gift to a son when he came of age or a daughter on her marriage—a *maritagium* as it was called—a donor would stipulate that the land should return to him or his heirs if the donee's issue failed within so many generations.

Such settlements were immensely complicated by the rules and requirements of feudal enfeoffment. And during the thirteenth century the common law lawyers, with their fine and subtle definitions, adopted the view that, if land had been given "to X and the heirs of his body," this must mean to X and his heirs absolutely as soon as an heir of his body was born. By availing himself of this interpretation an unscrupulous person—the husband, say, of a daughter to whom a conditional estate had been given—could dispose of the property as though it was his own fee simple and not a mere life-interest. In this way both the issue of the marriage could be deprived of the gift intended for them and the donor's estate of the reversion.

Naturally donors and their heirs, unversed in legal subtleties, regarded such alienation as a species of fraud. It particularly out-raged the magnates, who, as tenants-in-chief of the Crown, had still to find out of their truncated fiefs the feudal services and aids due for the whole. Their plea that the king should redress the wrong that the operation of his own law had made possible was met by the first chapter of the second Statute of Westminster. This did not seek to establish a perpetually enduring entail—a thing the Common Law regarded as unreasonable and unattainable. Its aim, as stated in the preamble, was to ensure that where a gift had been made on certain conditions to provide what were called estates of curtsey, dower or frank marriage, the rights of both beneficiaries and reversioners should be respected and that "the will of the donor expressed in the charter of gift should be observed."

Named after its opening words, *De Donis Conditionalibus*

established a basic principle of English land law. Not only did it protect the reversion to the donor's heirs, but by forbidding alienation by the donee and so safeguarding the rights of his issue, it gave recognition to a new kind of heritable estate, inalienable as long as there was issue in tail of the original donee. Within practicable limits it ensured the primogenitary principle in the descent of both the parent estate and its offshoot. Owing to a flaw in one of its clauses, a generation later a loophole was found in the statute that enabled not the donee but his son to alienate the land and so disinherit his issue. But a great judge of Edward II's reign, Chief Justice Bereford, who had known what was in the mind of Hengham when he framed *De Donis*, insisted in a famous judgment on looking to the spirit instead of the letter of the statute and restored the entail in the grandson's favour, so establishing a precedent that was followed by the courts.[1] And though, a century later, lawyers had found other ways of enabling tenants-in-tail to bar the entail, by that time it had become established that the principle of English landed inheritance, in families of modest wealth as well as large, should be primogeniture and not, as was the case in other western kingdoms, partition. Instead of being divided among younger sons, landed property in England was to be transmitted dynastically.[2]

The effect of this on the nation's future can scarcely be exaggerated. It did not render the alienation of entailed estates impossible—for the ingenuity of lawyers proved inexhaustible—but it made it difficult. At a time when the rigid feudalism of the past was giving place to more elastic forms of tenure, a new landowning class was encouraged by the common law to adopt the feudal military device for preserving landed property intact by

[1] " He that made the statute intended to bring within it not only the donees but also the issue in tail until the entail was fully accomplished in the fourth degree, and the fact that he did not do so by express words concerning the subsequent issue was only due to his negligence; and so we shall not abate this writ." *Year Books of Edward II* (Selden Society) XI, 176-7. On this Professor Plucknett in his *Legislation of Edward I* comments, " Compared with Bereford's exploit it seems a feeble thing merely to drive a coach-and-six through an act of Parliament."

[2] *Plucknett* 52. " They took a dynastic view of the family, regarding it primarily as a chain of ancestors and descendants extending through time, rather than as a contemporary group of kinsmen. Primogeniture is the natural expression of the former view, as partition is of the latter." *Idem*, 129.

transmission through the eldest son. Read aloud in Westminster Hall on June 28th, 1285, the second Statute of Westminster subordinated the promptings of personal affection to the long-term interests of the realm. It helped to create landed families whose estates and traditions, preserved from generation to generation, formed a school for training men for public service and the capacity to rule.[1] It was from such lesser knightly or county families that Edward and his successors drew the local leaders who represented the shires in parliament, enforced the law in their native place, and, as magistrates—*custodes pacis* or keepers of the peace—took the weight off the shoulders of his overworked judges and sheriffs. The heads of such families looked after and enhanced their estates, making England in time to come the wealthiest farming country in the world, while relays of energetic and ambitious younger sons, educated for wealth but not endowed with it, went out from homes rich in transmitted standards of living and behaviour to make their fortunes and serve the State. *De Donis* helped to prevent the landed gentry from becoming, as on the continent, an exclusive caste divorced from responsibility. It made for an elastic as opposed to a rigid system of government, for enterprise and adventure instead of stagnation.

The reform of the law of entail occupied only one of the fifty chapters of this great legislative act. Besides creating the estate in tail the second Statute of Westminster dealt with dower and bills of exception, advowsons and mortmain, the writ of account and remedies for executors. It also imposed new checks on the power of the sheriff and his officers to delay the execution of writs and to arrest and blackmail men on false charges. Like all Edward's reforms of the law, it dealt with these things in a severely practical way. It made great changes, yet never for the sake of change, only

[1] In the church of Lydiard Tregoz in Wiltshire an eighteenth century triptych, setting out the genealogy of the St. John family, contains a commentary on this,

> " This course of time, by God's almighty powe
> Hath kept this land of Lydiard in one race
> Five hundred and forty-nine years, and now more,
> Where at this day is St. John's dwelling place."

In 1943 during the Second World War the Corporation of Swindon bought the land whose tenure was thus broken by purchase for the first time since the Conquest. M. D. Anderson, *Looking for History in British Churches*, 111.

for clarification and greater working efficiency. Its object was to make the law operate more justly and expeditiously.

It also gave relief to jurymen from the administrative abuses from which they were suffering. Not only did it prohibit the im-panelling of certain classes, such as men over seventy or those not resident in the shire, but it ended the practice by which ever-growing numbers of men were being summoned to Westminster. For while criminal offences requiring juries were tried by the itinerant judges at their assizes in the county town, civil cases were dealt with at Westminster by the court of Common Pleas, which had been permanently located there by a provision of Magna Carta. As it was a principle of English law that any case involving issues of fact or local knowledge must be tried by a jury of the county in which the cause of action arose, the increase of litigation in the central courts was imposing an intolerable burden on the limited number of freemen eligible for jury-service. Edward there-fore decided that, instead of civil juries coming to his judges, his judges should go to them. Yet rather than override Magna Carta he and his advisers outflanked it by what was known as the award of *nisi prius*. Henceforward, the writ to a sheriff directed him to cause jurors from his bailiwick to attend the court at Westminster by a certain date, unless first—*nisi prius*—the justices of assize came into the county, in which case they were to attend before them. By means of adjournments the return day was then postponed until after the next visit of the Assizes, so enabling civil actions to be tried by juries in the county to which they belonged. It is for this reason that civil cases set down for trial by the itinerant justices are still referred to as being in the *nisi prius* list.

The statute also helped to ease the path of litigants in their choice of writ. Under common law the bounds of every form of action and the remedy provided by it were most narrowly pre-scribed. Until the middle of the thirteenth century the Chancery clerks had been allowed to devise new writs to meet new needs, and the register of writs had been extended to cover ownership and possession, not only of land—or real property—but of personal or moveable property. Such were the writs of *trespass* which directed the sheriff to compel a man to answer a complaint that, "with force and arms" and against the king's peace—the essence of the action—he had carried off a plaintiff's goods or done him some other direct injury; of *replevin* for wrongful distraint of cattle; of detinue for detention of a specific chattel like a plough or horse, and of *debt* to compel the repayment of a fixed sum of which the plaintiff was alleged to have been "deforced." There was also an action of *account* to make a bailiff and, later, a partner, submit an account of moneys, and of *covenant* to enforce certain rights under seal, such as leases. But in 1258, sixteen years before Edward's accession, the Provisions of Oxford—imposed on the Crown by the barons—stopped the Chancery from sealing any new writ without the express consent of king and council. The creation of new writs and forms of action had virtually ceased.

Feeling himself strong enough, the king now sought to remedy this restriction. Not only did the second Statute of Westminster extend the scope of the possessory writ of *novel disseisin*, but by a provision called *consimilis casus* it authorised the Chancery clerks to formulate new writs in cases of a parallel kind where on technical grounds a plaintiff's case could not be fitted into an existing form of action. Though for political reasons this right was little used during the next two reigns, it made possible a widening of the action for *trespass* and, later, the provision of two new actions—*assumpsit* for breaches of general undertakings and simple contract not under seal, and *case* for any wrong or breach of legal duty which caused damage including libel and slander, hitherto unactionable at common law.

. . . .

Wishing to pay a long-deferred visit to his Gascon dominions, Edward placed before a parliament at Winchester in the autumn of 1285 a further statute to reform the police and defence of the realm. During the past thirty years England had suffered a baronial civil war and two wars against the Welsh, and there was still a grave undercurrent of disorder. Gangs of disbanded soldiers called clubmen or *trailbastons* were beating up travellers and breaking into houses; not only burglaries, rapes and arsons were passing unpunished but murders in alarming numbers. Again and again on the coroners' rolls the words appear: " he has fled and left no chattels." Of eighty-three persons charged with homicides in Northumberland in 1279 only three were hanged, seventy-one escaping, six taking sanctuary and one pleading benefit of clergy.

By traditional English law every able-bodied man between the ages of fifteen and sixty was obliged to take his share in the defence and police of the shire. With his neighbours he had to keep "watch and ward" against felons and peace-breakers and, whenever the village constable raised the "hue and cry," to help him pursue and catch them. Every township according to its size had one or more of these part-time officers, elected by the community from a rota of householders and, serving for a year or longer, responsible for the king's peace to the high constable of the hundred. The petty constable, as he was called, represented both the local community and the Crown. He was not only a policeman but a soldier, for in time of invasion, riot or rebellion he also had to see that every man turned out at the sheriff's summons in the fyrd or *posse comitatus* of the shire.

Edward's Norman and Angevin ancestors had used this rude national militia against their turbulent nobles, and his great-grandfather, Henry II, had reorganised it by his Assize of Arms.[1] At that time it had been confined to free men—for to the feudal mind there was something shocking in the idea of a bondsman bearing arms—but it had later been extended to all classes, including villeins. Having employed it in his Welsh wars to offset the falling numbers of the feudal host, Edward now placed it on a permanent basis. In every county, hundred and township muster-rolls were to be prepared from which Commissioners of Array could select and impress men in an emergency to serve as paid soldiers in the royal ranks. The arms they were to provide, according to their various ranks and degrees, were laid down by his statute, which also prescribed regular practice in their use and, twice a year, a "view of arms" by the constables of the hundred at which defaulters were to be presented to the sheriff's court for punishment. Freemen possessing goods or lands worth from £20 to £40 a year—what we should today call the £2000 p.a. class—who did not already owe knight's service were to come as knights and those worth more than £15 p.a. as troopers, with horse, lance and armour. Humbler folk, divided into four classes, were to serve as foot soldiers and either provide themselves or be provided by the constable with iron headpiece, quilted jacket, spear, dagger and bow and arrows. In the wooded lands near the Welsh border

[1] See *Makers of the Realm*, 260.

—in Shropshire, Macclesfield forest and Sherwood—rustic Englishmen of the better sort were already learning to handle, not the short bow whose string was pulled to the chest and whose arrows were shot into the air, but the longbow of Gwent, drawn to the ear, whose arrows of steel and goose-quill, aimed straight at the target, could strike down a mounted knight through his armour at more than two hundred yards' range. From this, in the next century, momentous consequences were to flow.

By the Statute of Winchester England obtained a reserve of amateur soldiers from which she was to draw in all her wars until the age of Napoleon. Before she had learnt to command the seas, it repeatedly saved her from invasion. Fyrd, *posse comitatus*, musters, fencibles, militia, by whatever name it was called, it remained a homespun body, affording from the days of Shakespeare's Falstaff to those of Rowlandson much material for humourists, but it sufficed. Of all its services the greatest—though one that such an autocrat as Edward can hardly have contemplated—was that, in times when royal despotism might otherwise have triumphed, it obviated the need for a standing army.

The statute also gave precision to the subject's duties as a policeman and preserver of the peace. " Every day," ran its preamble, " robbery, homicide and arson grow more numerous and felonies escape presentment by the oaths of jurors who would rather see the felonies committed on strangers than accuse the offenders."[1] For there was a natural tendency for a township to get rid of criminals and responsibility for their crimes by letting them escape into some other. Instead, therefore, of leaving it answerable only for felonies committed within its borders, Edward made it jointly responsible with other townships for all felonies committed in the hundred. He also fixed a tariff for every unpunished crime and breach of the peace to be levied on the offending hundred and its villages. The unit of policing was enlarged and made to conform to the requirements, not merely of the village, but the nation. As part of this policy the townships along the royal highways were also ordered, on pain of indictment before the justices on eyre, to cut back the brushwood on either side of the road to a distance of two hundred feet to reduce the risk of ambush from brigands and outlaws.

[1] Stubbs, *Select Charters,* 464.

To help enforce the statute a new local judiciary was created. In every shire a number of trusted knights and landowners were appointed to act, in an unpaid capacity, as conservators or keepers of the peace. This was an extension of the Plantagenet system of dividing and broadening the exercise of provincial authority, formerly centred in the hands of the sheriff. For, in days of feudal delegation and inadequate communication, it had been found that too much power in a sheriff's hands ended in his becoming an irremoveable and even hereditary magnate, as ready to defy the Crown as those he was appointed to control. It had, therefore, been the policy of every king since Henry II to entrust every new power of the Crown, not to the sheriffs, but to other officers—to county coroners, justices of assize, commissioners of array and taxes, knights of the shire, and now conservators or, as they became in the next century, justices of the peace. All worked within the traditional unit of local government, with all its binding ties of neighbourhood and regional sentiment. Yet all were subject, not to some provincial satrap whose interest it was to defy the Crown, but to the king's courts and officers at Westminster by whom they were appointed and in whose hands lay the power to dismiss them. The source of their authority was the king, the terms under which they exercised it those of the common law, the link between them and the government the royal judges on their periodic visitations of inquest, gaol delivery and general supervision of their master's interests. This interplay of central authority and local representation, of the rule of law and popularly delegated self-government is the key to English history.

All this was part of a process which Edward tirelessly pursued of establishing order in every sphere of government and, with it, rules and institutions to ensure its continuance. All unconsciously he was creating a national establishment to stand the test of time. Everything emanated from the authority of himself and his Council, yet the whole community above the ranks of the villein peasantry was made party to it. The modern distinction between executive, legislature and judiciary did not exist in his mind or in that of his subjects; all were manifestations of his royal will and the sovereignty of the law which he and his judges enacted and administered. His chancellor and masters and clerks in

Chancery—the supreme executive, secretarial and judicial office of the kingdom—sealed and issued his ordinances and writs, and his treasurer and Exchequer enforced through his sheriffs the payment of his customs, dues and taxes. His judges sat in his court of King's Bench to try pleas of the Crown and offences against his peace, in the court of Exchequer to collect his debts and fine and punish those who withheld them, in the court of Common Pleas to hear the civil suits of his subjects. Above them, whenever he chose to summon to it his magnates and the representatives of the estates of the realm, was the supreme court of appeal and forum of national debate, the king himself and his councillors in his high court of Parliament. And at the circumference, supervised by his perambulating judges in their courts of assize and *nisi prius*, gaol delivery, oyer and terminer and *trailbaston*, were the local courts of the county and hundred, in which his sheriff and bailiffs tried petty pleas of debt and trespass and exercised summary jurisdiction over brawls, affrays, minor crimes and breaches of the peace; and the coroners' courts which investigated sudden deaths and reported homicides and concealments of treasure trove. To them were now added the sessions of the keepers of the peace. Beyond them, now subordinated to the common law in all matters affecting the king's peace and the ownership of freehold land, were the private courts and honours of the greater feudal lords and the village manorial courts.

Outside the common law, yet subject, too, to the overriding authority of the king were the borough courts which administered the Law Merchant. Mercantile law had grown up as an affair of international convenience to settle disputes between traders of different nations and arrange for the collection of their debts. It operated wherever merchants congregated, in boroughs and seaports, markets and fairs. Its details varied from country to country and even from town to town. In England there was a growing tendency for it to approximate to the custom of London. Ever since the aftermath of Evesham, when his father had made him warden of the Cinque Ports and had given him control of the foreign merchants in England, Edward had realised that trade was something more than a mere milch-cow for extracting tolls and tallages. On his way home from the crusade he had visited the great manufacturing cities of Tuscany and Lombardy, whose merchant princes had presented him with hangings of cloth of gold and horses caparisoned with scarlet and whose people had acclaimed him in the streets as an emperor. Here in the past half century the Italian genius had wrought an astonishing transformation in the means of creating credit and, with it, of manufactured wealth. Maritime trade with the Levant and Egypt— terminals of the camel routes from the mysterious East—had brought to the capitalists of Venice, Genoa and Pisa riches unknown since the days of imperial Rome. The cloth-manufacturing republic of Florence had 300,000 inhabitants; the cities of Milan and Venice each nearly 200,000 or four times as many as London.[1] Already in the churches of little Apennine hill towns great artists were creating for their patrons paintings of a kind that heralded a renaissance of the human spirit.

To Edward all this had been a revelation. To finance his projects and, later, his Welsh wars, he had borrowed heavily from the Lucca and Florentine cloth-working houses of Riccardi and Frescobaldi and in return, by facilitating their purchases of English wool, had granted them opportunities for enlarging their profits and, with it, the credit they were able to offer him. Wishing to see a similar commercial growth in his own kingdom, he had consistently encouraged its merchants, employing them as bankers, brokers and collectors and farmers of the customs and consulting them both in parliaments and in *ad hoc* professional assemblies or *colloquia*. Believing trade to be dependent on mutual trust and fidelity to bond and contract, he had sought to enforce respect for contractual obligations and the commercial virtues of fair dealing and to offer those who lived by it quicker means of obtaining justice than the slow, formalistic procedures of the common law.

In the summer of 1283, during the parliament at Shrewsbury that had sentenced the Welsh patriot David to death, Edward had issued from his chancellor's Shropshire home, Acton Burnell, a statute giving traders a novel means of proving and collecting debts. "Whereas," ran the preamble, "merchants on lending their goods have incurred poverty because no suitable law was provided whereby they could speedily recover their debt on the day set for payment, and whereas on this account many merchants have ceased coming into this land with its merchandise to the

[1] C.E.H.E. II, 303.

damage of the whole kingdom, the king by himself and his council has ordained and established that the merchant who wishes to make sure of his debt shall cause the debtor to come before the mayor of London, York or Bristol to acknowledge it, . . . and the acknowledgement be enrolled so that it may be known.''[1] When the date for payment fell due, by producing the debtor's bond before the mayor on whose roll it had been registered the creditor could demand an execution against the defaulter's chattels and burgage tenements and their sale by the borough authorities. If his assets were not sufficient he could have him imprisoned in the borough gaol and keep him there on bread and water until his friends came to his rescue.

Now, in this great creative year of 1285, Edward went even further. Finding that, through the fraud and collusion of borough officials, foreign merchants were still having difficulty in obtaining justice, he and his chancellor issued a new enactment called the Statute of Merchants. By this, as soon as the bond was in default, the debtor could be committed to prison; if the keeper of the borough gaol refused to accept him or allowed him to escape he became liable for the debt. If after three months the debtor had still failed to sell his assets to satisfy his creditor, the latter was to be given possession, not only of his chattels but of his freehold land, whether inside or outside the borough—a revolutionary precedent at a time when the ownership of land was regarded as sacrosanct. He could then assign his possessory rights over it—tenancy by statute merchant, as it was called—to anyone prepared to buy them or keep it until the debt had been discharged out of its income.

For Edward was resolved to make every jurisdiction in his realm conform to his overriding authority and what he conceived to be the dictates of justice. Where it failed to do so, he respected the "liberty" of a corporation no more than that of a rebellious feudal noble. In the summer that saw the publication of the Statute of Westminster II he challenged the privileges of the most powerful city in England. He had already, after the first Welsh war, precipitated a head-on clash with the civic authorities of London by ordering the traditional meeting-place of the folkmoot outside St. Paul's to be enclosed with a wall and posterns to keep

---

[1] *Statutes of the Realm* cit. *Stephenson and Marcham,* 172-3.

out the nightly concourse of thieves and prostitutes who made it notorious. From time immemorial the city had governed itself; it was believed to have done so without interruption since Roman times. But those who exercised authority on its citizens' behalf were now supine and incompetent; members of a little group of aldermanic families, they had long ceased to be able to keep order among the unruly artisans and apprentices and criminal riff-raff who thronged the narrow streets and courtyards of the fast-growing capital. Twice in seventy years London had played a major role in rebellion against the Crown; the last hours of Edward's father had been rendered hideous by the howling of its mob as, in answer to the great bell of St. Paul's, it poured towards Westminster in the course of a disputed mayoral election.

Before his return to England Edward had secured the election as mayor of a *nouveau riche* vintner named Henry le Waleys, an energetic and efficient autocrat after his own heart who had put down proletarian insubordination with a rude, authoritarian hand. Later, after Waleys had been transferred to the king's other and equally unruly capital, Bordeaux, his place had been taken by a rich Kentish franklin, Gregory of Rokesley—a member of one of the ancient city families—who effected a number of administrative reforms, particularly in the keeping of civic and legal records. From his seven years' mayoralty dates the first of the city's line of Common Clerks. But Rokesley was too much hampered by entrenched municipal rights and liberties to be able to satisfy the king's exacting standards of public order. In 1281, two years before the outbreak of the second Welsh war, following repeated complaints of crimes, broils and escapes from justice he was replaced by Waleys, who introduced a series of drastic reforms which virtually subjected everyone in the city to police surveillance. In keeping with the king's policy of freeing trade from restrictions and assisting the Italian capitalists who provided him with credit, all foreign merchants in the city were also given full citizenship, a court to settle their own disputes and the right to provide half the jury in any case in which they were involved.

All this proved more than the city could stand. In the autumn election of 1284, a few months before the king returned from Wales, Rokesley was restored to the mayoralty by an almost unanimous vote. Once again the old civic disorders and crimes broke out, and in the summer of 1285, following a notorious faction murder in the sanctuary of St. Mary le Bow in which the Common Clerk was implicated, Edward appointed a judicial commission under his treasurer, John Kirkby, to investigate the state of public order in the capital. Kirkby, as masterful and adroit a negotiator as the king himself, ordered Rokesley to appear before him and the Exchequer barons in the Tower. When, on the grounds that no mayor of London need attend an inquest outside the city liberties, Rokesley divested himself of his robes before appearing, Kirkby promptly declared that, as the city was now without a mayor, its jurisdiction was forfeit and must revert to the Crown.

This was precisely what the king wanted; as on other occasions he had caused his adversaries to play into his hands. Without hesitation he took the city into his keeping and appointed a warden. The rule of the patrician families was brought to an end and governance by royal officials substituted. For the next twelve years there were no more elections for mayor and sheriffs, and the aldermen were appointed by the court of the Exchequer which took up residence in the Guildhall. Kirkby, who a year later became Bishop of Ely, built himself, on an eminence overlooking the Holebourn valley and the city's western walls, a splendid palace which he left on his death to his episcopal successors; its beautiful little chapel of St. Ethelreda's, designed on the model of the Sainte Chapelle in Paris, still survives among the Georgian houses of Ely Place.[1] Though thirteen years later London recovered its right of self-government and even during the royal wardenship the city courts continued to administer its ancient customary law, henceforward in all matters affecting crime and public order its citizens were subject like everyone else to the common law and the provisions of the Statute of Winchester. It became part of the realm and not, like the free cities of Italy, Flanders and Germany, an entity apart from it.

The capital was not the only town to feel Edward's strong creative hand. Lincoln, once England's second commercial city,

[1] Owing to the difficulty of demolishing its eight-foot-thick walls the chapel survived when the palace was pulled down in the eighteenth century. Williams, 1, 369. For a detailed account of Edward's relations with the city, see G. Williams, " London and Edward I." *Royal Hist. Soc. Transactions,* 5th series, Vol. II, 81-98.

suffered the same treatment. At Oxford, where the chancellor of the university complained that the city bakers and brewers were contaminating the river waters, rendering them "dangerous and noisome" to "the community of scholars," a royal commission appointed a more suitable site and forbade the makers of bread and ale to use their former watering places "under pain of grievous forfeiture."[1] Two ports, New Winchelsea and Kingston-on-Hull, owed their existence to the king's passion for planning. At the former he employed Henry le Waleys and Gregory of Rokesley to lay out streets, wharves, markets, churches, mills and walls on a jut of land a few miles from the ancient Cinque port of Winchelsea, which was threatened by floods owing to the erosion of the shingle-banks protecting the tidal lagoon at the mouth of the Brede and Rother rivers. Three years after the work began Edward's foresight was proved by the great storm of 1284 which swept away the island on which the older Winchelsea stood. Hull or Wyke, as it was formerly called, was transformed from a fishing village into a port a decade later to take the place of Ravenser where a similar encroachment of the sea had occurred. The course of the river Hull was diverted at its junction with the Humber to enlarge the harbour, a hundred and fifty acres were purchased by the Crown and laid out, two-thirds as building sites and the remainder as streets and markets on the same Roman grid system as at New Winchelsea. Roads were built to link the town with the Yorkshire hinterland and the place was given a royal charter, a mint, two weekly markets and the name of Kingston-on-Hull.[2]

Not since Alfred had any king taken such meticulous and comprehensive care of his subjects' concerns. Edward experimented with the cultivation of hops on the royal estates, provided for the preservation of the national archives in the Tower under a Master of the Rolls, and had a geographical survey made which resulted in the earliest extant map of England.[3] He even laid down a close season for salmon in the rivers. His passion for detail is shown in the ordinances he issued for the control of his household. Every

[1] *Select Cases in the Court of King's Bench under Edward I* (Selden Society) II, 151.

[2] J. A. Williamson, *The English Channel*, 22, 93-4, 102-3; *Speculum*, Vol. 22, pp. 305-8; see also F. M. Powicke, *Henry III and the Lord Edward*, 634; H. C. Darby, *An Historical Geography of England*, 301-2.

[3] The Gough map now in the Bodleian Library.

evening the treasurer, stewards, marshal, clerks, sergeants and
ushers of the hall were to check the day's issues of food and wine
from pantry, buttery, kitchen and cellar. The usher of the wardrobe was to weigh the wax and candle wicks, subsequently re-
weighing what was left over on the morrow; the marshals of the
hall were to make a circuit of the court to clear it of all "ribalds"
—disorderly persons—and to prevent unauthorised men or horses
from drawing rations. No-one was to sleep in the Wardrobe
except the comptroller, the treasurer's clerk, the surgeon, chief
usher and one footman. One can picture the king, sitting in his
solar[1]—the royal bedchamber that served for rest and audience—
receiving reports from his servants, supervising, consulting and
directing everything.

.   .   .   .

Edward was not only king of England. He was duke of Aquitaine and as such ruled a French province that stretched from the
Charente to the Pyrenees and at one time had constituted nearly
half the area of France. Inherited from his great-grandmother,
Henry II's queen, much of it, including Poitou, Limousin,
Périgord and the Auvergne, had been ceded in the past half
century to the kings of France, as a result partly of war and partly
of legal processes brought by their lawyers. But with its famous
vineyards and export of wine and corn, what remained—known
as the duchy of Guienne or Gascony—was still one of the richest
fiefs in Europe. Though nominally subject to the French king,
for nearly all practical purposes it was an independent domain and
Edward's to rule so long as he could command the allegiance of its
turbulent nobility and prosperous burghers. He had governed it
as his father's viceroy in his youth and on his way home from the
crusade had spent a winter in its capital, Bordeaux, settling its
troubled affairs and internecine wars. But it was now twelve years
since he had visited it. Having conquered Wales and restored
order to London, he sailed from Dover for Calais in May 1286
with his queen, chancellor and a splendid train.

At Paris, on his way south, Edward did homage to the new

---

[1] It was in this room that soon afterwards, while sitting on the bed and
attended by the ladies of the court, Edward and his queen narrowly escaped
death by lightning. *Medieval England* (ed. H. W. C. Davis), 53.

seventeen-year-old king, his cousin Philip the Fair, receiving back his fief from his hands according to the rules of feudal tenure. He safeguarded his rights and the limitations of his allegiance by the non-committal phrase he had used while doing homage to the young king's father, Philip the Bold, after his own accession twelve years before: " My lord king, I become your man for all the lands I ought to hold of you according to the form of the peace made between our ancestors." For now, as then, he was resolved to offer no loophole to the cunning jurists of the *parlement* of Paris who were always trying to enlarge their master's rights by whittling down those of his feudatories. He even succeeded in extracting from his royal cousin a promise that no more encroachments on his territories should be made by the French courts during his lifetime, even when their verdict was against him.

Angevin and Norman by descent, with a Provençal mother and accustomed since childhood to speak and think in French, Edward was completely at home in France—the strongest and most civilised state in Christendom and the fount and nurse of its chivalry, of which he himself was the greatest living exemplar. A century earlier his great-grandfather, Henry II, had controlled far more of France than the French king, ruling Normandy, Maine, Anjou, Touraine and Brittany by inheritance and Aquitaine by marriage. And though, thanks to the folly and obstinacy of King John and the weakness of Henry III, all had since been lost except Gascony and a small enclave called Ponthieu on the Channel coast which had come to him with his Spanish wife, he was still by far the most powerful of the feudatories of France—a power immensely enhanced because he was also king of England and Wales and lord of Ireland.

At that time, fresh from his conquest of Wales, Edward was the first monarch in Christendom. There was hardly a part of it from the Mediterranean to the North Sea with which he had not been closely concerned through marriage or chivalry. His wife's brother, Alfonso the Learned, was king of Castile and Leon, largest of the Spanish kingdoms, while he was planning to marry his daughter to the heir of its neighbour and rival, Aragon, whose fleet, from its new-won Catalan and Valencian harbours, controlled the western Mediterranean, as Castile's did the Biscay bay.

Eastward along the Mediterranean littoral lay Provence, home-
land of Edward's mother and now an appanage of the French
throne. In the mountains beyond was Savoy whose count, another
cousin, was begging him to adjudicate a disputed succession. And
at the other end of Italy was the kingdom of Sicily and Naples,
whose crown had been offered to Edward's brother by the pope
in return for his father's promise to wrest it from its Hohenstauffen
rulers. It had been Henry III's attempt to do so that had
embroiled him with his barons and led to the civil war in which
Edward had won his spurs; later his uncle, Charles of Anjou—
brother to the saintly Louis IX of France and a sharp, shrewd,
ambitious man—had won its crown from the last Hohenstauffen
emperor's bastard, Manfred. The French prince's victory had
been the culminating event in the long disastrous struggle between
the papacy and the Hohenstauffens—for nearly a century emperors of Germany and titular kings of Italy. For a moment, at
the time of Edward's return from the crusade, it had seemed as if
Christendom was about to revert to that older ideal, dear to King
Louis of France, of a family of Christian princes living in amity
under the spiritual guidance of a universal ecclesiastical institution
above and beyond politics. As Louis's nephew and the son of the
builder of the new Westminster abbey, Edward was a firm
believer in this idea. The then pope, Gregory X, who had been his
chaplain on crusade, was a churchman without worldly ambition
whose lifelong aim was to end the doctrinal schism between the
Roman Church of the West and the Byzantine or Greek Orthodox
Church of the East and so unite all Christendom in a campaign to
free the Holy Land. Edward had stayed with him on his way
home in the spring of 1273, securing from him the right to take a
tenth of the temporalities of the English clergy for three years
to reimburse his crusading expenses. But Gregory had died
soon afterwards, and under his successors the papacy had once
more become embroiled in the struggle for secular wealth and
power.

The European countries which most closely affected the commercial interests of Edward and his subjects were those of the
Netherlands or, as it was sometimes called, Low Germany. Here,
facing the Thames estuary and controlling the lower reaches of
the Scheldt, Meuse and Rhine—the great commercial riverways

of northern Europe—lay Holland and Zeeland, Brabant, Hainault, Gelderland, Julich, Cleves and the bishoprics of Liége and Utrecht. With the two largest of these Edward had sought matrimonial alliances, in 1284 affiancing his eldest son, Alfonso—who died, however, in the same year[1]—to the Count of Holland's daughter, and his eight-year-old daughter, Margaret, to the heir of Brabant. A major importer of English wool for its cloth-looms, and possessor of the port of Antwerp, Brabant had many links with England, though less important than those of its western neighbour, Flanders, whose great cloth cities, Ghent, Bruges—larger then than London—Ypres and Douai, could never buy enough of her fine wool. Unlike his Netherland neighbours, the Count of Flanders was a vassal, not of the shadowy German emperor but of the anything but shadowy King of France. This caused a perennial conflict in Flemish policies between her ruler's feudal ties and her merchants' dependence on England. Any interruption of their trade with her—and before Edward's settlement of a dispute with the Countess of Flanders in 1274 there had been such a break for five years—spelt ruin for the Flemish burghers and starvation for their swarming millhands. For what the cities of Tuscany and Lombardy were to southern Europe, those of Flanders were to northern—densely populated industrial centres importing raw materials and food from primary-producing countries like England and turning them into fine cloths for the possessing classes of a luxurious and expanding civilisation.

Because he thought of Christendom as a single polity and its rulers as a family of Christian princes, Edward was eager to end the feuds and divisions into which they had fallen since the day when, an ardent youth, he had followed his uncle, King Louis, on crusade. At fifty, with all the prestige of his victories over de Montfort, the Saracens and the Welsh, he was the doyen of Christian kings. His ambition was to lead them once more against the infidel who held the sacred places of their faith and threatened their common polity. For nearly three years after doing homage for his French dominions he remained at his southern capital, Bordeaux, trying to negotiate a peace between the warring princes of western Europe and mobilise them in a crusade to save Acre

[1] The beautiful Tenison psalter in the British Museum was probably made as a wedding gift for him. *Evans*, 10.

and the beleaguered Christian fortresses of Outremer, now again in deadly danger.

For Christendom's affairs were in a sadly confused state. Although its causes were clear neither to Edward nor his contemporaries, the same process of national consolidation which had taken place in England was occurring in France, Castile and Aragon, all of whose rulers had succeeded in merging large groups of adjacent fiefs into nation-states. In doing so they had come into conflict with one another and, though all acknowledged the overriding unity of Christendom, no pope could any longer restrain their rivalries. Indeed, by its illusory triumph over the Hohenstauffen emperors and its attempt to dispose of the crown of Sicily, the papacy itself had helped to plunge the West into a new kind of war, fought not between tribes and feudal lords but between national dynasties.

In the Easter of 1282, at a time when England was shaken by news of the second Welsh rebellion, another popular insurrection had occurred in southern Europe. Inflamed by the insolencies of the troops of their French king, Charles of Anjou, the Sicilians had risen and massacred every Frenchman in the island.[1] Dominating the Mediterranean narrows, conquered in turn by Greeks, Saracens and Normans and transformed by the latter and the Hohenstauffen emperors into the best administered realm in the south, Sicily with its great natural wealth was a prize coveted by all. When Charles attempted to reconquer it, its people offered their throne to Peter III of Aragon, husband of the heiress of their former ruler, Manfred. By using his naval power to hold the island against the combined forces of Charles and the papacy, King Peter precipitated a war between France and Aragon which put an end to all hopes of the crusade which Edward was planning. In that war the most bitter partisan was the pope himself who, in his fury at Aragon's seizure of a papal fief, proved more irreconcilable towards the Spaniards than even the French royal house.

It was this sterile conflict that the English king set himself to end. Its original participants were all dead, but it still raged with unabated fury under their successors. In his self-imposed mission Edward showed a tact, restraint and perseverance that impressed

---

[1] A rising known to history as the Sicilian Vespers.

everyone. By October 1288 he had negotiated a treaty between France and Aragon that made him the acknowledged arbiter of Europe.

While he was mediating in the disputes of his fellow princes he was also engaged in settling the affairs of Gascony. Here, too, he left behind him creation and order. His enduring legacy to the duchy were the little towns or bastides[1] that he built in the Garonne valley to restrain the feudal anarchy of the Gascon nobles, whose diet of "garlic, onions, radishes and the headiest of wines," it was said, made them the most quarrelsome in Europe. Some of these *villes anglaises*, as they were called, with their narrow straight-paved lanes laid out in rectangular-grids like Roman camps, their arcaded squares and sturdy walls and posterns, still survive—reminders of the good peace that an English king established in that lovely land of vineyards and rivers seven centuries ago. One of them was named Bath after the Somerset see of Edward's chancellor, Robert Burnell.

For more than three and a half years Edward remained in France while his council and judges ruled England. Once at least he was forced to make an important decision *in absentia*; when Archbishop Pecham again challenged the Crown's right to remove cases from the Church courts. This time it was the Crown that had precipitated the quarrel, its lawyers having tried to claim that, apart from purely spiritual cases, the courts Christian had no jurisdiction in any but matrimonial and testamentary cases. At first the king had supported them, appointing a judicial commission to try the canon-law clerks and judges who had resisted the royal writs of prohibition. But the uproar caused by this high-handed step was so great that Edward, who usually knew when he had gone too far, decided to withdraw. In the autumn of 1286 he addressed a writ to his justices beginning with the warning *Circumspecte agatis*—be careful how you act—ordering them to leave to the jurisdiction of the ecclesiastical courts matters which under canon law had always belonged to them, such as injuries to clerics, defamation and perjury and breaches of ecclesiastical

[1] Derived, like *Bastille*, from the word "*batir*" to build, *Speculum*, Vol. XXII, 301. A great town planner, Edward wrote from Bordeaux to ask for four experts to be sent him from London "who know how to divide, order and arrange a new town in the manner most beneficial to us and the merchants." *Medieval England* I, 243.

right affecting tithes, monasteries and churchyards. Seeking to rally Europe for a crusade and to obtain the pope's authority to raise money from ecclesiastical property for it, he did not wish to quarrel with the Church.

·   ·   ·   ·   ·   ·   ·   ·

In an age when without the personal presence of its ruler even a strong nation could soon relapse into anarchy, the king's long stay in Aquitaine was a measure of England's administrative maturity. But by the summer of 1289 his return to his kingdom could be delayed no longer. Two of the Marcher earls in the Welsh borderland were engaged in open war over a castle the one had built on the other's land. Edward himself was deep in debt to his Italian bankers, for no grant to supplement the ordinary revenues had been made since the thirtieth voted for the Welsh war six years before. When that February the treasurer had asked for a subsidy from a parliament called in the king's absence, the magnates, led by the Earl of Gloucester, refused to give anything until their sovereign met them face to face.

For throughout the country there was widespread complaint of malpractices by royal officers and judges. Men were not getting, or felt they were not getting, the speedy and impartial justice Magna Carta and its successor charters had promised. Sheriffs were failing to make returns to writs and to summon impartial juries, judges and their clerks were letting it be known that success in their courts would never attend any suitor who did not fee them, and the king's rights were being sacrificed to enrich his servants in flagrant defiance of their trust and the law. And while rich suitors could get their cases settled without delay, the poor could get no redress.

When the king landed at Dover in August 1289 he made his usual pilgrimages to Becket's tomb at Canterbury and his favourite shrines of Bury, Walsingham, Ely and Waltham. While he made his oblations and hawked and hunted in the East Anglian heaths and forests, he took account of his people's grievances and "listened to the cries of the wretched." On the day after his return to Westminster for the Michaelmas feast he issued a proclamation inviting all with complaints of extortion and misprision and denial of justice to lay them before a special commission of seven officials of his household presided over by the chancellor. Its findings during the next two years affected more than seven hundred officials, high and low, and disclosed the worst scandal in English judicial annals. Only two of the eight judges of the King's Bench and Common Pleas escaped disgrace, while five justices of eyre were also found guilty and dismissed. Thomas of Weyland, a chief justice, who had amassed vast estates in his native East Anglia, was accused of incitement to murder and, sooner than face trial, fled for sanctuary. After an attempt to plead clergy—for he had been a deacon in youth—he was allowed to abjure the kingdom, penniless, barefooted and cross in hand. Enormous fines were imposed on the other judges; Solomon of Rochester, a chief justice of assize, had to pay the equivalent of four thousand marks —over £150,000 in modern money. Even this was light compared with the 32,000 marks confiscated from Adam de Stratton, the chamberlain of the Exchequer—an office held as deputy for its hereditary holder, the litigious Countess of Albemarle, with whose help he had amassed the largest fortune of his time. Ten years earlier he had narrowly escaped disgrace; this time his wealth failed to save him and, found guilty of forgery, fraud and extortion, he was sentenced to imprisonment and total forfeiture. Among the hoard discovered in his house were £12,650 in bullion—more than half a million of our money—and a king's crown.

Altogether the fines imposed on Edward's servants helped to pay off a sixth of his debts to the Italian bankers. The most tragic casualty of all was the great jurist and chief justice of the King's Bench, Ralph Hengham. It may be because he had trusted him so much that Edward punished him so severely. Dismissed from office and fined seven thousand marks—more than a hundred times his salary—he seems to have been disgraced for falsifying a record to save a poor suitor from a fine that would have ruined him.[1] Though he had amassed great wealth—for he could not

---

[1] *D. N. B.* According to Coke's *Institutes* Edward used the fine to build a clock-tower in New Palace Yard just outside the entrance to Westminster Hall where the courts sat. It survived till the reign of George I when it was demolished and its four-ton bell, "Great Tom", removed to Wren's new St. Paul's. A century later, when the present Houses of Parliament were built, the clock-tower that houses "Big Ben" was raised in its place. An Elizabethan

otherwise have paid the fine—it seems inconceivable that a lawyer of such distinction would have been guilty of any major offence incompatible with the spirit of the common law he loved and administered so well. On none of the other eight charges against him was even minor illegality proved.

It seems probable, therefore, that Hengham aroused his master's passionate Angevin temper by defending himself too tenaciously. Exceptionally merciful to those who confessed and submitted themselves to his judgment, Edward was relentless when anyone whom he thought at fault argued with him and tried to justify himself. A king, Bracton had written, cannot be coerced, but he can be supplicated; Hengham may well have been too proud to do so. Another judge, accused of accepting bribes to take an inquisition in private from a jury composed of the defendants' friends, was let off with a nominal fine because he admitted his guilt and humbly sought a pardon. As ten years later Hengham was again employed in the highest judicial office, it may have been, as Maitland wrote, "that the king broke the man who stood up to him in the hour of his wrath for refusing to allow guilt to be imputed to himself." Technically, too, the chief justice had placed himself in the wrong by stretching the law against his master—a thing the latter, so insistent on the letter of his rights, always found hard to forgive. Edward's rage when he considered an injury had been done him could be very terrible; one judge, Henry de Bray, justice of the Jews, tried to drown himself on the way to the Tower and later dashed out his brains.

As some extenuation of the judges' conduct must be set the very modest salaries they received. Hengham and his brother chief justice were paid sixty marks a year, that is forty pounds, and their fellow judges only forty marks—the equivalent of less than £1500 p.a. today. The Church having refused to allow its members to plead in the lay courts,[1] the Crown could no longer maintain a sufficiently experienced judiciary out of ecclesiastical benefices. Since it could not afford to pay adequate salaries, it let

---

judge, asked to alter a record, remarked that he did not wish to build a clock-tower.

[1] As early as 1217 Bishop Poore of Salisbury laid down in a *constitutio*, " Neither *clerici* nor priests are to appear as *advocati* in a secular tribunal unless in their own cases or those of poor persons." *Cohen*, 159.

its judges supplement their income by fees. In an intensely litigious age, when every great landowner was almost continuously engaged in the courts, rich suitors felt no compunction in supplementing the fees of judges and their clerks. Between such bonuses and bribery was only a step.

The most important result of the judicial scandals was a reorganisation of the legal profession. The task was entrusted to the new chief justice of the Common Pleas, John de Metyngham —one of the two members of the original bench to escape the purge. In 1292 he and his fellow judges were commissioned to choose from every county a number of the more promising students of law to be officially attached to the courts either as attorneys or as apprentices to the serjeants or *servientes ad legem* who pleaded before the king's judges. They were to enjoy a monopoly and their numbers, fixed at first at a hundred and forty, were to be left to the judges to add to as required. In other words, the profession was to regulate its own recruitment, education and rules of practice.

It was the beginning of a new form of learned education, one outside the Church and independent of it. A century after Henry II had been forced to concede immunity for clerics from lay justice, his great-grandson established secular training for the common law as an alternative to the study of civil law which, like every other form of learning, the Church in its universities reserved exclusively for its own members. It was an education based on the practice of the courts and necessitating great precision of thought and speech. It was taught, not by theorists in lecture rooms and libraries, but in crowded courts of law where, under the eye of the king's judges, quick and trained professional wits were pitted against one another, as the masters of forensic science, thinking and arguing on their feet, sought to fit the conflicting facts of their clients' disputes into the sharply defined framework of the common law writs and procedures.

These tyros or apprentices assisted and devilled for their seniors as they do today, attended their consultations and listened to the thrust and parry of their contests from enclosures called "cribs" built at the sides of the courts. In the year in which the king entrusted their education to his judges there appeared the first of the Year Books—manuscript notes of cases, pleadings and forensic argument made for young advocates to help them master the intricacies of the law. Written in the legal French of the courts, they set out in staccato jottings the arguments and altercations, exceptions and answers of the great serjeants who dominated the courts at the end of the thirteenth and beginning of the fourteenth century—Lowther, Heyham, Howard, Hertpool, Huntingdon, Spigornel—and the interruptions and, often, caustic comments of the judges. " Leave off your noise and deliver yourself from his account," Chief Justice Hengham interrupts an over-persistent pleader. " Get to your business," his successor, Bereford enjoins, " you plead one point, they about another, so that neither of you strikes the other." And when learned counsel tried to gain the day by arguing, " We have seen damages awarded in similar circumstances," Bereford replied: " You will never see them so long as I am here." " Where have you seen a guardian vouch on a writ of *dower*," asked another judge and, when the incautious serjeant answered, " Sir, in Trinity term last past, and of that I vouch the record," there came the crushing rejoiner, " If you find it, I will give you my hat! "

The interest of these early Year Books—and no other nation has anything like them—is the greater because, in those formative years, judges were helping by their judgments and the precedents they created to shape the future course of the law. Some of them, like Hengham, had even drafted it in the king's council chamber; " do not gloss the statute," he remarked on one occasion, " we know it better than you, for we made it." " The judgment to be by you now given," counsel reminded the court in another case, " will be hereafter an authority in every *quare non admissit* in England." For all their insistence on the rigid rules of pleading and procedure, such judges were very conscious of the immense discretionary power to do justice and equity delegated to them by their royal master. " You wicked rascal," Staunton, J. interrupted a dishonest attorney who had prayed for a *postea* in defiance of the rules of just dealing, " you shall not have it! But because you, to delay the woman from her dower, have vouched and not sued a writ to summon your warrantor, this court awards that you go to prison."[1]

[1] Selden Soc. XXII, Year Book Series IV, 195.

The apprentice pleaders did not only learn together in the courts. They lived together in inns or hospices presided over by their senior members. In the leafy suburb of Holborn and in the Thameside meadows between Westminster Hall and London's western walls there sprang up, during the years of expanding litigation that followed Edward's legislative reforms, a whole colony of such bachelor establishments. Keeping an inn seems to have become a highly profitable source of revenue for leaders of the legal profession, for some of them kept several; a Chancery clerk named John de Tamworth had, in the reign of Edward's grandson, no less than four in the neighbourhood of Fetter Lane. Similar inns were kept for the clerks of Chancery. Nearly all were rented from the ecclesiastical corporations or dignitaries—Templars, Hospitallers, Black Friars, the priory of St. Bartholomew, the convent of Clerkenwell, the abbey of Missenden, the Bishop of Ely—who owned most of the land to the west of London. Though never formally incorporated like the Church's residential colleges and halls at Oxford and Cambridge, they helped to create esprit de corps and standards of professional conduct among those studying and practising the law. Many of them adopted a practice of holding legal debates or moots; when in 1344 Clifford's Inn was demised to a society of apprentices of the law, one of its rules was that "every member shall be obliged in his turn to carry on all manner of erudition and learning in the said inn that appertains to an outer barrister."[1]

.   .   .   .

In the spring of 1290, following his purge of the judicial bench, the king presided over another parliament at Westminster—"a deliberation," as he called it, "with our faithful men." It sat for the unprecedented time of nearly three months and gave its witness and approval to an immense volume of judicial and other business whose purport was to ensure that everyone—king, magnates, landed gentry and merchants—received their just due. It set the seal on Edward's legislative work, begun with the first Statute of Westminster fifteen years before, interrupted by the two Welsh wars and his visit to Gascony and continued at Westminster and Winchester in 1285. At a family conference in his

[1] *Williams,* I, 15.

mother's convent at Amesbury to discuss the arrangements for the marriages of his daughters to the heir of Brabant and the Earl of Gloucester, it had been decided to ask the Crown's feudal tenants for an increase in the customary aids payable on such occasions. For, owing to the break-up of the old feudal fiefs, the amount obtainable from them had drastically declined. But, as a similar shrinkage had occurred in the feudal revenues of the magnates, a bargain was struck between them and the Crown. By what became known from its opening words as *Quia emptores*, all owners of freehold land, both great and small, were given protection to prevent the practice of sub-infeudation from robbing them of the incidental rights of lordship. The most valuable of these were *marriage*, *wardship*—the right to enjoy the profits of a tenant's estate during the infancy of his heir—and *escheat*—the reversion if the tenant died without heirs or committed a felony, which, in a rough and violent age, often happened. Yet if a mesne tenant granted his fee to a purchaser of the land for some purely nominal service, like a pair of gloves or a rose at midsummer, his lord could claim nothing from him but the valueless service he had reserved should he leave an infant heir, die without heirs or commit a felony. To end such an obvious injustice—one caused by the separation of the monetary value of land from the feudal obligations attaching to it—*Quia emptores* forbade sub-infeudation altogether. A mesne tenant could still dispose of his land, and his right to do so was now expressly recognised, but the feudal duties and obligations of its tenure passed automatically to the purchaser. In the long run, by preventing any further extension downward of the feudal chain and by formally legalising the sale of land in fee simple, the statute hastened the demise of feudalism. For the present it served, as it was meant to, the just ends of facilitating freedom of purchase and upholding the rights of feudal lords and the Crown.

In a further and revisionary Statute of *quo warranto* issued at Whitsuntide the king also conceded the principle that time could run against the Crown. This put a stop to the extreme claims that his judges had been making against franchise owners under the earlier statute of that name. He did not go so far as to admit that long user could ever be a legal answer to a writ of *quo warranto*. But he met what had become a major grievance by offering to confer charters on all who could prove by a jury of neighbours possession of their franchises since the accession of King Richard in 1189—from time immemorial, as it was called. This character-istic English compromise, while continuing to prevent acquisi-tion by mere seisin, assured quiet enjoyment of long estab-lished rights to those unable to produce a royal charter in their support.

All this gave great satisfaction. So did a royal enactment in parliament that summer expelling the Jews and cancelling all debts owed to them. The poor creatures, who had been subjected to a ruinous tallage four years earlier to finance the king's visit to Gascony, were now too poor to be of further assistance to him. Those who refused to accept conversion to Christianity were, therefore, ordered to leave England, taking only their money and personal goods.[1] A devout populace hailed with delight the expulsion from their closely protected ghettos of these hapless unbelievers, whose extortionate rates of interest had for so long been used by the Crown as a means of mulcting the improvident and extravagant.

The king's reward for these concessions and for the punishment of his judges was a general easing of his financial situation. In addition to the increase in the feudal aids granted for the marriages of his daughters, Joan and Margaret—celebrated that summer with special solemnity because a parliament was sitting[2]—he received a grant of a fifteenth from the magnates and knights of the shire and burgesses and two grants from the convocations of Canterbury and York, of a fifteenth from the higher clergy and a tenth from the lower. This brought him during the next two years

---

[1] The Dunstable chronicler tells a terrible story of how some of the richest Jews hired—to quote Holinshed's translation—"a mighty tall ship. When the same was under sail and got down the Thames towards the mouth of the river beyond Queensborough, the master mariner bethought him of a wile and caused his men to cast anchor . . . till the ship by the ebbing of the stream remained on the dry sands. The master enticed the Jews to walk out with him on land for recreation; and at length, when he understood the tide to be coming in, he got him back to the ship, whither he was drawn up by a cord. . . . The Jews were swallowed up in water." It is said that the captain and sailors were afterwards hanged.

[2] Edward was said to have married them "*in parliamento*." Edward Miller, *Origins of Parliament*, 14.

more than £100,000 and paid off most of his debt to the bankers of Lucca and Florence.

. . . .

There was a still more important family matter to be settled that summer than the marriage of the royal princesses. Three years before, after crossing the Forth on a stormy March evening, Alexander III of Scotland had ridden over a cliff while galloping through the night to rejoin his young French queen at King-horn. Since all his children had died before him, including his daughter the Queen of Norway, his death at 44 left Scotland with no direct heir but the latter's infant child, the Maid of Norway.

Alexander's rule and that of his father, Alexander II, had given Lowland Scotland three-quarters of a century of compara-tive civilisation and freedom from the perpetual border wars with England which had raged in the days of Henry II and King David I. Its quarrelsome, warlike nobles, many of whom were of Anglo-Norman descent or allied by marriage to English families, had come to accept, with reservations, a monarchical and feudal organisation of society on the English and European pattern in place of the tribal system which still prevailed in the Highlands. The Celtic Church, too, had become latinized like that of northern England, whose monasteries had many links with the abbeys—Melrose and Jedburgh, Holyrood, Newbattle and Kelso—founded in the Lothians and Border country by Alexander's half-English great-great-grandfather, David I. The prospect of a return to the anarchy of the past appalled the more responsible Scottish leaders who, two years before their king's death, in an assembly of the estates of the realm, had sworn to accept the infant Maid of Norway as heir to the throne should Alexander die without offspring.

In their dilemma they turned to Edward, from whose sister, first wife of their dead king, the Maid was descended. It had become natural to Scottish nobles and prelates with English estates and affinities to look for support to the more civilised neighbour kingdom with whom their own had been linked in friendship for as long as men could remember. Soon after Alexander's death two friars arrived in London with a message from the Guardians of Scotland to suggest the possibility of a marriage between their child queen and the five-year-old son and heir of the English king, Prince Edward. After the king's return from Bordeaux in the autumn of 1289 he had received at Salisbury four of the Scottish regents—Robert Bruce earl of Carrick, John Comyn of Badenoch and the bishops of St. Andrews and Glasgow. Together with plenipotentiaries from King Eric of Norway, they had signed a treaty under which the infant Maid was to be sent to Britain within the next year, Edward agreeing to deliver her free to Scotland as soon as the latter was sufficiently pacified to receive her, and the Scots to accept her as their queen and not marry her without his consent.

In July 1290, a treaty was sealed at Brigham near Durham by commissioners representing the two countries. It provided that the rights of neither should be diminished by the proposed marriage and that, if the young couple should leave no issue to make the union of the two crowns permanent, Scotland should revert to the nearest heirs of its ancient throne, "free and intact of any subjection to the King of England." The latter was to guarantee that its "rights, laws, liberties and customs" should be "wholly and inviolably preserved for all time" and that it should "remain separate and divided from the kingdom of England by its right boundaries and marches . . . free in itself and without subjection." No parliament was to be held outside Scotland on any matter that concerned it and no taxes should be exacted from its people except to meet the common expenses of the Crown.[1] It was agreed, too, that until the pair could marry and take the oaths to preserve the customs of the realm, Edward should hold the Scottish royal castles to ensure peace and order.

Edward confirmed the treaty on August 28th at Northampton. He and his queen had left Westminster at the end of July for their usual summer progress to the Midland shrines, hearing suits and petitions and hunting the great forests of Whittlewood, Rockingham and Sherwood. A further parliament had been called at Clipstone in Nottinghamshire in the autumn to confirm the settlement of the kingdom's affairs that the king had so

---

[1] Stevenson, *Documents Illustrative of the History of Scotland*, i, No. cviii, cit. *Scottish History*, i, 124-5.

triumphantly achieved and to make arrangements for the European crusade which he had vowed to lead.

On October 25th, at his favourite hunting-lodge in the Nottinghamshire woodlands, surrounded by the magnates of the realm, Edward announced his plans for the knightly Christian adventure which was to be the crowning act of his life. It had been agreed with the pope that the crusade was to be launched in the summer of 1293, the fifty-seventh of the king's life. Shortly before, he had despatched a Yarmouth ship to Bergen, well provisioned with "walnuts, sugar, ginger, figs, raisins, and ginger-bread," to bring the child queen of Scotland from her father's court in Norway to her kingdom and future husband.

But a few days after Edward met his parliament at Clipstone a disturbing letter reached him. It was written by one of the strongest advocates of the union of the two crowns, William Fraser bishop of St. Andrews, who described himself as "his devoted chaplain, William, by divine permission humble minister of the church of St. Andrew." It reported a rumour that after a stormy voyage across the North Sea the Maid had died in the Orkneys at the end of September. What was still more ominous was that the Bruces and other Scottish nobles with rival claims to the throne were in arms and gathering forces. " There is fear of a general war and a great slaughter of men," the letter ended,

"unless the Highest, by means of your industry and good service, apply a speedy remedy. If it turn out that our foresaid Lady has departed this life (may it not be so), let your Excellency deign if you please to approach towards the March for the consolation of the Scottish people and for saving the shedding of blood so that the faithful men of the kingdom may keep their oath inviolate and set over them for king him who of right ought to have the succession if so be that he will follow your counsel."

Before confirmation could arrive, news even more dire reached the king. His queen had been taken suddenly ill at Harbey in Nottinghamshire. On November 28th she died in his arms. " My harp is turned to mourning," he wrote, " in life I loved her dearly, nor can I cease to love her in death." She had been his inseparable companion for thirty-six years and had borne him thirteen children, of whom seven had died before her. For the rest of his life nothing ever went wholly right for him.

As the stricken king followed his wife's body on its long journey to Westminster, at each town and village where the bier rested he vowed to raise a cross to her memory. At Lincoln, Grantham, Stamford and Geddington, at Hardingstone outside Northampton, at Stony Stratford, Woburn, Dunstable, St. Albans and Waltham, and in Cheapside and the hamlet of Charing close to his palace of Westminster, beautiful stone memorials rose during the next few years to express his love for his lost consort. Three of them still survive. Although much damaged by time and the iconoclast, with their canopied niches and delicately carved statues, their free-flowing foliage and tracery, their pinnacles, finials and delicate crowning crosses, they are exquisite examples of the new Decorated style which, under the influence of Edward's court, had begun to replace the austerity of early English Gothic.

In accordance with contemporary practice the embalmed organs of the queen were given separate burial. Her bowels were laid beneath the Lady chapel of Lincoln and her heart in the vast new Dominican or Blackfriars church at Bridewell, upheld by a golden angel made by Adam the goldsmith. A week before Christmas her body was laid in the Abbey where Edward afterwards employed the sculptor William Torrel to raise a gilt brass effigy over her tomb. Then, having bidden farewell to all that was happiest in his past, the king rode to the monastery of the Bonhommes at Ashridge which his cousin, Edmund of Cornwall, had founded. There, in the cold solitude of the Chiltern beech-woods, he spent his Christmas.

Chapter Four

SCOTLAND THE BRAVE

Scots be light of heart, strong and wild enough . . . . They be cruel upon their enemies, and hate bondage most of anything, and they hold it a foul sloth if any man dieth in his bed, and great worship if he die in the field. They be little of meat and may fast long, and eateth well seldom while the sun is up, and eateth flesh, fish, milk and fruit more than bread, and though they be fair of shape they be defouled and made unseemly enough with their own clothing. They praise fast the usage of their own fathers, and despise other men's doing.

HIGDEN

The awful thistle, . . . keep it with a bush of spears.

DUNBAR

DEATH had not only taken from Edward his queen. It had robbed him of a great opportunity. Yet it was not in his nature to despair. The Scottish leaders' request for arbitration revived his hopes. Though he could no longer achieve a single law for Britain by marrying his heir to Scotland's queen, he might still do so as *bretwalda* of the island empire over which he believed King Arthur to have ruled and over which his predecessors in title had once claimed suzerainty.

He therefore accepted the regents' invitation. From Amesbury, where he went after Christmas to visit his dying mother, he asked for extracts from the monastic chronicles to prove his right to Scotland's overlordship. Her last two kings, both of whom had married English princesses, had done homage for their English estates. In accepting such limited fealty Edward had expressly reserved the right to call for a wider. And there had been occasions when it had been rendered. William the Lion and Alexander II had both paid tribute, the first, after his capture, doing homage to Henry II for his Scottish fief and crown—a vassal-age renounced by Richard Cœur de Lion in return for money for a crusade. And before the union of the Scottish kingdoms two centuries earlier, homage of a kind had occasionally been rendered to England's Anglo-Saxon rulers by the princes of northern Britain, even though the circumstances were shrouded in the mists of war and antiquity. The difficulty was that, though such precedents might satisfy an English judge, they were unlikely to carry conviction to the Scots.

Armed with these records of hereditary right, which he had marshalled with his usual thoroughness, Edward summoned the claimants to the vacant throne to meet him at Norham in Northumberland. At the beginning of May 1291, accompanied by judges, monastic chroniclers and a papal notary and supported by the levies of northern England, he met the representatives of Scotland, announcing through his new chief justice, Roger Brabazon, that out of pity for their plight he had come "as the superior and lord paramount of the kingdom of Scotland" to do his lieges justice. Yet he could only do so, Brabazon explained, under the terms of feudal law. Before the king's court could adjudicate, the vacant fief must be surrendered and his right as overlord acknowledged. After which the judge read out the evidences collected by the English chroniclers, reciting all instances of Scottish homage up to the reign of Henry II and ignoring everything that had happened since.

At this point some of the Scots representatives asked if they might consult those who had sent them. In one reply, presented on behalf of "the community of the good people of Scotland," it was argued that while they did not doubt the king's sincerity, they knew of no right to his overlordship and could not bind their future sovereign to it.[1] Edward thereupon offered them three weeks for consideration. As the only alternative to his adjudication was civil war, none of the competitors in the end refused what he asked. At the beginning of June they all swore to submit to his judgment and abide by his decision.

Having secured his point, in accordance with feudal practice, Edward demanded the surrender of the Scottish royal castles while the claims were determined. He reappointed the regents, added

[1] This reply—summarised in (*Rishanger*, Rolls Series 244-5) *Annales Regni Scotiae*, and discovered in a fourteenth century MS. in Glasgow University Library—does not appear in the official roll of the Norham proceedings made by the papal notary. *Powicke*, 605; *A Source Book of Scottish History*, I, 127-30.

an Englishman to their number and proclaimed his peace, promising to govern Scotland according to its ancient laws and customs. Then, pending examination of the claims, he set out on a tour of the country. During July he visited Edinburgh, Stirling, Dunfermline, St. Andrews and Perth, installing constables in twenty-three castles and exacting as many oaths of fealty as possible.

The preliminary hearing took place at Berwick at the beginning of September. The full judicial resources of both kingdoms had been mobilised. There were twenty-four English judges or auditors and eighty Scottish assessors to advise them on Scottish law. As Edward prided himself on the good justice he offered, the utmost legal nicety was observed. Each of the competitors, who included the King of Norway and the Count of Holland, appeared before him and his auditors, in person or by attorney, in the chapel of Berwick castle and traced his descent from the ancestor from whom he claimed. After ten days the evidences were deposited in a sealed bag and the court adjourned to enable the Scottish assessors to prepare their replies. Then the king set off for Amesbury to attend his mother's funeral. His world was growing emptier, and justice and kingship were the chief things left him.

That October, at Abergavenny on the Usk in the heart of the Welsh Marches, Edward grappled with another potential threat to the peace and good order he was bent on establishing throughout Britain. It was nearer home and more dangerous than any beyond the Cheviots. For two hundred years the Marcher lords of South Wales and the Welsh borderland had been allowed by his predecessors to be a law to themselves and in their wild terrain to rule and wage war as they pleased as the price of keeping the Welsh at bay. Now that in two costly campaigns he had destroyed the last stronghold of Welsh independence, Edward was no longer prepared to allow these feudal anarchs a liberty that ran contrary to every principle for which, as lawgiver and pacificator, he was contending and for which, now that the Welsh were subdued, there was no further justification. As a result of marriage and succession most of the Marchers were not only lords in Wales but English landowners and magnates as well, and it seemed intolerable that those whom he had been at such pains to subject to the common law and common obligation of his realm—members of his own council and supreme court—should on the other side of the Severn behave as though they were independent princes and wage private wars of their own. It had been such a contest between the Earl of Gloucester—the richest and most powerful magnate in the kingdom—and the high constable, the Earl of Hereford, that had hastened his return from Gascony in the autumn of 1289.

Soon after his return Edward had issued a proclamation enjoining the two earls to cease fighting. Yet only a fortnight later Gloucester's retainers made a further raid into Hereford's territory, carried off a thousand head of cattle and killed some of his men. Two further raids followed. Then in the autumn of 1290 Hereford brought an action at law against Gloucester, and the king saw his opportunity to break the "custom of the March." His half brother, William de Valence earl of Pembroke—himself a Marcher—a bishop and two judges were commissioned to hear the case and all the magnates of the March were formally summoned to attend the court as suitors. When Gloucester—married only a few months before to the king's daughter—failed to appear, he was adjudged guilty of contempt.

As soon as he got back from Scotland in September 1291, Edward summoned a parliament of archbishops, earls, bishops and barons to try the case at Abergavenny. This time, with the king himself presiding, Gloucester dared not absent himself. As Hereford in the meantime had put himself in the wrong by impounding some of his adversary's cattle without awaiting the decision of the court, both earls were sentenced to imprisonment and forfeiture for having acted contumaciously, audaciously and presumptuously. When they had been allowed to purge their contempt they were released on Gloucester paying a fine of ten thousand marks—well over £300,000 in today's purchasing power —and Hereford a thousand. Gloucester's lands in Glamorgan and Hereford's in Brecknock were both taken into the king's hands for their lifetime, though later they were restored. The worst punishment of all was to their pride; they had been treated as though lordship in the March was as subject to the king and his officers as in England.

Having disciplined the proud earls of the March, Edward

returned to the problem of establishing law, order and kingship in Scotland. By the end of the summer of 1292 "the prodigious labours of Brabazon" and his fellow judges had been completed. When the hearings at Berwick were resumed in October all the claimants had been eliminated save three descended from the daughters of William the Lion's younger brother, David earl of Huntingdon—a tenant-in-chief of Edward's great-grandfather, Henry II. The nearest in blood and the most favoured by his fellow magnates was the son of the second daughter, the 81-year-old Robert Bruce, an Anglo-Scottish noble who had served Edward's father as chief justice of the King's Bench and who before the birth of the last Scottish king had been acknowledged as heir-presumptive. But under the rules of primogeniture that were coming to be accepted by the more settled kingdoms of the West, a better claim was John Balliol's, whose father had married the daughter of Huntingdon's eldest daughter. He, too, was an English as well as a Scottish magnate; his father, lord of Barnard Castle, had fought by Edward's side at Lewes and had founded an Oxford college for poor students from the north[1] that still bears his name.

The decision turned on whether the custom of Scotland gave the son of a younger daughter a better right than the grandson of an elder. As the eighty Scottish auditors—half chosen by Bruce and half by Balliol—failed to agree, the decision devolved on Edward's judges. After long consideration they followed the accepted English usage; that the issue of the elder line must be exhausted before the succession could pass to that of a younger. There still remained the question—already raised by the descendant of the third daughter, an English noble and Marcher, John Hastings, lord of Abergavenny—whether, as a feudal fief without male heirs, Scotland ought not to be partitioned between the representatives of its three co-heiresses. In this he was supported by the other and now unsuccessful claimant Bruce.

If its direct rule and incorporation in England had been what

[1] It was already thriving thirty years after its foundation, for in 1293, when its master and scholars appealed to the Bishop of Lincoln for a private chapel, Bishop Sutton, though a great stickler for the rights of his diocese, granted it on the grounds that many of the college's *alumni* had "gone forth distinguished for virtue and knowledge and borne much fruit in religion and elsewhere." Rosalind Hill, *Oliver Sutton*, p. 16.

Edward at this stage wanted, it would have been clearly to his interest to have allowed the northern kingdom to be split into its three original components of Lothian, Alban and Strathclyde and divided among the competitors. But Edward's lifelong object was not the fragmentation of lordship but its definition and stricter enforcement in some wider dominion. His judges pronounced Scotland to be an indivisible and impartible kingdom and, by doing so, unwittingly ensured its future independence.

On November 17th, 1292, after a six weeks' hearing, Brabazon awarded the throne to Balliol. Two days later Edward ordered his constables to deliver the Scottish castles to him. The magnates did homage to their new king, and the latter did homage to Edward as supreme sovereign lord. The unsuccessful runner-up, old Bruce, avoided acknowledging his rival's claim by relinquishing his rights to his son, the Earl of Carrick, who, with the same object, made over his Scottish estates to his own son, Robert Bruce, a minor, subsequently sailing to Norway to marry his daughter to the widowed King Eric—father of the little princess whose death had caused all the trouble.

Balliol was installed at Scone on St. Andrew's Day on the historic Stone of Destiny, brought, it was believed, by the ancient kings of Scots from their native Ireland. He was a quiet, unassertive man, little fitted to serve as a buffer between a turbulent native nobility and a suzerain as zealous for formal law and order as Edward. Trouble began almost immediately.

For on December 7th, only a fortnight after the "great cause of Scotland" had been decided and almost before Balliol had been crowned, one of his subjects, a Berwick merchant, appealed to the English courts against a decision of the Scottish justiciars. Edward, whose pride it was never to refuse any man justice, ordered the record to be brought before the King's Bench at Newcastle where he was keeping the Christmas feast. When Balliol reminded him of his undertaking at Brigham that no Scottish subject should be made to plead in any court outside Scotland, Edward replied that he was not bound by a marriage-treaty that had not been carried out. To put the matter beyond doubt he extracted a further homage from Balliol and made him seal a document releasing him from every "article, concession or promise" made at Brigham.

It was a major political blunder—one that arose from

Edward's lifelong view of the rights and duties of kingship and law. It was an age of defining and enforcing law, and he was one of the greatest definers of law ever to wear a crown. He had received Balliol's homage both as an English baron and as king of Scotland and, as his liege-lord, had pledged himself under the feudal compact to safeguard his rights in both. He had sworn to respect the laws and institutions of Scotland, as he had done to respect those of Gascony, Wales, Ireland and all his other dominions. But as a sovereign lord he was also bound to offer justice, according to the highest standards, to all his subjects alike. If any of them could not obtain it in the court of his immediate lord—even though that lord were a king—he was entitled to appeal to the supreme overlord and seek it in his court. It was the same right that Henry II had given to his English subjects when he had offered them writs entitling them to apply to the royal courts for justice unobtainable in those of their feudal lords. Nor could the king's courts do justice by rules less enlightened than those they habitually administered or by any that conflicted with the principles of natural law.

The same claim to override the primitive codes of a backward people in the name of justice had shipwrecked Edward's plans for a peaceful union with Wales. Once Balliol had renounced his kingdom's right to the conditions secured at Brigham, he was lost. During the next two years he was repeatedly called to answer appeals in his overlord's court at Westminster as though Scotland were an English barony. Because the English courts offered better justice than could be obtained in Scotland appeals were made to them from the Scottish courts not only by English and foreign litigants, like the Gascon vintner who sued Balliol for a wine bill of his predecessor, but by Scots dissatisfied with the judgments of their own courts. The most humiliating of all was an appeal by the son of a former Earl of Fife—one of the new king's chief magnates—against a judicial decision of the Scottish council or parliament. When, making a stand at last, Balliol refused either to answer at Westminster or to ask for an adjournment, on the ground that, as Scotland's king, he could do neither without the consent of "the good men of his realm," he was adjudged to be in mercy for contempt of his overlord's court and ordered to hand over his three strongest castles. Whereupon he gave way, once more acknowledging himself to be Edward's man. "The empty jacket," his subjects called him. Faced by their resentment and the English king's demands, he was between the devil and the deep sea. "A simple creature, he opened not his mouth," wrote a contemporary, "fearing the frenzied wildness of that people lest they should starve him or shut him up in prison. So he dwelt with them a year as a lamb among wolves."

He was to have an issue out of his afflictions, but not a happy one. For he was not the only king with an overlord. Edward had one, too. His cousin, Philip the Fair—over whose youthful affairs he had taken so much trouble—had promised to respect, as Edward had always done, the ties of family affection between the royal houses of England and France established by St. Louis and Henry III. Yet the policy pursued by the clever Provençal lawyers to whom this shrewd, calculating young man had entrusted his affairs was to enlarge his powers by every possible means. A realist, like his great-great-grandfather, Philip Augustus, Philip's aim was to continue the process—temporarily halted during the reign of St. Louis—of bringing the outlying and formerly independent fiefs of France under a single rule and law like that of England. Philip Augustus had wrested from Edward's grandfather the provinces of Normandy, Anjou, Maine and Touraine. Philip, whose marriage had brought him the great French fief of Champagne and the kingdom of Savoy, wanted to secure what remained of the Angevin empire in France—his English cousin's duchy of Gascony.

To this end he used the same legal processes as Edward in Scotland. Regardless of the undertaking he had given at the start of his reign to refuse appeals from the Gascon courts to his own, he now sought every occasion to force his cousin to answer them. His "legal knights," as he called them, were adepts at reclaiming fiefs by juristic finesse and judicial confiscation. In the summer of 1293 a pretext had arisen over a broil in a Breton port in which a Gascon seaman had stabbed a Norman. This had led to reprisals and a major sea-fight between the two kings' maritime subjects off Cape St. Mathieu, followed by the sacking of La Rochelle by the victorious Gascon and English sailors. Anxious to make amends, Edward offered to have the dispute adjudicated in an English court, tried by an Anglo-French commission or referred to papal arbitration. Philip rejected all his offers and insisted on his right as overlord to be sole judge in his own cause. When the mayor and jurats of Bayonne declined to give themselves up to his officers as a forfeit for the townsmen's misbehaviour and appealed instead to the international maritime "laws" or customs at Oleron—the famous salt port off the Gascon coast which was part of Edward's dominions—he cited the latter as a peer of France to answer before his supreme court or *parlement* of Paris.

Edward did everything he could to compose the matter. He authorised his cousin, Edmund of Lancaster, to make a formal surrender of Gascony in accordance with the rules of feudal law on receiving a private undertaking from Philip that it would be returned as soon as the original dispute had been settled. When an assurance to this effect had been given him by Philip's queen, Edmund authorised the lieutenant of Gascony to deliver possession of its castles to the constable of France, upon which a French army entered the duchy and occupied Bordeaux. When after waiting six weeks Edmund asked when Philip's part of the bargain was going to be fulfilled, he was told that his overlord would restore nothing. On May 5th, 1294, it was announced in the *parlement* of Paris that the duke of Aquitaine had forfeited his fief by his contempt.

Edward had been hoist with his own petard and, under the outward forms of law, tricked out of his French hereditary dominions. Only Bayonne and the wild Pyrenean land in the extreme south of Gascony and the little towns of Bourg and Blaye in the Gironde estuary remained in his hands. Moreover, as his sole means of communication with his stolen duchy was by water and Bordeaux was four hundred miles away, it was going to be exceedingly difficult, if not impossible, to recover it. What made it still more galling was that Edward was to have led a crusade that summer for the recovery of Syria, where three years earlier the Mamelukes had captured and driven the Christians from their last Asian foothold. Under a special papal dispensation large sums had been collected for the expedition and stored in church chests and the coffers of religious houses. But with the two strongest kingdoms of Christendom at loggerheads, a crusade was now out of the question.

Edward was furious. He placed an embargo on French shipping, closed his ports and ordered his vassal, the Scottish king, to do the same. When a parliament of magnates and knights of the shire met at Westminster at Whitsuntide he told them that, " had he no other following but a single boy and horse, he would pursue his right to the death and avenge his injuries."

．　　．　　．　　．　　．　　．　　．

With his geographical stranglehold on Gascony and a far larger feudal force available than Edward could muster from his English tenants, the French king was in an almost impregnable position. To make him relax his grip Edward had not only to raise an army and transport it across pirate-infested seas; he had also to find allies who could offer him a continental base, from which to operate, and military aid to offset France's superior manpower.

With his usual resolution he set about finding them. Most of France's northern and eastern neighbours were alarmed by her king's expansionist policy, especially the newly elected King of the Romans or rather Germans, Adolf of Nassau. In return for a subsidy of 100,000 marks he agreed to declare war on Philip. So did Edward's sons-in-law, the Duke of Brabant and the Count of Bar. But the one ruler of the Low Countries whose adherence could have made a coalition against the French king effective, his vassal the Count of Flanders, was too frightened of his suzerain to court the fate of his English fellow feudatory. Not even the offer of Edward's son and heir for his daughter could tempt him to run such a risk, though his clothworker subjects were faced with ruin by the English embargo on wool shipments to the French king's ports.

Edward's plan was to send an army to Gascony in three stages. The advance-guard was to sail in June 1294 under his nephew, John of Brittany earl of Richmond, a larger force under the earls of Lancaster and Lincoln in the autumn, while he himself was to follow with the main host before Christmas. To supplement the feudal fleet of the Cinque Ports he ordered his foresters to provide timber for two hundred ships. To command them he appointed admirals—the first so styled in English history—for the country's southern and eastern coasts. One of them, a Kentish gentleman named William Leyburn, was later given the title of "admiral of the King of England's sea."

All these preparations and alliances necessitated the export of currency and heavy fiscal demands on English, Welsh and Scottish taxpayers. For, as his Gascon subjects were now in the power of the French king, Edward could not finance the recovery of the duchy from its own revenues. However much credit he might obtain from the Italian bankers—and during the next year he borrowed a further 200,000 gold florins from the Frescobaldi—in the last resort the war had to be paid for by the feudal tenants, landowners and traders of his island kingdom. And for this, outside certain narrow and by now fairly well-defined limits, he needed their consent.

Nor was it easy to obtain, for they did not regard the defence or recovery of their sovereign's fief as their business. Yet Edward's importunity in a matter that he regarded as impugning his rights was hard to resist. In the end he obtained a tenth from the magnates and shire knights at his Whitsun parliament and a sixth, negotiated separately, from the London traders—a consent which he treated as a permission to tallage the burgesses of other towns at the same rate. He also secured from the wool merchants an extra duty on every sack of wool exported of no less than five marks—ten times as much as the modest "ancient and great custom" which had been agreed to at the beginning of the reign.[1] But the largest possessor of wealth in the country, the Church, had a strong objection to financing war between one Christian king and another. On the pretext of calling in defective coins to halt a debasement of the currency—a matter of some urgency in view of the need to export coin to Europe—Edward had already authorised his officers to "borrow" the money collected from the clergy and stored in religious houses for the crusade. In the absence abroad of the new Archbishop of Canterbury, he now summoned Convocation himself and confronted the assembled clergy in the chapter house of Westminster. When they at last reluctantly offered him a fifth of their temporalities—the income of ecclesiastical land held in feudal tenure—he flatly rejected the offer and demanded half. Nor, though he had no power to tax them

[1] In deference to public clamour it was later reduced to three marks. See p. 149.

without their consent, did they dare refuse. So great was the terror he aroused that the Dean of St. Paul's dropped dead at his feet.

In his resolve to enforce his rights Edward was growing increasingly oblivious of the rights of others. He had not only lost his wife's restraining hand but those of his wisest counsellors. His chancellor, Burnell, had died during the closing stages of the "great cause of Scotland," his treasurer, John Kirkby, two years earlier. Archbishop Pecham, who for all his struggles with him, had proved a true friend, had now followed them. Though he spent the summer in Hampshire supervising the preparations of his fleet and armies, Edward's plans were not going well. The advance-guard which had sailed for Gascony in July was driven back by gales and only reached France in October. The reinforcements which were to have followed never started, and in their absence the English proved too weak to retake Bordeaux or expel the French garrisons.

Little enthusiasm as the English felt for their king's war in Europe, his new Welsh and Scottish subjects and feudatories felt less. They had no wish either to fight or finance a campaign so utterly remote from them. They merely saw it as an opportunity to free themselves from a hated subordination. At the end of September alarming news arrived from Wales. Like everything from that mercurial land it was completely unexpected. The Welsh levies, who had been ordered to muster at Shrewsbury, had failed to appear and had suddenly swept down from the Snowdon hills under a scion of their old princely house, Madog ap Llywelyn, to surprise and storm Caernarvon castle. In the south-west Carmarthen and Pembrokeshire rose under a young chieftain named Maelgwyn; in the south a Morgan harried the estates of the Earl of Gloucester. At Flint, Rhuddlan, Conway, Criccieth, Harlech, Bere, Llanbadarn, Builth and Cardigan the English garrisons—seldom numbering more than thirty or forty men-at-arms and archers[1]—were surrounded by hordes of native warriors whom Edward's recruiting officers and commissioners of array had armed. An attempt by the Earl of Lincoln to relieve Denbigh ended in disaster and for a few weeks it looked as though Wales was lost.

---

[1] *Morris*, 265

Edward reacted with his usual terrifying speed. Abandoning his French projects and concentrating everything on the one thing essential, he prepared for a winter campaign in the Welsh hills. Early in November he met a parliament of magnates and knights of the shire at Westminster, obtaining a tenth on moveables and negotiating separate subsidies from London and the provincial cities. By the end of the month he had assembled an army at Worcester and established bases at Cardiff, Brecon and Chester. All the fighting earls were mobilised—Norfolk, Pembroke and Gloucester in the south, Hereford and Arundel in the Middle March, Surrey, Lincoln, Warwick, Lancaster and Cornwall in the north. Meanwhile the coastal castles were revictualled by sea.

From Chester, which he reached at the beginning of December, the king struck west into Denbighshire to clear his southern flank and avenge Lincoln's defeat before following the Clywd to the coast at Rhuddlan. By Christmas he was in his new castle at Conway, starting towards Bangor and Caernarvon early in January. But, pressing on too fast, in one of those steep wooded defiles that suited the Welsh genius for war, his baggage-train was ambushed and captured not far from the spot where de Tany's men had perished twelve years before. It had been a wet autumn and the harvest had failed, and the king and his bodyguard were cut off by floods from the main force and had to take refuge behind the walls of Conway. There was little in the castle to eat and only one small cask of wine, but the king insisted on sharing his men's meagre rations. " In time of need," he said, " all things must be in common and he who has caused the hardship should not fare better than others."

It was a grim fortnight. The Welsh tribesmen besieged the castle, and all round were flooded fields and rivers and the bitter winter of Snowdonia. Among the troops in the icy cold castle was a contingent of foot from Lancashire; in the great fourteenth-century epic, *Sir Gawayne and the Green Knight*, written by an unknown Lancastrian, there is a description of a North Welsh winter that may have been based on memories of this time:

" But worse than battle is the winter season,
   The cold clear water shedding from the clouds
   That froze ere it the fallow earth might freeze on,

In hail by night. In naked rocks he shrouds,
His limbs half-frozen into an heap he crowds;
Then streams fall clattering sharp and like flint-stone
Icicles hang."[1]

Before January was out the castle was relieved. Soon afterwards Madog, raiding Powys, was surprised by the Earl of
Warwick in a night attack at Maes Moydog. There is a contemporary account in the chronicle of the Dominican friar and
historian, Nicholas Trevet; by employing the tactics that had
proved so successful at Orewin Bridge of interspersing archers and
crossbowmen between his men-at-arms, Warwick shot gaps in the
Welsh spear phalanxes and then broke in with his horsemen.
Madog himself escaped but his force was annihilated.

After that the war turned against Wales as the full force of
England was deployed. With the valleys blocked, it was the
Welsh who starved while the English coastal castles were provisioned by sea, mainly from Bristol, Dublin and Wexford. By the
summer of 1295 Edward was able to march with 3000 foot from
one end of the country to the other, moving down the Merioneth
coast to Cardigan to force the surrender of Morgan and then
turning east into Glamorgan and the vale of Neath before returning through Powysland to Caernarvon and Anglesey. As usual,
when his foes submitted, he showed a clemency rare in that age
and there were few executions. At the end of July Madog himself
yielded, and, after leaving orders to build a castle at Beaumaris,
Edward returned to Worcester to offer thanks at the shrine of St.
Wulfstan.

But he had lost a year, was straitened by the cost of the campaign and had incurred a heavy debt. In his absence the war in
Gascony had gone badly and the French had harried the English
south coast. Scarcely had he resumed his preparations for
invading France than he was faced by a new threat to his rear.
When the war had first broken out Edward had demanded aid
from his Scottish feudatories. King John had offered the revenues
of his English estates for three years and had later been summoned
to join the feudal host at Portsmouth with his steward, eight earls

---

[1] *Sir Gawayne and the Green Knight* (transl. from Middle English by K.
Hare), 24.

and twelve barons. But, heartened by the news of the Welsh rising, he had failed to appear and in the summer of 1295, pressed by the anti-English party at his court, he had secretly received an embassy from Paris to discuss a marriage between his eldest son and the French king's niece.

For, seeing his chance to counter Edward's European coalition by another at his own back door, Philip had brought off a brilliant coup. And, by making an alliance with his overlord's enemy, Balliol was able to assert his country's independence. On October 22nd, 1295, a treaty of alliance was concluded between France and Scotland. To force Edward to abandon his "perverse and hostile incursions into France," it was agreed that the King of Scots should "begin and continue war" against him with all his power. If France was attacked Balliol was to invade England. In return Philip promised that, if Edward retaliated by attacking Scotland, he would distract the common enemy "in other parts."

In pursuit of his breach of fealty King John now seized the estates of all Scottish nobles with land in England, including those of his rivals, the Bruces. He also imprisoned and maltreated the English traders in Berwick. Having successfully put down a Welsh rebellion, Edward was now faced with a Scottish one.

He was not the man to let treason, as he deemed it, pass unpunished. In November 1295 he summoned the most comprehensive parliament yet assembled in England. Magnates, prelates, representatives of the lower clergy, knights of the shire and burgesses were all called "to provide ways to meet the dangers that threaten,... to consider, ordain and decide how such dangers are to be obviated and . . . to do whatever may be ordained by common counsel."[1]

Edward found it far easier to get money from "his beloved and faithful men" for a Scottish campaign than a French one. Gascony was their king's affair; Scotland, they felt, was England's. The former was remote and beyond the sea, the latter at their gates. The magnates and knights of the shire voted an eleventh, the burgesses a seventh, and the clergy a tenth with a promise of more if need arose. With such aid Edward was in a position to crush his perjured vassal and, by bringing Scotland under his rule,

[1] Palgrave, Parliamentary Writs I, 28-31, cit. *Stephenson and Marcham,* 159-61. *Powicke,* 673-4.

to end for ever the danger with which the French king had confronted him. The recovery of Gascony could wait.

By March 1296 he was ready to strike, with a fleet gathered from the eastern ports in the Tyne and a large army at Newcastle. Half the 10,000 infantry came from the militia of the northern counties, half from the Welsh hills, though among the officers were a number of volunteers from southern England—yeomanry men of substance drawn from the second category of the Assize of Arms, each bringing his own horse and armour and taking the king's pay and keep for the adventure of the thing. The cavalry was composed of the knights of the household bodyguard—the *servientes regis ad arma* or serjeants-at-arms—the traditional feudal quotas of the tenants-in-chief, and a number of smaller retinues, each of from half a dozen to a score of lances, raised by lesser barons and other landowners, mostly from the Welsh and Scottish Marches, who were coming to make war and the raising of men for war a profession. The old Earl of Surrey commanded the vanguard, and the Bishop of Durham, Antony Bek, whose palatine jurisdiction stretched from the Tyne to the Tees—headed his military tenants. At Wark the army was joined by a contingent of Anglo-Scottish nobles, led by the earls of Angus and Dunbar and the two Bruces. The old "competitor" had died in the previous year, but his son Robert lord of Annandale and the latter's son, young Robert Bruce earl of Carrick, had answered the lord paramount's summons. All of them did homage and fealty for their Scottish lands.

Balliol's force began the campaign with a raid across the border. Edward grimly observed that, since they had begun, he would make an end. On March 28th, crossing the Tweed at Coldstream, he called on Berwick to surrender. Even by medieval standards it was only a little place, with less than two thousand inhabitants.[1] But it was the chief royal borough of Scotland, with a trade in salmon, herrings, hides and imported wine and spices that made it a symbol of civilisation and national pride. When Edward offered its burghers his peace, they mocked him from the walls. Two of his ships, trying to force the harbour, were captured and their crews put to death, while his nephew, Richard of Cornwall, was killed by a bolt from a crossbow. When next day

---

[1] W. C. Dickinson, *A New History of Scotland*, I, 119.

the city was stormed, the angry king let it be sacked in accordance with the usual practice when a town refused to surrender. There was a massacre in which, according to Scottish accounts, women and children as well as men suffered, though the English chroniclers denied this. A week later the Scots retaliated with a raid through Coquetdale and Redesdale in which the barbarities of a century earlier were re-enacted.

Edward remained at Berwick for a month, impressing hundreds of craftsmen and labourers to rebuild its walls and, not only supervising the work, but, characteristically, taking a hand himself. Before he could advance across a desert he had to create a base as at Rhuddlan in his invasions of Snowdonia. Then the Scots played into his hands. Towards the end of April the wife of one of his Scottish supporters, the Countess of Dunbar, changed sides and surrendered the family castle on the road to Edinburgh. The Earl of Surrey was sent to recapture it, and the main army of the Scots marched to its relief. After a century of peace they had forgotten how formidable English discipline could be and, attacking at Spottsmuir, met with complete disaster. Their commander, John Comyn earl of Buchan, was taken prisoner together with three other earls and more than a hundred of Balliol's chief adherents.

Scotland was now defenceless. Ten days later another of its nobles, James the Steward, surrendered Roxburgh and did homage. By June 6th Edward was at Holyrood abbey watching his battering-train reduce Edinburgh Castle. On the 13th he reached Linlithgow; on the 14th he received the surrender of Stirling, the strongest place in the kingdom. The fall of Perth followed.

On July 2nd Balliol submitted. The unhappy man apologised for the French alliance—caused "through evil counsel and our own simplicity"—accepted Edward's terms and acknowledged himself in mercy. A week later he abdicated in the hall of Brechin castle. Edward sent him to England under escort and continued his march. On the 15th he reached Aberdeen; by the end of the month he was on the Moray Firth. No ruler of Britain had penetrated so far north since the Romans.

At lonely Invercharrad, "where there were no more than three houses in a row, in a valley between two mountains," the king halted. Then striking through the eastern Highlands he retraced his steps by Arbroath, Dundee, Perth and Edinburgh, reaching Berwick again on August 22nd. On the way he took the Stone of Destiny[1] from Scone abbey and the Black Rood of St. Margaret from Edinburgh and sent them, with the Scottish regalia and national archives, to Westminster, just as twelve years before he had robbed Wales of its most cherished symbol of nationhood by taking Arthur's iron crown and laying it on the high altar of St. Edward in his father's abbey church. In a chronicler's words he had "conquered the kingdom of Scotland and searched it through in twenty-one weeks."

At Berwick he held a parliament and received the homage of two thousand Scottish landowners—the entire "franchise" of the land. " There were all the bishops, earls, barons, abbots and priors," the chronicler recorded, " and the 'sovereigns' of all the common people, and there he received the homage of all and their oaths that they would be good and loyal to him. To the well-regulated he forthwith gave up all their own goods and those of their tenants; the earls, barons and bishops he permitted to enjoy their lands provided they came at All Saints to the parliament at Bury St. Edmunds." The king restored their estates in return for sealed submissions, copies of which were sent to Westminster on thirty-five parchment skins known as the Scottish Ragman roll.[2] He even provided Balliol with a home in England and a pension.

But Scotland itself Edward treated as non-existent or rather as though it had become part of England. Not even its name was included in his title of " King of England, Lord of Ireland and Duke of Aquitaine." Having achieved what he sought he left for the south, ordering Berwick to be rebuilt and settled with English traders.[3] He had done, he supposed, with Scottish intransigence for ever. " It eases one," he said, " to be rid of dirt." He left the

[1] Believed by some to have been Jacob's pillow and said to have been brought to Ireland by an Egyptian princess and subsequently transported, by way of St. Columba's Iona, to Scotland. It is of old red sandstone, not native to Fife, so may have travelled far.

[2] It constitutes a valuable record of nearly all the principal families of Scotland of the time.

[3] On September 21st, the city of London was ordered to appoint four experts in town planning to meet him at Bury St. Edmunds and advise him on the replanning of Berwick. Similar summonses were sent to twenty-three other boroughs. *Speculum* XXII, 307-8; *Powicke*, 636-7.

country to be governed by an English earl, treasurer and justiciar. " Now," wrote a ballad-maker, " are the two waters come into one and one realm made of two kingdoms. Now are the islanders all brought together and Alban is rejoined to its regalities of which Edward is lord. There is no longer any king except King Edward. . . . Arthur himself never had it so fully."

.   .   .   .

Edward was free at last to settle with France. A year earlier, with the west and north in rebellion, he had welcomed an offer of arbitration from the pope who wanted the warring kings to join a crusade against the still rebellious Sicilians and their Spanish king. But, as the war with England was going in his favour, Philip had refused. Now, with the whole resources of his realm available, Edward planned to attack him both from Gascony and Flanders whose count, under pressure of the English embargo and the clamour of his clothier subjects, had at last summoned up courage to defy his French overlord and join the alliance against him. In return Edward promised to go to his aid with a large army.

To raise money for this great opportunity, as Edward saw it, a parliament was summoned to Bury St. Edmunds. But the response of the previous year was not repeated. Though the magnates reluctantly granted a twelfth and the burgesses an eighth, the Church refused the fifth asked of it. The representatives of the lower clergy, repeatedly asked to pay both royal and papal taxes, complained that their pockets had been emptied by the last grant to the Crown, while the prelates pleaded a Bull which the new pope, Boniface VIII, had issued forbidding the payment of taxes to the temporal authority without his permission. Champion of the Church's most extreme pretensions and a prelate of autocratic temper, Boniface had framed his decree—called after its opening words, *Clericis laicos*—to stop the kings of England and France from draining ecclesiastical property to finance their secular war.

But Edward felt able to deal with the rebellion of the Church. After a century's evolution of the kingdom's secular institutions the Crown was in a far stronger position than in the time of his great-grandfather and Becket. The day had passed when a pope's displeasure could make an emperor stand in the snow or an English king bare his back to the lashes of avenging monks. The new primate—Robert of Winchelsey—was given two months by Edward to consider the matter. When in January 1297 the clergy met again in London and, pleading the papal Bull, refused the aid demanded, the king withdrew from them the protection of law. No cleric who could not produce a writ certifying that he had paid the tax was to be allowed to sue in the royal courts. No tenant of his need pay rents or services, and his property would lie at the mercy of anyone strong enough to seize it. " If they keep not the fealty they have sworn me for their benefices," Edward declared, " I will not be bound to them for anything."

By outlawing them the king faced the clergy with beggary. He was at Castle Acre on his way to Walsingham when he delivered his ultimatum, and he continued his pilgrimage as though nothing had happened. Within a few days submissions were pouring in. The Convocation of York, led by its metropolitan and the fabulously rich bishop of Durham, was the first to yield. To reconcile their obedience to the papal Bull with their duty to the Crown, its clergy were allowed to pay the fifth not as a tax but as a fine to redeem their property. Even Archbishop Winchelsey, who with the aged and much respected Bishop of Lincoln, Oliver Sutton, refused to give way, felt obliged to leave his subordinates to act as their consciences dictated.[1] " Let each man save his own soul," he said.

Yet, though Edward obtained his ecclesiastical fifth, the archbishop's defiance had started a train of dangerous consequences. On the day the clergy were outlawed the Earl of Lincoln suffered a disastrous defeat at Bellegarde in Gascony—a coincidence widely noted in that superstitious age. When a Scottish horde raided Tyneside, burnt abbeys and schools and carried off cattle, the Englishman, however little he liked paying taxes, felt he was doing so in a cause that concerned himself. He felt very differently when he was asked for money to enable the king to recover his private dominions in someone else's kingdom overseas, still more to finance a campaign in a land where neither he nor they had

---

[1] Edward allowed his officers to make an arrangement with the bishop's friends by which they took only as much of his goods as was needed to pay the tax. Rosalind Hill, *Oliver Sutton*, 4.

any property at all. And in the measures adopted to meet what he, not they, regarded as a national emergency and to which he had been driven by three years of war against the French, Welsh and Scots, Edward had gone far beyond what his subjects felt to be legitimate or bearable. The Gascon war had cost over £400,000; revenue had long ceased to balance expenditure, and the accumulating debt to the Italian bankers had become bottomless. The taxes demanded by the assessors of shire and hundred and the ceaseless requisitions of crops, beasts and goods to supply the armies—the ancient wartime right of "prise" and "purveyance"—touched even the humblest; in a contemporary ballad a landless peasant complained that he could no longer live by gleaning and ploughing, "for ever the fourth penny must go to the king." For three years running there had been a levy on moveables: a thing unprecedented. The tax on wool—the *maltote* or "evil toll," as it was called—crippled every sheep-farmer in the land. As a result of clamour it had been reduced from the original five marks a sack to three, but even this seemed intolerable, for the rich wool exporters merely passed on the burden to the producer in lower prices. Now, in February 1297 Edward ordered all existing wool-stocks to be exposed for sale within a month in assigned ports and then, after requisitioning it and giving only Exchequer tallies in exchange, shipped it to the Low Countries to finance his alliances and coming campaign.

In May he did an even more high-handed thing. Seeking to broaden the basis of his kingdom's military strength and take to the plains of Flanders—where heavy cavalry would be decisive— a larger number of knights than the attenuated feudal muster of England could produce, he ordered the sheriffs to summon to London not only his military tenants, but all freeholders with lands worth £20 a year, " so that they might," as he put it, " be fit to . . . go in the company of our own person for the salvation and defence of themselves and of all our realm . . . and ready to cross with us to foreign parts." Though such a summons was within the vast undefined powers of the royal prerogative, it ran counter to every rule and principle of feudal procedure. It was resented, not only by those called upon—many of whom possessed the financial resources to assume such knightly obligations—but by the magnates who saw in it an encroachment on their privileges and a threat to their power and independence. For if the king could raise mounted armour without relying on the feudal levy, their military monopoly—already impaired by Edward's new recruiting devices—would be at an end.

The greatest of the magnates, the Earl of Gloucester, had died a year earlier, tamed by his royal marriage and his humiliation in the Abergavenny trial. But his mantle of proud independence had fallen on two fellow Marchers, Roger Bigod earl of Norfolk and Humphrey de Bohun earl of Hereford. Both had suffered what they regarded as an injury at the king's hands, Norfolk the marshal because in the recent Welsh campaign he had been given a separate command instead of his hereditary post at the king's right hand; Hereford the constable because he felt he had been unjustly punished in his action against Gloucester five years before. Early in March there had been a scene at Salisbury when the king had ordered the marshal to lead an expedition to Gascony while he himself was planning to go to Flanders. Bigod had refused on the grounds that he was only under an obligation to serve abroad under the king's personal command.[1] Edward had lost his temper and, making play with his name, had threatened, " By God, Sir earl, thou shalt either go or hang! ", to which Bigod had replied, " By that same token, Sir king, I will neither go nor hang! " He had then withdrawn to his domains in South Wales where he had been joined soon afterwards by the constable. Together the two magnates called a private parliament of their fellow Marchers in Wyre Forest and agreed to take joint action against their over-lord's revolutionary demands. When in July the tenants-in-chief and £20 freeholders assembled in answer to the royal summons outside St. Paul's cathedral, both marshal and constable flatly refused either to enrol the latter or to carry out their hereditary duties, as they had not been formally summoned under the proper feudal terms. After some attempts to make them reconsider the matter, the king deprived them of their offices and appointed another marshal and constable in their place.

Determined not to be thwarted, Edward appealed over their heads to the nation and the conception of national or patriotic

[1] "I shall go with you willingly, my lord king, riding before you in the van, as is my duty by hereditary right." Walter of Hemingburgh (ed. H. C. Hamilton II, 121.) cit. *Barrow*, 379.

obligation which, unconsciously, he was seeking to substitute for the contractual feudal tie. " The matter is so great," he wrote, " and touches all and each of the realm so nearly that we can defer to no man." Making his peace with the archbishop, whose temporalities he restored without conditions, he made an impassioned speech from a hustings outside Westminster Hall to a crowd of his supporters with his son Edward, the primate and the Earl of Warwick at his side. Common dangers, he declared, must be met by common measures. With tears in his eyes he begged his subjects to pardon whatever he and his ministers had done amiss or unlawfully taken from them, explaining that it had been solely that they might enjoy their possessions in security. " Behold," he said, pointing to his thirteen-year-old heir, " I go to expose myself to danger on your behalf. I beg of you if I return, receive me as you have done today and I will restore to you all that I have taken. If I come not back, crown my son as your king."[1]

All who heard the speech were deeply moved. The archbishop wept and the onlookers swore fealty to the prince. Among those who prayed for Edward's success when a few weeks later he sailed for Flanders was Oliver Sutton, the venerable Bishop of Lincoln who had so staunchly opposed his tax demands earlier in the year.[2] But though, in return for a promise to confirm Magna Carta and abandon his scheme for compelling £20 freeholders to serve overseas, the knights of the shire whom his summons had brought to London voted the king a subsidy of an eighth, the bulk of the magnates remained ominously aloof and, declaring that " the whole community of the land was aggrieved," continued to appeal to the charters which their forebears had wrung from his father and grandfather.

Aware of the effect that the opposition of the earls was having, Edward issued on August 12th, from Udimore near Winchelsea

---

[1] *Flores Historiarum* III 294. Cit. *Wilkinson*, I, 212-13.

[2] Rosalind Hill, *Oliver Sutton*, 27-8. None the less, the collect of intercession which he enjoined on his diocese had certain reservations. "O Lord, the strength of them that hope in Thee and the glorious victory of them that strive, hear our prayers and grant that our king may devise with prudent mind and perform with strenuous labour only those things which are pleasing to Thy majesty, and that by Thy help and mighty governance he may bring to a prosperous and happy issue those things which he has undertaken to do, through Jesus Christ our Lord."

where he had gone to supervise the embarkation of his army, a national manifesto justifying his actions and relating the events that had led to his quarrel with them.

" The king always desires peace and quiet and the happy state of all the people of his kingdom. In particular, he wishes that after the voyage that he intends to go on for the honour of God and to recover his rightful inheritance, out of which he is being very fraudulently tricked by the King of France, and for the honour and common profit of his realm, all occasions by which the peace and quiet of his kingdom might in any manner be troubled may be completely removed . . . There is mention, so it is said, of certain grievances of which the king has caused his kingdom to suffer, of which he is very cognisant, such as the aids that he has frequently asked of his people. He has been obliged to do this because of wars that have been incited against him in Gascony, Wales and Scotland against which he could not defend himself or his kingdom without the assistance of his loyal subjects. He is much grieved that he has put such burdens and hardships upon them, and he begs them to be willing to excuse him as one who has inflicted these impositions, not to buy lands or tenements or castles or towns, but to defend himself and them and all the kingdom. And if God grants that he shall ever return from the voyage that he is now taking, he wishes all to know that he has the will and great desire to make real amends according to God's will and his people's wish."

Sent to the sheriffs and ordered to be proclaimed, the letter ended with a reminder of the dangers of civil war and the "great discord that formerly arose in this kingdom through disputes between the king and his subjects and the harm that resulted from them."[1]

Yet though Edward, as always, sought his people's co-operation and was ready to go to great trouble to obtain it, nothing would deflect him from his purpose. His cause, he felt, was just, the Flemish expedition offered a means of recovering what was rightly his, and it was his subjects' duty to help him. He continued, therefore, to turn a deaf ear to the magnates' protests.

[1] Rymer's *Foedera* cit. *Wilkinson I, 219*

A few days later, while riding along the ramparts of his new port at Winchelsea, his horse shied at a windmill and he was thrown down an embankment, narrowly escaping death.   He remained undeterred.   Though scarcely a quarter of the two thousand armoured horsemen he had hoped to take to Flanders were forthcoming, he sailed at the end of the month, leaving his kingdom in bewilderment and confusion.

.   .   .   .

Among the signs of opposition in every part of the country which the king had ignored had been a new kind of unrest in the remoter parts of Scotland. It had occurred, not among the landowning and military classes who had submitted to him, but among the small gentry, farmers and peasants who had never taken any part in the government of the north. Like the earlier discontent in Wales it had arisen through the tactlessness and corruption of the English officials who had been left in charge and who, contrary to Edward's ideals but in accordance with the general practice of the age, had seized the opportunity to feather their nests. The clerks in the English justiciar's court, it was said, took a penny a piece from every litigant, "whereby they became wealthy fellows." There was a general fear, too, born of the king's military preparations, that he meant to seize all the middling folk of Scotland, like their aristocratic betters, and pack them off to fight in his foreign war.

The risings, though small affairs, had occurred in widely separated areas, in Galloway and Clydesdale, Ross, Moray and Aberdeenshire. At Lanark the English sheriff and garrison had been overwhelmed and massacred in a sudden night broil by a gang led by a young man of gigantic stature named William le Walyes[1] or Wallace—son of a local knight from Elderslie, a few miles from the little city of Glasgow. Rendered desperate by his bloody exploit and heartened by the enthusiasm it aroused, Wallace had led his band of fellow outlaws across Scotland and, suddenly descending from the hills, all but captured the royal justiciar, William de Ormesby, as he was holding his court at Scone.

What made these risings of unaccounted folk more grave

[1] The generic English name for a Celt or Welshman.

than they would otherwise have been was the countenance they received from the Church. For in Scotland, even more than in England, clerical sentiment had been outraged by the royal demands on ecclesiastical property. The Bishop of Glasgow, Robert Wishart, openly sided with the Clydeside rebels. Partly as a result of his encouragement and partly from fear of being made to serve in France, several land-owners who had done homage at Berwick threw in their lot with the insurgents. Among them was Sir William Douglas of Galloway, James Stewart, the hereditary steward, and the twenty-two-year-old earl of Carrick, grandson and namesake of Robert Bruce, the competitor. Bruce's defection was the more surprising because his father, the lord of Annandale, was one of Edward's strongest supporters and had been entrusted with the custody of Carlisle.

This was too much for the king. Before he left for Flanders he sent a force under two North Country magnates, Henry Percy and Robert Clifford, to suppress the Galloway rising. They had little difficulty in dealing with the rebel lords who, incapable as always of agreeing among themselves, threw in their hands as soon as the English caught up with them at Irvine on the Ayrshire coast. The only condition they made was that they should not be sent to fight in France. But what Edward and his lieutenants failed to foresee was the resistance of the Scottish people. Most of their leaders were already in England waiting to sail with the host to France. But Wallace's outlaws, lurking in the trackless wastes of Selkirk forest between the Clyde and Forth, and other guerilla bands in the wild country north of the Tay continued to harry the English garrisons—notably one led by young Andrew de Moray, a son of Sir Andrew de Moray of Petty. During the summer of 1297 Aberdeen, Inverness and Urquhart all fell to these northern insurgents.

A new phenomenon, at first unperceived, had appeared in the world to confront the centralising encroachments of great organisers and legalists like Edward. It arose out of the regional loyalties of ordinary men and women and the instinct for personal liberty and dignity which the spread of Christian teaching had implanted in them. It was to become known as patriotism. Five years before, when Edward and his judges had been laboriously selecting the right king for the kingless Scots, the peasants of

three remote forest cantons in Alpine Swabia—one of the feudal
dukedoms of Germany—had made a league with the neighbouring burghers of Lucerne to resist the unifying attempts of the
Emperor Rudolph of Hapsburg to subordinate them to what
they regarded as an alien and oppressive vassalage. It was the
beginning of the Swiss Confederation which, helped by the wild
mountain terrain in which these sturdy hillfolk lived, was to
defy every assault of their Hapsburg and Austrian dukes. By his
disregard for the feelings of Scottish graziers and crofters Edward
had unconsciously aroused a similar resistance in northern
Britain.

.   .   .   .

What sort of a country was this "Scotsland" whose humble
folk, ignoring the surrender of their Anglo-Norman king and lords,
had so unexpectedly defied their English overlord? With a few
fertile plains and valleys along its eastern and south-western
coasts, it was a narrow, rocky peninsula, tapering away into a
remote, misty and inaccessible *ultima thule* of mountain, lake and
island. Across it, cutting off its inhabitants from one another yet
forming a series of formidable barriers to any invader from the
south, ran a succession of barren mountain ranges and of stormy
inlets or firths of the sea. Such livelihood as its stony soil afforded
could be won only by constant battle with the elements—snow,
gale and flood—an existence rendered the more precarious by
the lawlessness of its inhabitants and the difficulty of enforcing
central authority. Cattle and sheep-stealing was the most profitable activity in wide areas of Scotland—one which united chieftain
and laird with their clansmen and tenantry in continual forays
and feuds. In such a society human life was held cheap; courage,
hardihood and loyalty to the local leader in war were honoured
above all other virtues.

Partly English or Angle in the south-east and an inter-
mixture of Romanised Briton and piratical Irish settler in the
wet, wooded south-west, beyond the Highland line in the sparsely
populated mountains and mists of the Gaelic north and west—
the old Pictland—the Scots lived the same barbaric and pastoral
life as their ancestors a thousand years before. An enigma to
all who had tried to tame or rule her, Scotland had only known

political unity in the past two and a half centuries and even then of a precarious and incomplete kind. Its half million people —shepherds, graziers, crofters, fishermen—were as accustomed to violence as to wind and rain and, like the Spartans, were nourished in proud poverty from childhood. They lived in huts of turves and mud, usually of only a single room, with a pile of dung—their chief wealth—on the floor.

Such national sentiment as they possessed stemmed from their dynasty of kings ruling them from sea-girt Fife; such local unity from Gaelic earl or chieftain and, in the half-feudalised south, from the royal sheriffs and burghs which had grown up in the shadow of the king's castles. Scotland's sole contacts with the outer world were her Church, the dual allegiance of her Anglo-Norman lords for their English lands, and a trickle of trade across the North Sea with England, Flanders and northern Europe through the little eastern ports of Berwick, Leith, Kinghorn, Crail, Arbroath, Montrose and Aberdeen. Their rustic burghers, stiffened by a few English and Flemish immigrants, exported fish, hides, skins, wool and a little rough cloth, and imported salt, wine, honey, raisins, oil, thread, spices, wax and a few manufactured objects like cooking pots, swords and armour.

Of these links with European civilisation the Church was the greatest. Though Christianity had originally come to Scotland from Ireland and Iona, until the end of the twelfth century the Scottish Church had been a part, though only a loosely bound and fiercely disputed part, of the province of York and, as such, nominally subordinate to the northern English metropolitan. But after its quarrel with Henry II the papacy had taken the Church in Scotland under its direct control and, though no Scottish archbishop had been appointed, its eleven bishops under the primacy of St. Andrews had for the past century acknowledged no spiritual superior but the pope. This had ensured that though, as the champion of civilisation and opponent of war, the Church had at first welcomed a union with England through the marriage of the two crowns, its leaders were foremost in rejecting Edward's claim to suppress the nation's separate identity by force.

Since the country was at least a hundred years behind England in civilisation, Scottish Christianity was more monastic than episcopal, particularly in the south-east. Here in the first half of the twelfth century David I, inspired by his English mother, Queen Margaret, had established a chain of priories and monasteries—Augustinian at St. Andrews, Lochleven, Holyrood, Jedburgh and Cambuskenneth, Cistercian at Melrose, Newbattle, Kinloss and Dundrennan. Superseding the hermit communities of the primitive past, they had begun to perform for Lowland Scotland something of the cultural and artistic service that the great Cluniac houses had done for England in the days of St. Dunstan and the Anglo-Saxon kings. In that civilising mission David himself—greatest of Scotland's royal line—had played a major part. "He did his utmost," wrote the chronicler Fordun, "to draw on that rough and boorish people toward quiet and chastened manners, . . . looking after not only the great affairs of state, but all things down to the very least . . . in order that by his example he might stir up the people to do likewise . . . Hence all the savageness of that nation became meekness and was soon overlaid with so much kindliness and lowliness that, forgetting their inborn fierceness, they bowed their necks under the laws." Open to all from the highest to the lowest, a Scottish Alfred from whom, through his mother, he was descended, this great king had created a small hard core of civilisation on either shore of the Forth, which his successors, William the Lion and the two Alexanders, had consolidated and enlarged. It was this that Edward had attacked in his attempt to enforce English law and obedience. By striking at it he had broken such civilisation as Scotland possessed. As a result he found himself confronted by what lay beneath—the stark, savage, native turbulence of a people to whom feuding, violence and vengeance were second nature. Such was the detestation that he and his "southron" officers and soldiers aroused that, wherever the English penetrated, the Scottish people, for the first time in their history, seemed almost united.

From this rude, tough, resourceful community were drawn the followers of Wallace and his fellow hedge-knights, Andrew de Moray and Sir John Graham—"the guid Graeme" of the legends. Armed with home-made spears and axes, they wore animal skins and hessian cloaks and carried their rations of oatmeal and dried lentils on their backs or ponies' saddles. Even by the standards of that hardy age they were almost incredibly mobile, traversing vast distances of lonely moor, mountain and forest to waylay and fall on their foes. They were animated by a passionate hatred of the English; Wallace himself, it was said, as a matter of principle slew every "southron" who started an argument with him. According to the Scottish bard, Blind Harry, when the guerilla chief captured a batch of "English knaves" he made them drag his loot to his forest lair where he hanged them all on trees. Like all partisan warfare in primitive lands, his campaign was waged with merciless ferocity and intimidation. What was most disturbing to the authorities was that it became impossible to collect taxes. "Not a penny can be raised," the treasurer of Scotland, Hugh de Cressingham, reported to his royal master from Roxburgh, "until my lord the Earl of Warenne shall enter in your land and compel the people by force and sentence of law." For old Surrey, the warden of the North, resting on his laurels of Spottsmuir, had gone home for the winter to his English estates, leaving Cressingham—a fat cleric of the ledgers—in charge.

Thus, despite the surrender of the western lords at Irvine, by the time the king crossed to Flanders there was scarcely an English garrison left north of the Tay. By now, however, an army under Surrey, hastily recalled to his charge, was hurrying up the east coast to restore order. There was no doubt in official minds that, confronted by a regular military force, the Scots' resistance would crumble as quickly as it had done a year before. "As for the people on the other side of the Scottish sea"—the Firth of Forth—Cressingham wrote to the king, "we hope soon to have them at our pleasure."

With his ragged horde Wallace was by now besieging Dundee castle. He had no siege-train and could only hope to starve it out. Hearing of Surrey's advance, he broke off the siege and, joining his fellow rebel, Moray, took up a position on the southern-most spur of the Ochils, barring the road from Stirling to the north. Sooner than allow the invaders to penetrate to the liberated lands beyond the Forth, he decided to give battle about a mile from the point where the Stirling road crossed the river, here deep and tidal.

It was a bold decision. The royal forces were far better

trained, armed and disciplined. They were particularly strong in mailed cavalry—the dominant arm in war and one in which the Scots, a rabble of low-born, unaccounted men, were almost totally deficient. But the English leaders underestimated their humble adversaries. Wallace had gained an extraordinary ascendancy over his men and possessed a born soldier's eye for ground. The Earl of Surrey was old and infirm, and Cressingham —an Exchequer official of gross girth who had made himself universally hated by his meanness and greed—was notoriously impatient and arrogant. Against the advice of more experienced soldiers, including an Anglo-Scottish knight who urged that Wallace's position should be outflanked rather than attacked frontally, Surrey reluctantly yielded to the importunity of the treasurer who, in his obsession with financial considerations, viewed every day's delay as a waste of money. On September 11th, in face of a strongly-posted enemy, they committed the army to an advance across a narrow wooden bridge scarcely wide enough for two horsemen and with no room to deploy on the far side.

This was just what Wallace wanted. He had already rejected overtures for an armistice from the Steward of Scotland and the Earl of Lennox, who, trying to hunt with the hounds and run with the hare, had been offering their services as mediators. "Tell your people," he said, "that we have not come here to gain peace but for battle to avenge and deliver our country. Let them come up when they like and they will find us ready to meet them to their beards." He ordered his men not to move from their position among the rocks until he blew his horn. He waited till as many of the enemy had crossed as he felt certain he could destroy. Then he gave the signal.

The Scots' charge threw the English armour into confusion while it was trying to deploy in a swampy, congested meadow. A phalanx of Wallace's spearmen reached the bridge, cutting off those who had crossed from their comrades on the other bank. For the next hour Surrey was forced to watch the massacre of his cavalry, with an unfordable river behind them and the only bridge held by the Scots who hacked them to pieces with gusto. Cressingham was slain, and his skin afterwards cut into strips by the victors. Then panic set in, and the rest of the English army fled, not resting till it reached Berwick. Surrey himself continued all the way to York. "We understand," ran a letter from the Chancery, "that the earl is on his way to our dearest son Edward, who holds our place in England, to speak with him concerning this business of Scotland."[1]

Stirling Bridge restored the independence of Scotland. The Steward and the Earl of Lennox now threw in their lot with the insurgents. Dundee and Stirling surrendered, and by the end of September only the castles of Edinburgh, Dunbar, Roxburgh and Berwick remained in English hands. Wallace himself occupied Berwick town, putting to the sword the few English merchants who had been foolhardy enough to remain.

·   ·   ·   ·   ·   ·   ·   ·

While these events were taking place in the north, England herself was on the verge of revolution. For no sooner had the king left for Flanders than the marshal and constable, challenging his son's council, appeared at the bar of the Exchequer and forbade the collection of the eighth which Edward had induced the representatives of the shires to vote him but to which the assent of the magnates had never been obtained. In the name of the community of the realm they denounced it as a "tallage at will" —a symbol of servitude—and appealed to Magna Carta and the Forest Charters. In a document known as the Barons' Monstruances which they had sent to Edward at Winchelsea just before he sailed, they had already set out the king's illegal demands—the summons to military service abroad of the £20 freeholders, the high-handed tallages and prises imposed by his officers on the people—"of corn, oats, malt, wool, hides, oxen, cows and salt-meat without any payment on which they might live"—above all, the failure to consult and secure the consent of the taxed. However much they may have been influenced by their own grievances, they took their stand on the community's corporate right to be consulted, according to traditional forms and usages, before innovations affecting its liberties became law. By appealing over their heads to the commons—a section of the community too weak by itself to withstand him—the king had tried to divide the nation and destroy its rights piecemeal. As

[1] J. Ferguson, *William Wallace*, 93-4.

the guardians of the customs of the realm the magnates, like their forebears, were speaking and acting for all.

For a few weeks, while the regency council tried to call out the militia of the southern counties and summoned a parliament for October, it looked as though the civil war of thirty years before was about to break out again. But the barons had the support of all who had suffered from the exactions and arbitrary measures of the past three years and, most important of all, of the Londoners who for a decade had been without a mayor and had twice met with a refusal when they had petitioned for a restoration of their liberties. Despite the archbishop's reconciliation with the king they also had the support of the Church. On September 21st, preparatory to marching to Westminster at the head of their retainers, they held a preliminary parliament of their own at Northampton, at which they drew up an uncompromising list of demands against arbitrary taxation and government known as *De Tallagio non Concedendo*.

Then came the news from Scotland. The shock restored the nation's unity. On October 10th, the boy regent and his council met the baronial leaders and agreed to the more moderate of their demands. Pardon was granted to those who had refused to serve abroad, and the offices of the marshal and constable were restored to them. The charters were confirmed, official record of the illegal imposts and prises was erased, and the *maltote* on wool was abolished. Henceforward, it was agreed, no taxes other than the customary feudal aids and the "ancient and great custom" on wool granted at the beginning of the reign were to be taken without "the common consent of the whole kingdom and for the common benefit of the same." In November the first step was taken to restore London's civic liberties.

The king, who was at Ghent, after hesitating for three days accepted his council's surrender. There was nothing else he could do if he was to avert civil war and recover Scotland. In return, the magnates agreed to a subsidy of a ninth and the clergy to a "voluntary" offering of a fifth from the threatened northern province and a tenth from the southern. By now the Scots had crossed the border and were ravaging Northumberland and Cumberland. For three weeks "the praise of God ceased in every church and monastery from Newcastle-on-Tyne to

Carlisle." The invaders were only stopped from crossing the Tyne by a snowstorm and the bold front of the Bishop of Durham. At Hexham, it was said, the personal intervention of Wallace alone saved the lives of the monks at the altar.

His intervention had also saved England from civil war and forced her king to concede to his people the principle of consultation and consent of which in earlier days he had been the protagonist and on which the true strength of his kingdom depended. In the words of a constitutional historian, Edward had been "sharply reminded of the changing implications of the monarchical tradition and his increasing, not diminishing, dependence on the community of the realm. He had learned that the details of co-operation mattered as well as the principle. Each new demand of the ruler had still to be established with the consent of the people."[1]

All that he could now do was to return to England and re-conquer the Scots. It had taken him three years to achieve his aim of leading an army to the continent, and the only result had been to lose Scotland and alienate his subjects. The money he had wrung from them to subsidise his allies had effected nothing. Even the adherence of Flanders from which he had hoped so much had brought nothing but vain expense to himself and disaster to the Flemings, for Philip the Fair had reacted by invading their country and capturing several of their cities, including Lille, while Bruges had fallen into the hands of the *leliants*—"the men of the lily"—Philip's adherents. Even in Ghent, Edward's headquarters during the winter, the plundering proclivities of his Welsh troops had alienated the burghers.

Making a truce with the French king which left the latter in possession of all his gains, Edward returned in March 1298 to England. He proceeded at once to York, where he established his court, exchequer and law courts until such time as the Scots could be subdued. The northern barons had by now relieved the beleaguered castles of Berwick and Roxburgh, but the rest of Scotland was firmly in Wallace's hands. Despite his lowly rank

[1] *Wilkinson*, i, 61. "The dangers inherent in Edward's sectional appeals to the nation recreated a national opposition which, whatever its shortcomings, vindicated the ancient political ideals in face of the most powerful ruler England had ever seen."

the victor of Stirling Brig was the acknowledged head of the country, governing it as "guardian of the realm and leader of the armies" in the name of King John,[1] whose nephew, John Comyn the Red—son of another of the competitors—had now joined him. Though most of the other Scottish nobles still held sulkily aloof, they failed to answer the royal summons to York. Among them was young Robert Bruce earl of Carrick.

Edward ignored the malcontent lords and concentrated against Wallace. As the wagons carrying the records and rolls of government jolted along the rutted track to York, he mobilised the largest army that had entered Scotland since the days of the Romans. At Pentecost he held a parliament at which he gave the kiss of peace to the marshal and constable who had been demanding a further confirmation of the charters—a demand he had refused as impugning his honour. Not till the end of June, after a pilgrimage to the shrine of St. John of Beverley, were his preparations for the campaign complete.

Altogether some 2400 horse and 29,000 foot had been assembled. Not all were in arms at once for, both in the field and on the way to it, the rate of desertion in a medieval army was very high. But when Edward crossed the border at the beginning of July it was at the head of 12,500 infantry and archers and more than 2000 cavalry and with a huge train of baggage-wagons, artificers and camp followers. Eight of the earls accompanied him: the marshal and the constable, old Surrey the warden of Scotland, the Countess of Gloucester's new husband, Ralph de Monthemer, Arundel and Guy of Warwick who had just succeeded his father. All of them brought their quotas of knights and men-at-arms, as did the young earls of Lancaster and Pembroke, both minors and eager for glory—the king's nephew and cousin. Only one Scottish earl, Angus, was present, but the magnificent Bishop Bek led the military tenants of Durham, and Lord Percy of Alnwick the men of Northumberland and Westmorland.

It must have been an imposing spectacle with thousands of

[1] Among the records of the German Hanse is a letter written in October 1297 to the merchants of Lubeck and Hamburg in the joint names of Wallace and Andrew de Moray, who had died soon after Stirling Bridge of his wounds, inviting them to resume trade with Scotland, which "God be thanked has been recovered by war from the power of the English."

pennons and heraldic banners fluttering in the breeze—the knights on their war-horses, mailed from head to foot, with huge lances and blazoned kite-shaped shields, their hauberks and armour, polished by emulous pages, flashing a warning in the sunlight to watchers on distant Scottish hills. Behind them came the infantry, raised by veterans of the Welsh wars like Grey of Ruthin and William de Felton or picked by the king's commissioners of array from the sheriff's rolls of England's northern counties, with their millenars, centenars and vintenars—colonels, captains and lieutenants—riding in their midst: little, sharp-eyed, restless men armed with spears and long knives, the black sheep of their native homesteads and villages, trotting rather than marching and ready at the slightest opportunity to plunder, desert or join in a fight or mutiny with their polyglot comrades-in-arms. There were squads of dark, mounted Gascon crossbowmen and green-jacketed archers from Gwent and the Cheshire and Sherwood forests with enormous bows and sheafs of arrows; helmeted hobelars—or light lancers—riding ragged ponies and wearing iron gauntlets, leather doublets but no armour; smiths, armourers, fletchers, miners for siege operations and pavilioners to pitch the grandees' tents; cooks and butlers, musicians with long pipes, drums and glittering instruments; surgeons, chaplains and solemn clerks of the households of the king and magnates with pack-horses laden with rolls and boxes. And at some point in the long winding cortège that reflected all the elements of the ancient feudal and new national state with which Edward made war, surrounded by his bodyguard of knights and mounted archers the tall king, towering above everyone, with his broad forehead and noble head of silvery hair.[1]

As this great host moved up the coast to Edinburgh, Wallace, lying on its flank in Selkirk forest, fell back driving everything edible from its path. In marching a medieval army to battle there was one overriding need and three inescapable evils. The need was discipline, and the evils desertion, disease and dearth of rations. The size of the Anglo-Welsh host made it particularly

---

[1] Annales (ed. Hog) 281-2, cit. *Barrow*, 308; *English Government* 1, 337-64. (A. E. Prince, "The Army and Navy"); *Morris*, 282-305 *et passim*. *Medieval England* 1, 145-8.

dependent on its communications. The fleet which was to have provisioned it was delayed by adverse winds and, after advancing beyond Edinburgh, Edward was forced to halt for nearly a fortnight while the Bishop of Durham reduced Dirleton and two neighbouring castles which were holding out on the road behind. His temper during the enforced delay is revealed by a conversation he held with a knight whom the bishop had sent to explain his difficulties. "Go back," he said, "and tell the bishop that, in so far as he is a bishop, he is a good man, but that his goodness is out of place for this task. You are a cruel man and I have several times rebuked you for being too cruel and for the pleasure you take in the death of your enemies. But now go and exert all your frightfulness—I shall not blame but praise you. And mind you do not see my face again until those three castles are burnt." Asked how this was to be done, the king replied, "You will do it by doing it and give me your promise that you will."[1]

With Dirleton taken, the royal army was able to advance towards Linlithgow. But it was still dangerously short of food, for road transport in that wasted countryside could not supply so vast a host, and, until his wind-bound convoys could leave the Tyne, Edward's soldiers had only the barest rations. The Welsh archers threatened to desert and fighting broke out between them and the English men-at-arms. On July 21st the king was about to give orders to retreat on Edinburgh when news reached him that the Scots were moving out of the forest to attack. "God be praised who has brought me out of every strait," he exclaimed, "they shall have no need to follow me, for I shall go to meet them and on this very day."

That night the hungry English army bivouacked in the fields, the men pillowed on their shields, the tough old king among them, and the horses tethered beside their riders. During the small hours there was an alarm, and in the darkness Edward was trampled on by his charger as he was about to mount. With two ribs broken he rode among the troops to restore confidence before they resumed their march at daybreak. Shortly after dawn Scottish patrols were encountered near Falkirk, and Wallace's force was seen drawn up for battle on the lower slopes of a hill.

[1] J. Fergusson, *William Wallace*, 129.

Wallace was a magnificent fighter and had proved himself a brilliant commander. Only a few weeks earlier, with remarkable prescience, he had forestalled Edward's plans by sending a small mobile force to besiege Carlisle and prevent him supplying a march into the south-west, where young Bruce had once more thrown in his lot with the insurgents. But he was now committing himself to battle against as great a soldier as himself and one with far superior resources. He had been deceived by optimistic reports into supposing Edward's plight to be worse than it was. He made the mistake of quitting his forest fastness and challenging him instead of leaving him to starve.

Yet he had made his plans with his usual care. Knowing that he would again have to defeat armoured cavalry with infantry—a feat that before his victory at Stirling Brig had been considered impossible—he had trained his men to fight in dense oblongs called schiltrons[1] or shield-troops, with triple tiers of twelve-foot spears facing outwards which it was almost impossible for cavalry to break. With the front ranks squatting or kneeling and the rear rank standing, a schiltron resembled a vast steel hedgehog:

"Their spears point over point as sair and so thick,
    And fast together joint, to see it was ferlike;
    As a castle they stood that was walled with stone."

Wallace had drawn up his army in four of these bristling human fortresses, with palisades of stakes and ropes in front and archers between. Before his position, as at Stirling, was a boggy ground to slow down the attackers' horse. "I haif brocht you to the ring," he told his men, "hop if you can."

If Wallace had evolved a new technique of war to redress the balance between the armoured cavalry of the nobles and the "uncovered" infantry of the plebs, his adversary in his far longer military experience had evolved a still more formidable weapon. In his Welsh campaigns Edward had learnt the striking-power of the longbow of Gwent. Drawn with the whole strength of the body instead of, like the short bow, of the arm only, the "stiff, large and strong bow" of the South Welsh hillsmen could be fired at twice the speed of a crossbow to penetrate the strongest

---

[1] It has been suggested that the name derived from the rounded three-deep joints in the hand and foot. See *The Scottish Antiquary*, XIV, 185-8, cit. *Dickinson*, I, 159.

armour. It was for this that the English king always included in his armies a contingent of Welsh mercenaries, despite their cost and the troubles they caused by their quarrelsome ways.

On the morning of July 22nd, 1298, Edward took up the Scottish challenge. But in disobedience to his orders and contemptuously ignoring the advice of Antony Bek—who was told by one of them to go to his Mass—the arrogant young English lords of the advance guard began the day by attacking before the king could arrive or the archers had had time to deploy. As Wallace anticipated, they failed to break the schiltrons. But they rode down the Ettrick bowmen between them and drove Wallace's minute force of cavalry off the field. This left the Scottish infantry alone on the battlefield. Then Edward arrived to take control and played his trump card. Safe from cavalry attack or answering archery, his bowmen started to shoot down the schiltrons, concentrating against each one in turn until their arrows had cut a swathe of dead and dying through it. Then the heavy cavalry went in, slashing and slaying. Soon all was over. The flower of the Scottish army was left on the field, and, fighting desperately, Wallace withdrew with the remainder into the wood of Callander.

Falkirk ended Wallace's brief spell of power. The Scottish lords had only allowed the leadership to rest in his hands because of his record of success compared with theirs of defeat and surrender. It was hard for feudal lords with an hereditary monopoly of commanding in battle to think of such a man as a leader at all, let alone to serve under him. Soon after his defeat he either resigned his position as Guardian or was deposed, and his place was taken by Balliol's nephew, John Comyn the Red, and the young Earl of Carrick, Robert Bruce. Yet Wallace continued to serve his country under them and, as he never compromised or stopped fighting, his influence remained a decisive one in Scotland's struggle for independence.

Already by the past year's campaign he had shaped its future. If armoured knights, trained to war from childhood, could still ride down undisciplined and unmounted farmers and burghers, Wallace and his foot kerns had proved that, on ground of their own choosing, they could stand up to the proudest chivalry and, with scarcely a knight in their ranks, confound and destroy them.

Even against so famous a soldier as the English king they could survive in a war of endurance without giving battle at all. Had Wallace not tried to repeat his earlier success in the field he might have remained at the head of an undefeated army, while his adversary would have accomplished nothing save a succession of fruitless marches.

Even as it was, except for his one victory, Edward achieved little. He reached Stirling only to find it in ruins and the country-side beyond wasted. After recuperating for a fortnight and sending a raiding party to burn St. Andrews, he withdrew to Edinburgh as the only alternative to starvation. As Wallace had vanished, he reverted to his original plan of marching through the Selkirk forest to Ayr and Galloway to punish the Earl of Carrick. Yet here, too, he was thwarted by Wallace's fore-thought. For the provisions on which he had counted had been intercepted by the raiding party the great partisan had earlier sent to the Solway, and when he reached Ayr he found nothing but the charred ruins of the castle which had been burnt by Bruce. The young earl, copying Wallace's tactics, had vanished into the hills, and, though Edward occupied his castle of Loch-maben, he was forced at the beginning of September to with-draw to Carlisle, his men half-starved and deserting and his horses dying. He had been able to stay in Scotland little more than two months and, except for his defeat of Wallace, had achieved nothing except the capture of a chain of castles in the south-east, whose garrisons were now once more surrounded by guerilla bands and a hostile population.

.   .   .   .

Edward was under no illusions as to his failure. When he reached Carlisle he summoned the host for a new campaign in the following summer "to go forward in the Scottish business upon the enemies of the crown and realm of England and to put down their disobedience and malice." For the present it was all he could do, for the marshal and constable, standing on their feudal rights, insisted on returning home, grumbling at the time they had spent in the field and at the grants of Scottish land the king had given his more faithful followers without consulting them. Edward himself remained in the north for the rest of the year, keeping Christmas on his Holderness estates where he was rebuilding the harbour of Wyke-on-Hull.

In the Easter of 1299 he held another parliament at Westminster. It was a troubled one, for when, according to his promise, he confirmed his father's and grandfather's charters the barons took exception to the reservations attached to those of the Forest. Like all the Plantagenets Edward loved the wild forests he had hunted from childhood and hated to see encroachments made on them. And his sympathies lay with the woodland folk to whom the forests afforded a traditional livelihood and whose ancient rights, like his own, had been overridden by the constant assarts or enclosures of his richer subjects. Yet he had no choice but to give way, for his lords refused to grant any aid for a Scottish campaign unless he did so, and, after five years of war, his financial plight was desperate. He accordingly reconfirmed the charters and appointed a commission to carry out the perambulations they demanded, in other words to recognise the unlicensed assarts they had made and which they now regarded as their own. In his heart he made reservations against the day when he could recover freedom of action. For though he gave his magnates, so insistent on their rights, the kiss of peace, he meant to get his own back.

The first step was to prolong the armistice with France so as to end the intolerable drain on the country's finances of two simultaneous wars. Fortunately the French king, though reluctant to surrender his gains, was by now in a much more amenable frame of mind. For despite his easy conquests in Flanders and Gascony he was finding the prolonged war against Edward's German and Netherlands allies a serious burden to a country whose tax structure was far less elastic and adaptable than England's. The Church, with its concern for the unity of Christendom, was trying to compose the quarrel, and, at Edward's instance, the two kings agreed in the summer of 1298 to submit their dispute over Gascony to papal arbitration. The truce, therefore, was renewed, and, though still officially at war, the dynasties of France and England, so closely allied by blood, began to draw together again. Proposals put forward before the war were resumed for a double marriage between Edward and his heir and the French king's sister and daughter. In September

1299, the sixty-year old royal widower was married at Canterbury to the princess Margaret of France. It was a wedding that boded ill for Scotland.

In the spring of 1300 the bridegroom set out on his fourth invasion of Scotland. Before going north he stayed at Bury St. Edmunds where, as always, he delighted the monks by his punctilious devotions and splendid gifts. As he rode out of the gatehouse he bowed twice to the memory of the royal saint and sent back his standard to be touched by every relic in the abbey. His young queen went with him as far as Yorkshire where, at Brotherton on the banks of the Wharfe, she gave birth to the son who was to become the ancestor of the present ducal house of Norfolk. With the seventeen-year-old Edward of Caernarvon[1]— till now a stranger to war—the king joined his army at Carlisle, where a fleet of fifty-eight ships was assembled in the Solway. "On every side," an onlooker wrote, "mountain and valley were filled with carts and sumpter-horses, stores and baggage, tents and pavilions . . . At length, when all had arrived, they set out into Sulwatlandes which is the march between England and Scotland."

Edward's objective was Galloway where the rebels' main strength lay. Advancing by Ecclefechan and Lochmaben, he turned aside at Dumfries to clear his communications by capturing the little castle of Caerlaverock at the mouth of the Nith. The siege, which lasted until his battering-train arrived, was the subject of an heraldic poem in French, the Caerlaverock roll of arms. It listed the chivalry taking part, the pavilions, white or painted, with their bright pennons, the huts built with timber from the Nithsdale woods and carpeted with herbs and flowers, the huge engines hurling their stones against the walls, the knights going forward in turn to the attack, splendidly caparisoned and with bright-coloured banners. The castle fell after a week, on July 15th. During the campaign that followed it rained continuously. At Twynholm, near Kircudbright, an English skir-

---

[1] Before joining his father the prince had spent a further week at Bury St. Edmunds where he seems to have much enjoyed the abbey's pious and stately routine. "He became our brother in chapter," its chronicler records. "The magnificence of the place and the frequent recreations of the brethren pleased him greatly. Every day he asked to be served with a monk's portion such as the brothers take in refectory." cit. *Johnstone*, 46.

mishing party captured Sir Robert Keith, the hereditary marshal, and forced the Scottish army under the Earl of Buchan and John Comyn of Badenoch to take to the "mosses and the moors." Yet though the invaders penetrated as far as Wigtown they achieved nothing. By the end of August the English king and his army, hungry, drenched and dispirited, were back at Carlisle.

Meanwhile the Scots had been seeking support abroad. Their delegates had won the ear of Pope Boniface, always eager to advance claims to dispose of earthly kingdoms. While Edward was withdrawing from Galloway, Archbishop Winchelsey arrived at Sweetheart abbey with a letter from Rome declaring Scotland to be a papal fief and ordering the king to release Balliol and his fellow captives, make peace and withdraw from the country. Scotland neither was nor ever had been, the pope declared, a fief of England. Edward was furious. "By God's blood," he told the trembling primate who exhorted him in the name of Mount Zion and Jerusalem to obey, "for Zion's sake I will not be silent and for Jerusalem's sake I will not be at rest, but with all my strength I will defend my right."[1]

Though a parliament which met at Lincoln that winter proved far from amenable in other ways, insisting on the enforcement of the Forest Charters and making its grant of a fifteenth dependent on the suspension of the treasurer, Walter Langton— the able but unpopular pluralist bishop of Lichfield who had become Edward's chief adviser—its leaders were completely at one with the king in repudiating the papal claims. "It is the custom of the realm of England," he had replied to the pope, "that in matters touching the estate of the realm the counsel should be sought of all whom the matter concerns."[2] In a declaration bearing the seals of seven earls and ninety-seven barons, the magnates affirmed in the name of the community that no king of England had ever been responsible to any foreigner in matters affecting his temporal rights and that the overlordship of Scotland belonged to him both by right and present possession. If, they declared, their lord the king should ever think of submitting his rights over Scotland to his Holiness's decision, they would oppose with all their power an act tending so manifestly to the disinherison of the crown.

[1] *Powicke*, 229.　　[2] *Johnstone*, 53.

The long, wearing struggle to reduce the insurgent north, therefore, continued. In the summer of 1301 Edward once more invaded Scotland, this time with two armies. One, operating from Carlisle against Bruce's strongholds in the south-west, again advanced as far as Wigtown under the veteran Henry Lacy, earl of Lincoln, and the titular command of young Edward of Caernarvon who during the Lincoln parliament had been invested by his father with the title of Prince of Wales.[1] As, however, the Scots merely withdrew into the hills, removing everything edible from the valleys, the military effect was nil. "As none of the Scots would resist," wrote the disgusted Westminster chronicler, "nothing glorious or even worthy of praise was achieved." The other army under the king marched up the Tweed valley and through Selkirk forest into Clydesdale and to Linlithgow. Here with his queen Edward spent the winter in the ancient royal palace above the Forth. While his judges and officials ruled England from York, he organised the Scottish marches on the Welsh model, appointed wardens and sheriffs to administer the area south of the Forth as part of northern England and garrisoned its castles with English soldiers to whom he granted Scottish lands. As earnest of his resolve to subdue all "rebels and traitors" and as a symbol of his authority over the whole of Britain, he celebrated the New Year with a Round Table feast at Falkirk.

By this time King Philip had become involved in a still more furious controversy with the pope about their respective rights over the French clergy. It had resulted in Boniface calling a General Council "for the reformation of the kingdom and the correction of the king,"[2] and in Philip retaliating by convening a States General or national assembly to protest against papal interference. At the height of the dispute the French king and his chivalry suffered an unexpected disaster at the hands of the Flemings, who, like the Sicilians twenty years earlier, had risen against their oppressors. On July 11th, 1302, fighting on foot and armed with pikes, the burghers and weavers of Bruges and Ghent did at Courtrai what Wallace's crofters had done at

[1] It was the first time the title prince had been conferred on an Englishman. *Johnstone*, 55-62.

[2] It began with the words "*Ausculta, fili*," "Listen, son."

Stirling and to Europe's amazement defeated the proud feudal cavalry who had lorded it over the plebs for three centuries.

Heartened by the French humiliation the pope that autumn promulgated a Bull—*Unam Sanctam*—which marked the apex of papal pretensions, pronouncing it to be "necessary for salvation that all men should be subject to the Roman see." He followed it up with a threat of excommunication against the French king. To gain his support against Boniface, Philip now conceded to Edward what he had so long sought. He was having increasing difficulty in holding down the Gascons, who much preferred the rule of their English duke, and after the populace of Bordeaux had successfully risen against his officers in the winter of 1302, he offered to restore the duchy. At the same time he agreed to abandon his Scottish protégés, alliance with whom had hitherto prevented the truce with England being converted into a formal peace. On May 20th, 1303, a treaty was concluded at Paris, Edward doing homage by proxy for his restored fief.

France's defection left the Scots friendless. Needing Edward's good-will in his duel with Philip, the pope, too, had abandoned them, withdrawing his protection from Wallace's patron, the Bishop of Glasgow, whom he described as "stumbling-stone and rock of offence," and ordering the Scottish prelates to rebuke their flocks for their rebellion against his "dear son in Christ, King Edward." The Scottish envoys at Paris at first put a brave face on it, writing to the Guardians of Scotland to assure them that the French king was still privately their friend and urging them not to despair but to continue the struggle. "If you knew," they added, "how much honour has come to you from your last fight against the English you would greatly rejoice."

This was a reference to a skirmish that February in which John Comyn and Simon Fraser had ambushed a small force under Edward's viceroy, John Segrave, at Rosslin near Edinburgh. The viceroy himself had been captured and had only been rescued from ignominious death in the nick of time. But it was the Scots' last victory. With France out of the struggle Edward had them at his mercy. The entire resources of his realm, with seven or eight times their population, were mobilised to crush them. He had recently obtained from the foreign merchants trading with England an important new source of revenue to finance his campaign. Summoning their representatives to Windsor on February 1st, 1303, he had negotiated with them a charter —Carta Mercatoria—freeing them from tolls—"wharfage, pontage and pannage"—and from the city of London's restrictive and jealous anti-foreign regulations and giving them a court of their own and the right to a fifty per cent representation on juries in all but capital cases. In return they granted him increased duties on imports of wine and on their export of wool, leather and other goods. This new or "petty custom"—so called to distinguish it from the "great custom" granted by the English merchants in 1275—came to be known later as tonnage and poundage. Since it fell only on foreign traders and did not result in the tax being passed on in the shape of lower prices for English wool producers, it was far less unpopular than the *maltote* of six years before.

Thus provided for, Edward once more invaded Scotland. In June 1303 he crossed the Forth with the aid of three prefabricated floating bridges brought by sea from Lynn. By-passing Stirling, by the middle of the month he had taken Perth. By September he was on the Moray Firth. His advance was slow and systematic, and every place that resisted was burnt. Brechin castle alone held out, its commander, Sir Thomas Maule, defying the royal battering-engines for five weeks and cursing with his dying breath any successor craven enough to yield.

Even the stoutest rebel lord now made his peace. The young Earl of Carrick, weary of fighting for his rival, Balliol, had already returned to his allegiance, rejoining his father who had remained true to Edward throughout. The bishops of Glasgow and St. Andrews and the remaining guardians, Comyn and de Soulis, followed his example. From Dunfermline abbey—heart of the old royal Scotland—the victorious king offered life and freedom from disinherison to all who should lay down their arms. There were only seven exceptions. Of these six were sentenced to short spells of banishment. The seventh, William Wallace, was told to put himself unreservedly at the disposal of the king.

The stark heroic man refused. He remained in the forest and heather with his outlaw band and, when friends urged him to submit, quoted the lines in praise of freedom he had learnt as a child. "If all the people of Scotland," he said, "yield obedience to the king of England or depart each one from his own freedom, I and my companions who are willing to cleave to me will stand for the liberty of the kingdom."

For a few months Stirling castle—the one stronghold still defying Edward—held out with a garrison of fifty men under Sir William Oliphant. Its reduction by the royal siege-train was treated as a set piece, an oriel being constructed in one of the houses in the town from which the queen and her ladies could watch the army's *loup de guerre* or war-wolf battering its walls. After its surrender in August the king went south, ordering Wallace to be brought to him by Christmas. At the same time the Exchequer and law courts returned to Westminster. Here in February 1305 a parliament for the entire island was held, attended by Robert Bruce in his capacity as an English baron. With his advice and that of Bishop Wishart of Glasgow it was decided that ten representatives of the Scottish estates—two earls, two bishops, two abbots, two barons and two others chosen by "the commonalty"—should be elected to sit in English parliaments and serve, with twenty Englishmen, as a council for the conquered north until a permanent constitution had been issued. Meanwhile Bruce, Bishop Wishart and John Mowbray were appointed Guardians.

Late that summer Wallace was taken. The Scottish nobles joined in the search and, with the help of a money reward, the one patriot leader who would not yield was harried from hiding-place to hiding-place. On August 5th, he was betrayed near Glasgow. Brought south in seventeen days he was paraded through the London streets, preceded by the mayor and sheriffs. On the following day, August 23rd, 1305, he was tried in Westminster Hall—the spot where he stood, crowned with a derisory chaplet of laurel leaves, can still be seen—and charged with treason, murder and robbery. Forbidden to plead, he denied that he had ever sworn allegiance to the English king or done anything that could make him a traitor. Sentenced to be hanged, drawn and quartered, he was dragged for four miles on a hurdle to the Tower and thence by Aldgate to the gallows "by the elms" at Smithfield, where "he was hung in a noose and afterwards let down half living, his privates cut off and his bowels torn out and burnt." His severed head was stuck up on London Bridge and his quarters sent to the chief cities of the north—Perth, Berwick, Stirling and Newcastle[1]—for display.

Something went with them, to take root, in Andrew Lang's words:

> " like a wild flower
> All over his dear country."

Wallace was the first of a long line of Christian patriots who have died for the ideal of national independence. Abandoned by the lords and prelates of Scotland and by almost all the members of his knightly class, his memory lived on in the legends and ballads of the common folk he had led. In the fifteenth century the bard, Blind Harry, enshrined in the vernacular the ineradicable belief of peasant Scotland in his achievement:

> "Scotland he freed and brocht it off thirlage
> And now in Heaven he has his heritage."

It was this that, after a summer evening's walk to the Leglen wood in 1793, inspired the greatest of all Scottish peasants to write a song on his hero "equal to his merits." Burns's "Scots wha hae" is still sung wherever Scotsmen honour their native land or men decide to stand or fall for freedom.

[1] "Where the common sewers go down into the Tyne.

Chapter Five

TRIUMPH OF THE BRUCE

Liberty's in every blow!
Let us do or die.

BURNS

AFTER TWELVE YEARS OF WAR, Edward, at sixty-six, had overcome all his enemies. He had paid a heavy price for victory.
He was virtually bankrupt, his accounts, once so perfectly kept,
had fallen into utter confusion. His foreign bankers had taken
over control of the customs. Yet at the sacrifice of his kingdom's
finances and his people's goodwill he had regained his duchy,
subdued the Scots and imposed his will on those who had
humiliated him.

Time had given Edward his revenge on the constable and
marshal. Hereford had died soon after his successful defiance,
and in 1302 the king had married the princess Elizabeth to his
youthful heir, so making his earldom, for the time being, a royal
appanage. To win forgiveness the ageing Norfolk had been
driven to make a surrender of his estates, receiving them back on
condition that they should escheat to the Crown if he died without
heirs to his body. When this occurred in 1306, another of the
great feudal earldoms, with the hereditary office of marshal, fell
to the king, later being conferred on Thomas of Brotherton, his
eldest child by his second wife. The earldoms of Chester, Cornwall, Gloucester, Norfolk, Hereford, Richmond, Lancaster,
Derby and Leicester were all now held by Edward or his close
kinsmen.

One opponent remained—the Archbishop of Canterbury.
Against Winchelsey, who had led the opposition to his war
taxation and stiffened the baronial resolve to enforce the Forest
charters, the old king nursed an unappeasable grudge. It had
been deepened by the primate's intemperate support of charges

of murder, adultery and intercourse with the Devil brought against his faithful but much disliked treasurer, Walter Langton bishop of Lichfield.[1] Edward's opportunity came in the winter after Wallace's death. Both he and Philip the Fair had responded in kind to Pope Boniface's bid to make the Church an independent State within the State and to treat all disobedience to the papal power as heresy. Philip had reacted with such brutality that the conflict had ended, in the autumn of 1303, with the seizure of the pope in his own castle of Agnagni by French agents and his subsequent death from shock. Two years later the papacy passed to a Gascon, Clement V, whose name is still commemorated in the vineyard of Chateau Pape-Clement and who as archbishop of Bordeaux had been a subject of Edward's. The latter used his friendship to secure both a dispensation from his oath to observe the Forest charters and Winchelsey's suspension from office. In February 1306, the primate was summoned to the *curia* to answer his sovereign's charges, among them that he had falsely accused his fellow prelate, Walter Langton. "Merciless hast thou been to others," the king said in his farewell interview, "mercy to thyself we shall never show."

Edward was almost as unrelenting towards his own son. In the summer of Wallace's capture words had passed between the twenty-one-year-old heir and the treasurer. Edward would brook no disrespect for his ministers; in the reports of cases in the King's Bench there is an account of how a Marcher baron, William de Braose, who had insulted Chief Justice Hengham, was made to go ungirt, his head bare and without his coif, through a crowded Westminster Hall to implore the judge's pardon before being committed to the Tower. The same report spoke of how the king had lately "removed his eldest and dearest son, Edward Prince of Wales, from his household for almost half a year because

---

[1] He was said to have done homage to Satan and sealed his vassalage with a kiss. *Tout, Edward II*, 14. "The king," Edward wrote to the pope, "feels much anxiety and bitterness of heart when he sees Walter bishop of Coventry and Lichfield, a prudent man distinguished by many virtues, so persecuted by the evil tongues of his enemies . . . He has been known to the king familiarly from his boyhood, and the cleanliness of his life and the honesty of his conversation . . . ought to commend him to the pope and Holy See." *Williams*, I, 325-6.

he had spoken coarse and bitter words to a certain minister of
his and would not allow that son to enter his sight until he had
made satisfaction to the minister for the trespass."[1] For months,
until the young queen interceded for him, the offending youth—
forbidden to approach within thirty miles of the royal presence
and his household supplies cut off—had to follow the court as a
suppliant.

With Wallace out of the way the king issued his ordinance
for the administration of Scotland. It was to be ruled under a
royal lieutenant by an English chancellor and chamberlain
assisted by an advisory council of eight prelates and fourteen
magnates, including Bruce and the two Comyns. Judges,
coroners and sheriffs were to be appointed on the English model,
and, though the civil law of Scotland was retained, customary
laws, like those of the Celtic Highlands, "plainly against God
and reason" were abolished. Pleased at having set Scotland, as
he believed, on the road to civilisation and order, the king
graciously suspended the sentences on the remaining exiles.

Yet six months after Wallace's execution terrible news
arrived from the north. On February 11th, 1306, in a quarrel
in the Greyfriars church at Dumfries, Robert Bruce—the thrice-
pardoned Earl of Carrick—had slain his fellow councillor and
rival for the forfeit throne, John Comyn the Red—head of the
house of Badenoch.[2] Having committed murder and sacrilege,
broken the king's peace and involved himself in a blood feud with
the most powerful family in Scotland, he had then imprisoned
the royal judges who were holding an assize in the town and
appealed to the cause of national independence, not in the
dethroned Balliol's name, but in his own. Hurrying north, he had
sought the aid of old Bishop Wishart of Glasgow who heroically
gave him absolution, produced from its hiding-place the royal
standard of Scotland and accompanied him to the crowning-

---

[1] *Select Cases in the Court of King's Bench under Edward I* (Selden Society, ed.
G. O. Sayles), III, 152-4.

[2] The exact circumstances of the quarrel and Comyn's death are uncertain,
but according to one account he was despatched by Bruce's servants after the
latter had emerged from the church shouting, "I doubt I ha' slain the red
Comyn," upon which, drawing their swords, they cried, "We'll make sicker"
(sure). According to Edward, Bruce had proposed rebellion and Comyn had
threatened to tell the king. *Barrow*, 405.

place of the Scottish kings at Scone. Here on Palm Sunday, with a golden circlet made by a local smith and in the presence of Wishart and Bishop Lamberton of St. Andrews and a hundred disaffected lords and knights, mostly from the Celtic north and west,[1] he was crowned Robert I of Scotland by the Countess of Buchan, wife of Comyn's closest kinsman and sister to the young Earl of Fife with whom the hereditary right of crowning lay.

When the news of the rebellion reached Edward he was in Hampshire, travelling from hunting-lodge to hunting-lodge and seeking in the milder air of the southern counties relief for his failing health. He at once ordered the mobilisation of the northern levies and summoned a parliament to Westminster. Bruce and all concerned in the death of Comyn were to be castrated and disembowelled and those who aided him hanged. The king's mood is shown in a letter to his cousin, the Earl of Pembroke—husband of the murdered Comyn's sister—whom he had appointed to command in Scotland.

"As Sir Michael Wemyss has now shown in deed that he is a traitor and our enemy, we command you to burn his manor where we stayed and all his other manors, to destroy his lands and goods and to strip his gardens clean so that nothing is left, for an example to others like him. . . . And as for Sir Gilbert Hay to whom we showed much courtesy when he stayed with us in London recently and in whom we thought we could place our trust but whom we now find to be a traitor and our enemy, we order you to burn down all his manors and houses, destroy all his lands and goods, and strip all his gardens so that nothing is left and, if possible, do worse to him than to Sir Michael Wemyss." [2]

To finance the coming campaign an aid was demanded from all tenants-in-chief for the knighting of the king's eldest son— a ceremony long delayed because of the latter's shortcomings but now fixed for the meeting of parliament at Pentecost.

On May 20th, too ill to ride, Edward was carried to West-

---

[1] They included two of Scotland's seven earls—Lennox and Atholl—and young Sir James Douglas and Thomas Randolph, who were to be Bruce's greatest lieutenants. M. Mackenzie, *Bruce*, 165-6.

[2] National MSS. Scotland, ii No. XIV. Transl. *Barrow*, 309.

minster on a litter. Two days later, after an all-night vigil in
the Abbey, the Prince of Wales was knighted at the high altar
in the presence of the flower of his contemporaries. Nearly three
hundred young gentlemen were invested at the same time in the
church of the Knights Templar; so great was the excitement
that two of them were trampled to death in the crowd. Afterwards at a feast in Westminster Hall—the most splendid, a
chronicler recalled, since Arthur was crowned at Caerleon—two
swans, robed in cloth of gold and their necks encircled with
golden chains, were brought in by heralds to the sound of trumpets and laid before the king who swore "before God and the
swans" that he would not rest until "the Lord had given him
victory over the crowned traitor and perjured nation." Thereafter he vowed never to draw sword again except against the
paynims in the Holy Land. After which the prince rose and
swore that he would not sleep two nights in the same place until
he had fulfilled his father's vow and avenged his wrongs.[1]

As soon as the magnates and shire knights had voted a thirteenth and the burgesses a tenth, the king set out by litter on his
northward journey. His son had already preceded him. Meanwhile the vanguard under Pembroke had crossed the Forth. On
June 20th Bruce was surprised at Methven and all but taken,
only saving himself, like Wallace after Falkirk, by vanishing into
the heather; as his wife had remarked at their coronation, he and
she were but king and queen of the May. Many who had rallied
to him in the first flush of enthusiasm were by now on their way
to England in fetters. Several, including Simon Fraser and the
Earl of Atholl, suffered the fate of Wallace.

For Bruce, throughout that summer of 1306, disaster followed
disaster. In August he was defeated at Dalry by a Scottish force
under John of Argyll, lord of Lorne. Two of his brothers were
hanged, drawn and quartered; his queen—perhaps to her relief,
for she was more than half English—was taken, while his sister
Mary and the Countess of Buchan were imprisoned in cages in
the castles of Roxburgh and Berwick. And the familiar train of

---

[1] A ceremony is still enacted at the Swan Feast of the Vintners' Company
at which, preceded by a heraldic banner and to the sound of trumpets, a
cygnet is borne into the hall on a vast silver dish and presented to the Master.
See *Speculum*, Vol. XXVIII 128; *Powicke*, 514-15.

desertions, so characteristic till now of Scotland's wars of independence, began again.

> " Bruce durst not to the plainys ga
> And all the commons went him fra:
> That for their lives were full fain
> To pass to the English peace again."

In October Edward established himself for the winter at Lannercost priory, a few miles east of Carlisle. Most of the insurgents had by now been caught and hanged and their lands given to Englishmen; Bruce himself had disappeared into the glens and islands of the far west. No record of his movements during the next few months exists, but according to one account he spent some time in the little island of Rathlin off the Irish coast where, sheltering from his terrible adversary, he is said to have taken heart through watching the efforts of a persistent spider. In February, evading Edward's searching ships, he reappeared in Arran and in the middle of the month landed on the Ayrshire coast where he tried to surprise the English garrison of Turnberry castle and captured the governor's plate. Then he vanished once more into the hills and heather.

A month later his lieutenant, young James Douglas—a Dumfriesshire knight whose father had died in the Tower—surprised Castle Douglas while the garrison was at Mass, slew every man and, leaving their bodies and stores to roast in the blazing keep, disappeared again into the moors. The "Douglas larder," as it was called, caused a tremendous sensation. The tall, dark, sallow young knight, with his lisp, courteous ways and daring imagination, possessed just the qualities to mystify and terrify the English and inspire his followers. "The maist coward", it was said, "stouter he made than a leopard." In him Bruce possessed what Wallace had never had: a lieutenant as bold as himself and loyal to the Scottish cause as the heather.

That March an English parliament met at Carlisle to protest at the high-handed papal tax-collectors who had descended on England as the price of the king's bargain with their master. Edward, who left Lannercost to meet his magnates, was eagerly waiting for news of Bruce's capture as he had waited for Wallace's; in April his armies closed round the Scots king in the lonely glen of Loch Trool among the Galloway hills. Yet just when he seemed in the net Bruce broke the ring of his pursuers by a sudden charge and again vanished. A month later, on May 10th, he encountered the viceroy, Pembroke, "in a fair even field" at Loudon in the valley of the Ayrshire Avon and defeated him. Three days later he fell on another searching party under the Earl of Gloucester and drove them into Ayr castle. Scotland in arms was once more a reality.

Edward was now sinking fast. But, resolved to put himself at the head of his troops and capture the hated will o' the wisp, he left Carlisle on July 3rd, mounting his horse for the first time for a year. The agony proved insupportable. For three days he struggled on, reaching Burgh-on-Sands six miles from his starting point on the 6th. Here on July 7th, 1307, within sight of the Scottish border, he died in the arms of his attendants. His last command was that his son should carry his bones at the head of his armies till every Scot had surrendered. Then his heart was to be borne to the Holy Land on the crusade he had sworn to lead.

So died in his sixty-ninth year a king whom his queen described as "terrible to all the sons of pride but gentle to the meek of the earth." Passionate in pursuit of law and order, in the early part of his reign he had carried out a great work of constructive legislation, stirring up, in the words of the Statute of Westminster, "ancient laws which had slumbered through the disturbances of the realm." In doing so he had taken the nation into partnership and, by regularly consulting its representatives and seeking their consent, had gone far to create the greatest of all English institutions—a royal parliament in which king and subject could meet to treat, co-operate and, if necessary, dispute over matters of common concern. He had fostered, too, the development under the Crown of a self-governing legal profession that in later centuries was to become a bulwark of liberty. Yet, in seeking to enlarge the frontiers of law, his obstinate insistence on his rights had involved him in struggles which had exhausted his financial resources and forced him to make demands on his people incompatible with his own good intentions and their faith in him. Only at the end, in the Statute of Carlisle of 1307, had he once more become leader of the whole nation, identifying himself with his subjects' protest against papal encroachment and proclaiming that he could only act "by the counsel of the earls, barons, magnates, *proceres* and other nobles and of the commons of this realm."

But to the Scots and Celts Edward remained the object of an unrelenting hatred. To them he was "le roy coveytous" of Merlin's prophecy, the bringer not of order but of eternal discord. On his tomb in Westminster Abbey, inscribed by some later hand, are the words "malleus Scotorum—hammer of the Scots." They epitomise his unwitting service to a great people. For by hammering them, as he thought, to his will, he had welded them into unbreakable nationhood.

. . . .

Had Edward lived another year Bruce could not have survived. By Comyn's murder he had aligned against himself England, the papacy and half Scotland and had alienated, not only those of his fellow nobles who were loyal to Edward, but those who had been loyal to Balliol. Now, in place of the greatest soldier of his age, command of the forces of vengeance had passed to an overgrown, self-indulgent youth of twenty-three. For the first time since the Conquest a king sat on the English throne with no feeling for arms. His distaste for the hardships of campaigning was in shameful contrast to his father's Spartan ways. He lay long in bed, wore fantastic, extravagant clothes and took a tame lion round with him in a cart. Instead of Arthurian tournaments and the martial pursuits of his class he delighted in digging, thatching and farriery, horse-racing and rowing, swimming and wrestling. He also liked acting and playing the kettledrums. To his lords who thought of themselves as the prototypes of the knights of the Round Table—outside the Bible story their only literary mirror —these were childlike and contemptible frivolities. Their new sovereign had nothing in common with Arthur or Lancelot, Galahad or Sir Gawain. He appeared to them eccentric, effeminate and a fop.

For if Edward I's accession had proved the virtue of hereditary kingship, that of his son seemed to disprove it. The second Edward had the same name, the same stature, the same superb Plantagenet physique as the first. But the golden-haired young giant who had inherited his father's throne had no interest in government except as a means of extending his own liberty and enjoyment. From infancy he had been starved of affection. A few months after his birth his parents had been plunged into mourning by the death of his ten-year-old brother, Alfonso[1]— heir to the throne and their hopes. Soon afterwards they had left England for their long sojourn in Gascony and within a year of their return, when Edward was five, his mother had died. Left to the care of a preoccupied and increasingly tyrannical father, who was for ever campaigning in Wales, Flanders or Scotland, he had grown up without systematic education or discipline. Much of his boyhood had been spent in meaningless peregrinations after the royal court, and the only home he had known had been his manor of King's Langley among the Hertfordshire elms and water meadows, where he had acquired an early love for the rustic and mechanical pursuits of the country folk around him. His affections, which were strong and undiscriminating, were given to the officers and clerks of his household, to whom, in later years, he remained touchingly loyal, like the rather disreputable Windsor baker's son, Walter Reynolds, whom he was to make Archbishop of Canterbury, and that other and worthier clerk of humble parentage, William de Melton, whom he made Archbishop of York. His companions were grooms and gardeners, blacksmiths and watermen, jesters, jugglers, actors and singers.

"Fair of body and great of strength," Edward had remained a child, frivolous and emotionally unstable. Denied all share in the counsels of his father, of whose terrible rages he stood in dread, he had only one ambition, to lead his life in his own way. When still in his teens he had conceived an inordinate love for a handsome but penniless Gascon knight a few years his senior, named Piers Gaveston, whose father's loyalty in the Anglo-French wars had been rewarded by his appointment to the heir-apparent's household. The influence acquired by this quick-witted, accomplished but arrogant adventurer had become a major concern to the old king and his ministers. Twice he had been banished the realm—the last time only a few months before Edward's death when the prince had tried to bestow on him his maternal patrimony of Ponthieu—a proposal which so enraged

[1] Two older brothers had died in infancy.

the dying king that in his fury he had torn tufts out of his son's hair.

The first thing Edward II did on his accession was to recall his favourite. Disregarding his father's request that his bones should be borne at the head of the army, he made a brief perfunctory march into south-western Scotland. At the beginning of September he returned to London, where he invested Gaveston with the royal earldom of Cornwall and bestowed on him the hand of his niece, Margaret, daughter of the princess Joan and sister of the young Earl of Gloucester. Simultaneously he dismissed his father's treasurer, Bishop Langton of Lichfield, and sent him to the Tower.

The new king's abandonment of the campaign gave Bruce a breathing-space to settle accounts with his Scottish enemies. Leaving Douglas in the Galloway hills, he turned north to harry the lands, first of Dougal MacDowell and then of the Earl of Buchan, head of the house of Comyn. The valleys were swarming with English troops and the principal strongholds were in their hands, while half the Scottish nobles, adherents either of Balliol or the English king, were bitterly opposed to the Bruce claim. But the lesser gentry and common people, smarting under the invaders' injuries, turned instinctively to this God-given champion of their cause. Though as yet only a king of the heather, in their eyes he was Wallace's successor. And though surrounded by enemies and with a price on his head Bruce was already thinking in terms of hunting his hunters.

For weak and divided though she had long been, with all but two or three of her great families in the pay of England, Scotland was now to enjoy real leadership. Bruce had all the traits which the world has learnt to associate with Scottish character, magnified to the point of genius: dogged courage, persistence, unshakable loyalty to friend and unrelenting enmity to foe, tenderness to women, genial ironic humour, logical, uncompromising ruthlessness in pursuit of his purpose. The story of the spider in his Rathlin cell reveals the man. This king in the heather, this mountain-fox with the mist in his beard— "King Hobbe in the mures," as the English contemptuously called him—was one of the great national leaders of all time. Never commanding more than a few thousand men and at first only a few hundred, he evaded every attempt at capture. Whenever his foes thought they had beaten him he reappeared and, in the end, inflicted on them one of the decisive defeats of history.

At the beginning of the winter of 1307 he moved north into the land of Moray to deal with the earls of Ross and Buchan. The latter, whose cousin he had slain and whose young wife had crowned him and, according to scandal, granted him other favours, was his bitterest enemy. In November Bruce fell ill on the borders of the Comyn country and for weeks his cause seemed doomed. Yet when Buchan attacked, thinking him dying and at his mercy, the outlaw king and his partisans turned on their pursuers and routed them:

> " They chasit them with all their main,
> And some were tuk and some were slain,
> The remanand was fleaned ay,
> Wha had good horse got best away."

Again, having survived, Bruce vanished. He and James Douglas, who was waging the same will o' the wisp campaign against the English in the south-west, followed the rules taught by Wallace and improved on them. By mounting their men on moorland ponies they gave them an astonishing mobility. They trained them to disperse after a fight in small companies, to join again and fall on the foe whenever he was momentarily at a disadvantage before vanishing once more into the hills. "Better," said the good Sir James, "to hear the lark sing than the mouse cheep," and his leader, who knew that certain death awaited him in captivity, held the same philosophy. Yet when the hour of opportunity came, no man could be swifter or bolder. Nor, in adversity, more wily.

> " On foot should be all Scottish war,
> By hill and moss themselves to fight.
> Let wood for walls be, bow and spear
> And battle-axe their fighting gear.
> That enemies cause them no dread,
> Let them keep all their stores in strait places
> And burn the plains them before.
> Then shall they pass away in haste,
> When that they find nothing but waste,

With wiles and waking in the night
And much noise made on height,
Then shall they turn with great fright
As if they were chased with swords awa.
This is the counsel and intent
Of good King Robert's testament." [1]

When 1308 began, Bruce was lord of little more than Moray, with Buchan still in superior force to the east, a hostile Ross to north and west, his enemies of Lorne and the Isles between him and Douglas in the south-west. The English were in control of every major fortress in Scotland. That February, after bringing home his twelve-year-old bride, the princess Isabella, from France, King Edward was crowned with every circumstance of pomp at Westminster, Gaveston—"his brother Peter"—at his side "so decked out that he more resembled the God Mars than an ordinary mortal." Scarcely were the celebrations over when Bruce, recovered by now from his fever, struck at Buchan, routing him at Inverurie. Then, seizing Aberdeen and Forfar, he harried the lands of Buchan, teaching by fire and sword the partisan's unchanging lesson that, in the hour of revolution, no man, however peaceable, can adhere to the powers-that-be with safety. Neither Comyn nor England, Scotsmen discovered that summer, could give protection against Bruce's vengeance. A stark, primitive people, who honoured resolution and hardihood and had no love for the English and little for their own predatory nobles, observed the fact with relish. Bruce's "harrying of Buchan" became a national legend, establishing his claim to the throne in the Scottish heart. Balliol's cause never recovered.

Meanwhile the English were at sixes and sevens. The king's childish irresponsibility and dependence on Gaveston infuriated the feudal nobility. "If anyone of the earls or magnates," wrote a chronicler, "had to ask a special grace of the king in the forwarding of any business, the king would send him to Peter and whatever Peter said or commanded would be immediately done." Yet three times in the last century the proud magnates of England had taken up arms, with the support of the Church, capital and

---

[1] Barbour, *The Bruce*, Modern rendering by W. Notestein, *The Scot in History*, 39-40.

people, to enforce the ancient national principle that the king should govern with the counsel and assent of his "chief men." Edward's father, who at the start of his reign had been scrupulous to honour this practice, had tended in his autocratic latter years to rely solely on his chosen ministers and judges and only to seek the counsel of the greater feudal lords when he knew they agreed with him. Now that his masterful rule had been succeeded by the feckless governance of his son, the magnates still found themselves excluded from their share in advising their sovereign by an irresponsible foreign favourite.

Before the king was crowned they consulted as to what should be done. It was their duty to support the Crown but also to ensure that its wearer maintained the basic laws and liberties of the realm of which, under God, he was the guardian. Before they did fealty and homage to him as the representatives of the community he was expected to swear, in the traditional coronation oath, that he would confirm to the people the laws and customs given to them by his predecessors, "the just and god-fearing ancient kings of England," preserve the liberties of Holy Church and cause justice to be rendered rightly, impartially and wisely in compassion and in truth." And in the coronation Order it was laid down that

" early in the morning of the day on which the new king is to be consecrated, the prelates and nobles shall gather in the royal palace at Westminster to treat together concerning the confirming and firm enactment of the laws and statutes of the realm." [1]

Because they did not trust him, in performing this duty the magnates added a clause to the coronation oath by which Edward was made to swear that he would "grant to be held and observed the just laws and customs that the community of the realm shall determine." In other words, as the price of their homage he was to leave it to them to determine what the fundamental laws of the kingdom were or should be. This unprecedented undertaking—one to which his father would never have agreed—was given by the young king, according to one account,

[1] L. G. W. Legg, English Coronation Records 85-6, cit. *Wilkinson*, II, 107-8.

in return for his lords' not insisting on Gaveston's banishment.

Two days after the coronation, meeting in the refectory of Westminster Abbey the magnates asked their sovereign for a written confirmation of his promise "to consider as firm and settled"—as their doyen, the old loyalist Earl of Lincoln put it —"whatever, by the inspiration of God," they should be led to ordain. When at the instance, as they suspected, of Gaveston, Edward procrastinated, they drew up a declaration in which they announced that their own oaths, rendered in return for the king's, were binding in respect of the Crown rather than of his person and that, if he should not "be guided by reason" they, his liege subjects, as the protectors of the people were bound by their oaths "to guide him back again by reason and amend the estate of the Crown." If necessary, they must do so by force, as "he cannot be directed by course of law, for there are no judges but such as are the king's."

This was reaching back to the days of de Montfort. Yet as Edward had virtually transferred his prerogative to Gaveston, insisting that he had a right to consult whom he pleased, it was hard to see how else the magnates could reconcile their homage with their obligation to the community or perform their feudal and national function of giving the king "good counsel." Whatever he might have sworn to, the only counsel he heeded was that of his favourite—the "king's idol," as the people called him. And to the magnates Gaveston was now a red rag to a herd of bulls. Soon after the coronation the hated upstart held a tournament at Wallingford in which he and his gay young friends defeated and humiliated several of the earls, including Surrey, Arundel and Hereford. With his Gascon swagger he loved to mortify their pride. The magnates were swaggerers, too, but in a more restrained, stolid and unimaginative way. They took their immeasurable superiority for granted as a law of nature. Gaveston's family was old and honourable but of the petty *noblesse* of a foreign province, and, though he was as much Edward's subject as they, he had no place in the community of England of which they were the pillars. To have made him earl of Cornwall seemed a gross insult to their pride and patriotism. If he had accepted his elevation with humility and tried to ingratiate himself, they might have borne with him. But he did no such thing and exulted over and taunted them. With no backing but the king's favour he was committing the most perilous crime in the political calendar and recklessly flouting a vested interest.

Early in the summer of 1309, while Bruce was harrying Buchan, the English lords met in parliament and demanded Gaveston's banishment. He had disinherited the Crown of its estates, they declared, separated the king from his rightful counsellors and bound adherents to himself by unlawful oaths. In an attempt to appease them Edward bestowed the stewardship of the realm on his cousin, Thomas earl of Lancaster, who, though of royal blood, was also the greatest of the magnates. He reluctantly, too, agreed to Gaveston's banishment as viceroy of Ireland. In June, after Archbishop Winchelsey—now back in England and the mainspring of the opposition—had pronounced the favourite excommunicate if he should return without parliament's permission, the king sadly accompanied him to Bristol to watch him embark for Dublin.

Yet Gaveston's departure settled nothing. His master intended to recall him at the earliest opportunity and the magnates knew it. And the insoluble problems created by Edward I's wars remained unsolved. The financial system devised by his treasurer Walter Langton and the keeper of the Wardrobe, John of Droxford, had completely broken down. The Wardrobe officials and the chamberlains of Scotland who had to finance the campaign against Bruce were for ever trying to obtain the wherewithal from an exhausted Exchequer to meet their accumulating debts. For years their accounts had ceased, not merely to balance, but even to be made up. Despite every expedient to raise more money, the yield from the taxpayer had steadily diminished. Most of the receipt of customs stuck to the fingers of the Crown's Italian and Gascon creditors to whom it had had to surrender its fiscal powers to obtain cash to pay and feed its armies. The great Florentine financier, Amerigo dei Frescobaldi, was receiver of the customs, keeper of the king's exchanges and constable of Bordeaux. After the favourite he was the most influential, and unpopular, man in the kingdom. And Gaveston's banking kinsmen, the Calhaus, who controlled the revenues of the royal duchy of Cornwall, were almost equally hated.

Meanwhile the run of Scottish successes continued. While the English king was escorting Gaveston to the waterside, Bruce's brother, Edward, won a spectacular victory on the Cree; by the summer he and Douglas were in control of the entire south-west except the fortresses of Dumfries, Dalswinton, Caerlaverock and Lochmaben. In August King Robert defeated the men of Lorne and Argyll in the Pass of Brander. In October he received the submission of Ross in the far north. Even in the border country south of Edinburgh guerrilla bands threatened the English convoys as they made their way through moor and forest to revictual the royal castles.

By the year's end Bruce was *de facto* ruler of almost all Scotland north of the Tay; only Banff and a few castles on the north-east coast, provisioned by sea, held out for England. Early in 1309 he liberated the major part of Fife and in March held his first parliament at St. Andrews. Three of the Scottish earls—Ross, Sutherland and Lennox—now supported him, while the earldoms of Menteith and Caithness, held by infants, were represented in his parliament. After three years of continuous peril and struggle he was a real king at last, enthroned in the hearts of a people resolved to fight to the death for their freedom. "His mishaps, flights and dangers, hardships, weariness, hunger and thirst, watchings and fastings, nakedness and cold, snares and banishments," wrote one of them, recalling those years, "the seizing, imprisonment, slaughter and downfall of his near ones, and—even more—dear ones, . . . no-one now living, I think recollects or is equal to rehearsing." They formed his royal title-deeds.

Even now the might of England could have crushed him; every major fortress in Scotland was still in her hands. Again Edward's infatuation for Gaveston saved Bruce. The host had been summoned for September and two armies were massing at Berwick and Carlisle. Before they could strike the favourite was back in England, the king meeting him on his landing at Chester like a brother. In the hope of conciliating the baronage Edward had agreed in July, in a parliament at Stamford, to eleven articles repudiating certain actions of his officers which had been denounced by the magnates: purveyances, the levying of his father's "new" customs, the deliberate depreciation of the

currency, judicial delays and the sale of pardons to criminals.
Yet within a few weeks of his return Gaveston had everyone by
the ears. He had a witty mocking tongue and a way of ridiculing
the magnates that delighted his childlike master. The most loyal
of the earls, the sallow, hook-nosed Pembroke, was nick-named
Joseph the Jew, Guy of Warwick "the black hound of Arden",
Gaveston's own youthful brother-in-law, Gloucester, one of the
Crown's few remaining supporters, "the cuckoo's chick" or
whoreson—an ungallant allusion to the speed with which his
mother, the king's sister, had married the young knight Ralph
de Monthermer after the old Earl of Gloucester's death. And the
Earl of Lancaster—Edward's first cousin—with his heavy frame
and clipped, bristly hair, was christened the "black hog" or
"churl." Everyone, including their owners, heard of these labels;
Gaveston's gay young accomplices saw to that.

In the autumn, the five of the greatest magnates in the kingdom
—Lincoln, his son-in-law Lancaster, Warwick, Oxford and
Arundel—refused to attend the council at York because the favourite was to be there. Even Gloucester informed his royal uncle
that, as the Articles of Stamford had been broken, the collection of
the aid voted by parliament for the Scottish war would have to
be suspended. Early in the new year the barons appeared in the
council chamber in arms. The king, they affirmed, led by evil
counsellors, had wasted the moneys granted by parliament, had
reduced his revenues till he was forced to live by extortion and,
by losing Scotland, had disinherited the Crown. They demanded
the immediate appointment of an executive of "Lords Ordainers"
to reform the kingdom. When the king hesitated they told him
that they would "no longer hold him as their king nor keep the
fealty they had sworn to him since he himself would not keep
the oath which he had sworn at his coronation." Petulantly
Edward agreed. On March 17th 1310, in the Painted Chamber
it was announced that for the next eighteen months the Archbishop of Canterbury and six bishops, the earls of Lincoln,
Lancaster, Gloucester, Hereford, Warwick, Pembroke, Richmond
and Arundel and five barons were to "ordain and establish
the estate of the realm and the household according to right and
reason."

Yet in his own eyes and those of the great mass of his subjects the king remained a king. The magnates could constrain him by arms; they could only permanently prevent him from exercising his functions by depriving him of his liberty as their predecessors under de Montfort had deprived his grandfather. Whatever titles they might compel him to grant them, the royal prerogatives remained his and his alone. No sooner had the Lords Ordainers set themselves up at Westminster than Edward, accompanied by the favourite, removed himself and his court to York under pretext of preparing the reconquest of Scotland. And as the chancellor, Bishop Langton of Chichester, was an Ordainer, the king resumed control of the great seal, the supreme instrument of executive power, by appointing to his place another prelate who was not—Walter Reynolds bishop of Worcester, his former chaplain who was said to have won his favour by his facility in writing plays.

All this accrued to Scotland's advantage. Five of her earls— Buchan, Atholl, Ross, March and Angus—still adhered to the English king or to Balliol, and her twenty strongest fortresses were held by English garrisons. But not even a new papal excommunication for "damnable perseverance in iniquity" could shake King Robert's standing with the Scottish people. Early in 1310, disregarding the pope's anathemas, a general council of the Scottish Church, meeting in the Greyfriars kirk at Dundee, recognised him as the "true heir to the crown." And as the Ordainers refused to support it, a further invasion of Scotland that autumn only strengthened his position. On September 16th Edward crossed the Tweed and entered Roxburgh, with Nicholas Segrave acting as marshal in the absence of the hereditary holder. Of the greater nobles only Surrey and Gloucester accompanied him. When he advanced through the forest of Selkirk and Lanarkshire to Linlithgow, Bruce merely withdrew to Stirling, wasting the country. By the beginning of November the hungry invaders were back at Berwick.

Nor was a second invasion by the king and Gaveston in the spring any more successful. Even at sea the English were harried by Scots privateers, operating not only from their own harbours but from Flanders. For as long as possible the king remained at Berwick, postponing the evil day when he would have to meet the Ordainers. Then, at the beginning of August 1311, leaving

Gaveston for safety in Bamborough castle, he was forced by lack
of funds to return to London.

Here after an unavailing pilgrimage to Becket's shrine at
Canterbury he met the lords of parliament, offering to agree to
anything they ordained if only Gaveston were spared. But the
favourite's enemies were adamant. On September 27th Archbishop Winchelsey and the earls of Lancaster, Warwick, Pembroke and Hereford published the Ordainers' articles at Paul's
Cross. On October 5th it was announced that the king had
accepted them.

The Ordinances transformed the king into an official of state
committed to carrying out the will of the magnates through
officers controlled by parliament. They sought to transfer the
royal power from Edward and his existing household officers—
the chamberlain and the keepers and controllers of the Wardrobe
—to their own nominees who were no longer to be responsible
to the king personally but to the king in parliament, an abstrac-
tion which they made the corner-stone of their reformed system
of government instead of the Council favoured by de Montfort
fifty years before. "Inasmuch," they proclaimed, "as the king
has been misguided and advised by bad counsellors, we ordain
that all the bad counsellors shall be removed, so that neither they
nor others like them shall be near the king nor kept in the king's
service, and other suitable persons shall be put in their places
. . . by the counsel and assent of his baronage in parliament."[1]
The Ordainers were an aristocratic body, but by their insistence
on ministerial responsibility to parliament and their reliance on
that institution to make an erring king fulfil his obligations to
the community, they took a first step on the long stony road to
parliamentary control of the executive. They ordained that the
king should not engage in any foreign war or leave the country
without consent of parliament which was to meet in some convenient place at least once a year. All his officers were to swear
to maintain the Ordinances, and a committee of lords was to
hear and adjudge complaints against them in every parliament.

The Ordainers also decreed that all taxes imposed since 1274,
including the "new" custom on wool, were to be abolished, while

[1] *Tout, Edward II,* 93.

the Italian bankers and foreign merchants were to be banished. So was Gaveston. "All the evil counsellors," it was laid down, "shall be put out and utterly removed." The favourite who had "estranged the king's heart from his people and replaced the royal ministers by his own gang or coven" was to sail from Dover by All Saints Day or be treated as a public enemy.

It was the end, and ruin, of the Frescobaldi, but the effect on the Scottish war was disastrous. For by suddenly cutting off the supply of foreign credit the Ordainers made an early reconquest of Scotland impossible. While this was happening at Westminster, Bruce once more took the offensive. Free at last from the threat of invasion he crossed the Solway, eleven days after the king left Berwick, to raid the farms of upper Tynedale. A month later he returned and, wasting Coquetdale and Redesdale, penetrated as far as Durham. Scotland, after six years of war, was starving behind him; northern England, he intended, should taste the same medicine. By the end of the month, despairing of help from a divided and preoccupied government, the men of Northumberland offered him a ransom for their homes and crops. When he recrossed the border it was with £2000 of English money paid for a truce till February.

Such was the price of the Ordainers' triumph. Nor had they rid themselves of Gaveston. Though he had sailed from the Thames two days after the day appointed for his banishment, rumours soon reached London that he had been seen in Cornwall and the south-west. In November, after the Ordainers had ordered the removal of several more of his household officers, the king himself left London with them, complaining that he was being treated like an idiot. Uninterested in government though he was, their interference with his personal servants infuriated him. He might lack the Plantagenet genius but he had his full share of the Plantagenet temper and obstinacy. Before the end of the year Gaveston had openly rejoined him at Windsor where they kept the Christmas feast together.

Civil war was now unavoidable. On January 7th, 1312, Edward left for the north "to escape bondage," ordering the great seal to be brought to him at York. There were now two governments, one composed of the king and his Wardrobe officers, the other of the Lords Ordainers and the older departments of state at Westminster. From York Edward announced that "the good and loyal" Piers had been restored to all his offices and estates. The Ordainers accepted the challenge, formed a confederacy to defend their Ordinances and, under a pretence of tournaments, called out their retainers. The archbishop excommunicated Gaveston, while Lancaster wrote to the queen promising that he would not rest till he had rid her of the hated favourite's presence.

For the moment the country was whole-heartedly behind the magnates. Gaveston was a foreigner; so were the Italian and Gascon extortioners, personal friends, it was rumoured, to whom the collection of the customs had been entrusted. The Charter, men said, was being "melted away." Because "might was right," ran a popular ballad, "the land was lawless," because light was darkness it lacked doctrine, because "fight was flight" the kingdom was without honour.

In April the king and Gaveston moved from York to Newcastle, ostensibly to chastise the Scots, in reality to escape the barons. But on May 4th Lancaster, advancing across the Pennines, surprised and all but captured them. The queen was taken with part of the royal treasure, while Edward and the favourite fled down the river to Tynemouth, thence escaping by boat to Scarborough. Leaving Gaveston in the castle—one of the strongest in the kingdom—the anguished monarch hurried to York to raise an army to relieve him.

But the barons forestalled him. Marching south Lancaster barred his path, while Pembroke, Surrey and Henry Percy laid siege to Scarborough. After a fortnight, running short of supplies, Gaveston surrendered on terms. His captors promised to deliver him unharmed on August 1st in York minster to abide the judgment of parliament.

The barons meant to keep their word. But their fellow Ordainers—Lancaster, Warwick and Hereford—having missed their quarry at Newcastle, took the law into their own hands. When, removing the favourite for safe custody to his castle at Wallingford, Pembroke left him for a night in the rector's house at Deddington, the three earls pounced on him and carried him off to Warwick. After keeping him there a few days Warwick allowed Lancaster—a Front-de-Boeuf of a man with no scruples

—to have him beheaded by a pair of Irish assassins on Blacklow Hill. His corpse was contemptuously refused admission to Warwick castle and was only given burial by those friends of the poor and outcast, the friars.

By their act of violence the murderers split the baronial opposition. Lancaster had burnt his boats; any real trust or co-operation between him and his royal cousin was henceforth unattainable. Feeling their honour compromised, Pembroke and Surrey now gravitated to the king's side. So did the country which, for all its hatred of Gaveston, was shocked by the brutal act.[1] The English were a rough pugnacious people and much disliked upstarts and aliens, but they were used to the rule of law. Nor did they want civil war.

The result was a royalist reaction. London rallied to the king; in any case Gaveston was dead and could do no more harm. On November 13th a son—the future Edward III—was born to the king and his young French queen at Windsor. The danger of a disputed succession, with Lancaster as king designate, seemed over. During the next few weeks, with the help of a papal mediator, some kind of understanding was reached between the king and magnates. Gaveston's murderers were prevailed upon to make a public apology in return for an amnesty and the measures against the officers of the household were tacitly suspended.

Yet under the surface the fissure in the ruling establishment continued. So did the tale of Scottish successes. In the spring of 1312 Edward Bruce had carried Dundee castle. In August, while his lieutenants were reducing the last English fortresses of the south-west, King Robert again crossed the border and harried Tynedale, penetrating to the walls of Durham and sacking Hartlepool. The north was in a panic, and the border counties paid £10,000 for a truce till the spring. With a long trail of hostages and the loot of five towns Bruce returned to his ravaged, poverty-stricken land well content. At the end of the year he all but took Berwick in a surprise attack.

---

[1] Sir James Ramsay called Gaveston's murder "the first drop of the deluge which within a century and a half carried away nearly all the ancient baronage and a great proportion of the royal race of England." Ramsay, *Genesis of Lancaster*, i, 46.

During the early months of 1313, under cover of his truce with the northern counties and while Edward and his queen were paying a ceremonial visit to France, Bruce struck at the royal garrisons in Scotland. On January 8th, after a seven weeks' siege, he led his men neck-deep through the icy waters of the moat to capture Perth in a midnight escalade. A month later his brother Edward took Dumfries and the Bruce castle of Lochmaben. And at the end of the summer a farmer named Binnock, who was in the habit of supplying the garrison of Linlithgow with hay, blocked the main gate with a wagon, enabling armed men concealed in it to rush the portcullis and capture the fortress.

At this point, Edward Bruce, who lacked his brother's Fabian sense of strategy, brought the long-drawn-out war to a crisis. He made a truce with the governor of Stirling, Sir Thomas Mowbray, by which the latter agreed to surrender the castle if it was not relieved by midsummer. This put both kings in a dilemma. Edward could not ignore the challenge without ignominy, while Robert could only allow Stirling to be relieved at the expense of laying northern Scotland once more open to invasion and jeopardising the successes of the past six years.

During the opening months of 1314 the summons went out to all English fighting men. The greatest army England had ever sent forth was to march to the castle's relief before the day agreed for its surrender. Unable to secure from an Exchequer controlled by jealous magnates all the money required for the campaign or, as a result of the Ordinances, to make the same use as his father of the Wardrobe—the royal department responsible for financing war—the king had started to raise money through another branch of his household, the Chamber, using his secret seal or signet to authorise its operations. Part of the funds to equip the expedition is said to have come from the confiscated wealth of the great international crusading Order, the Templars, which Philip the Fair had seized after his victory over Pope Boniface by accusing its rich bachelor brethren of heresy, black magic and perversion—charges of which they were almost certainly innocent but which were supported by confessions wrung out of them by torture. Having secured the election of a French pope and his removal, in 1309, from Rome to a French enclave at Avignon,

Philip had prevailed on him to dissolve the Order and have the Grand Master, who had retracted his confession, burnt as a relapsed heretic. Not only was the dowry of Philip's daughter, Edward's queen, found out of it, but the huge income of the Templars in England, though ultimately assigned to the Knights of St. John, remained for many years in the hands of the Crown. In this way endowments originally intended for fighting the Moslems of the eastern deserts helped to finance an English crusade against an excommunicated Scottish king.

While Edward was mobilising England's might to crush once and for all "Robert de Brus who calls himself king of Scotland," the latter was wresting from him his last bases in the north. On the night of Shrove Tuesday Douglas captured the chief fortress of the marches, Roxburgh, while the garrison was keeping the feast in the great hall:

"at their dancing,
Singing and otherwise playing."

A month later Bruce's nephew, Thomas Randolph, to whom he had given the earldom of Moray, secured an even greater prize. Scaling Edinburgh castle from the ravine which today divides the new city from the old, while a frontal attack engaged the garrison, Randolph and his men wearing darkened armour reached the ramparts by a track down which one of them in his youth had been wont to visit his lady-love. Rigid discipline, silence and the use of a twelve-foot collapsible ladder did the rest.

Having dismantled the captured castles Bruce withdrew into the Torwood, close to the Roman road to Stirling up which the English would have to march. Here, training his men for the battle which was now inevitable, he awaited the supreme test of his own and his country's life. He had to pit the fighting forces of a nation of less than half a million, desperately impoverished by twenty years of invasion and civil war, against those of a kingdom with more than eight times its population and resources. Once more he was helped by the English king who, though determined now to destroy him, again failed to unite his country behind him. Instead of letting a parliament approve the measures for crushing the hated Scots he persisted in acting independently of the magnates and at the last moment, fearing their criticism, cancelled the session he had called. Instead, he spent the Easter feast at his favourite abbeys of St. Albans and Ely. As a result, a number of leading magnates, including the earls of Lancaster, Surrey, Warwick and Arundel, refused to answer the summons, insisting that under the Ordinances the king's departure from the realm was illegal until a parliament had been consulted.

Even without their presence it was an immense array that assembled at Wark on June 10th. There were probably between 2000 and 3000 knights and nearly 20,000 archers and spearmen. Hereford the constable, Gloucester, Pembroke, Clifford, Despenser, Nicholas Segrave, the half-Northumbrian, half-Scottish earl of Angus and the murdered Comyn's son, were all there. On the 17th they set out, advancing up Lauderdale to Edinburgh and the Forth, while their supplies followed by sea to Leith. This time there was no indecision; the king meant to make a speedy end of Scotland's defiance. By the evening of June 22nd—two days before Stirling had to be relieved—he reached Falkirk, having covered nearly a hundred miles in six days.

That night Bruce's scouts brought news of the English host— "so great that it was ferly." The whole glittering panoply of a rich nation's chivalry was displayed in the summer twilight as the armoured horses and men passed in endless procession through the streets of Falkirk:

" Banners right fairly flaming
And pencels to the wind waving."

So impressive was the sight that Bruce forbade those who had seen it to speak of it to their comrades. His own force numbered little more than a quarter of the English: some 5000 infantry, mostly spearmen equipped with twelve-foot spears, padded coats, steel helmets and mail gloves, together with a few archers from Ettrick forest and about 500 lightly armed horse. Another 2000 auxiliaries,[1] "small folk" from the neighbouring farms and boroughs, roused by the magnitude of the country's peril, had recently joined him. Save for these, his men were all veterans who had been drilling for many weeks for the battle they would have to fight. And they were defending all they held dear. Sir

[1] The figures are based on General Sir Philip Christison's "Bannockburn," published in 1960 by the National Trust for Scotland—with John Morris's study of fifty years ago the best military account of the battle.

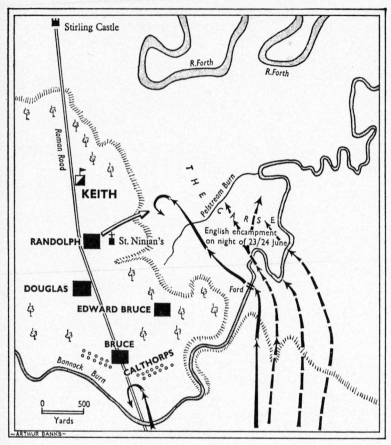

Stirling Castle

R.Forth

R.Forth

Roman Road

KEITH

THE

Pelstream Burn

C
R I S E

RANDOLPH   † St. Ninian's

English encampment
on night of 23/24 June

DOUGLAS

EDWARD BRUCE

Ford

BRUCE
CALTHORPS

Bannock Burn

0   500
Yards

~ARTHUR BANKS~

A Plan of Bannockburn

James Douglas, acting for young Walter—the Steward's heir—led
the men of Clydeside and the western Border, Randolph the men
of Ross and Moray and the burghers of Inverness, and the
king's brother, Edward, contingents from Buchan, Mar, Angus,
Menteith and Lennox. Bruce himself commanded the reserve,
made up of his tenantry from Carrick and a strong force of clansmen from the western Highlands and the Isles. These four
divisions or "battles"—Douglas on the left, Randolph in the
centre and Edward Bruce on the right—each consisted of two
or more schiltrons capable, thanks to their king's training, of

manœuvre as well as of passive defence. The small force of cavalry was under Sir Robert Keith, the marischal.

Soon after midday on Saturday June 23rd, hot and weary from its twenty-mile march from Falkirk, the English army reached the little Bannock burn that, crossing the Roman road to Stirling, serpentined north-eastwards through pools to the Forth. The beleaguered castle, clearly visible on its height, was now only three miles away. The Scots were posted on rising wooded ground barring the road, their front protected by rows of carefully dug pits or *pottis* concealed by turf and branches, with steel calthrops for maiming horses strewn between them. The governor of Stirling had ridden out to warn the king of these. He also pointed out that, as he was within three leagues of the castle, it was already technically "relieved" and that there was therefore no need for haste.

But, inexperienced in Scottish warfare and believing Bruce's hopelessly outnumbered army to be at their mercy, Edward and the younger English lords were impatient for victory. Despite the long morning's march they decided to attack at once. Through the hot afternoon haze the armoured knights under the constable and Earl of Gloucester pressed forward across the burn on their great war-horses without waiting for the rest of the army to deploy.

The Scots were not expecting this move, which, after so long a march and so late in the day, seemed contrary to every prudent rule of war. Bruce himself was in front of his outposts, reconnoitring the English positions. At the top of the rise, near the Borestone on the Stirling road, Sir Humphrey Bohun, the Earl of Hereford's nephew, suddenly encountered him. Seeing the crown over his helmet and a chance of immortal glory, he put his horse into a gallop and bore down. But Bruce, mounted on a small grey palfrey, was too quick for him. Rising in the stirrups as the English knight thundered past, he cracked open his skull with his battle-axe. Then he galloped back to join his waiting men in the wood.

Here the English cavalry, confronted by the pits and calthrops, were soon in difficulties. The Earl of Gloucester himself was thrown and unmounted, and, after some ineffective skirmishing, the exhausted knights and their heavily laden horses fell back in confusion without having penetrated the Scottish position at any point. Meanwhile a smaller contingent of six or seven hundred horse under the lords Clifford and de Beaumont had been feeling its way northwards towards Stirling round the Scots' eastern and retracted flank where, immediately below the escarpment, a narrow corridor of firm ground lay unguarded between Bruce's left and the carse that stretched between the Bannock burn and the Forth. Lacking the strength both to hold the road through the wood and bar this alternative approach to the castle, Bruce had deliberately left it open, hoping that, if Edward's troops were to advance along it without first dislodging him, he might, by descending on them while they were still strung out, force them into the carse where their armour would be helpless and unable to manœuvre.

Confident of being able to drive Bruce from the wood, Edward had ordered Clifford to take up position between Stirling and the Scots' rear, ready to cut off their retreat and destroy them. This manœuvre fared no better than Hereford's frontal attack. Randolph's division, posted near the little chapel of St. Ninian's on the left of Bruce's line, moved down from the escarpment to intercept the intruders. Instead of obeying their orders and continuing their march, the English wheeled left and engaged the schiltrons who at once halted, closed and confronted them with the usual impenetrable hedgehogs of spears. Though the riders flung their maces and battle-axes into the Scottish ranks in the hope of breaking them, nothing would make the horses face those steady, glittering circles of steel. Clifford was killed and his lieutenant, Sir Thomas Grey—whose son wrote an account of the action—was dragged, dismounted, into one of the schiltrons and made a prisoner. In the end the attackers dispersed, some taking refuge in Stirling castle and the remainder galloping back to the English host beyond the Bannock burn, spreading dismay.

A council of war was now held. As no hope remained of driving the Scots from the wood that day, the more prudent urged a halt. But Edward, anxious to obtain water for his horses, fell into the very trap Bruce had baited. Intending next day to attack from the east the position that he had failed to carry from the south, he ordered his entire army to move down into the valley of the Bannock burn and the boggy carse beyond. Here, its morale badly shaken, it passed the night, as one present described it, "in a deep, wet, evil marsh." The lights of the Scottish camp-fires could be seen shining through the trees about a mile away on the higher ground to the west.

That night Bruce had to decide whether to stand and fight or fall back on the old evasive tactics of withdrawal and dispersal which under his leadership had brought his country through so many perils. His decision to stake all on a single throw is said to have been reached after a Scottish deserter from the English host, Sir Alexander Seton, had brought news of the demoralisation that had set in after the defeat of its advance-guard. "Now," he urged, "is the time and now the hour and Scotland shall be free." Bruce needed no prompting, for his enemy at last was where he wished him.

Sunday, June 24th, Midsummer Day, 1314 was the feast of St. John the Baptist. At the first light the Scottish priests, moving from schiltron to schiltron, celebrated Mass at the head of each division. Afterwards the men knelt in prayer while the abbot of Inchaffray, armed with sacred relics, blessed them. A Scottish historian, Dr. Muir Mackenzie, has recalled that the lesson for the day was from the 40th chapter of Isaiah, "Comfort ye, comfort ye, my people," and the gospel the prayer "that we should be saved from our enemies and from the hands of all that hate us."[1]

Meanwhile the trumpets were sounding in the English camp along the burn, and thousands of knights, assisted by their pages, were buckling on their armour and mounting their huge barded horses after their comfortless night among the pools and peat. But before the ranks could be marshalled the Scots were seen to be on the move. To the amazement of the invaders, instead of awaiting their attack on the higher ground or withdrawing into the forest westwards, the schiltrons were descending the slope towards them in three great battles of massed spears. "Will these men fight?" asked the incredulous Edward of Robert de Umfraville earl of Angus,[2] his most trusted Scottish adherent. And de Umfraville, who knew his countrymen, replied that they

---

[1] M. Mackenzie, *Bruce*, 272.

[2] His grandfather, a Northumbrian baron, had married the heiress of the ancient Celtic earldom of Angus.

would and begged him to order a retreat to tempt them to open their ranks and expose themselves to the English armour.

But like Cressingham before Stirling Brig the English king despised the Scots. Disregarding those who wished to give the army time to form battle array, he ordered his nephew Gloucester to charge the advancing spearmen. Angered by his taunts and without waiting even to don his surcoat, the young earl flung himself against the foremost schiltron commanded by Edward Bruce. Here on the hedge of spears he met his death like every other knight brave enough to follow him. Behind, the rest of the English army tried desperately to deploy. But while King Robert knew what he was doing, the invaders were without plan or leadership. The archers, whom Edward's father had used at Falkirk to shatter the schiltrons before his cavalry charged, were still where they had bivouacked in the rear and could only shoot over the heads or into the backs of their countrymen.

All this, like the great commander he was, Bruce saw. It was why, instead of awaiting the English attack, he had chosen to anticipate it. Using his schiltrons as a slowly moving wall of steel, he sought to compress the vast, unprepared mass of invaders into a steadily diminishing space with the marshes of the carse and the reaches of the Forth behind them. As he brought his right forward and swung his steady footmen northwards along the course of the burn, without the English realising it he was driving them into the one place where he could destroy them.

Hitherto, in their nine years of trying to bring him to book, the leaders of England's chivalry had encountered only the cautious side of Bruce—the Fabian general who had repeatedly survived by vanishing into his native mists, leaving them to starve amid barren mountain and flood. Now, like their subordinate garrison commanders who had long experienced his sudden lion pounces on lonely moor and midnight escalade, they discovered his other side. For once he had chosen his moment, no man could be bolder. His chief danger were the English and Welsh archers who, so long as his schiltrons kept their ranks, alone possessed the power to break them. He had only five hundred horse, but knew that the time had come to use them. Most of the enemy's archers were still in the rear of the dense, confused English armour as it struggled to hold back the advancing spears, and their arrows were falling impartially on friend and foe alike. But a number had by now taken station on the English left and were starting to shoot at the densely packed Scottish infantry. Seeing that they were unprotected by pikesmen, Bruce ordered the marischal to move his horsemen round their flank and charge.

The move was a brilliant success. In a few minutes the archers had been cut to pieces and the English were without one of their two principal weapons. The other, their armour, unable to deploy and with its horses getting more and more out of control, was by now unusable. Unable either to break or stop the contracting ring of Scottish spears, it was gradually pushed back in confusion into an ever-smaller area of firm ground as Bruce's wheel cut it off from the south and pressed it towards the bogs and marshes of the Forth. Now, King Robert saw, was the moment to throw in his reserve, hidden in the wood to the west of the Stirling highway. Calling on Angus Og, MacDonald of the Isles, in the words still borne on the Clanranald coat-of-arms, "My hope is constant in thee," he launched the islemen against the receding English flank where, a mile or more to the east of St. Ninian's chapel, the Bannock burn narrowed into a small precipitous gorge. Into this the English cavalry were driven as the Scottish officers repeatedly called out, "Press! Press!", and the pikesmen, keeping their steady ranks, raised the shout of, "On them, on them, they fail! they fail!"

As the mêlée of falling knights and terror-stricken horses continued in the narrowing space left by the Scottish spears, a further force was seen to be entering the battle. Emerging from the wood on the hill beyond St. Ninian's church, "the small folk" and camp followers of Bruce's army moved into the fight to take their share of whatever slaying and plundering there might be. They had made themselves banners of blankets slung on saplings, and the sight filled the by now demoralised invaders with despair. The burn was choked with English knights and horses, struggling and sinking under the weight of armour into the peat, while the spearmen pressed the survivors into the loops of the stream and the archers and camp followers, entering the fray, hacked at them with swords and daggers.

By this time panic had set in; it was Stirling Brig over again. The English were far from home in a wild hostile land, and their line of retreat was cut by relentless enemies and the bogs of the carse. The only way open was northwards across the narrowing plain to Stirling. The first thought of those immediately about him was to save the king. The tall Plantagenet, his horse stabbed under him, helped to clear a way with his battle-axe, while his entourage hustled him through the milling mob towards the north. Sir Giles d'Argentine, after Bruce and Douglas the most famous knight on the field, guarded him till he was clear of the throng, then turned and rode back to die. "For me," were his parting words, "I am not of custom to fly; nor shall I do so now. God keep you!"

When Edward reached the walls of Stirling castle he was reminded by the governor that any stay there would be fatal, since he was obliged to surrender it by the terms of the truce. There was nothing for it but to make a wide detour to the west round the rear of the Scottish army. With five hundred followers the king set out into the unknown, vowing to endow a college of Carmelite friars if he reached England in safety. Riding day and night, with Douglas in pursuit, he reached Dunbar castle where he took boat to Berwick.

Others were less fortunate. The constable, flying towards Carlisle with the Earl of Angus and other Balliol supporters, was handed over to his pursuers by the governor of Bothwell castle. Those taken on the field included the keeper of the Privy Seal, which itself fell into Scottish hands. In all some five hundred men of high rank were made prisoner. Thousands more, including seven hundred knights and many of England's greatest lords, perished in the carse or in the waters of the Forth or were slaughtered by the country folk. Of the magnates who had accompanied the king to Scotland, only Pembroke—flying on foot with a handful of Welsh archers—reached England.

Had Bruce commanded a substantial force of cavalry it is unlikely that any of the invaders would have got away. His booty included the royal wardrobe, a vast haul of jewels and ecclesiastical vestments—brought to celebrate an English victory —and over £200,000 in bullion, worth many millions in modern money. The whole of the royal siege-train and military chest remained in his hands. He treated his prisoners with magnanimity and courtesy like the great gentleman he was. Sir Marmaduke de Twenge, the English hero of the rout of Stirling Brig who, after a night hidden in a bush, surrendered to him personally next day, was sent home without ransom. For nearly a year after the Battle of the Pools, as the English called it, a stream of agents visited Scotland under safe conducts to negotiate the exchange of prisoners. In return for the release of Hereford, Bruce secured the return of his queen, his daughter Princess Marjorie, the young Earl of Mar, and Wallace's old patron—blind after seven years' captivity—Bishop Wishart.

. . . .

After Hastings, Bannockburn was the greatest military disaster in English history. It ended any real hope of reconquering Scotland by arms. For a generation the Scots had suffered invasion. Now, under Douglas and Randolph, they took the offensive. Having expelled the English from every corner of their land save Berwick, they swept across the border, burning Appleby and almost reaching Richmond before they returned with their booty. Before Christmas they were back to waste Tyneside. And as the government at Westminster was neither prepared to recognise their independence nor able to oppose them, the people of northern England had to make what terms they could. Cumberland and Durham paid ransom for a truce, and Tynedale did homage to the Scottish king. It was almost like the days after the fall of the Roman wall.[1]

In the summer of 1315, an offer by Bruce of a permanent peace having been refused, the Scots again attacked. They were joined by many English bandits and outlaws, for, with the Crown's weakness, northern society was disintegrating. Douglas raided Durham and burnt Hartlepool; Carlisle was only saved by the courage of its governor, Sir Andrew Harclay, and the departure of the main Scottish army for Ireland. For in the winter after Bannockburn, roused by his fellow Celts' victory,

---

[1] Such was the devastation of the north that in a papal valuation made in 1318 of ecclesiastical property in the dioceses of Durham and Carlisle, both were found to have lost about five-sixths of their value since the last valuation in 1291. *Tout, Edward II*, 236.

Donal O'Neill, titular king of Tyrone, renounced the English allegiance and invited Bruce's brother to assume the Irish crown. On May 26th, 1315, unable to resist the gamble, the Scottish heir-presumptive landed in Larne bay.

Always ready for a knock at the English, the Irish rose. Under the rule of Edward I's justiciar, Sir John Wogan, the eastern half of the island had been enjoying comparative peace and had exported troops to feed the king's Scottish campaigns. Now, heartened by the news of Bannockburn, the west and south relapsed into their traditional anarchy, and the English of the Pale were forced to fly from Ulster. Even in Leinster the O'Briens, O'Tooles and O'Carrols turned out with their wild kerns to sack the coastal towns of Arklow, Newcastle and Bray. In May 1316, after defeating Edward Butler the justiciar at Ardswill, Edward Bruce was crowned high king of Ireland at Dundalk. Later in the summer he was joined by King Robert who, secure from attack by a divided England, left Scotland and the harrying of the marshes to his son-in-law, Walter the Steward, and the redoubtable Douglas. Such was the terror which the latter inspired that for generations North Country mothers rocked their babies to the refrain,

> " Hush thee, hush thee, do not fret thee,
>   The Black Douglas shall not get thee! "

Yet the dream of a Bruce dynasty ruling the Celtic north and west of the British Isles under a single crown proved as insubstantial as Edward I's dream of union under the Plantagenets. Though the Bruces advanced to within five miles of Dublin they were halted by its English mayor who arrested the great Anglo-Norman magnate, Richard de Burgh—the "red" earl of Ulster —to forestall any risk of his siding with his son-in-law, King Robert. And in the face of reinforcements from England a Scottish march to Limerick ended in a winter's retreat across a wasted, starving land. "The combatants," wrote the chronicler, "left neither wood nor crop nor house nor barn nor church without burning and wholly destroying." By the time King Robert withdrew to Scotland the Irish had discovered that the Scots could be as big a curse as the English. When in 1318 Edward Bruce was defeated and killed at the Hill of Faughart

while attempting a new invasion of Leinster, Irish disillusionment was complete. A native annalist wrote that "there was not
done from the beginning of the world a deed that was better
for the men of Ireland."

Meanwhile England remained in the doldrums. Afraid after
Bannockburn even to appear before a parliament, the king left
his enemies to do as they pleased and spent his days at his anvil.
At Christmas 1315 he was reported to be "rowing in the Cambridge fens with a great company of simple people," refreshing
his soul "with the solace of many waters." He and "his silly
company of swimmers" roused the scorn of the feudal barons
who could not understand how a prince bred to arms, instead of
seeking revenge on his enemies, could busy himself with "childish
frivolities." So far as the country at this time had a ruler it was
Edward's cousin, Thomas of Lancaster, who, having escaped the
odium of defeat by refusing to accompany him to Bannockburn,
found himself a national hero. Son of a queen, nephew of the
late king and inheritor of five earldoms, this surly and unattractive
magnifico behaved as though the throne were his property. He
insisted on the dismissal of the chancellor, treasurer and keeper
of the Wardrobe and the appointment of his own nominees in
their place. At the Lincoln parliament of 1316 he kept his
cousin and his fellow magnates waiting for more than a fortnight before he chose to appear and allow the proceedings to
start.

Yet though the king and council were forced to obtain the
earl's assent for every administrative act, he proved as incapable
of governing as Edward. Enjoying greater nominal powers than
de Montfort, appointed chief of council and commander of the
campaign against Scotland and with the right to repudiate any
action of the Crown that did not meet with his approval, he
spent his time on his northern estates, where, isolated by his pride
and splendour, he maintained a royal state without any of the
responsibilities of kingship. His sole object was to keep the king
a puppet and humiliate him. When in the summer of 1316 the
Scots again ravaged the north, sacking the iron-works at Furness
and reaching the walls of Richmond, the army assembled to
repel them achieved nothing since Lancaster refused either to
serve under the king or to advance without him. For fear of

treachery the cousins were afraid of approaching one another except in the midst of armed retainers.

Because of this sterile rivalry England was hamstrung. Not only did her Crown fail her, but her harvests. In the years 1315-17 a cycle of wet summers brought, in the words of the Bridlington chronicler, "misery such as our age has never seen." At the height of the famine wheat rose to six times its normal price and men ate horses and dogs and even, it was said, children; "thieves that were in prisons did pluck in pieces those that were newly brought amongst them and greedily devoured them half alive." All over the Welsh marches and in the north private war raged unchecked; in revenge for the shelter given to his wife who had eloped, Lancaster ravaged the Earl of Surrey's Yorkshire estates and plundered his castles. Even during a session of parliament in Lincoln cathedral a knight attacked one of the household officers, Hugh Despenser, with a drawn sword. Gangs of disbanded soldiers roamed the country, and in the moors and Midland forests brigands and outlaws held up travellers to ransom. In the autumn of 1317, while journeying from Scotland to England in a vain attempt to negotiate a peace, two papal legates—both cardinals—were waylaid by a Northumbrian knight and his robber band, stripped and sent on their way stark naked.

By 1318 the English had recovered sufficiently from Bannockburn to plan a new invasion of Scotland. Edward Bruce's death had left that country's dynastic future as precarious as ever, for the only heir of royal blood left was the infant son of Walter the Steward whose wife, the Princess Marjorie, had died after giving him birth. But the little sandy king as usual was two moves ahead of his enemies. Before the spring he pounced on Berwick, which he had failed to take by surprise two winters before, carrying the castle after an eleven weeks' siege. In May, before the avenging English host could assemble, his columns were a hundred and twenty miles across the border, burning Northallerton, Boroughbridge and Knaresborough and coming within fifteen miles of York itself. Ripon only escaped destruction by paying a £1000 ransom after its terrified inhabitants had stood a three days' siege in the minster. Then the victors returned by Wharfedale, plundering as they went. King Edward never got further than York, where his generals quarrelled with one another until the money for paying their troops gave out and they had to disband them.

All this served to discredit Lancaster, who could no longer cast the blame for everything that went wrong on the king. Both were far more concerned with thwarting one another than the country's enemies; "whatever pleases the lord king," it was said, "the earl's servants try to upset, and whatever pleases the earl the king's servants call treachery." Since someone had to govern, a middle party arose to fill the vacuum. Its leader was Aylmer de Valence earl of Pembroke, the most moderate of the Ordainers—an honourable man who embodied the ordinary Englishman's dislike of political violence and extremes.[1] He was backed by the leaders of the Church, including the primate, Archbishop Reynolds, and by most of the barons who were becoming increasingly alienated by Lancaster's arrogance, boorishness and persistent refusal to shoulder responsibility. The middle party was also supported by the permanent officers of the Exchequer and Chancery and the curialists of the royal household whose aim, like that of all officials, was to strengthen the power and efficiency of their departments—a desire in their case immensely stimulated by the Ordainers' attempts to deprive them of all influence and power. Its objects were, while keeping the wayward, impulsive king under control, to restore the royal dignity, enforce what was good in the Ordinances and reduce the overmighty Lancaster to his proper size.

Under such guidance the country now enjoyed a brief recovery. Following the "treaty" of Leake in the autumn of 1318 between the royal councillors and Lancaster, there was an outward reconciliation between the king and his cousin. The latter, it was agreed, should no longer attend meetings of parliament as a rival prince but as an ordinary peer of the realm "without encroaching sovereignty towards the others," while the king was to observe the Ordinances, grant pardon to his cousin for all former offences and govern through a council, one member of

---

[1] The son of Henry III's Poitevin half-brother, he was descended on the distaff from William the Marshal. His countess, who survived him by half a century, founded Valence Mary or Pembroke College, Cambridge, in his memory in 1347.

which should always be nominated by Lancaster. The rivals
publicly exchanged the kiss of peace and in the ensuing calm it
almost looked as though the ship of state had found a helmsman.
A number of important administrative reforms were set in hand
by the household officers and an accommodation reached with
France over the question of homage for Aquitaine and Ponthieu.
There was even an improvement in the weather and an end to
the disastrous harvests of the past few years.

Yet the country's refusal to accept Scotland's independence
continued to bedevil all. In June, 1319, following the king and
Lancaster's reconciliation, the host assembled at Newcastle. All
the earls were present—Pembroke, Surrey, Hereford, Arundel,
even Lancaster and his brother Henry "Wryneck." There was
a fleet from the Cinque Ports, a siege-train that included a ship with
a drop-bridge for storming city walls and a movable mine or
"sow" with a concealed storming-party in its belly. Impressed
by the new accord in England, the pope granted a subsidy from
the crusading fund to finance the expedition that was at last to
punish Bruce's sacrilege. Yet it achieved nothing. Walter the
Steward continued to hold Berwick with the help of a Flemish
engineer named Crab, who mounted a stone-thrower on the
walls that "caused the English sow to farrow." And, instead of
advancing to the city's relief and giving England's chivalry the
chance to avenge Bannockburn, the Scottish king sent Douglas
through the western marches to threaten York, where he all but
captured Queen Isabella with the royal Exchequer and judges.
On September 20th, at Myton-in-Swaledale, Douglas's Highlanders routed the army which the northern metropolitan had
hastily raised from the tenants of the Yorkshire monastic houses
to defend his capital. During the "white battle" or chapter of
Myton, as it was called from the number of Cistercian dignitaries
taking part, the mayor of York was killed and the Master of the
Rolls taken prisoner. Then, with their plunder, which included
the archbishop's plate, the invaders marched on Lancaster's
castle at Pontefract.

The result was as Bruce had foreseen. The earl hurried south
to save his estates, and the king and the rest of the host, feeling
themselves betrayed, abandoned the siege of Berwick. Three
days before Christmas Edward concluded a two years' truce with

the Scots who obtained everything that they sought except a
formal recognition of their national sovereignty, which was still
more than the English stomach would concede. And though the
pope launched yet another proclamation of excommunication
against Bruce and summoned him and the Scottish prelates to
Avignon, he too got more than he bargained for. For in April 1320,
meeting in parliament in the monastery of Arbroath, the Scots
answered him with all the crushing logic—and eloquence—of
their race.

Issued in Latin in the name of the lay community and attested
by the seals of eight earls and almost every leading magnate, the
Declaration of Arbroath was the first great appeal for national
independence in modern history. It opened with the story of the
Scottish people's past, of how "by victory upon victory and
travail upon travail" they had won for themselves their "abodes
in the west"; how, "assailed again and again by Norseman,
Dane and Angle," they had kept themselves "free from servitude,"
living under "one hundred and thirteen kings of native royal
stock, never an alien upon the throne," and how, "dwelling at
the limit of the world," they had been among the first to receive
the Christian faith. Then, the declaration continued, "the
masterful prince Edward, king of the English, father of him
who now reigns," had come "in the guise of a friend and an ally
. . . against a people with no thought of ill or fraud, unused to
the assaults of war" and had subjected them to "slaughter,
violence and pillage, . . . sparing neither age, sex, order of religion
or priesthood," until "from these unnumbered ills, with the aid of
Him who heals the wounded and makes whole," they had been
delivered by the strong arm of their king, the lord Sir Robert,
"who, that he might free his people and his heritage, endured
cheerfully toil and weariness, hunger and peril." Nothing could
shake them from their allegiance to the man who had preserved
their liberties, though, if he were now to surrender their kingdom
to the English, they would, they declared,

> "thrust him out forthwith as our enemy and the subverter
> of right and take for our king another who would suffice
> for our defence, for so long as an hundred remain alive we
> are minded never to bow to the dominion of England. It
> is not for glory, riches or honour that we fight; it is for

liberty alone which no good man surrenders but with his life."

The petitioners ended with an appeal to the pope to exhort the English king to suffer them to live in peace "in this narrow plot of Scotland beyond which we have no habitation." Such was the declaration's effect that the pope suspended the process of the *curia* against Bruce and urged Edward to make peace.

It was not only Scotland that continued to wreck everything England did, but her king's incorrigible irresponsibility. For a short while after Lancaster's surrender of power Edward displayed an unwonted application to affairs, getting up, according to one bishop, early in the morning "contrary to his wont" and showing a "cordial countenance" to prelates and magnates at the council table and even occasionally contributing something useful to their discussions. But the improvement was short-lived. He had now got a new favourite—a particularly grasping young Marcher baron named Hugh Despenser whose father, an old servant of the Crown, had incurred the distrust of the magnates by supporting Gaveston against the Ordainers. The Despensers were not, by Marcher standards, a family of the first rank, being descended from the dispensers of the former earls of Chester. Hugh, who had been a member of Edward's household when he was Prince of Wales and had been knighted with him, had married the eldest sister and co-heiress of the last Clare earl of Gloucester. Since the latter's death at Bannockburn, he had become embroiled with his brothers-in-law over the division of his property, of which, with the king's backing, he claimed the lion's share, including the county of Glamorgan. Edward, who could never love or hate by halves, doted on him and loaded him with favours. As chamberlain of the household, young Despenser was accused of undermining every other influence and leading the king "like a cat after a straw."

By the spring of 1321 Despenser's greed and the resentment of the Marchers had broken up the middle party and precipitated a private war in South Wales of the kind that Edward I had tried to make impossible. Infuriated by the favourite's use of the royal prerogative to encroach on their rights, the great lords of the March invaded and wasted the Despenser lands under the Earl of Hereford and the Mortimers. They were backed by Lancaster, himself a Marcher. When the king ordered Hereford and his confederates to disperse, he was openly defied, while Lancaster, on the ground that no justice could be obtained in the king's court, held a parliament of the northern lords in the chapter-house of Pontefract abbey at which the Despensers were formally condemned. The civil war spread from Wales to England, and in July, so that, as they put it, "universal peace might better be fostered . . . and the peace and profit of the people be more safely kept," the Marchers entered London in arms and quartered their troops in the suburbs. Warned by Pembroke, who alone remained faithful to him, that, if he failed to banish the Despensers, the magnates would withdraw their allegiance and appoint another ruler in his place, the king delayed for a fortnight and then surrendered. On August 19th, in his presence, the lords in parliament sentenced the Despensers to banishment for having "accroached to themselves the royal authority, estranged the heart of the king from his people and kept the magnates from having access to him."

Yet, as with Gaveston ten years before, it was one thing to force the king to banish the man to whom he had given his heart, another to prevent him from recalling him. Unable to keep their retainers permanently away from their homes, the Marchers dispersed. And, as Edward had done what his subjects wanted and was still their anointed king, public opinion once more veered towards him. In October one of the confederates, Lord Baddlesmere, grossly insulted the queen by refusing her admission to Leeds Castle. This was too much, and when Edward besieged the castle and hanged its constable there was a general feeling that the Marchers had gone too far and that he was only behaving as a king should.

That January Edward acted with a resolution that recalled his father. Having regained the support of the more moderate magnates, he struck at the Marchers in Wales. Crossing the Severn at Shrewsbury, by the end of the month he had forced the Mortimers to surrender while an irresolute Lancaster remained inactive in the north. Then, after reducing the castles of Ludlow, Hereford, Gloucester and Berkeley, he got the Archbishop of Canterbury to declare Despenser's banishment illegal.

At that moment his chief opponent made a fatal blunder. Beguiled by that prince of diplomats, the Earl of Moray, into a secret correspondence with Scotland in which he figured under the flattering soubriquet of "King Arthur," Lancaster agreed to recognise Bruce in return for the aid of a Scottish army. By inviting their arch enemy to invade England he alienated the Border lords and played straight into the king's hands.

Through his failure to support the Mortimers in their hour of peril Lancaster had left himself friendless. Only Hereford remained, having gone too far to withdraw. Proclaiming them both traitors, calling out the militia and summoning a parliament to meet in May at York, the king now marched against them. On March 16th, 1322, while attempting to cross the Ure, Lancaster was intercepted at Boroughbridge by the warden of the Western March, Sir Andrew Harclay, with a force of Westmorland men-at-arms and archers. Hereford was killed and Lancaster, hesitating as usual, was captured a few hours later by the pursuing royal forces. Brought before the king in the hall of his own castle at Pontefract and forbidden, like Gaveston, to speak in his defence, Earl Thomas was sentenced to death and summarily beheaded in the presence of a jeering crowd.

Having avenged himself on Gaveston's murderer, Edward met his parliament at York. The tide was now running strongly in his favour; his sheriffs had done their business well. A representative assembly of magnates, knights of the shire, burgesses and clerical proctors[1] annulled the Ordinances on the ground that the Ordainers had acted without the king and were therefore no true parliament. Since "the power of the lord king" had been "wrongfully limited to the injury of his lordship and contrary to the estate of the Crown," they enacted that "every kind of ordinance or provision made under any authority or commission whatsoever by subjects . . . relating to the royal power" should be "null and void and have no validity and force." Instead, they laid it down that all matters affecting "the estate of the king and his heirs" should "henceforth be granted and established in parliament by our lord the king and with the con-

---

[1] It included a contingent of twenty-four discreet men from "the communities of the principality of Wales." The burgesses were sent home after the first three weeks. *Tout, Edward II,* 151.

sent of the prelates, earls and barons and of the commonalty of the kingdom, as has been accustomed in times past."[1]

The Statute of York was an attempt to stabilise the realm, not by a compromise embodying the best of two opposed principles like the young Lord Edward's Statute of Marlborough after the baronial wars, but by a denial of everything for which the magnates had been contending. It repudiated, not only the distinction made in the declaration of 1308 between the monarch and the Crown, but Edward's coronation oath to uphold the just laws and customs determined by the representatives of the community. Instead, the ruler alone was to "treat, grant and establish" such laws in parliament. The only function of "the prelates, earls, barons and commonalty of the realm" was to "consent". The statute harked back to the benevolent paternalism which had worked so well and with so broad a measure of agreement in Edward I's early years but which had broken down under a successor as idle, irresponsible and easily swayed as his son. It postulated a just and active king and a willing people. But it made no attempt to deal with the question of what was to happen if the king was not just and active and the subject not willing.

Yet, like the Ordinances it repealed, the Statute of York set the powers it restored to the king in the framework of parliament, even though a parliament that could do nothing without him. And, unlike the Ordinances, it took cognisance of the Commons as part of that parliament. The war with Scotland and the royal need for money were making the humble representatives of the shires and merchant towns increasingly necessary. In the twenty years of Edward II's reign they were summoned by writ to no less than twenty-five parliaments.

The king had beaten Lancaster and the Marchers; he had still to conquer the Scots. Once more in the summer of 1322 he appointed a muster at Newcastle for July 22nd. Once more Bruce was in the field before him. On June 19th, he swept past Carlisle to raid Allerdale, put Furness Abbey to ransom and burned Lancaster and Preston, recrossing the border with the usual tribute and plunder on July 24th. When at last, in August, Edward advanced to Melrose and Edinburgh the Scottish king withdrew behind the Forth, wasting the country and evacuating

[1] Statutes of the Realm I, 189, cit. *Wilkinson*, II, 155-6.

the inhabitants. As before, he put his trust in Edward's commissariat breaking down, and it did. He let the heather and the
long Scots miles fight for him. After a fortnight in a barren
wasted Lothian, Edward fell back on England, burning Dry-
burgh abbey and sacking Holyrood and Melrose. The only
booty taken in the campaign was a lame cow—"the dearest
beef," grumbled the Earl of Surrey, "he had ever seen."

Then Bruce took his revenge. On September 30th, 1322, he
again crossed the Solway and struck eastwards into Yorkshire to
ravage the Cleveland farmsteads and the lonely villages of the
North Riding. King Edward himself, journeying homewards by
Barnard Castle, was surprised and defeated at Byland, where
the captain of his guard, John of Brittany, was taken prisoner.
He and his half-brother, the Earl of Kent, only saved themselves
by flight to Bridlington and thence by boat to Holderness.
Meanwhile Bruce's Highlanders pursued the English to the gates
of York, exacting ransom as far as Beverley and again plundering
Ripon.

After this the northern English made what terms they could.
The Archbishop of York empowered the heads of the Cistercian
houses to ransom themselves, the Bishop of Durham treated with
the Scots and even the gallant Harclay—victor of Boroughbridge
and now Earl of Carlisle—bowed to the inevitable and, seeking
out Randolph at Lochmaben, proposed negotiations for a peace
between the two countries. Its basis was to be the recognition
of King Robert and his marriage to an English princess in return
for an indemnity of 40,000 marks provided Edward approved the
terms within a year. Harclay made the proposals openly and
with the full support of the Border, but they were represented
to his royal master—still smarting from his defeat—as treason.
On his orders Harclay was seized and hanged as a traitor.

Though he had destroyed his most faithful servant, it availed
Edward nothing. Within a few weeks he was forced by the state
of the Border to send an envoy to Berwick. On May 30th, at
Newcastle, a thirteen years' truce was concluded between the
two countries. The issue of recognition was left open, Bruce
signing as King of Scots, and Pembroke and Despenser
accepting his signature on behalf of the English king. It was the
only way to save the North from complete ruin. By the treaty

England also agreed to offer no impediment to the Scots' reconciliation with the papacy. After this, Randolph was sent on an embassy to Avignon where he succeeded in obtaining the pope's recognition of his sovereign and his country's independence. Two years later at Corbeil he secured a renewal of what was henceforward to be known as "the auld alliance" between France and Scotland. Any truce or peace between France and England, or England and Scotland, it was mutually agreed, was to terminate immediately England attacked either.

King Robert's struggle for recognition was ending at last. Though the final acknowledgement by England was still wanting, the truce offered Scotland freedom from invasion and a chance to rebuild her shattered economic life. "It hadna'," it was said, "been burnt this year or more." The succession, too, now seemed secure, for in March 1324 the queen had unexpectedly given birth to a son, David. Two years later a parliament held at Cambuskenneth and attended by representatives of the Scottish boroughs granted the king a tenth of all the country's rents and profits for the rest of his life. He was even able to build himself a country house at Cardross on the Clyde, with glazed windows and painted chambers, where in view of his failing health, he spent much of his time, hunting and sailing.

England, too, gained from the cessation of a war so costly and inglorious. It enabled the Despensers to start to restore the authority of the Crown. Though out to feather their own nests, their fortunes were entirely bound up with their royal master's and their survival depended on his strength. Their recipe for dealing with Edward's deficiencies was, not to limit his prerogative but to use it to make the royal executive so efficient that his personal inability to rule would no longer matter. Pembroke had died in 1324 soon after the negotiation of the Scottish truce, and the Despensers, the elder now made Earl of Winchester, were left with almost untrammelled power. They used it—for they were able men with a strong feeling for efficiency—not only to build up a vast private principality in South Wales from Milford Haven to Chepstow, but to improve the administration. As the Ordainers had restricted the royal use of the Wardrobe by endeavouring to make it, like the Exchequer and Chancery, a public rather than a private department, accountable to parliament, they did everything possible to revive the power of that other household department, the Chamber—originally the king's bedroom, as the Wardrobe had been his clothes-closet—which the younger Despenser controlled as chamberlain, and which, taking the place of the Wardrobe, increasingly managed the royal manors and their revenues. With its third royal seal, the *sigillum secretum*, by-passing the privy seal, which now, like the great seal, was becoming a seal of state, Despenser and its zealous officials issued a continuous succession of royal writs and letters designed to bring as much as possible of the nation's business and revenue under their control. Simultaneously the new treasurer, Walter Stapledon bishop of Exeter, effected reforms in the Exchequer and its recording methods to enforce the Crown's rights and speed the settlement of accounts: "to deliver our people more quickly for their easing and our profit,"[1] as a warrant put it. It was to this orderly-minded prelate—builder of the beautiful nave of Exeter cathedral and founder of Exeter College, Oxford—that England owed the re-arrangement of the memoranda rolls of the Exchequer. It is a testimony to the strength and continuity of the English administrative system that this departure should have been taken in such a troubled time.

How much the country needed firm rule can be seen from the London coroners' rolls. Men resorted to force on the most trifling provocation. On Monday October 19th, 1321, at vesper-time, a squire of the Earl of Arundel named Thomas Church, riding with a companion down Thames Street, knocked down a woman with a child in her arms. Because a porter begged him to ride more carefully, Church drew his sword and, striking the man a mortal blow, rode off before the passers-by could apprehend him. A few weeks later a Broad Street shopkeeper, roused at midnight by a passing roysterer, smashed in his skull with his staff and left him to die on the pavement. Another citizen took a crowbar to a minstrel who kept him awake and was himself killed by a knife which the flying musician plunged into his breast, while a vendor of eels who had thrown some skins on the roadway opposite the premises of two shopkeepers in Cord-wainers Street was kicked to death as he lay in the churchyard

[1] J. C. Davies, *The Baronial Opposition to Edward II*, 533.

of St. Mary le Bow where he had fled for refuge. Gangs of apprentices and law students fought in the streets with swords; prisoners made mass escapes from jail; county magnates intimidated monastic chapters with arms to elect the candidate for office they favoured; a baron of the Exchequer was assaulted and killed in the king's highway. Though all this was part of the general violence of the age, disorder was growing daily stronger. So was the readiness of men to cheat the Crown and intimidate their neighbours of their rights. In a medieval State, when a king was too weak or idle to govern, anarchy was never far away.

.   .   .   .

The Despensers' attempts to restore public efficiency and order did not make them popular. There was only one person whose authority could be stomached by a proud aristocracy trained to arms from childhood. If the wearer of the crown delegated authority to a favourite, whether an upstart like Gaveston or an hereditary magnate like Despenser, that favourite was certain to be detested. The king had to rule in person if the realm was not to disintegrate. In outward appearance Edward was everything his people expected a king to be: as magnificent a figure as his father. Despite all they had had to endure during his reign he was still popular with the common people, whose rustic sports he pursued so enthusiastically in his Hertfordshire retreat and who were too far removed from him to realise his inadequacy. But those who were brought into daily contact with him or saw or heard accounts of his childishness, levity and undignified behaviour were profoundly shaken in what, after religion, was medieval man's deepest conviction—veneration for God's consecrated vice-regent, the king. It began to be rumoured that Edward was a bastard or changeling. And hatred of the favourite and of his master's doting and indecent besottedness grew apace; one king, it was said, was enough; three were intolerable.

Though the opposition had been silenced, it only needed time and opportunity to bring the general malaise to a head. The government had become a tyranny; nobody dared withstand the king's wishes, wrote the Malmesbury chronicler. Substituting the prerogative for justice, Despenser used it to commit the gravest of all medieval secular offences: disinherison of property by illegal means "without the assent of the peers of the land being asked for." In the autumn of 1323, aided by friends who had drugged the warders' drink, his most dangerous enemy, Roger Mortimer of Wigmore, escaped from the Tower by a rope-ladder and took refuge in France. About the same time a summons reached Edward from the new French king, Charles IV, demanding the homage due for his fiefs of Gascony and Ponthieu. As earlier, trouble arose from a feudal relationship that had caused no difficulty before the development of national feelings in England and France. For while the English king could not bring himself to admit that his sovereignty over the French provinces inherited from his ancestors was less absolute than that over his own kingdom, his French cousin and their ministers were equally resolved to extend their rule over all the hitherto independent fiefs that geographically and linguistically were part of France.

After consulting his council Edward gained a six months' respite on the ground that he could not leave his kingdom with safety in its present troubled state. But by the time he was due to appear at Amiens to do homage a situation had arisen in Gascony almost identical to that which had caused war between England and France in his father's reign. During the winter of 1323-4, having burnt a new French frontier fortress and hanged a French serjeant-at-law for an encroachment on his jurisdiction, Sir Ralph Basset, the English seneschal of Gascony, failed to answer a summons from the French king to appear in his court at Toulouse to answer for his contempt. When in July 1324 Edward's ambassador in Paris refused to hand over the offending seneschal and asked for a further postponement of homage, the French king acted as his father had done thirty years before, declared Gascony and Ponthieu forfeit under feudal law and sent an army into the Agenais and other outlying districts of the duchy. Prevented by French privateers and the weakness of his naval forces from sending reinforcements to his outnumbered garrisons, all Edward could do in his impotent rage was to arrest French traders in England and dismiss his French queen's attendants. By September his half-brother, the Earl of Kent, had been forced to surrender La Réole and to agree to a six months' truce to save what remained of Gascony.

There was little love between Edward and Isabella. She bitterly resented his devotion to Despenser. Their matrimonial relationship had become so strained that it was said that "the king carried a knife in his hose to kill the queen and had said that if he had no other weapons he would crush her with his teeth." The dismissal of her ladies and the substitution of the favourite's wife in their place completed the estrangement.

As, however, she was the French king's sister, Edward and the Despensers adopted a suggestion of the papal nuncio that she should be sent to France to plead for the return of his lands. Isabella seized the opportunity to escape from the humiliation of her position. All, however, she obtained was an extension of the truce till the summer of 1325. For King Charles not only retained the Agenais pending the decision of his courts but insisted on the personal appearance of either Edward or his fourteen-year-old heir to do homage for the rest of Gascony. And as, fearful for his unpopular favourite's safety, Edward did not dare to leave England, the young prince was sent to France to be invested with his father's truncated fief. Once there, his mother refused to let him return and openly defied her husband and his ministers.

By doing so she opened the floodgates of rebellion. Everyone was thirsting to overthrow the Despensers and everyone turned against the king. At Pontefract the country people flocked to the tomb of Thomas of Lancaster who, only three years after his unmourned death, had become a popular martyr; there was already talk of miracles at his shrine and even a demand for his canonization.[1] More even than the avarice and despotic efficiency of the royal favourite his ruthlessness shocked the country. In a parliament at the end of the year petitions were presented in the name of the "commonalty" complaining of lawless imprisonment, corruption, arbitrary forest laws and grave miscarriages of justice; feeling was particularly strong over the indecency of

[1] A memorial tablet portraying him which was attached to a pillar in St. Paul's was believed to possess healing virtues and attracted such crowds that the king ordered the Bishop of London to remove it. G. H. Cook, *The English Cathedral*, 34.

leaving rebels' bodies hanging indefinitely without Christian burial. In Paris English exiles flocked to the queen's court, among them Roger Mortimer who soon became not only her adviser, but her lover. And though this caused so much scandal that after a protest from the pope, she was forced to leave Paris for Hainault, she obtained there an even more favourable base for her campaign against her husband, offering its count, who was also ruler of Holland and Zeeland, the hand of her son—England's future king—for his twelve-year-old daughter, Philippa, in return for ships, men and money for invading England.

When news of this reached the king and the Despensers they ordered the coasts and castles to be put in a state of defence and issued commissions of array. But they did not dare call out the host, for they knew the barons would turn against them. Even the Earl of Kent, and Edward's cousin, the Earl of Richmond, threw in their lot with the queen. When in September 1326 she and Mortimer sailed from Dordrecht with a company of English exiles and Hainaulters, no attempt to intercept them was made by the men of the Cinque Ports who hated the favourite whom the king had made their warden. Landing at Orwell the invaders advanced without resistance to Bury St. Edmunds and Cambridge where they were joined by a great concourse of magnates and gentry, including the king's eldest half-brother, Thomas Brotherton earl of Norfolk, Henry "Wryneck"—brother and successor of the murdered Earl of Lancaster—and Adam of Orleton bishop of Hereford, an old opponent of the royal power. Meanwhile Edward and the Despensers withdrew to the Tower whence they poured out proclamations calling for a national rally and offering rewards for Mortimer's head. But no one took the slightest notice, and, in the middle of October, finding that "the whole community of the realm" adhered to their enemies, they fled to the west. After which the London mob rose, seized the late treasurer, Bishop Stapledon of Exeter, and beheaded him with a butcher's knife on the Cheapside cobbles.

By the end of the month the queen's army was at Gloucester, where it was joined by the Welsh Marchers and northern lords. A few days later, aided by its citizens, Mortimer captured Bristol where the elder Despenser had taken refuge. Brought before his fellow magnates he was sentenced to immediate death. "This court," he was told,

"denies you any right of answer because you yourself made a law that a man could be condemned without right of answer. This law shall now apply to you and your adherents. You are an attainted traitor, for you were formerly banished as such by assent of the king and the whole baronage . . . By force and against the law of the land and accroaching to yourself royal power, you counselled the king to disinherit and undo his lieges, and notably Thomas of Lancaster whom you put to death for no cause. You are a robber and by your cruelty you have robbed this land, wherefore all the people cry vengeance upon you. You have traitorously counselled the king to undo the prelates of Holy Church, not allowing the Church her due liberties. Wherefore the court awards that you be drawn for treason, hanged for robbery, beheaded for misdeeds against the Church, and that your head be sent to Winchester, of which place, against law and reason, you were made earl. . . . And because your deeds have dishonoured the order of chivalry, the court awards that you be hanged in a surcoat quartered with your arms and that your arms be destroyed for ever."[1]

It was a dangerous precedent, but a more perilous one was to follow. On November 16th Lancaster captured the king and Hugh Despenser in Neath abbey where they had taken refuge after an attempt to escape by sea. Next day, forbidden like his father to plead, Despenser was hanged fifty feet high while his royal master was removed under guard to Kenilworth castle. Here he remained till the new year when a parliament, called in the name of his son, the Duke of Aquitaine, met in Westminster Hall. The proceedings were opened by the Bishop of Hereford, who, declaring that the queen's life could never be safe in her husband's hands, asked whether the magnates and representatives of the realm would have the father or son to reign over them. Overawed by the London mob in the hall, the king's friends remained silent save for four brave prelates—his old servant, William of

[1] *McKisack*, 85-6.

Melton of York, Stephen Gravesend of London, Hamo Heath of Rochester and John Ross of Carlisle. Then the prince was brought in and shown to the people with the cry of "Behold your king!"

By making the personal monarchy legally impregnable the framers of the Statute of York had left the nation's representatives only one remedy if the king infringed the liberties of the subject. That was to dethrone him. The grounds for Edward's deposition as set out in the articles of accusation were that he was incompetent to govern, that he had been controlled by others who had given him evil advice, that throughout his reign he had been unwilling to hear or adopt good counsel, that he had given himself up to unseemly works and occupations, neglecting the needs of his realm, and through lack of good government had lost Scotland and territories and lordships in Gascony and Ireland which his father had left him in peace. "He has stripped," it was said, "his realm and done all that he could to ruin his . . . . people, and, what is worse, by his cruelty and lack of character, he has shown himself incorrigible and without hope of amendment."[1]

Yet those set on changing their ruler—and at that moment they seemed to include almost the entire nation—wished to do so by legal means. Having resorted to force, they now sought to cloak it under the forms of law. But the king could only legally be dethroned with his own assent. And when Orleton and another bishop waited on him at Kenilworth to ask him "to concur in some just and suitable arrangement with respect to the Crown," the angry, lonely prisoner refused, cursing them as traitors. Only five years had passed since the York parliament had decreed that any matter affecting the king's estate and power must be granted and established by him in his parliament. There was no such thing in English law as a parliament without the king. But those resolved on his dethronement refused to be deterred. Once more a delegation rode through the muddy roads to Kenilworth to interview the royal prisoner. Intimidated by threats that if he did not comply the people would crown his wife's paramour instead of his son, the wretched man, weeping

---

[1] Twysden, *Historiae Anglicanae Scriptores Decem*, col. 2765; Rymer's *Foedera*, ii, 650, transl. by Adams and Stephens, 99, cit., *Wilkinson*, ii, 170-1.

and groaning, gave way. The delegation returned to London with the royal insignia, and a new reign was proclaimed on January 25th, 1327.

When, "speaking in the name of all the earls and barons of the realm of England" as "procurator of all in the land and of the whole parliament," Sir William Trussell of Peatling renounced the nation's allegiance to Edward II, a new chapter in parliamentary history had begun. Though without the king's presence neither a court of law nor a legislative assembly, a parliament that had not even been constituted had virtually dethroned one king and set up another in his place. And, though the first had abdicated under duress and the other was in the lawful line of succession, the order assigned for the young king's crowning showed what had been done. "The earls, magnates and eminent citizens," it laid down, were to gather in the king's court to "treat about the election of the new prince and the confirmation of the laws and customs of the kingdom." When they had agreed to these they were to acclaim him with united voice and "exalt him with all gentleness and reverence as the custom of the kingdom" demanded. Then, having lifted him up and replaced him in his chair, still unrobed, unspurred and uncrowned, four of the earls were to inform the clergy of his election and demand that, "as he has been elected by the people, so he may be . . . consecrated to be king."[1] First introduced into the coronation of Edward II and now reinforced by the presence of representatives of the *plebs* at the meeting to choose his successor, the rite of Elevation, followed by that of Recognition, symbolised the dependence of the king on his people and the participation of the community in the "regnum" or rule of the state.

.   .   .   .

With the young king in their charge and his father imprisoned, the queen and Mortimer had now to face the problems Edward II had failed to solve. To win the support of the wool producers the Despensers in an earlier bid for popularity had transferred to England the staple on exported wool which had been set up

---

[1] Maskell, *Monumenta Ritualia Ecclesiae Anglicanae*, III, 3-48 cit., *Wilkinson*, III, 97.

by Edward II in the Low Countries; now it was abolished altogether. At the same time ambassadors were sent to France to make terms with the queen's brother, King Charles. By agreeing to everything he asked, the question of the king's fiefs and the homage due for them was settled on the basis of the French retaining the Agenais and the other lands they had seized north of the Garonne and the English king agreeing to abide by the decisions of the French courts in matters under dispute or, in default, to pay an indemnity of 50,000 marks. In consideration of this the French king restored to his nephew Ponthieu and the coastal strip between Bordeaux and Bayonne—all that was now left of the once vast inheritance of Eleanor of Aquitaine.

There remained Scotland. Edward's deposition had made a renewal of the truce necessary, for in such a matter no king had power to bind his successor. With the North so vulnerable, the English badly needed the truce. But they were still not prepared to acknowledge Bruce as king. When, in re-proclaiming peace on the Border, they referred to "Robert Bruce and his adherents," the Scots seized on the insult as a pretext for renewing their raids. Even Mortimer could not afford to ignore such provocation, and in April 1327 orders were given for the feudal host to muster at Newcastle in the summer under the nominal command of the fifteen-year-old king.

It was the latter's first experience of war and it was not a happy one. It began with a racial riot at York against the mercenaries from Hainault whom Queen Isabella had brought over. While the king was feasting their count and his officers a fight broke out in the streets outside over a dicing dispute between the strangers' grooms and pages and the English archers. When the Hainault knights sallied out to rescue their men they were met by a shower of arrows and chased to their lodgings. Nor did they feel safe, as one of them recorded, "until they lay again at Wissant in their own country."

When at last, armed with a new weapon—some small "crakys of war" or cannon—the royal host marched into Northumberland it never got within bow-shot of the Scots. With their hardy mounted infantry living on oatmeal carried on their ponies' backs, Douglas and Randolph led the English from one inaccessible position to another across what the Hainault chronicler, Jean le Bel, described as "a savage and a wild country full of deserts and mountains, and right poor country of everything save beasts, through which there runneth a river full of flint and great stones called the water of the Tyne." When, in imitation of their adversaries' supply arrangements, the English knights strapped flour-loaves behind their saddles they found the horses' sweat made them uneatable. Edward's luxuriously-equipped army crawled on its belly along the valleys; the invaders flitted across the hills like deer. When, following the trail of smoking farms and villages, the English thought they were about to catch their invisible foes, Douglas raided their camp at night with two hundred savage Highlanders yelling, "Douglas! Douglas! you are all dead men!" and, in the confusion, all but captured the king in his tent. Yet when next day the English occupied the Scottish camp all they found were the bones of some stolen cattle and five prisoners tied to trees with their legs broken. Young Edward was so mortified by his failure that he burst into tears.

The moorland rain did the rest. After three weeks' campaigning and a week's continuous downpour the English withdrew with sodden saddles southwards, grumbling furiously— a "*grande murmuration*," the chronicler called it. Thereupon Douglas overran Durham. Three weeks later Bruce himself joined his lieutenant for one last glorious raid on England. He was now a very sick man, dying, it was believed, of leprosy. Yet, while Douglas and Randolph laid siege to Alnwick and Norham, he hunted Northumberland as though it was his private park. When Henry Percy, warden of the Marches, retaliated with a raid on Teviotdale, Douglas chased him home like a stag.

That same September saw the death of the king whom fourteen years before Bruce had routed at Bannockburn. Taken in the spring from the gentler custody of his cousin, Henry of Lancaster, he had been carted by hired ruffians from dungeon to dungeon— to Gloucester, to Berkeley, to Corfe and back again to Berkeley. Lodged over cesspits filled with stinking carcasses and mocked as a madman in a crown of plaited straw, his Plantagenet physique survived every attempt to break it until in the autumn, fearful lest the Church might force her to return to her husband, the queen

allowed her paramour to end the brutal farce. A few nights later
appalling screams of agony were heard echoing through Berkeley
castle. No marks were found on the body, but after it had been
taken to Gloucester abbey for burial the rumour spread that a
red hot iron had been inserted into the bowels through a drench-
ing-horn.

About the same time a parliament met at Lincoln to discuss
ways and means of raising money for the Scottish war. The
humiliations of the campaign and the bill for the Hainaulters'
hire proved too much even for English stubbornness. Early in
October secret envoys were despatched to Bruce's camp at
Norham to ascertain his terms for a permanent peace.

The Scottish king and his nobles were adamant; nothing but
full and unqualified recognition would do. In February 1328
a hundred Scottish knights brought to an English parliament at
York terms drafted at Holyrood abbey in Bruce's presence, it is
believed, by Bishop Lamberton. Sealed in the spring by the two
kings and ratified by a further parliament in the summer, the
treaty of Northampton gave the Scots everything for which they
had fought. "Since we and some of our predecessors," ran the
English king's acknowledgement, "have tried to obtain the
rights of rule or lordship over the kingdom of Scotland, on
account of which dire dangers of wars have long afflicted the
kingdoms of England and Scotland,

"mindful of the slaughters, deaths, misdeeds . . . and innumerable evils which by reason of this kind of wars have
happened to both kingdoms, we have conceded, by the
common consent and assent of the prelates, magnates, earls
and barons and of the commons of our realm in our parliament, that the kingdom of Scotland should, within its
rightful borders, . . . remain in perpetuity to the magnificent prince, the lord Robert, by the grace of God
illustrious King of Scots, our most dear friend and ally,
and his heirs and successors separately from the kingdom
of England, whole, free and quit of any subjection, claim
or demand."

All charters or pacts impugning Scotland's independence
were declared null and void, all State documents " touching the
subjection of Scotland to the King of England " were to be

restored,[1] and, in return for an indemnity of £20,000, the English king's seven-year-old sister, Joan of the Tower, was to be married to the Scottish king's five-year-old son, David.

Nearly forty years had passed since the death of the Maid of Norway and the treaty of Brigham and close on a quarter of a century since Wallace had died defying the conqueror's might. After a generation of war Bruce had accomplished his work and freed his country. He died a year later, on June 7th, 1329, at his favourite hunting palace of Cardross on the Clyde. His body was embalmed and carried, by way of Loch Lomond and Cambuskenneth abbey, past the scene of his greatest victory, to Dunfermline and there laid among the Scottish kings. In accordance with his crusader's vow, his heart, enclosed in a silver casket, was entrusted to his old lieutenant, Douglas, for burial in the Holy Land. On the way Douglas, never able to resist a fight, was persuaded by the King of Castile to join in an attack on the Moors of Granada. There, mortally wounded and encompassed by paynim hordes, he flung the heart into their midst crying, "Go first, as thou wert wont to go." Rescued and brought back to Scotland, it was buried in Melrose Abbey.

[1] The Black Rood—Scotland's most sacred relic—was restored but there was no provision in the treaty for the return of the coronation stone of Scone. *Common Errors in Scottish History* (Historical Association) 8.

Chapter Six

THE GREY GOOSE FEATHER

No warring guns were then in use
They dreamt of no such thing;
Our Englishmen in fight did use
The gallant grey-goose wing.

And with the gallant grey-goose wing
They shew'd to them such play
That made their horses kick and fling
And down their riders lay.

OLD BALLAD

EARLY ON THE NIGHT of October 19th, 1330, three years after the murder of Edward II, a band of armed men silently crossed the courtyard of Nottingham castle. Admitted by two household officers of the young king through a secret passage under the moat, they were on their way to the Queen Mother's apartments where her paramour, the hated dictator Mortimer, was unrobing for the night.

For, in overthrowing the Despensers and ridding herself of a weak, impulsive sovereign, England found that she had merely exchanged the rule of one ruthless Marcher lord for that of another. When after twenty years of misrule Edward II had been forced to abdicate, it had seemed as though a great principle of government had been asserted. Henceforward no royal favourite could forget that, while the king's ministers owed their authority to his will, they were answerable to the Crown and law of the realm, as established and interpreted by a king, not acting in isolation or through irresponsible favourites, but with the advice and common counsel of his "natural counsellors" and the representatives of the community in parliament. On his last sad journey to Berkeley castle, crowned with hay and shaved with

234

ditchwater by mocking jailers, the fallen king who had flouted this principle had seemed without a friend and less privileged than his poorest subject.

Yet it had not been against their hereditary Crown that Englishmen had rebelled, but against a failure to wear it as usage and justice dictated. No sooner had Edward been murdered than he became a martyr and his tomb in Gloucester abbey a place of pilgrimage. And the whole nation had turned against the rapacious lord of Ludlow who, usurping his former sovereign's bed and adding barony to barony, ruled England through his mistress and kept her son, the king, his prisoner. The peace he had made with Scotland—the "shameful treaty of Northampton" —was seen as a national betrayal and the vast grants of land he had obtained from the queen as the price of it. A few months after the crime of Berkeley, to the indignation of his fellow Marchers he took upon himself the proud title of Earl of March. Claiming descent from the legendary heroes of British chivalry, Arthur and Brutus of Troy, and enthroned by the queen's side he kept a royal state. "He honoured", it was said, "whom he liked, let the king stand in his presence and was accustomed to walk arrogantly beside him."

No-one felt this more deeply than the young Edward III. Forced by Mortimer and his mother to surrender his claim to Scotland, he had also suffered humiliation at the hands of his cousin of France. In the year after his accession the death without male issue, of his uncle, Charles IV, had ended the elder line of the House of Capet which had ruled France for three and a half centuries. As the only surviving child of Philip the Fair—father of the late French king and his two immediate predecessors— Edward's mother had been left the nearest direct successor. But to avoid the dangers of female rule the French royal lawyers had revived an ancient law of the Salian Franks denying the crown to a woman. And though Edward claimed that this Salic law did not bar the succession to Isabella's son, his claim had been ignored in favour of his cousin, Philip of Valois, a son of Philip the Fair's younger brother. This was inevitable, for the French aristocracy would never have brooked the rule of an English sovereign, and in any case Edward's claim was merely presumptive, since it could be extinguished—as a few years later it was—by the birth of a son to his young cousin Jeanne, daughter of the late Louis X, Queen Isabella's eldest brother. What rankled with Edward far more, was that after his Valois cousin's accession he was made to do homage to him in Amiens cathedral for his hereditary fiefs, notwithstanding the fact that they had been unjustly shorn of the Agenais and the lands of the middle Garonne under the abject bargain which Mortimer and his mother had made with the late French king.

In the summer of 1330, Edward, now nearly eighteen, became a father. A year after his accession he had been married in York minster to Philippa of Hainault—"a most beautiful creature, the mirror of her sex and scarce fourteen years old"—who had fallen in love with him during his visit to her father's court two years before. The young queen's grace and charm only accentuated the unpopularity of her mother-in-law and Mortimer— now universally regarded as regicides and usurpers. But though everyone looked to the youthful pair to rescue the country from a hated dictatorship, Mortimer was not the man to let power slip from his hands. He and his Welsh guards—men of the kind who had committed the Berkeley murder—kept the king under ceaseless surveillance. When in 1329 the Earl of Lancaster— brother of Edward II's old enemy and the richest man in England —tried to break Mortimer's stranglehold by threatening to impeach him in parliament for his treaty with Scotland, the dictator retaliated by wasting Lancaster's lands, seized his borough of Leicester and forced him to make an abject surrender of half his estates to save his life. A year later, Mortimer had forestalled another attempt to overthrow him by the murdered king's half-brother, the Earl of Kent. Tricked into the belief that his brother was still alive in Corfe castle,[1] the earl was arrested

---

[1] "Certain men, to the intent to try what friends . . . the King of England, lately murdered, had in the land, pretended that he was living magnificently in Corfe castle. . . . Wherefore they caused dancing to take place on many nights on the walls and turrets, bearing before them tapers and flaming torches so that they might be seen of the yokels of the countryside as if they guarded within some great king to whom they did these solemnities. . . . The Earl of Kent therefore sent a certain Dominican friar to find out the truth of the matter who, thinking that he had corrupted the doorkeeper of the castle by bribes, was himself deceived." *Baker's Chronicle* (ed. E. M. Thompson).

on a charge of treasonable correspondence and, after an unavailing plea for mercy, beheaded at Winchester.

By that autumn those who hated and feared Mortimer were desperate. They knew that they were being watched and resolved to strike before they were struck down. "Better," said one of them, "to eat the dog than be eaten by him." Their chance came with the meeting of the Council at Nottingham. The young lords and knights who with the king's connivance gained admittance to the castle included a brother of the constable, the Earl of Hereford, and representatives of most of the great feudal families. Ignoring Queen Isabella's cries of, "Have pity on the gentle Mortimer," they seized him and sent him in fetters to the Tower. Tried by his fellow peers "as judges of parliament," he was condemned as he himself had condemned the Despensers. Forbidden to plead and drawn on an ox-hide to the common gallows by the elms at Smithfield, "the same measure which he had meted out to others was measured to him."[1]

At eighteen Edward became king in fact as well as in name. He had suffered greatly. When four years earlier he had returned to England it had been at a time of national shame, eclipse and disunity and in circumstances of what, for him, must have been peculiar horror. Within a few months of his accession his father had been murdered by his mother's brutal paramour to whose tyranny he had been forced to lend his name. Having seen one parent the instrument of a despotic and lawless Marcher, he had seen the other become the slave of a worse one. Both had brought the Crown into utter disrepute and the nation to the verge of civil war and anarchy.

When at the coronation Mortimer and his fellow magnates bathed the young king and dressed him in spotless apparel before elevating him in the presence of the people, it must have seemed to the boy a mockery of all that kingship meant. In their triumph over his irresponsible and incompetent father they appeared to have destroyed almost everything that the Norman and Plan-

[1] His partner in iniquity, Queen Isabella, was relegated by her son to an honourable retirement. She lived till 1358, mostly at her favourite residence, Castle Rising, in Norfolk. In old age she took the habit of the Poor Clares. *McKisack,* 102.

tagenet kings had done to unify and strengthen the realm. Rebellion in a medieval State could never take the place of stable government and justice. Great as had been parliament's part in preserving the national tradition of common counsel and consent at a time when, with its growing and increasingly efficient bureaucracy, the monarchy had threatened to become a despotism, an assembly of feudal nobles could not rule England. As the repository of executive power it was incapable of controlling its own members or of being anything but a discordant oligarchy. Like the nation whose divergent forces and estates it represented, to operate effectively it needed a king capable of ruling.

For all his youth Edward was such a king. Like his grand-father, he meant to rule. Since childhood he had seen the fatal consequences of a breach between a sovereign and the lords through whom so much of the administration of a feudal kingdom had to be exercised. He recognised that there could be no governing England without its greater nobles. With its mechanism of judges, Exchequer barons, Chancery and Wardrobe clerks, sheriffs, escheators, coroners, constables and militia a strong royal government could prevent baronial anarchy. Yet without the co-operation of the feudal magnates and their courts and retainers, the kingdom could never be at unity with itself. In an age when a journey from London to York took nearly a week, devolution of authority was essential. As the attempt to impose it on Scotland and Wales had shown, centralisation in the fourteenth century could not produce either liberty or order.

After the struggles and tragedies of the past forty years what was needed was a compromise—a reconciliation between royal authority and the liberties of the subject. It was the supreme merit of this conciliatory yet shrewd young king to realise and achieve it. By doing so he saved for his country the strong, binding monarchy of his forebears. A few weeks after assuming control of the kingdom he proclaimed that his conception of rule was partnership. "Our affairs and the affairs of our realm," he wrote to the sheriffs, "have been managed in the past to our damage and dishonour and that of our kingdom and to the impoverishment of our people. We wish all men to know that in future we will govern according to right and reason as is fitting our royal dignity, and that the matters which touch us and the estate of our realm are to be disposed of by the common counsel of the magnates of our realm and in no other manner."[1]

Edward was both a realist and a romantic. Brave, handsome, with magnetic appeal, a brilliant performer in the tournament lists and a model of knightly deportment, he embodied all the qualities that the young aristocrats around his throne admired. His queen, nursed in the graces of the cultured courts of the rich Flemish plain, was the ideal partner for such a ruler. For the next quarter of a century she became the arbitress of English fashion. It was said of her that she "ordained and changed every year diverse shapes of disguising of clothing, of long, large and wide, . . . and another time short and tight-waisted, dragged and cut on every side, slashed and loose with sleeves and tippets." Patroness of scholars and artists, her countryman Froissart, the chronicler of fourteenth-century chivalry, was for a time her secretary, writing of her as "his noble and valiant lady," while her chaplain, Robert de Eglesfield, founded Queen's College, Oxford, in her honour.

Generous, impulsive, profuse in display, a laggard neither in love or war, with a boyish charm which won the hearts of warriors and fair women, Edward III was the beau-ideal of chivalry and of the elaborate code of knightly conduct and manners known as courtesy that had grown up in the French-speaking courts of western Christendom. A few months before he and his companions made their coup against Mortimer they had taken part together in a three days' tournament in Cheapside at which, dressed as Tartars and each leading a lady robed in ruby velvet by a silver chain, they had ridden to the lists through the London streets to the sound of trumpets, challenging all comers. In an age when for the great mass of men life was harsh and bleak and, even for the favoured few, perilous and uncertain, princes and great lords who could afford such costly pageantry loved to re-enact in costly habiliments the legends of an imaginary past. Splendid in armour and emblazonry, Edward seemed to the young English nobles the very reincarnation of their hero, King Arthur. It was so that he saw himself—the crowned leader of a brotherhood of Christian knights.

[1] *Foedera*, II, 799, cit. *Wilkinson*, II, 173-4.

In the aristocratic society of lance, pennon and heraldic shield and surcoat over which the king presided, the long rambling tales of the Arthurian legend were the favourite hearing or reading of every lord and lady. Transmitted from the dark ages by Celtic bards and invested by later generations with a background of giants, magicians and enchanted forests and fountains before which moved a company of heroic knights with high-sounding names, challenging foes of fabulous strength and rescuing king's daughters of incomparable beauty, these stories of a primitive tribal folk presented their heroes as patterns of the civilized virtues which a warlike society of *nouveaux-riches* conquerors had grafted, through the Church's influence, on to their forefathers' blood-thirsty fighting code. The ideal of chivalry enshrined in them was an immense advance on that of the brutal horsemen who had conquered at Hastings and carved out the young kingdoms of western Europe with their swords. For the paladins of Arthur's court were judged "worshipful"—to use the Arthurian phrase—not merely by their feats in battle but by their fidelity to a code far removed from that of Frankish warriors. Valour in battle and loyalty to the feudal overlord were still the basic virtues: treason the most despicable of crimes. But in place of the old suicidal law of tribal vengeance and the bloody anarchy of might is right had been substituted an elaborate code of chivalry and even, within the narrow bounds of class, of gentleness; of comradely tenderness towards one's knightly companions, of mercy and magnanimity in victory, of fidelity to vows, of fine manners. Above all—and this was something that had been added to the Arthurian legend by the troubadours of southern France—was a feeling and conduct towards women which the pagan world had never known. Constancy to one's lady— for it was courtly, rather than married, love the troubadours idealised—and devoted service to her were elevated, in these fables of knight errantry, into a virtue which no man could sit at King Arthur's table without possessing. In the kingdom of Logres—as Arthur's Britain was called in the French romances —"if a knight found a damsel or lorn maid alone and he cared for his fair name, he would no more treat her with dishonour than he would cut his own throat."

Sung in French by wandering minstrels in the tapestried halls of Marcher lords and the castles of the Ile de France and former Angevin empire, the legends of the Arthuriad had created an image of ideal kinghood that made an irresistible appeal to a romantic young sovereign like Edward III. It seemed a talisman for solving the problems of his kingdom after civil war and anarchy. Heroic, tireless, compassionate, magnanimous to his foes, evoking in all who served him admiration and loyalty, Arthur was the unifying symbol of medieval kingship—"a king whom all true knights were glad to serve, . . . liberal to all, knight with the best, . . . to the young for father, to the old for comforter. . . . Wrong to him was exceedingly loathsome and the right ever dear." Those admitted to his knightly order feasted with him at a round table, "it being ordained of Arthur that when his fair fellowship sat to meat their chairs should be high alike, their service equal and none before or after his comrade."

This ideal took little account of those outside that hereditary warrior society.[1] Yet within its narrow bounds it made its members proudly conscious of their privileges and obligations. It was the age of high chivalry when the devices painted on the warrior's shield and surcoat as distinguishing marks in battle and tournament and transmitted as family honours from father to son had become the subject of an elaborate science. Its priests were the heralds who assisted the marshal and constable in tournament and tilt-yard, proclaiming the name of every champion by his arms as he entered the lists and officiating in the courts of chivalry which adjudged the right to bear coat-armour. From the shield of golden lions borne by the Plantagenet kings to the rustic coat-of-arms of the humblest shire knight,[2] these devices reproduced on banner and helm, horse-trappings and pavilion,

---

[1] Vinaver points out that the only time a peasant appeared in Malory's Arthurian tales he received a great buffet on the head merely for refusing to lend a knight his cart.

[2] The wheatsheaf and the three green hillocks of the fourteenth century Lancashire family of Shakerley derived from the wheatsheafs of the earls of Chester, from whom they were descended on the distaff side, and from the three small hills—now overbuilt with grimy houses—of the manor of Shakerley.

gatehouse and seal, were the symbols of knightly honour and lordship. They appeared in churches and chantry chapels, on the tombs of knightly benefactors and of prelates and abbots and even in representations of the Holy Family; an altar-picture of the education of the Virgin, executed in the early years of Edward III's reign and now in the Musée de Cluny in Paris, shows Mary and her mother studying against a background of heraldic lion tiles, while in the de Lisle psalter the crucifixion is set against the leopards of England and the fleurs de lys of France. Every great lord employed a private herald or pursuivant who, as his ceremonial messenger or ambassador, bore his heraldic title; Leopard and Windsor for the king, Hereford for the constable, Warwick for the Beauchamps of Warwick. Other heralds called kings-of-arms regulated the chivalric affairs of different parts of the kingdom, Norroy king-of-arms of the north, Surrey, and later, Clarenceaux of the south.

All this fostered enthusiasm for the outward and visible forms of status, which, as always with any human ideal, tended to be more eagerly pursued by the generality of its adherents than the sacrificial virtues it enjoined. Costly armour, richly furred robes, jewelled belts and coronets, tapestries and cloth of gold were now regarded as essential to noble status as fighting prowess, broad acres and castles. Even the latter, their design constantly elaborated by Edward I's engineers under the stimulus of his Welsh and Scottish wars, were ceasing to be thought of as exclusively functional and were being designed as places in which rich men and their retinues could live lives of elegance and comfort. Edward I's chancellor, Robert Burnell, added a hall and chambers to the bishop's palace at Wells, and his contemporary, Bishop Bek, built himself a princely abode within the walls of Durham castle. Like those other once purely functional buildings—the monasteries—the castles of the king and aristocracy were beginning to be furnished, however sparsely, with artistic treasures.[1] At Castle Rising Queen Isabella had the cushions of

[1] When in the sixteenth year of Edward I's reign Walter of Kent brought an action against two guests who "by their foolishness and lack of care and through a badly guarded candle" set fire to his house and granaries, among the two hundred pounds' worth of goods which were destroyed with his home were silver spoons, gold rings, wool and linen cloths and household utensils. *Select Cases in the Court of King's Bench under Edward I,* (Selden Society) Vol. 1, 181.

her private chapel embroidered with monkeys and butterflies; King Edward possessed silver ewers adorned with enamels of monkeys playing harps and children riding pick-a-back and a chest decorated with swans and ladies bathing. A lady's girdle of the same period—which today forms part of William of Wykeham's mitre—was set with enamels of dogs, stags and hares and of monkeys walking on all fours blowing horns. The earliest piece of medieval silver extant in England—the Swinburne pyx—dates from Edward II's reign: the loveliest—the Lynn cup, still preserved in the guildhall of that ancient Norfolk town—from the opening years of his son's.

Books, too, formerly owned only by monastic houses and a few great churchmen and princes, were becoming, with the advance of civilization, a treasured possession of rich lords, knights and even merchants. They were being made, in ever increasing numbers, not only in monastic *scriptoria* but by schools of professional illuminators who during the thirteenth century had organized themselves in a stationers' guild for producing vellum bibles and works of devotion. A lady travelling on the king's highway between Boughton and her home at Wereham on Easter Day 1285 was robbed of a missal worth twenty shillings—about fifty pounds in the money of today —of a manual worth 6s. 8d. and two rolls of songs worth respectively sixpence and twopence.[1] The books most coveted by connoisseurs were the folio psalters and apocalypses—picture books with accompanying French or Latin texts, illustrated usually in burnished gold and brilliant reds, blues and greens though sometimes in more subtle colours. One of these, the Tenison psalter, was commissioned by Edward I as a wedding-gift for his eldest son, Prince Alfonso. Its beatus page contains the coats-of-arms of the royal houses of England and Holland and, in addition to full-page pictures, the borders of the text are illustrated with delicately coloured drawings of men and angels, beasts and birds, biblical and contemporary hunting scenes. Another made a little later was the Ormesby psalter, now in the Bodleian Library, with its margins full of wonderful monsters and fantastic conceits—a trumpeter blowing a fanfare among dragons,

[1] *Cam*, 182. See also H. H. Glunz, *History of the Vulgate in England*, 269, and the *Holkham Bible Picture Book*, Intro. (ed. W. O. Hassall).

a centaur combing his hair, a fox dressed as a friar paying court
to a rabbit, a unicorn taking refuge in a lady's lap from a pursuing knight. Closely allied to the gargoyles on the corbels and
roof-bosses of medieval churches, these drolleries have something
in common with the drawings of Edward Lear and the giants
and comic beasts of Victorian pantomime. After the accession
of Edward II, who reacted so strongly against the austerities of
his stern father and, with his raffish court of mountebanks and
jesters, delighted in the frivolous and absurd, these grotesques
or babewyns, as they were called, became highly fashionable.
In a series of early fourteenth century illuminated manuscripts
of the East Anglian school—the Gorleston psalter, the St. Omer
psalter with its tiny miniatures, the lovely Queen Mary's psalter
saved for England by a discerning Tudor customs officer, and
the later and better-known Luttrell psalter—an extraordinary
assemblage of elephants, lions, monkeys, pigs, foxes, peacocks,
geese, cats, rabbits and mice, often in human clothing and
enacting human parts, with dragons, mermaids and strange
creatures with human heads and beasts' bodies, float and gyrate
round the margins of the pages.

During the sixty years since Edward I's accession, despite the
wars against the Scots and his son's misrule England had been
growing steadily richer in beautiful things. The art for which
its people were most famous outside their own country was
ecclesiastical embroidery. Ever since Saxon times the *opus
Anglicanum* had been treasured throughout western Europe. In
France, Italy, the Low Countries, Germany and even Spain,
altars and the clerical dignitaries who officiated at them were
draped in cloth of gold with silken panels, medallions and roundels
delicately embroidered by the fingers of English nuns. In a
Vatican inventory of 1295 no less than a hundred and thirteen
specimens of such work were listed. Among the few that escaped
the savagery of latter-day Puritans and still survive in the land
that made them are the Sion cope in the Victoria and Albert
Museum and the chasuble that bears the shield of Edmund of
Cornwall and his wife Margaret de Clare, with its scrolls of lions
and griffins worked on a blue ground and an orphrey stitched in
gold, silver and silk threads on its back, and quatrefoils showing

the Virgin and Child, the Crucifixion, St. Paul and St. Peter and the martyrdom of St. Stephen.[1]

. . . .

All the greatest art in England still centered round the Church. For more than a century the enormous columns, rounded arches and massive wall spaces of Romanesque architecture had continued to be replaced by the delicate pointed Gothic arching evolved by the French and Anglo-Norman masons in the age of the crusades. With its airy clustered shafts, soaring vaults and slender lancet and rose windows grouped together in geometrical patterns and filled with brightly-coloured glass, this pointed architecture, born of greater technical knowledge, had brought a new dimension of light into churches where formerly the walling needed for the support of roof and tower had made adequate fenestration impossible. Yet except at Salisbury, where the cathedral had been rebuilt on a fresh site, this revolution had supplemented rather than superseded the country's older ecclesiastical architecture, so that everywhere, in the English mode, new Gothic mingled with old Norman and even, in places, Saxon. At Malmesbury, where the nave of the abbey church was rebuilt in the thirteenth century, the Norman doorway was preserved inside a new porch; at Ely, Norwich and Peterborough Romanesque pillars blended with Gothic vaulting.

Much of this building was to accommodate the shrines and relics which the greater religious houses accumulated to enhance their prestige and attract the offerings of pilgrims. Every large monastic and collegiate establishment tried to outsaint and outbuild its neighbour, and in the competition the artistic heritage of the country was being continually enhanced. When after the murder of Edward II none dared bury him for fear of Mortimer, Abbot Thokey of Gloucester marched his monks to Berkeley and bore the corpse back to St. Peter's, making the splendid tomb he raised there the most popular place of pilgrimage in the west and crowning it, first with a wooden, and later, as pilgrims' contributions poured in, a magnificent alabaster effigy.

---

[1] Perhaps the finest of all examples of *opus Anglicanum* is the cope in the Museo Civico in Bologna embroidered with scenes from the life of Christ.

The most famous shrines in England were those of St. Thomas at Canterbury, where the jewels were as large as goose-eggs and "gold the meanest object to be seen," and of St. Edward in the rebuilt abbey at Westminster. Made of mosaics of marble and gold, with delicate twisted columns and set with emeralds, rubies and precious stones, the Confessor's shrine was "placed high like a candle upon a candlestick so that all who enter into the house of the Lord may behold its light."[1] Above it hung a vast corona with innumerable candles burning continuously, while on the shrine itself stood silver basins containing lamps. Such shrines and their chapels, fitted with apertures for the crippled limbs of pilgrims, were usually sited in an ambulatory behind the sanctuary so that worshippers could approach without disturbing the liturgical services in the choir.

Enriched by service to the Crown, the "courtier" bishops and the chapters of secular cathedral canons had now taken the lead in building from the Benedictine monks, the pioneers of medieval culture. Edward I's reign had seen the culmination of the rebuilding of Lincoln's glorious cathedral—its towers crowned with three immense spires, one of them said to be the tallest in England—in an extension of the presbytery to house the shrine of St. Hugh. The king himself had been present at the translation of the saint's bones to their new resting place. With its huge traceried east window and double-banked lights extending the full width of every bay, the new choir was more brilliantly lit than any building yet erected. Beneath the windows of the clerestory, filling the spandrels of the triforium arches, thirty smiling stone angels looked down, some like those carved a generation earlier in Westminster Abbey with musical instruments, others holding crowns, scrolls and censers. Some had their feet on monsters, others presented souls at the Judgment seat, one with stern face expelled a crestfallen Adam and disdainful Eve from Paradise. These exquisite figures, saved by their great height from the iconoclasts of a later age, were painted in vivid colours and patterned with stars. "Flooded with light," a historian has written, "the Angel choir stands like a halo at the head of St. Hugh's darker sanctuary and with its radiance

[1] *Annales Monastici*, Thos. Wykes, R.S., xxxvi, iv, 226, cit. *Brieger* 121.

. . . comes nearer than any other building to the poet's vision of the temple of the Grail."[1]

It was light above everything else that the new architecture sought—the crying need of the sunless north. One after another the great churches of northern England followed the lead of the Angel choir. At Ripon, where every canon contributed a tenth of his prebendary income until the work was done, the east end of the choir was rebuilt during the closing decade of the thirteenth century with a huge window; at York a few years later a new nave was begun in which, in the search for greater light and space, the upper windows of the clerestory were extended downwards to incorporate the triforium, so that the two stories, though divided by the concealed roof of the aisle, presented a continuous double bank of light along the church's entire reach. The work took more than half a century to complete, and during that time, like almost every major church in the land, the minster must have been full of scaffolding and of the sound of hammer and chisel. At Southwell, too, in the new Lady chapel at Lichfield, in the choir at Chester—rebuilt between the end of Edward I's Welsh wars and Bannockburn—the triforium was wholly or partly incorporated into the window scheme of the clerestory.

In the south the most important additions to English architecture in Edward I's reign had been the commencement of St. Stephen's chapel in the palace of Westminster—the English counterpart to the Sainte Chapelle at Paris—and the completion of the Gothic work at St. Paul's. The cathedral's new choir, added to the Norman nave and the vast double-aisled transept, made it the largest church in Europe, with a length of nearly 700 feet and an area of 100,000 square feet—nearly half again as big as England's next two largest churches, Lincoln and Bury St. Edmunds, which themselves equalled the largest of the French cathedrals. At its eastern end, towering above the roofs of the city, was the biggest single group of lights in the country— an enormous rose window filling a space equal to the height of the combined clerestory and triforium, and, below, seven conjoined lancets separated only by thin mullions linked by trefoiled heads. Above the cathedral rose a five-hundred foot

[1] *Brieger*, 191.

tower and spire, crowned by a ball and cross filled with sacred relics.[1]

As remarkable, on a smaller scale, were the beautiful polygonal chapter-houses of Salisbury and Wells, completed at the end of the thirteenth and beginning of the fourteenth century. Here, debating the business of the chapter, the canons sat in a circle, enthroned on stone niches under traceried windows, every one an equal, facing the graceful multi-shafted central pillar which bore the vaulted roof. In the north the new chapter-houses at York and Southwell were vaulted without a central pillar, the former having a free-standing span of nearly sixty feet.[2] At Southwell the naturalistic carving which had recently taken the place of the more formal stiff-leaf reached its zenith in the wonderful variegated leaves and flowers carved on the capitals during the years when Edward I was trying to subdue Scotland. Like Pygmalion's Galatea they possess all the qualities of life except actual movement, though made of stone.

Carved figures as beautiful, wrought in metal and stone, had risen at Edward's behest in his father's rebuilt abbey at Westminster. Soon after his return from the second Welsh war he had commissioned William Torel the London goldsmith to make a bronze effigy of his father to lie on his tomb at Westminster above a stone base engraved with royal leopards. Beside it a decade later he placed the effigy of his wife, Eleanor of Castile, recumbent with sceptre in hand and jewelled robe and crown under a canopy of Purbeck marble. Two other noble examples of the sculptor's art were added to the abbey's treasures in the old king's last years —those of his brother, Edmund Crouchback earl of Lancaster, under an elaborately carved canopy guarded by painted and gilded regal mourners and angels holding candlesticks; and of his uncle, William de Valence. With his copper-plate armour

---

[1] Owing to its dangerous condition the cross had to be renewed in the year of Bannockburn, when the relics inside it included a fragment of the true Cross, a stone from Christ's sepulchre and another from Mount Calvary, and some of the bones of the eleven thousand Virgins. *Lambeth Palace Library MS.* 590. *Transactions of The London and Middlesex Archaeological Society*, v (1881), 316-17, cit. *Rickert*, 47.

[2] Of the twenty-five polygonal chapter-houses in England and Wales and two in Scotland, less than half have survived. J. Harvey, *English Cathedrals*, 34.

coloured with rich enamels, his mailed hands crossed in prayer and his expression of serene confidence that the aristocratic society he had adorned on earth must be mirrored in Heaven, William's effigy was the forerunner of a whole army of recumbent knights in stone, metal or brass. During the fourteenth century there everywhere appeared in the parish or collegiate church enriched by his benefaction or bequest the likeness of some local worthy, clad in the armour and heraldic trappings of his warrior craft, with his lady in long trailing mantle, kerchief and wimple at his side and his hound or supporting heraldic beast at his feet. Though those that survive constitute only a fraction of the splendid knightly company that once glittered under the painted roofs and windows of England's churches, owing to Edward I's law of entail they proved more enduring than the statues of saints and holy personages that shared their resting places. For when the latter were smashed as idols these memorials to bygone bene-factors received the protection of those who had inherited their blood or lands.

The brightness of a Gothic cathedral, with its painted walls and jewelled shrines—the gleaming or *nitens* of the monkish chroniclers' phrase—is hard to visualise from the bare, grey stone interiors of today. We see the noble skeleton but not the flesh and blood with which our forefathers clothed it. The walls were frescoed with paintings, telling the Christian story by masters whose names, like their works, have been obliterated by time, though from the few that remain, faint and resuscitated from agelong layers of neglect and defacement, we can dimly apprehend their glory.[1] The paintings on the sedilia in the sanctuary of Westminster Abbey—of the Virgin's blue robe and pink mantle and of Gabriel in mauve and green of a lovely limpidity—executed when the first masterpieces of the Italian artistic renaissance were beginning to appear at Siena, Pisa and Florence; the scenes from the life and Passion of Christ in the little Northamptonshire church of Croughton; the East Anglian

---

[1] Of the wall painting of St. Faith in the south transept of Westminster abbey it has been written: "The noble and severe quality of style of the art here seen is such as to leave a profound impression upon the spectator and make us realise what the world has lost by the almost complete destruction of the works of the Westminster School of the 13th century." *Borenius and Tristram*, 10-11.

figures of saints on the vaulting of the north ambulatory of Norwich cathedral and others recently discovered at Little Missenden in Buckinghamshire and in the beautiful circular room at Longthorpe Tower—once the home of the stewards of Peterborough abbey—are among the survivors of thousands of pictures that told the Bible story to a people unable to read but able to behold and adore.   Among the most beautiful is the thirteenth-century roundel in the bishop's palace at Chichester of the Madonna in robe of rose and jewelled crown holding her infant son against a background of blue, powdered with golden fleur-de-lys.

As rare today is the coloured glass that filled the windows. These, too, like the frescoes, told in picture the story of Christ and His saints and martyrs.   Divided by uprights of stone or lead, each pane—medallion, lozenge, circle or square—formed part of a continuous pattern of colour and light.   Most of the glass was imported, either through the Channel ports from Normandy and the Ile de France, where the French *verrours* had recently presented mankind with the splendours of Chartres, Bourges and Rouen, or from Hesse and Lorraine by way of the Rhine and Meuse to England's eastern rivers.   Owing to the very richness of this early glass, with its deep reds, blues, greens and golden yellows, some of the quality of light sought by the Gothic window-builders was lost, and towards the end of the century a whitish grey or grisaille glass began to be used.   One of the few examples that survives is the Five Sisters window in the north transept of York, whose huge lancets are paned with plain glass framed in thin strips of red and blue, patterned with a delicate and scarcely perceptible scroll and leaf design.

In all this there was a growing elaboration unknown in western Europe since the days of imperial Rome.   As the old century merged into the new, a richer architectural sumptuousness began to succeed the simplicity of "Early English," pointed arch and geometrically traceried window giving place to flowing curvilinear lines, fantastic pinnacles, crockets and finials decorated with carved globular buds known as ball-flower.   Pierced balustrades, wave parapets and foliate stone tracery radiated from the mullions of window-heads like the branches of a tree. And everywhere were niches filled with statues of the heavenly

family, angels, saints and martyrs, Christian princes and prelates, brilliantly gilded and painted. Such was the passion for
carving and ornamentation that the mason, working high above
column and clerestory among the roof trusses and rafters,
fashioned whole legions of tiny figures on the bosses—foliage
masks of men and monsters, fauns, satyrs and beasts, and the
leaves and flowers of their native woods and fields—here the
Lamb of God, here St. George wrestling with the dragon, here a
peasant with toothache or two lovers kissing, here the face of a
king or bishop or of a fellow workman, here David with his harp
or the Virgin crowned—all carved with a care that must have
been born of creation for its own sake, since, once the carver's
work was done and the platform of scaffolding removed, no eye
but that of some unborn craftsman repairing the roof in similar
solitude would ever see them again. In Exeter alone, rebuilt
between 1301 and 1338, there are more than five hundred carved
bosses; in the great late fourteenth century Bristol church of St.
Mary Redcliffe over eleven hundred. When two centuries later
the might of the medieval Church was broken and fanatics swept
through every place of worship with axe and hammer, smashing
and defacing the sculptured masterpieces that to them seemed
only painted idols, this invisible host of carved roof-bosses remained, unknown for nearly four hundred years until the tele-
scopic lens of the modern camera revealed their forgotten
testimony to the genius of English medieval craftsmanship.

The first great cathedral to be rebuilt wholly in the decorated
style was Exeter. Between Edward I's accession and that of the
early years of his grandson's reign, through the zeal of five great
building bishops—Walter Bronescombe, Peter Quinel, Thomas de
Bitton, Walter Stapledon who was murdered by the London
mob for his loyalty to Edward II, and John Grandison who
negotiated the treaty with France for his son—the old dark
Norman structure was transformed into the broad graceful
edifice of today with its multiple-shafted marble pillars, the
flowing tracery of its windows, its pinnacled sedilia and bishop's
throne, statued screen and reredos and carved roof-bosses representing every kind of man and angel, angel and demon known
to the medieval imagination. Another West Country cathedral,
Bristol, was rebuilt about the same time, with a feature, unique

among English cathedrals, of three aisles of equal height and a vault of lierne ribs of a completely novel pattern.

During the early decades of the fourteenth century almost every great church in England was added to or partly rebuilt in this richly ornamented style. There was Selby with its crocketed gables and parapet adorned with wave mouldings and little figures, Carlisle whose flamboyant east window was made during the sieges and raids of the long Scottish war, the south aisle of Gloucester with ball-flower blossom climbing like roses all over it, and the prior's door at Norwich with saints and angels grouped round the seated Christ against a background of intricate lace-like arcading. During the same period many of the larger parish churches were rebuilt with arcades and windows of curvilinear tracery, elaborate ball-flower ornamentation and decorated parapets and towers. To these years belong the towers of Wells and Hereford and the West Country abbeys, Leominster, Ledbury and Ludlow, rising above apple orchards and sheep pastures; the traceried windows of St. Wulfram's, Grantham, modelled on the Angel choir of Lincoln; the spire of the university church of St. Mary's Oxford and the Tree of Jesse window at Dorchester-on-Thames. Most of the ports and upland towns that were growing rich from the export of wool built or refashioned their churches in the new style: Newark, Donington and Sleaford, Beverley and Hull, Boston, Holbeach and Great Yarmouth, Deal, Rye and Winchelsea, of which last only the choir remains with its canopied statue of Stephen Alard, admiral of the Cinque Ports. All were decorated with the same profuse wealth of carving; at Heckington in Lincolnshire the exterior sculpture alone included thirty-one statues in ogival niches, eighty carved corbels and a hundred and ninety-eight gargoyles.

Though the greater Benedictine houses were comparatively little affected by the new style—only Milton Abbas, destroyed by lightning in 1309, was completely rebuilt in it—the Cistercians, with their wealth from wool, had by now abandoned their former austerity and started to build in the grand manner on the sites of their primitive encampments in the wilderness. Fountains had already been rebuilt in Henry III's reign, but Tintern, Rievaulx and Byland were refashioned in the enriched architecture of the Edwardian age. Even the friars had left their squalid abodes in

the city slums and were raising great churches out of the benefactions of merchants who recalled with gratitude the days when
they or their fathers had fled from villeinage to the hovels of the
nearest town and were there befriended by the mendicants. As
with their evangelical mission the Franciscans and Dominicans
had no need to provide for the elaborate liturgical and processional services of the monastic Orders, their churches were usually
built without aisles and with naves larger than the choirs to
accommodate the middle-class congregations who flocked to
hear the sermons for which they were famous. Having no aisles,
these preaching or hall-naves were far easier to light. The most
celebrated of all was the vast Greyfriars church in London
founded in 1306 by Edward I's second queen, who was buried
in it.[1] Almost as large were the Whitefriars churches which the
Carmelites built at Gloucester and Plymouth and the one at
Blakeney on the lonely Norfolk coast, with its groined roof,
clustered shafts crowned by carved bosses, and glorious east
window. Another was built by Edward II for the Dominicans
at King's Langley in Hertfordshire in memory, and to house the
dust, of Piers Gaveston.

In 1321 the monks of the Benedictine abbey at Ely began to
build a Lady chapel with the largest span of vaulting yet seen
in England and, under its traceried roof and wide decorated
windows, arcaded niches filled with hundreds of gilded and
painted statues, today mutilated and headless, telling the story
of the Virgin in sculptured stone. Scarcely had the work begun
when the central tower of the abbey church fell, crashing into
the choir below and destroying three of its bays.[2] Faced by the
problem of revaulting so large a space, the sacrist, Alan of
Walsingham, who later became prior, employed a London mason
referred to in the abbey accounts as Master John, who, it is con-
jectured, may have been John of Ramsey, member of a famous
family of Norwich masons. He and one "Peter Quadraterius"
built, instead of a new tower, an octagonal lantern of revolutionary design with four traceried windows to flood the centre of

[1] It was destroyed at the Reformation.
[2] A few years later, following the addition in 1321 of the decorated central
tower, a similar disaster at Wells was only averted by the building of the
inverted supporting arches which are such a unique feature of this cathedral.

the Norman church with light. And, as the seventy-foot span proved too wide to bridge with stone, the monks called in William of Hurley, the king's master-carpenter, at a fee of £8 a year to vault it in timber with eight gigantic hammer-posts and hammer-beam trusses. The work took twenty years to complete and, when finished, constituted, as it still does, the only Gothic dome in Europe.

Though the new style was decorative rather than structural, in its seeking for ever greater illumination it continued the trend which had begun more than a century before with the evolution of the Gothic arch. Even before Edward III's accession there were signs that English masons were beginning to feel their way towards an architectural revolution. There was a sense of ever-growing light and unity in the many-ribbed vaults that broke through the older vaulting system of each separate bay and in the marriage between piers, vaulting and roof. The pillars of the new nave of York were like the trunks and branches of a beech wood, and the lierne vault of the choir at Ely like the stars on a winter's night.

.   .   .   .

The realm over which Edward III reigned was rich not only in architecture but in the vigour and enterprise of its people. At the time he assumed power the population of England and Wales, which had been rising during the thirteenth century, was probably somewhere between three and four millions—far lower than that of Italy and France. Most of it was concentrated in the south-east, notably in the wheat-growing and sheep-raising districts of East Anglia and the southern Midlands. The taxation yield of Norfolk was almost twice that of the next highest yielding county, Kent; after which followed, in order, Gloucestershire, Wiltshire, Lindsey in south Lincolnshire, Suffolk, Oxfordshire, Somerset and Essex. Hampshire, Northamptonshire, Sussex, the East Riding of Yorkshire, Berkshire and Cambridgeshire came next. The yield of the three northern counties of Lancashire, Cumberland and Northumberland was less than a tenth that of Norfolk.[1]

The capital had a population of between 40,000 and 50,000. It was only a quarter the size of Milan and much smaller than

[1] W. G. Hoskins and H. P. R. Finberg, *Devonshire Studies*, 215-16.

Paris, Florence, Bruges or Ghent. The next largest cities—York, Bristol, Plymouth and Coventry—had probably around 10,000 inhabitants, and Norwich, Gloucester, Newcastle, Salisbury and Winchester about half this number. These are only estimates, for no complete statistical record exists.

The country was still predominantly agricultural; a rich primary-producing land, exporting vast quantities of fine wool and, in good years, grain and dairy-produce. It also exported hides, leather-goods, dried and salted fish, embroideries, metalware, tin, coal and lead, mostly to the overpopulated Low Countries in exchange for manufactured cloth, to Gascony and the Rhineland for wine, and to the Baltic for timber and ship-building stores. Wool was its main source of wealth. The finest —the short wool of the Ryeland sheep and the long of the Lincolns, Leicesters and golden Lion breed of the Cotswolds—came from the Severn valley and the limestone belt between Somerset and Lincolnshire. But almost every part of the country, except the far north and extreme south-west, exported wool of some kind. It was reckoned that on an average 30,000 sacks or eight million fleeces went abroad every year, mostly to northern Italy and the cloth-manufacturing towns of Flanders, Artois, Brabant, and Hainault.

Though England was primarily a supplier of raw wool to others, cloth was manufactured on a small scale for home consumption in most of the larger towns. Edward's marriage to a Hainault princess brought a new stimulus to native manufacture, and one of his earliest acts—probably at his wife's instance—was to grant letters of protection to a Flemish weaver named John Kempe.[1] Other colonies of Flemish weavers, attracted by the cheap and abundant supplies of the raw material of their trade and the social stability of England, established themselves during the early years of the reign at Norwich, York and Cranbrook in Kent. Queen Philippa herself made a practice of visiting one of these settlements in Norwich whenever her husband went on progress in East Anglia. Another Fleming named Thomas

[1] In his invitation to Kempe—today a common English name—the king wrote "that if he will come to England with his servants and apprentices, his goods and chattels, dyers and fullers and exercise their mysteries in the kingdom, they shall have letters of protection and assistance in their settlement." *An Historical Geography of England* (ed. H. C. Darby) 230.

Blanket founded at Bristol the first regular factory in England, posthumously giving his name to a household article of universal use.

Export of wool and the increased imports which it paid for of spices, wine, silks, furs, timber, pitch, tar, oil, salt, alum, rice and fruits proved a great stimulus to English shipping and ship-building. The merchant capitalists of London, the country's leading port, were by now, after the magnates, the richest lay tax-payers in the country. Southampton, Bristol, Plymouth and Falmouth were the chief ports of the west, Lynn, Boston, New-castle-on-Tyne, Kingston-on-Hull and the Cinque Ports of the east. After London the most important was Southampton, whose deep and quiet water, protected by the Isle of Wight from Breton, Gascon and Flemish pirates, rivalled the Thames estuary as the starting-point for the convoys of sailing-ships, mostly of less than a hundred tons burden, which carried England's wool to the continent. It was a terminus port, too, for the wine fleets from Bordeaux, Bayonne and La Rochelle, and for the Genoese and Pisan carracks which during the early years of the fourteenth century started to export wool-fells from the Solent and Thames to the mills of the *Arte della Lana* of Florence in return for luxuries from Italy and the Orient. To Southampton came by barge down the Itchen—then navigable as far as Winchester—the wool of the Wiltshire, Berkshire and Gloucestershire downs, while coastwise vessels from Poole, Melcombe Regis, Bridport, Lyme and Exeter brought that of Dorset, Somerset and Devon. Other wool travelled down the Severn and Warwickshire Avon for ship-ment at Bristol. Carts and pack-horses took the canvas-wrapped bales and fells on their journey from the upland pastures to the nearest river.

In days when water provided by far the cheapest form of transport, England's commerce gained from two circumstances. Though her rivers were small compared with those of the con-tinent, the sea was never far away and her coast abounded in estuaries where goods could be shipped either abroad or to her own ports. And at a time when every petty ruler from the Vistula to Biscay was trying to fill his coffers by levying tolls on mer-chandise, with her strong, unified royal government England was the largest free-trading area in Europe. Almost her only internal transportation-tolls were petty portages and viages levied to recoup expenditure where a bridge or road had been provided by private enterprise. By contrast with the passage of Thames, Humber or Severn the movement of goods along the European rivers added enormously to their price. When the century began there were more than thirty toll-stations on the Weser and even more on the Elbe, nearly fifty on the Rhine and over eighty on the Austrian reaches of the Danube.[1] Nor were the French rivers and roads much better; the great Champagne fair, which for centuries had provided the principal trade-mart of northern Europe, was being strangled by the highway tolls imposed after the fief's merger with France. Only at the courts of Brabant and Hainault and in the Italian and Flemish trading-cities was the value of the free movement of trade appreciated as it was in Edward I's England. At the Cinque Ports the dues and tolls on wine ranged from between 2d. and 4d. a cask, while at Southampton the average charge on imported merchandise was only 2d. in the pound. At most ports English goods were exempted from tolls, either by royal charter or by treaties between one town and another.

With a coastline longer for her size than that of any western kingdom England possessed a substantial maritime population living by fishing, coastal trade and deep-water voyages to the Baltic, Low Countries, France and Biscay—already sometimes called "the sea of the English." Though most of her ocean carrying-trade was still in the hands of foreigners and her ships were of much smaller tonnage than those of the Mediterranean trading states—Genoa, Pisa, Venice and Aragon—her seamen, accustomed to the Channel and North Sea tides and storms, were tough, skilful and notorious for their pugnacity. Constantly involved in harbour broils with their Norman, Breton, Flemish and Basque rivals, they fought as often among themselves. Whenever the seamen of the Cinque Ports met the fishermen of Yarmouth, whom they viewed as interlopers, they engaged them, "on lond and strond," in pitched battle. With their seven chartered ports—Winchelsea, Romney, Hythe, Dover, Sandwich, Hastings and Rye and their outlying "limbs"—the "portmen"

[1] *C.E.H.E.*, II, 135. A thirteenth-century English chronicler, Thomas Wykes, described this as "the raving madness of the Teutons."

of the Sussex and Kent lagoons and inlets had long been the aristocrats of the narrow seas, producing their feudal quota of ships for the king in time of war and living in peacetime by a well-tried blend of fishing, piracy and trade with northern France and the Low Countries. But, with the gradual silting up of their harbours and the development of sail their ascendancy was beginning to be challenged by the west country seamen. With the richest fishing grounds in the world at their gates and a Catholic country to feed that lived on fish all Lent and Fridays, coastal Englishmen were learning the business of mastering the watery wastes in which their island was set. Though they seldom ventured further than Spain or Norway—Chaucer's shipman in the next generation knew the coasts from Jutland to Finisterre—the stormy and changeable seas they sailed were well adapted for teaching them the finer points of seamanship. A race of men apart, transmitting their sea-lore from father to son, they introduced into the make-up of a stolid rustic people a certain adventurous, carefree strain which was to have far-reaching consequences.

Equally important in its effect on the nation's character was buying and selling. The merchant town with its life of freedom and opportunity had already gone far to transform the racially divided society that England had become after the Norman conquest into a fluid one in which every social grade shaded imperceptibly into the next. Many of the leading merchant families, especially in London and the larger ports, traced their descent from foreign traders who had settled in England, like the Bocointes and Buckerells who had come from Italy and the Arraxes who took their name from Arras. Far more were enterprising English countrymen, often of villein blood, who had fled from bondage on their paternal acres to seek their fortunes behind the walls of the self-governing chartered boroughs. Many who did so perished of poverty or disease in overcrowded slums before they could force a way through the monopolistic restrictions with which the established burgesses protected themselves and their crafts and trades. Others passed, sometimes in less than a generation, from the harsh, unchanging life of the manor to affluence, the dignity of aldermanic or mayoral status and even office under the Crown —always in England quick to avail itself of the services of men of business and financial experience. Merchants unknown to the hereditary feudal hierarchy with rustic names like Dunstable and Haverill and Piggsflesh served as royal chamberlains, butlers and purveyors, loaned money to the Crown or some great magnate, arranged for the transfer of funds from one part of the Plantagenet empire to another and offered mortgages to supply their social superiors, lay and ecclesiastic, with the ready cash to cater for their increasingly luxurious tastes. In doing so, though many fell by the way, they made fortunes for themselves, investing their gains in land and founding landed and knightly families.

Such merchants were of many kinds—woolmongers, vintners, grocers, fishmongers, goldsmiths, mercers, drapers, haberdashers and leathersellers—associated for mutual protection in corporate gilds which regulated and controlled the local conditions and practices of their trades as well as in the government of the borough of which they had acquired or inherited the freedom. Once they had attained burgess status they could not be touched by their former lords and enjoyed the protection, not only of the borough, with its jealously guarded rights, but of the royal courts. How quickly the transformation could be effected is shown by an action for assault and imprisonment during Edward II's reign by a London mercer and alderman, one Simon de Paris, against Walter Page, bailiff of Sir Robert Tony, lord of the Norfolk manor of Necton, the place from which the plaintiff had originally come and to which he and his forebears had belonged. While paying a visit to his former home this rich, proud man had been seized and detained by the manorial authorities, presumably in the hope of blackmail. Their defence was that, though he might now be a burgess, he had been born a villein and, being found at Necton "in his villein nest," was bound to perform the servile services of his hereditary status. When the lord's bailiff tendered to him the office of village reeve he had refused it and so had been arrested under the law of the manor and detained "in custody from the hour of terce until vespers," when the uproar he made seems to have secured his release. The alderman's case was that he was a free citizen of London, had been so for the past ten years, acting as the king's sheriff in the city and "rendering account at the Exchequer," and "to this very day" was an alderman against

whose person no man could allege villeinage. To which counsel
for the defence replied that

> " with what they say about his being a citizen of London
> we have nothing to do; but we tell you that from grand-
> dam and granddam's granddam he is the villein of Robert,
> and he and all his ancestors, grandsire and grandsire's
> grandsire and all those who held his lands in the manor of
> Necton; and Robert's ancestors were seized of the villein
> services of Simon's ancestors, such as ransom of flesh and
> blood, marriage of their daughters, tallaging them high
> and low, and Robert is still seized of Simon's brothers by
> the same father and same mother . . . Whereas he says
> that we were not seized of him as our villein, he was born
> in our villeinage and there our seizen began, and we found
> him in our nest."

Upon which the presiding judge, Bereford, C.J., observed:

> " I have heard tell that a man was taken in a brothel and
> hanged, and if he had stayed at home no ill would have
> befallen him. So here. If he was a free citizen, why did
> he not remain in the city? "[1]

It took four years before, after repeated adjournments, the case
was finally decided in the alderman's favour and judgment for
£100—an enormous sum in those days—was given against the
lord and his bailiff.

＊　　＊　　＊　　＊　　＊

The greatest single factor in the growth of English capitalism
was war. The conflicts with Wales, Scotland and France that
followed Edward I's breaches with Llewelyn and Balliol, acted
as an enormous stimulus to the development of the merchant
class. Though no English trader could yet offer the Crown the
credit-facilities of the great banking and cloth-manufacturing
houses of Florence and Lombardy, there were already native
financiers rich enough to play an important part in equipping
Edward's armies. It was to those who dealt in wool, "the
sovereign merchandise and jewel of this realm of England," that

[1] F. W. Maitland, *Year Books of Edward II*, (Selden Society) I, 11-13.

he turned. For alone of England's rustic commodities wool could always be converted into cash; Flanders and Italy could never have enough of it. It was on its export that in 1294 Edward I had clapped the hated *maltote* to finance his war against his French overlord. And it was with the help of the dealers in wool, led by the great Shropshire woolmonger, Laurence of Ludlow—"*mercator notissimus*", as the royal lawyers described him —that three years later he had equipped his expedition to Flanders. When Laurence was drowned in an over-loaded ship taking the wool to Holland, the monastic chroniclers saw in it the hand of God avenging the lowered prices to the home—and ecclesiastical—producer with which the financier and his fellow monopolists, cheating Holy Church, passed on their losses. Laurence's memorial is the beautiful little castle of Stokesay which he built for himself near Ludlow. Two other wool merchants of the time remembered for their wealth were Gilbert of Chesterton and Thomas Duraunt of Dunstable. The latter's loans to the priory of his native place were so large that the prior dared not refuse his invitation to a feast which the presumptuous fellow gave to the magnates of the county, all of whom were in his debt on the security of their future wool-sales.

The bargaining power which the collection and export of wool gave to the rich subject in his dealings with the Crown played an important part in the development of national taxation and of parliament. The right to levy customs had always been a royal prerogative but, in an age of primitive economy, if the Crown wished to raise money quickly it could do so only with the co-operation of those who dealt in the goods it wished to tax. Hence it was to the wool-merchants in their corporate capacity that Edward I, his son and grandson turned when they wanted cash. Sometimes, instead of summoning a parliament and asking for a subsidy from the merchant class or estate as represented by the elected burgesses, the king convened an assembly of leading wool-merchants and negotiated with them a levy on exported wool. In either case he applied the principle of obtaining the assent of those who were to be taxed. But as soon as it became realised that the woolmongers invariably passed on the tax by lowering prices to the wool-producers, the latter's representatives in parliament began to demand that the Crown should negotiate with them instead of with those who paid the tax only in name. In doing so they put forward as a *quid pro quo*, however at first humbly and tentatively, demands not only for redress of grievances but for control over the expenditure of the money raised and of the royal officers who administered it.

The means by which the wool tax was collected was the customs staple. It had been first set up in London and thirteen other English ports at the beginning of Edward I's reign to collect the "ancient or great custom" of half a mark—6s. 8d.— a sack granted to him by a parliament in 1275. When in 1297 he forcibly borrowed all the available stocks of English wool to finance his expedition to the Low Countries, a foreign staple had had to be set up, first at Dordrecht and later at Antwerp, both to weigh and price the commandeered wool and levy the *maltote* on that of the merchants. Here and in the domestic staple towns in England the royal officials—collectors, controllers, searchers, surveyors, clerks, weighers and crane-keepers—administered both the ancient and great custom and the so-called petty custom which Edward at the end of his reign imposed on foreign exporters only and which, abolished by the Ordainers in 1311, his son reimposed after his short-lived triumph in 1322. In the year before Bannockburn, after an earlier attempt to do so had been foiled by the Ordainers, Edward II had made this preferential foreign staple—then at St. Omer—a compulsory one through which all wool exported to the Low Countries had to pass. During the next thirteen years this royal staple had been moved from one Flemish town to another. In 1326, to still growing criticism from the wool-growers and smaller traders, it was brought back to England, and two years later Mortimer and Queen Isabella, in their search for popularity, abolished it altogether.

But, though freedom in trade increased both the export of wool and the prices paid to the producer, the Crown could no longer subsist without the revenue of the customs and the credit that could be raised from it. Early in Edward III's reign the foreign staple was revived to become a permanent feature of the wool-trade and the national system of taxation. It both enabled the king to borrow money on the security of the customs and directed the export of wool to whatever city in the Low Countries suited his foreign policy of the moment.

The raising of wool was the concern of almost the entire rural community. Not only were the owners of the great feudal and ecclesiastical estates dependent for ready money on their fleeces, but so were knights of the shire, rich franklins and even humble villeins whose communal village flocks helped to swell the flow of wool from the manorial demesnes to the quays and warehouses of the collecting merchants. Travelling with their pack-horses to grange, village and monastery and buying up the year's produce to sell to the exporters who shipped it to Flanders or Italy, the "woolmen", by offering credit in exchange for low prices, earned a high rate of concealed interest without infringing the Christian rules against usury. Many larger landowners, as well as keeping flocks, engaged in this collecting trade, buying the wool of their smaller neighbours who lacked the capital and know-how to dispose of their own produce. The Cistercian abbeys of the northern and western dales were particularly active in such business, drawing from it and their flocks the revenues that enabled them to replace the austere and primitive habitations of pioneer days with the magnificent buildings that still, after centuries of desolation and decay, make the ruins of Fountains and Tintern, Rievaulx and Byland places of pilgrimage.

Picturing fourteenth-century England one sees the traces of this rural industry everywhere—the open downlands nibbled close by immense flocks of tiny sheep with their shepherds, tinkling bells, sheepcotes and dewponds; the fells and fleeces stacked in great barns of stone and timber; the up-country towns and the market-places of York and Lincoln, Grantham, Louth, Ludlow and Shrewsbury, Winchester and Andover crowded with dealers and factors; the trains of packhorses and barges moving towards the sea; the London merchants in their furred robes doing business with the king's officers; the English cogs and tall Italian carracks beating out from the Thames estuary and southern ports towards the hungry mills of Flanders and distant Tuscany.

> " The sward the black-face browses,
> The stapler and the bale,
> The grey Cistercian houses
> That pack the wool for sale."

The pastoral economy of shepherding and tending "the silly sheep," of sheep-shearing and dispatching the wool-fells to their remote destinations made a lasting impression on the nation's character. It embraced both the solitude and meditation of the shepherd's life, and the journeyings and bargainings involved in selling the wool that the mills of Ghent and Arno transformed into raiment for Europe's rich. It helped to make a race both of merchants and poets. The lonely sheepcotes and farms of western and northern England, the epitaph in the downland church,

> " Faithful lived and Faithful died
> Faithful shepherd on the hillside,
> The hill so high, the field so round,
> In the day of judgment he'll be found"

is one side of the medal; Chaucer's merchant off to Bruges at break of day and the bustling wife of Bath at her clothier's trade the other. Wool-growing, wool-carrying and wool-mongering all tended to make men more thoughtful and resourceful than the uneventful life of communal arable agriculture by which peasant Christendom lived.

They made, too, for a sense of freedom. The man who owned or tended sheep on the uplands felt himself to be more his own master than the man of the three-field village closely bound by manorial custom and watched always by prying neighbours. "Because," ran the report of a case in the King's Bench,

"it was testified before the sheriff of Nottingham and Derby . . . that Sir Thomas Folejambe was accustomed to make rescue and offer resistance to the king's ministers and bailiffs who wished to distrain him for debts and other things due to the king, the aforesaid sheriff with our lord king's bailiff of the Peak . . . came to Tideswell to make distraint . . . And because he did not find any distress save sheep, he caused his sheep which he found there to be taken. And while he was elsewhere, there came people, who are still unknown, and rescued the said sheep and drove them away no one knew where. The sheriff, when he heard this, caused the hue and cry to be raised up to the vill and through the vill of Tideswell, but the people would not come at the hue and cry as they ought to do. The sheriff was then told that the forenamed Sir Thomas had other sheep in a sheepfold outside the vill. The sheriff went there and found some of Sir Thomas's sheep, but his men went into the sheepfold and would not allow the sheriff to have the sheep as a distress but held the sheepfold against him and against the king's peace by force and arms.

"Wherefore the sheriff, in order to assemble more people to witness his action and to fulfil the king's command and preserve his estate and peace, raised the hue and cry by horn again from the said sheepfold up to the vill of Tideswell . . . And whilst the sheriff was doing this, Sir Thomas came to the said sheepfold and harshly abused those of the sheriff's men whom he found . . . And Sir Thomas demanded of the sheriff by what warrant he had done this, and the sheriff showed him the king's writ under his privy seal. And Sir Thomas, biting his nails on his palfrey, read the writ and looked at the seal and said that he knew it well, and further said, 'A fig for that! produce another warrant.' "[1]

Subsequently, after the sheriff had caused the hue and cry by horn and mouth to be raised a third time, Sir Thomas, taking counsel with his friends, surrendered himself with his three shepherds and sheep. Yet he came to no ultimate harm by doing so, for after two years a jury found him and his collaborators not guilty.

The sheriff of Nottingham, with the great forests of Sherwood and Rockingham at his door, had more trouble than most with those who did not show much concern for the law. Shortly before the overthrow of Edward II, a Leicestershire gentleman named Eustace de Folville and his three brothers, one of them a chaplain, with a band of fifty followers murdered an Exchequer judge in a roadside ambush near Melton Mowbray. Outlawed, since no-one could find him, he was subsequently pardoned by the new government whose adherent, in that time of warring factions,

[1] *Select Cases in the Court of King's Bench under Edward I* (Selden Society ed. G. O. Sayles), III, 194-6.

he may well have been. But it soon transpired that he respected no government, for a few months later complaints were lodged with the sheriff of Nottingham that the Folvilles were again pestering the highways, waylaying rich travellers and holding them to ransom. In January 1332, fifteen months after Edward III had seized the reins from Mortimer, another of the king's judges, a man widely suspected of corruption who was said to have sold the law "like cows", was taken by the same gang as he was travelling from Grantham to Melton and, carried "from wood to wood," held to ransom for the immense sum of 1300 marks. Subsequently the "brotherhood," as they called themselves, transferred their activities to the Peak where, warned by local sympathisers of every attempt by the sheriff's officers to apprehend them, they continued to evade capture. The chief justice of the King's Bench, Sir Geoffrey le Scrope, drew the attention of parliament to their depredations. A year later Eustace and his men, being notable archers, were pardoned in return for service with the royal army in Scotland. But as soon as the campaign was over they returned to their old ways in the greenwood. And though one of the Folvilles, the chaplain, was captured and beheaded in 1345 after a dramatic siege in a Rutland church where he had fled for sanctuary, Eustace was still untaken when he died a year later.[1]

Without widespread sympathy for the Folvilles,[2] who were men of great courage and possibly victims of injustice or supposed injustice, they could hardly have remained at large in the heart of England for nearly twenty years. The vast woodlands of the midlands and the north were full of fugitives from justice—outlaws who could look for no protection from the king's judges and lived by defying them. People whose homes were near the royal or baronial forests often had a bone to pick with authority,

---

[1] *Keen,* 197-8.

[2] In Langland's *Piers Plowman* ("B" Text, Passus, xix, transl. and ed., D. and R. Attwater), there are three lines which, though not mentioned by Mr. Maurice Keen in his brilliant *Outlaws of Medieval Legend,* seem to connect the Folvilles with the Robin Hood legend.

> "And some (he taught) to ride and recover what unrightfully won;
> He taught them to win it again through quickness of hands,
> And fetch it from false men with Folville's laws."

For another view recently advanced see J. C. Holt in *Past and Present.*

for the forest laws and the verderers who enforced them gave no mercy to a poor countryman who took his dog or longbow into their sacred preserves to fill his pot with venison. There was a natural affinity between poachers and outlaws which helped to protect the latter's hide-outs in the greenwood. When ambush of "the king's liegemen and the goods of Holy Church" meant a proud woolmonger, a grasping landowner or a fat abbot held to ransom, country folk's hearts warmed to the outlaws who plundered them and who gave, if tradition and legend did not lie, some of their surplus wealth to the poor.

It was during the fourteenth century that the first written references appeared to Robin Hood—the North Country outlaw who lived with his merry men in the greenwood and robbed the rich but spared the poor. Though the form in which most of the ballads have come down to us is that of a later age, they all stem from legends originally transmitted by recitation and singing. They may even have derived from the wars of de Montfort or the troubled reigns of Richard I and John. But the king who figures in them and who is ready to do justice to the outlaws when the truth becomes known is usually called Edward and is presented as a splendid figure of a sovereign able to hold his own at wrestling and fisticuffs with Robin himself. The three Edwards who reigned from 1272 to 1377 were all physically outstanding, two of them famous warriors and the other, though despised by his own class, a man who delighted in the rough pleasures of his rustic subjects and loved to be familiar with them. It was no accident that after his murder Edward II became a popular hero and even a saint to the simple folk of the Severn valley.

Certain features recur in all the Robin Hood tales. In all of them the hero—a man denied justice and a dauntless champion of the poor and oppressed—asserts his rights and theirs through his wonderful skill with the longbow, a weapon that first came into use in England at the end of the thirteenth century, notably among the yeomen of the Cheshire and Midland forests who had learnt its mastery from the Welsh hillmen during the wars of Edward I. Local place-names called after Robin Hood are found in almost every northern county but occur most frequently in Sherwood in Nottinghamshire and in Barnedale in the Pennines.

In some of these legends the leader of the outlaws is a real personage like Hereward the Wake, Fulk Fitzwarin the baron who defied King John, or Adam of Gurdon who held out against the future Edward I in the Hampshire forests after the fall of de Montfort. Even William Wallace of Scotland figures in one. Most of them, however, carry names that cannot be identified with any historical character, such as Adam Bell of the Clough, William Clowdisdale and Robin Hood himself—a name that may have come down from pagan folk-lore and been derived from Hodekin the Saxon wood-sprite or Robin Goodfellow the fairy. Despite the Church's power the myths of the heathen past were still dear to country folk. So was the cult of the "Green Man," enshrined in many a traditional morris dance and in the garlanding of church towers in the spring, and whose effigy can be seen on a boss in the cloisters of Norwich cathedral and on a capital in the transept of Llantilio Crossenny church in Monmouthshire.[1]

Antiquarians have also sought to associate Robin with persons of the same name who flit, at different times, through court rolls and other records, like the Robin Hood who was a tenant of Wakefield in the time of Edward II's victorious campaign against Thomas of Lancaster and whose name reappears as a valet in that king's service shortly afterwards. But as a reference to an ancient Robin Hood stone in south Yorkshire occurs in a monastic cartulary of almost exactly the same date, this person cannot have been the hero of the legends. Perhaps the nearest to a real Robin Hood in recorded history is one Roger Godberd, an obscure follower of de Montfort who held out as an outlaw in Sherwood long after everyone else had yielded and, for several years at the end of Henry III's reign, gave a great deal of trouble to the sheriff of Nottingham and to rich travellers in that district. On one occasion, after the steward of Sherwood had caught two men with bows and arrows in the forest, they were rescued by a band of twenty outlaws armed with swords and bows.

[1] In April 1577 and again in 1578 the General Assembly of the Church of Scotland requested King James to prohibit plays of "Robin Hood, king of May" on the Sabbath. Half a century later, in his translation of a Latin history of Scotland, John Bellenden wrote that Robin Hood was the subject of "mony fabillis and mery sportis soung amang the vulgar pepyle." *D.N.B.*, IX, 1152-5.

All that is certain is that in every version of this saga of the plain and oppressed man's dream,[1] the hero, defying the law from his forest fastness, becomes the leader and champion of all who have suffered injustice. "Look," Robin bids his followers,

> " ye do no husband harm
> That tilleth with his plough;
> No more ye shall no good yeoman,
> That walketh by greenwood shaw."

While, like the Arthurian knights in contemporary legends of chivalry, he enjoins an almost exaggerated courtesy and chivalry towards the weak and needy, against their oppressors he preaches ruthless and unrelenting war:

> " These bishops and archbishops,
> Ye shall them beat and bind;
> The high sheriff of Nottingham,
> Him hold you in your mind."

He pits his wits, his courage and his skill at archery against the "establishment"—against unjust judges and greedy prelates and all who have usurped the property and rights of others, and, in the end, after many a heroic fight in which no mercy is given or taken, wreaks punishment on his oppressors, restores every man, including himself, to his own, and wins the pardon and favour of the king whose officers he has shown to be false rogues.

For this champion of the people is no traitor to his sovereign, to whom, for all his wrongs, he is a faithful and loyal subject. Despite his popular sympathies, he usually turns out to be a man of noble blood, a dispossessed landowner, and, in some of the later ballads—for his rank, like his feats, tended to grow with the years—an earl. Nor, though a terror to greedy evil-living abbots and bishops, was he other than a devout son of Holy Church. One of his chief followers was a friar, and he always showed a particular veneration, characteristic of the time, for the Virgin, who was the inspiration of chivalry and courtesy to the weak.

---

[1] "What he and Little John did to the sheriff was what the common man would have liked to have done." *Keen*, 190.

> "Robin loved our dear Lady,
>   For doubt of deadly sin
>   Would he never do company harm
>   That any woman was in."

If Robin Hood was the personification of the common English-man's resentment against oppression and injustice, he was also the model of the fighting virtues he admired. What Arthur and his Round Table knights were to the feudal classes he and his followers were to the common folk of England. What the one did with sword and lance, the other did with longbow and cudgel. Robin had the pugnacity of a terrier. When he encountered an antagonist worthy of him, a Nottingham tanner called Arthur, he fought him all day:

> "'I pass not for length,' bold Arthur reply'd,
>   'My staff is of oak so free;
>   Eight foot and a half, it will knock down a calf
>   And I hope it will knock down thee.'

> "... And about and about and about they went
>   Like two wild boars in a chase,
>   Striking to aim each other to maim,
>   Leg, arm or any other place."

Robin's lieutenants were all chosen for their ability to stand up to him and give as good as they took; only when they had proved themselves did he open his heart to them and trust them:

> "Then Robin took them both by the hands
>   And danced about the oak tree,
>   'For three merry men and three merry men
>   And three merry men we be!'"

Like him the English loved a man who stood his ground and never asked for quarter. It was the way they learnt to respect one another.

Unlike the peasants of the continent, where fighting was the preserve of the nobility and their retinues, the English country-man was trained to arms under Edward I's statute of Winchester and the old Anglo-Saxon rule by which every man between fifteen and sixty had to turn out with his weapons in the *posse comitatus* to defend the realm and maintain the peace. For the

poor man the chief of these weapons were a longbow and a
sheaf of arrows. In all the ballads Robin is a superb marksman.
At Whitby in Yorkshire travellers used to be shown two stone
pillars a mile apart, said to have been set up by a medieval abbot
to commemorate one of the outlaw's shooting feats. Thrice, we
are told, at the sheriff's archery competition at Nottingham,

> "Robin shot about
> And always sliced the wand."

And when he and his followers switched their aim from the butts
to the sheriff's men who had tried to apprehend him at the
moment of his triumph, the latter had to run for their lives under
a hail of arrows.

In all this Robin symbolised his race. Even during the wars
of Coeur de Lion it was said of the English archers at Messina
that "no man could look out of door but he would have an
arrow in his eye before he could shut it." By the time of Edward
III, after half a century of almost continuous campaigning
against the Welsh and Scots, skill at archery in rustic England was
becoming widespread. Practice at the village butts after service
on Sundays was enjoined by the law, and archery competitions
were the favourite recreation of the commonalty on feast days
and holidays, when

> "They showéd such brave archery
> By cleaving sticks and wands."

Often, the ballads tell us, they did so in the presence of their
warlike lords and princes. "Bend all your bows," Robin bade
his men,

> "and with the grey goose-wing,
> Such sport now show as you would do
> In the presence of the king."

The longbow—originally in its native Wales made of rough,
unpolished wild elm—was in England usually made of yew. It
was drawn not by strength of arm but of the whole frame. Bishop
Latimer in a later century was taught as a boy to lay his body
to the bow and was given weapons of increasing size as he grew
bigger, "for men shall never shoot well unless they be brought
up in it." The arrows, a cloth-yard long, were plumed with the
feathers of the geese that fed on the village greens and commons:

" Their arrows finely pared, for timber and for feather,
With birch and brazil pierc'd to fly in any weather,
And shot they with the round, the square or forked pile,
The loose gave such a twang as might be heard a mile."

In some verses of a later period there is a picture of an archer
taking aim—

" a youth of clean compacted limb
Who, with a comely grace in his left hand
Holding his bow, did take his steadfast stand,
Setting his left leg somewhat forth before,
His arrow with his right hand rocking sure,
Not stooping nor yet standing straight upright;
Then with his left hand, little above his sight,
Stretching his arm out with an easy strength
To draw an arrow of a yard in length."

.   .   .   .

By the time of Edward III's accession the longbow had
become the English weapon *par excellence*—one which no other
people could use and which seemed designed for the Englishman's
physique. A century later a foreign visitor noted that the bows
employed by the island commonalty were "thicker and longer
than those used by other nations, just as their bodies are stronger
than other people's." In the hands of such masters as the Sherwood and Cheshire foresters the weapon was far more deadly and
accurate than a generation earlier. Without anyone realizing it
except a few fighting men—one of whom seems to have been
Edward himself—it had introduced into the nation's life an
element of power which was soon to have effects, not only on the
destiny of nations but on the structure of English society.

The first to feel its power were the Scots. Bruce and Douglas
were dead, and of the patriot trio who had saved Scotland only
Thomas Randolph earl of Moray remained, governing the
kingdom as regent for Bruce's six-year-old son, David II. Much
though he resented Scotland's independence, Edward at first
showed no sign of repudiating the treaty of Northampton. Yet
he could not disregard the demands of his northern adherents—
the "disinherited," as they were called—who, it had been agreed,
were in certain cases to have had their Scottish lands restored to

them. Some were friends who had risked their lives in the *coup
d'état* against Mortimer, others had fought loyally for Edward's
father or grandfather. Though nearly all were either English
nobles with Scottish estates or members of the Comyn-Balliol
party opposed to Bruce, they were entitled by inheritance to
properties and titles in Scotland which her rulers, who regarded
them as traitors, persisted in denying them, having given them to
their own adherents.

Soon after he assumed the government Edward asked for
their reinstatement. Fifteen months later, as nothing had been
done, he asked again. As his request was still ignored, he connived at the disinherited taking the law into their own hands
and let them prepare an invasion of Scotland on English soil.
He had already given shelter to Edward Balliol, son of the former
king, and it was in Balliol's name and under Balliol's command
that on July 31st, 1332, a little force of expatriates, including
the anglicised earls of Angus and Atholl, sailed from Ravenspur.
They were accompanied by several hundred English archers.
Shortly before they started the regent died at Musselburgh, some
said of poison.

Landing at Kinghorn in Fife and meeting only mild opposition, the invaders occupied Dunfermline. But on August 10th
they came up against a large Scottish force on Dupplin Moor
commanded by Randolph's successor, the Earl of Mar. That
night, while the Scots were recalling Bannockburn and singing
ribald songs about the English having tails, Balliol's men secretly
crossed the water of Earn and fell on them at dawn. So fast and
furious was the shooting of the English bowmen and so accurate
their aim that Mar's troops were virtually annihilated. "The pile
of dead," wrote the Lanercost chronicler, "was greater in height
from the earth towards the sky than a whole spear's length."

After their victory the invaders entered Perth and crowned
Edward Balliol at Scone. It proved, however, a grim affair, at
which those participating sat down to the coronation feast in full
armour. Afterwards at Roxburgh, where he had withdrawn to
be near the border, Balliol secretly acknowledged Edward as
overlord and promised to cede him the town and county of
Berwick.

Before the year ended, Balliol and his adherents had been

driven from the country. On this, still protesting his peaceable intentions, Edward moved his court to York and prepared to invade Scotland on Balliol's behalf. In the spring of 1333 he laid siege to Berwick. For two months the town held out until, faced by starvation, its commander agreed to surrender unless relieved by July 19th. The position was the same as that which had faced England nineteen years before in the summer of Bannockburn. Only now it was the Scots who had to relieve a beleaguered fortress, the English who had to fight a battle to prevent them.

When on July 19th, responding to the challenge, the new regent, Archibald Douglas—brother of the great Sir James— came within sight of the starving town, he found the English barring his path on the northern slopes of Halidon Hill. They were drawn up in a long thin line of dismounted knights and men-at-arms marshalled in three brigades, between each and on either flank of which were projecting salients formed by archers with huge six-foot bows and sheafs of arrows. The apexes of these four salients stuck out in advance of the main line so that between each pair was a gradually narrowing and rising funnel at the end of which stood a line of armoured men with banners and pennons fluttering above the sheen of their levelled lances. Behind them was a reserve brigade to deal with any attempt to drive in the archers on the wings, while a small force of mounted knights and troopers was stationed nearby to intercept any Scottish horse that tried to reach Berwick by by-passing the hill. In the rear, encircled by baggage-wagons, were laagers packed with horses awaiting a summons from their riders in the battle-line and guarded by the pages and *valets aux armes* who looked after their masters' steeds and armour.

It was the gallant Harclay—executed by Edward's unjust father as a traitor—who ten years earlier at Boroughbridge had first applied the teaching of Bannockburn, confronting the flying Lancaster and his knights with a line of dismounted men-at-arms and archers. Since then, in the ill-fated Stanhope Park campaign of 1327, Edward had seen for himself the fatuity of trying either to attack the Scottish pikesmen with heavy cavalry or to catch them on their moorland ponies as they flitted across the northern hills and dales. This time, by ensuring that they could reach

Berwick in no other way, he intended to make the Scots attack him. Nor did he mean to let himself be driven, like his father, by their inexorably moving pikes into a position where his men would be at a disadvantage. Instead, he had designed a battle-field exactly suited to his means.

For the trap he had set for them was more deadly than the bogs of the Bannock burn or the pits which Bruce had dug on the road to Stirling. In the hands of English archers the long-bow of Gwent had come of age, and Edward and his warrior lords had found a way to turn it into a military arm with a mobility and mass killing-power till now undreamt of. One of them, the crusader Henry of Grosmont—son of the Earl of Lan-caster and known to his fellow knights as "the father of soldiers"—had fought at Bannockburn, and it may have been this imagin-ative and brilliant commander who first saw how the longbow could be used to revolutionise the art of war. What seems certain is that during those waiting weeks while the English army was blockading Berwick, the archers whom Edward's commissioners of array had gathered from the northern and midland counties were being trained to manœuvre and exercise their art under orders, just as Bruce's pikesmen before Bannockburn had been trained to fight the battle he had foreseen. Brigaded with the men-at-arms of their native shires and disciplined by grizzled veterans who had learnt war the hard way on the Welsh and Scottish hills, they were taught to operate, not only as individual marksmen, but in massed phalanxes from which, at the word of command, rhythmic volleys of arrows, travelling at incredible velocity, could be directed first at one part of an attacking force, then at another, until every living thing in the target area had been killed or maimed. In their metal helmets and padded deerskin jackets these light, active men had been trained to manœuvre in extended order, to enfilade a column from flank or even rear and, combining fire and movement, at a bugle call or other signal to reform, under cover of their comrades' volleys, in massed ranks in which, so long as their ammunition lasted, they were virtually unapproachable. Among them—pardoned by their sovereign—were the outlaws of Sherwood Forest, the Folvilles and their ilk. Adepts at approaching and destroying their foes unseen, it was not the high sheriff of Nottingham and his bailiffs who were now their target but the king's enemies.[1]

It was at this moment in time—on a summer's morning in 1333—that a Scottish army experienced on the slopes of Halidon Hill what was to happen to other and more famous armies at the hands of this disciplined combination of English archers and men-at-arms under their young Plantagenet king and his lieutenants, many of whom were to win fame by applying the same tactics on the battlefields of Europe. As the pikesmen in their dense schiltrons and the accompanying columns of mounted knights moved forward across the marshy ground at the foot of the hill, they suddenly came into range of the archers. Though hundreds fell as the showers of steel-tipped arrows struck home, recalling their fathers' triumphs they pressed stubbornly on. Lowering their heads against the blinding hail and closing their ranks, they instinctively edged away from the archers on either side and started to climb the hill. Packed together till they were almost suffocated, riven and tormented by the shooting of the marksmen and the massed volleys from the formations into which the archers withdrew at every attempt to attack them, they stumbled up the slope towards the waiting line of English armour and the one place on the battlefield where no arrows were falling. When, breathless from the ascent, the survivors reached that hedge of levelled lances, the knights and men-at-arms, fresh and eager for the fray, started to hack at them with great swords and battle axes, forcing them down the slope where they came once more into that terrible enfilading hail.

The same fate attended the mounted lords and knights. A detachment that tried to work round the flank towards Berwick was intercepted by Edward's cavalry, while the rest were shot down as they tried to drive their terrified horses up the hill, falling in tangled masses of writhing men and beasts, transfixed and pinned to one another or the ground. When even their courage could endure no more and they broke, the English knights called up their pages and horses and pursued them across the rolling Berwickshire hills until nightfall, "felling the wretches," in the Lanercost chronicler's words, "with ironshod maces." The

[1] There is a brilliant study of the bowmen's tactics and of Halidon Hill in the last chapter of John Morris's *Bannockburn* and in his article on the Archers of Crécy in the *English Historical Review*, Vol. XII.

regent himself was mortally wounded and taken prisoner and six earls were left dead on the field. Altogether seventy Scots' lords and five hundred knights and squires fell and almost the entire infantry. The defenders lost one knight, one man-at-arms and twelve archers. In a single morning the patient work of a quarter of a century had been undone, and Bruce's spider's thread had been shot through by English discipline and the "grey goose feather."

Chapter Seven

THE GARTER KNIGHTS

"There are periods at which the history of its wars is the true history of the people, for they are the discipline of the national experience."

BISHOP STUBBS

NOT ONLY BERWICK, but Scotland now lay at Edward's mercy. He did not incorporate it in England as his grandfather had done after Spottsmuir, but, reverting to the latter's original policy, delivered it, as lord paramount, to Balliol as his feudatory. An Anglo-Scottish parliament of the latter's supporters reversed all the acts of the Bruce dynasty and ratified the obligations to the English king undertaken in the previous year. The counties of Dumfries, Selkirk, Peebles, Roxburgh, Berwick and the Lothians were made over to "the royal dignity, crown and kingdom of England with all their towers and castles, rights and appurtenances." Of Scotland south of the Forth only Stirling, Lanark, Dumbarton, Ayr and Galloway remained. Edward also obtained the Isle of Man, which he gave to his friend and comrade-in-arms, William Montague.[1]

Yet somehow the Scotland of Bruce and Wallace survived. The disinherited quarrelled over the spoils, and the people's contempt for Balliol reduced his authority to little more than the place where he happened to be. Within a year he had been forced to take refuge again in England, while the boy king, David II, was smuggled by his adherents to France. And though in 1335, when Edward again invaded Scotland, most of the Scottish magnates made their peace with the usurper and "none but children in their games dared to call David Bruce king," guerrilla resistance continued. As fast as the English built forts to overawe

---

[1] From whom it passed, after various vicissitudes, to the Stanleys, who sold it back to the English Crown in the eighteenth century.

the countryside the Scots pulled them down. Like Wallace and Bruce before them, "they kept in the wild country, among marshes and great forests, so that no man could follow them." Bruce's sister held out in Kildrummie and, when the turncoat earl of Atholl laid siege to her castle, Douglas's heir, the "black knight of Liddesdale," and Sir Andrew Moray—the third regent of the stricken kingdom in three years—marched to her rescue, slaying Atholl under an oak in Kilblain forest.

Yet it was France that saved Scotland. Edward sought nothing from that country except his hereditary lands in the Agenais which her kings had seized on a legal pretext from his father and failed to restore. So anxious was he for friendly relations with his Valois cousin that in the summer of 1331, paying a secret visit to Arras disguised as a merchant, he had done a second and fuller liege-homage for his duchy. He had even offered to surrender his Gascon revenues for a number of years in return for justice in the Agenais and had proposed a marriage between his son and Philip's daughter. He also offered to go on crusade with him.

As a result an Anglo-French legal commission had been set up to investigate the dispute. But the Process of Agen, as it was called, though at first conducted in a spirit of learned enquiry, soon degenerated into the legal bickerings on which all earlier attempts at a settlement had shipwrecked. Both sides, intensely suspicious, began to insist on safeguards to which the other was afraid to agree and, as a chronicler put it, "to gnaw the bone of contention with the tooth of temarious cavilling." The English refused to surrender certain castles, and the French king threatened Gascon nobles in the disputed territories with disinheritance and even death unless they transferred their allegiance. He also hinted that he might seize Edward's inheritance of Ponthieu—an enclave in northern France impossible to defend—unless he surrendered the castles. The trouble was that the commissioners were not trying merely to adjudicate points of feudal law but to reconcile the claims of contending national sovereignties. The old loose feudal relationship no longer satisfied either side. Edward, a sovereign in England, was resolved to be one in his French dominions; Philip and his lawyers were not prepared to concede him more than the rights of a subject. No agreement was reached, and the disputed lands remained in French hands.[1]

Meanwhile the two countries had fallen out over Scotland. After granting David the same hospitality that Edward had given Balliol, the French king insisted that the Scots must be included in any settlement between France and England. The Franco-Scottish alliance of seven years before became a reality. If Edward wished to be master of the British isles like his grandfather it was clear that he would first have to settle with the French king, whose price was a like control of France.

Though feudal ideology was giving place to a more national ideal, lordship was still an enormously important conception to the medieval mind, hallowed both by the Church's precepts and the dictates of chivalry and honour. Part of the land which Edward regarded as rightfully his under the compact made between his great-grandfather and Louis IX was being withheld from him. Yet the overlord who detained it—his own cousin and a prince whose right to the French throne was, in Edward's eyes, no better than his own—was encouraging the Scots to repudiate their fealty. Whenever Edward had seemed on the point of making the Scots acknowledge his suzerainty and recognise his vassal, Balliol, as their king, Philip had covertly or openly come to their aid. When in the summer of 1336, having obtained a grant for a Scottish campaign from parliament— always readier to vote money against the Scots than against any one else—Edward marched as far north as his grandfather had done and burnt Aberdeen and Forres, Philip moved from the Mediterranean to the English Channel the transports he had been assembling for a crusade and forced him to hurry south again. French money and supplies encouraged Robert the Steward and Andrew Moray to defy the English and enabled the Countess of Dunbar—Randolph's daughter—to hold out for many months in her husband's castle on the road between Edinburgh and Berwick against a large army under William Montague. When told that her brother, the Earl of Moray— then a hostage in English hands—would be put to death if she continued to resist, "black Agnes," as her countrymen called

[1] There is an interesting account of the Process of Agen in *Speculum*, Vol. XIX, 161-71.

her, replied that in that case she would inherit his earldom. And when the besiegers blasted the walls with battering-ram and stone-thrower, she and her ladies appeared on the battlements, gorgeously attired, and wiped away the dust with their napkins. Thanks to French provision ships she was able to defy all Montague's attempts to dislodge her for half a year and in the end forced him to retire. "Came I early, came I late," a Scottish ballad-writer made him complain, "I found Annot at the gate."

It was not surprising, therefore, that when an aggrieved French exile, Robert of Artois, who had taken refuge at Edward's court, urged him to defy the French king he should have been given encouragement. He was even allowed in the course of a swan feast in Westminster Hall to draw attention to Edward's right to the French throne by serving up a heron at the royal table—a cowardly bird, he explained, that, like the English, would not fight for its inheritance. For others had suffered from the encroachments of Philip of Valois and feared his power. Since the days when Henry III had made his family pact with Louis IX of France great changes had taken place in the map of Europe. At that time its dominant secular power had been the feudal German and Italian empire of the Hohenstauffens, then engaged in a life-and-death struggle with the papacy. But when that struggle had ended in the latter's triumph, it was France that reaped the fruits of a victory which had destroyed the reality both of the Empire and of the papal temporal dominion. While England was engaged in her long, costly attempt to conquer Scotland, Philip the Fair of France, seeking to extend her frontiers to the Pyrenees, Alps, Rhine and North Sea, had brought Champagne, Brie, Franche-Comté, the Lyonnais, Navarre and much of Lorraine under his rule. When he died in the year of Bannockburn, of the great outlying provinces of France only Flanders, Brittany and Gascony—the rump of the once vast duchy of Guienne or Aquitaine—remained independent fiefs.

In 1337 France was by far the greatest state in Christendom with a population of over twelve millions, at least four times that of England. She was the cultural, artistic and military leader of Europe, with immense agricultural wealth and a fast-expanding industry and commerce. The papacy itself had been transferred from Rome to a French enclave on the Rhone where, in their palace at Avignon, a succession of French popes, controlled by a college of French cardinals, wielded the authority of their mighty Italian predecessors. Despite German colonial expansion in the Baltic and Ostmark and the commercial and artistic achievements of the Italian cities, both Germany and Italy had lost all political cohesion. And the poet Dante's dream of a universal Christian monarchy centered in Rome had faded before the ugly reality of city-state after state falling under the ruthless dictatorship of some popular or oligarchical tyrant and warring against one another.

It was in the plain between Picardy and the Rhineland that alarm at France's expansion was greatest. Every few years some new encroachment, legal or military, had pushed her dominion a little further eastwards and northwards. Since the French victory at Cassel in 1328 over the Flemish peasants and weavers who a quarter of a century earlier had defeated France's chivalry at Courtrai, Flanders had become a French fief in reality as well as in name. But though her count and many of her rich capitalists, in their fear of the despised "blue nails" of their factories, adhered to the lilies and were prepared to pay the price of an embargo on English wool, the other countries of the Netherlands—fiefs not of France but of the Empire—had a common interest to resist French aggression.

It was through a coalition of these and the princes of northern Germany that Edward sought to provide the necessary base and man-power with which to humble Philip of Valois. Early in the summer of 1337 a splendid embassy under the Bishop of Lincoln and Earl of Salisbury left England to negotiate alliances with Hainault, Brabant, Gelderland, and Juliers, all of whose rulers were already allied to Edward by marriage. The Count of Hainault, who also reigned over Holland and Zealand, was his father-in-law; the Count of Gelderland and the Margrave of Juliers were his brothers-in-law. The Duke of Brabant was his cousin, and the Emperor or king of the Germans himself, Lewis the Bavarian, whose titular vassals they all were, was married to a sister of Queen Philippa.

Yet, as his grandfather had found before him, European alliances had to be paid for. The English, however, were now far readier to finance a war for their French king's fiefs than in

Edward I's time. After the humiliations of the late reign their young sovereign's victories over the Scots, his generosity and the gallantry of his bearing had made him very popular, especially among the merchants of the capital who benefited from the lavish expenditure of his brilliant court.[1] There was a general sense that the French king was treating him shabbily. In the autumn of 1336 a great council of the realm had granted him a tenth and a fifteenth and, when in the spring of 1337 Philip declared his French fiefs forfeit and sent his troops into Gascony and Ponthieu, a parliament voted a further tenth and fifteenth for three years, so virtually doubling the peacetime revenue. Simultaneously an assembly of merchants agreed to a special levy on every sack of wool exported, enabling the king to raise a loan from the woolmongers in return for a monopoly of exporting wool through the staple which, to encourage the Duke of Brabant, was re-established at Antwerp. Edward also received a clerical grant from the convocations of Canterbury and York. The feeling that Edward I had vainly tried to generate in the English people was at last taking shape. Men no longer thought of the king's foreign business as a private feudal obligation remote from themselves. Conscious of a common destiny, they felt an obligation to help him.

As for the chivalric classes on whom the brunt of a war would fall, far from opposing the royal plans as their predecessors had done in the days of Bigod and Archbishop Winchelsey, they were eager to prove on the battlefield the prowess they had so often displayed in the tournament lists. In the spring of 1337 at his Westminster parliament Edward held a splendid gathering at which he granted earldoms, as well as estates to support them, to six of his closest friends, including his two chief lieutenants in Scotland: his cousin, Henry of Grosmont who was made earl of Derby, and William Montague who became earl of Salisbury. He also conferred the dukedom of Cornwall—a title new to England—on his six-year-old son, Prince Edward. And in the presence of their ladies forty young bachelors of rank, all wearing

[1] In 1331 the king's pavilion-maker, a member of the Merchant Taylors' guild or fraternity, bought a mansion which, until it was destroyed in 1940, was the oldest existing City Company hall in London. E. Pooley, *The Guilds of the City of London*, 10.

silk covers over one eye, vowed never to remove them until they had performed some knightly deed in France.

The king did not appeal only to the chivalric classes. He took the whole nation into his confidence. In a manifesto read in every county court he set out the story of his negotiations with Philip and his repeated attempts to secure an honourable peace and offered, if any man knew of a better way, to follow it. A muster was appointed for the end of September and all sports were forbidden except archery.

Hostilities began in November with a spirited raid on Cadzand at the mouth of the Scheldt by Sir Walter Manny—a gallant Hainaulter who was a great favourite of Edward and his queen and who, adopting England as his country, was later to become the founder of the London Charterhouse. "When the Englishmen saw the town before them," wrote Froissart, "they made them ready and had wind and tide to serve them. And so in the name of God and St. George they approached and blew up their trumpets and set their archers before them and sailed toward the town." The archers "shot so wholly together" that the Flemings, after a stout fight, fled and the Count of Flanders's brother was taken prisoner. But the French and their Genoese and Spanish allies were stronger at sea than the English and the raid was repaid with interest. Hastings, Rye, Portsmouth and Plymouth were all plundered and burnt. Southampton suffered particularly severely, being raided by fifty galleys, one of them equipped with a *pot de fer* which fired iron bolts into the houses. "They came on a Sunday in the forenoon while the people were at mass and . . . robbed and pilled the town and slew divers and defouled maidens and enforced wives and charged their vessels with the pillage and so entered again into their ships. And when the tide came they dis-anchored and sailed to Dieppe and there divided their booty and pillages."[1]

None of this deterred the chivalry-loving king. With lavish subsidies his ambassadors in the Low Countries negotiated alliance after alliance. His cousin of Brabant was promised £60,000—a sum equivalent to nearly two years of the peacetime revenue—and a still larger sum was distributed among seven other rulers, including the Count Palatine of the Rhine and the Mar-

[1] *Froissart*, I, 108.

grave of Brandenburg. In the summer of 1338, "well accompanied with earls and barons" Edward crossed the North Sea to Antwerp and, travelling with splendid and costly pomp through Brabant to Cologne[1] and thence up the Rhine to Coblenz, was invested by the Emperor as his vicar-general of the imperial lands west of the Rhine for the war against France. Yet, though it all seemed very glorious and hopeful at the time, it did not produce results. It took more than a year and a vast expenditure on feasts and tournaments—"giving great rewards and jewels to the lords, ladies and demoiselles of the country to get their good-will"—before Edward could get his allies to take the field. And when at last, in the autumn of 1339, they did so, nothing came of it but expense and frustration. For though, eager to repeat their exploits of Halidon Hill, the king and his English knights and archers "rode against the tyrant of the French with banners displayed," ravaging frontier villages and crops in revenge for the burning of south coast towns by Norman and Breton privateers, Philip merely watched the proceedings from behind the walls of Amiens. Despite the presence in his host of the kings of Scotland and Navarre and the dukes of Bourbon, Brittany, Burgundy, Normandy, Lorraine and Athens he ignored all Edward's taunts and challenges. And after a brief investment of Cambrai—a former imperial fief—the Hainaulters, Brabanters and Germans insisted on returning home to their families for the winter. "Our allies," Edward wrote in disgust to his son, "would no longer abide."

By this time he was £300,000 in debt with nothing to show for it, while the French had taken Bourg and Blaye in Gascony and the Scots had recaptured Perth. Even his crown had had to be pledged and his ten-year-old heir engaged to a Brabantine princess to stave off his foreign creditors. Yet Edward still persisted in his dream of bringing the French king to terms through a grand alliance. And in the winter of 1339/40 he achieved an unexpected success. For, driven desperate by the embargo he had placed on the export of English wool to Flanders, and incited

[1] To the rebuilding of whose cathedral he contributed at the instance of his confessor, the Merton theologian and mathematician, Thomas Bradwardine. Modern scholars believe that some of the wall-paintings in the choir were inspired by English artists of that time. *Borenius and Tristram*, 24-5.

by a rich Ghent merchant, James van Artevelde—a patriot rabble-rouser of the type that had risen to power in the Italian city-states[1]—the people of the Flemish cloth-towns rose against their pro-French count and drove him from the country. Then under van Artevelde's leadership they appealed to Edward to assume the crown of France and become their suzerain and protector.

It had been the defeat of the French chivalry by the Flemish townsmen at Courtrai that had enabled Edward I to recover his Gascon dominions. Regardless of his debts his grandson now promised them arms, the removal of the wool-staple from Antwerp to Bruges and a subsidy of £140,000. And to legalise their repudiation of homage and protect them from an interdict for their breach of feudal faith he laid formal claim to the throne of his Capet ancestors. On January 24th, 1340 he entered Bruges and was acclaimed by the burghers as king and overlord. Two weeks later, in a proclamation to "the prelates, peers, dukes, counts, barons, gentle and simple dwelling in the realm of France," he announced that Philip of Valois "had intruded himself by force" onto his throne while he had been "of tender years", and that he was now resolved to regain it and "with unshakeable purpose do justice to all men."[2] Henceforward he quartered the fleurs-de-lys of France before the leopards of England, bearing them in the senior position on both seal and surcoat.

Having secured his alliance Edward hurried home to obtain the wherewithal to finance it. So desperate were his straits that he was forced to leave his queen and children and the earls of Derby and Salisbury at Antwerp as a pledge for his debts. His expenditure had by now almost drained England of specie. Yet his popularity was still sufficient to rouse the country. Though in the autumn, after being told by the Council that unless they helped him he would have to surrender himself to his foreign creditors, the Commons had asked for time to consult those they

---

[1] According to Froissart "he had always going with him up and down in Ghent sixty or four-score varlets armed, . . . so that if he met a person that he hated or had him in suspicion, incontinent he was slain. . . . He had in every town soldiers and servants at his wages, ready to do his commandment and to espy if there were any person that would rebel against his mind."

[2] *Chronicle of Robert of Avesbury* (ed. E. M. Thompson), 309.

represented, they now joined with the magnates in giving him a
ninth of every sheaf, fleece and lamb for two years, a ninth from
the royal boroughs and a fifteenth from the rest of the community.

Yet they made their grant dependent on his answer to four
petitions, one of which, by finally ending the Crown's right to
tallage merchandise at will even in the royal demesnes, was a
major step on the road to parliamentary control of taxation. In
return for allowing Edward to collect the hated *maltote* for
another fourteen months they received a promise that it should
never be levied again "except by common consent of the prelates,
earls, barons and other lords and commons of the realm." They
also asked for limitations on the right of purveyance, for the
abolition of the ancient process against men of Anglo-Saxon
ancestry called "presentment of Englishry," and for the king's
assurance that his French title should never entail the subjection
of England to France.

Having obtained supplies for a new campaign, Edward prepared to return to the continent where the French were burning
the towns and villages of Hainault and threatening Flanders.
In his absence a fleet of nearly two hundred French,
Genoese and Spanish ships had arrived off Sluys at the mouth
of the Zwin to bar his passage and blockade the Flemings.
Throughout the past year the position at sea and the raids on England's southern ports had been causing increasing anxiety; in the
autumn of 1339 several of the king's own ships had been seized
in the North Sea. In its debates parliament had stressed the
country's maritime weakness and "how the sea should be guarded
against enemies so that they . . . should not enter the kingdom
to destroy it."

As it seemed that the king would have to fight his way back
to Flanders, every ship that could be requisitioned was assembled
at Orwell and packed with archers and men-at-arms. Apart
from a few royal cogs and galleys specially built for fighting,
—kept normally at Winchelsea and Portsmouth and administered
from the Tower by an officer called the clerk of the king's ships—
the fleet consisted of one-masted, single-decked merchant and
fishing boats, most of them of under a hundred tons. Impressed
by the sheriffs of the maritime counties, they had been adapted

for battle by the addition of fighting-tops to the masts and timber superstructures at bow and stern called "forecastles" and "after-castles", from which archers and slingers could shower arrows, darts and stones on adversaries' crews and rigging and boarding parties could take off. In honour of the king these were brightly painted and adorned with golden lions. The two largest vessels were the flagship, the cog *Thomas*, and a 240-ton ship called the *Michel* contributed by the Cinque Port of Rye.

Yet England was only in the second rank as a naval power. Her fleet was far inferior to the armada lying off the Flemish coast. To cautious minds it seemed insanity for the king to attempt to break through it to Sluys by ramming and boarding its taller and more heavily manned ships—then the only known method of fighting at sea. Appalled by the shortage of money and reports that the French and Spaniards intended to capture his royal master, the chancellor, Archbishop Stratford, begged him to abandon the voyage. Both admirals backed the arch-bishop's request. When the king refused, Stratford, to his indignation, resigned the seal. "I will cross in spite of you," he said, "and those who are afraid where no fear is may stay at home."

The fleet sailed on Thursday June 22nd, 1340, reaching the mouth of the Zwin next day. "About the hour of noon," Edward wrote to his son, "we arrived upon the coast of Flanders before Blankenberghe where we had a sight of the enemy who were all crowded together in the port of Sluys. And seeing that the tide did not serve us to close with them, we lay to all that night. On Saturday, St. John's Day, soon after the hour of noon at high tide, in the name of God and confident in our just quarrel, we entered the port upon our enemies who had assembled their ships in very strong array." There were so many of them, an eye-witness wrote, that "their masts seemed like a great wood."

Both sides fought as if on land.[1] The English went in to attack, with wind, sun and tide behind them, in three columns, the king leading the centre in the cog *Thomas*, and each ship manned alternately with men-at-arms and archers. The French and Spanish ships were chained together in four lines across the estuary like the walls of a castle. Built for the Atlantic with high

[1] The site has long since silted up and is now a sandy plain.

seaboards, they towered above their adversaries, their decks crowded with knights armed with lances and the rigging with stone-throwers and crossbowmen.

It was the English archers who decided the day. As they came into range, they loosed such a storm of arrows that the enemies' decks were strewn with dead before the boarding-parties reached them. So deadly was the marksmanship that many threw themselves into the water. Thousands were killed or drowned; only the Genoese, who had refused to anchor, managed to escape to sea. By morning two-thirds of the allied fleet had been taken or destroyed.

His victory at Sluys sent Edward's prestige soaring. Hitherto he had seemed to his fellow princes only a king of the tournament field and the Scottish moors; now he had proved himself in a major European battle. Though its consequences had still to be realised, he had broken the command of the Channel by the Atlantic seamen. What mattered to him most at the moment was the opportunity offered by his victory for an invasion of France. On July 10th he entered van Artevelde's capital, Ghent, as a conquering hero. His queen was there to greet him with a new-born son, who was to go down to history as John of Gaunt.

Together the two men—king and clothier—drew up plans for freeing the cities of Artois from the Valois. At the end of July they crossed the French frontier. While Robert of Artois, the exiled claimant to the fief, attacked St. Omer, Edward and the German and Netherland princes laid siege to Tournai. But quarrels soon broke out between the allies. When, with the brusque impatience of the self-made, van Artevelde reproached the Duke of Brabant for failing to storm the walls, the duke, furious at such low-born insolence, threatened to march his army away. It took all Edward's tact to restrain him. Meanwhile, instead of advancing to the relief of the town, Philip once more refused battle. When the English king challenged him to single combat he merely reminded him of his broken homage.

The final blow to Edward's hopes came when money to pay his allies ran out just as Tournai seemed on the point of surrendering. At that moment the Abbess of Fontenelle—his mother-in-law and a dowager Countess of Hainault—appeared in the allied lines with the Church's proposals for a truce. As there was no hope of any more English money, everyone except Edward welcomed her mission with enthusiasm. Such was her immense prestige, the respect felt for the pope's wishes and the longing of the Netherland princes to return home before the winter that in his penniless condition Edward was unable to stand out against them. By the truce of Esplechin the combatants agreed to withdraw for a year to their own boundaries, leaving everything as it was before the war, everything, that is, except the English king's and taxpayers' money which had gone beyond recall.

Furious, Edward laid the blame for everything that had happened on the ministers in England who had failed to send him the money for want of which the campaign had collapsed. Two summers before, when he first sailed for Brabant, he had issued from Walton in Suffolk a series of administrative ordinances which virtually placed the great permanent offices of state, the Exchequer and Chancery, under the control of the household officers of the Wardrobe and Chamber who accompanied him abroad. The great seal itself had been entrusted to his keeper of the Privy Seal, William Kilsby. Kilsby was an ambitious and not over-scrupulous clerk who had pleased his master by his ingenuity in raising money. He was on bad terms with the chancellor, John Stratford—the mentor of Edward's early years as king—who since 1333 had also been archbishop of Canterbury. This dislike was reciprocated by Stratford—the son of a Stratford-on-Avon burgess—who with his brother, the Bishop of Chichester, and his nephew, the Bishop of London, formed a powerful family group within the Church and administration. When the archbishop resigned the chancellorship before Sluys he had been succeeded by his brother and, after the king's return to Flanders, they had been left virtually in charge of England.

There were thus two governments, one at home representing the traditional elements, lay and ecclesiastical, through whom the country was normally governed and the other—in Flanders —composed of courtier-soldiers and the officers of the royal household. But in Edward's eyes the sole function of the former was to keep him supplied with money. Owing to the difficulty of obtaining payment from the overburdened taxpayer and the disappointing results of the wool subsidy, this had now become almost impossible. The growing arrears in the remittances from England and the "anguish and peril in which the king, queen and magnates of the host lay for lack of money,"[1] made the correspondence between the two branches of government increasingly acrimonious.

By the end of November, getting nothing but excuses in reply to his demands and reproaches, lacking the wherewithal to pay his troops and household and dunned beyond endurance by his creditors, Edward decided to return, unannounced, to Westminster. Stealing away from Ghent with only eight followers— including Kilsby—he took boat at Sluys and, after a stormy three days' voyage, landed on the night of St. Andrew's Day just before cockcrow at the Tower watergate. His temper was not improved by finding the governor absent. He at once ordered his arrest and began a furious investigation into the miscarriages of his ministers. Among those whom he summarily dismissed were the chancellor, the Bishop of Chichester, and the treasurer, the Bishop of Coventry, the chief justices of the King's Bench and Common Pleas and several other judges, as well as a number of Chancery and Exchequer officials. He also arrested the financiers, William de la Pole and John Pulteney, who had failed to sell the wool he had requisitioned at a sufficiently high price. But his chief anger was reserved for Archbishop Stratford. Accusing him of having counselled him to "cross the sea without provision of money and horses"[2] and of then withholding supplies in order to bring about his ruin, he was only with difficulty, and after being reminded of the penalties that would follow such an outrage, prevented from forcibly shipping him and his fellow bishops to Flanders as a pledge for his debts.

As it was, he laid charges against the primate of treason and conversion of public moneys and summoned him to answer at the Exchequer. In place of the dismissed ministers he appointed a lay treasurer, Sir Robert Parving, and a lay chancellor—the first in English history—Sir Robert Bourchier. Both had served as knights of the shire, held judicial appointments and could be trusted to do his will. Never again, he declared, would he em-

---

[1] Rot. Parl. ii 122, cit. *Tout, Chapters,* III, 113.
[2] "I believe that the archbishop wished me, by lack of money, to be betrayed and killed." *Idem* III, 120.

ploy anyone as chief minister whom he could not hang if guilty
of felony.

Believing, or affecting to believe, that his life was in danger,
Stratford took shelter with the monks of Christ Church, Canterbury. On the anniversary of Becket's death he preached a sermon
in the cathedral on his martyred predecessor. And on New Year's
Day 1341 he addressed a long letter to the king. "You have had
victory of your enemies of Scotland and France," he told him,
"and at this day are held the most noble prince of Christendom.
Consider well your great undertaking and the strong adversary
you have, and the great peril of your land . . . Take it not ill,
sire, that we send you so largely the truth, for we are moved to
do this by the great affection which we have towards you, the
safety of your honour and of your land, and because it belongeth
to us, for that we are, all unworthy though we be, primate of all
England and your spiritual adviser."

For while he protested his affection for his royal master,
which seems to have been genuine, the archbishop did not shirk
from telling him home truths. Though a worldling and a con-
ciliator, he was also a man of courage who in the past had stood
up to both Edward II and Queen Isabella and, at the risk of his
life, defied the dictator, Mortimer. The veiled menace in his
letter was unmistakable. "Very gentle lord," he wrote,

"may it please you to know that the most sovereign thing
which holds kings and princes in due and fitting estate is
good counsel. And let it not displease you to remember it
in your time, for, by the evil counsel which our lord your
father had, he caused to be taken, against the law of the
land and the great charter, the peers and other people of
the land and put some to shameful death and of others
he caused their goods to be seized . . . And what happened
to him for that cause, sire, you know well." [1]

The archbishop was resolved not to let the underlying
constitutional issues be obscured by the royal accusations against
his honesty or by his dispute with the household "intimates" who
had poisoned the king's mind. Having been an Oxford doctor

[1] Robert of Avebury, *De gestis Mirabilibus Regis Edwardi Tertii, Rolls Series*
1889, p. 324.

of law, a Chancery clerk and dean of the Court of Arches, he knew how to put the issue in its clearest and most compelling form. As in the crisis of 1297 and the days of the Despensers, the principle at stake was whether a king of England, either good or bad, could govern without resort to established law and to those who could speak for the nation. "By evil counsel," he told the king, "you begin to seize divers clerks, peers and other folk of the land. You make suit, quite unfitting and against the law of the land, which you are bound by the oath taken at your coronation to keep and maintain, and contrary to the great Charter." The only place for judging such charges as Edward had brought against his chief subjects was parliament—the national assembly in which an English king could look into the hearts and minds of his people. "For the salvation of your enterprise," he urged, "be willing to take to you the great and the wise of your land . . . Be willing, sire, if it please you, therefore, to cause them . . . to assemble in a fitting place where we and others may securely come." The archbishop had been accused by his master; he was entitled to be judged by his peers in parliament.

It was a tremendous claim going to the root of the problem men had been trying to solve since the days of Magna Carta; of how to allow a king the overriding executive power on which the peace and safety of the realm depended and at the same time to safeguard the rights and liberties of the subject. And though the angry king denounced Stratford as "a wily serpent and cunning fox," and, with Kilsby's help, published a venomous attack on him, the *libellus famosus*, it soon became clear that the archbishop had judged the issue rightly. Once again, as in 1297 and 1327, magnates, knights of the shire and Londoners came together under the archbishop's lead to protest at a royal attempt to rule by personal will instead of by established law. Stratford's demand to be tried by his peers was a shrewd stroke, for it was a right that every magnate in the land wished to secure for himself.

So it came about that the national crisis set in motion by the king was resolved, as Stratford had proposed, in "a full parliament." Edward's need for supplies to meet his debts and maintain the Scottish war forced him to yield, and at the end of April the magnates and commons met at Westminster. When Kilsby tried to bar the primate from the House of Lords, John de Warenne earl of Surrey, doyen of the independent magnates, and his nephew, the Earl of Arundel, protested that those who by their rank should be foremost in parliament were being excluded while others who had no right there were being admitted. "Lord king," Warenne is reported to have said after the manner of his famous grandfather of *quo warranto* fame, "how goes this parliament? Things were not wont to be thus. They are all now turned upside down."[1] And though Stratford never received the trial *in pleno parliamento* which he had been demanding, since the king dropped his charges and, later, even had them annulled as contrary to truth and reason, the principle for which he had contended was triumphantly vindicated. It was Edward who, needing the support of his people, had had to submit to the judgment of parliament. Seeing that, if he was to have their support in his wars, he must conciliate them, he yielded with grace and good sense.

Before the session ended in May, in reply to petitions from both lords and commons the royal assent was given to an act which not only conceded the right of peers to trial by their fellow magnates in parliament before suffering imprisonment or forfeiture, but made all ministers and officials of the Crown liable to answer to the same high court for breaches of *Magna Carta* and the statutes. The commons also obtained a promise that parliamentary commissioners should audit the moneys voted for the war and that the lords should share in the appointment of ministers. Though the magnates later allowed the king to withdraw this last radical concession as unworkable and incompatible with the custom and law of the realm and the prerogative, Edward made no further attempt to govern without consultation with the nation's traditional leaders and his customary constitutional advisers.

·   ·   ·   ·   ·   ·   ·   ·

So far, except for his victory at Sluys, the king's war to recover his French fiefs had been a costly fiasco. Nor, since France came

[1] *French Chronicle of London* (ed. G. J. Aungier, *Camden Soc.* 1844), 90, cit. *Wilkinson*, II, 193.

to Scotland's rescue, had his campaign to reduce the Scots to
vassalage fared any better. While parliament was discussing the
royal charges against the archbishop, Douglas's son, the knight
of Liddesdale, captured Edinburgh castle by the old ruse of
blocking the drawbridge with a supply-wagon. A few weeks
later Bruce's son, King David, now eighteen, returned from
France. When at the end of 1341 the truce expired, Edward
took the field against him, spending Christmas at Melrose
abbey and afterwards "riding" through Ettrick forest in what the
chronicler described as "a very ill season," his foray into that
war-wrecked, starving land achieved nothing. By February 1342
the Scots were once more over the border, raiding Northumberland where they "brent much corn and houses." And at Easter,
Alexander Ramsay of Dalhousie captured Roxburgh, the last
English stronghold in Scotland.

Yet that year, with the death of the Duke of Brittany, a new
opportunity opened for England. When his younger brother,
John de Montfort, visited Windsor to obtain the earldom of
Richmond to which, under English law, he was heir, he secured
from Edward a promise of support for his claim to Brittany
against the late duke's son-in-law, Charles of Blois, who was
backed by the French king and French-speaking aristocracy
against the Celtic-speaking peasantry and townsfolk who favoured
de Montfort. The crippling of France's naval strength at Sluys
had made the maintenance of an English base in Brittany possible,
and in the spring of 1342, after a French army had overrun the
duchy and captured de Montfort, a small expedition was despatched to rescue his countess who was besieged at Hennebont.
Arriving just in time its commander, Sir Walter Manny, took the
offensive. Later in the summer he was joined by a larger force
under the constable, William Bohun earl of Northampton.
With him came Edward's French protégé, Robert of Artois, and
his cousin, Henry of Derby—heir to the royal earldom of Lancaster and the most famous English fighting man of his day.

In Brittany the English had no longer to wait on their allies
as in Flanders. They were free to fight when they chose. If the
enemy outnumbered them they could apply the tactics that had
proved successful at Halidon Hill—a well-chosen defensive
position, the men-at-arms dismounted in the centre, the horses

and baggage wagons in laager in the rear, the archers on either flank, behind projecting hedges of stakes, to enfilade the attacking cavalry. Landing near Brest and forcing Charles of Blois to abandon the blockade of that town, Northampton laid siege to Morlaix. Here against a French relieving army seven or eight times as large as his own he won on September 30th, 1342 the first English victory on the continent since the days of Coeur de Lion. Fighting with their backs to a wood, his troops were at one time surrounded, but, with their incomparable archery, shot their way out and put the French to flight. Morlaix fell almost immediately, while a hundred miles away, by a use of amphibious power, Robert of Artois captured Vannes, the second city of Brittany. A few weeks later this brave French exile, with his handful of Englishmen, was overwhelmed by superior force and died of his wounds.

By this time Edward himself was in Brittany. Having waited for several weeks at Sandwich for the return of Northampton's transports which were held up by adverse winds, he had marched his troops to Portsmouth and seized enough ships to take them to Brest. Though it was now the end of October he at once took the field. Sweeping across the peninsula in two columns, one under his personal command, he occupied Vannes and laid siege to Rennes, while a small flying force reached the walls of Nantes on the Loire.

With southern Brittany lost, King Philip was compelled to intervene. Gathering an army at Angers far larger than Edward's sea-borne expedition, he marched to the relief of Nantes and Rennes. The long-awaited test between the rival kings seemed imminent when two cardinals arrived from Avignon to negotiate an armistice. As both armies were now running short of supplies, their mission proved successful. By the three-years' truce of Malestroit or Morbihan it was agreed that both sides should keep what they had won. De Montfort's supporters retained the southern and western parts of the country and those of Charles of Blois the northern and eastern. The truce was also extended to the chief participants' clients, Scotland and Flanders.

Though the war had now gone on for six years Edward had still made no impression on France, while Scotland was almost as free as in the days of Bruce. He had neither recovered his lost lands in Guienne nor unified Britain. Yet his dream of doing so and of winning immortal fame by arms remained. It may have been during his long and stormy voyage home, in which he narrowly escaped shipwreck on the Spanish coast, that he conceived the idea of founding an Order of Christian chivalry to perpetuate the ideals of his hero, King Arthur, and give expression to his desire for knightly glory. Nine months after his return, in January 1344, he held a tournament at Windsor "for the recreation and solace of men of war who delight in arms." During it he and nineteen of his bravest knights jousted for three days against all comers. "After the end of the jousts," the rector of Wraysbury wrote,

"the lord king caused to be proclaimed that no lord or lady should presume to depart but await until the morning to know the lord king's pleasure . . . About the first hour the king caused himself to be very solemnly arrayed in royal and festive vestures and the crown placed upon his head. The queen was likewise most nobly adorned. . . . Mass having been celebrated, the lord king went out of the chapel to the place appointed for the assembly. In which place the lord king, after touching his gospels, took an oath that he himself, whilst the means were possible to him, would begin a Round Table in the same manner as the lord Arthur, formerly king of England . . . To observe, sustain and promote which the earls of Derby, Salisbury, Warwick, Arundel, Pembroke and Suffolk . . . made a like oath. Which being done, the trumpets and nakers sounding all together, the guests hastened to a feast . . . complete with richness of fare, variety of dishes and overflowing abundance of drinks; the delight was unutterable, the comfort inestimable, the enjoyment without murmuring, the hilarity without care."[1]

When Edward of Windsor set his heart on a project no trouble or expense was too great. Within a few weeks workmen were covering the bridges of the castle with sand for the passage of stone and timber to build a round tower crowning the Norman mote. On February 16th letters patent were issued to William

[1] Adam de Murimath, cit. W. H. St. John Hope, *Windsor Castle*, i, 112.

of Ramsey, the king's master-mason—designer of the new octagonal lantern at Ely—and the royal carpenter William of Hurley, empowering them to choose as many masons and carpenters from "the cities, towns and other places in England" as they might need. Over seven hundred workmen were engaged at wages ranging from 4s. a week for master-masons to 2d. a day for labourers.[1] And within the castle a huge circular table was made, to accommodate the companions of the knightly brotherhood at an annual Whitsuntide feast.

Yet Fate had more in store for England's king than to preside at tournaments. Before the year ended, contending with the same Celtic separatism in Brittany as Edward in Scotland, Philip seized de Montfort's chief supporters and put them to death. Escaping to England, de Montfort did homage to Edward as king of France and appealed to him to avenge the broken truce and recover his duchy. The challenge was accepted. While the constable, Northampton, returned to Brittany with de Montfort, Edward himself, using his new-found freedom of movement at sea, prepared a triple attack on France from north, west and south. Despatching his cousin Derby as lieutenant of Aquitaine to rally the loyal forces in Gascony, he sailed in July 1345 for Flanders with the fifteen-year-old prince of Wales to take counsel with van Artevelde.

Once again the allies on whose aid he had counted failed him. After conferring with Edward on board his flagship at Sluys for a joint invasion of Artois, van Artevelde on his return to Ghent was murdered by a mob of discontented weavers. Though, bound to England by their need for wool, the Flemish burghers eventually remained loyal to their alliance, Edward was forced to return home with his plans for attacking France from the north still-born. In Brittany, too, his hopes miscarried. For though on reaching Brest the constable's lieutenant, Sir Thomas Dagworth, struck swiftly at the forces which had overrun southern Brittany and, marching a hundred miles in seven days, defeated a French army near Ploermel, de Montfort soon afterwards fell ill and died, while his countess, unhinged by her sufferings, went mad, leaving the English to wage war on behalf of her six-year-old son unsupported.

[1] W. H. St. John Hope, *Windsor Castle*, I, 113-18.

But at this juncture events in south-western France took a spectacular turn. Landing at Bayonne in June 1345 and marching to Bordeaux, Derby, with five hundred men-at-arms and two thousand archers, had been received with immense enthusiasm by the Gascons, who after six years of resisting the French had developed an almost passionate loyalty to their absent English duke. A soldier in the tradition of William the Marshal, simple, pious and courteous,[1] Henry of Derby had fought in every English campaign since Bannockburn and had been a crusader in Cyprus, Prussia and Granada. He was now forty-six—an age at which most men were then considered past fighting. But he had lost none of the fire and speed of youth. Assembling his little force at Libourne he suddenly struck eastwards at Bergerac, fifty miles up the Dordogne, where the French had withdrawn after his landing. Keeping the ramparts under continuous attack by his archers, he stormed the town at the end of August. Then, having regained most of the Agenais, he turned north against Perigord where he established an outpost at Auberoche, only nine miles from the capital, Périgueux, before returning to Bordeaux with his prisoners and booty.

Derby's six weeks' campaign made an immense impression on southern France. So did his courteous treatment of his prisoners and the civil population. It aroused, too, the French military authorities to action. Early in October they laid siege to Auberoche with 7000 men. Receiving an urgent appeal from its garrison, Derby at once gathered 400 men-at-arms and 800 archers and, ordering his second-in-command, the Earl of Pembroke, to follow, marched at high speed to the relief of the town. Hiding his men in a wood, he waited for twenty-four hours for Pembroke, then decided to attack without him rather than fail the garrison. Having made sure that every man knew what to do, he fell on the besiegers as they were cooking their evening meal, his archers spraying them with arrows and his men-at-arms charging out of the wood with shouts of "A Derby! A Derby!" In the confused fighting that followed, the enemy's

[1] At a time when literacy was only beginning to reach the aristocratic laity Henry was remarkable for writing two widely read works of devotion, in one of which, "Mercy Gramercy," he set down all the sins he could recall having committed and all the mercies he had received, asking God's forgiveness for the first and giving thanks for the second.

superiority in numbers was beginning to tell when the garrison threw themselves on the besiegers' rear. By nightfall the French commander and all his lieutenants were prisoners, including eight viscounts and the flower of the Languedoc nobility. "There was many a proper feat of arms done," wrote Froissart, "many taken and rescued again . . . If the night had not come on, there had but few escaped. No English man-at-arms but had two or three prisoners."

Striking once more, Derby turned south to take La Réole in the Garonne valley, thirty miles above Bordeaux. Without a proper siege-train he succeeded after ten weeks, not only in capturing the town—for years a standing threat to the capital—but in bluffing the garrison into the belief that the walls had been undermined, whereas his miners had found them so strongly built as to be impregnable. According to Froissart, the governor, Sir Agout des Baux, asked for an interview with Derby, upon which there ensued the following conversation:

"My lord, you know the king of France sent me to this castle and town to defend them to the best of my ability. You know how I have acquitted myself and would wish to continue. But a man cannot always stay where he wishes. If it will please you to let us depart with our lives and goods, I and my men will yield you the castle."

"Sir Agout, you shall not go so easily. You know well we have you where we wish and that your castle stands upon stays. Yield unconditionally and we shall receive you."

"My lord, if we were to do so, I think you have honour and gentleness enough to deal courteously with us . . . For God's sake blemish not your nobility for a poor sort of soldiers that be here within, who have won with much pain and peril their poor living. For if the least of us should not have mercy as well as the greatest, we would rather sell our lives."

At this Derby and his lieutenant, Sir Walter Manny, withdrew and pretended to confer, returning with the answer that the garrison might depart with their armour and no more. In this way they made themselves masters of the strongest fortress on the Garonne.

With Aiguillon, thirty miles up the river, already taken by Lord Stafford, the entire Agenais had been cleared. In four months two provinces and fifty towns and castles had been regained by a few thousand archers and men-at-arms. Derby, who that autumn had inherited his father's earldom of Lancaster, had proved that France was no longer invulnerable. For the first time since John's loss of Normandy a French king had been forced to take England's military threats seriously. By the spring of 1346 the whole chivalry of southern France was mobilised at Toulouse under Philip's eldest son, the Duke of Normandy, to recover his lost province.

.   .   .   .

Meanwhile, fired by the success of his soldiers and resolved to share in their glory, Edward was preparing to strike. His brilliant cousin had given him the chance for which he had been waiting for nine years. While the dauphin that April laid siege to Aiguillon, and Derby, with only a fraction of his force, watched from La Réole for a chance to relieve the tiny garrison, Edward started to assemble on the Hampshire coast the largest army that had ever sailed from England. He raised it, not by the feudal levy of the past nor even by over-much reliance on the commissions of array which Edward I had adapted to conscript the shire militia for war, but by offering those willing to fight high wages and still more tempting prospects of ransom and plunder.

He was able to do so because he had learnt from experience the value of the representative taxing assembly that his grandfather had created out of the Great Council of the realm. By observing the forms of parliamentary consultation and ruling with the advice of the great officers of Church and state in whom the taxpayers' representatives reposed their trust, he could obtain the wherewithal to raise a professional army far superior in quality to anything feudal France could put into the field. Developed during the past half century in the course of many a bitter tussle between Crown and taxpayer, a system of taxation by consent gave to the English king financial resources unknown to his Valois rival, though the latter ruled a kingdom far richer and more populous.

It was a system that assured the maximum fiscal support for the Crown with the minimum of hardship for the subject. Assessed for every shire and township by local commissioners on a nominal and by now standardised valuation much below the value of the real wealth taxed and so capable, in a time of rising wealth, of being repeated without arousing too much popular resentment, a parliamentary subsidy of a tenth from the royal demesne lands and boroughs and a fifteenth from the rest of the country brought in approximately £38,000. A tenth granted at the same time by the representatives of the clergy—voted, not in parliament but, as they preferred it, in their provincial councils—produced a further £13,000, five-sixths of it from Canterbury and the remainder from York.

Such wartime subsidies, lay and ecclesiastical, together with the continuance of the *maltote*, enabled Edward to obtain credit on far less ruinous terms than in the past. He was still the same extravagant spender, refusing to be bound by any considerations of economy in pursuit of his darling objectives of war and chivalric splendour and display. His Italian creditors, ruined by his borrowings, had by now gone bankrupt,[1] but by offering an exclusive licence to export wool through the Bruges staple, he had raised a loan of £100,000 from a group of native financiers who included his old accommodator, William de la Pole of Hull, the London merchants Walter de Cheriton and Thomas de Swanland, and two great East Anglican factors, John de Wesenham and Thomas de Melchbourn of Lynn.

Since composing his quarrel with the archbishop, Edward had made no further attempt to dispense with ecclesiastical ministers. His chancellors, treasurers and keepers of the Privy Seal were now once more all clerics. In 1344 he appointed as treasurer William de Edington who for the past three years had been keeper of the Wardrobe and formerly collector of the ninth south of the Trent. A West countryman who, after promotion to the see of Winchester, began the reconstruction of the cathedral's nave and built the lovely collegiate church of Edington in his native Wiltshire, the service to his time and country of this dis-

---

[1] He is said to have owed the Bardi and Peruzzi half a million pounds.

creet, efficient prelate statesman was that he weaned the king
from his earlier and disastrous reliance for financing the war on
his private household department, the Chamber. By confining
the latter's functions to those of a subordinate pay-office to serve
the army in the field and bringing it and every other branch of
royal expenditure under the control of the Exchequer, he assured
that concord between Crown and taxpayer, government and
parliament which for the rest of the present war was the basis
of England's strength. For the next nineteen years he served the
king in the highest offices, first as treasurer, then, after 1356, as
chancellor.

Having the nation's financial resources behind him, Edward
was able to make a royal campaign a national one. He raised
his army by indentures made with local leaders with a vocation
for war, under which they recruited, at agreed rates of pay, the
precise numbers and types of fighting men required. Each indenture specified the number to be raised, the time for which
they were to serve and the contribution to be made by the
Exchequer. Thus, for the first Brittany campaign William
Montague contracted to bring into the field six knights, twenty
other men-at-arms and twenty-four archers for £76 for every
forty days, the king maintaining them while in the field.[1]

The contingents thus raised were known as "retinues." An
earl, who was paid 8s. a day for his services, would contract to
raise, say sixty men-at-arms, of whom ten should be knights and
a hundred and twenty bowmen, all equipped and with horses, for
three months to a year "at the accustomed wages of war," together with pages called *valets aux armes* who served as apprentices
to the knights, cleaned their armour and looked after their horses
when dismounted. A commander-in-chief like the Earl of Lancaster would contract on an even larger scale; on one of his
campaigns he provided six bannerets, ninety knights, 486 men-
at-arms and 423 mounted archers.

The rates of pay were high. At a time when in some places
land let for as little as fourpence an acre a year, a mounted

[1] On a grander scale was the Earl of Salisbury's "regard" from the
Exchequer of £2000 17s. 7½d. for the services from 7th December 1337 to
13th June 1338, of himself, one banneret, 23 knights, 106 men-at-arms, 30
mounted archers, 56 Welsh footmen and 60 sailors, calculated at the set rate
of 500 marks for 100 men-at-arms for a quarter of a year. *Speculum*, XIX, 144.

archer received sixpence a day if he provided his own horse or threepence otherwise. Even the Welsh spearmen, the lowest grade of professional fighting men, were paid twopence. The wage of a mounted man-at-arms was a shilling a day, of a knight-bachelor twice as much, of a banneret four shillings a day or about £10 in modern money. Bannerets were knights of proved valour and experience who, distinguished by a rectangular banner, arrayed and directed contingents in the field, commanded castles and acted as staff officers to the commanders-in-chief. Such were Sir John Chandos and Sir Robert Knollys, the Cheshire yeoman who rose to be one of the most famous captains of the age and, through ransom and plunder, one of the richest.

Knights carried a triangular pennon and led the men-at-arms or armoured troopers who, like them, usually provided their own horses and horse-armour. They were armed with a long sword and either a lance or battle-mace, with a dagger for in-fighting. The mail-armour of the past was now giving way to plate-armour; a knight in the thirteen-forties wore a short sur-coat marked with his armorial bearings and a baldric or sword-belt over a metal breast-plate, plate-guards for his arms and legs, and on his head a heavy helm crowned with his crest and closed, when in action, with a vizor. There is a picture of one in the Luttrell psalter, bidding farewell to his lady before a tournament, his charger magnificently decked in heraldic trappings.

The archers, who, as a result of their spectacular successes, had become the largest part of every English army, wore either light steel breast-plates or padded hauberks of boiled leather, rough frieze cloaks and steel caps, not unlike the splinter helmets of modern infantrymen. In addition to their bows and sheaves of goose-quill arrows, they carried short swords, knives and steel-tipped stakes for building protective hedges against cavalry. Though they fought in separate contingents or phal-anxes, for purposes of recruitment and discipline they served under the lords or knights who paid them, the army's disciplinary unit being a "lance"[1]—a professional team, rather like the crew of a modern aircraft, consisting of a knight or man-at-arms, two archers, a swordsman or *courtillier* and a pair of pages armed with daggers.

[1] From this the title of lance-corporal derives.

The army was also accompanied by auxiliaries: Welsh spear-men and light unarmoured horsemen called hobelars—often drawn from Ireland—for reconnaissance and terrorising the country; miners from Durham or the Forest of Dean for siege-operations, smiths, armourers and pavilioners, carpenters for making bridges, *cementarii* for building fortifications, and wagoners for the baggage-train. The king himself was accompanied by a bodyguard of personal knights and archers and a band of min-strels—a dozen trumpeters, a clarioner, fiddler, pipers, a wait or two, a nakerer, a citole and a man playing a shawm.[1] For their services to morale these musicians ranked as archers.

Running through this English army and transcending differ-ences of rank and class was a new-found pride in common nationhood. Two-thirds of those who served in it were yeomen armed with a weapon which, as Morlaix and Auberoche had proved, could match and more than match the proud feudal cavalry which had lorded it in Europe for three centuries. Leading them were the representatives of all the great feudal houses—Bohun and Beauchamp, Warenne and Arundel, Morti-mer, Despenser, Ufford, Hastings, de Vere—whose ambitions and jealousies in the last generation had all but wrecked the realm, but who, won over by their young king's generosity and magnanimity, were now united behind him and ready to follow him anywhere. Among them were his father's one-time jailers, the lords Berkeley and Maltravers, and the sixteen-year-old grandson of Roger Mortimer, to whom he had restored the fallen traitor's castle of Radnor and other lands.

Such was the force, prepared with all the king's tireless drive and attention to military detail, that with its bright pavilions and banners encamped that May and June on Southsea common, waiting for a wind to carry it to the continent. Some imagined

[1] A naker was a kettledrum; a citole a plucked-string instrument, the ancestor of the guitar; and a shawm a wind one, ancestor of the oboe.

"Then saw I in another place
Standing in a largë space
Of them that maken bloody sound
In trumpet, beam and clarion;
For in fight and blood-shedding
Is usëd gladly clarioning."
Chaucer, *The House of Fame.*

that its destination would be Brittany, where, after surprising
Roche-Derrien during a twenty-four hours' winter's march of
forty-five miles, Northampton and Sir Thomas Dagworth had
opened the summer campaign with a flying-raid across the
duchy; this had culminated on June 9th in the victory of St.
Pol-de-Leon when Dagworth's archers, surrounded by a vastly
superior army under Charles of Blois, shot their way out of a
hopeless predicament. Others thought that the king would sail
to Flanders where that June the men of Ghent, Bruges and Ypres
had agreed to invade Artois and to whose help he had recently
sent six hundred archers. But most supposed that the king and
his host were bound for Gascony where the Earl of Pembroke
and Sir Walter Manny were still holding out in Aiguillon against
the dauphin's vast army and the strongest siege-train in Europe,
while Lancaster with a few thousand archers and men-at-arms
at La Réole barred the road to Bordeaux.

Yet Edward intended none of these things. When at long
last on July 11th, 1346 the south-westerly winds changed and the
great armada of seven hundred vessels sailed from St. Helens,
sealed orders opened at sea revealed that its destination was the
Cotentin peninsula of Normandy, the rich duchy once owned by
Edward's Norman ancestors and lost by King John. One of its
nobles, Godfrey de Harcourt, who had taken refuge at Edward's
court, had told him that its people, being unused to war, would
be unable to resist and that he would find there great wealth
and cities not even walled. By ravaging it and threatening Paris
he could draw the dauphin's army from Aiguillon and, linking
hands with the Flemings in Artois, strike at France from three
sides.

By the secrecy with which he had cloaked his plans Edward
had kept the French guessing. Having to guard eight hundred
miles of coastline from the Garonne to the Scheldt their fleet was
strong nowhere; Edward's, concentrated in one place, was able
to put the army ashore on July 12th at St. Vaast near La Hogue
almost without opposition. Once ashore he wasted no time. On
the 18th, after knighting the Prince of Wales and some of his
young companions, he began his march on Rouen. Crossing the
marshes at the south-eastern foot of the Cotentin peninsula,
where his pioneers and carpenters repaired the demolished

bridges over the Vire, he reached St. Lo on the 22nd. By keeping abreast with the army's left flank the fleet provided a moveable base, while the troops lived on the countryside, avenging the raids of Norman seamen on the English south-coast towns by burning their harbours and ships. The Welsh spearmen and Irish hobelars particularly distinguished themselves in this atrocious business—the usual accompaniment of fourteenth-century warfare—though after a few days, the king, as claimant to the French throne, issued an order threatening death to any soldier who should "set on fire towns or manors, . . . rob churches or holy places, do harm to the aged, the children or women of his realm."

Edward's new French subjects, however, showed no enthusiasm for their would-be sovereign. The peasants fled in terror from his march, and, when on July 25th he summoned Caen, the Bishop of Bayeux tore up the summons and imprisoned his messenger. Yet, though a formidable town—larger, a chronicler wrote, than any English city save London—the invaders carried it in a day after the archers had out-shot the crossbowmen defending the Orne crossings, and the fleet, sailing up the river from Ouistreham, had joined in the fight. They took a rich haul of prisoners and a treaty made eight years before by King Philip with the Norman authorities for an invasion of England. This Edward sent home to be read in parliament.

On the last day of July the march to the Seine was resumed. On August 2nd the army reached Lisieux. But on the same day the French king entered Rouen forty miles ahead, interposing his force between the English and their Flemish allies who, two hundred miles to the north, were just setting out from Ypres. As soon as news had reached him of Edward's landing he had raised the oriflamme at St. Denis and, summoning his son from Aiguillon to join him, had hurried to the Norman capital, gathering troops as he marched. The Seine here was three hundred yards wide and, with the city held in force, the English could not hope to cross.

Instead, on reaching the river at Elboeuf, twelve miles above Rouen, they turned upstream to seek a narrower crossing. By doing so they abandoned their communications with England but threatened Paris. For the next six days the rival armies marched south-westwards along opposite sides of the Seine. Everywhere the English found the bridges demolished or strongly held. But on the 13th, when they were only a dozen miles from the capital, Edward allowed the French to outmarch him and, by a sudden feint, turned back to Poissy where the bridge, only partially destroyed, was lightly guarded. Crossing by a single sixty-foot beam only a foot wide, Northampton, the constable, got a detachment to the far side. For the next two days, while skirmishing parties set fire to St. Cloud and other villages under the western walls of Paris to deceive the enemy, the carpenters worked feverishly to repair the bridge. Meanwhile, though by now in far superior strength, King Philip remained in a frenzy of indecision, marching first to one side of his capital and then the other, uncertain whether the English were about to assault it or to move south to relieve Aiguillon.

On August 15th the carpenters finished their work, and during that night and next morning the army and its baggage train crossed the Seine. In the next five days it marched seventy miles due north, hoping to cross the Somme between Amiens and Abbeville and join hands with the Flemings who were besieging Bethune, fifty miles beyond that river. But though he had been temporarily outwitted, when he found that his foe had crossed the Seine King Philip acted with equal speed. Realising at last Edward's relative weakness, he covered the seventy-three miles from Paris to Amiens in three days, ordering the feudal levies of the north to join him there. With him were the flower of France's chivalry, together with King John of Bohemia and his son, Charles of Moravia — titular King of the Romans and the rival of Edward's former ally, the Emperor Louis.

The position of the English was grave in the extreme. Between them and their Flemish allies in Artois lay the marshy valley of the Somme, with the French king at Amiens only a day's march away and every bridge over the river in his hands. All contact had been lost with the fleet, whose seamen, with their usual indiscipline, had returned to England in the wake of the ships that had taken home the sick and the spoils of Caen. The army's food supplies were almost exhausted and in the closing stages of their march the troops had been living on unripe fruit.

After covering nearly three hundred miles their boots were worn out and the horses dying for lack of forage.

Edward had been far too bold. But he showed no sign of his anxiety; " he was so great hearted," a contemporary wrote of him, "that he never blanched or changed countenance at any ill-hap or trouble soever." On August 23rd he started westwards in the hope of finding a crossing above Abbeville, but, as the estuary here widened to two miles, the prospect was unpromising. Scarcely had he set out when news arrived that Philip had left Amiens and, moving up the south bank of the river to attack, was already within a mile of Airaines where the English had spent the previous night.

Cut off in a strange land and without maps—a military commodity then unknown—the king ordered the prisoners to be brought before him and offered a huge reward for anyone who would reveal a crossing place. A native of the district told him of a concealed causeway across the estuary at Blanchetaque, midway between Abbeville and the sea, where at low tide a man could cross waist-deep. Without hesitation Edward decided to take the risk.

It was a hundred and thirty years since his great-great-grandfather, John, had lost his baggage and treasure in the Wash in a similar crossing. Before dawn on the 24th, marching the six miles to the ford in single column his advance-guard reached the river. The far bank was held by a French force of between three and four thousand men. As soon as the tide was low enough for a man to stand without being swept away, the troops started to cross, led by Hugh Despenser whose father had been hanged on a fifty-foot gallows by Edward's mother. Carrying their bows above their heads to keep them dry, the archers struggled through a mile and a half of water, while the knights followed on horse-back. A few hundred yards from the northern bank they came within range of the enemy's cross-bowmen but continued to advance until they were within killing distance. Then, standing ten abreast on the causeway and shooting over one another's heads, they loosed their usual devastating hail. When their arrows were exhausted they stepped into the deeper water on either side and let the mounted armour splash past them into the shallows where, after a brisk skirmish, it put the French cavalry to flight.

Meanwhile on the south bank Edward's rearguard had been holding off the advance echelons of Philip's host until the baggage wagons, with their precious load of arrows and cannon, had passed through the water, now starting rapidly to rise. Save for a few stragglers who were caught by the tide the whole army passed over in safety. The enemy, barred by the rising flood, could only watch in amazement.[1]

After crossing the Somme the English fanned out. The constable pursued the enemy towards Abbeville, while Hugh Despenser pushed down the estuary as far as the little port of Crotoy where he seized some wine-ships. By nightfall the whole army was encamped in the forest of Crécy, a few miles north of the ford. Edward was now in his hereditary fief of Ponthieu. Though his troops were still short of rations, their morale was high, for in a deeply religious age the passage of the river had seemed a miracle. The king therefore decided to stand and give battle. The odds against him were immense, but with so cautious an adversary such an opportunity might never recur.

All day on Friday the 25th, while the French were recrossing the Somme Edward searched for a defensive position. He found it on a low ridge facing south-west, between the villages of Crécy and Wadicourt. Behind lay a wood—the Bois de Crécy-Grange —into which and the forest of Crécy on his right his woodland-trained archers could withdraw in case of need.

On the morning of August 26th, 1346, having attended Mass and "committed his cause to God and the Blessed Virgin," Edward marched his army to its position. Allowing for losses he had now about 13,000 men, of whom more than half were archers, and, at the outside, some three thousand knights and men-at-arms. Under his directions the marshals deployed the latter in three divisions or "battles," two of them a little way down the forward slope of the ridge, which was about a mile long, and the third under his personal command in reserve. He himself took up his station in a windmill in the centre, with an extensive view of the valley which the French would have to cross. The right-hand

[1] The man who led the archers and who died three years later, during the Black Death, lies in his armour of alabaster, his hands crossed in prayer and a lion at his feet, in the Despenser tomb in Tewkesbury abbey whose glorious vaulting posterity owes to his and his wife's munificence.

division was under the earls of Warwick and Oxford with
the sixteen-year-old Prince of Wales in titular command,
and the other commanded by the constable. As usual, the
knights and men-at-arms were dismounted in single line, their
horses being taken by the pages to the wagon-leaguer in the
rear.

Forming four projecting salients on both flanks of each of the
forward divisions were the archers, with Welsh spearmen in
support. Before retiring to the leaguer the baggage-wagons
unloaded a supply of arrows along their lines. In front, to protect themselves from cavalry, they hammered in iron-pointed
stakes and dug pot-holes as the Scots had taught their predecessors to do. Such a formation, like that at Halidon Hill, was
calculated to force the attackers into two narrowing gulleys where
they would have to contend with the English armour while raked
by arrows from the flanks.

When the troops were all posted, the king rode along the
ranks on a small palfrey, carrying a white wand and wearing a
crimson surcoat of golden leopards. To each contingent he spoke
a few words. Beside him was Sir Guy de Brian,[1] bearing the
dragon banner of Wessex—the standard under which the
English had fought at Hastings. It was a symbol of the national
character Edward had given his army—so different to that of the
feudal hosts of the past. "Next to God," it was said of him, "he
reposed his confidence in the valour of his subjects." Norman,
Angevin, Saxon and Celt, his men all thought of themselves as
Englishmen.

After the king's inspection the army dispersed for the midday
meal which the cooks had been preparing in the baggage-
leaguer, the men-at-arms leaving their helmets to mark their
stations and the archers their bows and arrows. It had been
arranged that the trumpets should recall them at the first sign
of the enemy, who were now believed to be moving up from
Abbeville. During the afternoon there was a heavy shower,
which brought the archers scurrying back to their lines to guard
their bowstrings, each man unstringing his and placing it in a

---

[1] His effigy, still coloured in faded Garter blue, can be seen in Tewkesbury
abbey. He married the widow of Hugh Despenser, hero of the Blanchetaque
crossing.

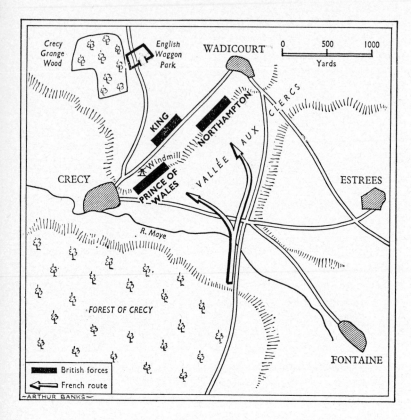

A Plan of Crécy

coil under his helmet. Afterwards the sun came out and the
men sat down in their lines with their weapons in front of them.
There was still no sign of the French, and it was felt that there
would be no battle that day.

But a little before four o'clock the trumpets sounded and
everyone stood to arms. Coming out of the woods three miles
to the south-east along the track still known as *le chemin d'armée*
was the French vanguard. For a whole hour the English watched
as Philip's immense host moved into view, "the fresh shining
armour, the banners waving in the wind, the companies in good
order, riding a soft pace." According to the lowest estimate that

has come down from the fourteenth century, they were 40,000 strong, of whom more than 12,000 were mounted knights and men-at-arms. They rode forward in eight successive divisions, so that there seemed no end. The advance-guard was commanded by the blind King John of Bohemia—a romantic figure and world-famous warrior—who was accompanied by the French king's brother, the Count of Alençon, and the Count of Flanders whom Edward's allies, the burghers of Ghent, had driven from his country. The centre was under the Duke of Lorraine with Philip's nephew, the Count of Blois, as lieutenant.

The king—"Philip Valois tyrant of the French", as the English chroniclers called him—followed with the rearguard, together with the German King of the Romans, Charles of Moravia, and the exiled King of Majorca. There were nearly a score of ruling counts, French, German, Luxemburger and Spanish. It was not so much a national army as the embodiment of the international chivalry which for three centuries had dominated the battlefields of the continent, commanded by the greatest monarch in Christendom. Above him waved the ori-flamme—the sacred banner flown when no quarter was to be given to France's enemies. For there had been disputes on the previous night about the allocation and ransom of the prisoners, and to prevent quarrelling the king had given orders to slay them all.

In addition to this array of chivalry there marched among the vanguard six or seven thousand Gascon crossbowmen, the best trained troops on the continent and the only professionals in the host. The rest of the army was composed of peasant levies—the "communes" as they were called—low-spirited serfs considered incapable of standing up to gentlemen, but useful to follow in the wake of their mounted superiors and help crush the foe by sheer weight of numbers. In the French army infantry were despised; it was knights—"the crested helmets"—who counted.

Goliath was pitted against David, but David had a sling. David, too, had discipline which Goliath lacked. When the French vanguard reached the valley in front of the English position the sun was already starting to sink, and Philip's advisers urged him to halt for the night and deploy for battle in the morning. To this, the only sane course, the king, who had not expected to find the English barring his path, agreed. But his vassals had other views. Seeing the English with their banners on the ridge, the young knights—arrogant and inexperienced—pressed forward, impatiently confident that they were at their mercy. Before even a blow had been struck the French army was out of control and committed to an attack undeployed.

The vanguard, therefore, came straight on, halting only to let the Genoese bowmen open the attack. With trumpets and clarions sounding they started to climb the ridge. The setting sun was in their eyes and it was hard to focus their target, waiting motionless and ready.

At this point, wrote Froissart, "when the Genoese began to approach, they made a great leap and cry to abash the Englishmen. But they stood still and stirred not for all that. Then the Genoese again the second time made another leap and a fell cry and stept forward a little, and the English removed not one foot. Thirdly again they leapt and cried and went forward till they came within shot; then they shot fiercely with their crossbows. Then the English archers stept forth one pace and let fly their arrows so wholly together and so thick that it seemed snow." Firing four or five times faster than the crossbowmen, they shot them out of the field. To add to the Italians' confusion and terror, two or three English cannons—a novelty from the Tower armoury which had been dragged round France and concealed among the archers—opened fire, sending their balls of iron and stone[1] rolling through the densely packed ranks amid flames and smoke.

As the Genoese broke, the French knights, with a cry of, "Ride down the rascals," charged through their ranks, trampling down the wounded and dying. They rode in a dense, glittering line of solid armour, waving plumes and levelled lances. Everyone expected them to crush the thin, defending line of the Prince of Wales's division before them. But they never reached it. For once again the English archers stepped forward.

As their arrows, aimed at the chargers, struck home, the stately advance dissolved into disorderly heaps and clusters of dead and wounded horses and of dismounted knights weighed down by their armour. Those who went forward on foot or

[1] Several of the balls have been found buried on the battlefield. *Burne*, 197-8.

succeeded in driving their terrified beasts through the hail of arrows came up against a solid line of English men-at-arms, as steady as the archers who continued shooting down each new batch of attackers as they struggled up the hill through the fading light.

The fight had now become general, with the second French wave assailing the constable's division. But everywhere the result was the same; the mounted knights struggling to reach and break the line of the English armour opposed to them and the archers continuing to massacre their horses. There was no-one to give them orders and no-one to co-ordinate the attack. For five hours, though darkness had fallen, the mêlée continued, wave after wave of knights entering the fight only to meet the same fate. At one moment it seemed as if the Prince of Wales's slender force would be overwhelmed, and Godfrey de Harcourt hurried across to the nearest unit of the constable's division to beg its commander, Lord Arundel, to make a flanking attack to relieve the pressure. But when a similar appeal reached the king, he only remarked, "Let the boy win his spurs," for he knew that the moment to throw in his reserves had not yet come. When the messenger returned he found the prince and his companions leaning quietly on their swords, taking breath as, amid mounds of French corpses, they waited for the next attack.

Soon after midnight, after fifteen or sixteen assaults had failed, the French army began to dissolve. The dead were now piled in walls before the English lines. Among them was the blind king of Bohemia, the reins of his bridle tied to those of the knights with whom he had charged. Two archbishops, the royal Count of Alençon, the Duke of Lorraine and the counts of Blois and Flanders had all fallen. King Philip himself, his horse shot under him, was led from the field as Edward II had been from Bannockburn. There was no pursuit, for the English king, who had never once lost his grip on the battle, had forbidden his men to break rank.

As the French melted away into the darkness and no more attacks came, the exhausted victors lay down, supperless and waterless, to sleep where they had fought. When, on the misty morrow they counted the dead they found the bodies of more than 1500 knights and 10,000 common soldiers[1]. The French army had ceased to exist. Edward himself with his son attended the burial of John of Bohemia—a paladin after his own heart who had long predicted that he would die in battle against the bravest knights in the world. His helm-plume of ostrich feathers has ever since graced the arms of the princes of Wales.

A new phenomenon had appeared in the western world: the military power of England. "The might of the realm," wrote the astonished Froissart, "most standeth upon archers which are not rich men." First in Brittany, then in Guienne and now in the north, the English had shown that on their own ground they could conquer against any odds and almost without cost. Their losses at Crécy were fantastically low; the official figure was forty dead, only three of them men-at-arms.

At that moment it was in Edward's power either to lay waste the Ile de France to the walls of Paris or march south to join Lancaster. But France was a land of fortresses and castles and these could not be reduced without catapults and a siege-train. Since leaving Caen his hungry men had been without a base, and they were still without any communication with England, for Crotoy in the Somme estuary was too small to serve.

Edward therefore used his victory to achieve his primary need. Fifty miles north of Montreuil, where he marched his army after Crécy, lay the port of Calais. Commanding the Dover strait, the haunt of pirates who preyed on the traffic between London and Flanders it was the nearest continental harbour to England. If it could be turned into an English settlement the islanders would possess a permanent door into France.

On the last day of August the king wrote asking for all available cannon in the Tower to be sent to join him before Calais. By then his army was already on its way north. By the middle of September the city was invested. Joined by his allies, the Flemings, and a fleet from England, Edward settled down to starve the place into surrender before the feudal forces of France could recover and march to its relief.

·   ·   ·   ·   ·   ·   ·   ·   ·

---

[1] The valley below the ridge is known to this day as the *Vallée aux Cleros* after the English clerks who, on the king's orders, made the grim tally.

While these events were taking place in the north Henry of Lancaster had resumed the offensive in the south. For five months his lieutenants, Lord Stafford and Sir Walter Manny, had held out in Aiguillon against the entire feudal force of southern France, while Lancaster from La Réole succeeded, at least once, in running supplies into the town. But in August, on receipt of his father's urgent summons, the Duke of Normandy had proposed a truce, which Lancaster contemptuously refused. The French heir-apparent was forced, therefore, to abandon his camp and supplies to the English. The blow to French prestige was shattering.

Having revictualled Aiguillon, Lancaster set out with a thousand men-at-arms and two thousand archers to reconquer Saintonge, the seaboard province beyond the Garonne. Crossing the Charente on September 20th he covered forty miles in just over a day to take St. Jean d'Angelys, where some English soldiers had been detained in breach of a safe-conduct. "We assailed the town," he wrote, "and it was won by force, thank God, and the men brought forth from prison."[1] Then, having won golden opinions by his clemency and moderation, he struck at Poitou which his great-grandfather, Henry III, had lost a century before. Covering fifty-five miles in three days he stormed Lusignan on October 3rd, and next morning, marching fifteen miles more, assaulted the capital, Poitiers. By evening, despite its immense strength, he had broken into it in three places under cover of the usual arrow storm. As the city had refused his summons to surrender it was sacked.[2] But the burning of churches and houses was forbidden under pain of death.

At the end of October Lancaster returned to Bordeaux. "Le comte d'Erbi," as the people called him after his earlier title, was now a legend. In three campaigns, all fought against vastly superior numbers, he had recovered four provinces, overrun half Poitou and carried the English power almost to the gates of Toulouse. Then, having completed all and more than all he

[1] *Burne*, 123, from Lord Derby's despatch in French in Robert of Avesbury's Chronicle, *Rolls Series*.

[2] Froissart's much repeated allegation that the entire population was put to the sword is contradicted not only by Lancaster's contemporary despatch but by Froissart's own omission of it from later editions of his work. See *Burne*, 126.

had been sent to do, this modest, brilliant soldier handed over his lieutenancy to his successor and, at the end of the year, sailed for England to take possession of his father's earldom and estates.

The *annus mirabilis*, 1346—not to be equalled in English military annals till the days of Chatham—ended with one more victory. To save his country from the cumulative disaster threatening it Philip invoked the Franco-Scottish alliance and called on David of Scotland to invade England. Early in October, in the belief that Edward had drained the country of troops, the young king crossed the border. After burning Lanercost abbey he struck eastwards across the moors into the Durham plain. Here on October 17th, just outside the cathedral city at what became known as Neville's Cross, he encountered an English army under Archbishop de la Zouche of York, the warden of the Marches, Lord Percy, and Lord Neville of Raby. For with his foresight in military matters, in recruiting his forces for France Edward had exempted the northern barons.

According to Froissart the queen was present and before the battle went from battalion to battalion, "desiring them to do their devoir to defend the honour of her lord the king of England and, in the name of God, every man to be of good heart and courage." But as the queen was at Calais it was probably the king's cousin, the Countess of Salisbury—the nineteen-year-old princess Joan, who in the queen's absence, was the first lady in the land.[1] Once more the English archers proved irresistible, annihilating every schiltron in turn as, with stubborn courage, the Scots spearmen in their packed ranks faced that hail of driving steel and goose-quill. The royal bodyguard fought almost to the last man. By nightfall both the young king, wounded in the face by an arrow, and the famous Black Rood of Scotland were in the victors' hands. The constable, the marshal and two earls were among the dead and three other earls taken prisoner. Only the Steward escaped. The Rood was hung with the royal standard of Scotland before St. Cuthbert's shrine in Durham, and King David was taken in triumph to London where he was

[1] That Froissart's royal lady was "the Fair Maid of Kent" is further suggested by her subsequent reception in the king's camp at Calais as a heroine. Margaret Galway, "Joan of Kent and the Order of the Garter," *Birmingham University Historical Journal*, Vol. 1.

lodged in the Tower. The campaign ended with Lord Neville and the disinherited Earl of Angus invading Scotland.

.   .   .   .

Meanwhile Edward was systematically reducing Calais. Like his campaign of the summer, he made the siege a national effort, raising his expeditionary force to more than 30,000 men and requisitioning more than half the country's ships and 16,000 seamen. To house his troops during the winter he built a town of wooden huts with radiating streets and a market to which the country people could bring their produce. Here, joined by his queen and her ladies, he directed operations with his usual meticulous care for military detail. His pay-roll for the siege has survived, with its allowances for different ranks, from the Prince of Wales at a pound a day and the Bishop of Durham and thirteen earls at six and eightpence, to 15,480 unmounted archers at threepence and 4,474 Welsh pikemen at twopence. There were also 5,104 mounted archers and 500 hobelars at 6d., gunners to serve the iron bombards which flung stone balls into the town, carpenters, engineers, pavilioners and armourers at rates ranging from 3d. to 12d. a day, as well as vintners, cooks and camp followers. For nearly a year a stream of supplies poured into France—food, horse fodder, clothing, tools, pikes, lances, arrows, and saltpetre and sulphur for making gunpowder.

Unable to breach the city's double circle of walls owing to its surrounding marshes, Edward was forced to rely on starvation to overcome the resistance of its gallant governor. When in the spring a fleet from Normandy with supplies succeeded in running the blockade—impossible to maintain with the single-sail ships of the time in the Channel tides and gales—he built a fort on a spit of land dominating the harbour's mouth and mounted cannon on it. He also erected piles along the coast to stop inshore vessels and sent the constable and the Earl of Pembroke to sea to keep his admirals up to the mark. A fleet of forty-four supply-ships, which made a further attempt to reach Calais in June, was intercepted in mid-Channel and driven back with heavy loss.

By this time attempts were being made to relieve the town by land. By the spring of 1347 the French king had sufficiently recovered heart to gather a new army at Arras. But it was curiously slow to take the field, and when in July it at last moved, Calais was starving. A ship trying to escape from the port was intercepted by the English with a message from the governor that read: "Everything is eaten up—dogs, cats, horses—and we have nothing left to subsist on unless we eat each other." Edward forwarded it to Philip, leaving him to choose between another Crécy or the dishonour of letting the town fall without a fight. When on July 27th a French relieving army came in sight the English were entrenched in its path in an almost unassailable position. For three days Philip encamped before them while his emissaries vainly tried to negotiate a truce which would allow the garrison to be revictualled. Declaring himself ready to treat on any other matter, Edward refused to allow Calais to be even discussed. At daybreak on August 2nd, the French king set fire to his camp and withdrew.

"When the defenders of Calais saw this," wrote the Oxfordshire clerk, Geoffrey le Baker, "they took their standard down and with great sorrow cast it from the tower into the ditch. And . . . John de Vienne, their captain, . . . opening the gates of the town, came out to the king of England, sitting on a little nag . . . with an halter about his neck, and the other burgesses and soldiers following on foot, bareheaded and barefooted, having halters about their necks. Thus coming before the king, the captain offered him the sword of war as to the chief prince of arms among Christian kings and one who had taken the town from the mightiest Christian king by noble chivalry. Then he delivered to him the keys of the town. Begging of him pity, he asked pardon and offered him the sword of peace wherewith to give right judgment, treat the humble and lowly with forbearance and chasten the proud-hearted . . . The king, receiving that which was offered him, sent the captain with fifteen knights and as many burgesses into England, enriching them with gifts."[1] According to her countryman, Froissart, Queen Philippa knelt before her lord and pleaded for them. One cannot understand the cruel wars of the fourteenth century without this background of chivalry.

Edward could now make Calais, not only a base for con-

[1] *Chronicon Galfride le Baker de Swynbroke* (ed. Thompson), p. 367. cit. *Rickert*, 306.

quering France, but an English town. He sent those of its inhabitants likely to oppose his rule to the nearest French territory
and offered English traders incentives to settle in their stead. He
left the town its old franchise under which magistrates were
elected by the leading householders, promised to respect its
customs and appointed an English governor. He also transferred
the staple there, making it the sole port for the export of wool,
tin, lead and cloth to northern Europe. With both sides of the
Straits of Dover in his hands he could now claim with justice to
be ruler of the narrow seas. On his new gold coin, the noble,[1]
which he had issued four years after his victory at Sluys, he
appears standing in a ship crowned with sword in hand.

Before Calais fell the English had won another victory in
Brittany. De Montfort's death and his countess's insanity having
once more tilted the scales in favour of the French, Charles of
Blois had laid siege to La Roche-Derrien with a large, well-
equipped army. The fortress, with its minute English garrison,
lay in the heart of Charles's country. But Sir Thomas Dagworth,[2]
setting out on June 19th with less than a thousand men from
Carhaix, 45 miles away, fell by night on the besiegers' camp and
routed them. Charles himself was taken prisoner and sent to
join the King of Scots in the Tower.

Having gained Calais and assured Brittany's independence,
Edward was ready to accept Philip's proposals for a truce. He
had been absent from England for more than a year and, the
threats to Gascony and the Scottish march having been eliminated,
his faithful commons needed a respite from taxes. Two cardinals
from Avignon had been trying to effect an accommodation all
the summer, and in September, on the basis of everyone keeping
what he had won, a truce was concluded till June of the following
year.

[1] Worth 6s. 8d.—half a mark—it was the first gold coin to be successfully
put into general circulation since the Conquest. Its beautiful predecessor, the
golden florin issued in the previous year, had been withdrawn for technical
reasons. *Medieval England*, 292.

[2] The name of this brave man does not even appear in the Dictionary of
National Biography. " We came, my comrades and I, upon them," he wrote
in his despatch to the chancellor, "about a quarter of an hour before daybreak, and by the grace of God the business went in such a manner that they
lost the field and were discomforted." Robert of Avesbury, *De Gestis Mirabilibus Regis Edwardi Tertii* (*Rolls Series*, 1889, p. 389).

In October 1347, therefore, Edward returned to England. For two dazzling years victory had crowned her every effort; a few thousand of her sons, most of them humble countrymen armed with a weapon which they alone could use, had again and again overcome almost inconceivable odds and laid the chivalry of the greatest kingdom in Christendom in the dust. Nor was it only in arms that England at that moment was great. In the years that saw her triumphs in Picardy, Aquitaine and Brittany one magnificent ecclesiastical building after another was being raised by the genius of her craftsmen. The Lady chapel at Lichfield, the cloisters at Norwich, the retrochoir and St. Andrew's arches at Wells, the choir of Bristol, the exquisite decorated nave of Exeter were all completed or partly completed in the same decade as Crecy. So, in the north, was the lovely Percy tomb at Beverley and the west front and nave—finished in the year of Edward's victory—of York minster. And at Salisbury Richard of Farleigh was crowning the thirteenth-century cathedral with a decorated tower and spire whose proportions have never been surpassed.

It was the thirteen-forties, too, that saw the first flowering in England of the Perpendicular style. Hitherto, with their broad bases and close relationship to the earth, her cathedrals had not sought to emulate the perilous height of the Gothic churches of the Ile de France. But now, under the lead of William de Ramsey who had become the king's chief mason in the 'thirties, English architects began to evolve a new technique which produced the effect of height without sacrificing structural proportion or safety. Like England's battle tactics, it was an art not of mass but of line, in which the vertical mullions of vast rectangular windows extended upwards and downwards to form, with the horizontal lines they crossed, continuous rectilinear panels of wall and glass. First essayed by the London masons in the new chapter-house and cloisters of St. Paul's and the royal chapel of St. Stephen's, Westminster,[1] its end—a reaction against the excessive ornamentation of the Decorated style—was an all-embracing unity in which the separate parts, arch, pier, vault, window and wall, were subordinated to a single whole.

It is in the west country abbey which sheltered the murdered

[1] Both since destroyed by fire, in 1666 and 1834.

body of Edward's father that the earliest surviving example of the new style can be seen. Aided by the gifts of pilgrims to the king's shrine, the monks of Gloucester began in the 'thirties to transform the dark Norman south transept by substituting for the end wall an enormous eight-light window crowned with a lierne vault. During the next decade they rebuilt the choir, marrying the massive Norman pillars to delicate vaulting shafts and encasing the walls in a framework of Perpendicular panelling beneath clerestory windows designed to flood the interior with light. And at its east end, in place of the Norman apse, they made the largest window in Europe, canting the walls of the last bay outwards to increase its size. This great wall of glass, seventy feet high and nearly forty wide, with over a hundred lights, was glazed, through the munificence of a local lord, with the shields and likenesses of his fellow commanders at Crecy, the king and Prince of Wales in their midst, and, above them, Christ surrounded by apostles, seraphim, saints and martyrs singing the *gloria in excelsis* for the crowning of the Virgin. In the foreground, high above the choir, the masons carved on the bosses of the vault fifteen angels, each with a different musical instrument, to accompany that chant of praise sung by figures poised in painted glass between the glittering interior and the grey Gloucestershire skies.

The Crécy window at Gloucester was not the sole memorial to the battle. To commemorate it Edward on his return to England resumed his project for an Order or fellowship of chivalry. It was to be dedicated now, not to King Arthur, whose victories he and his companions had surpassed, but to St. George —the patron saint of all Christian warriors and, henceforward, of England. It was to consist of the king and twenty-six of his most renowned knights, linked together by vows of eternal friendship for the "advancement of piety, nobility and chivalry." Associated with them and sharing a St. George's chapel in the royal castle at Windsor was to be a college of the same number of canons and of poor knights chosen from the humbler ranks of chivalry for their valour and need. And for the Order's badge and name the king, gallant in bower as in battle, chose a lady's garter, dropped by mischance at a ball at Calais by the loveliest woman in England, the princess Joan of Kent—heroine of

Neville's Cross and wife of the Earl of Salisbury—and which, as he bound it round his knee, the Sovereign is said to have immortalised with the words, "*Honi soit qui mal y pense.*"[1] Two months after his return from Calais he ordered for himself and the first knights of his Order twelve garters of royal blue embroidered with the words and the cross of St. George.

This band of "knights of the blue Garter," composed of "the valyantest men of the realm" and dedicated to the pursuit of "truth and honour, freedom and courtesy", in which was comprised courtesy to women, became the model of almost every Order of European chivalry. "Tie about thy leg for thy renown," each knight was enjoined at his installation, "this noble Garter; wear it as the symbol of the most illustrious Order, never to be forgotten or laid aside, that thereby thou mayest be admonished to be courageous, and, having undertaken a just war, . . . that thou mayest stand firm and valiantly and successfully conquer." The knights wore their insignia for the first time at a tournament at Eltham in January 1348 when nine of the original founders jousted before the king, among them the Prince of Wales, Henry of Lancaster, the constable Northampton and the young Earl of Salisbury whom some supposed to be the king's bastard. During the course of the nineteen tournaments held that winter and spring—at Bury St. Edmunds and Eltham, at Canterbury, Lichfield and Lincoln, and at Windsor for the churching of the queen after the birth of her youngest son—the Order was formally constituted. At one of them the purveyor of the wardrobe issued for Edward's wearing "a mantle, surcoat, tunic and hood of long blue cloth powdered with garters and furnished with buckles and pendants of silver gilt." Seventy-two standards with the king's arms "purfled and painted" were also ordered, two hundred and forty-four standards of worsted and English cloth with "a leopard entire at the head and underneath the arms of St. George," and "eight-hundred pennocells of the arms of St. George for the lances of the king's esquires and other men-at-arms." Even the nine-year-old prince Lionel, recently betrothed

---

[1] The evidence for this story, long discounted, has now been supported by convincing evidence in an article by Margaret Galway, "Joan of Kent and the Order of the Garter," published in Vol. 1 of the *Birmingham University Historical Journal.*

by his father to the heiress of the great Anglo-Irish house of Clare, appeared at the jousts at Windsor in "a doublet of yellow and blue velvet."

It was a time of jousting, feasting and pilgrimages in which the nobles and ladies of the Court moved resplendent in the finery of French cities and castles—furs and silks, jewels and cloth of gold. At the Christmas revels at Guildford the king appeared in a suit of dazzling white, his shield inscribed with the motto,

> "Hey, hey, the whyte swan,
> By Gode's soule I am thy man."

For the masques that followed there were eighty-four tunics of buckram of divers colours, forty-two vizors of elephants', dragons' and satyrs' heads, swans' heads with wings, tunics painted with peacocks' eyes, tunics ornamented with stars of beaten gold and silver. As 1348 dawned, all aristocratic England made merry in hall and tilting-yard with Edward, her "cumly" king, "that famous and fortunate warrior." In the words of the St. Albans chronicler, it seemed as if a new sun had risen on the land, "because of the abundance of peace, the plenitude of goods and the glory of the victories."

Chapter Eight

HOLY CHURCH

'Holy Church I am,' quoth she,
'thou oughtest to know me,
I was the first to nurse thee,
and taught thee the Faith.'

WILLIAM LANGLAND

The kingdom of England has always been governed principally
and for the greater part by clerks spaciously endowed with
ecclesiastical benefices and honours; by whose assistance the
interests not only of the kingdom of England, but also of the
Church are consulted with healthful circumspection, and the
indemnity of both is looked after.

Manifesto to the pope on behalf
of the kings' clerks, 1279

WHEN the king sailed to France before Crécy the most famous preacher in England—the great theologian Richard FitzRalph, dean of Lichfield and archbishop elect of Armagh— bade the people pray, not that he should overcome his enemies, since that might be contrary to Christ's laws and offend God, but that he should "be directed with prudent and sane counsel to obtain a just and happy issue and a just peace" so that his subjects might live "a quiet and tranquil life . . . piously and chastely."[1] For above his allegiance to king or lord the medieval Christian had one loyalty transcending all others. It was to the Christian faith and the teaching of the Church that was its repository.

In the dark ages after the dissolution of the Roman Empire

---

[1] "Men often err greatly when they pray for the king and his nobles, demanding from God that he give them corporal triumph in battle over their foes." Lansd. MS. 393. f. 26b. cit. *Owst, Preaching*, 204.

the tribal peoples of Western Europe found, in their acceptance of a common religion and Church, a solution for the mutual hates that were impoverishing, brutalising and destroying them. The union of faith so formed was known as Christendom. It was, in the nature of things, imperfect, for no common creed could make an end of all the savage and irrational enmities, greeds and distrusts that divided men. Yet it had enabled them to climb an appreciable way out of the anarchy of fear, uncertainty and cruelty in which they lived. Whatever wars Christians might wage against one another, the portals of the Church were open to every believer. A traveller in a foreign land could not approach a town in any part of Christendom without seeing the familiar sight of the church-towers and spires rising above its walls and houses. Under those vanes men were celebrating, with the same rites and in the same words, the supreme event in which every Christian believed—the Passion of Christ through which, daily renewed in the sacrament of the Mass, the Church, under the successor of St. Peter, mediated man's salvation from eternal death and Hell—what a great English theologian described as "the perpetual loss of the vision of God."

For all the divisions of class, allegiance and language in an age of slow, primitive communications, the Church's doctrine and ordinances were accepted by the entire West from the Mediterranean to the Celtic and Scandinavian islands in the Atlantic mists. It had its own international language—the Latin that the ecclesiastical scholars of the Dark Ages had retrieved and adapted from the fallen Roman Empire—its monopoly of education, its canon law by which it disciplined not only clerks but laymen. From morning to night, throughout its seventy provinces and seven-hundred dioceses, its bells marked the divisions of the day and the hours of prayer—a sound to which Christian ears were so habituated that, when in 1384 the Italian, Leonardo Frescobaldi, landed in Egypt, the first thing he noticed was their absence; "we found none," he wrote, "in all pagandom."[1] Nowhere was this music so continuous as in England, "the ringing isle" whose bell-founders

[1] Frescobaldi, G, and S. *Visit to the Holy Places* (transl. T. Bellonini and E. Hoade), 41.

were said to excel all others and where, save in the moors of
the north and west, the bells of some neighbouring parish
could usually be heard sounding across the dividing waste and
woodland.

Within the Church, set to guide both rulers and subjects in
their spiritual duties, was a vast hierarchy of clerics—cardinals,
archbishops and bishops, abbots and priors, deans and archdeacons, monks, vowed to perpetual prayer and contemplation;
parish and chantry priests, confessors and chaplains, learned
doctors expounding the lore of the universe of which the Church
was the sole interpreter, wandering friar and solitary hermits.
In England, with a population of three millions, there were
between eight and nine thousand parishes, each with at least
one priest or deacon and many with an unbeneficed chaplain
as well; seventeen or eighteen thousand regulars—monks,
canons, nuns, friars, Knights Hospitallers and, before their
dissolution, Templars—living under corporate vows and rule;[1]
and a large but uncertain number of unbeneficed priests and
chantry chaplains. York, with at the outside 10,000 inhabitants,
had forty-one parish churches and over five hundred clergy;
Norwich, with a population of about 6000, twenty churches
and forty-three chapels. Even in the overcrowded capital
there was a church for every five hundred people, while the
average country parson's flock cannot have exceeded three
hundred.

In addition to priests and deacons in holy orders who were
forbidden to marry and who alone, with their attendant acolytes,
officiated in the presbytery or eastern portion of the church shut
off from the congregation by the rood-screen, there was a huge
army of clerks in minor orders. These had received the Church's
initial tonsure—the small round patch cut in the centre of the
head by the officiating bishop as a reminder of Christ's crown of
thorns and which, by bringing its wearer under the Church's
protection, secured him "benefit of clergy". Among them were
the acolytes who tended the church-lights and helped the priest
at the altar, parish-clerks, readers who read and sang the lessons,
exorcists who laid evil spirits, door-keepers who looked after the
church and its bells. They included, too, the students of the

---

[1] *Knowles*, II, 256.

universities who numbered at least another two thousand. Probably one in every fifty of the population was a cleric. The Poll Tax returns of 1381 listed more than 29,000 inferior clergy in England, exclusive of friars.[1]

There were two provinces and seventeen dioceses in England, fourteen under the southern metropolitan and three—York, Durham and Carlisle—under the northern, whose jurisdiction was virtually independent of the southern and who, in his vast diocese, was served by the departmental cathedral-minsters of Beverley, Ripon and Southwell. Eight bishops, including the primate, were the titular heads of monasteries, all save one of them Benedictine. In these the episcopal throne was the monastic church, served by monks and presided over by the prior who controlled, with a jealous insistence on their independence, both monastery and cathedral, leaving the bishop free for his episcopal duties. The cathedrals of the nine secular bishops were served by chapters of canons presided over by a dean. There were also four Welsh sees—St. Asaph, St. David's, Llandaff and Bangor.

By the middle of the fourteenth century, as "universal ordinary" the pope in theory "provided" all bishops to vacant sees. He also claimed, and exercised, the right of translating them from one diocese to another. In England, however, they were nearly always nominated by the king, and none were appointed without his consent. As all English bishops were feudal tenants-in-chief—a peculiarity of the English Church imposed on it by William the Conqueror—he alone, as overlord, could invest them with the temporalities or revenues of the land supporting their sees, which, like other feudal estates lapsed to the Crown during a vacancy. It was useless, therefore, for the pope to provide someone unwanted by the king, though he could refuse to appoint anyone ecclesiastically unsuitable.[2] Subject to this right of veto the choice of bishops was left by tacit

---

[1] *Maynard Smith*, 38; *Green*, 40.

[2] In 1345, Pope Clement VI observed, "If the King of England were to petition for his ass to be made a bishop, we must not say him nay." *Walsingham I*, 255. cit. *Stubbs*, III, 324. "Where the pope showed opposition, a compromise was arranged . . . The dignity of the pope was saved by the bull of provision which marked his final acquiescence in the appointment and gave it final validity." *Hamilton Thompson*, 16.

agreement to the king in return for his leaving the pope the right of providing nominees to benefices less directly concerned with the royal administration. In deference to the principle of canonical independence the normal procedure was for the cathedral chapter to elect a candidate whose name had been submitted to it in a royal *congé d'élire*.[1] After repairing to Rome to be examined and approved by the pope he was formally "provided" to the see on payment of a fee to the *curia* and of the annates or first-fruits of the benefice. On his return to England he was then consecrated by his fellow bishops and enfeoffed by the king with his temporalities.

Under this characteristically English compromise a spiritual magnate, who was *ex officio* a peer of the realm, was selected by the head of the State subject to the veto of the head of a supranational Church. It provided not only leaders for the English Church but the chief administrative officers of the Crown. It was part of a system that everywhere financed the higher direction of Church and State in an age of growing administrative complexity for which earlier endowments—designed for a simpler form of society—had made no provision. Instead of taxing the community, lay or clerical, to provide salaries for the growing number of royal and ecclesiastical administrators needed by an advancing civilisation, the less unpopular device was adopted of deflecting to their maintenance some of the more lucrative ecclesiastical benefices—bishoprics, deaneries, archdeaconries, cathedral and collegiate offices and prebends—leaving it to the beneficiaries to provide deputies to perform their canonical functions.

From time immemorial it had been the Church's task to guide and counsel the State and its rulers, and it seemed only natural that some of its wealth should be used to maintain those who performed this part of its duties and that the descendants of the princes and lords who had endowed it should be able to call on churchmen for those administrative services which only churchmen were trained to give. When in 1340 Edward III appointed for the first time a lay chancellor, he had to make him an allowance of £500 a year—more than £25,000 in modern money—out of the inadequate royal revenues so that he could

[1] See *Makers of the Realm*, 224.

support his office without a bishop's emoluments.[1] It seemed
only just, too, that some of the Church's endowments should be
used to maintain the servants and officials of the papacy, whose
work of organisation and regulation served the ends of all
Christians. The benefices of the richer cathedrals and collegiate
churches, whose liturgical duties could be performed by salaried
vicars-choral, were much employed in this way by both Crown
and pope, particularly the latter who had to provide, not only
for the members of his own growing court, but for deserving
churchmen in every country in Christendom, a continual succession of whom flocked to the *curia*, in person or by deputy, to
petition for benefices.

However shocking to modern minds, this deflection of ecclesiastical endowments to the administrative ends of Church and
State gave to their beneficiaries—since an ecclesiastical benefice
was a life-freehold—a measure of economic independence which
enabled them to become something more than mere creatures
of their donors' will. Used by pope and prince, earl and baron
to reward the clerics who served them, it also helped to preserve
a balance of power in the governance of society and to provide
that brake on despotic power which the medieval Church was
always seeking.

During the fourteenth century more than half the English
bishops were employed in offices of state. Many were chosen
from the clerical administrators of the royal household. In 1300
there were only two civil servants on the episcopal bench; a
quarter of a century later there were twelve, most of them
Wardrobe or ex-Wardrobe officials. Under Edward III it was
the keepers of the Privy Seal who were most favoured; in 1350
six out of the seventeen bishops had held this office.[2] Though
there was never in England an aristocratic monopoly of high
ecclesiastical office as in some continental countries, about a fifth
of the bishops came from the land-owning and warrior families
who surrounded the throne—Beaumont, Cobham, Berkeley,
Burghersh, Courtenay. Most were of middling and, in some

---

[1] This was in addition to the normal allowance of £500 towards the
expenses of the office, £80 of it for robes and £420 "for the table of the said
household." *Tout, Chapters*, III, 156.

[2] *Pantin*, 12; R. Highfield, "The English Hierarchy in the Reign of
Edward III." (*R.H.S.T.* 5th series, VI 133.)

cases, humble birth. Something like two in every three had had a university education, usually in canon law—the subject most useful for a royal or baronial administrator.

Such prelates no longer tramped the countryside preaching and baptising like the pioneers from Rome and Iona who had first brought the faith to England. A bishop was a great territorial magnate, enjoying the revenues of numerous manors and knights' fees, who wore princely attire and lived in state. His income of two or three thousand pounds a year was fabulous compared with the yearly wage of forty or fifty shillings earned by a shepherd or ploughman. The Bishop of Durham's castle above the Wear was the greatest fortress in the north; the Bishop of Exeter had nine residences in Devon alone.[1] The archiepiscopal palace of Bishopthorpe, where Edward II recuperated after Bannockburn, was only one of a score of similar homes owned by the northern metropolitan; the Bishop of Lincoln had ten palaces and forty manor-houses including, like every other prelate, a mansion in London from which to perform his duties as a peer of the realm and attend meetings of parliament and the royal council. When a bishop travelled it was on horseback or in a litter with a retinue of thirty or forty mounted clerics and attendants, including knights and men-at-arms drawn from his tenantry to guard him from robbers.

Even in his purely ecclesiastical functions a fourteenth century bishop was an administrator, managing the wealth and exercising the jurisdiction of his see and the estates with which the piety of past ages had endowed it. If not employed in the king's business he was expected to make visitations to every part of his diocese, investigating either in person or through his diocesan officials the discipline of every parish and of every religious house not exempted by papal bull from his jurisdiction. He had to ordain priests and institute incumbents to benefices, confirm the young, hold synods of the diocesan clergy, consecrate churches and issue licences for chantries and private chapels, and excommunicate or otherwise punish laymen who withheld their tithes, refused to do penance for their sins or committed crimes or sacrilegious acts

---

[1] The name of Exeter Street in the Strand still commemorates his London palace, as Ely Place off Holborn, does that of the medieval bishops of Ely.

on consecrated ground. His office was not so much to teach and
comfort his flock as to discipline it. He was the judge ordinary
—*judex ordinarius*—of his diocese. As its "father in God" it was
his business to enforce the Church's law and correct and punish
the erring. In the poet Langland's words, his pastoral staff was
"hooked at one end to hale men from Hell . . . and pull down
the wicked."

To help him was a whole range of courts administering the
canon or ecclesiastical law. His own episcopal court, over which
either he or his chancellor presided, tried major clerical crimes
and such moral offences by laymen as perjury, usury, assaults on
nuns and violation of sanctuary—the Church's right to offer a
limited and, in some cases, indefinite refuge on holy ground to
fugitives from justice. Matters not requiring the bishop's personal
intervention were dealt with in the diocesan consistory court
under a trained canon lawyer called the official-principal, while
in each of the main divisions of the diocese another ecclesiastical
dignitary, an archdeacon, exercised, in person or by deputy, the
bishop's visitorial and penal powers over its parishes. In the
largest English diocese, Lincoln, there were eight archdeacons;
in others, like Rochester, Ely and Carlisle, only one. Smaller
jurisdictional sub-divisions, corresponding often with the hundreds or wapentakes of the shire, were administered by rural
deans, whose powers, however, were now falling into disuse.

Surrounding the bishop was his *familia*—chaplains, registrar,
notaries, clerks, household knights, yeomen and grooms. Its
most important member was the vicar-general to whom he delegated all functions which he could not perform in person, except-
ing only those for which episcopal orders were necessary such as
ordinations, confirmations and consecrations. For these, if absent
or employed at court, he would employ a suffragan, usually
drawn from the ranks of unemployed missionary bishops, who,
having been provided by the pope to sees in heathen lands—"*in
partibus infidelium*"—or in the wilder districts of Ireland, were
unable to exercise their episcopal functions and obtain the emoluments of their sees.[1] Even with such help a conscientious bishop
who was not permanently employed at court was kept continually
travelling round his diocese, staying at one or another of his

[1] *Hamilton Thompson,* 48-9.

episcopal manors or at religious houses and rectories. Oliver Sutton, a prelate with a strong sense of pastoral duty, who reigned over Lincoln during the last two decades of the thirteenth century, lodged under a different roof on an average of once a week throughout his entire episcopate.

. . . .

Between the life of such a magnifico and the poor parson who ministered to the ordinary Englishman was a gulf almost as wide as that between Caesar Augustus and the founder of the Christian Faith. The incumbent of a country parish was usually a peasant's son, living the same rustic life as his flock. Taught, at best, in monastic or grammar school enough Latin to read the scriptures and declaim the services in a language his parishioners venerated but could not understand, and usually the only literate person in the parish, he lived, like any other peasant, by cultivating the glebe or "parson's close"—a holding, usually, of some fifty or sixty acres in the village common fields. He also received dues and offerings from his parishioners for baptisms, weddings, churchings, death-bed visitations and burials—the traditional soul-scot paid at the open grave. By the fourteenth century almost every village possessed its own rector or parson—the *persona* of the place—serving an ecclesiastical unit known as a parish and entitled by law to an annual tenth or tithe of the produce of every parishioner. But in the case of many of the richer livings the right of presentation or advowson, as it was called, had been given by its patron—a descendant, perhaps, of the church's original donor—to a monastery, college, cathedral or other ecclesiastical foundation which, retaining the bulk of its revenues, paid a deputy to exercise the cure of souls. In other cases the owner of the advowson, a species of legal property, conferred the living on someone with family claims or on some promising youth marked out for preferment, who, by obtaining an episcopal dispensation to reside out of the parish, was allowed to employ a resident vicar or "perpetual curate" while he completed his education or performed some more eminent ecclesiastical function elsewhere. Usually the absentee rector kept the "great" tithe on crops, sheep and cattle while allocating to his vicar the farm of the glebe and the "lesser" tithes on pigs, geese, poultry, eggs, garden-produce, flax, honey and fish. In other cases the incumbent, who by canon law was at least assured of his share of the benefice for life, was paid a stipend in cash or kind. Thus the vicar of Stixwould in Lincolnshire received every week fourteen loaves and fourteen gallons of beer, with seven less good loaves for the servant who helped him cultivate the glebe.

In this way much of the wealth that had been left to provide for the cure of souls—the Church's primary duty—had been deflected to other ends.[1] By the end of Edward I's reign nearly a fifth of the country's churches had been appropriated. As only about a third of their income filtered through to the incumbents and, as the holder of a cure was supposed by canon law to devote two-thirds of the tithe to the upkeep of the chancel and relief of the parish poor, both the latter and the church fabric tended to suffer. Deprived of the "great" tithes, the vicar was tempted to press his parishioners too strictly for the lesser ones—those that most affected the bondsman and small-holder—and to spend too much time cultivating the glebe and looking after his livestock. The pre-occupation of the humbler parish clergy with agricultural pursuits constantly figures in the episcopal records of the time. During an archdeacon's visitation the sidesman of one Devonshire church complained that the vicar, though in other ways a worthy man, had stabled his beasts in the churchyard—"whereby it is evilly trodden down and foully defiled"—appropriated churchyard timber for his farm buildings and made his malt and stored his corn in the nave, "whereby his servants in their exits and entrances open the door and, at time of tempest, the wind comes in and is wont to uncover the church."[2]

Yet there was a compensation. To the average countryman the Church was represented by one of his own class, accustomed from childhood to the same agricultural pursuits and way of life as himself. Though he might not be able to construe the Latin prayers and services he chanted by rote at the altar and though he might have had some difficulty at his ordination in satisfying the bishop that he possessed the necessary means or sureties,

[1] Thus the great tithe of Ashby in Northamptonshire was assigned to the maintenance of the choir-boys in the new Angel choir at Lincoln, causing the village to become known as Ashby Puerorum or Boys Ashby. Rosalind Hill, *Oliver Sutton*, 5.

[2] *Medieval Panorama*, 177-8.

"title" it was called, to prevent him from becoming a charge on the diocese, he understood the problems of those to whom he ministered. In the market towns and a few of the richer country parishes the incumbent might be a man of substance like the parson of Trumpington in Chaucer's tale who gave his daughter —he should not, by rights, have had one—a dowry when she married the miller. Usually he was a small freeholder's son or a manumitted villein—for a bondsman could not be admitted to holy orders until he had been freed by his lord—with an average income in the prosperous eastern counties of £10 or £11 a year, equivalent to about the same sum a week in the money of today. In some cases his emoluments amounted to only £3 or £4 a year, no more than the earnings of a peasant farming twenty acres of ploughland. His sympathies and interests were those of his parishioners even if his poverty sometimes led to disputes about his dues or involved them in that much-resented form of parochial excommunication, "a cursing for tithes."

To a moral reformer like the great preacher, Dr. Rypon of Durham, or a famous philosopher and university doctor like Roger Bacon of Oxford, such a poor rustic priest seemed little better than a "brute beast" who, immersed in mercenary calculations about crops and beasts, could scarcely expound an article of the Faith and was fit only to "patter up his Matins and Mass." To his parishioners he was invested by his calling with mysterious powers on which rested their hopes and fears of reward or punishment after their hard, brief lives on earth had ended. When as the sanctus bell sounded he stood before the altar and officiated at the Mass, bringing about by virtue of his priestly office the miraculous transformation of the bread and wine into Christ's body and blood, he seemed almost a creature of another world. And when death struck and he hastened to the side of the dying, carrying lantern and bell, holy water for sprinkling, oil for anointing and the pyx containing the sacred elements, on him and his power to grant absolution and administer the sacrament of Extreme Unction depended the lonely, bewildered soul's readiness for its passage to salvation or eternal damnation.

The fear of the Church's wrath that could leave a sinner unshriven and exposed to everlasting torment was very real to the medieval Christian. His life was short and precarious and death a constant visitant. He knew how cruel nature and his fellow men could be; what destructive forces lurked in wait for him and them. To the pain and suffering of this world the imagination of his pagan forebears had added the dread of worse terrors beyond the grave; the old heathen gods lived on for him under new names. His mind was haunted by thoughts of demons that "fly above in the air as thick as motes in the sun," of diabolical tempters who might appear at any moment under any guise, animal or human—an ape, a woman, a spider, a dog, a witch, even a bishop in his pulpit—and beguile him into some fatal sin that could rob him of his hope of salvation. Such fears were strengthened by the pictures on the walls of every church: of the pit into which sinners were cast, with its "fire and brimstone," "venmous worms and nadders" and fiends with blazing eyes and mocking laughter, pitch-forking their victims into everlasting torture. "Some shall burn," ran the words of one medieval sermon, "in the great flaming of fire which is ten times hotter than any fire in this world; some shall be hanged by the neck, and devils without number shall draw their limbs asunder and smite their bodies with fiery brands . . . There shall be flies that bite their flesh and their clothing shall be worms . . . There is no sound but horrible roaring of devils and weeping and gnashing of teeth and wailing of damned men, crying, 'Woe, woe, woe, how great is this darkness!' "[1]

All this enormously enhanced the priest's power over his flock. Having learnt to understand a little Latin he was the sole interpreter of the Bible story and of the Judaic and Christian truths recorded in that work—one to which, in an age when all books had to be copied by hand and were fabulously expensive,[2] only the better educated of the clergy and a tiny minority of rich laymen had access. It was he or his clerk or acolyte who taught the village children the rudiments of their faith, the creed, commandments, catechism and Latin prayers of Pater Noster and Ave Maria in the loft that often served for school above the

[1] *Owst, Preaching,* 336-7.
[2] Dr. Hughes has pointed out that before the invention of printing a bible would have cost roughly ten years of the average village priest's income. P. Hughes, *The Reformation,* 9n.

church porch, who joined husband and wife at the church door in view of the community, who received once a year, usually at Easter, the confession of every parishioner in the shriving-pew, thereafter admonishing and, if satisfied of a genuine repentance, granting absolution. There were other times when, with the bell tolling in the tower above, he stood before his congregation to read the dreaded sentence of excommunication, casting out the accursed with book and candle from the Church's communion as he blew out the flickering taper and flung it, at the end of his anathema, to the ground.[1]

Every great event of a poor man's life, everything that raised it above that of the beasts and invested it with beauty or significance, centered round the parish church. Here every Sunday and on the more important of the thirty or forty holy days of the year which were his holidays and the occasion of his feasts and fasts, he listened, in awe and with bowed head, to the "blessed mutter of the Mass" and took part in the ritual dramas and processions which told for an unlettered people the Gospel story— the lighted candles carried round the church by the congregation at Candlemas, the distribution and blessing of the ashes on Ash Wednesday, the hanging of the Lenten veil before the altar, the distribution of branches on Palm Sunday, the dramatic creeping to the Cross in the darkened church on Good Friday, the triumphant procession with vestments and banners on Easter Sunday as the Host and Cross were borne, amid pealing bells and the chanting of the Resurrection anthem, from the Easter Sepulchre where they had lain since Good Friday to the High Altar. At Pentecost a dove was loosed from the rafters amid clouds of incense, at the feast of Corpus Christi—instituted during the fourteenth century in honour of the Real Presence— the entire community knelt in church and village street while the Sacrament was borne in procession through their ranks. At Rogationtide the fields were blessed by the priest, at Lammas

---

[1] "We curse them sleeping or walking, going and sitting, standing and riding, lying above earth and under earth, speaking and crying and drinking ... that they have no part of Mass nor Matins nor of none other good prayers that be done in Holy Church ... ; but that the pains of Hell be their meed with Judas that betrayed our Lord Jesu Christ, and the life of them be put out of the Book of Life till they come to amendment and satisfaction made." *Instructions for Parish Priests* (E.E.T.S.) 24, cit., *Medieval Panorama*, 163.

the loaf—first-fruit of the harvest—was presented by him at the altar, on New Year's Day he led his parishioners round the apple orchards to bless the fruit of the coming summer.

Some of these rites and the superstitions that attached to them had been adapted by the Church from the heathen worship of pre-Christian times. Others, like the exorcising of witches, ghosts and fairies and the lighting of fires on Midsummer eve, had never become part of the Church's doctrine and ritual but were tacitly accepted by a rustic clergy who had grown up with such beliefs and had to reconcile their parishioners' ineradicable loyalty to them with the Christian faith and discipline they were paid to teach. So incense had taken the place of pagan burnt offerings, holy water of haunted wells and streams, Christian incantations of sorcerer's spells.

Despite the manuals and instructions for parish priests issued by reforming bishops, the dividing line between religion and superstition was never clearly marked in medieval religion. The church bells were rung to still the approaching storm, "that the Devil hearing the trumpets of the Eternal king that be the bells may flee away through fear and cease from raising the tempest." When vermin infested a church or caterpillars the village orchards an anathema would be pronounced against them by the priest, while old women suspected of witchcraft were often accused of stealing the consecrated elements to destroy the pests in their gardens or put spells on their neighbours. It was popularly believed that, when at the supreme moment of the Mass the Host was elevated, whoever gazed on it with a pure and penitent heart would be granted freedom for the rest of the day from the normal misfortunes and mischances of life.

Except in Lent and on the occasions prescribed by Archbishop Pecham's constitutions the ordinary village parson seldom preached. Four times a year he was expected to expound in English the Creed, the Gospel precepts and Ten Commandments, and expatiate, like Chaucer's "poor parson of the town," on the seven deadly sins and their consequences, the seven virtues and the seven sacraments of grace. For the rest he relied, like every parish priest from Calabria to Scandinavia, on the dramatic ritual of the Catholic Church, the rites at the altar, the sonorous Latin prayers and incantations, the statues, images and pictorial representations of Christ crucified or risen in majesty, of saints and martyrs and angels, of the Last Judgment and Harrowing of Hell depicted in brilliant colours and terrifying detail over the chancel arch, of the stories from Bible and Apocalypse that covered wall, window and roof-space of even the humblest church.

In weaning pagan man from his primitive and bloodstained creeds of terror and human sacrifice the Church's supreme achievement was to domesticate and humanise the conception of Eternity. Everywhere he was confronted, in church and wayside shrine, with homely and familiar reminders of the Heaven he was enjoined to earn through the virtues of love, faith, compassion, humility, truthfulness, chastity, courtesy—virtues that came so hard and were so much needed by a passionate, hot-tempered, primitive people. To help them on their way to Paradise and make them shun temptation were the likenesses of men and women, who, the Church told them, had struggled and overcome the infirmities of human nature and were now, like the Master whose example they had followed, blessed spirits enthroned in Heaven yet ready to intercede for struggling mortals who called on them for aid. So human were the saints, Christians were taught, that they would help them in their humblest concerns. So St. Christopher, who once carried Christ on his shoulders, was the patron and protector of porters; St. Bartholomew, who was flayed alive, of tanners; St. Apollonia, whose jaw was smashed by his torturers, of those with toothache; St. John, who had been plunged into a chaldron of burning oil, of candlemakers. St. Giles looked after cripples, St. Crispin cobblers, St. Katherine little girls, St. Eustace and St. Hubert huntsmen, St. Cecilia the makers of music, St. Blaise sufferers from sore throats. And because she had anointed Christ's feet with aromatic oils Mary Magdalene was the protectress of perfumers. If one's oxen were sick one called on St. Corneille, if one's pigs on St. Anthony, if one's chickens on St. Gall. There was even a patron saint, St. Osyth, for women who had lost their keys.

So, too, there were saints for countries and places—St. George for England, St. Denis for France, St. Andrew for Scotland, St. Patrick for Ireland; St. Hugh of Lincoln, St. Swithin of Winchester, St. Chad of Lichfield. It was the function of the saints to intercede with Christ for the forgiveness of mortals, to protect them from the demons who were lying in wait for their souls, to assist them when they acted righteously and craved their succour in misfortune. One had to earn their protection by penitence and prayer as one knelt before their images and altars or called on them in toil or travail, but for those who sought it with humility their aid was always to be had. "Matthew, Mark, Luke and John," English children were taught to pray,

> "Watch the bed I lie upon:
> Four corners to my bed,
> Four angels there to spread,
> One at head and one at feet
> And two to guard me to Heaven's gate,
> One to sing and two to pray,
> And one to fetch my soul away."

Most loved of all who interceded for man was the Virgin. The Gabriel bell rang at evening to call Christians to recite Ave Maria, and the pilgrims flocked to see the replica of her house in the Augustinian priory at Walsingham, believing that the heavenly galaxy, the Milky Way, had been set to guide them there. The cult of supplicating Mary to intercede for human weaknesses which only a woman could be expected to forgive was then first reaching the height of its immense popularity. The great events of her life, the Annunciation, Purification, Visitation and Assumption, had taken their place among the feasts of the Christian year; at the Purification in February, known as Candlemas, everyone walked through the streets carrying candles blessed at the altar in her honour. She was thought of as the embodiment of every womanly virtue; tender, pure and loving and so pitiful that even the most abandoned could hope for forgiveness through her aid. "A woman clothed in the sun with the moon under her feet and upon her head a crown of twelve stars," a preacher called her: "this great sign and token stretched down into the depths of Hell, for all the devils there dread the name of this glorious Virgin."[1]

In no land was Mary so honoured as in England—our Lady's dowry, it was sometimes called. The number of churches and

[1] *Owst, Literature and Pulpit,* 19.

shrines dedicated to her was past counting; no other name figures so often in the lists of the royal oblations. When William of Wykeham founded his colleges at Winchester and Oxford he placed them under her protection, and at both the bishop still kneels in stone with outstretched hands before her to beg a blessing on his endowments. Nearly every church of importance possessed her image in silver, gold or alabaster given by some benefactor, and along the highroads and pilgrim ways were wayside chapels where travellers could tell their beads and say their Ave Marias to the Queen of Heaven.

Indeed, on this subject the English, usually less inclined to religious extremes than their neighbours, if anything outdid them. Sir Miles de Stapleton, a tough soldier who was sent to Normandy to stir up rebellion against the French king, was described as "a man of great integrity, much devoted to the Blessed Virgin and experienced in warlike affairs"; the valiant Sir John Chandos wore her figure embroidered on his surcoat. Her image with the child Christ in her arms was even set beside the cross on the king's crown.

It was not only England's fighting men who found inspiration in the Virgin. Much of the earliest English lyrical poetry that has come down to us from this time was written in her praise.

> "I sing of a maiden
>   That is matchless;
> King of all kings
>   To her son she ches . . .
>
> He came all so stillë
>   To his mother's bower
> As dew in Aprillë
>   That falleth on the flower."

No-one knows the author of this or of other poems in her honour —English counterparts of the Latin hymns composed for the Church's services, often with a liturgical phrase breaking through the vernacular,

> "Of one that is so fair and bright,
>   *Velut maris stella,*

> Brighter than the day is light,
> *Parens et puella . . .*"

The names on our parish maps, Ladygrove and Ladysmead, Mary's Well and Maryfield, and the flowers that country folk called after her, marigold and ladysmantle, bear witness after four centuries of Protestantism to the homage paid by our Catholic ancestors to Christ's mother.

Out of this worship of the Virgin sprang, in a harsh brutal age where force ruled and rape was a commonplace, the recognition that woman was entitled to respect and courtesy and that the test of civilisation was that she received it. "No man," a preacher declared, "should have woman in despite, for it is no wisdom to despise that which God loveth."

> " Love a woman with heartë true,
> She will change for noë new;
> Women beth of wordës few;
> Witness on Mary!
>
> Women beth good without lesying;
> From sorrow and care they will us bring;
> Woman is flower of allë thing;
> Witness on Mary!"

In his account of his travels in Christian lands nothing so amazed the pious Moor, Ibn Jubayr of Granada, as the sight, amid the refuse and excrement of Acre—"it stinks and is filthy; may God destroy it!"—of a Christian bride attended, with every accompaniment of honour, by a *cortège* of warriors. "Proud she was, walking with steps of half a span, like a dove or in the manner of a wisp of cloud. God protect us from the seduction of the sight!"[1] It was not thus that the faithful of a harem polity treated their womenfolk.

. . . .

It was this union of earth and heaven, matter and spirit, the assumption that the other world and this were in continual contact, that made medieval Christianity such a germinating and educative religion. For the ordinary man his parish church was

[1] *The Travels of Ibn Jubayr* (tranls. R. J. C. Broadhurst), 318-20.

the centre both of his spiritual and terrestrial life. It was the place where the whole community met. Its nave and aisles were the setting not only for prayer and liturgical processions but for proclamations and business transactions. Its porch was used for coroners' inquests and betrothals and for the payment of legacies; its oaken chest for depositing wills, charters and title-deeds. In the churchyard where the village children played and the dead, carried in the parish coffin, were laid in their shrouds to await the reunion of all Christians on Resurrection day, the parishioners met to beat the parish bounds, fairs were held and miracle plays or "mysteries" enacted by bucolic actors in which rustic exuberance and horse-play mingled, incongruously, with the piety of unquestioning faith. If by our standards such entertainments were crude and profane—if the shepherds at Bethlehem lauded the local ale or God appeared with a tiara, beard and gilded face—it was because the Christian faith was a part of the life of plain, unlettered men.

Medieval Christianity was an intensely human religion. It had place for comedy and farce. In the Palm Sunday procession a boy dressed as an angel standing above the west porch threw down cakes for which the congregation scrambled, while a wooden ass was drawn along behind the choir with a man belabouring it with a whip. Even in the deeply impressive Tenebrae services in Passion week when, one after another, the lights on the altar were darkened, the rustic singers in the loft were sustained during their long ordeal by wine and beer provided by the churchwardens, while the resurrection on Easter morning was hailed by the entire congregation banging on clappers. The very children had a place in the liturgy; on St. Nicholas' or Holy Innocents' Day the boys of the cathedral choirs conducted the service, and a boy-bishop with mitre and crozier preached while dean and chapter knelt to receive his blessing.[1]

[1] How touching some found this reversal of functions is seen by a bequest of one Joan Symonds of Coventry in the following century. "To the childe bisshop for the tyme being my cloke of scarlet to make him a robe on the condition that the byshop with the children shall come to my husband's grave and myn and there say *De Profundis* for my husband's soul and myn the same day as they do at the grave of Thomas Wyldegresse in the Drapers' chapel." A. W. Reed, *Early Tudor Drama*, 4.

Even for the lowliest—and many were so lowly that their
material life was little better than that of the brutes—the church
offered a nursing-ground for two attributes which raise and dignify
human nature. All the corporate life of the community that was
not purely economic centred round the church and was supervised by the churchwardens—the May Day dances when the
children went round the village collecting money, the bonfires
lit on the vigils of saints' days when the houses were illuminated
with candles and the wealthy spread tables of wine and sweet
cakes before their doors for their poorer neighbours, the watches
on Midsummer and St. Peter's eves when the parish was peram-
bulated and, in the cities, men and apprentices marched through
the streets in the liveries of their guilds. It was the churchwardens
—elected annually by the parishioners at the Easter vestry
meeting—who organised, in churchyard or in church-house if
the parish possessed one, church-ales to raise money for parish
expenses, bride-ales to help young married couples set up house,
bid-ales for those in need and distress. When a church was
rebuilt or added to—and throughout the fourteenth and fifteenth
centuries almost every town and village was refashioning and
refurbishing its church—the churchwardens raised the money by
arranging archery meetings and door-to-door collections. They
appointed a village "Robin Hood" and "Little John" to lead
the way to the butts after Mass on Sundays and holy days and
collect the fees of the competitors, and organised the annual
Hocktide collection when the young men and wives and maidens
went in turn to one another's houses to rope in those of the other
sex and make them pay forfeits for the church's benefit—"the
devocyon of the people on Hoke Tuesday," as the churchwardens
of St. Edmund's, Salisbury, called it. They held, too, the annual
church audit when the parishioners, grouped under their respective trades and callings, came in turn to present their gifts
and collections—"comyth in the yonglings and maidens,"
"comyth in the weavers," runs the account of the proceedings
in one Somerset parish.[1] It was then that the churchwardens
received any bequests left to the parish: the keep of a cow for
the poor, a swarm of bees to provide wax for candles and honey,

[1] Bishop Hobhouse, *Churchwardens' Accounts.* (Somerset Record Society,
1890), 3-18.

a woman's wedding ring, clothing for making into vestments and coverings. They were also responsible for the decoration of the church—with spring flowers on Palm Sunday and Easter, garlands of roses for Corpus Christi and holly and ivy at Christmas.

In his pride in and care for his place of worship the rustic parishioner found an outlet for another attribute which distinguishes man from the beasts: artistic creation. At a time when most men lived in bare, almost unfurnished mud and wattle huts little bigger than those in which a smallholder today keeps his farrowing sows, the wealth that was lavished on the church by even the poorest village seems little short of miraculous. As the inventories of the next century show, small and remote churches, with no rich benefactors to endow them, possessed chalices, patens, mazers, censers, candlesticks of silver and silver-gilt, panelled and gilded reredoses and altars, jewelled processional crosses and pyxes for the Host, embroidered vestments and altar-cloths of cloth of gold. They were furnished with carved rood-screens, misericords and bench-ends, stone and alabaster statues, finely cast and engraved bells, and windows blazing with glass brought from the *verreurs* of France and Germany. Much of it was art of high quality, inspired by faith and intense corporate pride. All was paid for and accumulated from generation to generation by the village community, many of whose members —carpenters, masons and smiths—helped to fashion it.[1]

. . . .

In their civilising mission the parish church and priest, however imperfectly, were continuing the work performed in an earlier age by the monasteries of carrying the Christian message to widening circles. The great conventual houses which had transmitted the legacies of Christianity and Latin civilisation to the warrior classes of western Europe had long ceased to be proselytising agents. So had the chapters of rich canons regular—the black Augustinians and white Premonstratensians—who served such splendid collegiate churches as Southwark, Waltham, Smithfield St. Bartholomew, Welbeck and Christ Church, Hampshire, though some of these had originally been founded to perform the work of missionary stations. No longer recruited

[1] *Maynard Smith*, 121-3; *Hughes*, 30-1; *Evans*, 211-16.

from men with a burning sense of mission but mainly from the younger sons of the lesser landowners and burgesses, the regulars were far removed from the lives of the peasants at their gates whose tithes and rents sustained their magnificent institutions. In their churches they still kept up a continuous sequence of services, prayer and chanting. But, though royal and noble personages frequently visited the more famous houses, making their stay and devotions memorable by benefactions of jewels and relics, except in a few of the larger abbeys, where part of the church was screened off for parochial use, the ordinary laity had no part in their secluded life. At Bury St. Edmunds the monks provided two churches on either side of the gateway, one for townsmen and one for pilgrims, to keep their holy of holies to themselves. The monks of Westminster built St. Margaret's to avoid having to use the south aisle for parochial worship. In this the abbeys differed from the secular cathedrals, where many canons and prebendaries were non-resident and whose naves the local people used as centres for their civic life, as at Exeter where booths were erected in the cathedral during fair-time and at St. Paul's where merchants settled the rates of exchange and even prostitutes plied for hire and where at every pillar a serjeant-at-law stood ready to interview clients.

Apart from those who lived inside their franchises and liberties and were so subject to their jurisdiction, the public's contact with such great monasteries was confined to the payment of rent, tithes and services to their officers and bailiffs, the carefully graded hospitality they offered to the various classes of travellers, and the broken meats their almoners distributed to the poor at their gates. Their premises—which included most of the largest habitable buildings in the land—were also occasionally used for sessions of parliament; the chapter house of Westminster Abbey was the usual meeting-place for the knights and burgesses of the Commons. At Gloucester the monks had to vacate their home and encamp in an orchard when a parliament met there; another, held at Cambridge, met in the priory of Barnwell just outside the town.

In the middle of the fourteenth century there were about seven hundred monasteries, colleges of canons, and nunneries in England. They ranged from great and ancient Benedictine houses like Christ Church Canterbury, Reading, Glastonbury, and St. Albans, with anything from sixty to ninety monks, to minute cells with only four or five. A century earlier the largest houses had been those of the Cistercians whose white-robed monks and lay brethren or *conversi* lived and worked together to farm the lonely dales and moorlands of the north and west. Rievaulx had once housed a hundred-and-forty choir-monks and six-hundred *conversi*; Fountains about a third as many.[1] But, though their buildings were now grander, the place of the lay brothers had been taken by paid workers and tenants, and the Benedictine foundations had regained their former primacy. While they, too, showed a slight falling off in numbers, their wealth was prodigious. From its manors, rectories and the offerings at its shrines Christ Church, Canterbury, enjoyed an income of £3000 p.a.—one equal to that of all but the greatest earls and equivalent in modern purchasing-power to over £150,000 p.a. Under the great prior, Thomas Chillenden, who ruled it at the end of the century, its revenues rose to £4000 p.a. Before Bruce's harrying of the north, those of Durham had been as large, though the long disastrous Scottish wars had since halved them. Though Mortmain had regulated the flow of legacies which had earlier threatened to undermine the kingdom's feudal system, under pressure of rising costs the monasteries were still managing to add to their wealth, chiefly by applying for licences to appropriate churches. Floods, drought, murrain, damage to crops,[2] too many travellers and guests, pestilence and war were all used as pretexts; after the battle of Neville's Cross the abbeys of Easby and Eggleston each acquired an additional rectory on the grounds that the English army had billeted itself on them and consumed their resources, "leaving them destitute."

Monks were members of an exclusive, self-renewing society. Subject to the rules of their Orders, and save in the few cases where their church was a bishop's throne, they elected their own heads and admitted to their privileged circle only those they approved. An abbot or presiding prior of a great monastery

---

[1] *Knowles*, II, 258.

[2] *Hamilton Thompson*, 173. In 1358 Pipewell abbey secured the appropriation of Geddington as a compensation for the devastations of deer and other game from the royal forest of Rockingham.

was a peer of the realm, sitting like a baron, by virtue of his house's lands, in parliament. In some of Edward I's experimental assemblies nearly a hundred heads of houses were summoned, more than half of them Cistercians and Premonstratensians on account of their interests in wool. By his grandson's time most of the white monks and canons had dropped out and the number of abbots attending had become standardised at just under thirty; with the bishops they still slightly outnumbered the lay lords, though their political influence was fast declining. Apart from the prior of St. John of Jerusalem and two abbots of Austin canons, Waltham and Cirencester—the last Cistercian house, Beaulieu, ceased to attend parliament after 1340—they were all black monks. Among them, in addition to those of the largest houses, were the abbots of Peterborough, Colchester, Abingdon, Gloucester, Evesham, Ramsey, Malmesbury, Croyland, St. Mary's York and St. Augustine's Canterbury and the prior of Coventry whose church was the joint throne or *cathedra* of the bishop of Lichfield. Nearly all wore the mitre conferred by the pope on important abbots.[1]

Such dignitaries lived in palatial lodgings, entertained princes at their table and, like bishops, had parks, studs and country manor-houses where from time to time favoured members of the chapters were invited to stay for recreation and sport. At St. Albans the abbot dined on a dais fifteen steps above the rest of the hall, while the monks who served him sang a grace at every fifth step. The abbot of St. Augustine's Canterbury had a chamberlain, a seneschal, a marshal of the hall, a carver, a waiter, a pantler, a master of the horse, an almoner and half a dozen other retainers. Yet sometimes such great men, who for the honour of their houses kept a lord's state, lived austere and devout lives, fasting, rising for the midnight office, sleeping on penitential beds and wearing horsehair under their magnificent garments, like Richard of Wallingford, the blacksmith's son who became abbot of St. Albans at thirty-one and died, still young, of leprosy, and Thomas de la Mare who reigned over the same house for nearly half a century and built its great gateway and King's hall. To enrich the architectural heritage of his house was a natural occupation for a fourteenth century abbot; Simon Langham of

[1] *Knowles*, II, 304.

Westminster, the last monk to become archbishop of Canterbury, endowed the Abbey with its cloisters and much of its present nave.

The age of monastic saints had passed; what was now admired in conventual circles was a dignified, shrewd man of the world who combined the conventional Christian virtues with a keen eye for his house's interests. There is a picture of one in Knighton's chronicle: William of Clown of the Augustinian abbey of St. Mary's in the Meadows, Leicester. The friend both of Henry of Lancaster and Edward III, he ruled it for thirty-three years to its great enrichment.

"He was a lover of peace and quiet, a reformer of quarrels and wrongs, . . . kind and obliging to his underlings and persons of the lower orders, unspeakably amiable to great men and the magnates of the realm . . . In his days two churches were appropriated, . . . two manors acquired, likewise rents and possessions. He also obtained a charter from the king for himself and his successors, excusing them from attending parliament . . . To this kindly abbot, William, God gave so great grace in the eyes of all men, lords and others, that there was scarce a man who could deny him what he asked. On such good terms was he with the lord king that he asked him in jest to grant him a fair for buying and selling harriers and hounds of all sorts. The king actually thought that he meant it seriously and granted him the fair; but he would not insist on the matter. In hunting of the hare he was reckoned the most notable and renowned among all the lords of the realm, so that the king himself and his son, Prince Edward, and divers lords of the realm had an annual engagement to hunt at his entertainment. Nevertheless he would often say in private that the only reason why he took delight in such paltry sports was to show politeness to the lords of the realm, to get on easy terms with them and win their goodwill in matters of business."[1]

Except in a few secluded priories and cells, where monks with a vocation for solitude were wont to retire for contemplation,

[1] *Hamilton Thompson*, 168-70.

and in the few houses of the Carthusians—a hermit Order where
the old strictness and monastic silence still prevailed and whose
motto was, "Never reformed because never deformed"—monks
were no longer dedicated men living austere lives, but comfortable members of a rich bachelor fraternity, proud of their corporate traditions and treasures and exceedingly jealous of their
rights. Though their lives for the most part were decorous and
orderly, they were seldom ascetic. In theory, vegetarian diet,
silence at meals and strict fasts were still the rule; in practice, the
"pittances" of meat and luxuries formerly only allowed to monks
in sickness had become part of the normal monastic dietary,
though, to avoid desecrating the refectory, meals on "flesh days"
were usually taken in a parlour or in the misericord of the
infirmary. The table of a rich, well-found monastery was like that
of a nineteenth century Oxford or Cambridge college, a by-
word for good food and drink.

Monks no longer did their own manual work; at the little
priory of Bicester twenty-five menials looked after eleven canons.
In the larger houses servants seem to have outnumbered the
brethren by three to one. At Durham the prior's staff, in light
green and blue liveries, included a butler, a cup-bearer, valets,
pages, grooms, gardeners, washerwomen, even a jester.[1] Nor
were monks any longer confined to the cloister. In a large house,
with numerous manors and distant estates, there was ample
excuse and scope for travel for any brother with a flair for affairs.
Langland depicted such a one as

> "a rider, a roamer by streets,
> A leader of law-days and a land buyer,
> A pricker on a palfrey from manor to manor,
> An heap of hounds at his arse as a lord were."

The monk in Chaucer's *Canterbury Tales*, whose passions were
inspecting farms and hunting, had "many a dainty horse in
stable"; his bridle, when he rode, jingled

> "so clear
> And eke as loud as doth the chapel bell
> Where that this lord was keeper of the cell.
> The rule of St. Maur or of St. Beneyt,
> Because that it was old and somewhat straight

[1] *Knowles*, II, 325.

This ilkë monk let pass the oldë day
And held after the newë time alway."
"A lord full fat and in good point," with sleeves rounded with
the finest fur, his favourite food was "a fat swan roast."

Paradoxically, despite their wealth the monasteries were
often in financial trouble, especially the smaller ones. With the
falling rents and farming profits of the latter fourteenth century
and with growing royal and papal taxation, even the greater
abbeys had difficulty in maintaining their costly expenditure and
were forced to borrow at exorbitant rates of interest. The open
house they kept for their rich patrons and for itinerant lords—
for no place was so comfortable as a monastery—was a heavy
strain on their resources; often some pious prince or earl would
descend on his favourite abbey for the Christmas or Easter feast
with two or three hundred retainers and, perhaps, a pack of
hounds. In many cases, too, monasteries were saddled with what
were called "corrodies," compelling them to maintain a number
of idle and sometimes highly embarrassing pensioners, either of
founders' kin[1] or the nominees of some benefactor. It was a
common practice for houses in need of cash to sell for a lump
sum a life pension or annuity to be paid in the form of food, drink,
clothing and lodging during the pensioner's life, sometimes
even with remainder to his widow.

All this tended to make the monks harsh landlords, enforcing
their rights against their tenants and villeins and the burghers at
their gates with more than ordinary rigidity, which they were the
better able to do owing to their habit of keeping records. They
were great sticklers for the privileges which had come down to
them from their historic past and which they regarded as the
private property of the saints in whose honour their houses had
been founded; as Tyndale later wrote, " It is God's, not theirs,
they say; it is St. Hubert's rents, St. Alban's lands, St. Peter's
patrimony."

This rendered them unpopular, except in the remote, wilder
parts of the country where their houses were still the chief centres

---

[1] On the assumption, so characteristic of medieval justice, that by his
pious gift or bequest the founder had deprived his descendants of what they
would otherwise have inherited. See *Knowles*, ii, 283, 286-7; *Hamilton
Thompson*, 174-5; *Pantin*, 109.

of local culture, piety and charity. Though their magnificent churches and famous relics were a source of regional pride—

> "In Holland in the fenny lands
> Be sure you mark where Croyland stands"—

they had become in southern England a synonym for easy living. The "Order of Bel-Ease" was the name given to the regulars in one satire. The real charge against them was that they no longer fulfilled any essential part in the country's polity or justified the huge proportion of the national wealth they controlled. They had even ceased to set its artistic standards, for, except in a few of the greater Benedictine houses like Gloucester and Ely, they were surpassed as architectural patrons and innovators by the rich statesmen-bishops of the royal court, while most of the lesser arts, like the illumination of manuscripts, were increasingly executed by lay professionals instead of in the cloister. Only in the keeping of historical chronicles were the monasteries still leaders. They survived and continued to exercise great social, and to a much lesser degree political, influence because they were an integral part of the ruling establishment and fabric of society and, as such, constituted an irremovable vested interest.

What was true of the monasteries was true, on their much smaller scale, of the nunneries. Most of them were very small, though a few like Wilton, Romsey, Wherwell and Sempringham were rich and famous; it was a saying that if the abbot of Glastonbury were to marry the abbess of Shaftesbury their heir would be richer than the king. Convents did a good deal of teaching, though seldom of a very strenuous kind, taking young girls of good family as boarders and sometimes keeping an infant school for the neighbourhood.[1] They were renowned, too, for their needlework—the much coveted *opus Anglicanum*. They provided dignified places of retirement for dowagers of the upper class, a vocation and home for unmarriageable daughters and a devout finishing-school for young ladies. The cachet given by membership of a fashionable convent was considerable, and rich merchants and franklins would pay high premiums for their womenfolk's admission. The prioress of such was a woman of distinction and breeding, like Chaucer's Madame Eglentine who

---

[1] "Abstinence, the abbess, taught me my A.B.C." *Piers Plowman.*

wore an elegantly pleated cloak, a coral bracelet, two necklaces of green beads—for saying her prayers—and a gold brooch engraved with the words, *Amor vincit omnia*.

> "Full well she sang the services divine
> Entunëd in her nose full seemëly.
> And French she spoke full fair and sweetëly
> After the school of Stratford-attë-Bowe,
> For French of Paris was to her unknowe.
> At meatë well i'taught was she in all;
> She let no morsel from her lippës fall,
> Nor wet her fingers in her saucë deep.
> Well could she carry a morsel and well keep
> That never drop upon her breast should be,
> For all her thought was set on courtesy . . ."

The poet's picture of the little dogs she kept as pets and on whom she lavished such affection seems to have been drawn from the life. An episcopal visitation revealed how Lady Audley brought to the convent at Langley "a great abundance of dogs, in so much that when she comes to church there follow her twelve who make a great uproar." As was to be expected in such purely female establishments, there was often more love of fine clothes than was compatible with a life of religious dedication, and an incurable tendency to tittle-tattle and back-biting. When during an episcopal visitation the nuns accused the prioress of Ankerwyke, Godstow, of making a private room for herself in the dormitory, she retorted that she had been kept awake at night by their chattering to Oxford scholars loitering on the river bank. And a fifteenth century prioress of Eastbourne, who might have been Madame Eglentine's sister, was accused by her flock of putting the convent into £40 debt because "she frequently rides abroad and pretends that she does so on the common business of the house—although it is not so—with a train of attendants much too large, and tarries too long abroad; she feasts sumptuously both when abroad and at home and is very choice in her dress so that the fur trimmings of her mantle are worth 100s."[1] Visiting bishops were always trying, though in vain, to moderate such shortcomings in the ladies religious.

The truth was that both monasteries and nunneries were

[1] *Hamilton Thompson*, 172; P. Kendall, *The Yorkist Age*, 269-70.

fighting against the trend of a thriving, vigorous age in which the instinct of the ordinary individual was to mingle with the world and emulate its rising standards of comfort and elegance rather than, as in earlier and more barbaric times, to seek refuge from it in the communal dedication of the convent. It was symptomatic that in many houses, not only the abbot and prior, but most of the obedientiaries had separate apartments. At Launceston, Bishop Grandisson of Exeter found every canon in possession, not only of a room, but of a page, a herb-garden, a dovecot and a dog of his own. Cash allowances to monks for personal expenditure, for spices, clothes, even for work done for the monastery, were all eroding the selfless spirit of the cloister; monasteries were approximating more and more to the less rigid ideals of the secular cathedral and collegiate chapters. It was symptomatic that most of the conventual houses founded in the fourteenth century partook of this looser character. Side by side with the monasteries, whose population was slowly declining, were springing up a growing number of collegiate chapters, whose prebends offered their founders a patronage similar to that of the secular cathedrals and which no monastery, with its basic rule of residence, could offer. Some of these were Crown foundations like the new chapels of St. Stephen's Westminster, and St. George's Windsor, and the older royal "peculiars" of Bridgnorth St. Mary Magdalene and Wimborne minster. Others were established by diocesan bishops, like Westbury-on-Trym and Ottery St. Mary which was founded during the French war by Bishop Grandisson out of a confiscated living that had belonged to the dean and chapter of Rouen. Great nobles like the earls of Warwick and Lancaster also endowed or added to similar collegiate foundations. Some of these possessed churches which rivalled those of the cathedral monasteries.[1]

If the conventual clergy mingled too much with the world they were supposed to shun, the uncloistered friars did so as a duty. For every monk on the road there were a dozen friars. They were to be seen in the king's court, in the baron's hall,

---

[1] In his *English Cathedrals* John Harvey reckons that before the end of the Middle Ages there were more than a hundred churches of cathedral type in England, a quarter of which have been totally destroyed while others survive only in ruins.

in the merchant's counting-house, on the village green, in the deepest haunts of vice and poverty. Wherever, it was said, there was a fly, there was "eke a friar." It was they who in the days of St. Francis and St. Dominic had brought Christianity from the sanctuary into the street and field. Since then, in the latter thirteenth and early fourteenth century, they had dominated the nation's theological life. But though the mendicants, as they were called, were still the chief missionaries of the age, they were no longer the selfless and penniless saints who had "followed the naked Christ" at their first coming a hundred and thirty years before. As their founders had bade them, they still begged their way wherever they went, but the need to do so had vanished. With their great international Orders—grey robed Franciscans, Dominicans in their white tunics and black robes, Carmelites, Austin Friars, all of them with forty or more houses in England— they possessed immense wealth, owning their friaries and churches, some of them like the famous three-hundred-foot-long Greyfriars church in London almost as splendid as those of the larger abbeys. For more than a century the benefactions and bequests of the rich had flowed into their coffers and, as the confessors of kings, nobles and merchants, they enjoyed vast influence. Though strongest in the trading and wool towns whose burghers thronged the great new preaching naves which had been raised with their wealth, they were to be seen everywhere, ministering to rich and poor alike and employing popular and even sensational devices to win converts to their faith and subscribers to their Orders.

Their universal appeal arose partly from their popular style of preaching—an art in which they were carefully trained and in which they far excelled the uneducated and untravelled parish priests—and from the understanding and ingratiating way in which they heard confessions and the readiness with which, according to their many critics among the secular and monastic clergy, they granted absolution, especially to those with money to compound for their sins. They were active at both ends of the social and cultural scale, playing a leading part in the teaching and theological and philosophical speculations of the universities of Oxford and Cambridge and tickling the fancy of the credulous and uneducated by their racy and often crude stories and similes.

Their genial, man-of-the-world approach was combined with a highly emotional appeal, and they were particularly popular with the ladies, to whom their gaiety, good humour and here-today, gone-tomorrow approach much endeared them—according to their enemies far too much.[1]

Because their sermons were changing the character of popular worship, pulpits, perched on long narrow stems like inverted wine-glasses and covered with painted canopies—until now only to be found in cathedrals and beside open-air preaching crosses —were becoming part of the internal furniture of the richer town churches. From these, hooded friars declaimed with lively gestures to rapt congregations, the ladies in wimples and 'kerchiefs grouped around on benches while their husbands stood behind or leaned against the pillars and humbler folk squatted on the rush-strewn stones. In an age when there were no newspapers and few could read, such sermons proved immensely exciting, being spiced not only with dramatic tales and jests but with news of the outside world. Their preachers had a way both of delicately flattering their auditors, even when they rebuked them, and of castigating the failings of others which made their sermons—at their best great and profound oratory—not only a religious experience but delightful entertainment. In the manuscript collections, some in the vernacular and some translated into more decorous Latin, that have come down to us from the fourteenth and fifteenth centuries one can follow their technique. "Do you want me to talk to you about worthy womanhood," says one, possibly with a wink to take the sting out of his rebuke: "I'm going to say something instead about that old dame whom I see asleep over there . . . For God's sake if anyone has a pin, let him wake her up." Another preacher tells of "the little black imp" that runs round in sermon time and "puts his fingers over the ears and eyes of the people, making them deaf and

---

[1] "When the good man is from hame
　And the friar comes to our dame,
　He spares neither for sin nor shame
　But that he does his will . . .
　Each man that here shall lead his life
　That has a fair daughter or a wife
　Beware that no friar them shrive."
Political Poems and Songs (ed. Wright),1, 263-8. cit. *Rickert*, 375-6.

sleep" or the small industrious devil who fills whole sacks with the words of those who "jangle and yap" in church and skip the prayers and responses.[1] One can see him doing so on a misericord in Ely cathedral; the craftsman who carved it must have heard just such a sermon.

This preaching had far-reaching social consequences. In days of wide regional differences it helped to create a common national sentiment, idiom and speech. Far more than writers of books could do before printing, the mendicants, with their similes, sayings and jests, familiarised men and women of all classes with words drawn from half the languages and dialects of the West. And at a time of staggering social injustices and ever-widening divisions of wealth, they produced a climate of thought in which the inequality of man could no longer be taken wholly for granted. The Church did not teach that all men were equal; on the contrary, it insisted that the world, like Heaven, was a hierarchy in which every man had his appointed place and must give reverence and obedience to those in authority. Yet the friars' vivid portrayal of the fate that awaited the unrighteous great made it clear to even the most humble-minded that no-one, from the king downwards, could hope to escape the pains of Hell if he flouted justice. The rich, the great Dominican preacher, Dr. Bromyard, declared in a characteristic friar's sermon, were deceived in thinking that they were the masters of their riches, since they were only for a short time its guardians. "All are descended from the same first parents, and all come from the same mud." Where, he asked, were the evil princes of the world, the kings and lords who had lived with pride and possessed great palaces, manors and lands, who ruled harshly and cruelly to obtain the pleasures of the world? "Of all their riches, their delicacies, they have nothing, and the worms have their bodies. Instead of palace, hall and chamber their soul shall have the deep lake of hell . . . In place of scented baths their body shall have a narrow pit in the earth and a bath more black and foul

---

[1] *Owst, Preaching*, 175-8, 186. His name was Tittivullus, and once, when caught at his business by a vigilant monk, he explained that he had to present daily to his master, the Devil, "a thousand pokes full of failings and of negligences and syllables and words that are done in your Order in reading and singing, or else I must be sore beaten." Eileen Power, *Medieval People*, 70.

than any bath of pitch and sulphur. In place of inordinate embraces they will have there the embraces of the fiery brands of hell . . . Instead of wives they shall have toads, instead of a great retinue and throng of followers their body shall have a throng of worms and their soul a throng of demons."[1] The friars were the pace-setters of the age, pointing to a world very different to that around them, where presently brother would no longer be able to ignore the claims of brother.

Yet though the mendicants exercised immense influence in the Church, they no longer monopolised its higher intellectual ranks as in the days of Aquinas and St. Bonaventura. Then a succession of great university doctors from the northern island, lecturing in the schools of Paris and Oxford, had contributed to the most remarkable flowering of abstract thought since the days of ancient Greece. Alexander of Hales, Adam Marsh "the illustrious doctor", Thomas of York and Roger Bacon had been among the foremost philosophers of the age; three other famous English scholastics, two of them friars, St. Edmund Rich, Kilwardby and Pecham, had sat in turn on St. Augustine's throne at Canterbury.[2] An even greater scholar, Duns Scotus—a Franciscan from Roxburghshire who inferred the rational probability of an Infinite Being by proving mathematically that infinity existed—had revolutionised philosophical thought by successfully challenging the conclusions of the great St. Thomas Aquinas, the "angelical doctor" who had set out to reconcile, in one intelligible, harmonious whole, all ascertainable knowledge with revealed truth. Another Franciscan born in a Surrey village at the beginning of Edward I's reign, William of Ockham, by proving, with a razor-like logic that no-one could refute, the impossibility of bridging the gulf between reason and faith, made a permanent separation between natural philosophy and theology and, leaving the Church the embarrassing legacy of thinking one thing and believing another, established ecclesiastical authority as the sole basis for religious conviction: a proposition loaded with peril should an age of scepticism ever arise.

[1] *Owst, Literature and Pulpit*, 293-4.

[2] "Any list of the dozen or so most influential masters of the period of 1200-1350 would be found to contain the names of more Englishmen than of any other nationality." D. Knowles, *The Evolution of Medieval Thought*, 279. For the beginnings of the universities in England see *Makers of the Realm*, 328-9.

During the fourteenth century there had been a reaction from the excessive intellectualism and subtleties of these great schoolmen. The main contribution of the universities had become not so much the production of philosophers and dialecticians as of men fitted for the highest offices of Church and State. Though still pursued to their logical end—sometimes so violently that archbishop, pope or king had to silence the disputants for the sake of peace—the theological controversies of scholars were now concerned with subjects more intelligible to the general body of Christians: dominion and grace, the salvation of the unbaptized, predestination and free will, the merits and dangers of apostolic poverty and mendicancy. In these debates the friars no longer had everything their own way but were challenged by secular masters trained in the little colleges of priest-fellows that had recently been founded both at Oxford and Cambridge, at that time about a third of the former's size.

These colleges were not intended for the swarms of undisciplined youths—most of them little more than children—who, while pursuing their studies under the nominal control of the diocesan bishop's chancellor or *magister scholarum*, lived in attics and cellars or crowded together in the lodging-houses or halls hired by the regent masters for their pupils.[1] Their object was to provide, in the tumultuous and squalid hurly-burly of a medieval university, a refuge where a few earnest scholars, most of them already graduates, could study in an atmosphere of quiet, free from material want and under ecclesiastical discipline. In theory the Church was responsible for the shifting population of hungry, ragged clerks, who, in pursuit of learning or hope of preferment, begged their way across England to fill the straw-strewn, draughty, barn-like lecture-rooms of the regent masters. Having received an educational grounding at an endowed grammar school—in Lincolnshire alone there were eight such foundations —or in one of the cathedral schools which the Lateran Council

[1] The meals in such hostels—some of which, like Brasenose and St. Edmund's Hall, grew later into colleges—were provided from a common fund called *commons*: a term still used at Oxford and Cambridge. Extra food bought individually was known as *battels*. *Social England*, ii, 64.

[2] By a later act of 1389 "scholars of the universities that go begging" were ordered to furnish themselves with a licence to do so from the chancellor on pain of being put in the stocks. 12. *Ric* ii *cap* 7. cit. *Jusserand*, 270-1.

had ordered to be kept by every major collegiate church, they
were under the Church's protection. Yet in practice neither it
nor the civic authorities from whom it so jealously shielded
them had any real control over them. Few of those unsupported
by private means or benefice were able to complete the long
exacting courses of dialectic, disputations and lectures—four
years for a bachelor's degree and seven or eight for a master's—
which were required to win the Church's coveted licence to
teach. Poverty, disease, the tavern and brothel, the night brawl
with knife and cudgel in Grope Lane or under the wall of Gutter
Hall, took their toll; as did the murderous faction-fights between
Town and Gown, North and South, England and Wales and
Ireland, which repeatedly broke out. At least twice—in 1264
when many masters and students migrated from Oxford to
Northampton, and in 1334, when a similar move was made to
Stamford—it looked as though a third university might arise.
But the Crown and ecclesiastical authorities forbade it and, by
supporting the monopoly of Oxford and Cambridge, ensured
that, while France had fifteen universities, England remained
with only two—a circumstance which in the future was to help
to create a national rather than a provincial culture for England's
professional ruling-class.

The earliest attempts to introduce stability into scholastic life
were made by the friars, all four of whose Orders established
convents for their own members at both universities. Despite,
however, the growing number of episcopal licences granted to
young incumbents wishing to attend the schools, little had been
done for those studying to be secular priests except a few elementary regulations for keeping order in the halls. Occasionally
some pious prelate or landowner would endow a scholarship or the
university's charitable chest to enable a lad of parts to study there
in return for saying masses for his soul, and towards the end of
Henry III's reign two small corporate establishments, University
Hall and the House of Balliol, were founded out of funds donated
for this purpose. The event that did most to determine the future
character of university education in England—though no-one
at the time could have foreseen it—was the publication in 1274
by the Bishop of Rochester, Walter de Merton, of statutes for an
Oxford college which he had founded and endowed out of his

Surrey property for training graduates for the priesthood. It was only a small affair of some twenty incorporated scholars or fellows, living together like monks with a common hall, chapel and dormitory under the rule of their own officers while studying for the university's higher degrees. But it became the model for a number of similar self-governing colleges, each under an elected warden, master, provost, rector or principal, and endowed with enough lands or appropriated churches to provide the fellows with lodging, food, clothing and a competence until they obtained a benefice.

The earliest Cambridge college, Peterhouse, was founded by Hugh Balsham bishop of Ely about ten years after Merton and with identical rules. It was followed in the reigns of Edward II and III by three other Oxford colleges and seven at Cambridge. At Oxford, Stapledon or Exeter Hall in 1314, Oriel—at first called the "house of Scholars of St. Mary"—in 1326 and Queen's College in 1340 were all founded by churchmen connected with the Court, the last two under royal patronage. At Cambridge, Michaelhouse in 1324 and King's Hall in 1336—both later incorporated in the Tudor foundation of Trinity—were established to train clerks for the royal service, the former by an Exchequer official and judge, the latter by a grant from the Crown. Clare was founded in 1338 by the last Gloucester heiress, and Pembroke in 1347 by the widowed countess whose husband had led the Middle party in the days of the Ordainers. Gonville or the "hall of the Blessed Annunciation of the Virgin" and Trinity Hall were founded by churchmen in 1348 and 1350; Corpus Christi in 1352 by two Cambridge guilds presided over by the victor of Auberoche, Henry of Lancaster.

From these little colleges d'élite great churchmen, trained in theology or canon law, went out into the world to organize and instruct their fellow clerics and govern the realm. Their numbers were small; at the six Oxford colleges in existence at the time of Crécy there were only forty masters, twenty-three bachelors and ten undergraduates.[1] It was their quality that counted. By creating a new kind of academic benefice they put the secular masters and doctors on a footing with the friars who, with their lectures and residential convents, had long dominated the uni-

[1] H. E. Salter, *Medieval Oxford*, 97.

versities. Their emoluments did not compare with the prebends of the great collegiate churches so sought after by pluralists, but they were sufficient to produce a remarkable sequence of scholar statesmen, both theologians and lawyers. Merton alone provided four archbishops of Canterbury between 1328 and 1366. Others almost as famous went out from this remarkable little college equipped to play their part in moulding the thought of the age, like the astronomers Simon Bredon, John Maudith and Walter Rede whose astronomical almanacs gave Oxford something of the position of Greenwich today, the logician and Aristotle commentator, Walter Burley—*doctor planus et perspicuus* —and the theologian, John Buckingham, who found "the eternal predestination, pre-ordination, prevolition and concourse of God" to be "consistent with the freewill and merit of the creature." From Balliol came a still more eminent theologian, Ralph FitzRalph archbishop of Armagh, who, born at Dundalk in the Irish Pale at the beginning of the century, became chancellor of the university in his early thirties—a man distinguished throughout Christendom for his eloquence, piety and penetrating powers of argument.

Though the monks at first stood aloof from the fierce intellectual life of the universities, they, too, established cells or small convents for their members, where specially selected monks could acquire the wider learning which the traditional carrel in the cloisters could no longer give and which they needed to be able to hold their own in sermon and writing against their rivals, the friars.[1] Following the foundation in 1280 by the Cistercians of the little abbey of Rewley for white monks at Oxford, the black monks of the province of Canterbury built a house of studies of their own on land owned by the abbey of Malmesbury. Known as Gloucester College, its staircases— some of which still form part of Worcester College—were leased by different monasteries as lodgings for picked relays of their monks.

[1] When the monks of Gloucester College, Oxford, asked the prior of Norwich for the return of Adam of Easton—their most promising scholar who had been recalled to organise preaching in the cathedral—the prior replied that he could not be spared, since without him "the mendicant friars, who are the enemies of our Order and indeed of all churchmen, loosing their backbiting mouths at everyone, . . . would at once come up like mice out of their holes." *Pantin*, 175-6.

Later, Thomas Hatfield bishop of Durham founded on the outskirts of Oxford where Trinity now stands a house called Durham
College for eight student monks from the great northern priory
and eight poor secular clerks to act as their servants and study
with them. Still later, in the third quarter of the fourteenth
century, Archbishop Islip founded Canterbury College for the
monks of Christ Church. From all these houses distinguished
scholars went out to play their part in the intellectual and
theological controversies of the time. One of them, Adam of
Easton, became a cardinal and, after suffering imprisonment and
torture during the papal schism, was buried in the church of St.
Cecilia, Trastevere, leaving six barrels of books—subsequently
exempted by the king from customs duty—to his old priory at
Norwich. Another famous scholar-monk was the Northumbrian,
Uthred of Boldon, who began his university career as a secular
clerk and, after taking the habit at Durham, returned to Oxford
as warden of Durham College and a regent master. Later, as
sub-prior of Durham and three times prior of its rest-house,
Finchale, he became known as one of the greatest preachers and
controversialists of the age and left behind him no less than
nineteen devotional works.

•   •   •   •   •   •   •   •

Though the "seven liberal arts"—rhetoric, grammar, logic,
arithmetic, geometry, astronomy and music—remained the basis
of the curriculum through which all university students passed
before proceeding to a degree in Grammar, Arts, Theology, Law
or Medicine, the two subjects most studied now were theology
and canon law. A doctorate in theology was a passport to ecclesiastical fame and promotion, in canon law to a wide range of
lucrative appointments. The entire organisation of the Catholic
Church—not only its relations with the laity and temporal
power, but those between its countless establishments and Orders
—its finances, taxation, the enforcement of its rights, both
spiritual and temporal, depended on and were regulated by this
intricate technical science.

Founded partly on the law of imperial Rome and partly on
the dictates of Christian conscience and natural reason and
justice—equity, as it was called—the canon law was binding on

every officer and servant of the Church and on all Christians. Growing in complexity with the advance of civilisation and the multiplication of bureaucratic functions, it operated through an ascending hierarchy of courts that stretched from the humblest rural deanery to the *curia* at Avignon or Rome and with rights of appeal at every level up to the Holy Father himself. It sought to adjudicate between nation and nation—for the Church was the great peace and truce maker of Christendom; it investigated and suppressed heresy; it dealt with the moral problems, offences and rights of princes and rulers. It tried, though with diminishing success, to enforce good faith and equitable dealing in economic matters and to decide and enforce the ideal of the just price and wage. Its officers had jurisdiction over every matter that concerned the salvation of souls.

In many respects the canon law affected the lives of ordinary men and women far more closely than that of the king's courts which normally touched only criminals and men of property. The ecclesiastical courts had cognisance of marriage, bigamy and divorce, intestacy, wills and probate,[1] provision for dower and orphans, libel, perjury and breaches of good faith, as well as sexual offences, including adultery, fornication and brothel-keeping. They dealt with sacrilege, blasphemy, failure to pay tithes and church dues or to attend Mass, and the crime of simony or trading in ecclesiastical preferments. Offences on consecrated ground also came within their jurisdiction. These ranged from poaching and cutting down trees to infringements of the right of sanctuary, for which tremendous penalties could be inflicted. In such cases the Church was both party and judge and could be a tyrant as well as the means of salvation.

Since the ecclesiastical courts also possessed wide, and in some cases overriding powers in matters affecting the individual rights of clerics, and since the term cleric included not only those who had been ordained but anyone who could claim "benefit of clergy" by the simple device of translating a verse of a Latin psalm known as the "neck verse,"[2] laymen often suffered what

---

[1] Wills were nearly always drawn up by churchmen and had to be proved in the bishop's court or in the Prerogative Court of Canterbury if the testator had goods in several dioceses.

[2] The first verse of Psalm 50 (Vulgate)—i.e. Psalm 51 (Authorised Version).

they regarded as gross injustice through the one-sided leniency of the ecclesiastical courts. Among those whom canon law protected were university students—a particularly unruly type —schoolmasters, professional men like doctors, and nearly all schoolboys. Nor was it only clerks in minor orders who were a menace to society. A canon of Walsingham was found guilty of stealing goods from the cellarer, breaking into the sacristan's box in a neighbouring church and committing a rape.

Though in some respects the canon law was more merciful than the law of the king's courts, it was in other ways less just. Under the latter a man was assumed to be innocent unless he could be proved by the testimony of others to be guilty. In the courts Christian he could be forced to take an oath of purgation and so either condemn himself or commit perjury. To fall foul of the Church and its legal officers was no light matter. Its courts could fine, imprison for life, sentence to whipping and scourging, excommunicate—a frightening penalty involving exclusion from the sacraments and all contact with one's fellow Christians under pain of like penalty for them, and, in cases of persistent obduracy, eternal damnation. It could also impose a whole range of penances. The only thing its courts could not do was to inflict the death penalty, for canon law forbade the taking of blood by churchmen. In cases, however, where death seemed the appropriate punishment, they could turn the criminal over to the secular arm and ask the Crown to deal with him.

It was the inquisitorial methods of the courts Christian and their petty interference in men's daily lives that aroused such resentment against them. Laymen could be convicted for brawling in the churchyard, for failing to attend Mass, for irreverent behaviour in church and disrespect to the clergy, for working on Sundays and holy days. Even work for the Church could not excuse Sabbatarian offences, as witness an indignant letter written at the end of Edward I's reign from the rector of Harwell, Berkshire, to his archdeacon, complaining that the Bishop of Winchester's harvester had called up all the latter's tenants on a Sunday morning to cut hay in the bishop's park.

"For this purpose, while we were at breakfast he called

them up to work by blowing a certain great horn through the whole village, as he is wont to do on working days. And this seemed to me unbearable, so I immediately sent Sir Thomas my colleague, chaplain of the parish, to prevent such work upon that day, but they would not listen to him or desist from their work. So I warned them three or four times to stop and afterwards threatened them with excommunication if they went on, but I laboured in vain; for the said H. . . . answered me mockingly that he was going to cart the hay whether I liked it or not, nor would he cease work or permit others to cease for my threats or warnings. I, therefore, being somewhat disturbed, summoned them generally and afterwards had them summoned . . . . to appear before you in your chapter held on Wednesday the vigil of St. James's day, to hear and receive the sentence which your discretion should declare according to justice. Wherefore I beg your discretion to give them a suitable sentence, punishing them so that others may not be tempted by the lightness of their sentence to follow their example, and let the harvester receive punishment for habitually working on holy days and encouraging others to do the same. He is a powerful man."[1]

The penances to which men could be subjected were of the most humiliating kind. A man might be sentenced to be whipped at the church door, to appear on consecutive Sundays barefoot and in shameful garments, to stand before the high altar holding a candle whilst his crime was proclaimed to the congregation. Thus for mowing a meadow on the feast of St. Oswald two labourers were sentenced to four whippings and to perambulate the village on the next saint's day bearing bundles of hay, while two women who had washed linen on St. Mary Magdalene's day were given "two fustigations with a hank of linen yarn." For the more serious offence of attacking a priest with a spade a Taunton man in the next century was excommunicated and, when he submitted himself for correction, was condemned

"to walk in procession with bare head and feet and clothed

[1] Rosalind Hill, "A Berkshire Letter-Book." *Berkshire Archaeological Journal*, vol. 41 (1937), 23.

only in a shirt and breeches, and holding in his hand the spade, round St. Mary Magdalene on two Sundays, and on one Sunday to walk round the chapel of James and also to walk once round the market-place and, when he comes to the middle of it, to stand still for a time at the discretion of the chaplain with a whip in his hand who follows him."[1]

The court which most affected the ordinary man was that of the archdeacon. Nobody much liked archdeacons—"the bishop's eyes", as they were called—not even their fellow churchmen; it was an old ecclesiastical jest to speculate whether an archdeacon could get to Heaven. A trained canon lawyer who had had to pay for a long and expensive education at Bologna or some other foreign law school, he could hardly avoid being a pluralist. The rest of his income came from fees which he, his deputies—if, as was often the case, he was an absent pluralist— and the proctors who pleaded in his court were popularly believed to augment by fomenting litigation. He was employed by the bishop to investigate and punish cases of embezzlement and misapplication of church funds, unchastity both of churchmen and laymen, and breaches of the Christian code. Chaucer has left us a picture of one of these functionaries at work:

"... an erchedeken, a man of high degree,
That boldly did execution
In punishing of fornication,
Of witchcraft and eek of bawdery,
Of defamation and adultery,
Of church-reeves and of testaments,
Of contracts and neglect of sacraments
And eke of many another kind of crime
Which needeth not rehearsing at this time;
Of usury and simony also,
But, certes, lechers did he greatest woe ...
For smallë tithes and for small offering,
He made the people piteously to sing."

In administering the law against sexual offences archdeacons'
[1] P. Kendall, *The Yorkist Age*, 244-5.

officers, if not archdeacons, were widely suspected of bribery. This applied particularly to cases against the rustic clergy, large numbers of whom, contrary to canon law but in accordance with immemorial English custom, kept an unofficial wife, usually under the guise of housekeeper—a *foccaria* or hearth-mate, as she was called.[1]   Though such unions seem to have been generally accepted by their congregations—for there was seldom any lack of parishioners to come forward as compurgators to swear away charges of "incontinence" against their parsons— they laid the latter open to blackmail by ill-disposed members of the flock, especially during the archdeacon's periodic visita- tions. No less than a quarter of the incumbents of seventy-two parishes visited on one occasion in Hereford diocese were pre- sented for incontinence. Most of them were able to escape a public penance by getting compurgators to swear to their innocence, but many must have been guilty, as the following entry shows:

"Sir William Westhope is incontinent with one Jane Stale whom he keepeth always in his house . . . The man appeared, denied and is given a day to purge himself with five compurgators: he was also admonished to remove her from cohabitation within six days."[2]

Despite repeated rebukes and fines such unions had a way of persisting; a Dawlish chaplain was stated to have "kept his concubine for ten years and more or longer still; and, though often corrected on that account, incorrigibly persists." England was a tolerant land and, provided the fines were paid and there was a show of obedience to the bishop's decree, authority was satisfied. A priest in whose house a child was born could usually compound by a fine of five shillings—a "cradle crown," it was called.

The chief agent, and often the instigator, of such petty per- secution, both of clerics and laymen, was the archdeacon's summoner. He was the most hated of all the Church's officials. Usually a clerk in minor orders, he seems all too often to have been a man of the lowest character who kept *agents provocateurs*, including loose women, and made his living by spying and

[1] See *Makers of the Realm*, 218, 281.
[2] *Medieval Panorama*, 174.

blackmail. The specimen in Chaucer's *Canterbury Tales*, with his
drunken bullying ways and fiery face, carbuncles, whelks and
pimples, knew the secrets of the entire neighbourhood and
would

> "allow just for a quart of wine
> Any good lad to keep a concubine
> A twelvemonth and dispense it altogether,"

yet would strip anyone of his possessions who was not prepared
to bribe him. "Purse," he used to say, was "the good archdeacon's Hell," by which he meant that any offender could
escape penance and punishment provided he paid enough. The
customary rate of what was known as "sin-rent" was £2 p.a.

The Church did not, of course, approve such abuses, but, by
its practice, it condoned them. In its need for ever more money
to support its huge bureaucracy and magnificent court, the
papacy countenanced ways of raising money which amounted
to a wholesale sale of indulgences for sins committed in return
for cash. The theory of an indulgence, as old almost as the
Church itself, was that punishment for sin could be partly remitted, with the aid of the Church's intercession, for any genuine
penitent who received absolution and did suitable penance.
With the advance of civilisation the ecclesiastical authorities had
tended to substitute for physical penances like flogging and
fasting such useful acts of public service and charity as the
building and repair of churches, the endowment of almshouses,
schools and hospitals and the provision of bridges and wayside
chapels. One of Oxford's earliest colleges, Balliol, owed its
existence to a penance imposed on a rich North Country baron,
John Balliol, father of the Scottish king, for an act of sacrilege.[1]
Penance could also take the form of money payments to provide
priests to say prayers and masses for an offender, securing, provided he confessed his sins and showed true contrition, remission
of so many days in purgatory—the "middle state" to which it
was believed that all not immediately translated to Heaven or
Hell were consigned after death until they had expiated their
sins and so become fit for eternal bliss. Such vicarious professional intercession in commemoration of their own good deeds,

---

[1] *Medieval England*, ii, 528. The original endowment was subsequently
increased by his widow, the Lady Devorguilla.

could, it was held, secure earlier forgiveness for a sufferer and shorten his pains. In practice, it proved a step to the tacit assumption by the unrighteous that, not merely punishment, but sin itself could be remitted and that a man could even buy from the Church a licence to commit sin.

In the days of the first Edward, when the standards of English churchmanship had been particularly high, indulgences had been granted only sparingly and in approved cases and had never been publicly hawked for sale.[1] But, in the general moral decline of the next century, the ecclesiastical authorities found the temptation of raising money in this way too great to resist. Among regular travellers to be met with on the highways of England during the reign of Edward III was the pardoner, a sanctified huckster licensed by papal or episcopal letter to sell indulgences at every price-range to anyone prepared to buy. These pardoners, with their wallets "brimful of pardons come from Rome all hot," not only sold their wares but, though not themselves in holy orders, preached sermons advertising them. Sometimes they sold them on behalf of some chantry or work of piety such as a hospital, the repair of a church or a new painted glass window; sometimes they were complete charlatans, pretending they had the power to absolve from any sin and travelling with a string of forged indulgences round their necks, like the one who was sentenced to ride through Cheapside with his face to his horse's tail and a penitent's paper hat on his head.[2]

As a sideline they also peddled faked relics which were supposed to secure for their purchasers remission from punishment or protection from accident. Chaucer's pardoner had a pillow

---

[1] See Rosalind Hill, *Oliver Sutton*, 26.
[2] *Owst, Preaching*, 109. So Langland wrote:
"There preached a pardoner, as if he were a priest,
    Dragging out documents with bishops' affidavits
    And saying he himself could absolve them all
    For having failed to fast or being false to their vows.
    Illiterates believed him and liked what he said,
    Came up and crossed themselves, kissing his charters;
    He bounced them with his brevets and bleared their eyesight
    And they gave up their gold to gorge the glutton."
Visions from Piers Plowman (ed. and transl. N. Coghill), p. 16.

"which he asserted was our Lady's veil:
He said he had a gobbet of the sail
St. Peter had, . . .
. . . a cross of brassë full of stones
And in a glass he haddë piggës' bones."

Similar shams were sold to pilgrims at the shrines of the saints—a small lead ampulla of Canterbury water, supposed to be coloured by a miraculously inexhaustible drop of Becket's blood, or Durham water from St. Cuthbert's shrine. Probably these were thought of more as mementoes and evidences of pilgrimage than as possessing the virtue of genuine relics. For pilgrimage was another way of winning remission of punishment in purgatory. To a true penitent a pilgrimage could prove a penance of the most onerous kind, one in which he bade farewell to kin and home for years, perhaps forever, facing untold hardships and perils in travelling, on foot and unarmed, to the Holy Land or some other remote place.[1] Many, however, acquired such merit by proxy, hiring professional pilgrims or "palmers" as they were called—complete with broad brimmed hat, cross on frock, staff, wallet, scallop and begging bowl—to go on pilgrimage for them, as Sir Richard Arundel did when in his will he instructed his executors to find a man after his death to journey for the good of his soul to Rome, our Lord's sepulchre, and the Holy Blood in Germany. So, too, John Blakeney, citizen and fishmonger of London, left twenty marks to employ a chaplain to go on pilgrimage to Rome "and there to remain throughout one year to celebrate and pray for my soul and the souls of those for whom I am bound to pray."

Yet for most a pilgrimage, though seen as a means of acquiring grace, was an excuse for a holiday, to be taken preferably
"when that Aprillë with his showers sweet
The drought of March hath piercëd to the root."
Every spring and summer the grassy tracks to Canterbury or Walsingham, Gloucester or the rood of Bromholm in Norfolk,

---

[1] Crossing the Sinai desert in 1384, Leonardo Frescobaldi met a caravan of French pilgrims of whom five were knights with gold spurs, who told him that, of twenty who had set out together, eleven were dead and buried in the sand. G. and S. Frescobaldi, *Visit to the Holy Places* (transl. T. Bellorini and E. Hoade), 41.

would be thronged with gay companies of both sexes making
their way to their chosen shrine with guides and in company and
beguiling the journey, as in Chaucer's *Canterbury Tales*, with tales,
singing and the playing of bagpipes. The innkeepers along the
pilgrim-ways did a roaring trade, coaxing travellers into their
houses and there, in the words of one of Friar Bromyard's sermons, "talking and gaming with them until the time comes for
reckoning." At other places there were hostels for pilgrims provided by charitable gilds or corporations. The "Bell" at Tewkesbury, the "New inn" at Gloucester, the "George" at Glastonbury were all built for this purpose. By the middle of the fourteenth century catering for pilgrims had become an immense
industry. At Christ Church, Canterbury, they were met by a
monk at a special door and, after being sprinkled with holy
water, were led into the north transept to an altar marking the
spot where St. Thomas was killed. Then, after inspecting the
relics of his martyrdom in the crypt and kissing the rusty blade of
his murderer's sword, they ascended the stairs to the shrine on
their knees—one can still see the worn steps—and made their
oblations to the custodians of that marvel of jewels and gold,
receiving in return tiny *ampullae* of Canterbury water, while those
suffering from rheumatism rubbed their limbs against the surrounding stones.[1]

There were fashions in pilgrimages as in everything else, but
Becket's shrine remained the most popular of all; during one
year the Christ Church monks took £954. 6. 3d. in offerings to
it while an adjoining shrine to the Virgin only brought in
£4. 1. 8d.[2] For those who wanted a trip abroad, the shrine of
St. James of Compostella in north-west Spain was a great magnet
for the English, much more so than the more accessible Our
Lady of Boulogne or the head of St. John the Baptist at Amiens.
The shipmen of Bristol provided a continuous summer service to
the Galician ports, packing the pilgrims in rows in their little
ships, their feet extended, like those of the negro slaves of a later
age, towards the centre. The discomforts of the voyage, which

[1] Cook, *The English Cathedral*, 34-5; S. C. Carpenter, *The Church in England*,
181.
[2] *Maynard Smith*, 168.

generally took at least a week each way, are eloquently described
in a contemporary poem:

"Meanwhile the pilgrims lie
And have their basins by,
And after hot malmsey they cry,
    'Help us to restore!' ...

When that we shall go to bed,
The pump was nigh our bed's head,
A man were as good as dead
As smell thereof the stink."

Despite such miseries, in a single year more than two thousand
licences were issued in England to visit the Spanish shrine, and
sometimes more than thirty English pilgrim ships could be seen
at a time in Corunna harbour.

.   .   .   .

The part of the laity in worship and religious activities was
steadily growing. In earlier times the Church had borne the
sole responsibility for almost every charitable activity—hospitals,
education, the care of the aged and indigent, alms at the convent gate, even bridges and causeways for travellers. Now,
though such work was still done in its name, laymen were
taking an increasing share in it. The most popular form of
religious endowment in the fourteenth century was the chantry
—a small chapel, either inside an existing church or, more
occasionally in one built for the purpose, in which masses,
prayers and chants were offered in perpetuity for the donor's
soul in return for his provision of some continuing work of
charity—an almshouse, a school, an annual distribution of food
and largesse to the aged and crippled poor, the provision of
marriage dowries for destitute girls or apprenticeship-fees for
orphans, a bridge or a rest-house for pilgrims. Sometimes such
endowments were made by one man, like the chantry with eight
chaplains which Guy Beauchamp earl of Warwick founded at
Elmley Castle in Worcestershire a few years before the murder
of Gaveston. More often they were contributed by a self-renewing guild or fraternity of pious laymen who, having bought a

licence from the Crown to transfer land to mortmain, vested it
in their corporate heirs for the use of charitable and religious
objects. They were particularly popular among the town
merchants who, having grown rich, were as eager as lords and
landowners to use their wealth to ensure the future welfare of
their souls. Such was the fraternity which John Enfield and
other London citizens founded in 1343 to restore the roof and
steeple of All Hallow's, London Wall, and another of the same
date established by a group of wealthy fishmongers to provide a
chaplain to sing the anthem, *Salve Regina*, every evening in the
church of St. Magnus, London Bridge, "to the honour of God
and his glorious Mother our Lady Mary the Virgin . . . for in-
citing the people to devotion at such an hour, the more to merit
their souls."[1]

Most cities and country towns possessed similar guilds by the
end of the century. At Ludlow—centre of the west Shropshire
wool trade—a brotherhood founded in honour of St. John the
Evangelist maintained a hospital or alms-house for thirty poor
folk and a house for its chaplains, while another provided a free
school and schoolmaster. The grammar-school at which one
day Shakespeare was to be educated was founded by the guild of
the Holy Rood of Stratford-on-Avon. Sometimes guilds were
even founded by working folk, like the one dedicated to Our
Lady at Ellesmere in which every married man paid fourpence
a year and every servant earning more than five shillings p.a.
twopence, or that of St. Helen and St. Mary, Beverley, in which
the members marched in procession to the church on St. Helen's
Day headed by an old man with a cross, another with a spade
and a youth dressed as Queen Helen, and where, after hearing
a solemn mass, each man contributed a penny.[2]

All this was symptomatic of the relationship between Church
and lay community—one closer, perhaps, in England than in
any land in Europe. The *Ecclesia Anglicana* was part of the
Catholic Church of Christendom, yet it was also part of the
English State. Its bishops and abbots were not only fathers in
God but feudal magnates, leaders of the local community and
royal advisers. Clerics administered the Chancery and
Exchequer, sat on the judicial bench and headed diplomatic

[1] *Rock*, ii, 442-3.   [2] *Hamilton Thompson*, 140; *Rickert*, 235.

missions and fiscal enquiries. King and community had
showered and continued to shower wealth on the Church yet,
by doing so, had made churchmen servants as well as spiritual
leaders of the realm, subject, as owners of national land and
property, to the same common law as everyone else. England
was a country in which the sanctity of canonical doctrine and
law was scrupulously respected so long as it did not override the
legal rights of Crown and subject. Its very churches were
proprietary ones, whose lay owners, having given and endowed
them, retained the right to confer their emoluments on any
qualified priest who conformed to the spiritual requirements
demanded by the Church.

Everywhere was a tacit collusion between God's law and the
king's, in which divided loyalties did not so much clash as merge.
It was not logic that the English looked for in the leaders of
Church and State but the spirit of accommodation and compromise. Both supported one another; every re-enactment of the
great Charter began by guaranteeing the freedom and rights of
Holy Church, while anyone who infringed Magna Carta or the
Forest charters incurred the penalties of excommunication. From
the king and primate down to the humblest hedge-priest and his
tithe-paying parishioners there existed an acceptance of the fact
that it was better to work together than to insist on the last letter
of incompatible and conflicting rights.

The ecclesiastical system was riddled with anomalies and
inconsistencies, founded on personal rights, both clerical and lay,
deeply rooted in history. In Chichester—a bishop's seat—the
city and close were the "peculiar" or private jurisdiction of the
dean and chapter, the outskirts were part of the diocese of
Canterbury, and the land adjoining the episcopal park belonged
to the canons of Bosham, a royal free chapel subject to the
spiritual supervision of the bishop of Exeter.[1] In none of them,
though his own palace was situated in the close, had the
diocesan bishop any rights save those of a stranger. Such
an apparent absurdity presented no difficulty to an English
ecclesiastic; he had been accustomed to similar ones from the
day of his entry into the Church.

In such matters, therefore, everyone tended to have a neigh-

[1] *Hamilton Thompson*, 75.

bourly yet wary respect for the conflicting rights of his fellows and to make them a subject for compromise and bargaining. The bargaining was stiff, but it usually was conducted with Christian courtesy. When the chancellor and treasurer of England wanted a Wiltshire living for a government official they wrote to the owner of the advowson, the Abbess of Wilton—who doubtless had protégés and ideas of her own—in the following terms:

> "Very honourable and very reverent lady of holy religion, we have heard that there is a church of the patronage of you and your convent named Berwick St. John which will apparently soon be vacant, so it is said, because the present parson is a man of great age and is now prostrate with so serious an illness that there is no hope of his recovery, as it is said. We therefore pray you, very honoured lady, that it may please you to present to the said church whenever it becomes vacant our very dear and well loved friend, H.H." (Henry Harborough?) "clerk, and to cause your letters of presentment to be made to him, on the understanding . . . that by such a deed we wish to be greatly beholden to you and shall be ready to do something agreeable another time for you in your house. Very honoured and very reverent lady, may the blessed Trinity keep and maintain you always for the good government of holy religion."[1]

. . . .

Such was Holy Church—the most venerated and valuable thing in the English polity—as it appeared to the ordinary man on the morrow of Edward III's victories in Europe. It had created the society and civilisation of which he was part. Full of imperfections its faults were open and confessed, but they did not touch, or seem able to touch, the validity of its faith and institutions. Individual failures there were in plenty and criticisms of churchmen. But neither the failures nor the criticisms could impair the Church's strength. "Something to which every man or woman could respond and at all levels," Sir Maurice Powicke

[1] *Anglo-Norman Letters and Petitions*, ed. M. D. Legge, Oxford, 1941.

has written, it had existed for centuries, was universally accepted and it worked.

Yet there was now to fall on the Christian and triumphant realm of England, with its magnificent churches, pious foundations and victorious knights, a testing disaster greater than that which befell Job when, dwelling in the land of Uz with a hedge about him and all his works blessed, there came a great wind from the wilderness and smote the four corners of his house and destroyed his substance and children.

Chapter Nine

BLACK DEATH
AND BLACK PRINCE

Death came driving after and all to dust pashed
Kings and knights, caesars and popes. . . .
Many a lovely lady and leman of knights
Swooned and swelted for sorrow of Death's dints.
WILLIAM LANGLAND

THE SUMMER of 1348 was exceptionally wet. The Leicester chronicler, Henry Knighton, attributed the incessant downpour to the wanton behaviour of ladies at tournaments. Dressed in men's attire "in party-coloured tunics, one colour or pattern on the right side and another on the left, with short hoods that had pendants like ropes wound round their necks, and belts thickly studded with gold or silver," he complained, "a band of women would come to share the sport, sometimes to the number of forty or fifty ladies, of the fairest and comeliest (though I say not of the best) among the whole kingdom. There they spent and lavished their possessions and wearied their bodies with fooleries and wanton buffoonery . . . But God in this matter, as in all others, brought marvellous remedy, for He harassed the places and times appointed for such vanities by opening the floodgates of heaven with rain and thunder and lurid lightning and by unwonted blasts of tempestuous winds."

Yet, as the monastic historian was quick to point out, the rain that wrecked the tournaments in honour of the Order of the Garter was the least of the evils awaiting England that summer. God had prepared a far more awful punishment for her. Eighteen months earlier, while the English were besieging Calais, another army two thousand miles away had been blockading a small Genoese grain port in the Crimea where a band of silk-traders, operating at the end of the seven-thousand mile caravan route to China, had taken refuge from the Tartar horsemen of the Steppes. Suddenly the besiegers had been struck down by a pestilence which, spreading everywhere throughout Tartary and known as "the death," had begun, it was believed, in the putrefaction of unburied multitudes in earthquakes in China. Before they raised the siege the Tartars are said to have catapulted some infected corpses into the town.

What is certain is that the disease was carried into Europe at the end of 1347 or beginning of 1348 by Genoese ships trading with the Black Sea. No-one knew its cause or even its nature, but it is now believed to have been the bubonic plague— a flea-borne epidemic of the black rat[1] which had invaded Europe from Asia at the time of the crusades and with which the wooden trading-ships of the day were heavily infested. By the time vessels that had called in the Crimea reached the Bosphorus and Mediterranean the plague was raging among their crews, and every port at which they touched became infected. It struck so suddenly that at first no-one had time to escape; at Constantinople the Byzantine emperor's heir was among its victims. The symptoms were a gangrenous inflammation of the lungs, vomiting and spitting blood, vilely infected breath and the appearance, on the second day, of hard black buboes in the arm-pits and groin which were almost always the heralds of death. Few who caught the disease in its first onslaught outlived the third day.

By the end of January 1348 the plague was raging in all the great ports of southern Europe, including Venice, Genoa, Marseilles and Barcelona. In the Mediterranean ships were found drifting with every member of the crew dead. One after another, despite frantic attempts to isolate themselves, the Italian cities went down before the pestilence. Terrifying stories circulated of its supernatural origin; of how "in the east, hard by Greater India, fire and stinking smoke had burned up all the cities" and how "between Cathay and Persia there had rained a vast rain of fire, falling in flakes like snow and burning up

---

[1] The communication of plague by the bite of the rat-flea was only fully realized at the beginning of this century, during the succession of epidemics that between 1897 and 1907 carried off some four million people in India.

mountains and plains with men and women," and accompanied by a sinister black cloud that "whosoever beheld died within the space of half a day."[1]   Thence, borne by "a foul blast of wind from the south," the infection had invaded Europe.

In the spring, having made Venice and Genoa cities of the dead, the plague reached Florence. In the introduction to his *Decameron* Boccaccio left a first-hand picture of its horrors: the helplessness of the doctors, the stench of the sick, the cautious shutting themselves up in their houses until the infection crept in and the reckless drinking in taverns day and night, the multitude of corpses lying uncovered before every church and the pits into which the dead were packed in layers. The poor perished in the streets or among the crops, the swine that rooted in the deserted streets dropped dead as they nosed the bundles of rags stripped from the plague-stricken, and swarms of oxen, sheep and goats—"and even dogs, those most faithful friends to men,"—wandered untended through the fields. The dying were abandoned, the dead were dragged out of the houses and stacked by the road-side, the houses of those who had fled were left open to all, "the reverend authority of the laws, divine and human, being almost wholly ruined and dissolved." It was the same everywhere: in Siena, in Piacenza, in Parma, in Rimini, where the chronicler, Agniolo di Tura, carried with his own hands his five little sons to the grave.

While the plague was devastating Italy, it spread in widening circles from the Mediterranean eastwards into Istria and Hungary and over the Alps into Bavaria, westwards across Spain where it struck down the Queen of Aragon and, later, the King of Castile, and northwards from Marseilles[2] up the Rhone. It broke out in the convent of the Carmelite friars at Avignon before anyone even realized what it was, slaying Laura, the adored of the poet Petrarch, and the abbot of the great Canterbury monastery of St. Augustine's who was visiting the *curia* at the time. "When

---

[1] The chronicler of Este, cit. *Coulton Black Death*, 10-12. See also Gabriele de Mussi, *Ystoria de morbo seu mortalite qui fuit a 1348*, cit. *Gasquet*, 5, 15-16.

[2] Where an English doctor, William Grisant, of Merton College, was among the survivors. He had been studying medicine at the medical school at Montpellier and was practising in Marseilles at the time. J. Astruc, *Histoire de la Faculté de Médécine de Montpellier*, 184, cit. *Gasquet*, 40.

anyone who is infected by it dies," wrote a Flemish canon from the city, "all who see him in his sickness or visit him or even carry him to the grave, quickly follow him there. The sick are served by their kinsfolk as dogs would be; food is put near the bed for them to eat and drink after which all fly . . . Nor do priests hear confessions or give the sacraments." "Charity was dead," reported the pope's physician, who himself caught the disease and was one of the few to recover. "Even the doctors did not dare to visit the sick. As for me, to avoid infamy, I did not dare to absent myself but still I was in continual fear." The pope himself, ordering corpses to be dissected to find the cause of the disease, fled to his country seat near Valence, where he shut himself up in a single room, keeping fires constantly burning to stifle the infection and giving access to no one.

All that summer of 1348 the Black Death was drawing nearer to England. In the spring it reached Gascony where it struck down King Edward's youngest daughter, the Princess Jean, who was on her way to Spain to marry the heir of Castile. Soon afterwards it broke out in Paris where vast multitudes died, including the queens of France and Navarre. By July, creeping north through Poitou and Brittany and round the coasts, it was in Normandy, where "it came to such a pass that no-one could be found even to carry the corpses to the tomb. People said that the end of the world had come." All the while clouds and continuous rain poured down on England and, towards the end of the month as men watched the ports, Archbishop Zouche of York wrote to his deputy ordering processions and litanies to be held in all parish churches twice a week "for the stay of pestilence and infection." Only by prayer, he declared, could the scourge be turned away.

The archbishop—the victor of Neville's Cross—spoke of man's life being a warfare, where "those fighting amidst the miseries of this world are troubled by the uncertainty of a future now propitious, now averse, the Lord Almighty permitting those whom he loves to be chastised so that strength by the infusion of spiritual grace may be made perfect in infirmity." But though the Bishop of Bath and Wells, equally apprehensive, ordered processions and stations in all his churches to "protect the people from the pestilence which had come from the East into the neigh-bouring kingdom," life in England that summer seems to have gone on very much as usual. In days when news travelled only by word of mouth and was carried from village to village along the grass roadways by friars and pedlars, the people of an isolated northern island can have heard little of the fate that had befallen their fellow Christians beyond the Channel. Absorbed in their local affairs, they were more concerned about the weather, the ruin of their crops and the murrain that had broken out among the sheep and cattle. Even the king, who must have been fully aware of the danger, seemed obsessed with his magnificent build-ing projects for housing the college of his new Order of the Garter. On August 6th, he issued orders for the conversion of St. Edward the Confessor's chapel, Windsor, into one "of befitting splendour" and for the provision of accommodation for the additional canons and twenty-four "helpless and indigent knights" whom he and his companions were to present on the next St. George's Day "in honour of Almighty God and of his mother Mary the glorious Virgin and of St. George the Martyr."

It may have been on that very day that, despite every pre-caution by the port authorities, the plague crossed the Channel. Some time that August it broke out in the little Dorset coast town of Melcombe Regis, now Weymouth, "depriving it almost of inhabitants." Within a few weeks it reached Bristol, probably by sea, turning it into a cemetery. It treated England as it had treated western Europe, and the English reacted in the same way. At Bristol "the living were scarce able to bury the dead," and "the men of Gloucester would not suffer the Bristol men to have access to them." But no constable's guard could stop the swift-running rats from infecting one another, or their parasites from deserting their putrescent bodies for living men and women. Nor had anyone any idea what caused the mor-tality: the pallor, the sudden shivering and retching, the dreaded scarlet botches and black boils—"God's tokens"—the delirium and unbearable agony that came without warning and carried off its victims in a few hours.

During that autumn the plague struck down southern shire after shire. Dorset and its adjoining counties suffered terribly;

Poole was so depopulated that it did not recover for more than a
century—a hundred years ago a projecting strip of land known
as the Baiter was still pointed out as the burial-place of its victims.[1]
In some villages, like Bishopstone in Wiltshire, scarcely a soul
survived, and when life was renewed after the plague the site was
left deserted.   The crops rotted in the fields, the church bells
were silent, and everywhere corpses were flung, blackened and
stinking, into hastily dug pits.   At his lonely episcopal manor of
Wiveliscombe, where he and his *familia* remained during the
visitation, the Bishop of Bath and Wells instituted an endless
succession of incumbents to vacant benefices—some, like St.
Laurence's Shaftesbury, denuded of its parson more than once,
and one, Winterbourne St. Nicholas, no less than three times.   In
a pastoral letter to his flock, he enjoined the sick to make confession to a layman if no priest was available and, if need be, to a
woman.   When the sacrament of Extreme Unction could not be
administered, he concluded, "faith must, as in other matters,
suffice."

In the adjoining diocese of Winchester, comprising the
counties of Hampshire and Surrey which, by some miracle,
escaped the infection almost till Christmas, Bishop Edington,
the treasurer, ordered the cathedral chapter to say the seven
penitential and fifteen gradual psalms twice weekly and on
Fridays to lead a procession of the clergy and people through
the streets and market place, bare-footed and with bowed head,
"whilst with pious hearts they repeat their prayers and, putting
away vain conversation, say as often as possible the Lord's
Prayer and Hail Mary."   News most grave, he declared, had
reached him; the cruel plague which had turned the cities of
Europe into "dens of wild beasts" had "begun to afflict the
coasts of the realm of England."   Towns, castles and villages
had been "stripped of their population by the pestilence, more
cruel than any two-edged sword and become abodes of horror. . . .
We are struck with the gravest fear lest, which God forbid, the
fell disease ravage any part of our diocese."   Already it was
spreading through that of Exeter, falling first, as everywhere, on
the seaports and estuaries and then following the course of the
rivers inland. The clergy and laity of Devon and Cornwall went

[1] Hutchins, *History of Dorset* I, 5.

down like corn before the reaper; at the Cistercian abbey of Newenham twenty monks and three lay brothers died and only the abbot and two others survived. At the Augustinian priory of Bodmin two canons alone lived to tell the tale; the abbots of Hartland, Tavistock and St. Nicholas Exeter, all perished, the last house losing two heads in succession.

The plague reached London at the beginning of November— "about the feast of All Hallows." It took the great financier, Sir Thomas Pulteney—four times mayor and builder of the parish church of Little All Hallows, Thames Street—the princess Joan of Kent's uncle, Lord Wake of Liddel, four wardens of the Goldsmiths' Company, and the abbot and twenty-six monks of Westminster. The adjoining hospital of St. James's was left without inmates, all the brethren and sisters perishing; perhaps, like the brave nuns of the Hôtel Dieu at Paris, " tending the sick with all sweetness and humility, putting all fear behind their backs."[1] Of the Bishop of Rochester's household, four priests, five esquires, seven acolytes, six pages and ten serving-men died. The courts of Kings Bench and Common Pleas came to a standstill; a parliament, summoned for January, was prorogued indefinitely. All through the winter the pestilence raged in the rat-haunted streets and alleys until, having carried off nearly half the population, "by the intervention of the grace of the Holy Spirit on Whit-Sunday it ceased." "The cemeteries," a chronicler wrote, "were not big enough and fields had to be set aside for the burying of the dead. . . . Men and women bore their own offspring on their shoulders to the church and cast them into the common pit, from which there proceeded so great a stench that hardly anyone dared to cross." A croft near Smithfield given by the Bishop of London for the burial of the dead became known as Pardon church yard; another just outside the north wall of the city bought by the defender of Aiguillon, Sir Walter Manny, was endowed with a Carthusian cell which was to become the site of the Charterhouse and the great London school which still bears its name.

Owing to the speed with which the plague slew, the worst was over in the south before it struck the midlands and north. By the spring of 1349 it had reached Norfolk. In Acle church a

[1] *Coulton, Black Death,* 51.

contemporary Latin inscription relates how that summer "the brute beast plague" raged "hour by hour"; the Norwich Dominicans died to a man.[1] At Haveringland every member of the priory perished; in the little manor of Cornard Parva twenty-one families disappeared altogether. At Old Hunstanton 172 tenants of the manor died, 74 of them leaving no male heirs and 19 no single blood relation. Here, as in other places, if once a household was attacked, the tendency was for all to go. The midlands suffered almost as severely; the Leicester chronicler recorded that in the small parish of St. Leonard's 380 perished, in that of Holy Cross 400, in St. Margaret's 700. At Oxford, where the schools were closed for lack of students, two mayors died within a month.

Before the summer ended the plague had crossed the Humber. In the West Riding the incumbents of nearly half its parishes died; in the East Riding almost as many. The great Cistercian abbey of Meaux in Holderness lost its abbot and all but ten of forty-two monks and seven lay brethren; Fountains was so reduced that one of the twin fireplaces in the calefactorium where the quarterly bleedings took place was permanently bricked up. Scotland, protected by a hundred miles of moorland, escaped until the end of the year. At first the Scots ascribed the affliction of their neighbours to their wickedness, swearing "by the foul death of England" and congratulating themselves on their own immunity. But when they gathered in Selkirk forest to harry the border, "their joy turned to mourning as the sword of the wrath of God . . . scourged them in fury and suddenness, smiting them not less than the English with abscesses and pustules." Next year it was the turn of the Welsh mountain valleys, and "at last, as if sailing thither, the plague reached Ireland, striking down great numbers of the English dwelling there" and wrecking the precarious framework of the manorial system of the Pale. "It scarcely touched the pure Irish who dwelt in the mountains and upland areas until 1357, when it unexpectedly destroyed them far and wide in terrible fashion." For the Black Death spared neither nation nor creed but inflicted misery on ever-widening circles of humanity. After it had devastated the rich cities of the Rhineland, multitudes of Jews, driven from their homes by super-

[1] *Mitchell and Leys*, 55; *V.C.H. Norfolk* II, 241.

stitious and murderous mobs, fled eastwards across Europe to
the Polish plains where an enlightened king, less cruel than his
fellow Christians, offered them refuge.

Though the Black Death visited every part of England its
incidence was uneven. Some villages like Tilgarsley in Oxfordshire and Middle Carlton and Ambion in Leicestershire—site of
the future battle of Bosworth Field—were so depopulated that
they were never re-occupied. Other places seem to have escaped
almost unscathed. At St. Albans the abbot, prior, sub-prior
and forty-six monks died; at Christ Church, Canterbury, only
four. Those who suffered most were the poor in their overcrowded hovels, and the parish and regular clergy. The nobility,
living in comparatively clean and spacious conditions, escaped
lightly; in England at least they had had plenty of warning of
danger. Isolating themselves in some retired country place and
keeping a strict guard against strangers, they let the pestilence
pass them by. A few caught the infection; three archbishops of
Canterbury died in that terrible year, one of them, John Stratford, at the end of August 1348 possibly from natural causes, but
the other two of plague. The rest of the episcopal bench, immured
in their country manor-houses, escaped, though Gynwell of
Lincoln, true to his diocese's great tradition, toured his eight
counties throughout the epidemic as usual. Of the parish clergy
at least forty per cent died, most of them probably at their posts,
though to remain must have been certain death. Others, we
know from contemporary testimony, succumbed to the general
panic and fled. The episcopal registers—better preserved and
more complete in England than in any other country—suggest
that, including monks and friars, nearly half the personnel of the
Church was taken.[1]

Of the general public it is impossible to estimate with any
certainty the proportion who died; the verdict of modern
scholarship is that the first outbreak probably carried off about

[1] *Knowles* II, 256. Statistics worked out by Dr. A. Hamilton Thompson for the
dioceses of Lincoln and York—an area covering a quarter of the parishes in
England—show that roughly forty-four per cent of the vacancies filled during
the plague year 1348/9 were caused by death. On this basis Dr. Coulton, in
his *Black Death*, estimated an ecclesiastical plague casualty-rate of forty per cent.
The general view of modern scholars is that, counting the regulars, about half
the clergy perished.

one in three of the population. Contemporary chroniclers and eye-witnesses believed the casualty-rate to be much higher: Thomas Walsingham of St. Albans reckoned "well-nigh half of all mankind," and others as much as two-thirds or even three quarters. As the authors of such first-hand accounts were mostly writing of places where the plague was fiercest and from which many of the inhabitants had already fled, the fatality-rate of those who remained may have been almost as high as they supposed. What is certain is that, once established in the soil, the plague remained endemic. Dormant for perhaps a dozen years it would suddenly flare up, first in one city, then in another, at least once in a generation. For three hundred years—a period of time as great as that which divides us from the last outbreak in Charles II's reign—the red cross on the stricken door, the cart piled with corpses on its way to the plague-pit, the cry of "Bring out your dead!" formed a recurrent part of the background of English life. During the three centuries since the Norman Conquest the population of England had probably doubled. The generation born in the middle of Edward III's reign saw it halved.

For anyone who has not experienced it, it is hard to realize the impact of a cataclysm carrying off one in every three, perhaps one in every two, of a civilised community. Its immediate effect, and of the shock and terror that accompanied it, was chaos. In the dirt and squalor of medieval life men were used to epidemic disease, but this had been no ordinary epidemic. While it continued all activity was suspended. The harvest could not be gathered, taxes or rents collected, markets held or justice done. At the Bishop of Durham's halmote court at Houghton on July 14th, 1349 it was recorded that "no-one will pay the fine for any land which is in the lord's hands through fear of plague; and so all are in the same way of being proclaimed as defaulters until God shall bring some remedy."[1] Everywhere there were vacant holdings and uncultivated farms, and for a time it was almost impossible to sell anything. In the Leicester chronicler's words, "everything was low in price because of the fear of death, for few took care of riches or property of any kind. A man could have a horse that had been worth 40s. for half a mark, a fat ox

[1] *R. O. Durham Cursitor Records. Bk. ii ff 2b* cit. *Gasquet,* 185.

for 4s., a cow for 12d., a heifer for 6d., a fat wether for 4d., a
sheep for 3d., a lamb for 2d., a large pig for 5d., a stone of
wool for 9d. Sheep and cattle ran loose through the fields and
among the crops, and there was none to drive them off or herd
them; for lack of care they perished in ditches and hedges in
incalculable numbers." To aggravate matters, a murrain,
popularly attributed to the infection of the air, carried off vast
numbers of livestock; in one Leicestershire pasture more than 5000
sheep died, "so putrid that neither beast nor bird would
touch them."

Indeed, to some, the immediate aftermath of the Black Death
seemed almost as ominous as the plague itself. "Only the dregs
of the people survive," an unknown hand inscribed on a stone
of Ashwell church against the date 1349. "Throughout the whole
of that winter and spring," wrote a Rochester monk, "the bishop,
an old and decrepit man, remained at Trotterscliff, saddened
and grieving over the sudden change of the age. And in every
manor of the bishopric buildings and walls fell to ruins. In the
monastery there was such a scarcity of provisions that the community was troubled with great want of food, so much so that the
monks were obliged to grind their own bread." When the bishop
visited the abbeys of Malling and Lesnes he found them so poor
"that, as is thought, from the present age to the day of Judgement
they can never recover."[1]

Nor did the pestilence have the purging effect hoped for by
moralists of making men work harder and become more
charitable and helpful to one another. A few serious Christians
were stimulated to good works and greater thoughtfulness like
that imaginative warrior, Henry of Lancaster, who not only
endowed a collegiate church at Leicester but, after going on a
crusade against the Baltic pagans, wrote in 1354 a long devotional
treatise entitled *Le Livre de Seyntz Medicines*—an allegory of self-
condemnation, "written," as he put it, "by a foolish wretched
sinner who calls himself Henry duke of Lancaster—may God
pardon his misdeeds."[2] But the world as a whole was not changed
for the better. "People," as a French chronicler wrote, "were
afterwards more avaricious and grasping, even when they

[1] *B. M. Faust, B.v.f. 99,* cit. *Gasquet,* 123.
[2] Ed. J. Arnould, *Anglo-Norman Text Society* 1940.

possessed more of the goods of this world than before. They were more covetous, vexing themselves by contentious quarrels, strifes and law-suits . . . Charity, too, began to grow cold, and wickedness with its attendant, ignorance, was rampant, and few were found who would or could teach children the rudiments of grammar." The Rochester monk, William Dene, tells the same story:

> "The people for the greater part ever became more de-praved, more prone to every vice and more inclined than before to evil and wickedness, not thinking of death nor of the past plague nor of their own salvation . . . Priests, little weighing the sacrifice of a contrite spirit, betook themselves to where they could get larger stipends than in their own benefices, on which account many benefices remained un-served. Day by day, the dangers to soul both in clergy and people multiplied . . . The labourers and skilled workmen were imbued with such a spirit of rebellion that neither king, law nor justice could curb them."

For most people it was its impact on labour that constituted the chief post-plague problem. "So great was the deficiency of workmen of all kinds," wrote Dene, "that more than a third of the land remained uncultivated." At an inquest on the estate of a Wiltshire landowner who died in June 1349 a jury found three hundred acres of pasture valueless because all the tenants were dead. At another manor near Salisbury only three tenants remained, all the rest having been carried off by the pestilence. At Cliffe in Holderness the joint rents from the customary tenants and tenants-at-will, normally worth £10. 5s. p.a., brought in a mere two shillings. At Drakelow in Derbyshire only 13s. 9¾d. was collected from seventy-four tenants, and the harvest, instead of being gathered free by customary services, cost £22. 18. 10d. —more than a thousand pounds in modern money—in hired labour.

In an age when all work was manual and the wealth of the ruling and fighting classes rested almost entirely on agriculture, the consequences of the labour shortage were revolutionary. In the course of a few months the charges for ploughing, mowing and reaping, for shepherding and carting, doubled, and at a time when rents and land-values had fallen disastrously. The competition for man-power affected both the demesne dependent on hired labour and the older type of manorial unit in the corn-growing villages of East Anglia and the midlands where the lord's land was worked without wages by a tied peasantry whose individual strips in the common fields were held in return for so many days' weekly or seasonal labour under the surveillance of the lord's bailiff and manor court. Legally the villein's position and obligation had not been changed; in practice, like the free wage-earner, he found himself in a position to better himself and, in an unpoliced community, obtain freedom if he was ready to forsake his familiar home and tramp to some distant but labour-hungry district where he was not known. Though the older workers with family ties remained in their wonted homes and bondage, the younger and more active ones and the landless labourers seized their opportunity.

As early as June 1349, when the plague was still raging in the north and midlands, the Council issued an emergency ordinance against what it called "the malice of labourers." Reinforced by a further ordinance in November empowering those who had paid wages in excess of pre-plague rates to recover such over-payment from their employees in order to defray their taxes, it laid down that "every man and woman . . . of whatsoever condition, free or bond, able-bodied and below sixty years of age, not living by trade or practising any craft nor having the means of livelihood from their own resources," should accept any employment suitable to their status and at the wages formerly prevailing in the locality. If the offence was proved by two law-worthy men before a sheriff, bailiff, lord or constable, anyone refusing could be summarily arrested and sent to the nearest gaol. If he left service before the end of his term without reasonable cause, no other employer was to give him employment. Anyone offering him wages higher than the authorised rate was to pay the original employer double.

This high-handed attempt to stay the hand of time applied not only to workers on the land but to "saddlers, pelterers, layers, cobblers, tailors, smiths, carpenters, masons, tilers and boatmen." The ordinance also attempted to regulate the prices charged by "butchers, fishmongers, hostlers, brewers and bakers, poulterers and sellers of victuals." Special justices of labourers were appointed, too, in every county to carry it out.

It was one thing to issue regulations, another to enforce them. When in February 1351, a parliament met for the first time since the plague, the Commons petitioned the Crown for a formal statute of Labourers, strengthening the penalties against those— employees and employers alike—who were everywhere disobeying the ordinances. The statute, which was granted, is believed to have been drafted by Sir William Shareshull, chief justice of the King's Bench and himself an Oxfordshire landowner,[1] and the demand for it came from the knights of the shire who represented the substantial franklin or freeholding middle class—less able than the magnates with their vast sheep-runs to pay high wages. In their petition they dwelt on "the malice of servants . . . unwilling to serve without outrageous wages" and to their having no regard to anything but "their ease and singular covetousness." "Carters, ploughmen, drivers of the plough, shepherds, swineherds, dairymen and all other servants," it was enacted, should take the wages paid immediately before the plague and should serve by the year and not the day. No-one should pay for haymaking more than a penny a day, for mowing a meadow more than 5d., for reaping corn more than 3d., "without meat or drink or other courtesy." Workmen seeking employment were to attend what became known as "statute sessions" in the nearest market towns, bearing in their hands the tools of their trade and "be hired in a common place not privy."[2] Those who refused were to be put in the stocks, which were ordered to be erected in every village, or kept in gaol till they conformed.

How unpopular these regulations were can be seen from the proceedings of the justices appointed to enforce them. They had been framed to combat one of the strongest forces in the world— the stubbornness and independence of the native English who, having survived three centuries of alien rule, had emerged more stubborn and independent than ever. So the constables of Kirkeby in Warwickshire presented to the magistrates that

---

[1] *The Place in Legal History of Sir William Shareshull*, 51, 68-72.
[2] As five centuries later Thomas Hardy's Gabriel Oak stood with his sheep-crook in the market place at Casterbridge.

William Martyn had long been out of work and could work "but refused absolutely to do so." In Lincolnshire the story was the same: William de Caburn of Lymbergh, ploughman, would not take service except by the day or month and would not eat salt meat but fresh, and, since "no-one dared to hire him after this manner against the statute of the lord king," had unlawfully left the town. So detested was the machinery for putting the law into effect that at Tottenham in Middlesex, as well as in Northamptonshire and Lincolnshire, the justices were driven from their sessions by crowds of angry labourers. And self-interest caused employers as much as employed to break the law. "The jurors of the hundred of Barlichway," runs the record of a Warwickshire assize, "present that Alice Portreve, wife of William Portreve of Henley, gives excessive salaries to spinning women. Item, they present that Geoffrey de Welneford, rector of the church of Kineton, gave to his two household servants for the winter term eight shillings with their liveries and with their daily food to be taken in his hall."[1]

Grossly selfish though such legislation was and bitterly though it was resented, with the universal fall in rents the owners of land, particularly the smaller ones, were faced by very serious difficulties. In 1353, four years after the Black Death, twenty-five Northumberland parishes were still finding it impossible to pay any taxes, while from the other end of the country the Prince of Wales's receiver in Cornwall reported that for two years he had been unable to let or raise anything from parts of the duchy because of the "want of tenants who died in the mortal pestilence." In the same year the sheriff of Bedfordshire and Buckinghamshire claimed back from the Exchequer moneys paid in the previous year for farming the hundreds, the latter's bailiffs having refused to take them on the usual terms owing to the fall in their revenues.[2]

Yet, though even as late as 1354 the vice-sheriff of Cumberland complained that the greater part of the manor lands of the royal castle of Carlisle were still lying waste and uncultivated "by

[1] See B. Putman *The Enforcement of the Statute of Labourers*, 196-7, 227; *Rickert*, 77.

[2] *Rot. Claus.*, 27 Ed. III m. 10d; *L.T.R. Memoranda Roll*, 28 Ed. III (Trinity Term) 27 Ed. III (Hilary Term), cit. *Gasquet*, 185, 202, 207.

reason of the mortal pestilence lately raging in these parts," the remarkable thing is how quickly the country recovered from its ordeal. Despite a mortality rate higher than that expected today from a nuclear war, England showed an astonishing resilience. In the work of the greatest English poet of the age there is only one reference, and that an oblique one, to the Black Death which three times swept across the England of his youth and early manhood. But men were far more used than now to the contemplation of death, and Chaucer grew up as a page in the royal court which almost entirely escaped the fate that overwhelmed the rest of the community. Even as early as St. George's Day 1349, while the plague was still raging in London, the first service of the Order of the Garter was held at Windsor, every knight in plumes and garter-blue robes taking his place in his stall; the great two-handed sword which the king carried on that day still hangs behind the altar of St. George's Chapel.

Nor did England's buoyant and extravagant monarch allow the universal labour-shortage to halt his building projects. The master-mason from Christ Church, Canterbury, was summoned to take the place of the dead William de Ramsey; five-hundred stone-masons, carpenters, glass-makers and jewellers were requisitioned by the sheriffs of the southern counties for the works at Windsor and were equipped with scarlet caps and liveries lest they should escape and take other employment.[1] In the year the Black Death subsided, English painters under the supervision of Hugh of St. Albans—a contemporary of Giotto—began to cover the walls of the royal chapel of St. Stephen's, Westminster, with a frieze of angels with peacock wings and pictures of Job and Tobias and the adoration of the Magi, the figures in contemporary court dress set against a background of gilt gesso. All round the walls were arcades with silver-gilt statues, the chapel's crowning glory being a golden image of the Virgin—famous for working miracles—and a painting by Hugh of St. Albans of the king and his sons being presented to the heavenly throne by St. George.

Elsewhere, too, after a pause, the work of church-building

---

[1] The six master-glaziers who in 1351 were set to draw and paint images for the windows of St. Stephen's chapel were paid 1s. a day. Those who refused the king's very liberal wages were ordered to be imprisoned. J. D. Le Couteur, *English Medieval Painted Glass*, 23-4.

was resumed. At Gloucester the cloisters, the earliest example of English fan-vaulting and a masterpiece of the new Perpendicular style, were begun in 1351 under the auspices of Abbot Horton—"beautiful," the seventeenth century antiquary, Stukeley, described them, "beyond anything I ever saw." In the following year the exquisite carved figures of the Church and Synagogue—one of the few specimens of English middle Gothic sculpture to survive the Puritan iconoclasts—were added to the doorway of Rochester cathedral, while two years later the nave of York received its vault. Building also started again at Exeter, Winchester and Ely.

In other places shortage of money and labour brought church-building to a stand; both at Worcester and Chester the work on the cathedral church of the priory was halted for years. At Cley in Norfolk the magnificent new church, begun in 1330, was not resumed till the next century. And the effect of the Black Death on the nation's religious life was grave and prolonged. Of the regular and beneficed clergy half had perished and the problem of filling so many vacancies with men of the requisite qualities was considerable; like the landless labourers, too, the lower ranks of the clergy were asking for more pay. Reduced to penury by the reduced size of their congregations and fees, the incumbents of many of the poorer benefices threw up their livings and sought more profitable employment as chantry clerks or chaplains.

" Parsons and parish priests   complained to the bishop
    That their parishes were poor   since the pestilence time,
    And asked leave and licence   in London to dwell,
    And sing *requiems* for stipends   for silver is sweet."[1]

The prevailing ecclesiastical poverty, too, accentuated the growing sense of grievance at the pope's canonical right to provide foreign nominees to the more lucrative benefices. Though papal provision was an essential part of the Church's machinery for promoting churchmen of merit, and though most of those for whom the pope provided were natives, a substantial proportion of the richer canonries and deaneries usually went to foreign

[1] W. Langland, *Piers Plowman*, Prologue (ed. D. and R. Attwater), 3.

cardinals and other papal dignitaries. This became increasingly resented after the removal of the papacy of Avignon and the outbreak of war with France. At the time of Crécy about a third of the higher cathedral clergy were alien absentees, including half the chapter of York; one cardinal was precentor of Lichfield, treasurer of York and archdeacon of both Buckingham and Nottingham.

Three times in the decade before the plague the Commons petitioned the Crown against the abuse, addressing in 1343 a courteous but firm protest to the pope himself, complaining of the intrusion into English benefices of strangers ignorant of the language and habits of the people. This, they declared, dried up the flow of domestic charity, drained the realm of currency and exposed its "nakedness" to the king's enemies. When in 1351 parliament met again after the Black Death, one of its first measures was to petition the Crown for legislation to stop this alienation of the country's richer benefices. Needing money for financing the war, the king met the Commons' wish by a statute of Provisors under which anyone bringing into the country a papal bull of provision could be imprisoned until he had compensated the owner of the advowson for the loss of his rights of collation and presentation. Two years later, in 1353, another parliament secured from the Crown a statute of Praemunire, adding outlawry and forfeiture to the existing penalties for suing in a foreign court on a plea whose cognisance belonged to the royal courts. But though these acts tended to reduce the number of rich benefices going to foreign cardinals and members of the papal household, and though they strengthened the king's hands in his dealings with Avignon, he only enforced them when it suited him, which was when the *curia* laid claim to patronage that belonged either to himself or his lay subjects. Needing papal provision for his episcopal appointments and for other royal nominees, Edward made little attempt to disturb his tacit understanding with the papacy over purely ecclesiastical patronage. The real significance of the statutes lay in their recognition of parliament's right to participate with the Crown in regulating ecclesiastical appointments.[1]

[1] The importance of these two acts was formerly much exaggerated. See Cecily Davies, "The Statute of Provisors of 1951," *History* xxxviii (1953),

Another victim of the Black Death was the foreign Staple which had been revived at the beginning of the war. For one of the plague's immediate consequences had been to complete the ruin of the capitalists who had advanced money to the Crown in return for a monopoly of the wool export. Unable any longer to offer advances or even to meet their commitments, the great syndicalists of London and the east coast ports—the Cheritons and Wesenhams and Swanlands who in the 'forties had succeeded the Peruzzi and Bardi as royal bankers—ceased like their foreign predecessors to be of use to the king. Instead, he turned to the woolgrowers and smaller traders who were represented, not by an assembly of great merchants, but by the knights of the shire and burgesses in parliament. The chancellor's address to the parliament of 1351 dwelt on Edward's gratitude to his magnates and commons for the love they bore him and the aids and subsidies they had made, his awareness of all they had suffered for the maintenance of the war and defence of the realm, and his wish to do all in his power for their "ease, comfort and favour."

Complaints about "irregular grants" of taxation by merchants other than "in full parliament" had become an increasing grievance of the Commons, not because they saw in them an infringement of their constitutional rights—they were still far too humble for that—but because the monopolies given by the Crown in exchange had enabled the big wool-exporters to force down the prices paid to native growers and exclude small traders from the market altogether. In return for the abolition of such monopolies the Commons in 1351 granted the Crown the hated *maltote* for two more years. Recognizing that the king could not wage war without it, they accepted its continuance as the price for their right to control it. At a further parliament held in September 1353 and attended by one knight from each shire and two burgesses from the thirty-eight chief trading towns, the king conceded what was known as the Ordinance of the Staple in exchange for the continuance of the wool subsidy for another three years. By this measure, in order to prevent any revival of

---

116-133; E. B. Graves, "The Legal Significance of the Statute of Praemunire of 1353" (*Haskins Anniversary Lectures*). See also *Hamilton Thompson* 10-12; *Pantin*, 47-75.

monopoly, English traders were forbidden to export wool, the Staple in Flanders was abolished, and foreign merchants were given leave to compete freely with one another in buying from the home producer subject to their bearing the full burden of the *maltote*. This was henceforward to be levied on them and them alone at fifteen domestic Staples—ten in England, one in Wales, and four in Ireland.[1]

This experiment in free trade delighted the wool-growers who, selling to competing foreign buyers, were able to raise their prices. Wool exports soared to 40,000 sacks in a single year, rivalling those of the great era of free trade under Edward I, and reached an annual average of more than 32,000 sacks during the next decade. So long as the war with France was waged on only a minor scale, as in the years immediately following the pestilence, and the king could do without large loans, the change suited the Crown and, by bringing an influx of foreign purchasing-power into the realm, helped to restore its depleted reserves of gold and silver. Its drawback was that, by giving the export trade to foreign merchants, it discouraged the building of English ships and so reduced the nation's fighting strength at sea. It was some time before the effects of this became apparent, but it was to have serious repercussions.

·   ·   ·   ·   ·   ·   ·   ·

Though both France and England had been denuded of a third of their people, the war had not ceased. While the Black Death was raging, the truce made in 1347 had been extended by mutual consent to the summer of 1350. But that spring word reached King Edward at Windsor of a French plot to surprise and recapture Calais. A Lombard knight deputising for the

---

[1] "Because the Staple of the wools of England, which are the sovereign merchandise and jewel of his realm of England, has been held outside the realm, people of foreign lands are enriched, and the profit which ought to have come in his realm to the common people by the sale of their wool has been acquired by certain persons . . . to the great injury and impoverishment of the common people, . . . our lord the king . . . has ordained that the Staple of wools, woolfells, leathers and lead should be held in his realm of England and in his lands of Wales and Ireland in certain places." Rot. Parl. II, 246. The English staple towns were London, Bristol, Canterbury, Chichester, Winchester, Exeter, Norwich, Lincoln, York and Newcastle.

governor, who had died of the plague, was bribed to admit a French raiding party into the castle by night. But the plot was betrayed and it was the raiders who were surprised. For, having secretly crossed the Channel in disguise with a band of picked companions, Edward and the Prince of Wales fell on the intruders as they were being admitted to the castle and took them all captive. Afterwards the royal victor feasted his prisoners and, signalling out a knight who had long resisted him in single combat, crowned him with a chaplet of pearls and set him at liberty.

In August of the same year the king and prince took part in a more important action, this time at sea. A Castilian fleet, bringing merino wool to Flanders, had taken advantage of the depopulation of the Cinque Ports to plunder English merchantmen in the Channel. To intercept it on its return voyage a squadron of fifty small vessels and pinnaces was assembled at Sandwich and manned by the flower of England's chivalry. Among them were nearly all the original knights of the Garter; even the king's ten-year-old son, John of Gaunt, was there. Sailing from Sandwich they sighted the Spanish fleet off Dungeness on the afternoon of August 29th and at once went in to attack. "As much larger than our ships were theirs as castles are than cottages," wrote Geoffrey le Baker. "Dressed in a black velvet jacket and a beaver hat that well become him," the king flew his flag in the cog, *Thomas*, while young John Chandos and the royal pipers beguiled the waiting minutes before action with a new German dance. Like Sluys the battle was a triumph for the English archers who, outshooting the Spaniards' crossbowmen and catapult-men, made their decks a shambles before the knights and men-at-arms swarmed up their sides to complete the slaughter. Though both the king's and the prince's ships were sunk, the day ended in the capture of seventeen galleons and the flight of the remainder, while crowds cheered the victors from the Winchelsea cliffs. That night the queen, who had spent the day praying in Battle abbey, was joined by Edward and his sons at Pevensey castle, "where the lords and ladies passed the night in great revel, speaking of war and love."

The victory helped to restore England's sea communications with her depleted garrisons in Gascony. For the plague had left the country dangerously short of military man-power. There were not enough seamen to man her ships, of archers and men-at-arms to guard her gains in Guienne and Brittany. A small country suffers more from attrition than a large, and the disproportion between the populations of France and England now mattered far more. In 1353 every holder of land to the value of £15 a year was ordered to accept knighthood and its military responsibilities or be fined in default, and two years later half the men of fighting age in two Derbyshire villages were at the wars.[1] With her population reduced to between two and three millions, England was forced to fill her foreign garrisons with Gascons, Bretons, Flemings, Irish and Germans.

In August 1350, a week before Edward's naval victory off Winchelsea, having taken to himself a bride of eighteen, Philip of Valois, died at the age of fifty-eight. He was succeeded by his son, John II—"*le Bon*" or good fellow. A devotee, unlike his father, of chivalry and martial glory, he refused to renew the truce. The war, therefore, continued in a rather desultory fashion while both countries recovered from the Black Death. In the south the French gradually built up a large army which at the beginning of 1353 invaded Saintonge. Henry of Lancaster, crusading in the Baltic with the Teutonic knights,[2] was no longer available to defend his sovereign's southern dominion. But the governor of Calais, Sir John Beauchamp—Lord Warwick's brother—was sent to save the threatened province. Reaching the beleaguered capital, Saintes, just in time, he won on April 7th another astonishing victory against odds. Two marshals of France were among the captives, the victors making a fortune in ransoms. Afterwards, hurrying back to his post at Calais, Beauchamp defeated the French at Ardres.

In Brittany, with Charles of Blois a prisoner and the de Montfort claimant a minor, the attempt of the English to rule the country in their protégé's name was growing increasingly unpopular. For the Bretons had not only to pay for their garrisons but were plundered by them into the bargain. English prestige

---

[1] *V. C. H. Derby*, II, 168, cit. *McKisack*, 253.
[2] On his way to the east, while passing through Calais, he had led a surprise attack on Boulogne, capturing the lower town and only failing to capture the upper through the inadequacy of the English scaling-ladders.

had suffered a serious blow in 1351 in a chivalric encounter called "the battle of the Thirty," when thirty Franco-Breton knights defeated thirty Anglo-Breton, Gascon and German ones, killing nine of them. But in 1352, when a French army under Marshal de Nesle invaded the duchy and, after regaining Rennes, advanced towards Brest, it was intercepted on August 14th at Mauron by Sir William Bentley. Bentley, who had succeeded Sir Thomas Dagworth as keeper of Brittany after the latter's death in an ambush, had been vainly trying to obtain reinforcements from England. But, though he had only a minute force, he drew it up in one of those strong defensive positions on which the English relied, with the men-at-arms dismounted in line and the archers in wedges on the flanks. There were not enough men even to form a reserve. The French attacked at four o'clock on a hot summer's afternoon; those waiting on the ridge long afterwards remembered the droning of the bees in the heather. Though the initial assault forced back the archers on the English right, their comrades on the left wrought the usual execution on the French horses, subsequently attacking their riders with their swords as they struggled to rise. Meanwhile the men-at-arms on the right, falling back up the hill to a belt of trees, put up so staunch a fight that the enemy was halted there too. When Bentley, dangerously wounded, was carried from the field crying, "Fight on, fight on," his lieutenant, Sir Robert Knollys, a rough Cheshire knight, took command and completed the enemy's rout. Marshal de Nesle was among the dead and more than six hundred knights and nobles were killed or taken prisoner, among them forty-five knights of the Order of the Star—the new Order of chivalry which King John had founded in rivalry of the Order of the Garter.

Mauron left the English masters of Brittany. It brought the little handful who fought there immense wealth. When two centuries later Shakespeare wrote of another Plantagenet victory against odds,

"the fewer men the greater share of honour,"

he might with truth have substituted the word "ransom" for honour. For the English army in France was raised on the same principle as that of a joint-stock company. Its officers and men received their king's or captain's pay during the waiting and marching months before battle, but the incentive to do or die was the knowledge that the survivors would share the fruits of victory—the booty of every city stormed and, for any man who took a prisoner, two-thirds of the ransom money, the rest being reserved for his commander who in turn paid a third of his gains to the Crown.[1] That, the use of the longbow and an iron discipline were the secret of the English success. How stern was that discipline was seen after the victory at Mauron when Knollys had thirty archers executed for retreating.

Probably at no time after the Black Death had the English more than ten thousand men in France. Their garrisons were only kept up to strength by recruiting from every western nation. But from earl to archer they were adventurers, with the plunder of the richest country in Europe as the prize for which they staked their lives. Chivalric honour in the higher ranks, loyalty to captain and comrade, even a kind of dawning and arrogant patriotism among the humbler English-speaking men-at-arms and archers were elements in their courage. But the strongest of all was the gambling spirit and passion for gain which they had inherited from their Viking progenitors and which made them ready for any risk. An archer named John Dancaster, a prisoner of the French in the castle of Guisnes, not having the money to pay for his ransom, secured partial freedom by working on the repair of the walls. Learning from his mistress, a laundress, that there was a submerged wall crossing the moat two feet under water, he got in touch with a band of thirty English deserters in the town outside. These "king's hard bargains" had scaling-ladders made to the right size, crossed the moat by night in blackened armour and, scaling the ramparts, killed the watchmen and threw them over the wall. Then they burst in on the garrison who were playing chess and hazard in the hall. "Breaking into the chambers and turrets upon the ladies and knights that lay there asleep, they so became masters of all that was within." Having released the English prisoners from the dungeons, they shut up the French in their place and got into touch with the local commanders of both countries with a view to ransoming the castle. The Count of Guisnes, we are told,

[1] See an article by Denys Hay in *R.H.S.T.* Fifth Series, Vol. 4, 91-109.

"demanded . . . in whose name they kept it. As they affirmed that they kept it in the name of John Dancaster, he asked whether the same John were the King of England's liegeman or would obey him and . . . offered for the castle, besides all the treasure found in it, many thousands of crowns in exchange and a perpetual peace with the King of France. To this the defenders replied that, before taking that castle, they had been Englishmen by nation, but, by their demerits, banished from the peace of the King of England. Wherefore the place which they thus held they would willingly sell or exchange, but to none sooner than to their natural King of England to whom they said they would sell their castle to obtain their peace. But if he would not buy it, then they would sell it to the King of France or to whosoever would give most for it. The count being thus shifted off, the King of England bought it."[1]

. . . .

Though the war brought fortunes to England's fighting men, it was proving a growing strain on the taxpayer. When having negotiated a year's truce with the war-weary French, the king in 1354 through his lord chamberlain asked the assembled lords and commons in parliament whether they desired a permanent peace, they answered with one voice, "Oeil! oeil!"—forerunner of the "aye, aye" with which the House of Commons still signifies its assent. Struggling with the dislocation of her economy by the plague, the country was having to contend not only against France but Scotland, with whom, on and off, she had been at war for half a century. That poor, insecure, war-ridden land, her king a captive and her treacherous nobles at constant logger-heads, was still determined not to acknowledge England's over-lordship and to fight to the last man to resist it. When two years before, having secured a provisional recognition of homage from his captive, King David, Edward sent him home on parole, a Scottish parliament unanimously rejected such terms and allowed him to return to captivity.

[1] *Chronicon Galfridi Le Baker de Swynebroke*, (ed. Thompson,) 284-6, cit. *Rickert*, 307-8.

Edward was no more successful in persuading the French
king to abandon his claim to his homage than in inducing the
Scots to acknowledge his right to theirs. For when in the winter
of 1354, through the mediation of a new pope, he opened peace
negotiations with France, his plenipotentiaries on arriving at
Avignon found the French, for all their defeats, unwilling to
surrender their sovereign's overall right of suzerainty over even
the smallest particle of conquered soil. Edward proposed that,
in return for renouncing his claim to the throne, King John
should release him from the obligation of homage for Guienne,
Ponthieu and the towns he had taken in Brittany and Normandy.
He also secretly instructed his ambassadors that he would be
prepared to abandon his Norman claims in return for the overlordship of Flanders. His terms were contemptuously rejected.
Despite twenty years of war neither monarch was prepared to
abandon his fundamental aim—the English king to full sovereignty
over his dominions beyond the Channel, the French to lordship
over all France.

The war, therefore, continued. Once more, as ten years
before, Edward planned a triple attack, from Gascony, from
Calais and, under his personal command, from Normandy
whose largest landowner, Charles of Navarre, had offered to
throw in his lot with him. The disgruntled son-in-law of the
French king and a descendant, like Edward himself, of the old
Capet line, Charles proposed that they should march on Paris
together with the idea of partitioning the Valois inheritance
between them. In September 1355 as a preliminary to the
combined operations planned for the following summer, the
Prince of Wales accordingly sailed for Bordeaux with a force of
3500 men, including a strong contingent of Cheshire and Derbyshire archers. He was received with immense enthusiasm just
as Lancaster had been ten years before. His mission was to win
back the territories and towns which the Count d'Armagnac
had recovered in south-western Guienne.

The prince had been brought up in the same school of war as
Lancaster and Dagworth. He was now twenty-five and at the
height of his powers. His recipe for dealing with superior force
was to strike with the utmost audacity and speed. By carrying
the war into the rich province of Languedoc and wasting it from

end to end, he meant to force d'Armagnac to dance to his tune. Though by the conventions of chivalric war the season for campaigning was over, the prince set out from Bordeaux on October 5th on a *grande chevauchée* with a mounted Anglo-Gascon force of 5000 men. For a hundred miles he marched south, crossing into French territory on the 11th. Then he turned east towards Toulouse, traversing the country through which Wellington's armies were to march three and a half centuries later. It was lovely weather and the cavalcade presented a brilliant spectacle, each of its captains, as Froissart described Sir John Chandos, riding "with his banner before him and his company about him, with his coat of arms on him, great and large, beaten with his arms." Strict discipline was observed, and while buildings, stores and crops were burnt as part of the plan of campaign, churches, monasteries and civilian lives were spared. Yet scarcely a day passed in that luxuriant countryside without some wealthy merchant or local landowner being brought in by the English patrols. Everyone down to the humblest archer was in high spirits, for there was ransom and plunder for all.

The army was equipped with portable pontoons for bridging the broad rivers of southern France, but not with siege-engines for reducing fortified cities. Toulouse was, therefore, by-passed, while d'Armagnac, not daring to give battle, watched from its walls the smoke of burning villages. Five more days of marching brought the English to Carcassonne, where they fired the lower town. On November 8th they reached Narbonne, only ten miles from the Mediterranean. All southern France was in panic; the pope at Avignon a hundred miles away barricaded himself in his palace and sent an embassy to the prince to plead for peace.

By this time two French armies were in the field. The Count of Bourbon was advancing south from Limoges to bar the passage of the Garonne while, under the pressure of an angry public opinion, d'Armagnac had at last ventured out from Toulouse. On November 10th, therefore, the prince began his homeward march, intending to fight d'Armagnac before Bourbon's army could join him. But though both were in superior numbers, neither French commander dared give battle, for the memory of Crécy still haunted them. Even when they had joined forces they left the raiders alone.

On December 2nd the prince returned to La Réole, laden with booty, after covering nearly seven hundred miles in nine weeks. Meanwhile his father had been conducting a similar *chevauchée* in northern France. Having waited all the summer for word from Charles of Navarre, who had now composed his quarrel with the French king, he crossed to Calais at the end of October. But nothing would induce King John to leave the shelter of Amiens, and Edward's march through Artois in November rain and mud proved a very different matter from his son's campaign in Languedoc. As winter fell on the Flemish plain he was forced by lack of forage to return to Calais.

Here he was greeted by news that the Scottish regent, William Douglas, had broken the truce and, with the help of a small French expeditionary force, had laid siege to Berwick castle, capturing the town. As both the warden of the March and the Bishop of Durham had withdrawn their troops from the border in order to join him at Calais, Edward was forced to return to England and hurry north. Having secured supplies from a parliament, he bought out Balliol's discredited claim to the throne for £2000 and a pension. Then obtaining from his captive, King David, a recognition of his suzerainty, he prepared to teach the Scottish nobles a lesson. In January 1356, in the depth of winter, he crossed the border to take "seisin," as he put it, "of his kingdom."

Yet though, with the twin banners of both nations borne before him Edward reduced to ashes every village and farm along the road to Edinburgh, driving out the inhabitants onto the wintry moors, the "burnt Candlemas," as it was long called in Scotland, produced nothing except a greater hatred of England. Like Bruce, the Regent Douglas cleared the country of everything edible and vanished into the hills and forests. Campaigning in such a land was an unrewarding business after the rich plains of France, and no one's heart was in it. Storms held up the supply-ships, and by March there was nothing left but to withdraw or starve. The Scots, still evading combat, hung on the flanks of the retreating army and murdered the sick and stragglers, while the English set fire to the beautiful friars church at Haddington—"the lantern of Lothian." Everyone was the loser.

Having safeguarded his northern border Edward resumed his

plans for conquering France. By this time the erratic Charles of
Navarre had quarrelled again with the French king and had been
arrested for treason at a banquet at Rouen. But his brother,
Philip, appealed to England for help. At that moment, back
from the crusade in Lithuania where he had taken part in the
battle of Tramassene,[1] Henry of Lancaster was about to sail from
Southampton for Brittany whose young duke, now sixteen, was
eager to take possession of the duchy. With 500 men-at-arms
and 800 mounted archers whom he was taking to reinforce the
English garrisons, Lancaster was now deflected to Normandy
with orders to relieve three rebel cities—Evreux, Pont Audemer
and Breteuil—which the French royal forces were besieging.

Landing at La Hogue on June 18th, the old warrior was joined
by a small Norman force and by Robert Knollys of Mauron
fame with 300 English men-at-arms and 500 archers. Lancaster,
who had been rewarded for his services with a dukedom, was
now fifty, but he acted as boldly as ever. With 2500 mounted
men he set out on June 22nd to relieve the insurgent cities, all
of them more than a hundred and thirty miles away and
threatened by an army which King John had assembled at
Dreux to overawe them. Covering sixteen miles on the first day
and thirty on the second, he reached Lisieux on June 28th. Next
day, after a twenty-three mile march, he relieved Pont Audemer,
surprising and capturing the besiegers' siege-train. Having revictualled the town and strengthened the garrison with some
English men-at-arms and archers, he set out again on July 2nd
and, by the morning of the 4th, after covering a further fifty miles
and storming the castle of Conches, had relieved Breteuil.

As Evreux had by now fallen, the duke completed his mission
by striking on the same day at Verneuil, the second city of Normandy. Using the siege equipment taken at Pont Audemer, he
carried the walls that night, all but one tower which held out till
the 6th. Then, on July 7th, with much booty and many prisoners,

---

[1] Like the knight commemorated in the *Canterbury Tales;*
  " In fifteen mortal battles had he been
    And foughten for our faith at Tramassene."
Chaucer, whose first patron was the duke's daughter, wrote the *Canterbury
Tales* about the time that his own sister-in-law married Lancaster's widowed
son-in-law, John of Gaunt, and may possibly have had Lancaster in his mind
when he described his "very parfait gentle knight."

he set out for home. For with John's huge army only a dozen miles away he was in grave danger.

By now the French king was in his path. At Turboeuf two heralds arrived with a challenge to battle. "Whereupon," wrote one of Lancaster's officers, "my lord gave answer that he was come into these parts to do a certain business which he had well accomplished, thank God, and was returning back to the place where he had business, and that if the said king of France willed to disturb him from his march he would be ready to encounter him."

With 2000 fighting men heavily encumbered with booty and prisoners, even Lancaster could not hope to defeat an army of 20,000. That night, in silence, the wily old duke vanished, leaving only a minute rearguard to deceive the French as they deployed next morning for battle. By nightfall he was thirty-five miles away at Argentan. On the 9th he covered a further fifty-two miles and by the 10th was across the Vire and safely back in the Cotentin, having marched three-hundred-and-thirty miles in fifteen days. At his base camp he found that Robert Knollys, with a handful of men-at-arms, had routed a force of local militia men who had tried to ambush him, slaying them all except three rich landowners whom he had kept for ransom.

Leaving the French king to resume the siege of the revictualled insurgent cities, Lancaster now marched south into Maine, while, three hundred miles away at Bergerac, the Prince of Wales set off north towards him. Between them the two English commanders hoped to pinch off a quarter of the French kingdom and, joining hands on the Loire, regain the Angevin inheritance which their ancestor, King John, had lost a century and a half before.

Since his *grande chevauchée* the Black Prince had been occupied in recapturing some fifty towns and castles on the northern and eastern borders of Guienne regained by the French during the years when the English garrisons had been depleted by the Black Death. By the middle of the summer of 1356, having established the English rule as far north as Périgueux, he was ready to strike. On August 4th, while Lancaster was laying siege to Domfront preparatory to marching on Angers, he crossed the Dordogne with 6000 men. Advancing at the rate of about ten miles a day, he crossed the old Aquitaine border into France at the end of the month and began to ravage the towns and villages of Touraine. "Taking care to send forward Sir John Chandos, Sir James Audley and others skilled in warfare to inspect the roads and discover the state of the enemy countryside lest our men might be suddenly attacked by ambushes," wrote the chaplain who accompanied the march and related the details afterwards to Geoffrey le Baker, " he moved his camp daily as if the enemy had been present, protecting it by night with watches . . . and marching with scouts in front, behind and on the flanks."

After covering 320 miles in just over a month, the prince reached the Loire at Amboise in the first week of September, hoping to make contact with Lancaster. Finding all the bridges held or down, he turned downstream towards Tours, before which he encamped for several days while his foraging parties reduced the neighbouring castles. The weather had turned wet and the river was in flood. Meanwhile the French king, making a hasty composition with his Norman rebels, hurried south to oppose the intruders. From Chartres he started during the second week of September to send advance-parties across the Loire.

On September 10th, when John was about to march on Blois, the prince gave orders to retreat. His supplies were running short and there was no sign of Lancaster. Without a bridgehead a crossing of the river was out of the question, and his little force was far from home and laden with plunder. During the next four days both armies raced south on parallel courses, the French gathering reinforcements and trying to cut off the English from their base. Yet even now the prince had not abandoned hope of a junction with Lancaster. On September 15th, disregarding the risk, he halted for two days at Chatellerault on the Vienne, waiting for tidings from the north while the French king continued to march ahead of him towards Poitiers which he reached on the 17th.

That evening there was a skirmish between the prince's scouts and King John's rearguard on the Chauvigny-Poitiers road, the English capturing two French counts and the steward of the household. But they were short not only of food but water, and their two days' wait for Lancaster—who, though he had now taken Domfront, was held up before Rennes—had placed them in deadly peril. They put, however, a bold front on it and on the 18th—a Sunday—took up a defensive position on a ridge near Nouaillé, just above the little hamlet of Maupertius, eight miles from Poitiers.

To the French it seemed certain that the English had tempted fate once too often. All that day two cardinals, sent by the pope to negotiate a truce, passed backwards and forwards between the armies with surrender-terms. The English position was so desperate that the Prince of Wales offered to give up his spoil and prisoners and even, according to one account, not to serve in France for seven years. But the French, who by now outnumbered his little force by something like five to one and were daily growing stronger, refused to let him off so lightly. Nothing but his unconditional surrender and that of a hundred of his best knights would content them.

That night the English commanders held a council of war. Sooner than accept such terms they decided to await the French in the defensive position they had chosen and give battle, and then, if the enemy failed to attack, to slip away by night and make a run for it. The prince had taken the precaution of sending his baggage and plunder across the Nouaillé bridge over the Moisson, and a day's delay would give them a sporting chance to get away. When, therefore, at dawn on September 19th the cardinals arrived in the English camp with the French king's final uncompromising terms, they were told that the sword must decide.

The truce ended at 7.30 a.m. on Monday morning. The English held a low ridge facing north-west, crossed by two roads, both from Poitiers, in an undulating, well-wooded countryside of small vine-clad hills. Before them lay a valley with a marsh protecting their left. Along the ridge ran a thick hedge behind which the prince drew up his dismounted knights and men-at-arms, with Salisbury's division on the right and Warwick's on the left. The archers were posted as at Crécy among vineyards on the flank of each division and protected from cavalry by stakes. A small reserve of mounted knights remained out of sight behind the ridge. On the extreme right, to avoid being enveloped, the prince had constructed a strong-point of wagons and trenches.

As the horses had to be watered in the valley, several hours elapsed before the whole army was in position—a circumstance which caused French observers to suppose that the English had already started to retreat. When everyone was assembled the prince rode along the lines, addressing his troops. His words have been handed down by the chroniclers. To the knights and men-at-arms he said: "Now, sirs, though we be but a small company, let us not be abashed. For victory lieth not in the multitude of people but where God will send it. If it fortune that the day be ours, we shall be the most honoured of all the world; and if we die in our right quarrel I have the king my father and brethren and you have good friends and kinsmen who shall revenge us. Therefore, sirs, for God's sake, I require you, Do your duty this day." To the archers he declared:

"You have made it plain that you are worthy sons and kinsmen of those for whom, under the leadership of my father and ancestors, the kings of England, no labour was too great, no place invincible, no mountain inaccessible, no tower impregnable, no host too formidable . . . Honour and patriotism and the prospect of the rich spoils of the French call you more than my words to follow in the footsteps of your fathers. Follow the standards, obey implicitly in body and mind the commands of your leaders. If victory shall see us still alive we shall always continue in firm friendship together, being of one heart and mind. If envious fortune should decree, which God forbid, that in this present labour we must follow the final path of all flesh, your names will not be sullied with infamy and I and my comrades will drink the same cup with you."

It was not till nearly midday that the French vanguard appeared. It came on in two divisions, led by the constable and two marshals of France, each following one of the roads from Poitiers. The left-hand column had some initial success, forcing its way through a gap in the hedge, until it was driven back by a counter-attack by the Earl of Salisbury. Before it reached the summit the right-hand column was shot to pieces by the archers, who, moving down with superb battle-discipline into the swampy ground on the attackers' flank, directed such fierce volleys at the horses' hindquarters that almost every rider was thrown to the ground and the marshal in command captured. On both

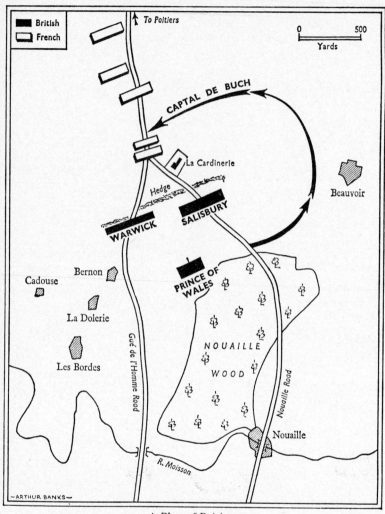

A Plan of Poitiers

flanks the survivors fell back in confusion. So perfect was English discipline that not a man moved in pursuit.

The larger part of the French host was now approaching, marching in three successive columns commanded by the Dauphin, the young Duke of Orleans and the king himself. Each division as it appeared seemed as large as the entire English army.

At the suggestion of a veteran of the Scottish wars, William Douglas, who was serving in the French host, the knights and men-at-arms had left their horses at Poitiers. But the long march and the weight of their armour had caused them to straggle and, by the time they neared the battlefield, there was a wide gap between the columns.

The Dauphin's division attacked first. Despite the fire of the archers, who were by now running short of arrows, it reached the hedge. Here a long and desperate encounter took place. "They went to it boldly on both sides," wrote Geoffrey le Baker, "with a clamour that rose to the skies of 'St. George' or 'St. Denis.'" But the French knights, who on Douglas's advice had cut down their twenty-foot lances to six foot, were unaccustomed to fighting without their horses and soon began to tire. In the end they, too, fell back in confusion.

After they withdrew there was a long pause. Fortunately for the English the Duke of Orleans's column never reached the battlefield at all, but, either through inadvertence or in a belief that the day was lost, made off in the wrong direction. Meanwhile the exhausted defenders replaced their broken lances, replenished their supply of arrows and fetched water from the stream in the valley, carrying the more seriously injured to the rear and placing them under bushes and hedges. "There was not one of them," wrote the chronicler, "who was not either wounded or worn out with great labour."

At this point, just as the English were beginning to think that the battle was over, the last and largest of the French columns, led by King John, appeared on the ridge on the other side of the valley. The effect on the tired defenders of this great host, glittering with steel and banners, was shattering. Almost everyone except their commander gave himself up for lost. The waverers started to leave the field, leading off the wounded, and the rest prepared to sell their lives dearly. "Then," wrote the chronicler, "came on the menacing swarm of crossbowmen, darkening the skies with the thick clouds of quarrels they shot, and their air reverberated with the glad storm of arrows from the English archers who were moved to fury because they were desperate. Out flew darts of ash which struck the French when they were yet some distance away, but the French host, composed of closely packed troops, protecting their breasts by shields held closely together, hid their faces from the missiles."

But as they moved up the hill the Black Prince showed himself the great commander he was. Instead of waiting to be overwhelmed he decided to attack along the whole front. Ordering the battle-horses to be brought from the rear, he made his exhausted knights and men-at-arms mount and, with a cry of "Banner, advance in the name of God and 'St. George'," launched them in open line against the enemy, himself leading. Simultaneously he sent a small detachment of cavalry which he had kept in reserve round the enemy's left flank under the Gascon, Captal de Buch, one of the founder knights of the Garter.

The archers, throwing aside their bows, had joined in the mêlée, striking at the French with their short swords. Suddenly, at the crisis of the fight, the captal's armour charged into the French rear. The result was devastating. Beset on both sides and fighting on uneven ground against mounted men, the French broke and fled, pursued by the English knights, hacking and slaughtering all the way to the walls of Poitiers. "Fortune turned her giddy wheel, and the Prince of Wales penetrated the ranks of the enemy and, like a lion with noble wrath, spared the lowly and put down the mighty and took the King of France prisoner." With him were one of the latter's sons, an archbishop, thirteen counts, five viscounts, twenty-one barons and nearly two thousand knights. So much potential ransom had never been taken at one time before. Another two-thousand five-hundred knights and men-at-arms were found dead on the field before the English lines, including two dukes. The oriflamme itself—the most sacred emblem of France—was barely saved.

That night the victor waited at supper on the French king in his tent, serving him on bended knee and saying that "he was not sufficient to sit at table with so great a prince." With exquisite courtesy he consoled him with praise of his gallantry. "You have won," he said, "high renown and have surpassed this day in valour all others of your party." Once during the feast the prince was called out by those collecting the dead and wounded to say that they had brought in Sir James Audley, one of the heroes of the day, who had been found wounded on the field.

The chivalrous prince conferred on him an annuity of five hundred marks and when he learnt that Audley, a knight of the Garter, had made it over to the four Cheshire squires who had fought so bravely by his side—Dutton of Dutton, Delves of Doddington, Fulleshurst of Barthomley and Hawkstone of Wrinehill--he doubled his award.

. . . .

When news of Poitiers and the French king's capture reached England anxiety turned to rejoicing. The prince's victory had transcended even that of Crécy. "The most valiant prince of this world throughout its compass," he seemed to a contemporary, "that ever was since the days of Julius Caesar and Arthur." And England herself was raised to a new pinnacle of glory. Foreigners noted "the proud mien of Englishmen everywhere"; "when the noble Edward first gained England in his youth," wrote the Liégeois chronicler, Jean le Bel, "nobody thought much of the English, nobody spoke of their prowess or courage. . . . Now they are the finest and noblest warriors known to man." Having found what seemed an infallible way of winning against almost any odds, they saw before them an endless vista of ransoms, loot and profit. The land of France was their oyster, and the long-bow had opened it.

For the wealth won was prodigious. The price put on the King of France was 300,000 crowns. "I am so great a lord," the prince told his officers after Poitiers, "as to make you all rich." Even the humblest returned with the sale of battle-horses, swords, jewels, robes and furs. There was hardly a woman in England, it was said, without some ornament, goblet or piece of fine linen brought home by the conquerors. Those fortunate enough to capture some great magnate became themselves lords. Sir Thomas Dagworth was offered £4,900—an enormous fortune —for the ransom of Charles of Blois. The north country squire who had taken David prisoner at Neville's Cross received an annuity of £500—equivalent to an income of more than twenty thousand pounds today—with the rank of a banneret.

Perhaps the most romantic of all the fortunes won on French battlefields was that of Thomas Holland, a cadet of an obscure Lancashire family who, after winning early favour, though not wealth, in the tournament-lists, became what would now be called a millionaire through capturing the Count of Eu at the storming of Caen in 1346. Nor did his success end there. Emboldened by his riches, he claimed the hand—he already possessed the heart—of the lovely princess Joan of Kent with whom, when she was a girl of twelve, he had contracted a secret marriage which she had been afraid to reveal when she was forced by her cousin, the king, to marry the Earl of Salisbury. And though there was a great scandal and her husband imprisoned her, Holland's wealth proved sufficient to secure a papal annulment of her second marriage, her restoration to his arms and, with her, the earldom of Kent.

The pageantry that accompanied the bringing home of the French king in the summer of 1357 outshone even that of the year when the Order of the Garter had been founded. Attending him on a small black palfrey, the prince paraded his prisoner through the London streets on a white charger while bells clanged, fountains spouted wine and thousands of liveried guildsmen marched behind their mounted wardens and aldermen through streets hung with tapestry. When the procession reached Westminster Hall, King Edward rose from his throne to embrace his fellow sovereign. Lodged in the Duke of Lancaster's new palace of the Savoy—rebuilt from the spoils of Guienne—the fallen monarch took part, with the captive King of Scots, in a succession of feasts and tournaments—the most splendid, it was said, held in England since the days of Arthur. The poor man was under no illusion as to their purport; "he had never seen or known," he said, "such royal shows and feastings without some after-reckoning for gold and silver." When the money asked for his ransom was not forthcoming, he was moved from his luxurious captivity in the Savoy to Somerton castle in the depths of Lincolnshire.

For though the Scots were able to ransom their king by selling on his behalf their entire wool export, France was in no condition to meet England's demands. Not only were large parts of Normandy and the north in rebellion against the government of the eighteen-year-old Dauphin, but hordes of professional soldiers, ignoring the two-years' truce after Poitiers, refused to return home and, taking service with anyone who would hire them, continued to live at large on the country. One such mercenary band or "free company," led by the Cheshire knight, Robert Knollys, descended on the rich countryside south of Paris and made itself master of forty castles. The charred gables that marked its progress were known as "Knollys's mitres;" "*qui Robert Canolle prendera,*" this ferocious Englishman had engraved on his banner, "*cent mille moutons gagnera.*" Another band under a Welshman, John Griffith, ravaged the Loire valley, while a Gascon, nicknamed "the archdeacon," plundered Provence, making even the pope pay blackmail. A French prior, forced to take to the woods, left a picture of life under these hateful bands.

"In the year of our Lord 1358 the English came to Chantecocq, captured the castle and set fire to almost all the countryside. Afterward they brought the whole country under their rule, ordering all the owners of both great and small estates to pay ransom for their lives, goods and chattels or their house would be burned. Roused and terrified, many came to the English and agreed to buy themselves back if they would cease for a little while their persecutions. . . . Some they kept in unknown prisons, threatening them every day with death, and some they tortured unceasingly with scourgings and blows, hunger and dire want. Others having nothing with which to redeem themselves, . . . made huts in the woods, there eating their bread in fear, sadness and grief. . . . Among them I, Hugues de Montgeron, prior of Brailet in the parish of Domats, . . . daily saw and heard of the base and horrible deeds of our enemies, of houses burnt and of the many dead left lying about the villages and hamlets."

"The vines," wrote another eye-witness, "were not pruned or kept from rotting by the labours of man's hands; the fields were not sown or ploughed, there were no cattle or fowls in the fields. The pleasant sound of bells was heard, not as a summons to divine worship but in order that men might seek out hiding places."[1] The poet Petrarch, when he revisited France, wrote that it was so wasted that he could scarcely believe it to be the land he had known.

[1] "Récit des tribulations d'un religieux de diocèse de Sens pendant l'invasion Anglaise de 1358," *Bibliothèque de l'École des Chartes* III, ser. 4. 359-60, cit. *Rickert,* 292; *Chronicle of Jean de Venette* (ed. R. A. Newhall), 91.

With all this misery, and her king and so many nobles in captivity, France dissolved into civil war and anarchy. While the Dauphin and his government were struggling against a bourgeois revolution in Paris, the starving peasantry of the Ile de France and Picardy rose and avenged themselves on their rulers with massacre, torture and rape. Under the circumstances, all attempts to ransom the king and conclude a peace with England broke down. The only terms Edward would consider were the surrender of all French rights over the whole of the lands he had conquered. And though, in return for the abandonment of his claim to the French throne, King John himself was now ready to agree to even this, Edward's subjects in parliament, intoxicated by his victories, insisted on demanding the cession of Poitou, Anjou, Maine, Touraine and Normandy. This was more than any French government would concede, however desperate its plight.

Edward prepared, therefore, to give his enemies a further taste of what he could do. "He said plainly that his intention was to pass over into the realm of France and not to return again until he had made an end of his war or else a sufficient peace to his great honour and profit."[1] To bring matters to an issue he proposed to march on Rheims and have himself crowned in its cathedral as king of France. Once more he collected a great army. Not only Englishmen, but Flemings, Hainaulters, Brabancons, Germans and even Frenchmen flocked to his standards to share in the spoils of victory. Eleven hundred ships were assembled at Sandwich and unprecedented quantities of food and stores. There were more than six thousand wagons and carts, mobile workshops for armourers and smiths, handmills and field-ovens, even portable leather coracles from the Severn for supplying the army with fish during Lent from the French rivers, and thirty falconers and sixty couple of greyhounds for the king's sport. For contrary to every rule of medieval war, Edward meant to invade in the autumn and campaign through the winter.

At the beginning of October 1359, the advance-guard under Lancaster landed at Calais. The king followed at the end of the month. Never before, it was said, "departed out of England

[1] *Froissart* II, 36.

such an army nor so well ordered." Nearly all the great figures of English chivalry were present—the king's sons, Edward of Woodstock, John of Gaunt, Lionel of Clarence and Edmund of Langley; the earls of Warwick, Suffolk, Hereford, Northampton, Stafford, Salisbury, March and Oxford; the lords Despenser, Percy, Neville, Mowbray, Grey, Fitzwalter, Hastings, Burghersh, Cobham and the Garter knights, John Chandos and James Audley. Early in November they set forth, marching out of Calais "with all their company and carriages in the best order that ever any army issued out of any town; it was a joy," wrote Froissart, "to behold them. The constable had five hundred knights armed and a thousand archers before his battle. Then came the king's battle with three thousand men-at-arms and five thousand archers in good order riding after the constable's battle; and next came all the carriage, two leagues in length, more than five thousand chariots and carts, every cart at least with four good horses brought out of England, making provision for the host with all things necessary. Then next after them came the prince's battle and of his brethren, wherein were two thousand spears nobly horsed and richly bedizened . . . and five hundred varlets with mattocks and axes to make even the ways for the carriage to pass."

It rained all the way. They rode through Artois and past the city of Arras and over the chalky Somme uplands that one day were to be the battlefield of another and greater English army. "The country," wrote Froissart, "had been long poor and sore wasted and it was a drear season in the realm of France and great famine ran generally through all the country . . . Also the season was sore raining and wet, the which did them great trouble and their horses also, for most part day and night it rained without cease so that wine that year was little worth." Nor, though strict march-discipline was enforced and the army was kept in constant readiness for action, did any enemy appear. The Dauphin had learnt from his father's folly, and his orders were that no-one was to challenge the English in open field. When, after four weeks marching, they arrived, wet and dispirited, at the gates of Rheims, they found them barred. Nor, despite repeated summonses, would the archbishop and citizens open.

The English could still destroy any army feudal France could put into the field. But they could not reduce a strongly fortified city except by surprise or starvation, and Rheims was prepared for a long siege. For nearly two months in bitter weather they occupied the surrounding heights while patrolling parties scoured the countryside as far as the walls of Paris, trying to provoke a relieving force to battle. But none came. In William Langland's poem, *Piers Plowman*, the first part of which was written soon afterwards, the allegorical Lady "Meed"—the spirit of corruption on trial before the king—apostrophised her accuser as one who had served in that bitter campaign, reviling him that while there he had

> " crept into a cabin for cold of thy nails,
> Thinking that winter would have lasted for ever
> And dreadest to be dead because of the downpour."

"The city was strong and well kept," wrote Froissart; "the king of England would not suffer any assault to be made because he would not travail nor hurt his people. They had not at all their ease, for there they were in the heart of winter, about St. Andrew's tide, with great winds and rain . . . and no forage to get abroad."

In the middle of January, unable to maintain his troops on the frozen Champagne plain any longer, Edward abandoned all idea of being crowned in Rheims and marched south into Burgundy, hoping to find early grazing for his horses. But the winter of 1360 proved the longest of the century. After capturing the wine-town of Tonnerre he remained in the Burgundian uplands for most of Lent, hawking and keeping the fast while he waited in vain for the grass to grow. Finally, having extracted an indemnity of 200,000 florins and a three years' truce from the young Duke of Burgundy, he struck north again for Paris, still hoping for the weather to turn and for a chance to force the issue. On the way he learnt that a Norman raiding party had sacked and burnt the royal port of Winchelsea, raping some unfortunate ladies who had taken shelter in St. Thomas' church and killing several hundred townsmen before being driven off by the local militia. In his fury, while he halted at Corbeil for Holy Week, the indignant king set fire to every village in sight of the French capital.

But though after Easter he paraded his army in battle array under its walls, the garrison never stirred. The Dauphin was

wiser than his years. After waiting for four days, while the
heralds issued challenge after challenge, Edward was again forced
to retreat. For, with April as cold as March, there was still
nothing for his horses to eat and, thanks to the Free Companies,
very little for his men. His only resort was to seek the milder
country to the south-west and re-provision the army in the Loire
valley or Brittany until he was able to resume the siege of Paris
in the autumn. Nor, even now, had winter done with him, for
on the first day of the retreat, April 13th, long remembered as
Black Monday—"a foul dark day of mist and of hail, so bitter
cold that sitting on horseback many died"—an icy storm swept
over the army, causing hundreds of vehicles to be abandoned.
A fortnight later, when it was moving down to the Loire, a
thunderstorm, with hailstones as big as pigeons' eggs, struck it as
it traversed the stony heaths beyond Chartres: "Such a tempest
of thunder, lighting and hail that it seemed the world should
have ended." Helpless in their armour, more knights were said
to have been killed that day by lightning than fell in the English
ranks at Crécy and Poitiers. It was this storm, according to one
chronicler, that caused the English king to "turn toward the
church of our Lady at Chartres and devoutly vow to the Virgin
that he would accept terms of peace."

Even in retreat Edward continued to try to tempt the French
to battle. "Certain knights in the following of the Duke of Lancaster," wrote Gray of Heton, "disguising themselves as brigands
or pillaging soldiers without lances, rode in pretended disarray
in order to give the enemy spirit and courage to tackle them.
Some . . . overdid the counterfeit to such an extent . . . that they
came to grief and were taken." It was in such a foray earlier in
the year that a young squire named Geoffrey Chaucer, in the
service of Prince Lionel of Clarence, had been captured, subsequently having to be ransomed for £16 together with many
other officers of the Household.

But if Edward had failed to be crowned at Rheims or to
tempt the Dauphin to another Crécy, the French on their side
could no longer endure the war. Almost anything seemed better
than its indefinite continuance, for, so long as the English remained, the country could not rid itself of the Free Companies
and the misery and anarchy they caused. Even before Edward

had landed in France Knollys had offered him the services of his Great Company and had been taken back into favour, and all over the land he and his like were continuing their enormities.

At the end of April, therefore, plenipotentiaries arrived at the Black Prince's headquarters at Chartres. This time they were ready to concede the principle for which Edward had contended for a quarter of a century—the complete independence of his French dominions. And thanks to their experiences of that winter and Lancaster's moderating influence the English were at last ready to be reasonable. "My liege," the wise old duke is reported to have said, "this war you are waging may be wonderful to all men; it is not so favourable to yourself! If you persist, it will last you a lifetime, and it seems to me doubtful that you will gain your desires. You are wasting your time."

Negotiations were opened on May 1st at the village of Brétigny. A week later, "eight days into the sweet month of May," as Chandos' herald put it, "when the birds were no more in dismay," the terms of a provisional treaty were announced. Under these, Edward renounced his claim to the French throne and to the overlordship of Normandy, Anjou, Maine, Touraine, Brittany and Flanders. He also promised to restore any castles and cities held in these provinces. In return he was to receive the unconditional cession, free from the French king's suzerainty, of Calais, Ponthieu and the whole of Aquitaine—nearly a quarter of France. It was to include the Limousin, Agenais, Angoumois, Poitou, Périgord, Quercy and Rouergue and the cities of Limoges, Poitiers, Angoulême, Cahors, Tarbes and La Rochelle, the headquarters of the European salt trade. France also agreed to pay the full 300,000 gold crowns for her king's ransom in six instalments, the first of which was to secure his release on royal hostages being given for the remainder. She was to renounce the Scottish alliance, and England the Flemish. The question of the Breton succession was to be left to discussion. Provision was also made for the subjects of both kingdoms to study once more at each other's universities.

.   .   .   .

On the morning of May 29th 1360 Edward and the Black Prince returned to Westminster, after galloping through the night from Rye. It was a day of pealing bells, Te Deums and rejoicings. Edward himself announced the good news to his royal prisoner; "you and I," he declared, "are now, thank God, of one accord." Five weeks later, after three and a half years' imprisonment, King John took leave of him at Eltham palace. But on his arrival at Calais, the poor man was detained for a further three months owing to delays in carrying out the treaty's preliminary terms. Even when on October 25th, the two kings formally ratified it, kneeling together before the altar of St. Nicholas church and swearing perpetual friendship, the transfer of territories was still not complete, the people of La Rochelle proving particularly reluctant to change their allegiance. In consequence both Edward's renunciation of the French throne and the French king's of his claim to allegiance were omitted from the treaty and left to letters of ratification to be exchanged later. From this much trouble was to follow, though none seems to have been anticipated, at least by the English. Three of the French king's sons accompanied Edward back to England as hostages, but were subsequently released on parole in return for a promise of 200,000 more crowns.

For the English king felt he could afford to be generous. In his fiftieth year he had obtained all he wanted of France—military glory transcending even his romantic dreams and full dominion over territories far larger than those he had inherited. He was regarded, by foreigners and subjects alike, as the most victorious, chivalrous and magnificent king in Christendom—an Arthur, it seemed, reincarnated. There is a picture of him at the time drawn by a contemporary chronicler, "his face shining like the face of a god, so that to see him or dream of him was to conjure up joyous images." Never, except in the brief interlude after the fall of Calais before the Black Death struck her, had England seemed so thriving. Her nobles and commons—knights, franklins and merchants—were united behind her sovereign, and under the administration of his discreet chancellor and former treasurer, William of Edington bishop of Winchester, the governance of the realm was conducted more smoothly than at any time before.

Chapter Ten

THE NEMESIS OF WAR

There is full many a man that crieth "War, war," that wot full little what war amounteth. War at his beginning hath so great an entering and so large that every wight may enter when him liketh and lightly find war. But, certes, what end that shall thereof befall, it is not light to know.

THE MELIBEE

WELDED by the comradeship of the battlefield, by fifteen years of victory and the Arthurian splendour of royal tournaments and feasts, the magnates had become a single family under the king. Even the fierce Despensers and Mortimers of the March, who thirty years before had hounded one another to death like beasts of prey, were now brothers-in-arms and fellow knights of the Garter. Proclaimed when he first assumed power on the eve of his eighteenth birthday, Edward's ideal of a working partnership between himself and his nobles had been triumphantly vindicated. The reigns of his predecessors had been rent by strife between the Crown and magnates. King John had died a hunted and desperate man with his baronage in arms against him, Henry III had been made prisoner by de Montfort, and even Edward I, the greatest monarch of his age, had had to make a humiliating surrender to the lords who drafted the defiant *De Tallagio non Concedendo*. And after twenty tragic years of division, defeat and national humiliation the reign of Edward's own father had ended in revolution and regicide. Yet for a whole generation the victor of Crécy had achieved complete harmony between himself and his nobles. He had not tried to master them like the first Edward in his later years but to lead them. Seeking not to make them weaker but, by his generosity, richer and stronger, he had bound them to himself in affection and loyalty. To the men of his time, remembering his father's fate, it seemed almost a miracle.

This partnership rested not on the outworn feudal tie, with its unresolved conflict of rights and duties between vassal and lord, but on a conception of national kingship in which the magnates of the realm shared, like the knights of Arthur's Round Table, in their sovereign's achievements and glory. It was one in which the comradeship on the battlefield of monarch, lords, knights and yeomen had implicated the whole nation. The loyalty and duty to the Crown that sprang from it had been enshrined by parliament in the Treason Act of 1352, enacted at the request of both lords and Commons. Under this a traitor was defined as one who compassed or imagined the death of the king, his consort or heir, who levied war against him or aided his enemies, who counterfeited his seal or currency, or slew his chancellor, treasurer or chief justice "while in place and attending to his office." Having released himself from his own obligation to do homage for his French dominions, Edward, unlike his predecessors, could afford to denounce as treason any act by a subject of levying war against the Crown. Yet the statute gave protection, not only to the king and his ministers but to the subject from the summary political trials of the previous reign in which, on grounds of "accroaching" the royal power, opponents of the monarch had been arbitrarily sentenced to death for constructive treason. No one, it was enacted, was to suffer the penalties of treason, as distinct from those of felony or trespass, merely for riding "openly or secretly with armed men against any other to slay him or take him or rob him or retain him until he has made a fine or ransom for his deliverance." Nor if any alleged treason occurred which had not been specified in the act was it to be adjudged as such until it had been expressly declared so by parliament.

Not that there seemed to be any traitors in an England which, under her "clement king", had enjoyed a longer period of internal tranquillity than at any time in her history. "The bringer of peace to his people," was how Edward's epitaph in the Abbey was to describe him,[1] and it was thus that his subjects saw him during his life. There had been times when the greatest threat to an English sovereign's authority and his kingdom's peace had come from his own sons; the first Plantagenet had

[1] *History*, Feb. 1960. M. McKisack, *"Edward III and the Historians."*

been harried to the grave by them. Edward's were devoted to him. It was an essential part of his policy of national conciliation to marry them to the heiresses of the greater feudal families. Of his four surviving younger sons, the eldest, Lionel of Antwerp, had been betrothed to the only child of the Earl of Ulster, William de Burgh, who also represented on the distaff side the great Marcher house of Clare.   Shortly after the Treaty of Bretigny the young prince was sent to govern Ireland with the dual object of securing the profits of his wife's vast but largely illusory inheritance and of restoring order to that turbulent country which, since its invasion by the Bruces after Bannockburn, had been in a state of more than usual anarchy.   His younger brother, John of Gaunt, had made a still more splendid marriage with his cousin Blanche, daughter and co-heiress of Henry of Lancaster.   On the latter's death in 1361 and of the other co-heiress shortly afterwards, he acquired the whole of the vast Lancastrian inheritance, including the earldoms of Lancaster, Derby, Lincoln and Leicester. A year later to mark his own fiftieth birthday Edward created him duke of Lancaster and Lionel duke of Clarence. At the same time he promoted his fourth surviving son, Edmund of Langley, to the peerage as Earl of Cambridge. The youngest, Thomas of Woodstock, who was still only eight, he married later to the eldest co-heiress of the last Bohun earl of Hereford.

Yet in his matrimonial policy the king suffered one major disappointment. The Prince of Wales, now in his early thirties— the hero of Poitiers and the darling of the nation—had remained a bachelor. It had been Edward's wish, by espousing him to the heiress of the Count of Flanders and Burgundy, to secure for the Crown the succession of two of France's richest provinces. But the prince had ideas of his own. Like many others he had long been an admirer of his cousin, Joan of Kent, after whose blue riband, dropped at a ball, the Order of the Garter had been named, and the dissolution of whose marriage to the Earl of Salisbury and remarriage to Lord Holland had caused such a sensation twelve years before. The latter's death in November 1360 had left her a widow of thirty-two with four children. Six months later, to his parents' dismay, the prince announced his betrothal to her. They were married that autumn in St. George's

chapel, Windsor, by papal dispensation—for they were cousins—
the pope having been informed that grave scandal would otherwise ensue.

The autumn of 1361 brought England and her king worse
troubles than the heir apparent's love match. In August the
plague returned. Before it ceased in the following May it had
struck down the flower of another generation. This time it was
less discriminating, carrying off three of the war heroes—"the
good Duke" of Lancaster, the Earl of Hereford and Lord Cobham—and four bishops, including London. It fell with particular severity on children; "*la mortalité des enfants*" it was
called to distinguish it from its predecessor. While it was raging,
on January 15th, 1362, a terrible tempest struck the country.
"Wretched, savage and violent," the unknown writer on the wall
of Ashwell church recorded, "a wicked populace survives to
witness, and in the end with a violent wind Maurus thunders in
the world."[1]

Coming so quickly after the country's triumphs, these disasters
seemed to serious minds a sign of divine displeasure. In the
earliest version of his poem, *Piers Plowman*, probably written in
the following year, William Langland attributed them to the
seven deadly sins—pride, luxury, envy, wrath, avarice, gluttony
and sloth—into which, in their obsession with the plunder of the
French wars, his countrymen seemed to him to have fallen. In
particular, he laid the blame on the spirit of greed and corruption
—the Lady Meed,[2] typified in his allegory by a seductive but
evil maiden,

"crowned with a crown   the king hath no better;
All her five fingers   were fretted with rings
Of the purest precious work   that ever prince wore.
In red scarlet robes   and ribboned with gold . . .
Frail of her faith   fickle of her speech,
And making men misdo   many score times:
Tickle of her tail   and treacherous of tongue,
And common as a cartway   to every knave that walketh."
"All the rich retinues that reign with falsehood," he declared,
"courted her,

[1] M. D. Anderson, *Design for a Journey*, 93.
[2] The old English meaning of the word is "reward."

"assessors and summoners,   sheriffs and their clerks,
  Beadles and bailiffs   and brokers of chaffering,
  Forestallers and victuallers,   advocates of the Arches; . . .
  And the earldom of Envy   and of Wrath together, . . .
  The county of Covetousness   and all the coasts about, . . .
  . . . .   the borough of Theft,
  And the lordship of Lechery."

And when Meed had been arraigned and found guilty of cor-
rupting the realm, Langland made Reason preach with a cross
before the king:

"He proved that these pestilences   were purely for sin,
  And the south-west wind   at Saturday at even
  Was plainly for pure pride   and for no point else.
  Pear-trees and plum-trees   were puffed to the earth
  In example for men   that they should do better;
  Beeches and broad oaks   were blown to the ground,
  Turned upward their tails   in token of dread
  That deadly sin at doomsday   shall foredoom them all."

Though the poet stigmatised the court and city and, indeed,
the whole nation, he did not blame or criticise the king. To
Langland, as to most Englishmen at this time, Edward seemed
above reproach. He depicted him in his poem as a courteous,
merciful and just ruler, scrupulously fair in hearing the charges
against the Lady Meed and only condemning her and banishing
her from the realm when the case against her has been proved
beyond all doubt by her accuser, Conscience. Yet there was an
Achilles heel in the king's armour of which those who knew him
were well aware. To Edward's Windsor neighbour, the rector
of Wraysbury—an enthusiastic chronicler of his reign—it seemed
that no land under the sun had ever produced a monarch "so
noble, so generous, so fortunate, prudent and discreet in counsel,
affable and gentle in courtesy of speech, pitiful to the afflicted
and profuse in largesse, liberal in giving and lavish in spending."
Yet even the admiring de Murimath had to admit that "he controlled not, even in old age, the dissolute lusts of the flesh." Indulgent to others, the king was, above all, indulgent to himself.
It was a lack of self-control that, through his example, infected
his entire court. In a manual of instructions written about this

time an English doctor of canon law warned priests hearing the
confession of any knight, "to inquire if he is proud or an adulterer
or otherwise lecherous, as they almost all are nowadays, or if he
has put away his wife."[1] For in this, the modern Camelot at
Windsor and Eltham resembled the literary ideal on which it
modelled itself.

"Clement and benign, familiar and gentle to all men," as
de Murimath described him, Edward was not an iron man like
his grandfather. His supreme object was to please and excel,
and, being able, courageous and immensely energetic and possessed of wonderful charm, he was at first completely successful.
But as difficulties grew he became more and more apt to follow
the line of least resistance; to promise, and when promise became
impossible of fulfilment, to evade and equivocate. At this
time, either through a wish to gain a tactical point or through
some unaccountable negligence, he made a fatal blunder. In
February 1361, with his four sons and the French royal hostages
by his side, he had opened the parliament which ratified the
treaty of Brétigny, first marching in procession to the Abbey,
where Simon of Islip archbishop of Canterbury celebrated
High Mass in honour of the Holy Trinity. Yet the one essential
condition of the treaty for which England had fought for nearly
a quarter of a century was allowed to go unratified, ostensibly
on account of French delays in making the promised ransom-
payments and in handing over certain of the towns and territories agreed under the treaty. The final date fixed for the
exchange of the mutual renunciations of sovereignty had been
November 1st, 1361. Yet when, two days before, the French
envoys arrived in England they were told that the king was not
prepared to abandon his title to the French crown until every
detail of the treaty had been complied with. The envoys, therefore, refused to make a unilateral surrender of their master's
suzerainty over Aquitaine.[2] As a result, by far the most important
gain of the peace was lost, and the question of ultimate sovereignty
was left unsolved to bedevil future Anglo-French relations.

[1] *Pantin*, 206.
[2] *Camden Miscellany*, xix (1952). *Anglo-French Negotiations of 1361-1362*
(ed. P. Chaplais), 5-7. See also *R.H.S.T.* 5th Ser. 10: J. Le Patourel, *The
Treaty of Bretigny*. 19-39.

Without it neither the transfers of territory nor the huge ransom instalments were of any permanent use to England, even though, when delays occurred in the time-table for the latter and one of the French royal hostages—temporarily given leave to visit his wife at Boulogne—broke his parole and failed to return,[1] King John most honourably surrendered himself again to his former captors. Returning to England at the beginning of 1364, perhaps not without relief at exchanging his own war-harried and poverty-stricken realm for the luxury and chivalric splendour of the English court, he died there that spring at the age of forty-five.

The French were given another and better excuse for renouncing the terms of the treaty of Brétigny, should they ever wish to do so. For though the disbandment and withdrawal of the free companies had been one of its main conditions when, in Froissart's words, "their captains departed in courteous manner out of those fortresses they held . . . and gave leave to their men of war to depart," the latter "thought that to return into their own country was not to them profitable—and peradventure they durst not because of such villainous deeds that they were accused of there. So they gathered themselves together and made amongst them new captains and took by election the worst and most unhappy person of them all and so rode forth . . . and met together again." After which they continued to behave as they had always done and as though no peace had been made. "They wasted all the country without any cause and robbed without sparing all that ever they could get and violated and defiled women, old and young without pity, and slew men, women and children without mercy."

For the English army of which the French had been so anxious to be rid was neither a feudal array bound by social obligations nor a national militia defending its own soil. It was a collection of private war-bands raised by indenture by adventurous nobles and knights for the pursuit of

---

[1] According to Froissart the French hostages had a very easy time of it, "sporting them without peril or danger all about in the city at their pleasure, and the great lords went a-hunting and hawking . . . and rode about the country and visited the ladies and damsels without any controlling, they found the King of England so courteous and amiable." *Froissart*, II, 74.

profit. And when replete with their gains the larger share-holders withdrew, the smaller took over. Though many of these "great pillagers" were not English, but Germans, Brabanters, Flemings, Hainaulters, Gascons and even Frenchmen, they had all served England's king, and the blame for their evil doings was laid at his door. Even after their captains, now grown rich and respectable, had departed in obedience to their sovereign's commands, many of those who succeeded them were Englishmen. One of them, an archer named John Hawkwood —the son of an Essex tanner—after ravaging southern France, led his gang of desperadoes to Avignon "to see," as they put it, "the pope and cardinals." Later he transferred himself to Italy where for thirty years he lived by placing his trained and disciplined band—the "White Company," as it was called—at the disposal of first one warring city-republic, then another. After making an enormous fortune and marrying a natural daughter of Bernabo Visconti, tyrant of Milan, he died in 1394, in the service of Florence, whose grateful government gave him a funeral in the duomo and commissioned as his memorial a magnificent equestrian fresco by Paolo Uccello.[1]

Two years after the end of the war with England the "brigands" were still strong enough to destroy a French army under a royal duke at Brignais near Lyons. But the accession in 1364 of the twenty-five-year-old Dauphin as Charles V proved the turn of the tide for France. A few weeks later a rough Breton knight with a genius for war, Bertrand du Guesclin, won a victory at Cocherel in Normandy over the forces of the traitor, Charles of Navarre, and an English freelance captain, John Jewel. It was the first decisive French victory for a generation and ended the Norman rebellion. In Brittany, where civil war had again broken out, Sir John Chandos with a few hundred English volunteers again showed that autumn at Auray the unbreakable ascendency of his countrymen in pitched battle, defeating and killing Charles

[1] With Robert Knollys and Hugh Calveley he was one of the founders of the English hospital at Rome and, through a daughter who married John Shelley, M.P. for Rye, was an ancestor of the poet. *D.N.B.*, IX, 236-42. In the year before his death he wrote what is believed to be the earliest extant letter in English. C. L. Kingsford, *Prejudice and Promise in Fifteenth-Century England*, 22. See also *History Today*, May 1956: E. R. Chamberlain, *The English Mercenary Companies in Italy*.

of Blois and taking du Guesclin prisoner. But the new French king turned the defeat to his advantage by recognising the rival claimant, de Montfort, as duke in return for his homage. In doing so he regained Brittany for France and brought the war in that country to an end and, with it, any further pretext for English intervention.

Charles V had none of his father's love of knight-errantry. After his early experience at Poitiers he never took part in another battle. He was a delicate young man, matured by misfortune, with a sharp nose, quizzical look and, under his scholarly appearance, a will of iron. Devout, learned and immensely shrewd, he was a brilliant judge of men; it was he who raised the younger son of a Breton hedge-squire to the command of France's armies. He loved the company of scholars and artists and strove to make his court and Paris once more the centre and arbiter of western civilisation, identifying his throne with a stately ceremonial that recalled, in a more luxurious age, his hero and great-great-grandfather, St. Louis. Yet, though operating from the library and counting-house rather than the saddle, he proved the most successful director of war of his age, attaining his ends with a minimum expense of life and treasure. Knowing precisely what he wanted, he pursued it with cunning, patience and inflexible resolution. In his sixteen years on the throne he raised France from the depths of defeat and poverty to renewed wealth and grandeur.

Above all, he sought to identify himself with the needs and hopes of the French people. His supreme object was to unite all Frenchmen under a single throne and law. Where the feudal nobility, with their arrogance and selfish separatism, had left France wide open to her enemies, this young king set himself to show that, from the highest to the lowest, safety for life and property could only be won by rallying round the Crown. Little by little he gained his ends, letting Edward leave unratified the renunciation of his claim to the French throne and, with it, his right to untrammelled overlordship over Aquitaine, and, while there was peace with England, driving or bribing out of the country, first one, then another of the free companies. All the while, as he restored order and prosperity to France's long-tormented countryside, he built up her financial resources and reorganised her armies. The price he had to pay was a heavy one; the *gabelle* or salt monopoly, which he made permanent, and his system of farming the taxes led to grave social abuses and oppression. Yet the poor who felt them most saw in him their protector against the English and the lawless soldiery who had so long preyed on them, and, when he died at the age of thirty-eight, it was said that the lilies were engraved on every peasant's heart.

.   .   .   .

Though the return of the plague in 1361 had fallen with equal severity on France, striking down no less than eight cardinals in the court of Avignon, it was again the smaller of the two countries that suffered most from its attrition. Yet the area which England with her reduced man-power had to control had been trebled by her conquests. In 1363, faced by the difficulty of finding archers for its foreign garrisons, the government issued a proclamation deploring the nation's degeneracy and enjoining archery practice on saints' days and holidays for all able-bodied men.[1] About this time, too, Edward tried once more to forestall any renewal of a joint attack from France and Scotland by using the latter's poverty and internal anarchy to coax her king and nobles into a union with England. He made generous, if calculated, concessions to her merchants and pilgrims, re-opened English universities to Scottish students—for Scotland still had none of her own—and in the autumn of 1363 offered to remit the remaining instalments of King David's ransom and restore Berwick, Roxburgh, and Jedburgh and the Stone of Scone in return for the Scots' acknowledging him or one of his sons as David's heir should the latter die without children. The Scottish king, who had learnt to love the fleshpots of the Plantagenet

[1] "Whereas the people of our realm, nobles as well as commoners, usually practised in their games the art of archery, whereby honour and profit accrued to the whole realm and we gained not a little help in our wars with God's favour; and now the said art is almost totally neglected and the same people amuse themselves with throwing stones, wood or iron, or playing handball, football or stick-ball or hockey or cock-fighting, and some indulge in other dishonest games which are less useful or worthwhile, so that the said kingdom . . . becomes destitute of archers." Rymer, *Foedera*, 3: II: 79.

court, was ready to agree, as was also, for a time, his chief opponent, the Earl of Douglas, who hoped to recover his English estates. But when the treaty[1] was presented to the Scottish parliament in the spring of 1364, its members proved worthier of the great Bruce and Douglas than their degenerate successors. Notwithstanding "the dark and drublie days" through which their country was passing, they declared themselves "in no way willing to assent" and rejected the terms as "insufferable." A few years later, the issue, as Scotsmen saw it, was put by John Barbour, archdeacon of Aberdeen, in the prologue to his epic, *The Brus*, which he wrote round the story of Scotland's liberator.

> "Ah, freedom is a noble thing! . . .
> Freedom all solace to man gives,
> He lives at ease that freely lives!
> A noble heart may have none ease
> Nor ellës naught that may him please
> If freedom fail"

Edward's hopes, therefore, came to nothing, and Scotland, poverty-stricken, proud and racked by constant civil war, remained the independent nation that Bruce and Wallace had made her and, as a result, a standing threat to England's back door. Meanwhile, beyond the Channel, the latter continued to maintain her vast military empire, the new outlying districts of which, in contradistinction to a still loyal Gascony, were growing every year more hostile to her arrogant and predatory dominion. In the past the English kings—descendants of the ancient princes of Anjou and Aquitaine—had behaved as Frenchmen and governed their French provinces through the local nobility and bureaucracy. But with their victories over the Valois kings and the growing identification of England's French-speaking lords with her Anglo-Saxon yeomanry—a union

---

[1] The tentative treaty offered Scotland better terms than she secured by the unions of the two crowns and parliaments under the Stuarts—the coronation of England's and Scotland's kings at Scone as well as at Westminster, the preservation of an independent Scottish parliament, freedom from all taxation not imposed by it, and the autonomy of the Scottish Church and Courts. See E. W. M. Balfour-Melville, *Edward III and David II* (Historical Association 1954).

cemented on the battlefield—England's rulers were becoming increasingly insular. Pride in their common Englishry and, with it, contempt for foreigners, were beginning to transcend the unity of class, speech and ideology that had so long identified them with their parent lands across the Channel. On October 1362 the chief justice of the King's Bench opened the proceedings of parliament for the first time in English—a precedent followed at the opening of the next parliament by the chancellor. In the same year it was enacted that all pleadings should be in the vernacular on the ground that French was "too little known in the realm" and that "people who impleaded or were impeached in the courts knew not what was said for or against them by their serjeants or pleaders." And though lack of precision in the language—for so long the despised speech of "uplandish men"— made this technically impracticable, and for several more centuries lawyers continued in their pleadings to use French to express the exact concepts demanded by their profession, forensic argument in the king's courts was henceforward conducted in English. The old romance tongue of western chivalry was ceasing to be the speech of the ruling class; a generation later Chaucer's high-born prioress spoke French, not after the French of Paris, "which was to her unknowe," but "after the school of Stratford-attë-Bowe."

In 1363, partly to please the Gascons and partly to provide him with an establishment suitable to his new married state, the heir-apparent was sent to govern Aquitaine as a sovereign and independent prince, subject only to his father's overlordship. Here he maintained a splendid court where, in Chandos' herald's words, "abode all nobleness, all joy and jollity, largesse, gentleness and honour, and all his subjects and all his men loved him right dearly." Yet, however much the Gascons might admire their new duke as a model of knightly chivalry and the first warrior of his age, they loved neither the taxation he imposed to maintain his extravagant court nor the horde of English lords and officials he took with him to administer the duchy. Still less did the peoples of the new provinces added to England's French dominion. The new high seneschal of Aquitaine was a Cheshire knight, Sir Thomas Felton; the seneschal of Poitou his cousin, Sir William of the same name; of Saintonge Sir Baldwin Treville;

of Quercy Sir Thomas Walkfare; of Limousin Lord Ros; of Rouergue Sir Thomas Wetenhall; of Angoumois Sir Henry Hay; of the Agenais Sir Richard Baskerville. Even the chivalry, good sense and moderation of the high constable of Aquitaine, the universally loved Sir John Chandos, did not remove the sense of shame felt by the proud Gascon nobles that foreigners should hold the highest offices of their ancient dukedom.

"We will do the English honour and obey them," the towns-folk of La Rochelle had said after the treaty of Brétigny, "but our hearts shall never change." Yet little more than a century before, the same city had stoutly resisted the advance of the French into Plantagenet Aquitaine. The sense of outraged nationality and longing for revenge aroused in Gallic peasants and merchants by a generation of invasion and rapine by English bowmen had spread from France proper into the south-west and had even begun to show itself beyond the Garonne. This growing anti-English, pro-Valois feeling of a countryside that had hitherto preferred the remote rule of its French-speaking English duke to that of Paris was brought to a head by the romantic extravagance and belligerency of the Black Prince. In 1366 the kingdom of Castile became the scene of one of those periodic civil wars that reflect the inability to compromise, impassioned partisanship and fanatic valour of the Spanish temperament. Its king, Don Pedro "the Cruel," was challenged by his bastard half-brother Don Enrico of Trastamara. Repudiated by a large part of his people, excommunicated by the pope and opposed, though without open intervention, by the French king who, seeing an opportunity for getting rid of the free companies, sent off as many of them as possible under Bertrand du Guesclin to help the Bastard whom he saw as a future ally against England, Pedro was driven from his capital. Taking refuge at Corunna he appealed to the Black Prince for help. This challenge to his chivalry, as well as to the principle of legitimacy, was more than the prince could resist. He saw himself as the knight-errant of Christendom leading a righteous war. "It is not the right way of a true Christian king," he declared, "to disinherit a rightful heir and to inherit, by puissance of tyranny, a bastard. . . . France used to be the chief land of Christians. Now the Lord God has willed that we have the courage to win that title." Obtaining his father's unofficial consent and a promise of help from his brother, the young Duke of Lancaster, he assembled an army at Dax and, in the winter of 1366-7, prepared to cross the Pyrenees.

Though more than half his force was Gascon, its hard-core was English. Following the prince on his chivalrous venture were the heads of many of the great Anglo-Norman fighting families and the fierce mercenary captains, Calveley, Knollys, Felton, Winstanley, who with their veteran bands flocked from every part of Europe to his standards. Joined by John of Gaunt with a thousand archers from forest Cheshire and the north, the prince turned his back on his restless duchy, his debts and the watchful French king beyond his borders, and in February 1367 crossed the Ronscevalles pass, driving his heavily accoutred men, horses and wagons through the wintry gorges of Navarre to the Castilian border. "Bitter cold it was," wrote Chandos' herald, "with a sharp wind and snow; . . . the cold and the hail were such that every man was dismayed." In the vale of Pampeluna a Spanish-Franco army barred the way in an impregnable position dominating the road to Burgos. Advised by du Guesclin, the Bastard made no move, leaving the invaders to choose between retreat or starvation. For three weeks, in driving wind, rain and snow, the Black Prince's men waited in "that inhospitable place and season," hoping against hope that the Spaniards would attack, while dysentery ran through their ranks, and hordes of fierce light cavalry—javelin-throwing *genetours* trained in the Moorish wars—descended on them in murderous rushes from the surrounding heights. Then, when his supplies were almost exhausted and disaster stared him in the face, the prince vanished by night into the mountains and, after a brilliant flanking march across the Sierra de Cantabria, reappeared two days later in the Ebro plain at Najera.

Having turned the Spaniards' position, the initiative was in his hands, and it was for the enemy to elect whether to give battle to save Castile from invasion or make a strategic withdrawal to some more favourable position. Knowing what a few thousand English archers and men-at-arms could do on their own ground, du Guesclin strongly advised the latter. Only a week earlier an outlying English contingent under the two Feltons had defied a force twelve times as large on a hill still known, after six centuries, as "the Englishmen's hill," fighting almost to the last man and inflicting immense losses on their assailants before surrendering. But retreat in the face of an enemy was not a practicable manœuvre for the proud, ill-disciplined feudal host of Castile, and the Frenchman's counsel was disregarded. The English were known to be desperately short of rations and heavily outnumbered. The Bastard offered battle.

That night "the Spaniards took their ease and rest, for they had plenty of victuals and other things and the Englishmen had great default, therefore they had great desire to fight either to win or to lose all." When day dawned on April 3rd the Black Prince rode from company to company to give his hungry, tired troops courage and confidence; "it was a great beauty," wrote Froissart, "to behold the battles and the armour shining against the sun." Before the fight began "he regarded towards heaven and joined his hands together" and offered up a prayer:

"Very God, Jesu Christ, who hath formed and created
　me, consent by your benign grace that I may have victory
　of mine enemies, as that I do is in a rightful quarrel. . . .
　Because my heart yearns for a life of honour vouchsafe,
　I pray, to watch over me and my people this day."

Then he gave the familiar order, "Advance banners! In the name of God and St. George!"

Though the battle was "right fell and cruel," the issue was never in doubt. The chivalry of Spain fought on horseback, as they were accustomed, and the English archers slew the horses in thousands and then shot their riders as they lay in their armour on the ground. Before the steady discipline and aim of the bowmen the feudal nobility of another European kingdom broke under a hail of steel and goosequill. The chief resistance was made by the French who, taught by past disasters, fought in a dense phalanx on foot. But in the end they, too, were overwhelmed "as they felt the sharp arrows light amongst them," and by nightfall 16,000 Spanish dead strewed the battlefield and the road to Burgos, and "the water that ran by Navaret was of the colour of red with the blood of men and horses." Among the prisoners were the Spanish historian Ayala and du Guesclin, who was taken by his old adversary of the Breton wars, Sir John Chandos. It was in the spirit of chivalric war that his ransom was paid by a Cheshire knight, Hugh Calveley, who before the Black Prince's summons had been serving with his fellow free-lance in the Bastard's army and had pledged himself as his "brother-in-arms" to share the spoils of war.[1]

The Black Prince's Spanish crusade had begun in glory; it ended in disillusionment and disaster. The king he had restored tried to murder his prisoners and went back on all his promises. All that summer the victors waited on the burning Castilian plain for the gold that was to have paid for their services, while dysentery, contracted from stagnant pools, continued to reduce their numbers. When in the autumn the prince led the survivors back across the Pyrenees, they were a shadow of the splendid host that had set out at the beginning of the year. Not one man in five, it was said, saw England again. All that the prince had to show for his victory was a handful of jewels[2] wrung from Don Pedro in place of the million crowns he had been promised.

At thirty-seven, his giant frame emaciated by dysentery, the Black Prince returned to Bordeaux. His troops were unpaid and his duchy restless under taxation. So troublesome were the survivors of the free companies whom he was now forced to quarter on his subjects that, when he summoned the estates of the duchy to meet at the little hill-town of St. Emilion, the deputies of Rouergue were forced to turn back by the "companions" ravaging the Dordogne valley. To add to the miseries of Aquitaine its eastern border was harried by the very man its duke had defeated in the summer—the Spanish Bastard who, taking refuge in Languedoc, had secured aid from the pope and the French to finance a private crusade of revenge.

At the beginning of 1368, disregarding the advice of Chandos, the prince got the estates to impose a five years' *fouage* or tax on every hearth in the duchy to meet his war debts. It was

[1] *History*, February 1962. Maurice Keen, *Brotherhood in Arms*, 9.

[2] Among them a huge uncut ruby, seized by the Castilian king from a murdered Moor. Worn by Henry V at Agincourt and by the last Plantagenet at Bosworth, it now adorns the imperial state crown in which the sovereign leaves the Abbey after a coronation.

bitterly opposed by two of the leading magnates of Guienne, the
Count d'Armagnac and the Count d'Albret, who had till now
accepted the English connection. When the prince "insisted
that, right or wrong, his vassals should do his bidding," they
refused to allow the tax to be levied in their domains and appealed,
first to the King of England, and then, without waiting for an
answer, to the King of France.

It was the opportunity for which Charles had been waiting.
Yet he proceeded with his usual caution. Privately promising
the appellants that he would investigate their case but pledging
himself to nothing, he played for time and with the pope's aid
secured the release of the last hostages from the unsuspecting and
now ageing Edward—in return, it was said, for papal approval
of the appointment of the English king's favourite minister,
William of Wykeham, to the see of Winchester. Continuing the
pretence of non-intervention in Spain, he sent back the now
ransomed du Guesclin to restore the Bastard and, through an
alliance with Castile, Aragon and Navarre, to circle England's
southern dominion with enemies. By getting a French pope to
refuse a dispensation on the grounds of consanguinity, he had
already thwarted Edward's hope of marrying his son, Edmund
of Langley, to the heiress of Flanders. Now, when English policy
had suffered a further set-back through the death in Italy of
Prince Lionel of Clarence after his wedding to the niece of Bernabo
Visconti of Milan, he brought off a still greater coup by inducing
the Count of Flanders to give his daughter to his own brother,
Philip the Bold of Burgundy, thus bringing Flanders once more
into the orbit of royal France. All the while, as he concerned
himself with art and his projects for a national library, he observed
the letter while violating the spirit of the treaty of Brétigny. His
reform of France's finances and military administration was now
almost complete.

By the end of 1368 he was ready. He had already allowed
the Gascon appellants to lay their case before the *parlement* of
Paris, making a secret pact with them that if it came to war
they would stand together. Knowing that hundreds more of
the Black Prince's subjects were eager to appeal to him, he now
announced that his judges had found that, as Edward had failed
to ratify the renunciation of his claim to the French throne, his

own father's surrender of the overlordship of Aquitaine had never become effective and that province was, therefore, still part of France. As its overlord he was entitled, and morally bound, to pronounce judgment on the appeals.

In January 1369 Charles formally summoned the Black Prince as a peer of France to appear in person at Paris. The prince was taken completely by surprise. When he realised that all that he and his father had fought for had been in vain he swore a mighty oath. "We shall willingly," he said, "attend on the appointed day at Paris since the King of France sends for us. But it will be with helmet on head and with sixty thousand men at our back."

What the victor of Poitiers threatened and what he could now perform were, however, different things. It was not he who took the offensive, but his discontented vassals and the French king. The time had passed when, at the English approach, the French "hid themselves in their fortresses and fled before them as the lark does before the hawk." All round the 800-mile perimeter of Aquitaine bands of fighting men poured in to help their compatriots, while the clergy everywhere took the lead in preaching rebellion. Within a few weeks more than nine hundred castles and towns had repudiated allegiance to the English; most of Armagnac, Limousin, Rodez, Quercy and the Agenais was lost without a fight.

Yet the French king still proceeded with caution. In March his troops helped the Castilians to win a decisive victory over Don Pedro, who was taken prisoner and killed. With the Bastard back on the throne, Castile and her fleet, as well as Aragon and Navarre, were now aligned against England. At last, in May 1369, Charles took the decisive step, first declaring the Black Prince contumacious for failing to appear before the *parlement* of Paris and then informing the English king that, as he had failed to observe the letter of the treaties, his French lands were forfeit. Simultaneously he seized Ponthieu.

Furious, Edward appealed to parliament for money and resumed the title, discarded nine years before, of King of France. At this moment the Black Death broke out in England for the third time. Among those who died that summer were the bishops of Norwich, Hereford and Exeter, the earls of Suffolk and Warwick and the young Duchess of Lancaster—the lady Blanche,[1] wife of John of Gaunt. Not till the autumn was it possible to collect even a small force for France, when, to forestall an invasion of the Isle of Wight, Lancaster crossed to Calais with 600 men-at-arms and 1500 bowmen. By striking at Artois and Picardy he was just in time to stop the embarkation of an army in Normandy under the French king's brother. But though he marched to the gates of Harfleur, burning and ravaging, he was unable to tempt the French to battle. For Charles had resolved to give no chance to the English archers to repeat their holocausts of a generation before. By November, unable to supply his troops any longer, the duke returned to England, to find that he had lost not only his wife but his mother, Queen Philippa having died that month at Windsor. "The good queen," her countryman, Froissart, wrote of her, "that so many good deeds had done in her time and so many knights succoured and ladies and demoiselles comforted."

If 1369 was a disastrous year for England, it saved Scotland. Without enough men to defend both the northern marches and Aquitaine, a plague-riven England agreed to a fourteen-year truce. But for this, famine, baronial and tribal war and the crushing taxation to pay for her king's ransom would have forced the northern kingdom to accept Edward's terms and acknowledge him as David's successor. As it was, though England still held Berwick, Roxburgh and Annandale, the Scots, freed from danger from the south, were able to put down a rebellion of the Lord of the Isles that threatened to disintegrate their country. When eighteen months later, in February 1371, King David died, the son of Robert Bruce's daughter, Robert the Steward, succeeded under the terms of the settlement of half a century before. Without their involvement in a losing war with France the English would never have recognised him.

The campaign in Guienne fared no better in 1370 than in 1369. The English could not contend indefinitely against a nation several times their size. Though they still did not realise

[1] "Who died fair and young, at about the age of twenty-two years. Gay and glad she was, fresh and sportive, sweet, simple and humble semblance, the fair lady whom men called Blanche." *Froissart*. Daughter of the great warrior Henry of Lancaster, she was the heroine of Chaucer's earliest important poem.

it, the door of opportunity, once wide open, was now bolted against them. They could no longer finance the war from plunder, which, as they burnt, ravaged and wasted, brought in diminishing returns. In vain they called in their free companies—Hugh Calveley from Spain and the "terrible Robert" Knollys from Burgundy—and enrolled them to defend the duchy; unpaid and forced to live on the countryside, the companions only made the situation worse, arousing the hatred of every peasant and burgher. In vain they made *chevauchées* in the old familiar style to provoke the French to battle. In the summer of 1370, with 1500 men-at-arms and 4000 bowmen Knollys marched from Calais to Troyes and thence, passing under the walls of Paris, to Brittany. But the only result was a further growth of French national consciousness, while the young English lords, humiliated by their lack of success, grumbled furiously at having to serve under such a low-born commander; "the old brigand," they called him.

The French king's strategy was admirably adapted to his means. It was to avoid pitched battles at all costs, use his superiority in numbers and the growing French sympathies of the Black Prince's vassals to liberate first one district, then another, and, by strengthening the defences of every castle in French hands, to make it impossible for the English to recover their lost gains. Gone were the days when a few daring Englishmen could surprise and escalade supposedly impregnable but weakly guarded strongholds; once Charles's engineers had put the defences of any fortress or town in order, nothing but a major army with a siege-train could reduce it. And this was something far beyond the capacity of the English forces.

Early in 1370 Sir John Chandos—the most loved figure on either side—fell in a skirmish near Poitiers. "Courteous and benign, amiable, liberal, preux, sage and true in all causes," Froissart wrote of him, "nor was there ever knight better beloved nor praised of every creature." His death caused the defection of thousands of Gascons who, as long as he was constable, adhered to the English cause. With his passing the Black Prince lost his wisest counsellor and the last hope of an accommodation with the French king.

That summer Moissac, Agen and even Aiguillon, which

twenty years before had defied a French army for months, fell after sieges of only a few days. The Count of Armagnac was now less than fifty miles from Bordeaux. At the end of August came the crowning humiliation when the city of Limoges was surrendered to the Duke of Berri by its bishop after the townsmen had risen and overpowered the small English garrison under Sir Hugh Calveley. Bitterly resentful—for the bishop had been one of his closest friends—the Black Prince roused himself from his sick bed at Angoulême and, borne in a litter in the midst of his army, marched on the city. Breaching its walls by mining, he stormed it by night. In the sack that followed, dreadful things were done, though the story of a general massacre told by Froissart is probably untrue and is omitted from his later and revised accounts of the city's fall.[1] But the vengeance taken by the prince and his unbridled troops shocked even that unsqueamish age and marred his reputation for chivalry. It did the English cause untold harm.

A month later the French king raised Bertrand du Guesclin to the great office of constable of France and commander of all her armies. This short, squat, coarse-featured veteran, with his long experience of mercenary war, was exactly the lieutenant Charles needed for his Fabian strategy of wearing down the invaders. In the days of the arrogant feudal nobility that had perished at Crécy and Poitiers such a promotion would have been unthinkable. Now after a generation of civil war and anarchy it seemed inevitable, for the Breton knight had become the hero of France. But the chief credit for the collapse of the hitherto invincible English belonged to the unmartial, unspectacular sovereign who had seen so clearly and so cunningly pursued the means by which they could be defeated.

In November 1370, two months after the sack of Limoges and only three years after his victory at Nájera, the Black Prince, a sick, frustrated man, handed over his command and the lieutenancy of Aquitaine to his brother, John of Gaunt. In January 1371 he sailed for England where he found his father, once the hero of Europe, sunk in a doting dependence on his mistress, Alice Perrers, a former lady-in-waiting of the queen.

[1] See A. Deroux, Le Sac de la Cité de Limoges: A. H. Burne, The Agincourt War 20-2, 27-8.

Withdrawing to Berkhamsted castle and taking no further part in public life, he watched from a bed of sickness the continuing decline of England's fortunes.

His departure made no difference to the course of the war. John of Gaunt, an ambitious, hustling and habitually unlucky man, was no more able to stem the French advance than his brother. In the late summer of 1371, after six months' campaigning, he too relinquished his command and handed over the governance of what remained of England's dominion to the Gascon veteran of Poitiers, Captal de Buch. A few weeks later he married the eldest daughter and co-heiress of the dead Don Pedro and thereafter became increasingly preoccupied with a claim to the Castilian throne.

Yet though the duke now called himself a king the only dowry his wife brought him were "castles in Spain." French aid had by now re-seated the Bastard on the throne and aligned him permanently against England. Henceforward Castile's ocean-going fleet became a major factor in the war. In their obsession with military glory the English had omitted to remain strong at sea, and the command which Edward had won at Sluys and which had enabled his armies to ravage France at will had slipped from his hands. Ever since the first Black Death he had overstrained the country's maritime resources by impressing ships and seamen and neglecting to pay for them, while his grant to foreign merchants of a monopoly of exporting wool had led to a decline in English shipbuilding. He still held both sides of the Dover strait and called himself lord of the sea, but in the Atlantic waters between England and Gascony the great galliasses of Castile were a growing menace to his communications. In the autumn of 1371 Guy de Brian—the standard bearer at Crécy and a founder knight of the Garter—won an action against French privateers near Roscoff off the coast of Brittany where civil war had again broken out after a quarrel between the Duke John and his French overlord. But on June 22nd, 1372, a much larger English fleet attempting to relieve La Rochelle under the new lieutenant of Aquitaine, the Earl of Pembroke, was routed by the combined fleets of Castile and France, and Pembroke, and most of its crews made prisoner. A final attempt by Edward III and the Black Prince to lead a new army to Gascony in person failed in a terrible autumn storm that sent thousands to the bottom after six weeks of buffeting at the mouth of the Channel. It was the old king's last appearance in the war.

With La Rochelle in French hands and the Castilian and French navies in control of the Bay of Biscay, the English cause was lost. The Gascon wine trade was ruined and for the moment the age-long link between England and the Garonne all but broken. In the summer of 1373 John of Gaunt made an attempt to do by land what could no longer be done by sea, setting out from Calais on August 4th with an army of 15,000 men and crossing eastern France in a *grande chevauchée* which ended at Christmas at Bordeaux after a wintry march across the Auvergne. This feat of endurance, in which vast numbers of horses perished, was regarded as "most honourable to the English" and probably saved Bordeaux. But as the French avoided battle, it achieved nothing else.

With the fall of La Réole at the beginning of 1374 all that remained of England's overseas empire was Calais and a thin coastal strip between Bordeaux and Bayonne—smaller now even than at Edward's accession. Having awoken the French people to nationhood, her king and princes could no longer retain the willing allegiance of Frenchmen. But the English still could not see this; after so many victories their defeats seemed to them only explicable as a judgment for their rulers' failings. They looked with horror at the spectacle of their king—once the model of Christian chivalry—decking his concubine with the jewels of his dead queen and enthroning her in the tournament lists as Lady of the Sun. They learnt with pity of the plight of the great warrior, his son, bedridden in his castle at Berkhampsted. And they laid the blame on the king's ministers and, when they were able, through their representatives in parliament, hounded them from office.

The first to feel this anger were the courtier bishops through whom, since his short-lived quarrel with Archbishop Stratford thirty years before, Edward had conducted the kingdom's administration. The place of William of Edington, the great bishop of Winchester who had been the king's right hand during the victory years of Crécy and Poitiers, had been taken in the middle sixties by an equally able administrator, William of Wykeham—

a clerk of humble parentage who had not even been ordained a priest until his thirty-seventh year but who had made himself indispensable to his sovereign as surveyor of the works at Windsor and supervisor of his building projects. In 1364 Wykeham became keeper of the privy seal and, in 1367, chancellor and bishop of Winchester. Unfortunately for him his tenure of power coincided with the decline of England's fortunes in France and, though he was not responsible for her military disasters, he was driven from office in 1371 by the parliamentary clamour of the Commons and a group of magnates under the Duke of Lancaster and the ambitious young Earl of Pembroke, soon afterwards himself to be defeated and humiliated off La Rochelle. It was the first real breach in the national unity of the past three decades. For the next few years the country was virtually ruled by Lancaster's henchmen, with two successive lay chancellors, Sir Robert Thorp and Sir John Knyvet[1]—both jurists—and a lay treasurer, Lord Scrope. But as the disasters in France still continued, they, too, soon became unpopular and were charged by a public enflamed by war taxation with every kind of corruption and malversation.

.   .   .   .

In the spring of 1376, after governing England without a parliament for three years, Lancaster was forced to call one by impending national bankruptcy. Indignant at the humiliating terms of a truce he had negotiated with France just when the fighting in Brittany under his brother, the Earl of Cambridge, seemed to be taking a turn for the better, and resentful at the waste of the vast sums raised for the war, the nation's representatives were in a determined mood. They were supported by two members of the royal family, the Prince of Wales and Edmund Mortimer earl of March, husband of the Princess Philippa, the king's grand-daughter. Their ten weeks' session—the longest that had ever taken place—was marked by the daring of the Commons who dominated the proceedings. Summoned not by name like the lords but by general writs addressed to the sheriffs,

[1] Thorp, a Norfolk man and a benefactor of Cambridge university, had been chief justice of the Common Pleas; Knyvet, a wealthy Northamptonshire landowner, Chief Justice of the King's Bench. *D.N.B.*

the seventy-four knights of the shire and the two-hundred or so burgesses who, since the beginning of the reign had been called to almost every meeting of parliament, had behaved till now, as they had been treated, as very humble partners in the *universitas* of the realm. As late as 1348 they had declined to advise the king on the conduct of the war as being "too ignorant and simple to counsel on such important matters." Their function, as defined in the traditional words of the royal summons, was "with full and sufficient power for themselves and their respective communities to do and to consent to those things which in our parliament shall be ordained"—in other words, to commit the taxpayers to such subsidies and taxes as the king should require.

Yet so stubbornly had they insisted on their right to withhold consent to any new form of taxation—not only direct taxes on moveables but, after 1340, even custom duties in the royal demesnes[1]—that, with the government's incessant need for additional sources of revenue for the wars, they had become an essential part of the national machinery of "counsel and consent." Without it being fully realised, their power to withhold supply had made them indispensable to the management of the realm so long as the war continued and the costs of government continued to rise The Crown's repeated demands for money for war over a whole generation had caused the representatives of two very different social groups, the landowning warrior knights and the trading burgesses, to draw together for consultations on finance. However hesitantly at first, they had acquired the habit of meeting together to discuss matters that vitally affected both. In doing so they had unconsciously and, as it were, accidentally, created a single assembly—called into being with each successive meeting of parliament—representing the communities of shire and borough. Unique among the rigidly divided class "estates" which made up the parliaments of other European kingdoms, they already formed by the end of

[1] See p. 287. In an oddly prophetic and pseudo-historical treatise on the powers and procedure of parliament called the *Modus Tenendi Parliamenti*, probably written in 1321 by a supporter of Thomas earl of Lancaster, the claim was made that the two knights who represented a shire in parliament had a greater voice in granting and withholding aid than the greatest earl. This, though untrue in Edward II's reign, had become partly true before the end of his son's. *Wilkinson*, III, 64, 323-31, 356.

Edward III's reign a continuing body which in the next century was to become known as the House of Commons. Sitting separately from the lords in a chamber of their own—at one time the Painted Chamber of the palace of Westminster, at another the chapter house of the Abbey—they had come in the course of the fifty or so parliaments of the reign to develop a business and procedure of their own, distinct from the parliamentary procedure of earlier days which had been designed solely by and for the convenience of the king and Council. This had been largely due to the lawyers who were so often chosen by local communities to represent them because of their professional expertise, and who brought to the work of an evolving institution their habits of mental precision and insistence on procedure and precedent.[1]

Much of this business of parliament centred round the petitions to the king for justice and reform of the law which poured in before the beginning of every session and which were now increasingly being referred by the king and his councillors to the Commons. Those that concerned public rather than private interests and seemed, after sifting and examination, to call for legislative action, the latter endorsed with a recommendation—usually the words, "whereof the commonalty prays remedy"—for presentation by the clerk of parliament to the king. If he approved them they then became the subject of either a royal ordinance or, in more important cases, of a statute formally assented to by both magnates and Commons and entered on the rolls of parliament as permanent law enforceable in the royal courts. Sometimes such petitions were made the subject of a bargain between Crown and parliament, the Commons voting subsidies and taxes on condition that the king assented to such legislation as they required.

Above all, the members of the Commons had acquired a corporate sense and habit of acting together. Though with their superior social status the knights of the shire took the lead in their debates, they constituted a single estate—the commonalty or *populus* of the realm as distinct from the lords and not, as in

---

[1] "It was the lawyers who so developed the procedure of parliament that it became a workable assembly and the only one of the medieval representative assemblies which survived and became an integral part of the machinery of government." W. Holdsworth, *Makers of Law*, 55.

continental parliaments, separate estates of knights and burgesses. They represented, not classes or callings, but localities, and, by acting together for the "common good" made the needs and views of those localities known to the Crown and brought their influence to bear at the place where in England power resided—the royal Council or, as it was now tending to become in every major crisis of the nation's political life, the king in parliament. Their influence and prestige were the greater because, even when, as sometimes happened, they were cadets of baronial families, the knights sat with the burgesses as commoners. More perhaps than any other factor this created a sense of national identity and common interest. It made it easy for lords and Commons to act together and hard for the monarch to encroach on the community's liberties by setting class against class. Without this, the tendency to absolutism inherent in the growing power of national monarchy might have become too strong to resist, as it did in almost every other European kingdom between the fourteenth and seventeenth centuries.

When at the end of April 1376 the chancellor, Sir John Knyvet, addressed the assembled lords and Commons in the Painted Chamber in the presence of the king and his sons, councillors and judges, everyone realised that the nation's affairs had reached a serious pass. Declaring that the realm was in danger of being destroyed by its enemies of France, Spain, Gascony, Flanders and Scotland, he asked for a tenth from the clergy and a fifteenth from the laity and for additional duties on wool and other merchandise to provide defences against invasion and maintain the war in France. According to custom, he ended by directing the knights and burgesses, on their allegiance and under pain of forfeiture, that if there was anything to redress or amend or if the realm was badly ruled or treacherously counselled, by their good advice they should find remedy."[1] Both houses were then ordered to disperse to their separate meeting places, the lords to the White chamber of the royal palace and the Commons to the chapter house of the Abbey, there "to treat and counsel among themselves."

[1] The *Anonimalle Chronicle* (ed. V. H. Galbraith), 79-80 cit. *Rickert*, 163-4. With the parallel account in Thomas Walsingham's *Chronicon Angliae*, one can follow for the first time discussions in parliament. *Wilkinson*, II, 210.

As soon as the Commons met next morning they took an oath of mutual loyalty and secrecy. Then "a knight of the south country" went to the reading-desk in the centre of the chapter house and, pounding on it, gave vent to what was in everyone's mind. "You have heard," he said, "the grievous matters before the parliament, how our lord the king has asked of the clergy and the commons a tenth and a fifteenth and customs on wool and other merchandise. In my opinion it is much to grant, for the commons are so weakened and impoverished by the divers tallages and taxes which they have paid up to the present that they cannot sustain such a charge. Besides, all that we have given to the war for a long time we have lost because it has been badly wasted and falsely expended. And so it would be well to consider how our lord the king can live and govern his kingdom and maintain the war from his demesne property and not hold to ransom his liegemen of the land. Also I have heard that there are divers people who, without his knowledge, have in their hands goods and treasure of our lord the king amounting to a great sum of gold and silver, and that they have falsely concealed the said goods which through guile and extortion they gained."

After this, speaker after speaker went to the lectern to express the universal belief that Lord Latimer the chamberlain and his financial agent, a London merchant and highly unpopular speculator named Richard Lyons, had made enormous profits by moving the Staple from Calais, by advancing—needlessly—money to the king at outrageous interest rates, and by buying up old debts of the Crown from its creditors at a tenth or even twentieth part of their nominal value and then persuading their senile royal master to redeem them in full. Everyone, however, felt that, in the face of such great men as Lancaster and Latimer, it would be useless for the Commons to try to act on their own without, as someone put it, "the counsel and aid of those greater and wiser." It was, therefore, proposed that the lords should be approached and asked to nominate a committee of four bishops, four earls and four barons to consult with them how to obtain redress.

The day's proceedings ended with a speech by the Earl of March's steward, a knight of the shire for Hereford named Peter de la Mare. He summarised the debate and the feeling of the Commons with such ability that he was unanimously invited to become their spokesman or Speaker. He was the first to hold that office of whom there is any record. "Neither terrified," as the St. Albans chronicler testified, "by the threats of his adversaries nor confused by the plottings of the envious," he carried out its duties with firmness and resolution. When the Commons arrived at the door of the White Chamber and only their leaders were allowed in and the rest were pushed back, de la Mare, undeterred by the Duke of Lancaster's displeasure,[1] refused to speak until his fellow-members had been admitted. Nor would he make the slightest concession when the duke, confronted by his stubborn silence and "very ill at ease," observed, "Sir Peter, there is no need for so many of the Commons to come in to give a reply, but two or three at a time are enough as has been the custom previously." In the end, since it was clear that there was no hope of the Crown getting its grant unless the Commons were humoured, the duke gave way, and those shut out were let in.

Having obtained the appointment of the lords' committee, with both the Earl of March and Lancaster's episcopal enemy, William of Wykeham, to serve on it, the Commons on May 12th returned to the charge. Through their Speaker they insisted that, before they discussed the royal request for supply, those who had been guilty of wasting and embezzling the taxes already voted should be dismissed and punished for "having taken advantage by their cunning to deceive the king." When Lancaster asked, "How is this and who are they that have taken advantage?" de la Mare boldly pressed home his attack, accusing Latimer to his face, as well as his agent, Lyons, and the king's all-powerful mistress, Alice Perrers. Latimer, an able and formidable man who had fought at Crécy and Auray, pointed out that the removal of the Staple had been authorised by the king and council. But his accuser, "ready to suffer all things for truth and justice," answered "that it was against the law of England and against the statute made in parliament and that what was done

[1] "What," he is reported to have said, "are these degenerate knights of tallow undertaking? Do they think they are the kings or princes of this land? Or whence have they got their pride and arrogance?" Thomas Walsingham, *Chronicon Angliae,* cit. *Wilkinson,* II, 217.

in parliament by statute could not be undone without parliament and that he would show them the statute." Whereupon he produced a statute book and read the statute in question "before all the lords and Commons so that he could not be contradicted."

The upshot was that, supported by a majority of the lords, the Commons obtained the restoration of the Staple to Calais, the dismissal of the guilty ministers and the banishment of the king's mistress who was described as "a lady or damsel who has every year from the income of our lord the king two or three thousand pounds of gold and silver from his coffers without any notable return and to his great injury." When Latimer and Lyons denied the accusations and demanded a trial, de la Mare in the name of the Commons declared that they would maintain their charges as prosecutors "in full parliament" before a bench of Latimer's fellow peers. It ended in Latimer being declared infamous—possibly unjustly, for he had an arguable case—"by common decree of parliament." In this way the first process of impeachment in English history took place, parliament assuming a new judicial function, or rather an old one in a new form, with the lords as judges and the Commons as accusers. It was only possible because, as a result of Edward III's policy of conciliating and spoiling his magnates, the latter were now the predominant element in the king's Council in parliament—the supreme tribunal of the realm—instead of the ministers and professional councillors and judges who had dominated it in their master's interest in the time of Edward I. In this trial, conducted at the highest level against one of the king's chief ministers and advisers, the king himself had no part, though the charge was brought in his name. Petition to the Crown for remedy as a matter of grace was superseded by a judicial process which, since lords and Commons united against him, neither the king nor his councillors had the power to prevent.

Through this there ran the sense—first tentatively expressed by the magnates seventy years before in their opposition to Gaveston —of a distinction between the king as a person and the Crown exercising authority in a matter of concern to all with the counsel and consent of the nation's representatives in parliament. It was a conception which the humble Commons had now grasped like

the Lancastrian lords of Edward II's day. No attack was made
on the old king or even on his son and lieutenant, John of Gaunt,
who for all practical purposes had been acting as king for the
past three years. After the lords had decided that the Commons'
charges against Latimer and his collaborators had been proved,
the king was dutifully informed that it was "the advice of the
Commons and assent of the lords that he should banish from his
presence those who were neither good nor profitable and not give
faith to evil counsellors and evil-doers. The king benignly told
the lords that he wished entirely to do what would be for the
profit of his realm, and the lords thanked him, praying his very
excellent lordship that he would appoint three bishops, three
earls and three barons" — nominated by parliament — to
strengthen his Council. "And the king replied patiently that he
would willingly act by their advice and good ordinance." At
the same time Lord Latimer, and two other councillors, Sir
John Neville and Sir Richard Stafford, were dismissed from the
royal presence. Alice Perrers shared the same fate, the king
swearing "an oath before the lords that the said Alice should
never come into his company again."

While this momentous assembly, which became known as
the "good" parliament, was still sitting, the Black Prince died at
his riverside manor of Kennington. Though still remaining on
friendly terms with his brother Lancaster, whom he made an
executor of his will, he had travelled to London from Berkhamsted in April in a litter to support the opponents of mismanage-
ment and corruption. His death on June 8th, 1376, deprived
the Commons of their chief champion. Almost their last act
before parliament ended was to petition the king "that it would
please him as a great comfort to the whole realm to cause the
noble child Richard of Bordeaux, son and heir of the Lord
Edward to come before parliament so that the lords and Commons might see and honour him as true heir apparent to the
realm"—a request which, despite its implied insult to Lancaster,
was granted. Their champion and hero—"the chief flower of
chivalry of all the world," as Froissart called him—was buried in
the autumn at Canterbury, close to the shrine of St. Thomas.
His effigy, clad in gilt metal armour, still rests on his tomb of
Purbeck marble in the cathedral, his helmet open, his hands

folded in prayer, his dog at his feet and, above the canopy, his crested helm, surcoat and shield, gauntlet and sword.

Before parliament was dissolved on July 10th the knights of the shire gave a feast to their comrades, the burgesses. The king contributed two tuns of red wine and eight deer, and the lords gave "a great sum of gold and much wine." But as soon as the members had applied for the customary writs for their wages[1] and they and the magnates had departed for their country homes, the government of John of Gaunt and the old senile king took its revenge. Peter de la Mare was thrown into the dungeons of Nottingham castle, and William of Wykeham, who with the Earl of March had been the chief opponent of Lancaster's rule, was brought before the council at Westminster, charged with malversation of public funds during his chancellorship of five years before and, after a two days' trial, deprived of his temporalities—an act of political vengeance which brought to a halt his building operations in Winchester cathedral and the dissolution of the new college he had founded for poor students at Oxford. The Earl of March, notwithstanding his royal connection, was forced to resign his position as marshal, Lord Latimer was reinstated in office, the financier Lyons released from prison, and Alice Perrers restored to her lucrative place in the king's bed. The "good" parliament was declared no true parliament by another and its acts were annulled.[2]

All this, however, merely made John of Gaunt still more unpopular. Ruler of England in his now fast-failing father's place, claimant to the throne of Castile, duke of Lancaster and the richest man in the realm, he seemed after his brother's death to be aiming at the succession. Though at Christmas the Black

[1] 4s. a day for knights and 2s. for burgesses, including the time spent in travelling.

[2] What happened is described by William Langland, whose view of the Commons' temerity, not to say rashness, was probably shared by most of his contemporaries.

"With that there ran a rout   of rats all at once
And small mice with them   more than a thousand,
And came to a council   for their common profit;
But a cat of the court   came when he liked
And leapt over them lightly   and caught them at his will
And played with them perilously   and pushed them about."

Piers Plowman, Prologue

Prince's nine-year-old son, Richard of Bordeaux, was formally acknowledged as heir-apparent in Westminster Hall and invested with his father's titles of Prince of Wales, Duke of Cornwall and Earl of Chester, popular distrust was not allayed. A few weeks later it culminated in an outburst outside St. Paul's where a panel of his episcopal opponents was examining on a charge of heresy a protégé of the duke's named John Wycliffe, an Oxford doctor and lecturer whose radical views on church reform and apostolic poverty had provided him with a handle to attack William of Wykeham and his fellow prelates. When in an attempt to influence the proceedings and overawe the London apprentices, Lancaster and the new earl marshal, Lord Percy, tried to exercise their authority within the city liberties, they were forced by a furious explosion of mob violence to fly for their lives across the river and take refuge in the Princess of Wales's manor at Kennington. Meanwhile the apprentices set fire to the Marshalsea and tried to sack Lancaster's palace of the Savoy. And though, with the help of a packed parliament presided over by his seneschal, the duke was able to re-establish his position and take his revenge on the Londoners, outside his northern estates his authority now depended wholly on the life of the king.

On June 21st, 1377, a dotard with long white beard, deserted by his servants and plundered by his very mistress, Edward III died after half a century on the throne. His death marked the end of an epoch, for he had been born only a few years after the death of his grandfather, Edward I, who himself was the great-grandson of the first Plantagenet. During the close of his reign, in the words of a seventeenth-century historian, "he had seen all his great gettings, purchased with so much expense, travail and bloodshed, rent clean from him." Even before his body could be laid to rest in the Abbey, the war with France had broken out again and the French had landed at Rye.

Chapter Eleven

THE VISION OF PIERS PLOWMAN

For one Piers Plowman hath impugned us all
And set all sciences at naught save love alone.

WILLIAM LANGLAND

THE PROBLEM facing England at the end of Edward III's reign was a moral one. A succession of disasters had befallen her; defeat in war, loss of conquests, the death of princes. The harvests had failed, wool-prices had slumped, the pestilence had returned for a fourth time. The nation's rulers were accusing one another of treason and malversation of public funds, and, for all the display of wealth in high places, the poor groaned under taxation. Now, with a child on the throne, war had broken out again and the French were closing in on England's last overseas possessions, burning her ships and ports and threatening invasion.

There could be only one explanation. The kingdom had outraged the laws of God and was suffering retribution. For medieval man believed that divine justice ruled the universe and that sooner or later every breach of it would be punished. The thought of it haunted everyone, from the king on his throne to the peasant in the fields. The very brutes in the stinking city alsatias, the outlaws in the woods, the *routiers* as they murdered, burnt and raped in pursuit of their merciless profession could not escape its insistent, disturbing reminders.

God had ordained men to live in harmony with a divine order; the task of those who ruled was to see that order observed. The king's function as supreme judge rested on this belief; his judges, though no longer ecclesiastics, wore, as they still do, the churchman's gown.[1]   A ruler who failed to do justice was a

---

[1] To this day when he pronounces the death sentence a judge of the High Court places over his eighteenth century wig a small black cap as though to cover the Church's tonsure.

tyrant, one whose pride, greed or ambition exposed his realm to
the calamities which followed a breach of the divine order—
what Bishop Brunton of Rochester, preaching before the young
king in St. Paul's on the day after his coronation, called "the
open vengeances of God; the slaughter of the mighty, famine,
mortalities, the storms of winds, internal feuds and wars without."

To define justice—*justicia* or righteousness—medieval man
looked to the Church.   Religion permeated every political
activity.   When the king issued a statute "at the request of his
Commons and by their petition," the preamble stated that it was
"for the honour and gratification of God, for the reform of the
grievous wrongs and oppressions suffered by the people and for
the relief of their condition."[1] When the Commons debated the
state of the kingdom in the " good " parliament they sat in the
chapter house of Westminster Abbey like monks in a circle
while each speaker began his speech from the lectern with the
words, "Jube Domine benedicere"—"Lord let thy blessing"—
and ended it with the equally familiar liturgical phrase, "Tu,
autem, Domine, miserere nobis"—"Thou, Lord, have mercy on
us." And when the Speaker assumed his charge he declared it to
be "out of reverence to God."

Yet though the Church existed to teach men how to live
justly, it was all too apparent that this was what so many of its
ministers failed to do themselves. It was not, as the saints sought
to make it, above the world; it was part of the world itself. Since
every worldly activity was conducted in Christ's name and with
the Church's blessing, it followed that Christianity had become
a very worldly religion. The richer society grew and the more
men laid up for themselves treasure upon earth, the more
materially-minded grew the Church. Official Christianity had
grown into a gigantic vested interest. It was one that had made
existence richer and fuller, had fostered artistic and intellectual
achievement, and, at a time when life was harsh and precarious
and death a constant visitant, had given millions a sense of hope
and security. Yet, many, if not most of those who served the
Church were very ordinary men and women who, without any
particular sense of calling, had entered it as the only profession

[1] 36 Edw. III, cit. *Stephenson and Marcham*, 231-2.

offering advancement for anyone who was not a warrior, land-owner or merchant. It was the avenue to wealth, power and dignity and to every learned and intellectual pursuit.

For the ordinary cleric and layman the drama of Christ's life, death and resurrection, though universally credited, was seen less as a means to a spiritual end than as a wonderful success-story in whose honour the whole glittering edifice of medieval religion had been raised. The splendid churches and their trea-sures, the processions, pageants and thrilling rites, the familiar company of tutelary angels and saints ready to help all who propitiated them, and Holy Church itself, watching over man's spiritual fortunes like a wise and far-sighted banker over his client's securities, were all there for his enrichment. And on the principle that to those that have shall more be given, it was the rich and successful, the "possessioners", to whom the Church offered most.

For though entry to the Church was open to all, and even a bondsman's son, if his lord would free him, could rise, with the necessary parts and patronage, to the glittering top of the pro-fession, there was an unbridgeable gulf between those selected for preferment and the common ruck of poor clerks. Whether the successful aspirant owed his fortune to birth and aristocratic connections, or whether he was a youth of humble antecedents whose talents had brought him to the notice of authority, the pick of the Church's benefices were available to enable him to pay for his education and to support him for the rest of his life in comfort and even affluence. So far as it gave financial inde-pendence to men of ability the system had much to commend it and brought outstanding talents to the service of Church and state. But it was subject to grave abuses. Lords and rich land-owners with younger sons unfitted for arms or with a taste for clerkhood would present them to livings before they were in their teens; a brother of the Earl of Gloucester in Edward I's reign who entered the Church in this way accumulated in the course of his far from edifying career no less than twenty-four benefices, in addition to two canonries and three other collegiate and cathedral appointments.

Nor was there any point of contact between the untutored peasant priesthood and the university-trained ecclesiastics who by the end of the fourteenth century all but monopolised the higher ranks of the Church. In their subtle labours of theological and philosophical analysis and classification, expressed in language only intelligible to those trained in dialectic, the regent masters of Oxford and Cambridge were too busy disputing with one another to have time to popularise their learning for the rustic clergy from whom nine Englishmen out of ten derived their religion. The amorphous image conjured up for super- stitious parishioners by the Mass magic of bucolic priests bore little resemblance to the highly intellectualised God of the great doctors. Nor did the Church seem concerned by this double standard in its doctrine and teaching.[1] With reckless disregard of its own canon law it continued to dispose of parochial endow- ments as though the training and competence of the parish clergy were a matter of minor importance. Of the 376 rectors whom one bishop instituted to benefices in lay patronage only 135 were in holy orders; in another diocese of 193 parishes visited more than a third were held *in absentia*. Episcopal dis- pensations for non-residence were freely granted so long as a minimum provision was made by the beneficiary for paying a deputy. It was common form for bishops to issue licences to enable young incumbents to study at the university. Thus Philip de Stanton, rector of Codford St. Peter, was given a year to pur- sue theology or law at Oxford provided he visited his parish during Holy Week and presented a chaplain by Michaelmas. As the licence was issued in January this meant that for most of the year his cure was without an incumbent—a state of affairs epitomised in a sermon of the time describing a flock without a pastor: "He is at the court or the schools or is residing elsewhere and is nowhere else to be found."[2]

[1] When one of Wycliffe's Oxford disciples, answering a charge of sup- porting his heretical views on transubstantiation, pointed out to the masters in Congregation that there was no idolatry like the worship of the consecrated Host, the chancellor replied, "Now you are speaking as a philosopher." *Medieval Panorama*, 648.

[2] *History*, N.S., XXXIV. V. F. M. Garlick, "The Provision of Vicars in the Early Fourteenth Century"; *Owst, Literature and Pulpit* 261. When in 1368 Wycliffe was presented to the benefice of Ludgershall he was granted a two- years' licence of non-residence by the Bishop of Lincoln, *D.N.B.* It was the only way by which he could perform his Oxford functions, for university teachers, as such, had no salaries.

This separation of the clerical sheep from the goats—so damaging to the laity's interests—was aggravated by the Crown's demand for clerks of parts for the country's growing administrative machine. It was accepted as a necessity of state that the Church should train and support in a condition of dignity its ablest sons to serve the king; one of Edward I's clerks of the Exchequer held twenty-one livings. Pluralism seemed almost a civic virtue; "clerks in the king's service," it was laid down by statute, "shall be discharged of their residence."[1] Great nobles, too, needed clerical servants, not only for spiritual, but worldly purposes; at a later date an earl of Northumberland had ten priests in his service as well as a clerk of the signet, a clerk of the board of works, a surveyor, a private secretary and a secretary of his privy council, all in orders. Thanks to the pious bequests of their forefathers such territorial magnates seldom lacked the advowsons to provide for them.

Thus, though the Church owned so large a part of the country's landed wealth—according to the Italian, Andrea Trevisan, who visited England in the following century, 28,015 out of 96,230 knights' fees—there were calls on its endowments more pressing than the cure of souls. For centuries the rich and powerful had showered wealth on the Church; it was natural for it to feel it owed them a recompense. If a rich man, eager for salvation, offered to endow a chantry, a college, a hospital, a perpetual mass for the souls of himself and his relations, to give a stained-glass window, rebuild a church or provide a wayside altar or rest-house for pilgrims, the Church could not do other than accept it. Provided the rich made a show of conforming to its observances and dogma, it reserved for such benefactors a place in the heavenly as in the earthly kingdom, negotiating, as it were, a special relationship between them and the Almighty. With their endowments for obits, masses and private chantries, their magnificent benefactions to parish and collegiate churches, their gifts of gems and relics, altar-cloths, statues

---

[1] The king and his ancestors since time out of mind have used that clerks which are employed in his service, during such time as they are employed in his service, shall not be compelled to keep residence at their benefices." Statutes of the Realm, I, 342. cit. V. F. M. Garlick, "The Provision of Vicars in the Early 14th Century." *History*, N.S., XXXIV.

and painted windows, they were encouraged to buy
themselves into Heaven. A rhyme of the time depicts them
doing so:

> "Thou shall'st kneel before Christ
> In compass of gold,
> In the wide window westward
> Well nigh in the middle;
> And Saint Francis himself
> Shall folden thee in his cope
> And present thee to the Trinity
> And pray for thy sins."

So the friar in *Piers Plowman* held out an inducement to the wicked
Lady Meed:

> "We have a window a working,   will stand us full high;
> Would ye glaze the gable   and grave there your name,
> In Mass and in Matins   for Meed we should sing
> Suddenly and soothly   as for a sister of our Order."

In the Norfolk church of Burnham Norton the local donors of
the pulpit can still be seen, sharing its panels with the four great
doctors of medieval Christendom, St. Augustine, St. Gregory,
St. Jerome and St. Thomas Aquinas.

Pride and privilege not only helped to raise and sustain the
Church's fabric; they penetrated the very sanctuary. Instead
of having to confess to low-born parish priests, nobles were
allocated confessors of rank, and the lord of the manor and his
lady worshipped with the clergy in the chancel instead of with
the congregation in the nave. Even at the moment when all
christians, living and dead, were supposed to be united in the
sacrament of Christ's sacrifice, and when before Holy Communion
the pax-brede or picture of the crucified Saviour was passed
round to be kissed in token of brotherly love, there was jostling
and shoving for precedence. Such pomp and vain glory—the
sin of *superbia* as theologians called it—was most frequently to be
met in the fine new town churches raised by the merchant community and nobility. One indignant preacher spoke of "great
lords and ladies that cometh to holy church in rich and noble
apparel of gold and silver, pearls and precious stones and other
worldly, worshipful attire before our Lord God Almighty," each
fine lady "stirring up the dust with her train, making the good

laymen, the clerks and the priests all drink of it and making it fall upon the altar of the Lord."[1]

This identification of the Church with wealth and power resulted in a grave loss of spiritual influence. Since it had inherited, and insisted on retaining, so large a share of Caesar's goods, it was forced to render unto Caesar the things that were God's. Because its prelates were great landowners and magnates, it had had to concede to the Crown the right of appointing them. They were seen by the laity as servants of the State rather than of the Church and therefore as agents of the State's oppression and injustice. Whatever their gain in worldly dignity, their possession of excessive wealth and the luxurious display that accompanied it lost them the respect of true Christians. For the values that attached to the pursuit of wealth were not Christian values; by the Church's own tenets they were sometimes diabolical ones. The Bishop of Winchester was joint owner of the Southwark stews; even the wonderful new nave of Winchester cathedral and the William of Wykeham scholastic foundations of Winchester and New College, Oxford, were thus partly and indirectly raised on the profits of prostitution. Such confusion of worldly and spiritual values ran through the Church's structure like a flaw; among its hangers-on were a species of men known as chop-churches whose business was the sale and exchange of benefices, "for simony," as a poet put it, "is sweet." And at the base of its imposing establishment was a hungry, unruly mob of unbeneficed clerks, picking up a living with psalter and primer by pattering prayers for rich patrons and competing furiously for employment.

The Church's obsession with its wealth—with "Christ's land," "Christ's goods," "Christ's property"—had other consequences. It made it appear obese and conservative. It was no longer, as in the days of St. Bernard and St. Francis, on the march; it was resting on its endowments. The "possessioners" who enjoyed its wealth would admit of no change. Religion in their hands had become materialistic and mechanical; it was the quantitative in worship that mattered, not the spirit of the worshipper. Salvation was measured by the number of prayers and masses said— so many Pater Nosters an hour, so many Ave Marias, so many

[1] *Owst, Preaching*, 171.

candles lit, so many glimpses of God made at the altar, so many benefactions to Holy Church. Great men would hurry into church just before the elevation of the Host and then hurry out again, conscience and public opinion satisfied that they had rendered homage for the day. Outward and visible signs seemed everything, inward and spiritual grace tended to be forgotten.

Because the Church was worldly and most of those who professed and called themselves Christians were mere participators or spectators in a magnificent pageant beneath whose surface they never penetrated, it did not follow that it had failed in its mission of transmitting Christ's teaching. It might have done so with the many but, as in every age since its work began, it succeeded with the few. However entangled during centuries of pagan barbarism with lies, half truths and superstitions, the Christian record still caused men and women to try to model their lives on Christ's example. Humility and long-suffering, truth and honest dealing, chivalry and gentleness towards the weak, hatred of violence and cruelty were virtues that had grown out of Christianity, and it was the cumulative effect of the Church's teaching and worship that had caused them to do so. Christ's seat on earth remained, as ever, not St. Peter's throne but the heart of the individual Christian; yet without St. Peter's throne there would have been few hearts for Christ to lodge in.

Of what the Church of the latter fourteenth century at its best could be we have the testimony of Chaucer. For when, in his cavalcade of worldly pilgrims, lay and ecclesiastic, he reached the humble village priest, that cynical, tolerant but scrupulously honest observer of the contemporary scene paused in his amused catalogue of human frailty to draw the portrait of one who came as near to fulfilling the precepts of Christianity as a man can.

> "A good man there was of religión,
> And was a poorë parson of a town;
> But rich he was of holy thought and work,
> He also was a learnëd man, a clerk,
> That Christës gospel gladly would he preach;
> His parishioners devoutly would he teach.

Benign he was and wondrous diligent,
And in adversity full patiënt,
And such he was i-provëd oft to be.
To cursen for his tithes full loath was he,
But rather would he given out of doubt
Unto his poor parishioners about
Of his offring and eek of his substance.
He could in little thing have sufficience.
Wide was his parish and houses far asunder,
But yet he leftë not in rain or thunder,
In sickness and in mischief to visit
The furthest in his parish, small and great,
Upon his feet and in his hand a staff;
This noble example unto his sheep he gave,
That first he wrought and afterwards he taught.
Out of the gospel he those wordës caught
And this figúre he added yet thereto,
That if gold rustë, what should iron do? . . .
. . . And though he holy were and virtuous
He was to sinful man full piteous. . . .
He waited after no pomp nor reverence
Nor made himself spiced in conscience,
But Christës lore and his apostles twelve,
He taught, but first he followed it himself."

It was the parson's parishioner and brother, the ploughman, who shared with him and the old crusading knight the distinction of being the only completely Christian characters in that company of professed Christians. However unsatisfactory some parish priests might be—and it was largely the Church's fault that so many were—a good priest could still make a Christian village.

Though they were only a minority, there was no lack of devout laymen in the fourteenth century. It was the age of the mystic recluse, both clerical and lay, but particularly the latter— who, withdrawing from the world to a life of religious contemplation, found in the inner experience of the heart a new revelation. Some of these wrote treatises and books enshrining their experience for the benefit of their fellow Christians, to teach, as one of them put it, "simple men and women of goodwill the right way to

heaven."[1]   Such was the nameless author—one of the father
founders of English prose—of the two great devotional classics,
The Cloud of Unknowing and *The Book of Privy Counsel*, and Walter
Hilton, the Austin canon of Thurgarton in Nottinghamshire, who
wrote in his *Scale of Perfection*, "It needeth not to run to Rome
nor to Jerusalem to seek Christ, but to turn thy thoughts into
thine own soul where He is hid . . . and seek him there." Such,
too, was the unknown poet who left posterity the lovely lyric,
Christ's Complaint for his Sister, Man's Soul, with its haunting refrain
of *Quia Amore Langueo*,

> "I am true Love, that false was never;
> My sister man's soul I loved her thus;
> Because I would in no wise dissever
> I left my kingdom glorious;
> I prepared for her a palace precious,
> She fled, I followed, I loved her so
> That I suffer these painës piteous
> *Quia amore langueo.*"

Other verses as beautiful, A Song of Love-Longing,[1] may have
come from the pen of the Yorkshire hermit, Richard Rolle of
Hampole—"love's prisoner," as he called himself—who translated the psalter into English prose and in his lonely retreat on
the Richmondshire moors taught himself to hear the *musica
spiritualis* and, honoured by his neighbours as a saint, died in the
first Black Death. Of the same elect company were the wandering
evangelist, Margery Kempe—a middle-aged Lynn housewife
who made the pilgrimage to Jerusalem and half the shrines of
Europe as a barefoot tramp—and Juliana of Norwich, the
anchoress who, entering her cell in St. Julian's churchyard in
1373, remained there for nearly seventy years, leaving in her
Revelations of Divine Love the first work of English literature
written by a woman. So real and ever-present did the passion of
Christ seem to Margery Kempe that on one occasion, entering a

[1] "Jesus Sweet, now will I sing
To Thee a song of love-longing;
Do in my heart a quick well spring
Thee to love above all thing . . ."
Vernon MS. f. ccxcvii., cit. *A Medieval Anthology* (ed. Mary Segar), 16.

church at Norwich and seeing "a fair image of Our Lady called a *'pieta'*," she started "to cry full loud and weep full sore as though she would have died." And when a priest tried to stop her, saying, 'Damsel, Jesus is dead long since,' she replied, 'Sir, His death is as fresh to me as if He has died this same day, and so methinketh it ought to be to you and to all Christian people. We ought ever to have mind of His kindness and ever think of the doleful death He died for us.'[1]

It was among such true Christians that dissatisfaction with the Church was strongest. The contrast between Christ's life of poverty and the wealth and self-indulgence of so many of its leaders was too great to overlook. The better among the clergy repeatedly drew attention to it. William of Rymynton, prior of the Cistercian abbey of Sawley and at one time chancellor of Oxford university, asked in a sermon how a priest could correct layfolk if he was "the slave of gluttony and lechery, given over to filthy lucre . . . and engrossed in vain or illicit pursuits?"[2] In the manuscript sermons that have come down to us from this time of disillusion one can feel the intensity of resentment aroused by the scramble for pluralities and the debasement of those engaged in it—the young scholars of promise, "poor and often innocent in everything at first, who before they grow rich are devout in their attendance at the churches, in their prayers and the many things they promise to God, but who, as soon as they have increased and waxed fat and wealthy, repudiate God, their maker."

"They say—'If only I had . . . one church or prebend, I should never want any more.' But when they have got it, they start complaining that the place is in a bad atmosphere, or too near the high-road which brings them too many guests, or too far away from a good town, or else because there is no pasture or wood or fish there. Therefore they must have another place where they can have pastures for the summer and fire-wood for the winter, and a third, where they can spend Lent and have fish. In

<hr />

[1] *The Book of Margery Kempe*, ed. W. Butler-Bowdon. (World's Classics), 193, cit. *Pantin*, 258.

[2] *Owst, Literature and Pulpit*, 274-5.

addition, they must have another prebend in their own district."[1]

This sense of disillusion with the clergy had been intensified by the Black Death. Its inroads had undermined Christian society; the Catholic Church in medieval England never wholly recovered from it. Too often it had been those who remained at their posts who had died and those who survived who had discredited and betrayed their faith. That a priest out of fear for his life could refuse the last rites to the dying and rob them of their hope of salvation was a thing so shattering to the medieval mind that it struck at the very roots of belief.

Nor had the damage done to the Church by the Black Death stopped there. By demoralising weak natures it had driven men to a hectic pursuit of pleasure, including many of the clergy. "Where," asked one preacher, "will you find the priests of today? . . . Not mourning between the porch and the altar but playing lasciviously around the prostitute and the brothel; not praying in the choir but wandering about the market place; not in the sanctuary but in the tavern and alehouse where sometimes they imbibe so much that they can say neither vespers nor matins properly." A popular rhyme of the time put it even more forcibly.

> "At the wrestling and at the wake,
> And chiefë chanters at the ale;
> Market-beaters, and meddling-make,
> Hopping and hooting with heave and hale.
> At fairë fresh, and at wine stale;
> Dine and drink, and make debate;
> The seven sacraments set a' sale;
> How keep such the keys of heaven gate?"[2]

Those who suffered most in public repute were the friars. A parish priest could only escape the pestilence by openly running away, and most of them probably, for all their natural fears, died

---

[1] G. R. Owst, *Literature and Pulpit in Medieval England*, 255-6. It is difficult to overestimate the debt owed to this great and original scholar for his two volumes on medieval sermons.

[2] Political Poems (R.S.), 1, 330, cit. G. G. Coulton, *Chaucer and his England*, 281; *Owst, Preaching* 258.

at their posts. For a friar, with his vagrant commission, it was easy to evade his Christian duty; those who performed it were the bravest of all, going out of their way to succour the sick and dying but almost inevitably succumbing while the cravens survived. This survival of the worst did the mendicants untold harm. Their reputation, and with it their morale, were gravely tarnished. In the writings of the time, and in the renewed controversy in the 'fifties about apostolic poverty, there appeared an almost savage dislike of friars; the great Durham Benedictine, Uthred of Boldon, declared that mendicancy was an impediment to the teaching of the word of God. Richard Fitzralph archbishop of Armagh—the famous Anglo-Irish preacher and theologian who tried to reconcile Rome and the Armenian Church and from whose writings Wycliffe derived his doctrine of dominion—worked himself into a frenzy of denunciation in his treatises and sermons at Paul's Cross against the mendicants for their interference with the parish clergy's cure of souls and their abuse of the power of confession.[1]

For being all things to all men the wandering brethren had enemies on every front. And as they did not spare the failings of their fellow clergy, their scathing references to tithes and pluralities caused intense indignation among their possessors, the more so as the preachers were the most shameless beggars of the age. They were thought of as hypocrites and wheedlers who denounced money but flattered men of wealth in order to obtain it—"fawning hounds that wag their tails, not faithful sheep-dogs but lap-dogs, eating up the luscious tit-bits that lords and ladies throw them."[2] Their Order is founded in poverty," wrote one critic, "I will tell you how they seek poverty. When they travel through the country they take up their lodging with the chief baron or knight, but by St. Peter of Rome they will never lodge with a

[1] "I have in my diocese of Armagh," he told the pope, "as I suppose, two thousand subjects who every year are involved in sentences of excommunication on account of the sentences passed against wilful homicides, public robbers, incendiaries and the like, of whom scarcely forty in a year come to me or to my penitentiaries; and all such men receive the sacraments like other men and are absolved or are said to be absolved . . . by the friars, . . . for no others absolve them." Pantin, 156.

[2] *Owst, Preaching*, 67. See also *Pantin*, 159-60.

poor man so long as there are richer men to be found."[1] "Fatter men about the ears," wrote another, "saw I never than these friars." So Chaucer depicted one of the tribe,

> "Feigning him poor and himself feeding
> With goodë morcels delicious,
> And drinking good wine precious,
> And preaching us poverty and distress
> And fishing himself great richess."

It was a libel, yet it was widely believed.

Indeed, though friars had long filled many of the greatest offices in Church and State and were employed throughout Christendom as the pope's special missionaries in expounding the Faith, their ecclesiastical opponents could not find words too bad for them. "Friar Fickle-tongue and folk of that feather," they seemed to the poet Langland. When the friar in the sum-moner's prologue from the *Canterbury Tales* asked the angel who was taking him on an escorted tour through Hell why there appeared to be no friars there, his guide bade Satan lift up his tail:

> "Show forth thine arse and let the friar see
> Where is the nest of friars in this place.
> Ere the tail rose a furlong into space
> From underneath it there began to drive,
> Much as if bees were swarming from a hive,
> Some twenty thousand friars in a rout."

. . . .

Thus in the quarter of a century that followed the first Black Death, there had grown up a widespread feeling that the Church was failing Christ's people. Bishops seemed proud luxurious lords, archdeacons and proctors blackmailers, monks gluttons, friars scroungers and liars. The Caesarian prelates, in particular, came in for attack. "They leave their flocks and spend their days in the courts of the mighty to eat the flesh of fat beasts," thundered the great Dominican preacher, Dr. Bromyard. Another sermon of the time described them as living in "strong castles and manors as royal as the king himself," surrounded by knights, squires, yeomen and grooms as they sat at their meat "with

[1] *Political Songs, John to Edward II*, ed. Wright, 145.

precious vessels and royal cupboards of silver and gold, and their men falling down as to a god at every draught they drink." When one of them rode out,

"yea, though it be to visit his poor sheep, he must ride with four or five score horse, proudly apparelled at all points, his own palfrey worth twenty or thirty pounds all behanged with glittering gold as though it were an holy horse, himself above in fine scarlet or other cloth as good, and within as good a pelure as the queen hath in any of her gowns; his parsons and clerks riding about him, all in gilt harness with swords overgilt hanging by their sides as though it were Centurio and his knights riding towards Christ's death."

Yet Christ himself, the preacher recalled, had no house to cover his head and no ménage but "twelve silly poor men whom he served oftener than ever they served him." It was this contrast that caused Fitzralph of Armagh to denounce his fellow prelates "as plunderers, thieves and robbers, who seize the fruits of churches and despise the sacred service of them; who are always exercising the cry, 'Shear! shear!' and never fulfil the command, 'Feed! feed!' "[1]

This, though it represented a widely-held view, was unjust, for many of Edward III's bishops were great public benefactors as well as able and hard-working administrators.[2] William Edington of Winchester, who from an obscure origin rose to be successively treasurer and chancellor, rebuilt the presbytery of his cathedral in the new Perpendicular style partly at his own expense and endowed his native village in Wiltshire with a superb collegiate church. His successor, William of Wykeham, son of a small Hampshire freeholder, used the endowments of his see and the many benefices he held in plurality to continue the rebuilding of the cathedral and to found, first, New College, Oxford, and then his great school at Winchester in order to make good the wastage in the ranks of the clergy caused by the Black Death. Contemptuously described by Wycliffe as "a clerk wise in building castles and worldly doings" and the greatest

---

[1] Owst, *Literature and Pulpit*, 244-5, 282-3.
[2] See G. R. L. Highfield, *The English Hierarchy in the Reign of Edward III. R.H.S.T.* Fifth Ser., Vol. 6, 115-38.

pluralist of his day, he was none-the-less a generous and kindly man who faced misfortune when it came to him with philosophy and who used his power with moderation and humility. Bishop Richard Bury of Durham, another of Edward III's chancellors, was a bibliophile who corresponded with Petrarch, founded a famous library and wrote a hand-book on its use, called the *Philobiblon*, extolling the delights of reading. The most famous scholar of them all was the saintly Thomas Bradwardine—*doctor profundus*—mathematician, astronomer, philosopher and theologian—the humble-hearted Merton fellow who was the king's confessor at Crécy and, called to the primacy after two archbishops of Canterbury had died in the year of the first Black Death, hurried to England only to perish of the pestilence within a week of receiving the temporalities of his see. His successor, Simon Islip, though a comparatively poor man founded an Oxford college for monks, while his successor, Simon Sudbury, set in hand the work of rebuilding the nave of Canterbury and laid the foundations of its present glory. Grandisson of Exeter, a princely patron of art, completed the nave of the West Country cathedral and added the musicians' gallery.[1]

Yet all their learning, munificence, and industry in the service of the Crown availed the statesmen-prelates nothing. Their excessive wealth condemned them. Even a saint like Brunton of Rochester—the Norwich Benedictine and Balliol fellow who was probably "the angel of Heaven" who "loved to speak in Latin" mentioned in *Piers Plowman*—could not hope to bridge the gulf that divided such lordly hierarchs from ordinary mortals. As for the papacy, to which only a century before England and her rulers had been so loyal, it was even more fatally damned in the eyes of humble Englishmen by its wealth and the rapacity with which it pursued it. To provide for its luxurious court at Avignon and swollen bureaucracy it employed the techniques of the lawyer, tax-collector and money-lender. Since its failure in the previous century to enforce its proud doctrine of the "plenitude of power" on the secular rulers of Europe and its consequent humiliation at the French king's hands it had sought to impose

---

[1] Among the many treasures he left the cathedral was the magnificent silk chasuble bearing his coat-of-arms which is now in the parish church of Ponta Delgada in the Azores.

its highly centralized control, successfully but with still more disastrous results, on the Church itself, extending its grip on the ecclesiastical benefices and endowments of every country in Christendom. In the eyes of those who were coming to think of themselves as Englishmen rather than as barons, knights or burgesses, it no longer seemed the protector but the exploiter of the *Ecclesia Anglicana*.

In place of the apostolic and intellectual ferments of the twelfth and thirteenth centuries the papal problems of the fourteenth centred round ecclesiastical taxation, first-fruits, provisions to benefices and the sale of pardons and indulgences. Annates—part of the first year's revenue of a benefice—were demanded of all new incumbents, the ready cash to pay being advanced to them by the papal bankers at usurious interest-rates which were subsequently enforced—in disregard of the Christian prohibition against usury—by threats of excommunication. No papal debt, it was said, was ever remitted. And, because of the French war and the papal residence at Avignon the pope's canonical right to appoint to benefices was increasingly resented by an England that had become insular and self-sufficient. In 1376 the knights and burgesses of the "good" parliament presented a petition to the king and council complaining that "the court of Rome, which ought to be the fountain, root and source of holiness and destruction of covetousness, simony and other sins," had attracted to itself the collation of so many "bishoprics, dignities, prebendaries and other benefices of Holy Church in England" that it was drawing from the country more than five times as much as the total royal revenue from taxation. This was a gross exaggeration, but it showed how far popular feeling had been exacerbated by papal practices. Other items in the Commons' complaint were that bishops were so heavily indebted to the curia for the fees and first-fruits of their benefices that they were forced to cut down their woods, borrow from their friends and demand crushing aids and subsidies from their tenants and diocesan clergy; that, as a result of simony by "brokers of benefices who dwell in the sinful city of Avignon," "a miserable fellow who knows nothing and is worth nothing" would be advanced to an incumbency worth a thousand marks, while an English doctor or a master of divinity had to content himself

with a fiftieth of that amount, "so that clerks lose hope of preferment by their orders and talent for learning . . . and people are
ceasing to send their children to school, and the clergy, who are
the substance of Holy Church and our holy faith, fall into decline
and annihilation." It was also alleged that the papal tax collectors were French spies who sent out of the country "secrets to
the great prejudice of the realm" and that, whenever the pope
wished to ransom one of his French friends who had been taken
prisoner, he demanded a subsidy from the English clergy. "Let
it be considered," the petitioners concluded, "that God has
committed his sheep to our holy father the pope to be fed and
not to be fleeced."[1]

So unpopular had the papacy become with the English that
when, just before the little king's accession, the city of London
put on a pageant in his honour "with great noise of minstrelsy,
trumpets, cornets and shawms and many wax torches," the high-
light in the procession was a mock pope accompanied by twenty-
four cardinals and "eight or ten arrayed with black masks like
devils, not at all amiable, seeming like legates."[2] When, following
an attempt to re-establish the papacy at Rome, the French
cardinals in 1378 challenged the election of a fantastically ir-
ascible and autocratic Italian pope, Urban VI, on grounds of
intimidation by the Roman mob, and set up with the help of his
enemies a rival pope at Avignon under the name of Clement VII,
an English parliament assembled at Gloucester decided to support Urban and, by doing so, helped to perpetuate for the next
half century an even greater scandal than the seventy years'
Babylonish captivity—the simultaneous existence of two and, at
one time, three popes. The emperor and most of the German and
Italian states, with Bohemia, Hungary, Portugal and Scandinavia followed England's example; France, Castile, Aragon,
Naples and Scotland supported Clement. Each pope demanded
the payment of ecclesiastical taxes and each excommunicated
the other as anti-Christ, while both declared a crusade and hired
the terrible roving bands that had been left over from the Anglo-
French wars to devastate the lands and massacre the supporters
of the other. The "seamless robe of Christ," as a preacher put
it, was rent asunder, and, to the horror and bewilderment of

---

[1] Rot. Parl. II, 338.   [2] Harl. MS. 247 f. 172v., cit. *Rickert*, 233.

simple Christians, Urbanists and Clementists fought one another for His garments.

. . . .

The "great schism," as it was called, was the culmination of the scandals that during the fourteenth century shook men's faith in the Church. It was against a background of popular indignation against simony, papal provisions, pluralism, non-residence and the sale of indulgences that John of Gaunt's learned protégé from the Lancastrian honour of Richmond, the theologian and philosopher, John Wycliffe, raised his voice of protest. Like most university doctors an absentee rector, supporting his teaching and scholarship from successive livings at Fillingham, Lincolnshire, Ludgershall in Buckinghamshire and Lutterworth in Leicestershire and by a small prebend in the collegiate church of Westbury-on-Trym, this radical-minded Yorkshireman—at one time master of the little Oxford college of Balliol and "holden of many to be the greatest clerk then living"—began by opposing papal claims on native benefices on behalf of parliament, went on to denounce ecclesiastical wealth, and ended by attacking most of the institutional assumptions of the Church, including the priest's indefeasible power of performing the miracle of the Mass. He based his stand on the life and teaching of Christ as revealed by the scriptures, which he maintained to be alone necessary for salvation and capable of interpretation by the humblest. "No man," he declared, "was so rude a scholar but that he might learn from the words of the Gospel according to his simplicity." All that was necessary was that they should be made available in his native tongue. "To be ignorant of the Bible," he wrote, "is to be ignorant of Christ." With a handful of Oxford disciples he embarked on the task of translating the Bible from the Latin Vulgate into English.

Instead of relying on sacerdotal pomp and ritual and identifying himself with the rich and powerful, the founder of Christianity, Wycliffe insisted, had gone about preaching in "small uplandish towns" like Cana in Galilee. "Christ went to these places where he wist to do good and he travelled not for winning of money, for he was not smighted with pride nor with covetousness." He had ordained "that his shepherds should live with their sheep, teaching them the way of the Lord as much by works as by preaching." "Christ and his apostles did not demand tithes but were content with the food and clothing that were their due . . . Let a priest move his parishioners by patience, humility and all the works of charity so that they will give him of temporal things what is necessary for the support of life."

All that was comprised in the word lordship—dominion, authority, property—depended, in Wycliffe's view, on grace: on the observance of Christ's commandments by its possessor and nothing else. Every man, to borrow a feudal analogy, held of God directly; he had no need for a mediatorial Church or spiritual mesne lord. "All leadership of man, natural or civil, is conferred upon him by God as the prime author in consideration of his returning continually to God the service due unto Him." "A priest fallen into sin is not a priest; . . . before God he is no priest"; a sinful prelate could not be a bishop at all and should be deposed and deprived of his property by the secular ruler.

The "dowering of the Church with lordship of the world" had been a heresy, for "Christ came of poor folk." Its wealth and power were millstones round its neck, its over-elaborate conventual services "the religion of fat cows." Even the pope himself was only "a naked servant of God." Wycliffe spoke with contempt of what he called the "possessioners": of monks with "red and fat cheeks and great bellies" and gowns of superfine cloth big enough to clothe four or five needy men; of the blasphemous sale of papal indulgences, of the worship of relics and images, of excommunication for political and financial ends. In contrast, he set out in simple language what he believed to be the essence of Christianity.

"The beginning and the ending of God's law is love . . . He that loveth his life, saith Christ, shall lose it, and he that hateth his life in this world keepeth it to life without end."[1]

Wycliffe's indictment traversed the Church's whole position, that it was "the bride of Christ" exclusively entrusted with the salvationary powers won for mankind on the Cross. Against its

[1] *Select Works of John Wycliffe* (ed. T. Arnold), I, 172, 174, 179, 197-9 *et passim*. The spelling has been modernised.

claim that God's will could only be known through its sacraments and ordinances, this gaunt, uncompromising North
Country puritan set up, not only the right of every man to judge
the scriptures for himself, but the direct responsibility of the
individual conscience to God. The ministry was requisite for the
well-being of the Church but not for its existence; its business,
and sole business, was to teach the gospel. Everything that came
between the individual and Christ was evil, and that included
most of the ecclesiastical establishment of the day, including
episcopacy. Far in advance of his time Wycliffe foreshadowed an
age when family and congregational worship would take the
place of the ritual and mystery of the candle-lit altar and what
he indignantly called "the drawing of the people by curiosity of
gay windows, . . . paintings and babwynerie."

With the fleets of France, Castile and Aragon threatening
England with invasion and the pope seen by most Englishmen
as "the French king's tame cat," Wycliffe in the autumn of 1377
was the most popular man in the country. He voiced the pent-
up feelings of the nation. He was supported against the papal
charges of heresy by almost the entire community of Oxford,
masters and students—at that time, after Paris, the most important university in northern Europe—by the Duke of Lancaster
and Princess of Wales, by an anti-clerical parliament and the
London mob. The rising middle-class delighted in his defence of
national rights and opposition to foreign ecclesiastical taxation,
while the aristocracy applauded his proposal to confiscate the
surplus wealth of the Church and distribute it among deserving
noblemen and knights "that wolden justly govern the people and
maintain the land against enemies." But when, after the outbreak
of the great Schism in 1378, he carried his theological arguments
and attacks on the institutional side of religion to their logical
conclusion by a denial of its central mysteries, not only repudiating transubstantiation and insisting that the Host remained
bread and wine,[1] but also declaring that it was blasphemy to
pretend that Christ's body and blood could be made by the
incantations of an ignorant and possibly sinful priest, he lost

[1] He based his denial on the impossibility of accidents existing without
substance, but believed that Christ might still be present without any change
in the elements of bread and wine—the doctrine of "consubstantiation."

the support both of his powerful patrons and of the Oxford friars who constituted the most vigorous element in the university. The ordinary Englishman was ready to support an attack on excessive clerical wealth, papal interference and Caesarian bishops but took fright at the idea of challenging mysteries which were the special preserve and concern of the Church. He could see no sense in incurring the risk of excommunication and eternal damnation by arguing about an abstract theory that did not affect his personal life or pocket.

For this reason Wycliffe's attack on clerical abuses failed to make any impression on the Church establishment of his day. It was too sweeping and too academic. It not only challenged vested interests; it proposed to abolish them altogether. Papacy, episcopacy, endowments, monasteries, friars, images, even tithes and the sacrament of the altar, all were to go. Had he had his way nothing would have remained but the authority of the Bible as interpreted by the individual worshipper, a parish priesthood supported by voluntary offerings and a presbyterian system of church government under the ultimate authority of the Crown.

Though, after a long duel between the bishops and the university authorities who at first continued to defend him, Wycliffe's attack on the Church's eucharistic doctrines ended in his being forbidden to lecture and his enforced withdrawal to his rectory at Lutterworth, he refused to retract or make the slightest concession to public opinion. For all his immense scholastic reputation and former popularity, his uncompromising dogmatism and contempt for time-hallowed beliefs alienated even the keenest reformers. Among those who attacked him were the Durham Benedictine, Robert Rypon, who in one of his sermons had described the higher clergy as "glittering like a prostitute," and that unrelenting foe of ecclesiastical corruption, John Bromyard, soon to become Vicar of the English Dominicans. Not even Wycliffe had denounced the rich possessioners more fiercely than he; "better for their souls," he had declared "that they should be drawn by horses to the gallows of the world than they should ride thus to the gallows of Hell."[1] But heresy—a cancer till then almost unknown in England—was something that threatened

[1] Owst, Literature and Pulpit, 302-3.

Holy Church itself and the continuance of Christendom. That a man of Wycliffe's prominence, a famous doctor of the Church, should have used his position to attack, not only its independence and endowments, but its most sacred mystery and in such stark and shocking terms, placed him outside the pale. Even Brunton of Rochester condemned him.

Beyond being banished from Oxford and forbidden to preach, Wycliffe was not punished. Parliament's traditional jealousy of foreign jurisdiction and the protection of the Princess of Wales left the bishops without any means of enforcing a papal order to bring him before the Church courts. Until his death at the end of 1384 the great deviationist remained quietly at Lutterworth, supervising the translation of the scriptures and training a band of disciples to spread his heretical message. These russet-clad preachers, travelling on foot like Christ's apostles and conducting their evangelical mission in street and field when forbidden to preach in church, were one of Wycliffe's two legacies to his country. The other was his vernacular bible, the first to be made in England since Anglo-Saxon times. Some of the scriptural phrases that were to become familiar to later generations appeared in their first tentative form in his homilies, like the parable of the prodigal son, with its, "Father, I have sinned against Heaven and before thee; now I am not worthy to be clepid thy son," and its beautiful ending, "This thy brother was dead and lived again; he was perished and is founden."

Yet the man who saw furthest into the Christian predicament was not a philosopher or ecclesiastical dignitary but a poor chantry-clerk in minor orders, earning a precarious living saying masses for rich men's souls. Born, it is believed, in the village of Colwall near Malvern,[1] the illegitimate child of a peasant girl and an Oxfordshire gentleman named de Rokayle, William Langland was probably educated at the priory choir-school of Great Malvern and ordained as an acolyte in the winter of the

[1] There is still a field in the neighbourhood called Longlands after which the poet may have been named. In his poem he describes himself as "Long Will." A. H. Bright, *New Light on Piers Plowman*; Nevill Coghill, *Visions from Piers Plowman*, 127-8.

first Black Death, subsequently drifting to London. Here, soon after the Treaty of Brétigny and the second visitation of the plague in 1361/2, while living in a cottage in Cornhill with his "wife Kitty and daughter Calotte," he wrote, in the alliterative metre and south Midland dialect of his Anglo-Saxon forbears, his poem "The Vision of William concerning Piers the Plowman." Expanded fifteen years later during the revolutionary crisis between the death of the Black Prince in 1376 and that of the old king in the following year, and revised at least once before the poet's death towards the end of the century, it consists of a series of allegorical visions in which, before the background of contemporary England, he sought for the secret of the Christian life.

Starting as a moral satire of the kind then common both in sermon and verse, it opened, far from the roar of Cheapside, in the land of the poet's boyhood,

"in a summer season   when soft was the sunlight
. . . on a May morning   on Malvern hills."

Resting under a bank beside a brook, he saw across the Severn valley, outlined against the distant Cotswold edge, the tower of Truth and beneath it a dungeon surrounded by ditches, "dark and dreadful of sight." Between him and these types of Heaven and Hell lay a "fair field full of folk,"

"of all manner of men   the mean and the rich,
Working and wandering   as the world asketh."

There passed before him the king and his knights and "the might of the community," barons and burgesses, mayors and mace-bearers "that act as a mean between king and commons in keeping the law," lovely ladies whose long fingers had silks and satins to sew at leisure to "make chasubles for chaplains in honour of the churches," serjeants-at-law hovering like hawks in silken hoods and "pleading at law for pounds and pennies," "merchants—proud-hearted men, patient of tongue,"

"buxom in their bearing   to burgesses and lords,
But to poor people   having pepper in the nose"—

Bakers, brewers and butchers, weavers of wool and of linen, tailors, tinkers and tax-collectors; "Peter the pardoner, Bertie the beadle of Buckinghamshire, Reginald the reeve of Rutland and Mumps the miller," all were there.

"Some were putting out to plough   had little play-time,
In setting seed and sowing   sweated at their labour,
Winning wealth that the worthless   wasted in gluttony.
Some pranked themselves in pride   preciously apparelled,
Coming under colour   of costly clothing. . . .
Beggars and blackguards   went busily about
With their bellies and bags   all brimming with bread,
Feigning sick for food   and fighting in the ale-house; . . .
Cissy the sempstress   sat on a bench,
Robin the rabbit-catcher   and his wife with him,
Tim the tinker and two   of his apprentices,
Hickey the hackney-man   and Hodge the huckster,
Clarice of Cock's Lane   and the clerk of the parish,
Parson Peter Proudie   and his Peronella,
Davy the ditcher   and a dozen others.
A fiddler, a rat-catcher,   a Cheapside crossing-sweeper,
A rope-maker, a road-man   and Rosy the dishwasher,
Godfrey of Garlick-hithe   and Griffin the Welshman, . . .
Jack the juggler   and Janet of the stews,
Daniel the dice-player   and Denis the bawd."[1]

Mingling with them the poet saw his fellow churchmen. There was Sloth the parson who could neither sing nor read but could find a hare in a field or furrow better than a *beatus*, "curates under Christ with the tonsure for token" who lodged "lazily in London all the year round" or served the king, "counting his silver in Exchequer and Chancery," monks who had no pity on the poor, "though money rained on their altars," university doctors "putting forth assumptions to prove the truth" and "gnawing God with their gorge" while they dined on the dais on delicate dishes,

"And the cry of the care-stricken   calls at their gate,
The hungry and thirsty   that quake for cold,
With none to take them in   and tend their suffering."
There were friars,

---

[1] *The Vision of Piers Plowman*, trans. into modern English by Nevill Coghill, 15, 41, 50. Where otherwise not stated the transcriptions, with the spelling modernised, are partly my own, based on the text of Dr. Skeat and the admirable modern version of Donald and Rachel Attwater in the Everyman's Library edition.

"all the four Orders,
          Preaching the people   for their private profit,
          Glossing the gospel   as seemed good to them;"
pardoners pulling out briefs with bishops' seals to cozen poor
folk for their gold; hermits with hooked staves on the road to
Walsingham, "their wenches with them;" "long lousy lubbers
that were loth to labour", and squabbling nuns in convents with
Wrath as cook making

          "a pottage or prattling   that Dame Joan was a
               bastard,
     And Dame Clarice a knight's daughter   and her father
          a cuckold;
     Dame Peronelle a priest's wench   that could never be
          prioress,
     For she had a child in cherry-time   all the chapter
          knew it."

Bishops and bachelors, chancellors and masters, deans, archdeacons and registrars, "saddled with silver our sins to sanction,"
the whole personnel of the Church in England passed before the
poet's eyes.

     Langland saw that what was true of the laity was true of the
clergy.

          "The most part of this people   that passeth on earth
          Have worship in this world   and wish for no better."
Both were corrupted by the universal craving for worldly reward;
both had forgotten the purpose of Christianity. It was from the
true Church, as he encountered her in his dream, that he redis-
covered what that end was:
"Truth telleth that love   is the governance[1] of heaven.
     . . . The father that formed us all
     Looked on us with love   and let his son die
     Meekly for our misdeeds   to amend us all. . . .
     Yet meekly with his mouth   Mercy he besought
     To have pity on that people   that pained him to death . . .
     Therefore I warn you rich   to have pity on the poor
     Though ye be mighty in power   be meek in your works

     [1] Langland's actual word was triarchy (Skeat gives "triacle")—the rule
of the Trinity.

For the same measures   that ye mete to others
Ye shall be weighed therewith   when ye wend hence . . .
Unless you love liberally   and lend to the poor
Of such goods as God sends   gladly them giving,
Ye have no more merit   in mass nor in hours
Than Malkyn of her maidenhood   that no man desires."

Turning their backs on the world, the dreamer and a crowd of penitents set off on pilgrimage to find St. Truth—a saint whom a professional palmer, his hat and cloak covered with tokens of the shrines he had visited, assured them he had never heard of. It was at this point that the pilgrims encountered by the roadside a poor labouring ploughman whose simple faith in God and unseeking service to his fellow men stood out in contrast to the shams and vanities of Church and State. Because, uncomplaining, he bore the burden of others, because he was truthful, just and faithful to his word and spent his days tilling and toiling for the common profit "as a true life asks," he was able to point the way to St. Truth. "Look to the deed," he told the pilgrims,

"that thy word declareth,
Such as thou seemest at sight   be in the trial found."

His was an old-fashioned morality. He expected knights and lords to protect Holy Church and guard the husbandman from wasters and robbers, to hunt the game that damaged hedges and crops, to be merciful to poor tenants and refrain from taxing them unjustly.   He denounced idlers, beggars and ribalds and all who lived irregular lives; "Robert the runabout," he declared, "shall have naught of mine".

For Langland had no more liking for a needy rogue and idler than a rich one.   His father had been a vassal of the ancient Marcher house of Despenser and, for all his poverty, he seems to have inherited a respect for the feudal loyalties. He had no wish to overturn the polity in which he lived, only to make it more just. When in his poem a knight, his conscience touched by Piers's example of sacrifice and honesty, asked him what was his duty,

" 'By St. Paul,' quoth Perkin,   'ye proffer you so fair
That I shall swynk and sweat   and sow for us both,
And other labours do for thy love   all my lifetime,
In covenant that thou keep   Holy Church and myself

From wasters and from wicked men   that this world
   destroyeth."
There was no hate in this conservative moralist's creed, only a
longing for justice. "Christ on his Cross," he wrote, "made us
all blood-brethren."

Yet the contrast between ill-used wealth and undeserved and
unrelieved destitution shocked Langland deeply. To him, as to
later English idealists, it seemed a denial of Christianity that the
honest poor should be oppressed and defrauded. It was an outrage against the founder of his religion:

"Jesu Christ of heaven
In a poor man's apparel   pursueth us ever . . .
For on Calvary of Christ's blood   Christendom gan spring,
And brethren in blood we become there . . . and gentlemen
   each one."

His heart was stirred and his indignation roused for "prisoners
in pits and poor folk in cottages, charged with children and chief
lord's rent":

"Old men and hoary   without help or strength,
   And all women with child   that can work no more,
   The blind and bedridden   and broken in limb,
   That bear mischief meekly   as lepers and others; . . .
   For love of their lowly hearts   our Lord hath granted
   Their penance and purgatory   here on this earth."

While they were neglected, he could not reverence "lords and
ladies and persons in fur and silver." At the back of his vision
lay always the memory of the Cross and of all that Christ had
suffered in poverty and obscurity, that men might have life and
have it more abundantly.

"I fell once more asleep   and suddenly me met
That Piers the Plowman   was painted all bloody
And come in with a cross   before the common people,
And right like in all limbs   to our Lord Jesu.
Then called I Conscience   to ken me the truth.
'Is this Jesus the jouster,' quoth I,   'that Jews did to death?
Or is it Piers the Plowman?   Who painted him so red?'
Quoth Conscience and kneeled: 'These are Piers's arms,
His colours and coat-armour   and he that cometh so bloody
Is Christ with his cross   conqueror of Christendom.'"

It was a very different heraldry to that of the knights of the Garter feasting in the Round Tower at Windsor.

Stronger even than Langland's longing for justice was his sense of compassion. When idlers and wasters shirked their work in Piers's field and, as a result, were scourged by Hunger, the ploughman had pity on them and fed them, though he knew that, once the famine had passed, they would fall to their idle ways again.

"They're my brethren by blood, for God bought us all.
Truth taught me once to love them each one
And to help them in all things always as they need, . . .
Love them and loathe them not; let God take the vengeance."

The work, not of a highly educated man protected by inherited wealth from the harsh animal struggle and squalid barbarism of medieval poverty but of one living precariously on its fringe, *Piers Plowman* faces the full Christian challenge. It is far more than a protest against social injustice, though none more eloquent has been written. It is a profound religious poem—as remarkable in its content, if not in its literary form, as the *Divine Comedy*. For all his asceticism, the virtues its author prized were mercy and charity. When a priest read out a pardon which Piers had secured from Truth for all who had worked on earth honestly or suffered unmerited hardship or poverty, and it was found to contain only the harsh words,

"Do well and have well and God shall have thy soul; do
evil and have evil and after thy death the Devil shall have
thy soul; hope thou none other,"

the ploughman hero, confronted by this unrelenting piece of Old Testament justice, indignantly tore it up.

For when, after awakening "meatless and moneyless" on Malvern hills, the poet once more renewed his visionary quest of the Christian mystery, roaming alone "all a summer season," it was to discover something that transcended the standards of "Do-Well," exemplar of the stern saving virtues on which the priest had insisted. Halted by the "bliss of the birds" singing "by a woodside in a wild wilderness" and leaning under a linden "to listen to the lay of these lovely fowl," he fell into a dream in which a tall man, like to himself, called him by his name and revealed himself as Thought. From him he found the answer he was seeking.

" 'Do-well and Do-better   and Do-best,' quoth he.
'Are three fair virtues   and be not far to find.
Whoso is true of his tongue   and of his two hands,
And through his labour or through his land   his livelihood
    winneth,
And is trusty of his tallying,   taketh but his own,
And is not a drunkard or disdainful   Do-well him followeth.

' Do-better doth right thus   and he doth much more,
He is lowly as a lamb   and loving of speech
And helpeth all men   as they needeth . . .

' Do-best is above both   and beareth a bishop's cross,
It is hooked at one end   to hale men from Hell:
A pike is on that staff   to pull down the wicked."

Throughout the rest of the poem, most English in its lack of logical order, its whimsical incongruity and underlying strength of feeling, the poet is guided by allegorical characters to comprehend each of the three ascending types in the scale of Christian perfection. Of each Piers, like Christ in his life on earth, becomes the prototype, first in his original form representing

"all living labourers   that live by their hands
And take the just wages   they honestly earn
And live in love and law."

—a type that comprised for Langland all, in whatever walk of life, who did their duty by their fellow men. With Do-better the poem passed from the Old Testament to the New. Its essence is love:

"He bids us be as brethren   and pray for our enemies,
And love them that lie to us   and help them when need help
And do good against evil   for God himself commands it."

The virtues now demanded are mercy, forgiveness, patience in affliction and poverty, cheerful acceptance of whatever God sends. Men should take no thought for the morrow but, loving their fellows, learn from nature how Providence provides for all in its "kind," how "lent never was life but livelihood was given"

—a theme which enables the poet to reveal his passionate love of nature:

> "I saw the sun and the sea   and the sands after
> And where the birds and beasts   seek after their mates,
> Wild worms in the woods   and wonderful birds
> With flecked feathers   and of many colours."

Piers has now embraced the life of contemplation—one that made a strong appeal to a poor unbeneficed scholar like Langland—

> "For if heaven be on this earth   and ease to any soul,
> It is in cloister or in learning . . . ;
> For in cloister cometh no man   to chide or fight,
> For all is courtesy there and book   to read and to learn"

—a passage followed by his scathing indictment of what cloistered life had become in contemporary England. As Do-better, his hero's way of life follows the path of full Christian charity wherever it leads. "Whoso giveth not, loveth not," is his creed; there is no limit to its practical expression.

> "Jesus Christ of Heaven
> In a poor man's apparel   pursueth us ever
> And looketh on us in their likeness   and that with lovely
>   cheer
> To know us by our kind hearts."

In the final stages of his dream the poet encounters the supreme form of Christian virtue:

> "Do well, my friend, is   to do as law teacheth,
> To love thy friend and thy foe   that is Do-better.
> To give and to succour   both young and old,
> To heal and to help   is Do-best of all."

And suddenly we realize that Piers has become the prototype of Christ himself. We see him, as Do-best, riding into Jerusalem to do battle for man's soul:

> "This Jesus of his gentlihood   will joust in Piers's arms
> In his helm and in his hauberk   *humana natura*."

There follows the most wonderful scene in the poem, the Harrowing of Hell, when after the agony on the cross, the risen Christ challenges Lucifer in his dark realm and, heralded by Light, demands the souls of the damned:

" 'What lord art thou' quoth Lucifer,   *'Quis est iste?'*
' *Rex glorae,'*   the Light replied,
' And Lord of might and main   and all manner of virtues.
   Dukes of this dim place,   undo these gates
   That Christ may come in   the king's son of Heaven!' "
Then Piers, now God incarnate, himself speaks,
   "I that am lord of life   love is my drink,
   And for that drink today   I died upon earth. . . .
   Now shall I come as a king,   crowned with angels,
   And have out of Hell   all men's souls, . . .
   For I were an unkind king   unless I my kind helped."
In his belief in the ultimate redemption of all men, even the
damned, Langland went far beyond the Christian theology of
his age. It was no academic reasoning that had brought him to
this conclusion but his knowledge of mankind's inherent sinful-
ness and desperate need for forgiveness and regeneration, and his
unshakable faith in Christ's all-embracing mercy.

   So, as the Easter bells pealed out from London's steeples, the
poet awoke—
   "And called Kit my wife   and Calotte my daughter—
   'Arise and reverence   God's resurrection,
   And creep to the cross on thy knees   and kiss it for a jewel,
   For God's blessed body   it bore for our salvation.' "
Langland's vision of Christianity, like Wycliffe's, was a personal
one. He saw that the Faith depended not merely on conformity
to the Church's creed and ritual—in which no man believed
more firmly than he—but on the individual's pursuit of truth
and his performance of acts of Christian love. It rested not
merely on commemoration of Christ's sacrifice but on man's
readiness to follow in His footsteps. "Clerics have told me," he
wrote,
               "that Christ is in all places,
   Yet I never saw Him for certain   save as myself in a mirror."
Piers Plowman is a restatement of a mystery incarnate: that the
kingdom of Heaven is within everyone's reach yet can only
be won by love and sacrifice.

   In the closing stanzas of his work revised before his death—
no-one knows exactly when he died or where he lies—appalled
by the schism in Christendom and seeing Piers as the Peter to

whom Christ had entrusted his Church, Langland made a
passionate appeal for Christian unity:

"Cry we to the commons   that they come to unity
And there abide and do battle   against Belial's children."

Despite his realization of his fellow churchmen's failings, from his
lowly station among the ecclesiastical army's flotsam and jetsam
he realized, as Wycliffe failed to realize, mankind's need for the
Church's guidance, "for Clergy is keeper under Christ of heaven."
His final word was of refusal to despair and of faith that somehow,
notwithstanding the universal corruption and disintegration of
his time, the search for truth and the Christian virtues would in
the end triumph.

" 'By Christ,' quoth Conscience then, 'I will become a pilgrim
And walk as wide   as the world lasteth
To seek Piers the Plowman   that Pride may destroy.' "

Chapter Twelve

CHRIST OF THE TRADES

Englishmen suffer indeed for a season, but in the end they repay so cruelly that it may stand as a great warning. For no man may mock them; the lord who governs them rises and lays down to rest in sore peril of his life . . . There is no people under the sun so perilous in the matter of its common folk as they are in England.

FROISSART

FOR A SHORT TIME after the young king's accession, in the hopes inspired by a new reign the differences dividing the kingdom's rulers were buried. William of Wykeham's temporalities were restored, Peter de la Mare was released from Gaunt's castle at Nottingham, and Gaunt himself, the hated Duke of Lancaster, was reconciled to the Londoners, showing his loyalty and goodwill by falling at the boy king's feet and begging him to forgive the citizens for their riotous behaviour against him. Riding from the Tower through cheering streets with his fellow offender against the city's liberties, Lord Percy the marshal by his side, he had carried the sword *Curtana* at the crowning in the abbey of the little king, "fair as another Absalom."[1] "It was a day of joy and gladness," wrote a chronicler, "the long awaited day of the renewal of peace and of the laws of the land, long exiled by the weakness of an aged king and the greed of his courtiers and servants." Three months later, at the opening of a new parliament in October 1377, the duke met the accusations of his enemies with a speech in which he declared that none of his ancestors had been traitors but good and loyal men, and that it would be strange, indeed, if he were one, for he had more to lose than any other subject in the realm.

Yet though, because of the suspicion with which he had long been regarded, Lancaster withdrew from the central direction

[1] Walsingham, *Historia Anglicana*, cit. *McKisack*, 399.

of affairs, the council of regency which governed the country in his stead was soon in trouble. The war continued to go disastrously. The loss of sea power and the enemy's command of the Channel still vitiated all. The Isle of Wight was overrun and occupied by a French army; Fowey, Plymouth, Melcombe Regis, Poole, Hastings, Rye and Gravesend were sacked and burnt. The Yarmouth herring fleet was attacked, the mouth of the Thames had to be guarded by booms, and the prior of Lewes, leading the posse of East Sussex against French raiders, was carried off into captivity. Such was the alarm at the burning of Gravesend that London's gates were strengthened with portcullises and barbicans, and a chain was suspended across the river from two hastily built towers to protect the Pool and the score of little creeks and quays along the northern bank through which the commerce of the capital flowed. Even inland cities like Oxford were put into a state of defence.

Yet no invasion took place save the usual harrying of the Northumbrian dales by Scottish moss-troopers. The skill of the seafaring population of England's southern and eastern coasts and estuaries—long exploited in pursuit of continental conquests—little by little re-asserted itself. When a fleet of French transports appeared on Southampton water the governor, Sir John Arundel, put to sea with boats packed with archers and drove it off. And, angered by the seizure of a convoy of merchantmen by Scottish, French and Spanish pirates off Scarborough, a rich London grocer and member of parliament named John Philpot[1] fitted out a squadron at his own expense and won an action in the Channel, recovering most of the lost prizes and capturing fifteen Spanish ships and their Scottish commander.

For, though no longer enjoying the leadership that had made her so feared, at the lower levels of authority England did not lack stout hearts. Sir Hugh Calveley, one "who slept not on his business," and whose record of service went back almost to Crécy, sallying out from Calais burnt Boulogne and sacked the fair of Etaples. When in 1378 the Bretons rose against their Valois overlord and a landing-party sent to help them was trapped by a superior French force, the old freebooter, acting as admiral,

[1] His name is still commemorated in the City by a lane on the site of his former house. *D.N.B.* xv, 1047.

made the master of his ship turn back to rescue his men, "refusing according to his wonted valiancy to return till he saw all others in safety." His armoured effigy still rests in the noble collegiate church he founded at Bunbury out of the wealth he won in the wars. His friend and fellow Cheshireman, Sir Robert Knollys, serving as lieutenant to Edward III's youngest son, Thomas of Woodstock, also covered himself with glory, marching in the summer of 1380 from Calais to Brittany by the old familiar route of Artois, Champagne and the Loire, and saving the army from disaster at the siege of Nantes.

Yet the new Breton war brought no gains to England, only frustration and continued expense. An attempt by John of Gaunt to capture St. Malo was repulsed, while an Atlantic storm in the winter of 1379 sent to the bottom an expedition under Sir John Arundel.[1] The following year saw the death of the French king whose policy had raised his country from the abyss of defeat into which it had fallen, and of the great soldier, du Guesclin who, by his Fabian tactics had turned the tables on the invaders. Yet though neither country—both now ruled by minors—had anything further to gain from it, the war went on, chiefly because no-one seemed able to end it. The papacy, which might have performed its traditional role of mediator, was divided by the schism, the French pope, Clement, supporting France, and the Italian pope, Urban, England. Each denounced the partisans of the other and urged their own to pursue the war as a crusade against anti-Christ.

Only a small fraction of the English people were engaged in fighting. Yet their sense of national pride, born of the victories of Edward III and the Black Prince, was deeply affronted. Then, complained an indignant homilist, England was a great ship able to weather any storm: the king her rudder, the commons her mast, the good duke Henry of Lancaster her barge—

"Noble it was and tall of tower,
Through all Christendom it was dread."[2]

The man whom everyone blamed for her misfortunes was John of Gaunt, whose failure to capture St. Malo had been in such

[1] It was regarded as a judgment for an assault made by his men on a nunnery. Walsingham, *Historia Anglicana* (ed. Riley), 418-25.

[2] *Owst, Literature and Pulpit,* 75-6.

sorry contrast to his father's and father-in-law's victories and even to that of the merchant Philpot in the Channel. Living in open adultery with his children's governess—the great love of his life and ancestress of the future British royal line—he seemed to be calling down heaven's wrath on the realm. From his hermitage in the Tuscan hills the Cambridge scholar and Austin friar who was the disciple of St. Catherine of Sienna, William Flete, recorded his fears that his countrymen would be direly punished because of their sins. "Pray, pray for England," he wrote, "England is much in my mind and the English king."[1]

So distrusted was John of Gaunt that it was even rumoured that he had poisoned his first wife's sister for her inheritance and was plotting a similar fate for his nephew, King Richard. Though there does not seem to have been any ground for such suspicions, the duke's vast wealth, pride and autocratic ways told heavily against him. In the autumn of his repulse from St. Malo fifty of his followers broke into Westminster Abbey during Mass and dragged from the sanctuary two squires named Hawley and Shakell who had escaped from the Tower, where he had imprisoned them for refusing to hand over a young Spanish hostage whom he wished to use in support of his claim to the Castilian throne. For this outrage, in which one of the fugitives was killed, Lancaster's lieutenants were excommunicated by the Bishop of London and only escaped death through his intervention. Feeling against him ran dangerously high; it was said that he had threatened to ride into the capital at the head of an army and seize the bishop in the midst of his supporters.

Affronted patriotism and resentment against the king's uncle was reinforced by the indignation of the tax-payer. There was a general belief that the sums voted for the war by successive parliaments had been embezzled or, at best, wasted. The government did what it could to allay these suspicions, agreeing at the joint request of lords and Commons to the appointment of two London burgesses to supervise the expenditure of the war subsidies. Yet even this invasion of the king's exclusive right to control military expenditure failed to satisfy the Commons. At the beginning of 1380, after the shipwreck of Sir John Arundel's

[1] A. Gwynn, *English Austin Friars*, 203.

expedition, their Speaker demanded the appointment of a parliamentary committee to investigate the expenses of the royal household. They even requested—and obtained—the replacement of the chancellor, Sir John Scrope, by the Archbishop of Canterbury, Simon Sudbury, and the dismissal of the regency council on the ground that the thirteen-year-old king was "now of good discretion and fine stature."

It was never easy to make the English pay taxes. More even than most medieval people they regarded them as a form of robbery and injustice. The evolution of their government during the past two centuries had turned on their rulers' recognition that the consent of the taxed to new imposts could only be won by allowing them a share in their imposition. When, Magna Carta having placed limitations on the feudal taxation of land, imposts had been levied on personal wealth and merchandise, the same rule had been adopted. Superseding the feudal ruler's right to tallage at will, the principle that the subject should be party to the fiscal burdens imposed on him was applied at every stage of the tax structure. Whenever parliament agreed that a fifth, a tenth or a fifteenth should be levied on moveables, justices were sent into every county to assess the local proportion payable with representative knights from every hundred, who, in turn, met the representatives of every vill, where a jury of inquests wore to the number, quantity and value of taxable goods in the township.

By Edward III's reign, with the growing need for subsidies, this consultative system of assessment[1] had become so troublesome to everyone that, as a result of an agreement in 1334 between

---

[1] *Powicke*, 523-7; see also S. K. Mitchell, *Taxation under John and Henry III*, 164-5; T. F. Plucknett, *Concise History of Common Law*, 84. Of this complex but not undemocratic method of assessing taxes, Sir Maurice Powicke, with his profound understanding of English institutions, wrote: "Behind the scenes, where peasants and burgesses wrangled about what should or should not be taxed of their stores and clothes and household utensils, peace can only have been preserved by timely concessions and convenient oversights. . . . Beneath all their grumbling and evasions, these lords, knights, burgesses and peasants had become aware of a common obligation . . . They had learned that the natural and ordered activities in which they shared, in the fields, in the courts, on juries and commissions, in watch and ward, on hue and cry, were but parts of a greater whole and subject to a wider loyalty." *Powicke*, 525-6.

Exchequer officials and representatives of the localities, a fixed valuation proportionate to the subsidy rate was allocated to every county, hundred and township—an allocation which had since remained unchanged. During the reign more than £400,000 in lay subsidies was raised by this method. But the war, which in the victorious 'forties and 'fifties had financed itself, by continuing into the 'seventies, compelled government and parliament to seek new ways of raising money to maintain the royal forces and garrisons abroad. Every year the Crown fell deeper in debt, the auditing and payment of accounts more in arrears and the country was more drained of specie. The financial stringency was aggravated by a general scarcity of precious metals throughout Europe.

In 1371, two years after the resumption of the war, parliament adopted the novel device of a tax on every parish in England at a standard rate of 22s. 3d., differences in wealth being met by a proposal "that each parish of greater value should help another parish of less value." By this means it was hoped that £50,000 would be raised, it being assumed by the king's inexperienced ministers that there were fifty thousand parishes in the country. There turned out, however, to be only nine thousand—a fact of which the displaced episcopal ministers must have been well aware. As a result, the individual contribution of each parish had to be raised from 22s. 3d. to 116s.

Six years later a still more revolutionary innovation was adopted by Edward III's last parliament. This was a poll-tax of fourpence a head on the entire lay adult population except beggars. This "tallage of groats," as it was called, mulcting the poorest at the same rate as the richest, was intensely unpopular and very difficult to collect. But it appealed to a parliament of landowners and employers, since for the first time it imposed a direct fiscal burden on the peasants and unpropertied wage-earners.

Two years later the tax was reimposed, though this time on a graduated scale to alleviate its more obvious injustices. Earls. widowed countesses and the mayor of London, who ranked as an earl, were assessed at £4 a piece, and the Duke of Lancaster, the richest man in the kingdom, at ten marks, about half again as much. Barons, bannerets, knights, London aldermen and the mayors of the larger provincial towns were to pay £2, other well-to-do squires and merchants £1, lesser merchants and craftsmen according to their status from 6s. 6d. to 3s. 4d., tenant farmers and cattle dealers a shilling, and everyone else, as before, four-pence. The result, however, was disappointingly small, and, instead of bringing in £50,000 as expected, the tax only produced £22,000.

In the autumn of 1380, faced by the government's now desperate need, a new parliament, meeting at Northampton, imposed the tax for a third time. On condition that £33,000 were contributed by the Church, which preferred to tax itself separately,[1] the Commons agreed to raise £66,000 from the laity. This it did by trebling the poll tax in the belief that, as a groat a head had previously brought in £22,000, a shilling a head would bring in three times as much. The graduated scale, however, was dropped in favour of the original flat rate, lip service being paid to the principle of justice by a provision that the well-to-do should "according to their ability help the less." No one was to pay more than a pound for himself and his wife and no one less than a groat. A slight concession was made to poorer tax payers by raising the age at which tax was payable from fourteen to fifteen.

To a peasant there was a vast difference between a groat and a shilling. The latter represented nearly a fifth of a hired labourer's annual wage without his keep. Even a man and his wife without dependents had to pay 2s. tax—the equivalent of well over £5 today—while a householder with a large family might have to defray the tax of several aged or female relatives. The poll tax reflected the belief of landowners and employers that since the plague "the wealth of the kingdom was in the hands of artisans and labourers." It not only showed an astonishing ignorance of the circumstances of "the common people

---

[1] "The reply given by the clergy was that their grant was never made in parliament, nor ought to be, and that the lay folks ought not to constrain the clergy and cannot do so . . . And they prayed to our lord the king that the liberty of Holy Church should be entirely saved . . . For certainly the clergy wish for their part to do what they ought and are bound to do, having regard to this present great necessity and as they have done in days gone by." *Rot. Parl.* III, 90.

whose occupations standeth in grobbying about the earth"; it ignored the principle for which parliament had long contended in its claim to some part in the governance of the realm: that there should be no taxation without representation and consent. The peasantry and town artisans on whom the tax bore so hardly were completely unrepresented in a parliament of magnates, prelates, landowners, merchants and lawyers. And the former were already labouring under a sense of grave injustice.

At this time probably somewhere near half the English people were not legally free but tied by inheritance to the soil they cultivated.[1] They could not claim a free man's rights under the Common Law, let alone representation in parliament. Like the feudalism of which it was part the servile manorial system of the open-field villages of central and southern England was already in decline and giving way to an economy based on paid labour and rented farms. But it was still the basis of life for nearly a million men and women who, though not technically slaves, were bound by birth to the soil and compelled to perform unpaid menial services for its lord. From this servitude they could only gain release by a formal grant of manumission or by flight from their homes and fields to some chartered borough where servile status had been abolished and where residence for a year and a day gave a man his freedom.

Though he was protected by the king's courts against everyone except his lord, a bondsman could not sue in them in respect of his villein land, livestock or property, all of which in the law's eyes belonged to his lord, and his own right to which was dependent on the customs and judgments of the latter's manor court. In accordance with feudal practice he could still be tallaged by the lord "at will," unlike the freeholder whom parliament had relieved from such arbitrary claims. If he wished to sell a beast he had to pay a fine, for the lord had an interest in his property. If he wished to marry a son or daughter he had to pay what was called a *merchet*, for, villeinage being hereditary, the lord had an interest in them too; if his unmarried daughter became pregnant he had to pay a *leywrite*, to compensate for the

---

[1] *Bennett*, 277; *Kossaminsky*, 197-255. For an account of the manorial system at the end of the thirteenth century see *Makers of the Realm*, 359-69.

depreciation of her manorial value. Should a bondsman wish to reside outside the manor he had to seek the lord's licence and, even though he occupied no land in it, pay *chevage* to offset the loss of his services. On his death his widow or heir was called upon for a *heriot* whose value was traditionally that of the best beast and chattel on his holding. And though the land he cultivated and the cot he inhabited passed by customary right to his heir, the latter was only allowed to enjoy it when he had paid an entry-fine, usually equivalent to a year's services or rent.[1]

The extent of the services the villein had to perform for his lord varied with the size of his holding and the custom of the manor. But wherever the open-field system operated, as it did in most parts of England except the pastoral north and west and in Kent, the peasant was confronted by uncertain demands on his time and galling restrictions on his freedom of action. Among these were the obligation to grind his corn, bake his bread and brew his ale at the lord's mill, oven and brewery— "suit of mill" and "suit of oven," as they were called—which not only enriched the lord, but offered opportunities for every kind of chicanery and oppression by those to whom he leased his rights.[2] An equally resented monopoly was the lord's dovecot and "free warren" from which hordes of pigeons and rabbits descended on the peasant's crops, while if he retaliated by trapping such pests he faced a heavy fine at the next manorial court.

All this had come to be intensely resented. Villeinage was

[1] This, however, was not as heavy as the death duty his counterpart has to pay to the State today. R. H. Hilton, in *The English Rising of 1381* (p. 31) cites the case of a Wiltshire villein who had accumulated possessions to the extent of £2000—over £100,000 in today's money. On this he had to pay £140—that is, about £7,500 of our money compared with the £50,000 death duty levied on a comparable modern estate. The heriot on the dead man's best beast must have pressed far more heavily on the poorer villager; in March 1347, on the death of a serf, the lord seized his horse, cart, sheep and two pigs worth twelve shillings, the widow being given five months to buy them back for this sum. *Bennett*, 145.

[2] The usual practice was for the lord to retain from a sixteenth to a twenty-fourth part of all grain ground; the miller often took more. "What is the boldest thing in the world," a popular riddle asked, to which the reply was, "A miller's shirt, for it clasps a thief by the throat daily."

seen by the bondsman as an economic imposition and a degrading distinction. It was no longer taken for granted, and every opportunity was taken to escape or evade its burdens. Those who resented them most were the richer villagers who occupied the traditional yardlands—holdings of thirty acres or more in the arable fields with corresponding rights in the manorial meadowland, waste and woodland. A yardlander had to perform for his holding, in person or by proxy, not only a full half-day's labour on the lord's land for three or four days a week throughout the year but additional services called "love-boons" —given, in theory, out of love for his feudal protector—at the very seasons, haymaking and harvest, harrowing and sowing times, when he needed all the labour he could command to wrest a living from his own soil.

Those who could afford it, therefore, seized every opportunity to commute as many of such services as possible for money payments. In the expanding agricultural economy of the thirteenth and early fourteenth century many peasants were able to free themselves from the more onerous burdens, for progressive landowners often found it paid them to hire labour rather than depend on the unwilling services of disgruntled serfs. Without formal manumission by the lord, they could not, however, achieve complete freedom, for, irrespective of the obligations attached to it—a matter for the manor court—villeinage was hereditary, and the law would not uphold a sale which the purchaser paid for out of property in which the vendor held a residual right.[1]

Yet, though the taint of servile blood remained, a number of the more enterprising villeins had achieved an economic, if not a social, status comparable to that of the freehold farmer. Often such men rented freehold land in addition to the villein holdings they held under the custom of the manor. Even the contraction and recession which set in during the troubled reign of Edward II, though they retarded, did not stop the process of commutation and, with it, the gradual substitution for a servile system of agriculture of one partially based on a wage-economy.

[1] "A third person always had to purchase the charter of manumission which would make the serfs free." *Hilton and Fagan*, 63

The halving of the national labour-force by the Black Death halted this gradual emancipation. Labour suddenly became the most precious commodity in the kingdom. A landowner who had made no concessions to his serfs found himself able to cultivate his depopulated estates far more cheaply than one who had commuted his villeins' services for a cash payment. Bound by agreements to let their serfs enjoy their holdings at rents which now bore no relation to what they themselves had to pay for hired labour, and desperate for lack of workers, many lords tried to enforce rights that had lapsed or to stretch those that remained.

If the Black Death made lords more conscious of the value of compulsory services, it made every serf more eager to evade them. Shaking off the shackles of their ancestry, bondsmen fled from their homes and took service for wages with distant employers who asked no questions. It was the poorer members of the village community who had no land to lose who seized such opportunities—the young and those with no possessions but their tools and skill as husbandmen or craftsmen. The attempts of the Commons and local justices to keep down wages by branding, imprisonment and the stocks drove them to make common cause with their richer neighbours, who were confronted by demands from their lords for services which they regarded as unjust and oppressive. On both classes of villagers, landed and landless, yeomen farmers and day labourers, there fell the demand for a tax in whose making they had had no part and whose inequity was glaring.

.   .   .   .

It was against the lord's officers and agents that the peasant's indignation was directed. In the larger estates the lord was seldom seen; where personal contact existed it might be softened by neighbourly and Christian feelings. Even John of Gaunt excused his serfs tallages in times of need and distributed nearly two pounds worth of alms every week. But from the receivers and bailiffs who wrung from the peasant the services and rents on which the landowner lived, from the steward who presided at his manorial court and the lawyers who made extreme claims on his behalf, the peasant received little mercy. Times were bad, money hard to come by, a luxurious ruling-class in need of the income it could no longer obtain from victories abroad. The business of its agents was to exact the uttermost service and payment obtainable. In the process they often took—and even more often were suspected of taking—more than was due or than the lord himself received.

Some of the hardest task-masters were the monasteries who, hit by the economic recession and the plague, had never enjoyed, like the secular lords, the opportunity of making good their losses by the plunder and ransoms of war. Intensely conservative and, like all corporations, impersonal in business relationships, they had the justification that their exactions were for the service of God. More easily than most they were able to prove rights to long-lapsed services by the charters which every religious house preserved, added to by cultivating the friendship of the great, and sometimes, if their critics are to be believed, improved by a little pious and skilled forgery.[1] Nor, conscious of the sanctity of their claims, were they always very tactful with those whose labour they exploited; the abbot of Burton told his tenants that they owned nothing but their bellies.

Of all who enforced the lord's rights the lawyer was the most hated. Just as the thirteenth century had added to the English scene a new figure in the shape of the friar, the fourteenth century introduced another and far less popular one in the man of law. Since Edward I had placed the education of the legal profession under his judges and divorced it from the Church, its wealth and influence had grown rapidly. In an acquisitive and evolving society in which litigation had taken the place of private war, the brethren of the coif—the white silken hood worn by the king's serjeants-at-law and the judges who were chosen from their ranks —constituted a new aristocracy; "law," wrote Langland, "is grown lord"! Their wealth was a phenomenon; in the poll-tax of 1379 the judges of the King's Bench and Common Pleas were assessed at more than earls and more than twice as much as barons, with whom the serjeants and greater "apprentices at law," or barristers, as they later became called, were grouped

---

[1] The abbey of St. Albans was supposed to possess a charter granted by King Offa in the eighth century which, written in letters of gold, was regarded by its tenantry as the chief obstacle to their freedom. *Keen,* 163.

as equals. Even "lesser apprentices who followed the law" had to pay as much as aldermen.

The judges in their scarlet robes trimmed with white budge or lambskin and the serjeants in their long parti-coloured gowns of blue, green and brown, cut almost as great a figure now as the magnates and prelates. Their splendour did not make them or their profession popular. At no time were lawyers so distrusted as in the latter fourteenth century. To a simple Christian mind there seemed something indecent in making a livelihood, let alone a fortune, out of influencing judgment by forensic subtleties. "Whosoever speaks the truth for a price," declared a preacher, "or does justice for reward sells God who is himself both truth and justice."[1]   Lawyers were regarded as special pleaders who championed any cause for a fee and unsuited the innocent with technical tricks and quibbles and a jargon that no man but they could understand. In his epic on Christian justice, Langland depicted the serjeants-at-law in their hoods of silk hovering like hawks at the bar,

"Pleading for pence   and pounds the law,
  Not for love of Our Lord   unloosening their lips.
  Thou mightest better measure   the mist on Malvern hills
  Then get a mumble out of them   till money were shown."
They seemed to him outside the pale of salvation.

So widespread was this conviction that lawyers were hired partisans that in 1372 the Commons petitioned for an act to disqualify them from membership on the ground that they "procured and caused to be brought into parliament many petitions in the name of the commons which do not concern them at all but only the private persons with whom they are engaged." Directed in particular against the attorneys who were seen as rogues and adventurers hanging about the courts to inveigle the unwary into litigation in which they were certain to be fleeced, it was enacted that "no man of the law following business in the king's courts," should be returned as knight of the shire except royal serjeants, and that those who had been should have no wages since they were already being paid by their clients. Fortunately for parliament's ultimate future the measure was never strictly enforced, for shires and boroughs continued to find

[1] Master Ralph of Acton, *Owst, Literature and Pulpit*, 344.

lawyers indispensable in a polity where everything had to be done with a show of law.[1]

To a lawyer, absorbed in a fascinating intellectual pursuit and a member of a professional brotherhood which had already developed a sense of tradition and *esprit de corps*, all this appeared in a very different light. How different is shown by Chief Justice Thirning's claim that in the reign of Edward III "the law was of the greatest perfection that ever it was." Yet, though most of the judges and serjeants were men of probity, proud of their calling and of the law they administered,[2] to the layman the law seemed incomprehensibly complex and formalistic. Suitors found their writs abated and themselves unsuited for minute errors in Latin or even spelling, or quashed by the judges because they did not closely enough resemble those that already existed, however inadequate these were for the needs of

---

[1] In John Gower's *Mirour de l'omme*, there is an account through the eyes of a contemporary layman of a young lawyer learning his, as it seemed, mercenary trade.

> "The apprentices in their degree
> Taste blood from the beginning
> In pleading at the assizes;
> Like dogs they seize as their prey
> The silver that is given them . . .
> For wrong that gives a rich fee
> Takes from them the scent of the straight course.
> . . . And then after the apprentice
> A certain time has fulfilled
> What is sufficient for pleading,
> He wishes to have the coif placed
> Upon his head, and to his own honour
> Wishes to bear the name of serjeant.
> But if before this time
> In one thing he was greedy,
> Now he is a thousand times inflamed;
> For he becomes so ravenous
> That part is not enough for him;
> He must devour the whole country."

Rickert, 159-60.

Like Chaucer's "man of law"—believed to have been drawn from his friend, Thomas Pynchbeck, who, admitted serjeant in 1376, became chief baron of the Exchequer:

> "In terms of law had he the judgments all
> That from the timës of King Will were fall, . . .
> And every statute could he plead by rote."

a developing society. Earlier in the century a great judge like William de Bereford could still look beyond the letter of the law and insist that, if it outraged natural justice, the court should offer redress to a suitor injured by such formalism. "This is not properly a debt but a penalty," he told a plaintiff who was demanding the last penal ounce from his bond; "what equity would it be to award you the debt when the document is tendered and when you cannot show that you have been damaged by the detention?" Yet by the 'forties, judges were laying it down that equity was one thing and the common law another and that they were exactly bound by the wording of statutes and their predecessors' decisions. If as late as 1345 Chief Justice Stonor, who had first practised in the days of Edward I, could still declare that "law is that which is right," the spirit of the bench in the second half of the century was put by Hillary J., when he said, "We will not and *we cannot* change ancient usages."[1]

In the long run there was gain as well as loss in this, for, by walking closely in well-trodden steps, judges and pleaders were building up a body of precedent so strong that, so long as they stuck to it closely, even the king and his ministers would presently have difficulty in forcing them from it. This was to prove a safeguard for men's rights against tyranny. But at the moment the threat to the ordinary man was not from the king but from the over-powerful neighbour who, with the help of force and fraud, could use formalistic legal processes and the letter of the law to trick him out of his rights and property. From this inflexibility of the common law courts the only appeal was to the king and his Council—the original source from which the judges derived their power. As the remedies of a system of law made for a rural and feudal society became increasingly inadequate, the Council took to referring petitions for relief and redress to the chancellor who, as the chief executive officer of the Crown, possessed in the Chancery staff a body of clerks accustomed to framing and issuing writs. Usually himself a cleric and trained in the canonical principles of equity and, in theory, the "keeper of the king's conscience," he seemed the natural channel

[1] *Y. B.* 2 and 3 Edw. II (Selden Society) XIII, 59 cit. T. F. Plucknett, *Concise History of Common Law,* 639; C. K. Allen. *Law in the Making,* 181, 375.

through which the discretionary prerogative powers of justice could be granted. There thus begun to grow up, side by side with the ordinary courts, a Chancery court of equity transcending and overriding their rules wherever these manifestly outraged conscience and reason. Those who sought the king's grace could petition the Crown for a remedy, on which, if the chancellor considered the petition or "bill" justified, he would issue a writ to compel the party whose wrong was complained of to return a sworn answer under penalty or *sub poena*—of a heavy fine. By examining the petitioner and respondent and allowing them to interrogate one another under oath he would then adjudicate the case without the aid of a jury as natural justice dictated. At the time of Richard II's accession the procedure of what was to become the court of chancery was, however, still in an experimental stage.

Such a court was desperately needed. For though "persons having power and dread" had long ceased normally to employ force in open defiance of the Crown and law, they had learnt to use their wealth to bend and twist the courts to their will. Among the abuses of justice complained of in petitions to parliament were the securing by rich litigants of commissions of *oyer et terminer* for judges who were known to favour them; bribing sheriffs to pack juries and appoint days for trial without warning to defendants and in places where the latter were afraid to venture; financing suits for a share in the profits of successful litigation—the offence of "champerty;" influencing juries by bribes, promises or threats—"embracery;" and the corruption of judges. That this last was not altogether exceptional is shown by the number of judges who found themselves accused by "clamour of people" of "selling the laws." Among them during Edward III's reign were two chief justices of the King's Bench and a chief baron of the Exchequer.

As for juries, a regular profession had grown up in the provincial courts of persons called tracers who, according to the poet Gower, made a speciality of procuring jurymen to perjure themselves and to whom those who wanted a favourable verdict were well advised to apply. The Dominican, John Bromyard, spoke of jurors who, having "sworn to try whether persons were thieves or true men, falsely and wittingly acquitteth them" and mentioned a case where, when the judge asked the jury whether they had agreed on their verdict, one of them replied, "No, because each of my fellow jurymen has had forty pounds and I have only had twenty!" On this Bromyard commented: "Not he who shall do justly but he who gives and takes more is set in offices and juries. He who can bring in his train more thieves and murderers is master of all." Another preacher described a jury as "the twelve apostles of the Devil."[1]

Gravest of all the abuses of law was maintenance, the practice by which suitors procured the armed backing of a powerful neighbour. The country was full of captains and knights who had grown used to enriching themselves by plunder and ransom and of disbanded soldiers of the same mettle as the *routiers* who had ravaged France. By offering them their keep and the protection of his livery any rustic magnate, particularly in the unruly west and north, could raise a private army with which to coerce and fleece his weaker neighbours under the forms of law. With such a gang of liveried bullies—raised by the same system of indenture as the royal armies—it was easy in an unpoliced countryside to seize a neighbour's land or cattle on a trumped-up charge and then intimidate witnesses, procure false evidence, falsify records and suborn court officials to secure a verdict endorsing the *fait accompli*. The sermons of the time are full of complaints about "officers of great men that weareth their liveries, the which, by colour and assistance of law, robbeth and despoileth the poor, now beating, now slaying, now putting them from house and land." Every now and then, after some particularly notorious abuse of justice, an outraged parliament would force the authorities to act. One statute at the beginning of Richard II's reign spoke of the practice by which a lord would give his neighbours "hats and liveries . . . by such covenant that every one of them shall maintain him in all quarrels, whether reasonable or not"; another complained at those who, "desiring to make maintenance in their marches, do gather them together to a great number of men and archers to the manner of war . . . and, refusing and setting apart all processes of law, do ride in great routs . . . and take possession and set them in divers manors and lands, . . . and ravish women and damsels . . . and beat and

[1] *Cohen*, 481; *Owst, Literature and Pulpit*, 339-49.

maim, murder and slay the people for to have their wives and goods."[1] In 1378 the Commons procured a special commission to travel the country to restore order. Yet little came of it. For there was no national army or police force, and no-one dared incur the wrath of a neighbour who could use a private one to put the law on his side. The only prudent course was to seek the latter's protection.

The Edwardian device of replacing a disintegrating feudal military system by paying the rich and warlike to raise levies on a cash basis had created problems which were beyond the Crown's power to control. Nor did that other Edwardian innovation—a magistracy composed of local gentry—afford any solution. At the beginning of Edward III's reign, following the precedent set by his grandfather, it had been enacted that "in every shire good and lawful men who are not maintainers of evil barrators shall be assigned to keep the peace." A generation later these conservators of the peace, as they were called, had been given power to try felonies and misdemeanours, and in 1359 their functions had been combined with those of the justices set up to enforce the Statute of Labourers. Constituted as a court of Quarter Sessions to meet like the Commissioners of Labourers every three months, it took over much of the criminal jurisdiction performed by the shire courts. Directly responsible to the Crown and, after some petitioning by the Commons, paid like the shire knights during their sessions at the rate of four shillings a day for a knight, two for a squire and a shilling for their clerk,[2] "three or

---

[1] Jusserand, *English Wayfaring Life in the 14th Century*, 149-50; *McKisack*, 206-7; G. M. Trevelyan, *England in the Age of Wycliffe*, 59-60, 64-5; *Cohen*, 465-6.

   "And then Peace came into parliament and put forth a plea
   How Wrong against his will had ravished his wife
   And how he had raped Rose, Reginald's sweetheart,
   And had Margaret's maidenhood, much as she struggled . . .
   He borrowed the brown mare, but never brought her back;
   And never a farthing for her! Aye, he outfaced me,
   Maintaining his men to murder my servants;
   Forestalled me at the fair, fought me in bargaining,
   Broke down my barn-door and bore off my wheat,
   Tendering me a tally for ten quarters of oats!"
Visions from Piers Plowman (transl. into modern English by Nevill Coghill), p. 34-5.
   [2] *Tout, Chapters III*, 184.

four of the most worthy men" of every shire were appointed to sit as justices, together with a local lord and "others learned in the law." They were "to enquire concerning all those who have been pillagers and robbers in parts beyond the sea and have now returned and who go wandering and will not labour as they were wont to do, and put them into prison, to the end that people shall not be troubled or damaged nor the peace be blemished nor merchants or others passing on the king's highways be disturbed."

But in this the justices had small success. Wearing the livery of the local magnates, the disbanded soldiers proved a worse menace than ever. Having no police but the parish constables, the justices were powerless against such entrenched maintainers of lawlessness, who sometimes included the very lord with whom they sat on the bench, and invariably the neighbours to whom they looked for leadership in peace and war and to whose good-will they owed their appointments. The chief use of the new justices was in enforcing the enactments against villeins and artisans who took advantage of the labour shortage to better their condition. Yet as they themselves were the employers for whose benefit such enactments were passed, far from settling a disturbed countryside their intervention only filled the rural rank and file with bitterness.

. . . .

To the peasant the purpose of the law seemed to be to keep him down and enforce the servile status that deprived him of liberty and opportunity. In the thirty years after the first Statute of Labourers nearly nine thousand cases of enforcement were tried by the courts and, in nearly all, judgment was given in the employer's favour.[1] When a poor man appeared at the assizes or in Westminster Hall he found himself confronted by "a great rout" of clerks who sat writing and calling out names, was hustled by touting solicitors, janitors, ushers and beadles for fees and tips, and, like the suitor in John Lydgate's *London Lackpenny*, found, after doing reverence to the judge in his silken hood, that without means to fee learned counsel he could achieve nothing.

"I told him my case there as well as I could
How my goods were defrauded me by falsehood;

[1] *Hilton and Fagan*, 27.

I got not a move of his mouth for my meed,
And for lack of money I could not speed."

Yet the spirit of the common law did not favour serfdom. However strong the class bias and interest of its officers, it leant instinctively towards liberty. In this it differed from the civil law of the continental kingdoms which derived from Roman imperial law and a civilisation whose economic basis had been slavery. The English ideal was the "free and lawful man"— *liber et legalis homo*—entitled to equal justice, answerable for the acts of others only if he had commanded or consented to them, and presumed by the law to be a rational and responsible being and, as such, expected to play his part in administering justice by representing the local community before the king's judges and assisting them in the determination of fact. Though many once free peasants had become tied to the soil during the feudal anarchy of the Dark Ages[1] and their liberties had been further eroded under their grasping Norman conquerors, the genius of the common law was already granting to the bondsman rights which it regarded as the heritage of all. It treated him as free in his relation to everyone except his lord, protected him against even the latter's crimes and gave him the benefit of the doubt in questions affecting feudal status, holding, for instance, that the illegitimate child of parents, one of whom was free, must be free too, contrary to the practice elsewhere. Though it enforced serfdom where serfdom could be proved, it construed every sign of freedom as a proof of freedom. It allowed a lord whose bondsman had fled from his "villein nest" a writ, *de nativo habendo*, bidding the sheriff hand over the fugitive, but it allowed the latter another, *de libertate probanda*, which set him at liberty until the lord had proved in the king's courts a right to his return. "In the beginning," said Justice Herle in a judgment of Edward II's reign, "every man in the world was free, and the law is so favourable to liberty that he who is once found free and of free estate in a court of record shall be holden free for ever unless some later act of his own makes him villein."[2]

Nor was the peasant hostile to law; it was lawyers he hated.

[1] See *Makers of the Realm*, 119-23.
[2] *Y.B., 3 Ed. II*, 94 (Selden Society), cit. *Bennett*, 309.

He was the descendant of the Anglo-Saxon and Danish freeman whose proudest boast had been that he was "moot-worthy." In the manor court he still sat, like his forest forebears, as a dooms-man, served on its juries and, in his corporate capacity, helped to judge questions of law and fact. For though with its profits and fines the court belonged to the lord and was presided over by his steward, its judgments were given by the whole body of its suitors. When a bondsman offended against its rules and customs and those of the manor he was judged by his own peers, just as the lords in the great council or parliament of the realm at Westminster were judged by theirs. And the security of his holding was witnessed and assured by the testimony and judg-ments of the court. Within the limits set by his villein status, it was for him both a court of justice and a court of record, and the entry on its rolls—and the copy which he purchased from its clerk when he paid the lord's fine before entering on his father's inheritance—were the title-deeds of his property, even though that property, in the eyes of the king's law, was no freehold.

It was because he was not a slave, was conscious that he was the heir of men who had been free and was beginning to ask how he came to be otherwise, that the villein so resented servile status. During the last century his position had been steadily improving, whether he was a well-to-do yardlander farming two or three hundred acres or a mere landless cottar earning his daily bread by wages. Compared with the wretched peasantry of the con-tinent, he was not too badly off except when the harvest failed; the bowmen of Crécy had not been drawn from an oppressed populace. It was a commonplace to contrast the lot of the stalwart English husbandman with that of the French serf, wrapped in sacking and living on apples and bitter rye-bread, who had perpetrated the fearful brutalities of the Jacquerie. Yet all this made the English bondsman not more contented with his lot but less. His anger at those who put restraints on him was increased by the spectacle of expanding freedom in the chartered towns which had sprung up in every part of England and to which so many of the younger men of his village had fled to better their condition. Some of these, who had survived the harsh conditions and competition of the medieval town, had grown rich and famous.

Because of this and for other reasons there was a captious, bitter, disillusioned spirit abroad. The strain and cost of the war, with its latter disasters and humiliations and the successive visitations of the Black Death had all tended to shake men's faith in society. The pestilence which had driven weak natures to a hectic pursuit of pleasure, elevating the self-indulgence of the moment above duty and morality, had left only half the labour formerly available to do the nation's work and supply the luxuries of the rich. For a generation the burden of war debts and taxes had borne with what seemed insupportable severity on the survivors. The result was a widespread sense of frustration, of loss of familiar standards, of resentment between employer and employed, landowner and husbandman, government and taxpayer. Everyone tended to blame someone else for his sufferings.

Deep down the malaise of England after the Black Death was spiritual. It was the sickness of soul of a people who felt that justice was being outraged. The old static feudalism, in which every man knew and accepted his place, was disintegrating; the more fluid society that was replacing it was on the make and given to lavish and ostentatious luxury. The reign of Edward III had witnessed a steady rise in the standards of comfort, not only of the aristocracy but of new classes—financiers, merchants, woolmasters, franklins, master-craftsmen, millers, even farmers. Hearths with chimneys had taken the place in rich men's houses of sooty open fires; Flemish glass had appeared in traceried windows; dovecots, fishponds and nut-alleys were laid out in parks and gardens; manor-houses and fine merchants' dwellings, with private bedrooms and plastered walls, were rising in place of the old gloomy fortresses where men and beasts had slept together on filthy, rush-strewn floors in draughty halls, full of smoke and stink. Yet such signs of progress struck moralists like William Langland as symptoms of a diseased society; of a selfish decline from the virtues of austerer days:

"Ailing is the hall   each day in the week
Where the lord nor the lady   liketh not to sit.
Now hath each rich man   a rule to eaten by himself
In a privy parlour,   for poor men's sake,
Or in a chamber with a chimney,   and leave the chief hall
That was made for meals   and men to eaten in."

All this was the result of an advance in civilization, arts and sciences. Exchange of goods and merchandise had thrown the career open to the talents. In every city a race of men had arisen who pursued money-making as an end in itself, who bought and sold not primarily to supply the consumer with goods but to increase their stock of money and use it for making more. Usury, forestalling, regrating, making a corner in commodities, and artificially lowering market-prices in order to buy and raising them in order to sell—all the practices which the Church had taught were unchristian and unneighbourly—were pursued as a profession by men who made fortunes by doing so and put ordinary folk out of countenance by extravagant living and the grandeur of their ways. Merchants whose grandfathers or even fathers had been simple craftsmen or serfs were addressed by their fellow townsmen as worshipful or sire, wore scarlet robes and costly furs as masters and liverymen of monopolistic merchant companies founded originally to protect and foster honest craftsmanship. Instead of mixing socially with their employees they hobnobbed with lords and even princes; Sir Henry Pickard, Master of the Vintners Company, is said on one day in 1364 to have entertained four kings to dinner in the livery hall.[1] The bitterest hatred of the 'good' parliament was reserved for another vintner, Richard Lyons, whose memorial brass, as recorded by Stowe, depicted him with "a little beard forked, a gown girt down to his feet of branched damask wrought with the likeness of flowers, a large purse on his right side hanging in a belt from his left shoulder, a plain hood about his neck." With his patron, Lord Latimer the treasurer, he was accused of "buying up all the merchandise that came into England and setting prices at their own pleasure, whereby they made such a scarcity of things saleable that the common sort of people could scarcely live."

Not all great merchants were crooks; even Lyons was probably maligned. By their own standards most of them were worthy, if self-important, men whose bond could be trusted by their fellows; they could hardly have continued to succeeed otherwise. Yet there was a widespread feeling that vintners diluted wine, that woolmongers cheated wool-growers, that

[1] Of France, Scotland, Denmark and Cyprus—the first two being then prisoners in England.

grocers and corn-merchants sold false measure, that those who lent money to the Crown cheated the tax-payer, and that if a man had grown rich by trade he must be a rogue. And some of those who had made money out of the French war were vulgar upstarts with extravagant standards of display and notorious for jobbery and corruption. "Soapmongers and their sons for silver," wrote the indignant Langland, "are made knights." "Covetise hath dominion over all things," complained his fellow poet, Gower; "there is no city or good town where Trick does not rob to enrich himself. Trick at Bordeaux, Trick at Sevile, Trick at Paris buys and sells; Trick has his ships and servants, and of the noblest riches, Trick has ten times more than other folk."

Running through society, including the Church, was this sense of division, strife and covetousness. "Avarice," a preacher said, "makes men fight one another like dogs over a bone." By its side went "the foul sin of pride." Both the old ruling class and the new vied in the extravagance of their cloths, feasts and entertainments; "in such manner they spent and wasted their riches with abuses and ludicrous wantonness that the common voice of the people exclaimed." The age was marked by absurd fashions in clothes: peaked and curled shoes with toes so long that their wearers were sometimes forced to walk upstairs backwards or hand their shoes to their pages to carry[1]; ladies' fantastic and towering head-dresses; the mincing gait, long hair and trailing sleeves of the young courtiers who often squandered as much on their pampered bodies as would have fed and clothed a whole village. Contrasted with "the gay robes, the soft sheets, the small shirtes" of the rich was the peasant, with his garment of hodden grey, eating cold cabbage, bacon and penny ale; his wattle-and-log hut full of holes; the poor Norfolk deerstalker whose feet were so putrefied by the dungeons of Norwich castle that he could not walk at his trial, and his eight fellow-prisoners who died in Northampton gaol from hunger, thirst and want. "I have no penny," declared Langland's Piers Plowman,

> "pullets for to buy
> Neither geese nor gris   but two green cheeses,

[1] *Mitchell and Leys*, 199.

A few curds and cream   and a cake of oats,
And two loaves of beans and bran   to bake for my bairns."
To him it seemed a denial of Christianity that the honest poor
should be defrauded. His heart was stirred and his indignation
roused for "prisoners in pits" and poor folk in cottages "charged
with children and chief lord's rent," and country women "rising
with rue in winter nights to rock the cradle,"

"To card and to comb   to clout and to wash; . . .
Many the children   and nought but a man's hands
To clothe and feed them   and few pennies taken."

Out of the air of fourteenth-century England, with all its
glaring inequalities, arose the conviction—so strangely contrasted
with the assumptions of the warrior and prelate class—that "the
peasant maintained the state of the world" and was receiving less
than justice. It was put in its highest form by Langland, the
underlying theme of whose poem on the divine mercy and forgiveness of God was that Christ's sacrifice demanded from men
in return just living and just dealing—honest work and loving
kindness:

"For we are all Christ's creatures   and of his coffers rich
And brethren of one blood   as well beggars as earls; . . .
Therefore love we as true brethren   and each man laugh on
    the other,
And of that each man can spare   give aid when it is needed,
And every man help the other,   for go hence we all shall."

He himself examined his conscience on this issue, comparing his
idle life as a chantry clerk with that of the peasant folk among
whom he had grown up. "Can you," Reason asked him,

"cock up haycocks   and pitch them in the cart?
Or can you handle a scythe   or make a heap of sheaves?
Or keep my corn in my croft   from pickers and stealers?
Can you shape a shoe, cut clothes   or take care of cattle?
Can you hedge or harrow   or herd the hogs or geese?
Or any kind of craft   the community needs?"

His poem voiced the recurring English reaction to the contrast
between ill-used wealth and undeserved destitution, with its
characteristic resolve, not to destroy society, but to redress the
balance. Though it never seems to have attained the dignity of

an illuminated manuscript—the *imprimatur* of fashionable esteem in that intensely aristocratic age—for a work written before printing by a man without rank or fortune, it had an astonishing success; some sixty copies have survived and, since it circulated among the poor and lowly, many more must have perished. Overlooked by the rich like the *Pilgrim's Progress* of a later age, its readers and copyists were probably parish priests—for it is hardly likely to have appealed much to friars—and it may have been through them and their sermons that the name of its humble peasant hero and his identification with the crucified Christ became so widely known. At the end of the fourteenth and the beginning of the fifteenth century there appeared on the nave walls of parish churches in southern England a number of paintings, crude and almost certainly executed by local hands, of Christ naked, lacerated and bleeding, with a carpenter's tools—mallet, hammer, knife, axe, pincers, horn and wheel—haloed round his head. This figure of "Christ of the Trades," is to be found in churches as far apart as Pembrokeshire and Suffolk. Many more probably disappeared during the Reformation; among the best preserved are those at Ampney St. Mary in the Cotswolds—not far from the hillside on which Langland saw silhouetted the tower of Truth—at Hessett in Suffolk and at Stedham in Sussex. In the first, the labouring Christ faces a painting of the hero of knightly chivalry, St. George slaying the dragon; in the last, of the Virgin sheltering the congregation under her cloak.[1]

·   ·   ·   ·   ·   ·   ·   ·

There was a wide gap between the patient, Christ-like crafts-man and peasant of the wall-paintings, of Langland's dream, and the angry labourer refusing service for his lord, cursing land-lords, monks and lawyers and fingering his bow. It was not hard to inflame uneducated men with a sense of injury, and it was not the selfless side of human nature that was inflamed. The poet himself was well aware of it. "Then," he wrote,

"would Wastour not work   but wandren about . . .
Labourers, that have no land   to live on but their hands,
Deigned not to dine today   on yesterday's cabbage,

[1] *Borenius and Tristram*, 29-35; see also *Speculum*, vol. 22, p. 462-5.

No penny ale may please them   nor no piece of bacon,
But if it be fresh flesh or fish   fried or baked."

He depicted the runnagate villein, demanding ever higher wages, who, when refused,

"would wail the time   that ever he was workman born;
Then curseth he the king   and all his Council with him
That lay down such laws   the labourers to grieve."

Parliament was being flouted and the Statute of Labourers made a dead letter by surly villeins standing idle in the fields or tramping in angry companies to the nearest town to sell their labour to those who would pay highest for it. Phrases like "stand together!" "make a good end of what hath been begun!" passed from shire to shire, and wandering agitators preached incendiary sermons on village greens. "Things will never go well in England," proclaimed the defrocked hedge-priest and demagogue, John Ball, "so long as goods be not in common and so long as there be villeins and gentlemen. By what right are they whom we call lords greater than we?" "We are formed," he declared, "in Christ's likeness and they treat us like beasts."

It was an age of war and violence; war always breeds violence. Resentment amongst the labouring classes against their oppressors was not confined to England. In the middle of the century the Roman mob had risen under the demagogue Rienzo; a decade later occurred the terrifying Jacquerie in northern France. Wherever men were brought together in large numbers to serve masters who catered for the luxuries of the rich, the spirit of rebellion was present. In 1378 the oppressed woolcarders of Florence had revolted against the merchant oligarchs of the city, stormed the palazzo of the Commune and installed one of their members as Gonfalonier of Justice. A year later the weavers of Ghent and Bruges and the Flemish cloth towns had risen and, under a second van Artevelde, son of Edward III's old ally, were still defying their count and the French king.

In England unrest so far had mainly taken the form of mass withdrawals of labour-services, particularly in places where the lord was an impersonal ecclesiastical corporation. In 1378, after the jurymen of Harmsworth, Middlesex—the property of a Norman abbey—had defied the lord's steward by returning a

false verdict in favour of their fellow villeins who had absented
themselves from the previous year's haymaking, the villagers
deliberately opened the river sluices to flood the hay. There
were mob rescues of fugitive bondsmen as they were being haled
back to their "villein nests", and armed assemblies by night to
poach the lord's woods and slay his game. The labour laws, too,
help to explain the passion and vehemence of some of these
sudden explosions of rustic wrath, often on seemingly trivial
pretexts. Englishmen were not prepared to suffer the indignity
of being branded on the forehead with an "F" for "falsehood"
because they took day-hire or demanded more than the inadequate statutory wage allowed by parliament. As far back as the
year before Poitiers, when feeling against this form of class
legislation was running particularly strong, the peasants from the
villages round Oxford joined the townsmen in a murderous
attack on the university—later known as St. Scholastica's Day—
distinguishing themselves by their savagery and furious cries of
"Havak, havoc, smygt faste, gyf good knok."[1]

During the opening years of Richard's reign such riots had
grown ominously in number. They were fomented by the egali-
tarian sermons of friars and wandering priests like John Ball,
who for the past twenty years had been tramping the country
preaching, in defiance of the ecclesiastical authorities, against the
rich "possessioners" of Church and State. In the words of
the chronicler Walsingham, he preached "those things which he
knew would be pleasing to the common people, speaking evil
both of ecclesiastical and temporal lords, and won the goodwill
of the common people rather than merit in the sight of God.
For he taught that tithes ought not to be paid unless he who gave
them was richer than the parson who received them. He also
taught that tithes and oblations should be withheld if the
parishioner was known to be a better man than the priest." Forbidden to preach in church, he continued to do so in streets,
villages and fields until he got himself excommunicated. Nothing,
however, stopped him, and, though he several times suffered
imprisonment, as soon as he got out he started again. He also
took to circulating inflammatory letters full of dark riddles and
rhymes calling on the virtuous poor to prepare for the day

[1] *McKisack*, 204.

when they could fall on their oppressors. "John Ball, St. Mary's priest," ran one, "greeteth well all manner of men and biddeth them in the name of the Trinity, Father, Son and Holy Ghost, stand manlike together in truth, and help truth, and truth shall help you.

> "Now reigneth price in price,
> Covetise is holden wise,
> Lechery without shame,
> Gluttony without blame,
> Envy reigneth with reason
> And sloth is taken in great season.
> God do bote" (amend) "for now is time."[1]

On top of this increasingly strained situation came the demand for the shilling poll-tax in the winter of 1380/1. The result was a wholesale falsification by the villages of southern England of the tax-returns, so much so that when the latter reached the commissioners it appeared that the population of the country had fallen by a third since the last poll-tax. The amount collected fell far below what was expected and the Government was furious. On March 16th 1381 the Council found that the local collectors had been guilty of gross negligence and favouritism and appointed a new commission to scrutinize the lists and enforce payment from evaders.

The decision was received with universal execration. It was spoken of as a corrupt job engineered for the private profit of the head of the commission of revision, John Legge, a serjeant-at-law, and of the treasurer, Sir Robert Hales—"Hob the robber," as he was called. When news of a further descent of tax assessors reached the villages, the ignorant supposed that a new tax was to be levied on top of that already paid. Everywhere in the populous counties of the south-east, rustic opinion was at boiling point against tax-collectors, escheators, jurymen, lawyers and royal officials in general and against the archbishop and treasurer in particular and, illogically enough, for he was no longer actively engaged in government but absent on a mission in Scotland, John of Gaunt.

No-one in authority treated the dissatisfaction of the peasantry

[1] *Hilton and Fagan*, 102; *Steel* 58-73

very seriously. But when at the end of May the new poll-tax commissioner for Essex, Thomas Bampton, appeared at Brentwood with two serjeants-at-arms to open enquiries into the returns for the hundred of Barstaple, he was met by the representatives of the defaulting townships with a sullen refusal to pay. They possessed, they said, their receipt for the subsidy and would not pay a penny more. But it was the fishermen and fowlers of the Thames estuary—the men of the sea and salt-water creeks—who provided the spark that fired the revolution of working-class England. Summoning to their aid their neighbours from Corringham and Stanford-le-Hope, the men of Fobbing-by-Tilbury met Bampton's threats of arrest with open violence, and with sticks and stones drove him and his men out of the town.

This was more than the government could ignore. On Sunday, June 2nd, the chief justice of the Common Pleas, Sir Robert Belknap, descended on Brentford with a commission of trailbaston and an escort of pikesmen. His business was to punish the rioters and hang the ringleaders. He found the place in a ferment. For by now the rebellious fishermen had prevailed on the entire neighbourhood to rise. Armed with staves, pitchforks and bows, a mob surrounded the judge, seized and burnt his papers and made him swear on his knees never to hold another commission. They then murdered his three clerks and three local tax-assessors or jurymen whose names they had made him reveal. Sticking their heads on poles they bore them in triumph round the villages of south-east Essex, while the terrified Belknap fled back to London.

On the same day trouble began on the other side of the Thames. At Erith in Kent a band of rioters broke into the monastery of Lesnes and made the abbot swear to support them. The ringleaders then crossed the river to take counsel of the men of Essex. During the next few days rebellion spread northwards across the county as rioters carried their messages from parish to parish. Everywhere government agents were attacked, their houses plundered and their records and papers thrown into courtyard or street and burnt. The admiral of the Essex coast, Edmund de la Mare of Peldon, and the sheriff, John Sewall of Coggeshall, had their homes sacked, the former's papers being carried on a pitchfork at the head of the triumphant fishermen. At every manor visited, a bonfire was made of all charters and manorial rolls.

It was as though the whole system of law and government, built up over centuries, was being repudiated by the common people. Yet though damage to property was widespread, there was comparatively little loss of life, most of the local lords managing to escape. The chief escheator of the county was murdered as well as a number of Flemish merchants in Colchester where the mob rose at the approach of the peasantry. Had the treasurer been at his home at Temple Cressing instead of in London, he would certainly have been torn to pieces; as it was, his "very beautiful and delectable manor," as a chronicler described it, was burnt to the ground after the populace had eaten the fine fare and broached "the three tuns of good wine" which he had laid in for an impending meeting of the chapter-general of the Order of St. John of Jerusalem of which he was master.

Meanwhile trouble was growing in Kent. On the day after the assault on the chief justice at Brentwood two serjeants-at-arms acting for Sir Simon Burley, the king's tutor, arrested a respected burgess of Gravesend on the ground that he was a runaway serf. When the townsfolk declined to pay £300 for his manumission—at least £15,000 in today's purchasing-power—the poor man was sent to the dungeons of Rochester castle. Two days later, on Wednesday June 5th, heartened by the arrival of a hundred insurgents from Essex, the people of all the towns and villages on the south bank of the river between Erith and Gravesend rose in rebellion. They were careful, however, to stress in a proclamation listing the crimes of their young sovereign's ministers that, though there were "more kings than one in the land," they wished for none but Richard. Patriotically they added that, "none dwelling within twelve miles of the sea should go with them but should keep the coast of the sea from enemies."

Next day, June 6th, decided the fate of Kent. At one end of the county the men of Gravesend and Dartford marched on Rochester. At the other end a commission of trailbaston, directed against tax-evaders and accompanied by the hated John Legge, was prevented from entering Canterbury. Rochester Castle, though strong enough to withstand a siege for weeks, was surrendered by its constable that afternoon after several ineffective attempts to storm it. Probably it was under-garrisoned, but, like almost everyone else, the defenders were bemused by the fury and turbulence of the mob. For the rustic population of England to behave in such a way seemed something outside nature: it was as though the animals had rebelled.

Certainly the government seemed unable to grasp the situation. Like the local authorities it remained inert throughout that critical first week of June, helplessly watching the course of events. The chancellor, its head, was the gentle primate, Simon Thebaud of Sudbury—the son of a Suffolk trader whose family had grown rich supplying the local gentry with luxury goods and developing the new rural cloth industry. He was utterly without martial instinct or experience. The king's uncles were far away; John of Gaunt was in Edinburgh negotiating a truce with the Scots, Thomas of Woodstock was in the Welsh marches and Edmund of Cambridge had just sailed for Portugal. On news of the outbreak a messenger had been sent to Plymouth to countermand the expedition but arrived too late. Owing to the needs of the English garrisons in France and Brittany the country was almost denuded of troops except on the remote Scottish and Welsh borders. In the capital and the crucial south-east there were only a few hundred men-at-arms and archers guarding the king, and a small force which the old condottiere, Sir Robert Knollys, had started to collect in his London house to reinforce Brittany. Nothing was done to call out the country gentry and their retainers who in the insurgent counties to the east and north of London were paralysed with fear.

But if the government was without an active head, the insurgents had found one. On Friday May 7th the men of Kent marched up the Medway valley from Rochester to Maidstone, where they were welcomed by the populace who rose and plundered the richer inhabitants, murdering one of them. Here they chose as their captain one Wat Tyler. Little is known of his past, but according to Froissart he had seen service in the French wars and, it subsequently transpired, like many old soldiers, had since been earning a livelihood by highway robbery. He was clearly a mob orator of genius, for he immediately reduced to discipline the motley throng of excited peasants and artisans. And he quickly showed himself a man of action and exceptional military talent.

On the day he assumed command Tyler issued a proclamation setting out the insurgents' aims. They would admit, he said, no allegiance except to "King Richard and the true commons"— in other words, themselves—and have no king named John, a reference to the Duke of Lancaster. No tax should be levied "save the fifteenths which their fathers and forebears knew and accepted," and everyone should hold himself in readiness to march, when called upon, to remove the traitors around the king and root out and destroy the lawyers and officials who had corrupted the realm.

The rebels not only found a military leader. They acquired a spiritual one. Among the prisoners released from Maidstone gaol was John Ball. Only a few weeks before, the long-suffering archbishop had clapped him in again, describing how he had "slunk back to our diocese like the fox that evaded the hunter, and feared not to preach and argue both in the churches and churchyards and in markets and other profane places, there beguiling the ears of the laity by his invective and putting about such scandals concerning our person and those of other prelates and clergy and—what is worse—using concerning the holy father himself language such as shamed the ears of good Christians." The irrepressible preacher now found himself free again and with a ready-made congregation of twenty-thousand ragged enthusiasts after his own heart. According to Froissart, who, though often an unreliable witness, visited England soon after the rising and was clearly fascinated by the whole affair, he addressed them in these terms:

"My good friends, matters cannot go well in England until all things be held in common; when there shall be neither vassals nor lords; when the lords shall be no more masters than ourselves. How ill they behave to us! For what reason do they thus hold us in bondage? Are we not all descended from the same parents, Adam and Eve? And what can they show, or what reason can they give, why they should be more masters than ourselves? They are clothed in velvet and rich stuffs, ornamented with ermine and other furs, while we are forced to wear poor clothing. They have wines, spices and fine bread, while we have only rye and the refuse of the straw; and when we drink, it must be water. They have handsome seats and manors, while we must brave the wind and rain in our labours in the field; and it is by our labours that they have wherewith to support their pomp. We are called slaves and, if we do not perform our service we are beaten, and we have no sovereign to whom we can complain or would be willing to hear us. Let us go to the king and remonstrate with him. He is young and from him we may obtain a favourable answer, and, if not, we must ourselves seek to amend our conditions."

At the same time the preacher sent out to the villages of Kent and Essex more of his inflammatory missives:

> "John Ball
>
> Greeteth you all,
>
> And doth you to understand
>
> He hath rung your bell.
>
> Now with right and might,
>
> Will and skill,
>
> God speed every dell!"

Another, written under a pseudonym and addressed to the men of Essex, was subsequently found in the pocket of a rioter condemned to be hanged.

"John Schep, sometime Saint Mary's priest of York, and now of Colchester, greets well John Nameless and John the Miller and John Carter and bids them that they beware of guile in the town, and stand together in God's name, and bids Piers Plowman go to his work and chastise well Hob the Robber. And take with you John Trueman and all his fellows and more, and look sharp you to your own head and no more.

> "John the Miller hath ground small, small, small.
>
> The King's Son of heaven shall pay for all.
>
> Beware or you will be in woe
>
> Know your true friend from your foe.
>
> Have enough and say 'Hello!'

And do well and better and flee from sin,
And seek true peace and hold therein.
And so bids John Trueman and all his fellows."[1]

Tyler and Ball—brigand and hedgerow preacher—were the leaders "the true commons" needed. While Ball addressed himself to his sympathizers, Tyler acted. Sending emissaries to urge the surrounding villages to rise and join him at Maidstone, he set out with several thousand followers for Canterbury. By midday on the 10th he had reached the city, where he was greeted with enthusiasm by the inhabitants, all those, that is, who had nothing to lose. On enquiring whether there were any traitors in the town, he was directed to the houses of the local notables, three of whom he had executed on the spot. Then, having burnt the judicial and financial records of the shire, beaten up the sheriff and sacked the castle, letting out the prisoners from the gaols he and his followers poured, a vast tumultuous multitude, into the cathedral during Mass. Here with one voice they cried out to the monks to elect a new archbishop of Canterbury in place of Sudbury whom they declared to be a traitor and "about to be beheaded for his iniquity." They also extracted an oath of fealty to the king and true commons from the mayor and corporation and—for the summer pilgrimage season was at its height—recruited their ranks by a number of pilgrims. At the same time they dispatched agitators to the towns and villages of East Kent.

Early on Tuesday June 11th, having spent less than twenty-four hours in Canterbury and set the eastern weald and coast from Sandwich to Appledore aflame, Tyler set off again. Reinforcements poured in as he marched. By nightfall he was back in Maidstone, having covered eighty miles in two days. Then, pausing only for the night, he marched with his entire host before dawn on the 12th for the capital, sending messengers into Sussex and the western counties to summon the commons to join him and "close London round about." Simultaneously on the other side of the Thames the Essex insurgents, who by now had won

---

[1] T. Walsingham, *Historia Anglicana* II, 32; *Hilton and Fagan* 99 *et seq.* John Ball had begun his career as a priest attached to the abbey of St. Mary's and later worked at Colchester. *D.N.B.*

complete control of the county, began a parallel march under the captaincy of Thomas Farringdon, an aggrieved Londoner.

While the two hosts converged on the capital, terror reigned on either side of their march as village mobs smoked out royal and manorial officials, lawyers and unpopular landlords, breaking into their houses and burning every record they could find. They would have, they declared, "no bondsmen in England." Many of the gentry took to the woods, among them the poet John Gower, who afterwards recalled in his long Latin epic, *Vox Clamantis*, the pangs of hunger he suffered while living on acorns and trembling for his life in wet coppices. Others, less fearful or unpopular, made timely contributions to the "cause" and took the oath of fidelity to the "king and true commons." A few, but only a few, were murdered, while others, being persons of distinction who had not done anything to make themselves unpopular, were carried off as hostages to grace Wat Tyler's entourage, including Sir Thomas Cobham and Sir Thomas Tryvet, a hero of the wars.

Meanwhile the authorities had at last resolved to act. On either the Tuesday or Wednesday Tyler's men, pouring towards the capital, were met by messengers from the king at Windsor to ask why they were raising rebellion and what they sought. Their answer was that they were coming to deliver him from traitors. They also presented a petition asking for the heads of the Duke of Lancaster and fourteen other notables, including the chancellor, treasurer and every leading member of the government. On receipt of this the king and his advisers left hastily for London and the Tower to form a focus of resistance round which the forces of order could rally. The king's mother and her ladies who had been on a summer pilgrimage to the Kentish shrines, also set out for the same place of refuge. On the way they encountered the rebel vanguard. Yet, though greatly frightened, they were subjected to nothing worse than a little ribald jesting and were allowed to continue their journey to the capital. Here the mayor, William Walworth, after escorting his sovereign to the Tower, was busy putting the city into a state of defence.

That evening the Kentish host encamped on the Blackheath heights, looking down across the Thames to the distant city. On the opposite bank the Essex men took up their station in the Mile End fields outside the suburb of Whitechapel and about a mile to the east of the walls and the Aldgate. Some of the less exhausted Kentish rebels continued as far as Southwark, where, welcomed by the local mob, they burnt a bawdy house rented by some Flemish women from Mayor Walworth and let out the prisoners from the Marshalsea and King's Bench. Finding the drawbridge in the centre of London Bridge raised against them, they went on to Lambeth where they sacked the archbishop's palace and the house of John Imworth, the warden of the Marshalsea.

It was not only the proletariat of Southwark who sympathized with the insurgents. There were thousands of journeymen, apprentices and labourers inside the city walls who did so too. On the mayor's orders the gates had been closed and entrusted to the aldermen and watch of the adjacent wards. But there were bitter rivalries among the city's rulers. The victualling interests were at daggers drawn with the older merchants, drapers and mercers, who, employing labour on a large scale, favoured a policy of free trade and low-priced food in order to keep down wages and feed their journeymen and apprentices cheaply—a matter of vital importance to them since the labour shortage caused by the Black Death. Both were monopolists, but, to overthrow their rivals the victuallers had formed an alliance with the discontented city proletariat—wage-earners and small craftsmen—who regarded their employers and the capitalists who controlled the market for their handiwork in much the same light as the villeins regarded their lords. Among three aldermen whom the mayor despatched to urge the insurgents to keep the peace was a certain John Horne, a fishmonger, who, separating himself from his companions, sought a private interview with Tyler and secretly promised his support. When he returned to London he not only assured the mayor that the marchers were honest patriots who would do the city no harm but, under cover of darkness, smuggled three agitators across the river to stir up the mob.

Earlier that evening an emissary from the rebel camp had travelled by boat from Greenwich to London to seek an interview with the king and council. This was the constable of Rochester castle, Sir John Newton, who for the past week had been a prisoner of the insurgents. Brought into the presence and given leave to speak, he explained that, though his captors would do the king no harm, they were determined to meet him face to face to communicate certain matters of which he had no charge to speak. Since they held his children as hostages and would slay them if he failed to return, he begged for an answer that would appease them and show that he had delivered his message.

To this after some hesitation the Council agreed. Next morning at prime the king and his lords embarked in five barges for Greenwich. Here, on the shore below Blackheath, the Kentish men, after a hungry and sleepless night, were assembled in battle array under two great banners of St. George. While they waited, Mass was celebrated, it being Corpus Christi day, and afterwards John Ball preached, taking as his text the old popular rhyme:

"When Adam delved and Eve span
Who was then the gentleman?"

According to the St. Albans chronicler, "he strove to prove that from the beginning all men were created equal by nature, and that servitude had been introduced by the unjust oppression of wicked men against God's will, for if it had pleased Him to create serfs, surely in the beginning of the world He would have decreed who was to be a serf and who a lord. . . . Wherefore they should be prudent men, and, with the love of a good husbandman tilling his fields and uprooting and destroying the tares which choke the grain, they should hasten to do the following things. First, they should kill the great lords of the kingdom; second, they should slay lawyers, judges and jurors; finally they should root out all those whom they knew to be likely to be harmful to the commonwealth in future. Thus they would obtain peace and security, for, when the great ones had been removed, there would be equal liberty and nobility and dignity and power for all." "When he had preached this and much other madness," wrote the disgusted chronicler, "the commons held him in such high favour that they acclaimed him the future archbishop and chancellor of the realm."[1]

Whether it was this sermon or the presence of the archbishop in the royal barge or the fact that the Kentishmen had not breakfasted, they greeted the king's arrival with such a tumult of shouting that he was unable to make himself heard. "Sirs," he

[1] T. Walsingham, *Historia Anglicana* II, 32.

kept calling across the water as the rowers rested on their oars just out of reach of the frantic multitude, "what do you want? Tell me now that I have come to talk to you." But as the crowd steadily grew more threatening, fearing lest some of the bowmen might start to shoot, the Earl of Salisbury—by far the most experienced soldier present—ordered the boats to put out into midstream and return to the Tower.

At that both the Kentish host and the Essex men who had been watching from the other shore set up a great shout of "Treason" and, with their banners and pennants, moved off towards London. Access to the city's markets and provision shops had by now become essential if they were not to have to disperse through hunger—a fact on which the authorities were counting. Within the city, processions of clergy were marching through the streets praying for peace, while crowds of sympathizers with the insurgents were gathering in the poorer lanes and alleys. For, though the city gates were still barred against them, the agitators whom Horne had slipped into the city had not been idle. As Wat Tyler's men neared the southern approaches to the bridge they were again met by this liberal-minded fishmonger waving a royal standard which he had procured by a trick from the town clerk. And as, headed by this emblem of loyalty and respectability, they surged on to the bridge, the drawbridge in the midst of its shops and houses was lowered to them by the alderman of the Billingsgate ward. About the same time another alderman of the opposition faction let in the Essex men through the Aldgate.

Once the head of the rebel columns was in possession of the southern and eastern entrances the whole multitude poured in to the city, while the apprentices and journeymen and the labouring poor of the slums flocked into the streets to greet them. For a time the newcomers were too busy eating, drinking and gaping at the city sights to do much harm. But presently, refreshed by several huge barrels of ale which some rash philanthropists had broached in the streets and incited by the apprentices who had old scores to pay off against John of Gaunt, they set up a cry of "To the Savoy! To the Savoy!" The duke might be in Edinburgh, but the superb palace he had furnished from the plunder of France—and, as many supposed, of England—

stood a mile outside the western walls where the fields and gardens sloped down to the riverside from the Strand that linked London to Westminster. Thither the men of Kent, with thousands of excited apprentices—a great company with torches—made their way in an angry tumult, breaking into the Fleet prison on the way and letting out the criminals while the duke's servants fled as the shouting came nearer.

No time was wasted. In the general desire for justice or revenge even plundering was forbidden. Everything in the great house was hurled out of the windows—tapestry, sheets, coverlets, beds—and hacked or torn to pieces. Then the building was set on fire and burnt to the ground. At the height of the fire there was an explosion caused by three barrels of gunpowder, which were thrown into the flames in the belief that they contained specie. Some of the rioters afterwards continued towards Westminster where they destroyed the house of the under-sheriff of Middlesex and let the prisoners out of the gaol. Others, on their way back to the city, broke into the lawyers' home in the Temple, tore the tiles off the roof and took all the books, rolls and remembrances from the students' cupboards to make a bonfire. They also fired some shops and houses which had recently been built in Fleet street, declaring that never again should any house deface the beauty of that favourite country walk of the Londoners. Those who had gone on to Westminster returned by way of Holborn, setting light to the houses of several "traitors" pointed out to them by their London comrades and breaking open Newgate still further to enlarge their company. Meanwhile the men of Essex descended on the priory of St. John's, Clerkenwell, the headquarters of the Knights Hospitallers just outside the city's northern wall. Here they burnt the priory and hospital—"a great and horrible piece of damage for all time to come"—and murdered seven Flemings who had taken sanctuary in the church.

That night, while the insurgents camped round the royal fortress in the open spaces of Tower Hill and St. Catherine's wharf and while their leaders drew up lists of persons to be liquidated, the king and Council debated long and anxiously what was to be done. Since the morning their position had changed dramatically for the worse; instead of waiting behind London's walls while the rebels starved outside, they themselves were hemmed in the Tower, and the city it was supposed to dominate was in possession of a fanatic, uncontrollable mob. From a garret in one of the turrets into which he climbed the boy king could see twenty or thirty fires burning in different parts of the town. Beyond, the whole of the home counties to south and east were in revolt, while, unknown as yet to the beleaguered Council, the revolutionary ferment had spread that afternoon into Hertfordshire and Suffolk, where burgesses and bondsmen had risen together against the monks of England's two most famous abbeys, St. Albans and Bury.

The key to the situation lay, however, in the capital. If the mob who had taken possession of it could be defeated, the flames of revolt might be put out elsewhere. But, with London lost and the court imprisoned inside it, there was nothing round which the forces of order could rally. Mayor Walworth, a bluff and vigorous man, urged an immediate sally against the insurgents while they were sleeping off the effects of their evening's debauch. There were six hundred armed men-at-arms and archers in the Tower and a hundred or so more in Sir Robert Knollys's house and garden; with a bold front they would probably be joined by all the law-abiding in London. Only a small minority of the insurgents wore armour; if the loyal forces struck at once, thousands might be slain as they slept. But the Earl of Salisbury, who had fought at Crécy and Poitiers, thought otherwise. Once fighting began in the narrow streets and lanes, the rebels' immense superiority in numbers would tell and total disaster might ensue. "If we should begin a thing which we cannot achieve," he said, "we should never recover and we and our heirs would be disinherited and England would become a desert." Instead, he offered the Ulysses-like counsel that an attempt should be made to induce the rebels to disperse by fair words and promises, which could afterwards be repudiated as obtained under duress.

An earlier attempt that evening to persuade them to do so by putting up the king to address them from the ramparts and offer a free pardon to all who should go home had been shouted down in derision. Some more signal mark of royal trust was needed if the populace were to be appeased. It was, therefore, proposed that the king should offer to confer with the rebels in the Mile End fields and to ride out there next morning through their midst with such of his lords as were not expressly marked down for execution. While under cover of this bold move the crowds were drawn away from the Tower, the archbishop and treasurer and John of Gaunt's son and heir, young Henry Bolingbroke earl of Derby, could be smuggled out to safety by water.

The plan depended on the king's readiness to take the risk. But, though he appeared a little pensive, the boy was ready and even eager. He was now fourteen, and it was something to find that at last all the great lords and counsellors around him looked to him for leadership. As soon as it was light a proclamation was made from the walls and soon afterwards, surrounded by an immense multitude of excited country folk, the royal cortège set out along the Brentwood road for Mile End. But many of the Londoners stayed behind to watch the Tower, for the rebels' leaders were not so easily fooled. When the boat by which their intended victims attempted to escape appeared, it was forced to put back as soon as it emerged from the water-gate.

Nor did the royal ride to Mile End prove easy or pleasant. At one moment the Essex leader, Thomas Farringdon, a highly excitable man, seized the king's bridle, demanding to be avenged on that false traitor Prior Hales, the treasurer, who he said had deprived him of his property by fraud. So threatening was the crowd that the king's half-brothers, the Earl of Kent and Sir John Holland, finding themselves at the edge of the throng, seized the opportunity to gallop away and escape to open country to the north. When, however, the royal party arrived in the Mile End fields the simple country folk who were waiting there knelt before the king crying, "Welcome, our lord King Richard, if it pleases you we will have no other king but you." It was like the scene in the ballads when the sovereign whom Robin Hood and his men had captured revealed his identity and promised to restore every honest man to his own.

It must have seemed to many present that such a golden time had come when their young king—the son of England's hero, the Black Prince—announced that he would grant all their demands. He promised the abolition of serfdom, of villein services and seigneurial market monopolies, and that all holders of land in

villeinage should henceforth become free tenants at the modest
rent of 4d. an acre a year. Nor did he only promise them all
free pardons and an amnesty if they would return quietly to
their villages, but offered to give a royal banner to the men of
every county and place them under his special protection and
patronage. His words, as Froissart put it, "appeased well the
common people, such as were simple and good plain men." They
rather took the wind, however, out of their leaders' sails. The
latter, therefore, returned to the charge. "The commons," Tyler
told the king, "will that you suffer them to take and deal with all
the traitors who have sinned against you and the law." To
which the king replied that all should have due punishment as
could be proved by process of law to be traitors.

This, however, was scarcely what Tyler and his fellow-leaders
wanted. While the king, surrounded by the better disposed of
his humbler subjects, was helping to set them on their way to
their distant villages, the two captains of the commons of Kent
and Essex hurried back with a band of picked followers to the
Tower where a large crowd was still waiting outside the gates,
clamouring for the archbishop's and treasurer's blood. Pushing
through them they succeeded in bluffing their way into the
fortress itself either through the treachery of the guards or, more
probably, because, with the king and his lords expected back at
any moment, the portcullis was up and no one knew what to
do. Fraternizing with the soldiers, shaking their hands and
stroking their beards, the crowd pressed after their leaders into
the royal apartments, shouting for the traitors' blood. In their
search the king's bed was hacked to pieces and the Princess of
Wales subjected to such rude treatment that she was borne off
in a dead faint by her pages and put into a boat on the river.
John Legge, the serjeant-at-law who had drawn up the poll-tax
commission, and three of his clerks, the Duke of Lancaster's
physician, a Franciscan friar named Appleton, and several others
were found. The duke's son, Henry Bolingbroke—who eighteen
years later was to become king—was more fortunate, being saved
by the resource of one of his father's retainers. The archbishop
and treasurer were taken in the chapel, where, expecting death,
the former had just received the confession of the latter and
administered the last rites. Dragged by the mob into the court-

yard and across the cobbles to Tower hill, they were summarily beheaded across a log of wood. It was the third time in the country's history that an archbishop of Canterbury had been assaulted at the altar and brutally done to death.

After that, all pretence of moderation and order vanished. While the primate's head, stuck on a pike and crowned with his mitre, was being borne round the city before being set over the gateway to London Bridge—the traditional place for traitors— and the king, shunning the desecrated Tower, made his way with his escort to the royal wardrobe at Baynard's Castle near St. Paul's where his mother had taken refuge, the riff-raff of the capital and the peasants' army ran riot in the streets, forcing passers-by to cry, "With King Richard and the true commons" and putting everyone to death who refused. By nightfall "there was hardly a street in the city in which there were not bodies lying of those who had been slain."[1] The chief victims were the Flemish merchants who were hunted through the streets and killed wherever found; more than a hundred and fifty are said to have perished, including thirty-five who had taken shelter in St. Martin-in-the-Vintry and who were dragged from the altar and beheaded outside on a single block. Every disorderly person who had old grudges to pay off or property he coveted seized his opportunity; Alderman Horne, with a mob at his heels, paraded the streets bidding anyone who wanted justice against a neighbour to apply to him. Tyler himself hunted down and cut off the head of the great monopolist, Richard Lyons, whose servant he was at one time said to have been, while his lieutenant, Jack Straw, led a gang to burn the home of the murdered Sir Robert Hales, the treasurer, at Highbury. Far away in Suffolk at about the same hour the head of Sir John Cavendish, chief justice of the King's Bench, was being carried on a pike through the rejoicing streets of Bury St. Edmunds,[2] while his friend and neighbour, the prior of the great abbey, who had been hunted all day on the Mildenhall heaths,

[1] London Letter-book, H., fol. cxxxiii, Riley *Memorials of London* ii, 449-51 cit. *Rickert*, 365.

[2] He had been caught at Lakenheath as he was trying to cross the Brandon, a country woman having recognized him and pushed the ferry boat into midstream so that he should not escape his pursuers, who executed him on the spot.

cowered before his captors awaiting the trial that was to lead to his death next morning. Later, on the Saturday, when his head, too, was borne back on a pike to Bury, the crowd carried the heads of the two friends round the town together, making them converse and kiss one another.

Dawn on Saturday June 15th saw the nadir of the once proud kingdom whose princes a quarter of a century before had led the French king captive through the streets of London. From Lincolnshire, Leicester and Northampton to the coasts of Kent and Sussex its richest and most populous counties were aflame, while, as the news spread of London's capture and the king and Council's humiliation, other shires as far as Cornwall and Yorkshire crackled with rumours of impending rebellion. The greatest officers of state—the primate and chancellor, treasurer, and chief justice—had all been brutally done to death, and everywhere magnates and gentry were flying to the woods or, isolated and helpless in their homes, awaiting the sound of mobs and the light of torches. In London riot, plunder, arson and murder had continued all night and, though thousands of law-abiding peasants had returned to their homes on receiving the king's promise, thousands more, including their leaders and all the more violent and criminal elements, were in control both of the capital and what remained of the government.

The king spent the night at the wardrobe in Baynard's Castle, comforting his mother. His surrender at Mile End seemed to have achieved nothing, and though thirty royal clerks had been employed all the previous afternoon copying out pardons and charters, the hard core of the insurgents remained both unsatisfied and seemingly unsatiable. Yet, since there was no other way of loosening their stranglehold, Richard resolved, regardless of the risks involved, to try again. Accordingly on the morning of Saturday the 15th he proposed a further meeting with the commons and their leaders. This time the rendezvous was to be the cattle market at Smithfield, just outside the city's northwestern walls close to the church of St. Bartholomew the Great and the smoking ruins of the priory of St. John's, Clerkenwell.

Before proceeding there the king rode to Westminster Abbey to pray at the shrine of his ancestor, St. Edward the Confessor. Murder and sacrilege had been there that morning before him, a mob having broken into the sanctuary, tearing from the pillars of the shrine to which he had clung in terror the marshal of the Marshalsea—a man hated by the populace as being "without pity as a torturer." The monks of Westminster and the canons of St. Stephen's met the king at the abbey gates, barefooted and carrying their cross. For a while all knelt before the desecrated shrine while the young king confessed to the abbey's anchorite and received absolution, afterwards repairing to the little oratory in the royal closet of St. Stephen's chapel to pray before a golden image of the Virgin which had been a treasured possession of his family since the days of Henry III and was believed to have special protective powers.[1] It is possible that it is this deeply moving incident in the king's life rather than his coronation four years earlier that is depicted in the Wilton Diptych—the young Plantagenet, robed and crowned, kneeling before the figures of St. Edward, King Edmund the Martyr and St. John the Baptist whose hand rests on the boy's shoulder and all three of whom seem to be gazing fixedly and sternly as at some threatening force, while a winged galaxy of guardian angels, wearing Richard's badge of the hart, gather round the Virgin and her child beneath the banner of St. George.[2]

The king and his retainers, about two hundred strong, now mounted and rode on to Smithfield. Because of their peril they wore armour under their robes. They were joined at St. Bartholomew's church by Mayor Walworth and a small party, while on the opposite side of the market-place the entire insurgent

[1] See Maurice Hastings, *St. Stephen's Chapel*, 72-7. Many years later St. Stephen's chapel became the meeting-place of the House of Commons.

[2] In discussing the date and occasion of this lovely painting neither Dr. Evans in her volume of the *Oxford History of English Art* nor Margaret Rickert in her *Painting in Britain in the Middle Ages* seems to have considered this possibility, both inclining to attribute its occasion either to Richard's coronation at the age of eleven or his re-coronation in St. Stephen's chapel after his assumption of power in 1389 at the age of 23, while Mr. John Harvey in his paper read to the Society of Antiquaries of London in February 1957 attributes the painting to the closing years of the reign. Yet, whenever painted, the king depicted is neither a child nor a full-grown man, but unmistakably a boy in his teens. No event in Richard's life can have had greater significance to him than this occasion, and there seems a strong case for supposing that, though painted later—possibly for the ceremony in St. Stephen's in 1389—the artist had in mind this earlier and momentous occasion in the royal chapel.

army awaited in battle order. It must by now have been about five o'clock of the afternoon and the weather very hot.

Tyler now felt himself to be master of the kingdom. He was at the head of a host which outnumbered by many times the little royal band, and all day news had been coming in from every quarter of new risings. On the previous evening he had boasted to the rebel delegates from St. Albans that he would shave the beards—by which he meant slice off the heads—of all who opposed him, including their abbot, and that in a few days there would be no laws in England save those which proceeded from his mouth. "He came to the king," wrote the Anonimalle chronicler, "in a haughty fashion, mounted on a little horse so that he could be seen by the commons and carrying in his hand a dagger which he had taken from another man. When he had dismounted he half bent his knee and took the king by the hand and shook his arm forcibly and roughly, saying to him, 'Brother, be of good comfort and joyful, for you shall have within the next fortnight 40,000 more of the commons than you have now and we shall be good companions.'

"When the king asked Tyler, 'Why will you not go back to your own country?' the insurgent chief replied with a great oath that neither he nor his fellows would depart until they had their charter such as they wished to have, and such points rehearsed in their charter as they chose to demand, threatening that the lords of the realm would rue it badly if the points were not settled to their satisfaction. The king asked him what were the points that he wanted, and he should have them freely without contradiction written down and sealed. He then rehearsed points which were to be demanded. He asked that there should be no law except the law of Winchester, and that there should be henceforth no outlawry on any process of law, and that no lord should have any lordship . . . and that the only lordship should be that of the king; that the goods of Holy Church should not remain in the hands of the religious nor of the parsons and vicars and other churchmen; but those who were in possession should have their sustenance from the endowments and the remainder of their goods should be divided amongst their parishioners; and no bishop should remain in England save one, and that all the lands and tenements now held by them should be confiscated and shared amongst the commons, saving to them a reasonable substance. And he demanded that there should be no more bondsmen in England, no serfdom nor villeinage, but that all should be free and of one condition. And to this the king gave an easy answer, and said that he should have all that could fairly be granted saving to himself the regality of the Crown. And then he commanded him to go back to his home without further delay. And all this time that the king was speaking no lord nor any other of his council dared nor wished to give any answer to the commons in any place except the king himself.

"After that Tyler, in the king's presence, called for a flagon of water to rinse his mouth because he was in such a heat, and when it was brought he rinsed his mouth in a very rude and disgusting fashion before the king; and then he made them bring him a flagon of ale of which he drank a great deal, and in the king's presence mounted his horse. At this time a yeoman of Kent, who was among the king's retinue, asked to see the said Wat, the leader of the commons; and when Wat was pointed out to him, he said openly that he was the greatest thief and robber in all Kent. Wat heard these words and commanded him to come out to him, shaking his head at him in sign of malice; but the yeoman refused to go to him for fear of the mob. At last the lords made him go out to Wat to see what he would do in the king's presence; and, when Wat saw him, he ordered one of his followers, who was riding on a horse carrying his banner displayed, to dismount and cut off the yeoman's head. But the yeoman answered that he had done nothing worthy of death, for what he had said was true and he would not deny it, but in the presence of his liege lord he could not lawfully make debate without leave, except in his own defence . . . For these words Wat would have run him through with his dagger and killed him in the king's presence, and because of this, the mayor of London, William Walworth by name, reasoned with the said Wat for his violent behaviour and contempt done in the king's presence and arrested him. And because he arrested him, the said Wat struck the mayor with his dagger in the stomach with great anger; but as God would have it, the mayor was wearing armour and took no harm. But like a hardy and vigorous man the mayor drew his cutlass and struck back at Wat and gave him a deep cut on the neck and then a great cut on the head. And in this scuffle a yeoman of the king's household drew his sword and ran Wat two or three times through the body, mortally wounding him. And the said Wat spurred his horse, crying to the commons to avenge him, and the horse carried him some four score paces, and there he fell to the ground half dead. And when the commons saw him fall and did not know for certain how it was, they began to bend their bows to shoot."[1]

It was thirty-five years since Crécy and Neville's Cross and a quarter of a century since Poitiers, and even the youngest who had shared in these masterpieces of the bowman's art were now, by the standards of the fourteenth century, old men. Even Najera was fourteen years away, and few of the English archers who had wrought that Phyrric victory can ever have returned to England. Yet there must have been at least several hundreds in the insurgent host who had served in the French and Breton wars and many thousands more who had learnt to use the long bow at the butts after church on Sundays and were armed with the terrifying weapon—the most formidable in the world—which the Plantagenet kings had given the yeomanry of England. It seemed, as hundreds of bows were drawn in the rebel ranks, that it was going to cost the last of them his life and throne.

At that moment Richard clapped spurs into his horse and rode straight across the square towards the massed insurgents. "Sirs," he cried as he reined in before them, "will you shoot your king? I am your captain. I will be your leader. Let him who loves me follow me!" The effect was electric; the expected flight of arrows never came. Instead, as the young king slowly wheeled his horse northwards towards the open country, the peasants in ordered companies followed him like the children after the piper of Hamelin.

As they did so, the mayor galloped back into the city to rouse the loyalists and call them to rescue their sovereign. His chief adversary—Alderman Sibley who had lowered the river drawbridge two days before—arrived just before him, spreading the rumour that the whole royal party had been killed. But Walworth's appearance gave him the lie and, sickened by the plunder,

[1] *The Anonimalle Chronicle*, (ed. V. H. Galbraith).

murder and arson of the last forty-eight hours, the shopkeepers and wealthier citizens flocked with their arms into the streets as the sole hope of saving their homes and possessions. Mustered by the aldermen and officers of their wards and led by old Sir Robert Knollys with his archers and men-at-arms, they hurried in thousands out of the Aldersgate in pursuit of the imperilled king and his rabble following. They found them in the Clerkenwell cornfields with the boy, still unharmed, sitting on his horse in their midst, arguing with the insurgents, now leaderless and confused in the absence of Tyler who had been borne dying into St. Bartholomew's hospital. While they were so occupied, Knollys quietly deployed his men, outflanking and surrounding the multitude, while a band of heavily armoured knights pushed through the crowd to the king's side.

The threat to the Crown and capital was over. The insurgents made no resistance; it was the end of a long hot day and they must have been parched and exhausted. Encircled by armed men and appeased by the king's promises, even the extremists had no more fight in them and were ready to return home. He refused to listen to the proposal of some of his rescuers that, as his former captors were now at his mercy, he should order them to be massacred; "three-fourths of them," he is said to have replied, "have been brought here by force and threats; I will not let the innocent suffer with the guilty." Knollys, who was himself of yeoman birth, strongly counselled the course of mercy and helped to organize the march of the Kentish men through London to their homes.

The whole multitude now dispersed. When Richard returned to the Wardrobe amid the rejoicings of the Londoners whose mayor he had just knighted in the Clerkenwell fields, he said to his anxious mother, "Rejoice and praise God, for today I have recovered my heritage that was lost and the realm of England also."

Had the king fallen at Mile End or Smithfield there would have been no authority but that of the rebellious peasantry left from Yorkshire to Kent and from Suffolk to Devon. When he and Walworth so unexpectedly, and at the eleventh hour, turned the tables on Tyler, the revolution was on the point of complete success. For on the very afternoon that Richard, preparing for death, confessed and received absolution in the desecrated abbey, the fires of rebellion, fanned by the news of the previous day's massacre in the Tower and the insurgents' triumph, spread to St. Albans, Cambridge and Ipswich and into Bedfordshire, the Fens and Norfolk. At St. Albans, led by a local tradesman called William Grindcobbe—a brave man with a burning love of freedom—the townsfolk invaded the abbey, seized its charters and burnt them in the market place, ripping up the confiscated millstones—symbols of the abbey's monopolistic privileges —with which the abbot had paved his chamber, while the countryfolk drained the fishponds and trampled down the fences enclosing the monastic woods and pastures. At Cambridge, as during that Saturday village after village rose in the fenland, the bell of Great St. Mary's brought out the mob in a riotous crusade against the university and the adjacent priory of Barnwell. Corpus Christi College, the chief owner of house-property in the town, was gutted, and the university charters, archives and library were burnt next day in the Market Square while an old woman shouted, as she flung parchment after parchment into the flames, "Away with the learning of the clerks! away with it!" During the weekend other risings occurred at Huntingdon, Ely, Ramsey, Thorney, Peterborough, North Walsham, Wymondham and Bishop's Lynn, as well as in hundreds of villages in East Anglia, the Fenland and east Midlands. In all of them justices of the peace, tax commissioners, lawyers and unpopular landlords, particularly monastic ones, were attacked, their houses sacked or burnt and their charters and court-rolls destroyed.

The most formidable of all the risings outside the capital occurred in Norfolk, the richest and most populous as well as most independent-minded county in England. In West Norfolk, where it broke out during the weekend of the king's triumph and lasted for ten days, it was without a leader and apparently quite purposeless, the one common denominator being robbery under threats of violence. Many of the victims were persons in humble circumstances, farmers, priests and village tradesmen; in only two of the 153 villages in which felonies were committed did they take the form of attacks on landlords. But in the eastern half of the county, where a leader of Tyler's calibre appeared, rebellion took a political course, though a different one to that of the home counties. Its aim, natural in so remote an area, was not the reform and control of the government, but the setting up of an independent East Anglia.

Its leader was a Felmingham dyer named Geoffrey Litster. His lieutenant was a local landlord, Sir Roger Bacon of Baconsthorpe, an unruly spirit of the same family as the Carmelite philosopher of that name and the still more famous Roger Bacon. Yet though Litster was only a small tradesman he exercised an autocratic authority, not only over Bacon but over four other prominent Norfolk landowners whom he terrorised into obeying him and whom he constituted as his court—Sir William Morley, Sir Stephen Hales, Sir John Brewes and Sir Roger Scales. At the start of the rising, which began on June 17th with a rally of thousands of disaffected Norfolk villagers on Mousehold Heath—the traditional mustering-place of the county —Litster narrowly missed capturing the Earl of Suffolk whom he wished to make his constable. A knight who refused to serve him was put to death—a local miller's son named Sir Robert Salle, who had won his spurs in Edward III's wars.

By that evening the rebels were in possession of Norwich, the fourth city of the kingdom. They entered it, "with pennons flying and in warlike array," Litster and Bacon in armour riding at their head. The corporation paid a heavy fine in return for a promise that there should be no pillage, but many houses were sacked and burnt, and an unpopular justice of the peace was murdered. Litster took up his quarters in the castle where he styled himself king of the commons, kept a royal state and was served on bended knee by his hostage knights. He at once set about reducing the whole of eastern Norfolk to his rule, punishing "traitors," that is oppressive landlords, rich merchants, lawyers, and foreign merchants, of whom there were plenty, Norwich being the centre of the cloth-trade. On June 18th his lieutenant, Bacon, entered Yarmouth, burnt the town charters, let the prisoners out of the gaol and beheaded a number of Flemings. He also—for he was by no means disinterested—forced several of his fellow landowners to transfer their estates to him.

By this time, however, news of the re-establishment of royal authority in London had reached Norfolk. On June 21st—a week after the Mile End meeting—Litster despatched three personal henchmen, named Trunch, Skeet and Kybytt, with a large sum of money and two of the hostage-knights to lend respectability to the mission, to obtain from the king a charter and amnesty similar to those granted to the rebels in the home counties. But at Temple Bridge on the Suffolk border next day they had the misfortune to run straight into the arms of the Bishop of Norwich—Henry Despenser—who was hurrying back to his diocese with a force of men-at-arms and archers. This warlike prelate, a nephew of the Despenser who had forced the crossing of the Somme before Crécy and one who in his own youth had fought in the papal wars in Italy, had been staying at Burleigh-by-Stamford when news of the disorders in East Anglia reached him. Setting out homewards on June 17th—the day that the rebels took Norwich—he and the eight knights who constituted his escort entered Peterborough just as the townsmen and the tenants of the abbey were about to attack the latter. Without hesitation the bishop and his little band of armoured men fell on them and put them to rout; "some," wrote the monastic chronicler, "fell by lance or sword without the minster, some within, some even close to the altar; those who had come to destroy the church and its ministers perished by the hand of a churchman, for the bishop's sword gave them their absolution."[1]

Having saved Peterborough, Despenser collected as many local gentry and their retainers as he could and hurried on to Ramsey. Here on the 18th he routed a band of Cambridgeshire and Suffolk rioters who were terrorizing the monastery. Next day he reached Cambridge where he put down the rebellion that had been raging since the weekend, beheaded several ringleaders in the market-place and removed the mayor as "notoriously inefficient." Then, having restored the authority of the university—whose privileges and powers were subsequently enlarged at the expense of the town—he set off for Norwich, encountering Litster's emissaries on the morning of the 22nd. Finding how things were from their two hostages, he promptly cut off the heads of Trunch, Skeet and Kybytt and sent them to be stuck on the pillory at Newmarket.

Meanwhile in London the king and his reconstituted government had been acting with equal vigour. Having granted to the

---

[1] *Knighton's Continuator,* II, 140, cit. *Oman,* 130.

mayor and Robert Knollys summary powers to repress and punish the now quiescent rioters in the capital, Richard and his new chancellor, Lord Arundel, issued on the 18th a proclamation ordering the royal officers throughout the country to disperse and arrest all malefactors. Two days later Knollys with the constable of Dover castle and the sheriff of Kent left London to reduce that county to order, while the Earl of Suffolk, who after his escape from the hands of Litster, had joined the king in London, set off with five hundred lances for Suffolk. On the 22nd the king himself marched into Essex, announcing that those who claimed to be acting in his name had no authority. From Waltham Abbey where he set up his headquarters next day he sent forward against the still-armed insurgents his uncle, Thomas of Woodstock, who by now had arrived with reinforcements from Wales, and Sir Thomas Percy, a veteran of the fighting in France and the Channel. On the 28th they attacked them in their fortified camp at Billericay, driving them with heavy loss from their entrenchments. A day or two earlier the Bishop of Norwich, who had re-entered his cathedral city on the 24th, stormed the wagon-laager at North Waltham into which the commons of Norfolk had withdrawn. Litster had been captured and sentenced on the spot to be hanged, beheaded and quartered, the bishop personally superintending his execution but first confessing and shriving him. The Essex leaders, abandoned by most of their followers, fled to Colchester and thence, obtaining no support from the townsmen, to Sudbury where they were finally broken up by a force of local gentry. Elsewhere the rebellion, which had spread during the last week of June as far as Scarborough, York and Bridgewater, collapsed as suddenly as it had begun.

Except for the summary execution of a few ringleaders like Tyler's lieutenant, Jack Straw, and John Starling—the Essex rioter who had decapitated Archbishop Sudbury and who was taken still carrying the sword that had done the deed—the insurgents were tried and punished by the normal processes of law. The new chief justice of the King's Bench, Robert Tresilian, who succeeded the murdered Cavendish, presided over a special judicial commission, first at Chelmsford and then at St. Albans, meting out justice with great severity, the young king sitting by his side. But though a large number of persons were charged with treason or crimes of violence, only about a hundred and fifty[1] suffered the death penalty, nearly all of them after being found guilty by a local jury. Most of the ring-leaders perished including John Ball, who was found in hiding at Coventry, and John Wraw, another priest who had led the Suffolk insurgents and who tried to save his life by turning king's evidence. The noblest of all—the leader of the St. Albans townsmen against the tyranny of the great abbey that held them in bondage—died with sublime courage, protesting the righteousness of his cause. "If I die for the liberty we have won," he said, "I shall think myself happy to end my life as a martyr for such a cause."

Before the end of the summer the king put to a stop further arrests and executions, and in December a general amnesty was declared. The peasants' revolt and its repression were over. Only the smouldering ashes of anger and resentment remained; that and fear of its recurrence. But for two circumstances the king would have perished with his ministers. One was his courage, the other the deep-seated loyalty to the throne which transcended the sense of injustice and desire for revenge of the peasant multitude. Fierce as were the passions aroused during the "hurling time," and cruel and atrocious some of the deeds done during it, the majority of those who had marched under the banner of "King Richard and the true commons" sincerely believed that they were restoring the realm to justice and honest government and rescuing their young sovereign from traitors and extortioners. They did not seek to destroy either him or his kingdom, and even at the height of the rebellion provided for the defence of the country. And, though they released the criminals from the jails and allowed the more savage of their companions to wreak their will on those whom they regarded as oppressors, they made no attempt to massacre their social superiors like the French jacquerie of a generation before. When in their wretchedness after their rulers' defeat in war the French peasants had risen, they had loosed their vengeance on the entire ruling class, murdering, raping, torturing and mutilating every man, woman and

[1] Froissart's estimate of 1500 hanged or beheaded, like most of his figures, seems wildly inaccurate. In his detailed but unfinished study of the rising, André Réville made a list—admittedly incomplete—of a hundred and ten persons who suffered the supreme penalty. André Réville, *Le Soulèvement des Travailleurs d'Angleterre en 1381.* cit. Oman, 87.

child within their reach. In the contemporary accounts of the English peasants' revolt no instance is recorded of violence to a woman, though for three days the capital and for several weeks the richest parts of England lay at their mercy.

Yet they and their leaders came very near to overthrowing the government of their country, far nearer than the rebellious peasants of France, Flanders and Italy had ever come. They had done so because their cause was based, not on mere desperation or unthinking anger, but on certain principles of justice on which, when they could free their mind from class prejudice, all English-men were agreed. And though they seemed to have been defeated and to have been reduced once more to bondage, they had, in fact, as time was to show, achieved their object. When, a week after the Smithfield meeting, a delegation of peasants waited on the king at Waltham to ask for a ratification of the charters, he replied that his pledges, having been extorted by force, counted for nothing. "Villeins you are still," he told them, "and villeins ye shall remain!" He was wrong. For the present the lords might enforce their rights; they could not do so permanently. The magic of their old invincibility was gone. Given arms by the Statute of Winchester and taught to use them on the battlefields of France, the peasants had tested them on the manor itself and knew their strength. They would no longer brook servitude.

As an economic means of cultivating the soil for profit, villeinage was doomed. With such surly and mutinous labour and no police to enforce it, it proved impossible to make it pay. Faced by the growing competition of the towns the lord had to make concessions to keep his villeins on the land. And as the population began to rise again after the first-waves of Black Death, the process of commuting services for money payments was resumed and paid labour increasingly took the place of servile. In other places, lords found their demesnes so hard to work that to maintain their incomes they were forced to let them to the wealthier and more industrious peasants. Within half a century of the revolt, even in the open-field villages of the Midlands tenant-farming with hired labour had become the norm, and hereditary servile status had ceased to have any practical significance. It was only a question of time, before the common law, with its bias in favour of freedom, had transformed villein tenure into copyhold. The propertyless bondsman became the copyholder enjoying, by virtue of his copy from the manorial rolls, the same protection from the king's courts and the same right to enjoy or dispose of his hereditary holding as a freeholder.

.   .   .   .

Just as the English refusal to be constrained by force—so repeatedly shown during the past century—was turning the personal monarch into the king in parliament, the lord was dwindling into the lord of the manor. He might be an oppressor, but he could no longer be a wholly irresponsible one. With their deeply rooted instinct for the principle of consent and for the safeguarding and definition of rights by law, it was not in the nature of the English to endure power unbound by law. It was a lesson that the young sovereign whose courage had saved the realm had to learn if he was to keep what he had saved. In a sense, Richard's very success in taming the revolution of his poorer subjects, was to prove his undoing. The impressionable boy who had exorcized anarchy by the mystique of kingship was never to recover from this early intoxicating experience and the belief engendered by it that, as the lord's anointed, he could impose his will on whoever opposed it. Pitting himself, with rare patience and political astuteness, against the powerful lords who surrounded his throne, in the course of a decade he completely turned the tables on them and made himself more master of his realm than any king before him. Its laws and the property of his subjects were—or seemed to be—at his sole disposal. Yet within little more than eighteen months of his triumph all was in the dust.

No English king ever had a more splendid heritage than Richard. Son and grandson of the two greatest heroes of the age, "tall and fair among men even as another Absalom," happily married and surrounded by a brilliant court, he used a private army and political skill of a high order to destroy his enemies. His reign saw a flowering of native art and culture that anticipated that of fifteenth century Burgundy and rivalled and even promised to surpass that of contemporary Italy. He had Yevele for his architect and Chaucer for his poet. Yet, despite his virtues and ability, when he claimed that the laws existed only in his own breast he made the same mistake as the abbot who told his serfs that they owned nothing legally but their bellies. Because he failed to see that whoever claims absolute power in England will in the end be repudiated by her people, he was to lose everything and be dethroned by a parliament of his own subjects. Like his foolish great-great-grandfather—and others who came after him—he was to discover that the English could only be ruled by those who acknowledged the sanctity of their laws and liberties and their right to defend them.

List of abbreviations used in footnotes

Barrow. C. W. S. Barrow, *Feudal Britain*
Bennett. H. S. Bennett, *Life on the English Manor*
Borenius and Tristram. T. Borenius and E. W. Tristram, *English Medieval Painting*
Brieger. P. Brieger, *English Art 1216-1307* (Oxford History of English Art)
Burne. A. H. Burne, *The Crécy War*

Cam. H. Cam, *The Hundred and the Hundred Rolls*
C.M.H. *The Shorter Cambridge Medieval History* (ed. C. W. Previté-Orton)
C.E.H.E. *The Cambridge Economic History of Europe* (ed. M. Postan and E. E. Rich)
Chronicon. Geoffrey le Baker of Swinbrook, *Chronicon* (ed. E. M. Thompson)
Cohen. H. Cohen, *History of the English Bar*
Coulton, Black Death. G. G. Coulton, *The Black Death*

D.N.B. *Dictionary of National Biography*
Dickinson. W. C. Dickinson, *Scotland from the Earliest Times to 1603*
Douie. D. L. Douie, *Archbishop Pecham*

English Government. *The English Government at Work 1327-1336* (ed. J. F. Willard and
  W. A. Morris)
E.H.R. *English Historical Review*
Evans. J. Evans, *English Art, 1307-1461* (Oxford History of English Art)

Fergusson. J. Ferguson, *William Wallace*
Froissart. *The Chronicle of Froissart* (transl. Lord Berners) (ed. W. P. Ker)

Gasquet. Cardinal Gasquet, *Great Pestilence*
Green. V. H. H. Green, *The Later Plantagenets*

Hamilton Thompson. A. Hamilton Thompson, *The English Clergy and their Organization
  in the Later Medieval Ages*
Harvey. J. Harvey, *Gothic England*

Johnstone. H. Johnstone, *Edward of Carnarvon*
Jusserand. J. J. Jusserand, *English Wayfaring Life in the Middle Ages*

Keen. M. Keen, *Outlaws of Medieval England*
Knowles. D. Knowles, *The Religious Orders in Medieval England*
Kosminsky. E. A. Kosminsky, *Studies in the Agrarian History of England* (ed. R. H.
  Hilton)

Lapsley. G. T. Lapsley, *Crown, Community and Parliament in the Later Middle Ages*

Makers of the Realm. A. Bryant, *The Story of England*, vol. I, Makers of the Realm
Maynard Smith. J. Maynard Smith, *Pre-Reformation England*
Mitchell and Leys. R. J. Mitchell and M. D. R. Leys, *A History of the English People*
McKisack. M. McKisack, *Fourteenth Century* (Oxford History of England)
Medieval England. *Medieval England* (ed. A. L. Poole)

Medieval Panorama. G. G. Coulton, *Medieval Panorama*
Morris. J. E. Morris, *The Welsh Wars of Edward I*
Myers. A. R. Myers, *England in the late Middle Ages*

Oman. C. Oman, *The Great Revolt of 1381*
Owst, Preaching. G. R. Owst, *Preaching in Medieval England*
Owst, Literature and Pulpit. G. R. Owst, *Literature and Pulpit in Medieval England*

Pantin. W. A. Pantin, *The English Church in the Fourteenth Century*
Perroy. E. Perroy, *The Hundred Years' War* (ed. D. C. Douglas)
Piers Plowman. W. Langland, *The Vision of Piers the Plowman* (ed. W. Skeat)
Plucknett. T. F. T. Plucknett, *Legislation of Edward I*
Power. E. Power, *The Wool Trade in English Medieval History*
Powicke. F. M. Powicke, *The Thirteenth Century* (Oxford History of England)

Ramsay. J. Ramsay, *Genesis of Lancaster 1307-99*
Rickert. E. Rickert, *Chaucer's England*
Rock. D. Rock, *The Church of Our Fathers*
R.H.S.T. *Transactions of the Royal Historical Society*

Salzman. L. F. Salzman, *English Life in the Middle Ages*
Scalacronica. Sir Thomas Gray of Heton, *Scalacronica* (ed. J. Stevenson)
Scottish History. *A Source Book of Scottish History* (ed. W. C. Dickinson, G. Donaldson and I. A. Milne)
Social England. *Social England* (ed. H. D. Traill)
Steel. A. Steel, *Richard II*
Stephenson and Marcham. C. Stephenson and F. G. Marcham, *Sources of English Constitutional History*
Stubbs. J. Stubbs, *Constitutional History of England*

Thrupp. S. L. Thrupp, *The Merchant Class of Medieval London*
Tout, Chapters. T. F. Tout, *Chapters in the Administrative History of Medieval England*
Tout, Edward II. T. F. Tout, *The Place of the Reign of Edward II in English History*

V.C.H. *Victoria County Histories*

Wilkinson. B. Wilkinson, *The Constitutional History of Medieval England 1216-1399*
Williams. E. Williams, *Early Holborn and the Legal Quarter of London*
Wright, Political Songs. *The Political Songs of England* (ed. T. Wright) (Camden Soc.)

Y.B. *Year Books* (Selden Society)

I am greatly indebted to Dr. A. R. Myers for kindly allowing me to quote from translations and transcripts of contemporary documents which he has prepared for his forthcoming volume of *English Historical Documents*, 1327-1485, to be published by Eyre and Spottiswoode as Vol. IV of the series appearing under the general editorship of Dr. D. C. Douglas.

INDEX

Figures in italic type refer to passages giving a more detailed treatment of the subjects indicated

Bruce, Robert, [cont'd.]
Rathlin, 182; attacks Turnberry castle,
182; breaks ring of pursuers at Loch
Trool, 183; victory at Loudon, 183;
obtains breathing-space, 184, 186;
genius for leadership and war, 186-7,
187-8; harries Buchan, 188, 191;
strikes down enemies in the Highlands,
192; liberates Fife, 192; holds first
parliament at St. Andrews, 192; enthroned in hearts of Scottish people,
192; saved by English divisions, 192;
ignores excommunication, 194; wastes
country before English invasion, 194;
harries Tynedale and Durham, 196,
198; captures Perth, 199; wrests last
English bases in Scotland, 200; trains
army in Torwood, 200; victory of
Bannockburn, 201-8; magnanimity in
victory, 208-9; terrorises northern
England, 209; invades Ireland, 210;
captures Berwick, 212; threatens
York, 212; outwits Edward II and
forces him to conclude truce, 214-15;
praised in Declaration of Arbroath,
215-16; recognized by Lancaster, 218;
burns Lancaster and Preston, 219;
withdraws beyond Forth, 219-20;
raids Cleveland and North Riding,
220; signs truce with England as King
of Scots, 220; birth of a son, 221;
builds a palace at Cardross, 221; re-
news raids on England, 230; hunts
Northumberland, 231; recognised by
English as king, 232; dies at Cardross,
233; laid among Scottish kings at
Dunfermline, 233; heart saved from
Moors and buried in Melrose abbey,
233; other references to, 272, 273, 275,
277, 278, 279, 295, 296, 348, 406, 434,
442
Bruges, 114, 163, 172, 255, 264, 286, 302,
306, 516
Brunton, Thomas, b. of Rochester, 458,
472, 479
"Brutus of Troy," 29-30, 93, 235
Buchan, 187, 191;
countess of, 180, 181, 187;
earl of, see Comyn;
harrying of, 188
Buckerells, 258
Buckingham, 396
Buckingham, John, 363
Buckinghamshire, 250, 393, 475
Builth, 58, 86, 89, 140
Bulgaria, 68
Bunbury, 492
Burgh, Richard de, e. of Ulster (1283-
1326), 210
Burgh, William de, e. of Ulster (1330-3),
426
Burgh-on-Sands, 183
Burghersh, Henry, b. of Lincoln, 282, 331

Burghersh, lord, 419
Burgos, 27, 437, 438
Burgundy, 15, 16, 420, 426, 443;
d. of, 285
Burleigh-by-Stamford, 542
Burley, Sir Simon, 520
Burley, Walter, 363, 520
Burne, A. H., 314
Burnell, Robert, b. of Bath and Wells,
48, 61, 96, 106, 111, 116, 242; char-
acter, 31, 70, 77; death, 140
Burnham Norton, 462
Burns, Robert, 176, 177
"Burnt Candlemas," 406
Burton, abbot of, 501, 546
Burton-on-Trent, 52
Bury, Richard, b. of Durham, 472
Bury St. Edmunds, 146, 147, 226, 324,
530 533-4; abbey 24, 95, 117, 170,
247, 347, 530, 533, 534
Butler, Edward, justiciar of Ireland, 210
Byland, 25, 220, 252, 263
Byzantium, 17, 69, 380

Caburn, William de, 393
Cader Idris, 90
Cadiz, 27
Cadzand, 284
Caen, 307, 308, 316, 416
Caerlaverock, 170, 192
Caernarvon, 91, 93, 142;
castle of, 92, 140, 141
Caerphilly, 23, 59, 93
Cahors, 422
Caithness, e. of, 192
Calabria, 339
Calais, 111, 316, 321, 400, 404, 406, 418,
419, 422, 423, 442, 443, 446, 491, 492;
siege, 316, 318, 319-21, 323, 324,
379;
St. Nicholas church, 423;
Staple at, 321, 451, 452;
surprise attack, 398-9
Calhaus, 191
Callander, 167
Calveley, Sir Hugh, 431, 437, 439, 443,
444, 491-2
Cam, Helen, 95
Cambrai, 285
Cambridge, 226, 347, 540, 542;
e. of, see Edmund of Langley;
university, 12, 32, 122, 356, 360, 361,
362, 447, 460, 493, 542;
colleges and halls:
Clare, 362;
Corpus Christi, 362, 540;
Gonville, 362;
King's Hall, 362;
Michaelhouse, 362;
Pembroke, 213, 362;
Trinity, 362;
Trinity Hall, 362
Cambridgeshire, 211, 254, 542

Edward II [cont'd]

Despenser, 216-17; successfully counter-attacks barons, 217, 268; has Lancaster put to death, 218; meets royalist parliament at York, 219; again fails against Scots, 219-20; has Harclay hanged as traitor, 220; makes truce with Scots, 220-1; governs through Despensers, 221-2, 223; loses French dominions, 224; animosity of Queen, 225; kingdom invaded, 226; captured at Neath, 227; dethroned, 228-9; murdered at Berkeley castle, 231-2, 234; tomb at Gloucester becomes place of pilgrimage, 235, 245, 267; other references to, 230, 243, 251, 259, 262, 265, 292, 332, 362

Edward III:

birth, 198; sent to France, 225; affianced to Philippa of Hainault, 226; acclaimed king, 228; crowned, 229, 237; in Stanhope Park campaign, 230-1; humiliated by Mortimer, 235; does homage for French lands, 236; marriage, 236. 255; overthrows Mortimer, 234, 237; resolves to rule with common counsel, 238-9; character, 238, 239; love of chivalry and tournaments, 239-42; shelters Edward Balliol, 273; victory at Halidon Hill, 274-7; delivers Scotland to Balliol, 278; fails to conquer Scots, 279, 280-1; dispute with France, 279-80; entertains Robert of Artois, 281; negotiates alliances against France, 281-2; appeals to nation, 283; dealings with wool merchants, 283; fails to provoke French to battle, 284; financial difficulties, 285, 290; alliance with Flemings, 285-6; appeals to parliament, 286-7; victory at Sluys, 287-9; besieges Tournai, 289; forced to make truce, 290; returns to England, 291; dismisses ministers, 291; worsted in dispute with Archbishop Stratford, 291-4; governs henceforward through traditional advisers and ecclesiastical ministers, 294; intervenes in Brittany, 295-6; plans Round Table, 297-8; confers with van Artevelde, 298; raises army to invade Normandy, 301-5; lands in Cotentin peninsula, 306; march to Ponthieu, 307-10; victory at Crécy, 311-16; besieges Calais, 316, 319-20; claims command of narrow seas, 321; agrees to truce, 321-2; founds Order of Garter, 323-5; appointment of bishops, 325-6; friendship with Abbot Clown, 350; support for

university of Oxford, 361; loses daughter in plague, 382; projects for housing Order of Garter, 383; holds first Garter Service, 394; relations with pope over provisions, 396; expresses gratitude to parliament, 397; abolishes foreign staple, 397-8; thwarts attempts to surprise Calais, 398-9; naval victory off Winchelsea, 399; fails to obtain Scottish homage, 403; plans triple attack on France, 404; unsuccessful *chevauchée* in Artois, 406; invades Scotland in the "burnt candlemas," 406; fame after Poitiers, 415-16; entertains King John, 416; prepares new invasion of France, 418-19; thwarted by winter, 419-20; withdraws to Loire, 420-1; agrees to truce of Brétigny, 422; triumphant return to England, 423; seals peace at Calais, 423; his domestic achievement, 423-6, 428; matrimonial policy, 426; moral weakness, 428-9; fails to consolidate gains of Brétigny, 429-30; gives unofficial consent to son's intervention in Spain, 437; loss of Ponthieu, 441; loses queen, 442; moral enfeeblement, 444-5; driven back by storm, 445-6; enthrones mistress as Lady of the Sun, 446; dependence on William of Wykeham, 446-7; on mistress and John of Gaunt, 447, 452, 455; constitutional effects of policy, 448; forced by Commons to dismiss mistress, 454; dies in dotage, 456

Edward, Prince of Wales, made duke of Cornwall, 283; accompanies father to Flanders, 298; knighted in Normandy, 306; wins spurs at Crécy, 311, 314, 315, 316, 323; at siege of Calais, 319; jousts in Garter insignia, 324; in sea-fight off Winchelsea, 399; leads *grande chevauchée* in Languedoc, 404-6; marches on Loire, 408-9; retreats, 409; victory at Poitiers, 410-15; chivalrous conduct, 414-15, 416; in 1359-60 campaign, 419; negotiates truces at Brétigny, 422; marries Joan of Kent, 426; viceroy of Aquitaine, 435-6; aids Don Pedro, 436-7; victory at Najara, 438; contracts dysentery, 439; financial difficulties, 439-40; summoned before *parlement* of Paris, 441; worsted in war, 441-3; sacks Limoges, 444; returns to England, 444; withdraws from public life, 445; supports Commons in "good" parliament, 447, 454; death, 454; burial at Canterbury, 454-5

Egglesfield, Robert de, 239

Eggleston, 348

560

Kempe, Margery, 466-7
Kenilworth, 23, 52, 227, 228
Kenn, Walter of, 242
Kennet, R., 23
Kennington, 456
Kent, 65, 70, 108, 258, 498, 519, 520-1,
    522-5, 527-8, 532, 534, 539, 543;
        earl of, see Edmund of Woodstock,
        Holland,
Kidwelly, 64
Kilblain Forest, 279
Kildrummie, 279
Kilsby, William, 290, 291, 293, 294
Kilwardby, Robert, abp. of Canterbury,
    62, 70, 359
Kineton, 393
Kinghorn, 125, 156, 273
King's Langley, 185, 208, 223, 253
Kingston-on-Hull, see Hull
Kinloss, 157
Kircudbright, 170
Kirkby, John, bp. of Ely, 31, 32, 87, 89,
    109, 140
Kirkeby, 393
Kirkstead, 25
Kite, Robert, 36
Knaresborough, 212
Knighton, Henry, 350, 379, 388
Knights of St. John of Jerusalem
    (Hospitallers), 122, 200, 328, 349, 520,
    528
Knights Templar, 122, 181, 328;
    dissolution of, 199-200, 328
Knollys, Sir Robert, 304, 401, 402, 407,
    408, 417, 422, 431, 437, 443, 492, 521,
    530, 539, 543
Knowles, M. D., 359
Knyvet, Sir John, 447, 450
Kublai Khan, 18
Kybytt, 542

Lacy, Henry de, e. of Lincoln, 29, 86,
    138, 140, 141, 148, 172, 190
Lakenheath, 533
Lamberton, William, b. of St. Andrews,
    174, 180, 232
Lambeth, 526;
    council of, 78
Lanark, 153, 278
Lanarkshire, 194
Lancashire, 64, 141, 254, 415
Lancaster, 219
Lancaster, earls and dukes of, see Ed-
    mund, Henry and Thomas
Lancaster, Blanche, duchess of, 426, 442
Lang, Andrew, 176
Langham, Simon, 349
Langland, William, 12, 326, 333, 351,
    371, 379, 395, 420, 427, 455, 457,
    462, 470, 472, 479-89, 511, 513, 515-
    16
Langley, 354
Langton, John, chancellor, 31, 32, 194

Langton, Stephen, abp. of Canterbury,
    70, 71
Langton, Walter, b. of Lichfield, 31, 32,
    171, 178-9, 186, 191
Languedoc, 300, 404-6, 439
Lannercost priory, 182
Lantwit, 57
La Réole, 225, 300, 301, 317, 446
Larne, 210
La Rochelle, 136, 256, 422, 423, 436,
    445, 446, 447
Las Navas de Tolosa, 27
Latimer, Bishop Hugh, 271
Latimer, William, Lord, 451
Lauderdale, 201
Launceston, 355
Lavenham, 40
LAW COMMON: system on Edward I's
    accession, 32-40; his reform of, 40-50,
    52, 67-8, 93-107, 117-25, 183; attempts
    to extend to Wales and Scotland, 11,
    57, 59-60, 79, 80-6, 91-2, 131-2,
    134-6, 153; abuses of, 40-5, 48, 83-4,
    96-7, 99-100, 117-20, 266, 291, 505-7,
    508; relations with Canon Law, 72-5,
    76-8, 116-17, 119; legal education,
    120-2
    Attorneys, 33, 39, 121, 502;
    Constables, police, disorder and
        crime, 18, 94, 101-4, 108, 162,
        222-3, 238, 265-6, 270-1, 506-8,
        517, 519 et seq;
    Coroners, 36, 37, 101, 105, 179, 222,
        238;
    Courts, central 34-5, 38-9, 40, 53,
        100, 105, 118, 178, 435, 508-9;
    Courts, itinerant, 33, 37, 44, 67, 104,
        105, 179;
    Courts, local, 35-7, 43-4;
    Courts, manorial, 510, 546;
    De Donis, see under Statutes;
    Equity, Chancery court of, 504-5;
    Frankpledge, view of, 35-6;
    Inns of Court and Chancery, 122,
        503, 529;
    Judiciary, 32, 33, 39, 49, 50, 96, 117,
        118-20, 121, 178, 238, 260, 265-6,
        291, 392, 501, 502-4, 505, 509;
    Juries, 34, 37, 43-4, 100, 117, 505-6;
    Jurisdictions, private, 33, 43-4, 48,
        67-8, 123-4;
    Justices of Labourers and the Peace,
        99, 104, 392-3, 500, 507-8, 517;
    Language, legal, 33, 435, 502;
    Mercantile Law, 106-7, 174;
    Mortmain, see under Statutes;
    Nisi prius, 100;
    Outlawry, 35, 265-70;
    Quia Emptores, see under Statutes;
    Quo Warranto, 67-8, 123-4;
    Rigidity of law, 34, 81, 100-1, 503-4;
    Serjeants-at-law and narrators, 32,
        33, 39, 120, 121, 501-2, 503;

Rutland, 64, 266
Rye, 252, 257, 284, 288, 423, 431
  456, 491
Rymynton, William of, 467
Rypon, Dr. of Durham, 336, 478

St. Albans, 128, 387, 536, 540, 543, 544;
  abbey, 24, 201, 348, 349, 352, 387,
  388, 501 f.n., 530
St. Andrews, 127, 131, 156, 157, 168, 192,
  340, 420;
    bishops of, see Fraser; Lamberton
St. Asaph, 329
St. Cloud, 308
St. Columba's, 146
St. David's, 32, 56, 62, 329
St. Denis, 307, 340, 413
St. Emilion, 439
St. George, 251, 284, 323, 324, 340, 383,
  394, 413, 414, 438, 515, 527, 535
St. Helens, 306
St. Hugh of Lincoln, 246-7
St. James of Compostella, 373
St. Jean d'Angelys, 317
St. Jerome, 462
St. John family, 99
St. Lo, 307
St. Malo, 492, 493
St. Mathieu, Cape, battle of, 136
St. Neot, rood of, 94
St. Ninian's Chapel, 204, 207
St. Omer, 262, 289
St. Omer psalter, 244
St. Paul's, see London
St. Pol-de-Leon, 306
St. Scholastica's Day, 517
St. Vaast, 306
Saintes, 400
Saintogne, 317, 400, 435
Salisbury, 42, 150, 245, 255, 345, 390;
  cathedral, 19, 24, 69, 119, 248, 322
Salisbury, e. of, see Montague
Salisbury, countess of, see Joan of Kent
Salle, Sir Robert, 541
Samarkand, 17
Sandwich, 257, 296, 399, 418, 524
Saracens, 25, 114, 115
Savoy, 16, 113, 136, 416, 456, 528
Sawley abbey, 467
Saxony, 16, 17
Sayles, G. O., 45
Scales, Sir Roger, 541
Scandinavia, 17, 339, 474
Scarborough, 197, 491, 543
Scheldt, R., 113, 284, 306
Scone, 134, 146, 153, 180, 233, 273, 434;
  Stone of Destiny, 134, 146, 233, 433
SCOTLAND, early history, 55, 59, 125,
  129-30, 148, 155-7; national character,
  55, 155-8, 186; failure of royal line,
  125-6, 127; "great cause" of, 129-31,
  132, 133-6, 140; reign of John Balliol,
  134-6, 138, 140, 142-5, 199; suppres-

sion of nationhood, 146-7, 149, 152,
  175, 179, 238; first war of independence (1296-1305), 12, 153-60, 161-8,
  169, 170-7; second war of (1306-28),
  11, 12, 179-84, 186-8, 191, 192, 194,
  196, 197, 198-211, 212-13, 214-16,
  218-21, 228, 230-3, 235, 236, 244, 252,
  260, 311; third war of (1332-69), 12,
  266, 272-81, 283, 285, 292, 293, 294-5,
  296-7, 298, 318-19, 386, 403, 404, 406,
  433-4, 442; "auld alliance" with
  France, 143, 221, 279, 280, 285, 294-5,
  318, 413, 433, 442; captivity of David
  II, 318-19, 321, 403, 406, 416, 433-4,
  512; Black Death in, 386; succession
  of Robert II, 442; renewal of war in
  1377, 491, 518, 521; other references
  to, 23, 85, 248, 268, 359, 470. See also
  Balliol, Bannockburn, Barbour, Bruce,
  Douglas, Randolph, Wallace
Scrope, Lord, 447
Scrope, Sir Geoffrey le, C.J., 266
Scrope, Sir John, 494
Segrave, Nicholas, 194, 201
Seine, R., 307, 308
Selby, 252
Selkirk, 278
  forest, 154, 164, 168, 194, 386
Sempringham, 353
Seton, Sir Alexander, 205
Severn, R., 23, 25, 55, 65, 80, 132, 217,
  255, 256, 257, 267, 418, 480
Sevile, 513
Sewall, John, 519
Shaftesbury, 42, 384;
  abbey, 25, 353
Shakell, John, 493
Shakerley, 241
Shakespeare, William, 13, 375, 401
Shareshull, Sir William, C. J., 392
Shelley, John, 431
Shelley, Percy Bysshe, 431
Sherborne, 24
Sherwood forest, 103, 126-7, 164, 265,
  267, 268, 272, 275
SHIPPING AND NAVY, 65, 66, 88,
  136, 138, 170, 257-8, 284, 287-9, 296,
  298, 306, 307, 308, 316, 321, 373-4,
  380, 383, 384, 398, 399, 418, 420,
  445-6, 491, 492-3
Shrewsbury, 58, 59, 60, 90, 106, 140
  217, 263;
    Ralph of, b. of Bath and Wells,
    383, 384
Shropshire, 31, 57, 82, 90, 103, 106, 261,
  375
Sibley, Alderman, 538
Sicilian Vespers, 115, 172
Sicily, 16, 68, 69, 80, 113, 115, 147, 172
Siena, 249, 381, 493
Silesia, 18
Silverstone, 40
Sion cope, 244

574